GH00360764

STREI

Norfolk

First published in 2003 by

Philip's, a division of
Octopus Publishing Group Ltd
2-4 Heron Quays, London E14 4JP

Second edition 2006
First impression 2006
NORBA

ISBN-10   0-540-08959-1 (pocket)
ISBN-13   978-0-540-08959-8 (pocket)

© Philip's 2006

Ordnance Survey®

Contents

III   **Key to map symbols**

IV   **Key to map pages**

VI   **Route planning**

X   **Administrative and Postcode boundaries**

1   **Street maps** at 1⅓ inches to 1 mile

132   **Street maps** at 2⅔ inches to 1 mile

178   **Street map of Norwich city centre**
at 5⅓ inches to 1 mile

179   **Index** of towns and villages

182   **Index** of streets, hospitals, industrial estates, railway
stations, schools, shopping centres, universities
and places of interest

Digital Data

The exceptionally high-quality mapping found in this atlas is available as digital data in TIFF
format, which is easily convertible to other bitmapped (raster) image formats.

The index is also available in digital form as a standard database table. It contains all the details
found in the printed index together with the National Grid reference for the map square in which
each entry is named.

For further information and to discuss your requirements, please contact Philip's on
020 7644 6932 or james.mann@philips-maps.co.uk

PHILIP'S MAPS

the Gold Standard for drivers

◆ **Philip's street atlases cover every county in England, Wales and much of Scotland**

◆ Every named street is shown, including alleys, lanes and walkways

◆ Thousands of additional features marked: stations, public buildings, car parks, places of interest

◆ Route-planning maps to get you close to your destination

◆ Postcodes on the maps and in the index

◆ Widely used by the emergency services, transport companies and local authorities

For national mapping, choose **Philip's Navigator Britain** the most detailed road atlas available of England, Wales and Scotland. Hailed by Auto Express as 'the ultimate road atlas', this is the only one-volume atlas to show every road and lane in Britain.

Street atlases currently available

England
Bedfordshire
Berkshire
Birmingham and West Midlands
Bristol and Bath
Buckinghamshire
Cambridgeshire
Cheshire
Cornwall
Cumbria
Derbyshire
Devon
Dorset
County Durham and Teesside
Essex
North Essex
South Essex
Gloucestershire
Hampshire
North Hampshire
South Hampshire
Herefordshire Monmouthshire
Hertfordshire
Isle of Wight
Kent
East Kent
West Kent
Lancashire
Leicestershire and Rutland
Lincolnshire
London
Greater Manchester
Merseyside
Norfolk
Northamptonshire
Northumberland
Nottinghamshire
Oxfordshire
Shropshire
Somerset
Staffordshire
Suffolk
Surrey

East Sussex
West Sussex
Tyne and Wear
Warwickshire
Birmingham and West Midlands
Wiltshire and Swindon
Worcestershire
East Yorkshire
Northern Lincolnshire
North Yorkshire
South Yorkshire
West Yorkshire

Wales
Anglesey, Conwy and Gwynedd
Cardiff, Swansea and The Valleys
Carmarthenshire, Pembrokeshire and Swansea
Ceredigion and South Gwynedd
Denbighshire, Flintshire, Wrexham
Herefordshire Monmouthshire
Powys

Scotland
Aberdeenshire
Ayrshire
Dumfries and Galloway
Edinburgh and East Central Scotland
Fife and Tayside
Glasgow and West Central Scotland
Inverness and Moray
Lanarkshire
Scottish Borders

Northern Ireland*
County Armagh and County Down
Belfast
County Londonderry and County Antrim
County Tyrone and County Fermanagh

*Publishing autumn 2006

Symbol	Description	Symbol	Description
	Motorway with junction number	◆	Ambulance station
	Primary route – dual/single carriageway	◆	Coastguard station
	A road – dual/single carriageway	◆	Fire station
	B road – dual/single carriageway	◆	Police station
	Minor road – dual/single carriageway	✚	Accident and Emergency entrance to hospital
	Other minor road – dual/single carriageway	H	Hospital
	Road under construction	✛	Place of worship
	Tunnel, covered road	*i*	Information Centre (open all year)
	Rural track, private road or narrow road in urban area	🛒	Shopping Centre
	Gate or obstruction to traffic (restrictions may not apply at all times or to all vehicles)	P P&R	Parking, Park and Ride
	Path, bridleway, byway open to all traffic, road used as a public path	PO	Post Office
		⛺ 🚐	Camping site, caravan site
	Pedestrianised area	▶	Golf course
DY7	**Postcode boundaries**	✕	Picnic site
	County and unitary authority boundaries	Prim Sch	Important buildings, schools, colleges, universities and hospitals
	Railway, tunnel, railway under construction		Built up area
	Tramway, tramway under construction		Woods
	Miniature railway	River Ouse	Tidal water, water name
Walsall	**Railway station**		Non-tidal water – lake, river, canal or stream
	Private railway station		
South Shields	**Metro station**	⟨ ⊢ ⟩	Lock, weir, tunnel
⚍ ⚍	**Tram stop, tram stop under construction**	*Church*	Non-Roman antiquity
	Bus, coach station	ROMAN FORT	Roman antiquity

Acad	**Academy**	Inst	**Institute**	Recn Gd	**Recreation Ground**
Allot Gdns	**Allotments**	Ct	**Law Court**		
Cemy	**Cemetery**	L Ctr	**Leisure Centre**	Resr	**Reservoir**
C Ctr	**Civic Centre**	LC	**Level Crossing**	Ret Pk	**Retail Park**
CH	**Club House**	Liby	**Library**	Sch	**School**
Coll	**College**	Mkt	**Market**	Sh Ctr	**Shopping Centre**
Crem	**Crematorium**	Meml	**Memorial**	TH	**Town Hall/House**
Ent	**Enterprise**	Mon	**Monument**	Trad Est	**Trading Estate**
Ex H	**Exhibition Hall**	Mus	**Museum**	Univ	**University**
Ind Est	**Industrial Estate**	Obsy	**Observatory**	W Twr	**Water Tower**
IRB Sta	**Inshore Rescue Boat Station**	Pal	**Royal Palace**	Wks	**Works**
		PH	**Public House**	YH	**Youth Hostel**

87 **246** Adjoining page indicators and overlap bands
The colour of the arrow and the band indicates the scale of the adjoining or overlapping page (see scales below)

Enlarged mapping only

	Railway or bus station building
	Place of interest
	Parkland

■ The small numbers around the edges of the maps identify the 1 kilometre National Grid lines
■ The dark grey border on the inside edge of some pages indicates that the mapping does not continue onto the adjacent page

The scale of the maps on the pages numbered in blue is 4.2 cm to 1 km • 2⅔ inches to 1 mile • 1: 23810	0 ¼ ½ ¾ 1 mile / 0 250m 500m 750m 1 kilometre
The scale of the maps on pages numbered in green is 2.1 cm to 1 km • 1⅓ inches to 1 mile • 1: 47620	0 ¼ ½ ¾ 1 mile / 0 250m 500m 750m 1 kilometre
The scale of the maps on pages numbered in red is 8.4 cm to 1 km • 5⅓ inches to 1 mile • 1: 11900	0 220 yards 440 yards 660 yards ½ mile / 0 125m 250m 375m ½ kilometre

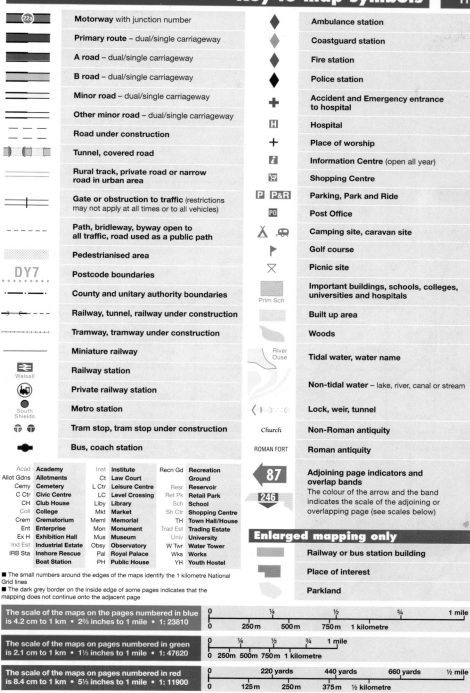

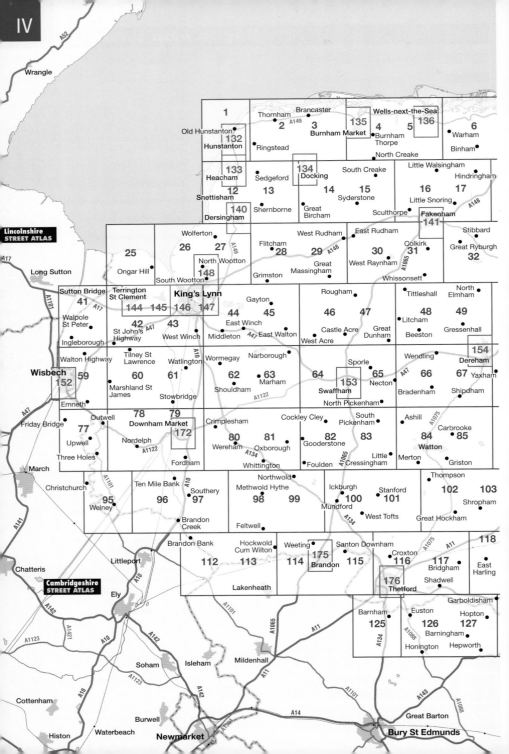

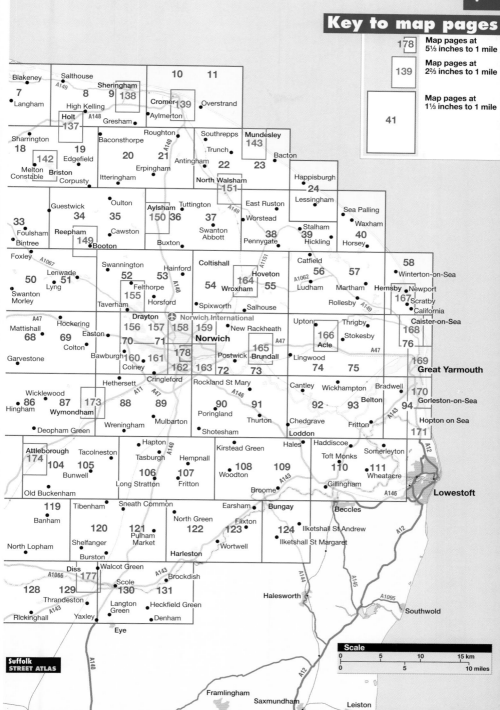

V

Key to map pages

178	Map pages at 5⅓ inches to 1 mile
139	Map pages at 2⅔ inches to 1 mile
41	Map pages at 1⅓ inches to 1 mile

Blakeney Salthouse Sheringham **10** **11**
7 *A149* 8 9 **138**
Langham High Kelling Cromer **139** Overstrand
Holt A148 Aylmerton
137 Gresham
Sharrington Roughton Southrepps Mundesley
18 **19** Baconsthorpe *A140* **143**
Melton **142** Edgefield **20** **21** Trunch Bacton
Constable Briston Erpingham Antingham **22** **23**
Corpusty Itteringham North Walsham Happisburgh
151 **24**
Guestwick Oulton Tuttington East Ruston Lessingham
33 **34** **35** Aylsham **150** **36** **37** Worstead Sea Palling Waxham
Foulsham Reepham Cawston Swanton Stalham **40**
Bintree **149** Booton Buxton Abbott Pennygate **38** **39** Hickling Horsey
Foxley *A1067* Swannington Hainford Coltishall Catfield **58**
50 Lenwade **52** **53** Hoveton **56** **57** Winterton-on-Sea
Swanton **51** Lyng Felthorpe **54** Wroxham **55** *A1062* Ludham Martham Hemsby Newport
Morley **155** Horsford Spixworth Salhouse Rollesby *A149* **167** Scratby
Taverham Drayton Norwich International California
A47 Hockering Easton **156** **157** **158** **159** New Rackheath Upton Thrigby Caister-on-Sea
Mattishall **68** **69** **70**—**71** **Norwich** **166** Stokesby **168**
Colton **178** *A47* Acle **76**
Garvestone Bawburgh **160** **161** Postwick Brundall Lingwood *A47*
Colney **162** **163** **72** **73** **165** **74** **75** **169**
Hethersett Cringleford Rockland St Mary Cantley Wickhampton Bradwell **Great Yarmouth**
Wicklewood **87** **173** **88** **89** **90** **91** **92** **93** Belton **94** **170**
86 *A11* *A47* **A146** Gorleston-on-Sea
Hingham Wymondham Poringland Chedgrave Fritton Hopton on Sea
Deopham Green Wreningham Mulbarton Thurton **171**
Hapton Shotesham Loddon
Attleborough Tacolneston Tasburgh Hempnall Kirstead Green Hales Haddiscoe Somerleyton *A12*
174 **104** **105** *A140* **106** **107** **108** **109** Toft Monks **110** **111**
Bunwell Woodton Gillingham Wheatacre
Long Stratton Fritton Broome *A143* **Lowestoft**
Old Buckenham *A146*
119 Tibenham Sneath Common Earsham Bungay Beccles
Banham North Green Flixton
120 **121** **122** **123** **124** Ilketshall St Andrew *A12*
Shelfanger Pulham Wortwell Ilketshall St Margaret
North Lopham Market Harleston
Burston
Diss Walcot Green *A143* Halesworth *A145* *A1095*
A1066 **177** Scole Brockdish *A144* Southwold
128 **129** **130** **131**
Thrandeston Langton Heckfield Green
A143 Green
Rickinghall Yaxley Denham
Eye

Suffolk STREET ATLAS *A140*

Scale

0	5	10	15 km
0		5	10 miles

Framlingham Saxmundham Leiston *A12*

Route planning

Scale

0	1	2	3	4	5	10 km
0	1	2	3	4	5	6 miles

BRANCASTER ROADS

Holkham Bay

Brancaster Bay

THE WASH

Lynn Channel

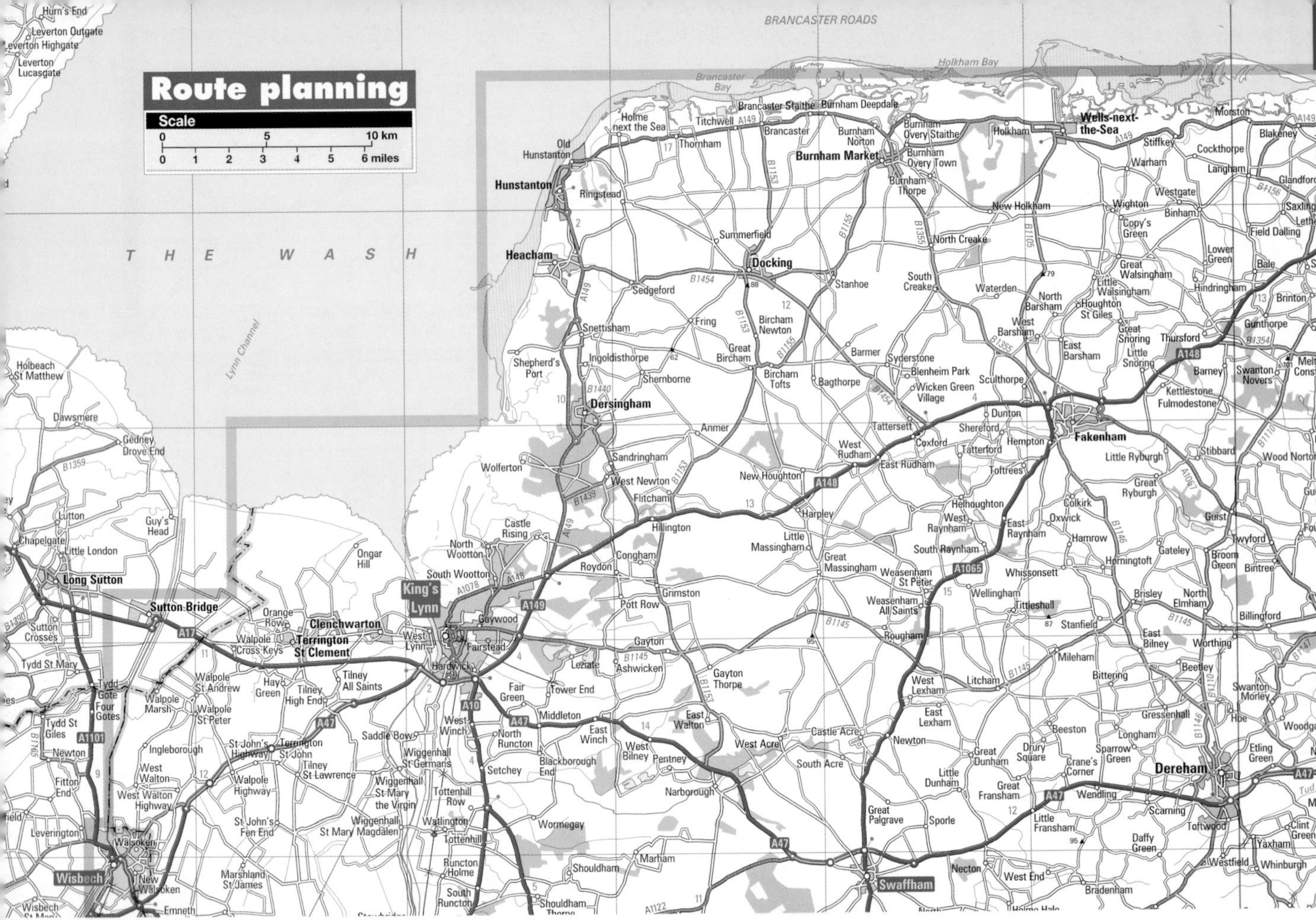

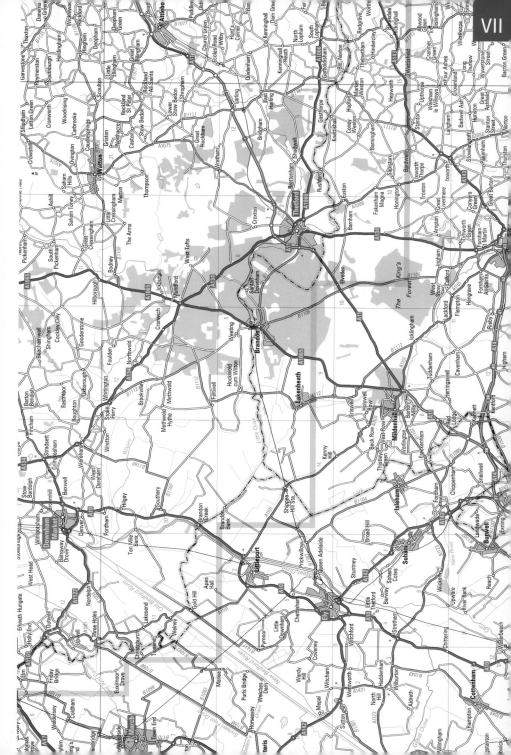

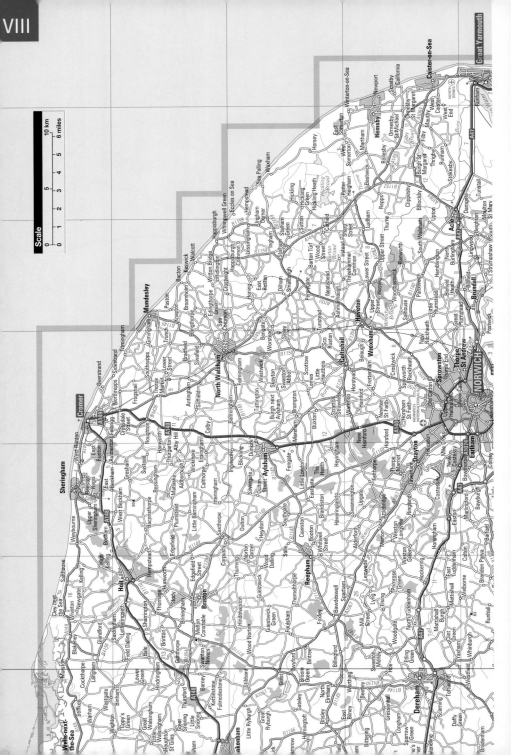

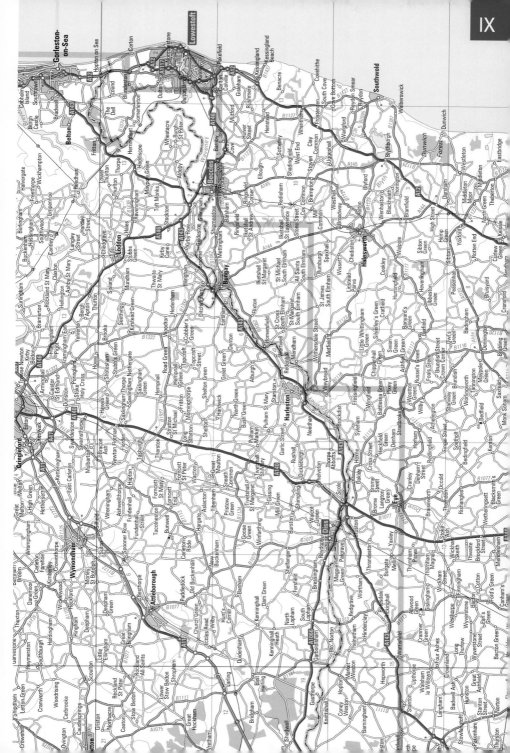

Administrative and Postcode boundaries

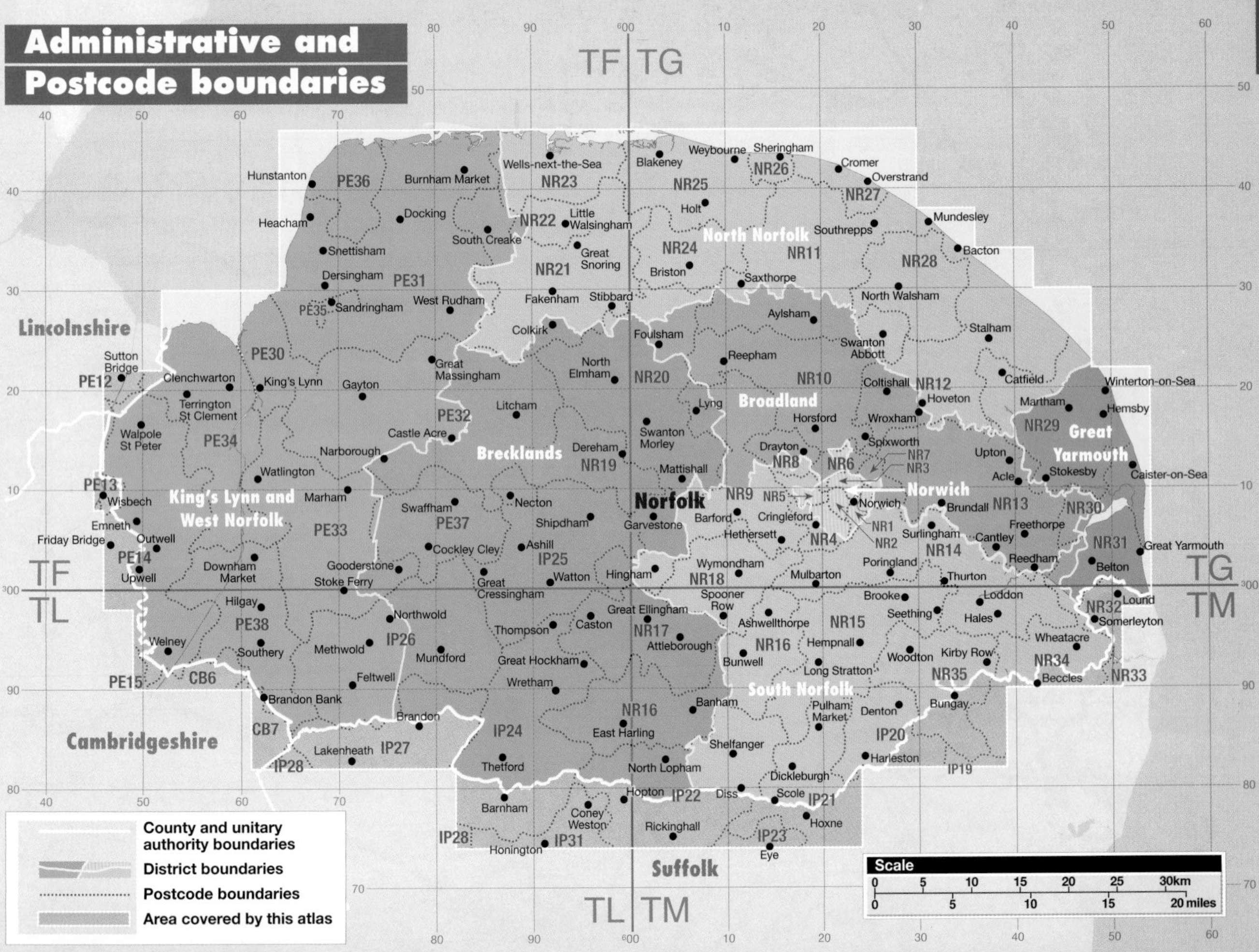

Scale

30km

20 miles

Great Yarmouth

Norwich

North Norfolk

Broadland

Norfolk

South Norfolk

Breckland

King's Lynn and West Norfolk

Suffolk

Lincolnshire

Cambridgeshire

TF | TG

TF | TL

TL | TM

TG | TM

County and unitary authority boundaries

District boundaries

Postcode boundaries

Area covered by this atlas

Winterton-on-Sea
Hemsby
Caister-on-Sea
Great Yarmouth
Somerleyton
Lound
NR31
NR32
NR33
Belton
NR30
Stokesby
Acle
NR13
Freethorpe
Cantley
Reedham
NR34
Beccles
Wheatacre
Loddon
Thurton
Hales
Kirby Row
Bungay
NR35
Woodton
Kirstead
Long Stratton
IP20
IP19
Denton
Harleston
IP21
Dickleburgh
Scole
Hoxne
IP23
Eye
Diss
Shelfanger
Rickinghall
IP22
Hopton
North Lopham
Coney Weston
IP31
East Harling
IP28
Barnham
Honington
Thetford
IP24
Wretham
Great Hockham
Brandon Bank
CB7
Lakenheath IP27
Brandon
IP28
CB6
CB7

Mundesley
Overstrand
Cromer
Sheringham
Weybourne
NR27
NR26
Southrepps
NR28
Bacton
Stalham
Catfield
Hoveton
NR29
Martham
NR11
North Walsham
NR25
Holt
Blakeney
NR24
Aylsham
Saxthorpe
NR10
Reepham
Briston
NR12
Wroxham
Cottishall
Horsford
Sprowston
NR7
NR3
Brundall
Surlingham
NR14
Porringland
Brooke
NR15
Seething
Hempnall
NR16
Barnham

Wells-next-the-Sea
NR23
Little Walsingham
NR22
Great Snoring
NR21
Fakenham
Colkirk
North Elmham
Stibbard
NR20
Foulsham
Lyng
Swanton Morley
NR19
Dereham
Mattishall
NR8
Drayton
NR1
NR2
Norwich
NR6
NR5
NR9
Barford
Hethersett
NR18
Wymondham
Spooner Row
Bunwell
NR17
Attleborough
Great Ellingham
Hingham
Garvestone

Hunstanton
Heacham
PE36
Burnham Market
Docking
Snettisham
PE31
Dersingham
PE35
Sandringham
West Rudham
South Creake
Great Massingham
Litcham
Castle Acre
PE32
Swaffham
PE37
Necton
Shipdham
IP25
Watton
Cockley Cley
Cressingham
Caston
Thompson
Mundford
IP26
Feltwell
Methwold
Northwold

Sutton Bridge
PE12
Wisbech
PE13
Emneth
Outwell
PE14
Upwell
Friday Bridge
Clenchwarton
Terrington St Clement
PE34
King's Lynn
PE30
Gayton
Narborough
Marham
PE33
Watlington
Stoke Ferry
Goodestone
Downham Market
PE38
Hilgay
Southery
Weney
PE15
Denver

For full street detail of the highlighted area see page 132

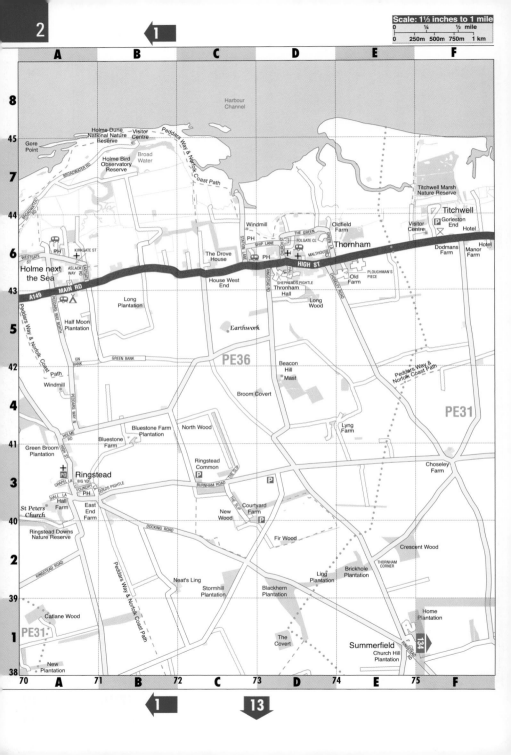

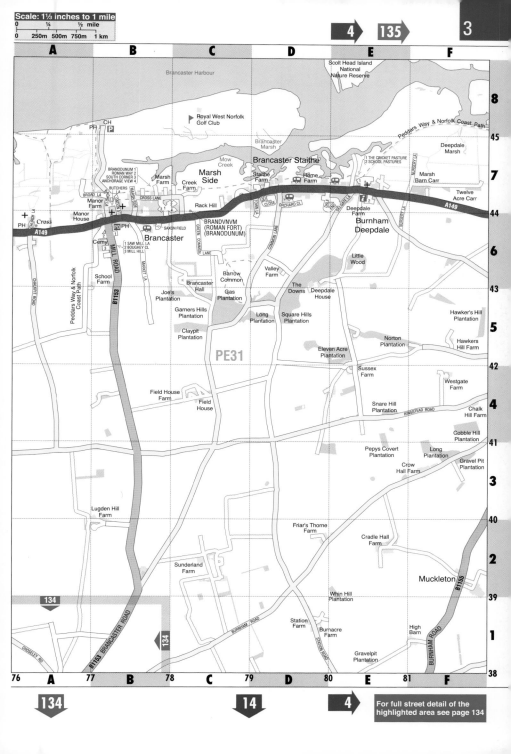

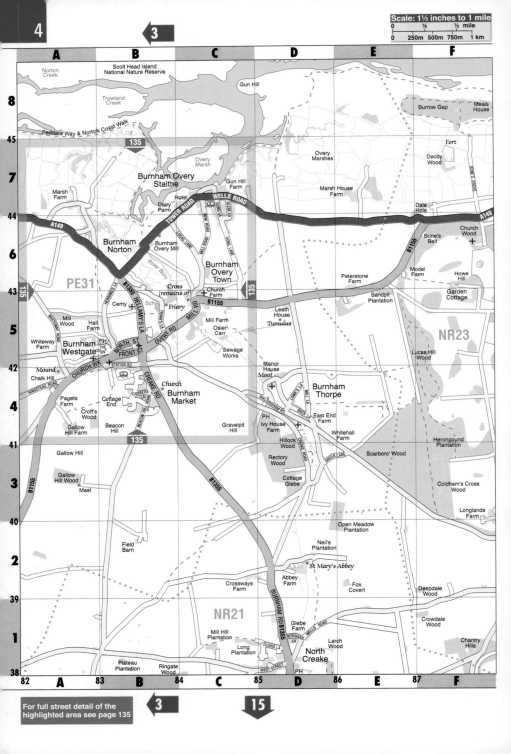

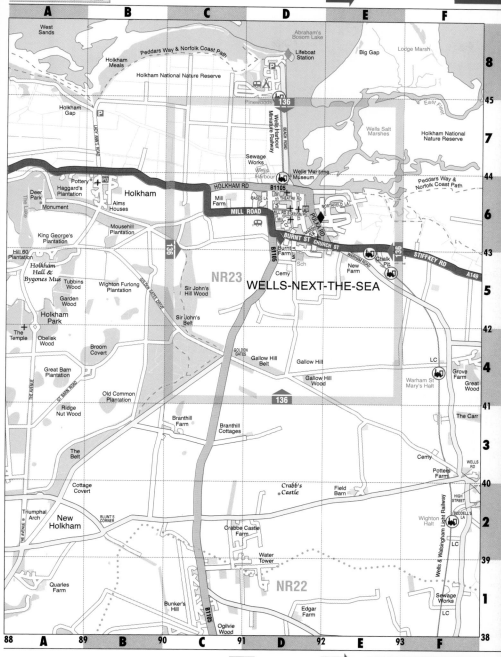

West Sands

Holkham Meals

Peddars Way & Norfolk Coast Path

Holkham National Nature Reserve

Abraham's Bosom Lake

Lifeboat Station

Big Gap

Lodge Marsh

Pinewoods

136

8

45

Holkham Gap

Wells Harbour Miniature Railway

BEACH ROAD

East Fleet

Wells Salt Marshes

Holkham National Nature Reserve

7

LADY ANNE'S ROAD

Sewage Works

Wells Harbour

Wells Maritime Museum

Peddars Way & Norfolk Coast Path

44

Pottery

Haggard's Plantation

Deer Park

HOLKHAM RD

B1105

GALES LA

THEATRE RD

Monument

Holkham

Alms Houses

Mill Farm

MILL ROAD

MIC

MILL RD STATION RD

NORTHFIELD LA

6

The Lake

Mousehill Plantation

POLKA RD

King George's Plantation

BURNT ST

CHURCH ST

Hill 60 Plantation

Holkham Hall & Bygones Mus

Tubbins Wood

Wighton Furlong Plantation

NR23

Burnt Farm

B1105

Sch

Cemy

WELLS-NEXT-THE-SEA

New Farm

WARHAM ROAD

Chalk Pit

STIFFKEY RD

A149

43

Garden Wood

GOLDEN GATES DRIVE

Sir John's Hill Wood

5

Holkham Park

The Temple

Obelisk Wood

Sir John's Belt

42

Broom Covert

GOLDEN GATES

Gallow Hill Belt

Gallow Hill

LC

Great Barn Plantation

Gallow Hill Wood

Warham St Mary's Halt

Grove Farm

Great Wood

4

THE AVENUE

ST BARN ROAD

Ridge Nut Wood

Old Common Plantation

136

41

The Belt

Branthill Farm

Branthill Cottages

Cemy

The Carr

3

Cottage Covert

Potters Farm

WELLS RD

40

Triumphal Arch

New Holkham

BLUNT'S CORNER

Crabb's Castle

Field Barn

HIGH STREET

Wighton Halt

BUDDELL'S LA

THE AVENUE

Crabbe Castle Farm

Wells & Walsingham Light Railway

LC

2

Quarles Farm

Water Tower

NR22

39

Bunker's Hill

B1105

Edgar Farm

Sewage Works

1

Ogilvie Wood

LC

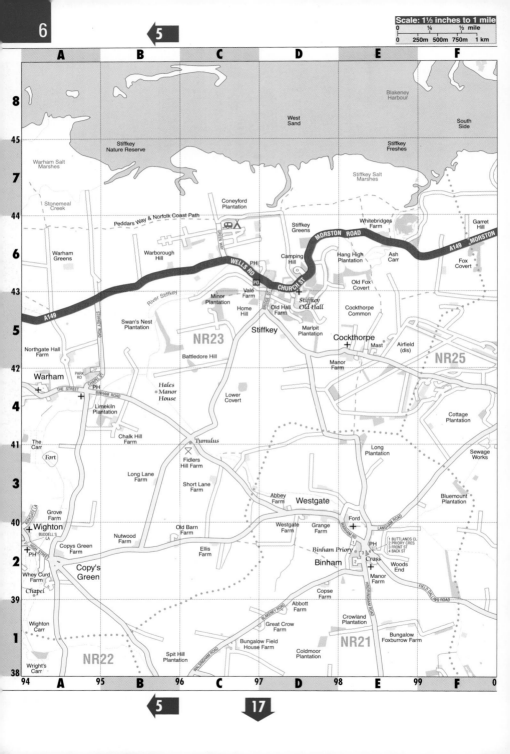

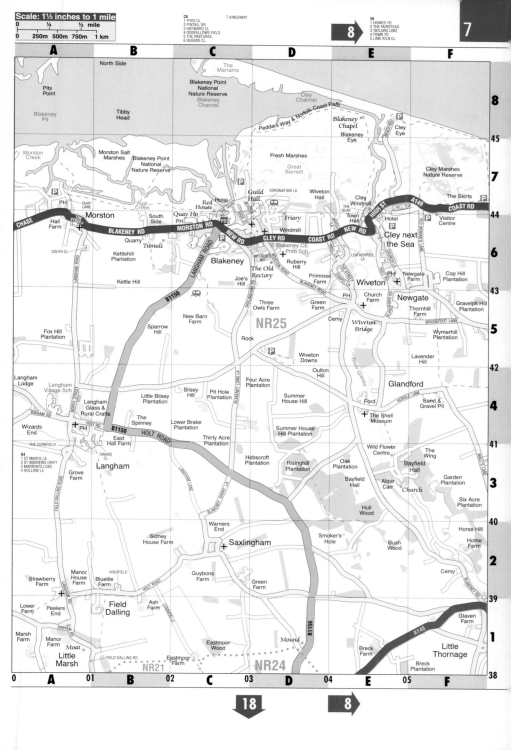

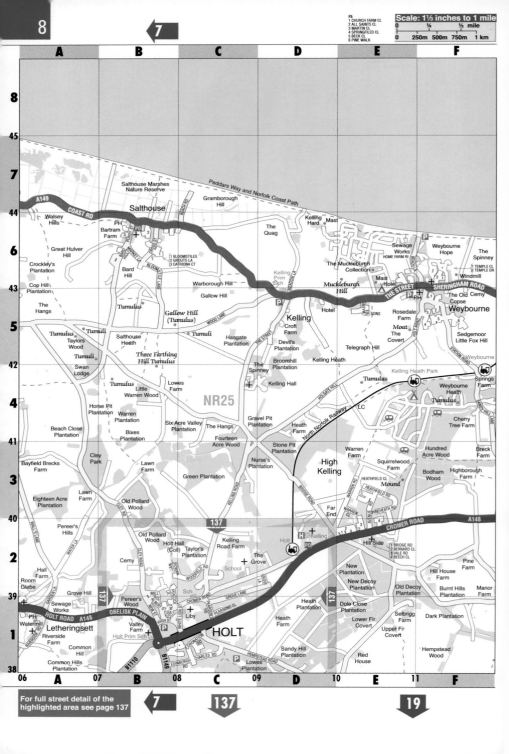

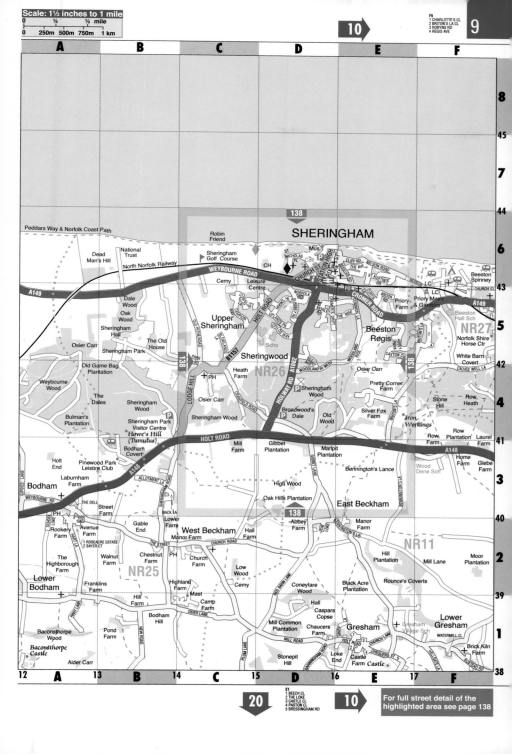

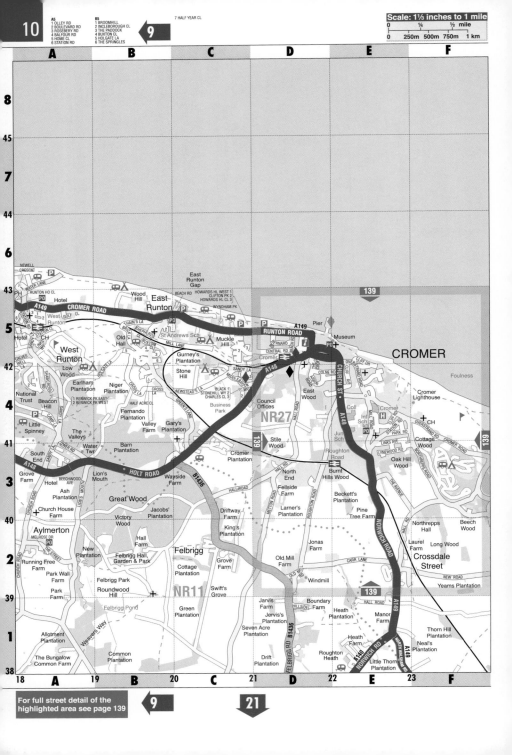

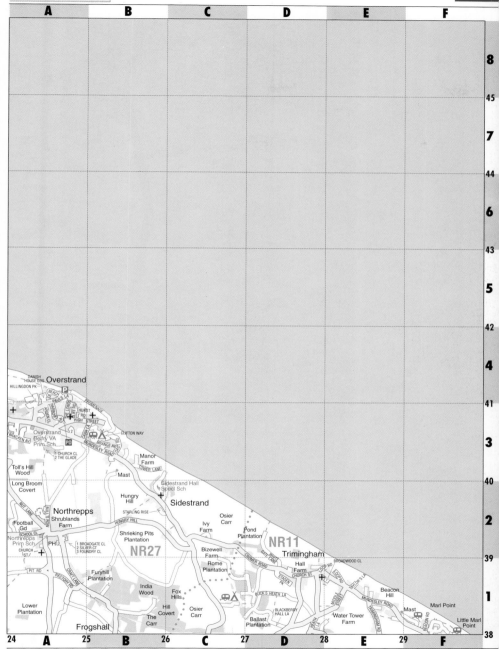

Scale: 1⅓ inches to 1 mile

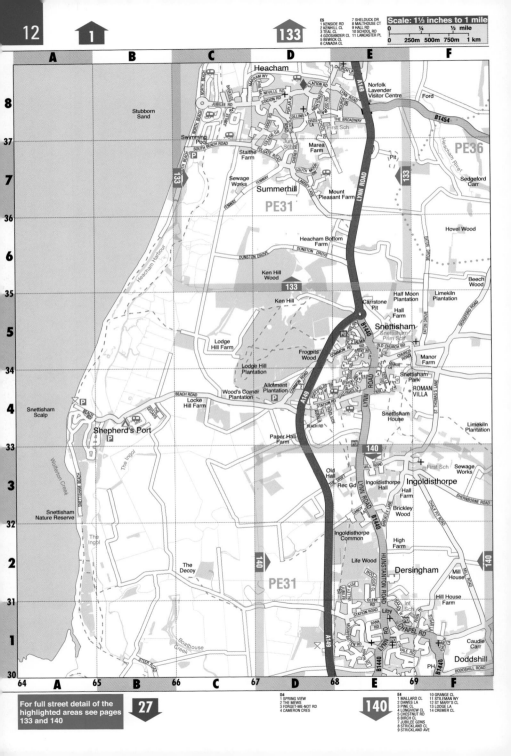

E5
1 KENSIDE RD
2 KENHILL CL
3 TEAL CL
4 GOOSANDER CL
5 BEWICK CL
6 CANADA CL
7 SHELDUCK DR
8 MALTHOUSE CT
9 HALL RD
10 SCHOOL RD
11 LANCASTER PL

Scale: 1⅓ inches to 1 mile

0   ¼   ½ mile
250m   500m   750m   1 km

Heacham

Norfolk Lavender Visitor Centre

Ford

B1454

PE36

Stubborn Sand

Swimming Pool

Staithe Farm

Marea Farm

Pit

Sedgeford Carr

Sewage Works

Summerhill

PE31

Mount Pleasant Farm

133

Hovel Wood

Heacham Bottom Farm

DUNSTON DROVE

Heacham Harbour

Ken Hill Wood

133

Beech Wood

Ken Hill

Half Moon Plantation

Limekiln Plantation

Carrstone Pit

Hall Farm

Snettisham

Snettisham Prim Sch

Lodge Hill Farm

Frogpits Wood

Manor Farm

Lodge Hill Plantation

Wood's Corner Plantation

Allotment Plantation

Snettisham Park

ROMAN VILLA

Snettisham Scalp

BEACH ROAD

Locke Hill Farm

Snettisham House

Limekiln Plantation

Shepherd's Port

The Ingol

Paper Hall Farm

140

Walkerton Creek

Old Hall

First Sch

Sewage Works

Ingoldisthorpe Hall

Ingoldisthorpe

Rec Gd

Hall Farm

Snettisham Nature Reserve

The Ingol

Brickley Wood

Ingoldisthorpe Common

High Farm

The Decoy

140

Life Wood

Dersingham

140

Mill House

PE31

Hill House Farm

Inf Sch

Boathouse Creek

Caudle Carr

CHAPEL RD

PH

Doddshill

DODDSHILL ROAD

For full street detail of the highlighted areas see pages 133 and 140

27

D4
1 SPRING VIEW
2 THE MEWS
3 FORGET-ME-NOT RD
4 CAMERON CRES

140

E4
1 MALLARD CL
2 DAWES LA
3 PINE CL
4 LONGVIEW CL
5 CHESTNUT RD
6 BIRCH CL
7 JUBILEE GDNS
8 STRICKLAND CL
9 STRICKLAND AVE
10 GRANGE CL
11 STILEMAN WY
12 ST MARY'S CL
13 LODGE LA
14 CREMER CL

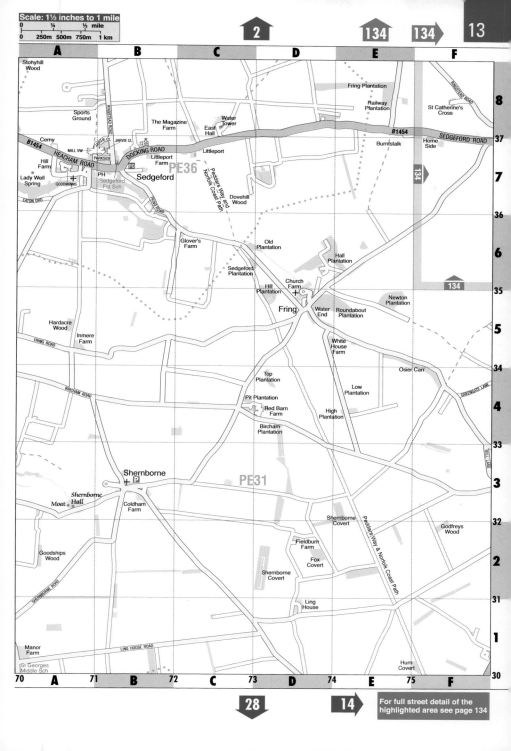

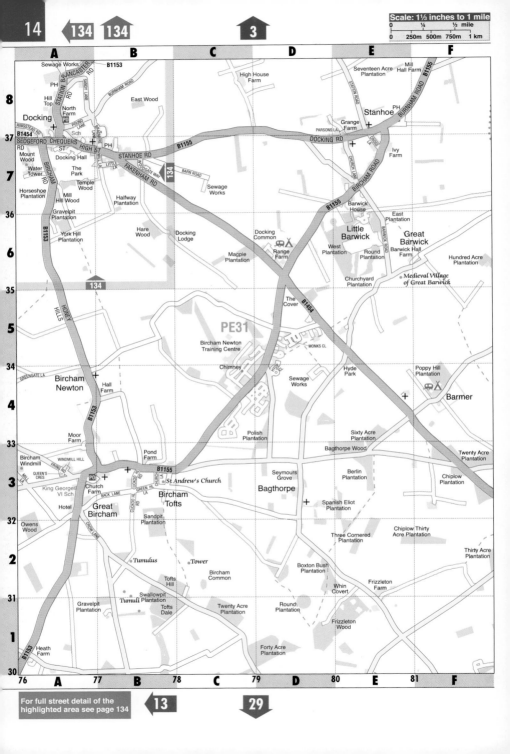

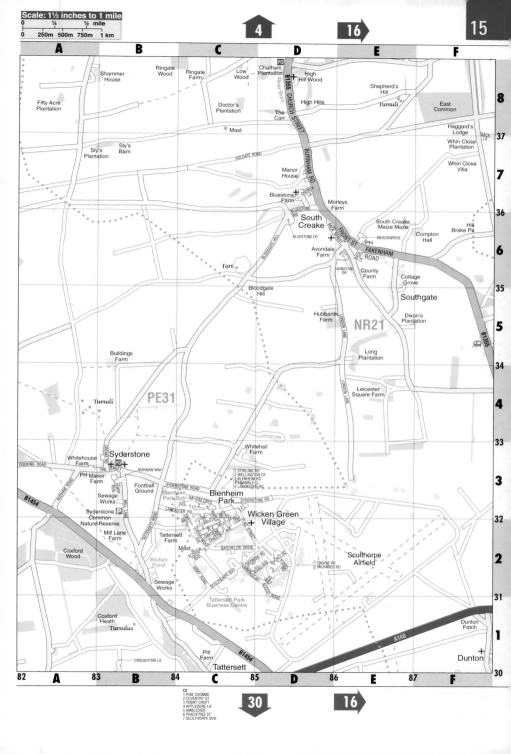

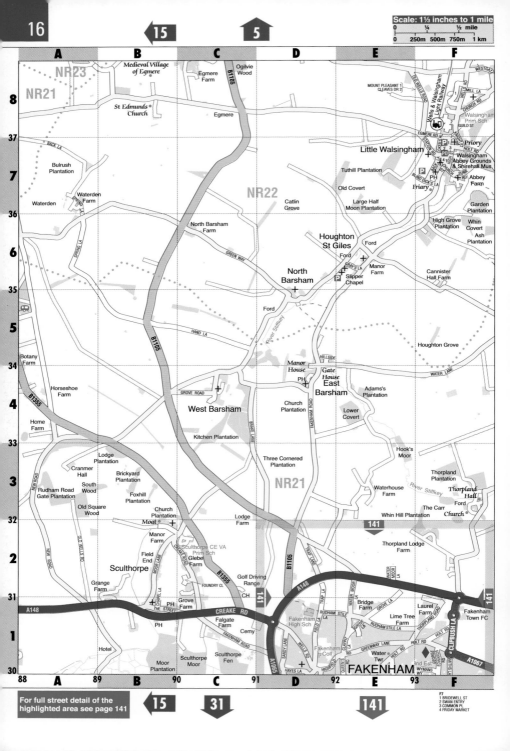

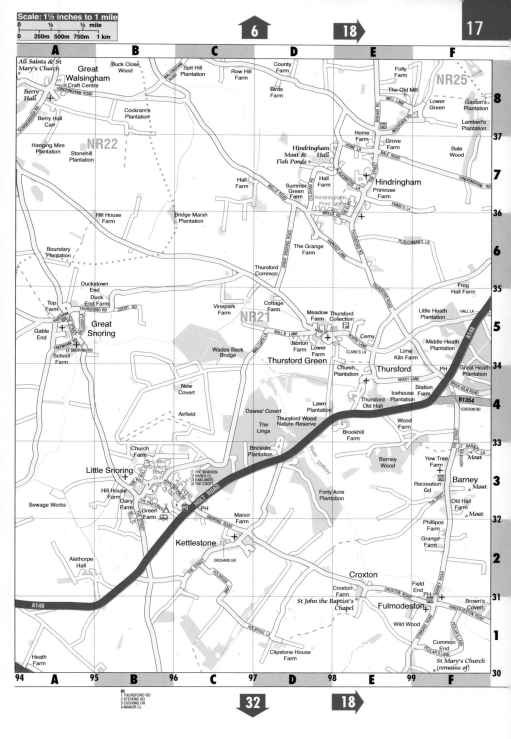

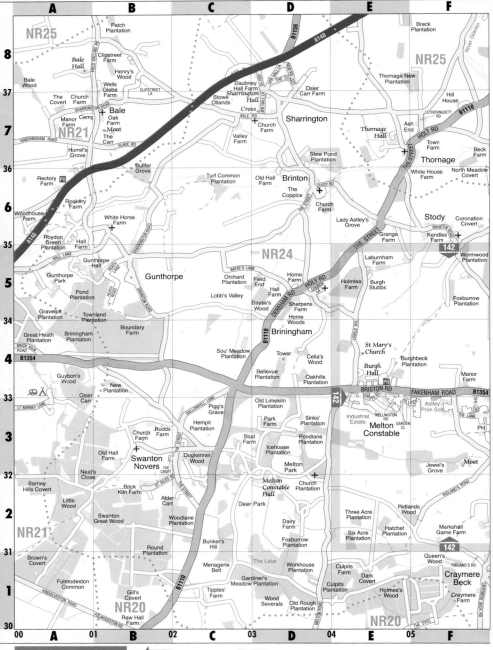

NR25

A148
B1156

Breck
Plantation

River Glaven

NR25

Patch
Plantation

Clipstreet
Farm

Bale
Hall

Henry's
Wood

Wells
Glebe
Farm

Daubney
Hall Farm

Stowe
Ollands

Sharrington
Hall

Osier
Carr Farm

Thornage New
Plantation

Hill
House

LETHERINGSETT RD

B1110

Bale
Wood

The
Covert

Church
Farm

CLIPSTREET
LA

SHARRINGTON RD

Sharrington
Cross

Sharrington

Ash
End

HOLT RD

THE STREET

Manor
Farm

Cemy

NR21

Bale

Oak
Farm

Moat

Church
Farm

Thornage
Hall

Town
Farm

Thornage

Beck
Farm

HINDRINGHAM ROAD

The
Carr

SLADE RD

Valley
Farm

White House
Farm

North Meadow
Covert

Hurrel's
Grove

Bulffer
Grove

Stew Pond
Plantation

Rectory
Farm

PO

Turf Common
Plantation

Old Hall
Farm

Brinton

STODY RD

Stody

Coronation
Covert

Woodhouse
Farm

Rookery
Farm

White Horse
Farm

The
Coppice

Church
Farm

THE STREET

Lady Astley's
Grove

Grange
Farm

BRINTON RD

Kendles
Farm

142

Royden
Green
Plantation

Hall
Farm

HALL LANE

HEATH LANE

Gunthorpe
Hall

BAYSE'S LANE

NR24

THE STREET

Laburnham
Farm

Wormwood
Plantation

Gunthorpe
Park

Gunthorpe

Orchard
Plantation

Field
End

Home
Farm

DEREHAM RD

HOLY RD

CHURCH LA

Holmlea
Farm

Burgh
Stubbs

Foxburrow
Plantation

Pond
Plantation

SWANTON ROAD

HEATH ROAD

Lobb's Valley

Hall
Farm

Bayse's
Wood

Sharpens
Farm

Gravelpit
Plantation

Townland
Plantation

Boundary
Farm

Home
Woods

Great Heath
Plantation

Briningham
Plantation

BRICK KILN ROAD

Sou' Meadow
Plantation

B1110

Briningham

Tower

Celia's
Wood

St Mary's
Church

Burghbeck
Plantation

Manor
Farm

B1354

Guybon's
Wood

New
Plantation

Bellevue
Plantation

Oakhills
Plantation

Burgh
Hall

PO

BRISTON RD

FAKENHAM ROAD

B1354

LT BARNEY LANE

Osier
Carr

Pigg's
Grave

Old Limekiln
Plantation

142

Astley
Prim Schl

THE LANE

PH

GALLOWHILL LANE

Hempit
Plantation

Park
Farm

Sinks'
Plantation

Industrial
Estate

WELLINGTON
RD

LAKESIDE

GARDEN
CL

Church
Farm

Rudds
Farm

THE STREET

Stud
Farm

Pondlane
Plantation

Melton
Constable

Old Hall
Farm

Dogkennel
Wood

Icehouse
Plantation

Melton
Park

Jewel's
Grove

Moat

Swanton
Novers

THE CROFT

ST GILES LA

Melton
Constable
Hall

Church
Plantation

Neat's
Close

Brick
Kiln Farm

Alder
Carr

Deer Park

Three Acre
Plantation

Ridlands
Wood

RIDLANDS ROAD

Barney
Hills Covert

Little
Wood

Swanton
Great Wood

Woodlane
Plantation

Dairy
Farm

Six Acre
Plantation

Hatchet
Plantation

Markshall
Game Farm

142

NR21

Round
Plantation

Bunker's
Hill

Foxburrow
Plantation

Queen's
Wood

RIDLAND'S RD

Craymere
Beck

Brown's
Covert

Menagerie
Belt

The Lake

Workhouse
Plantation

Culpits
Farm

Dark
Covert

CRAYMERE BECK RD

Fulmodeston
Common

HINDOLVESTON ROAD

Gill's Covert

FULMODESTON RD

Gardiner's
Meadow Plantation

Tipples'
Covert

Culpits
Plantation

Holmes's
Wood

Craymere
Farm

NR20

Raw Hall
Farm

B1110

MELTON ROAD

Wood
Severals

Old Rough
Plantation

THE DYES

NR20

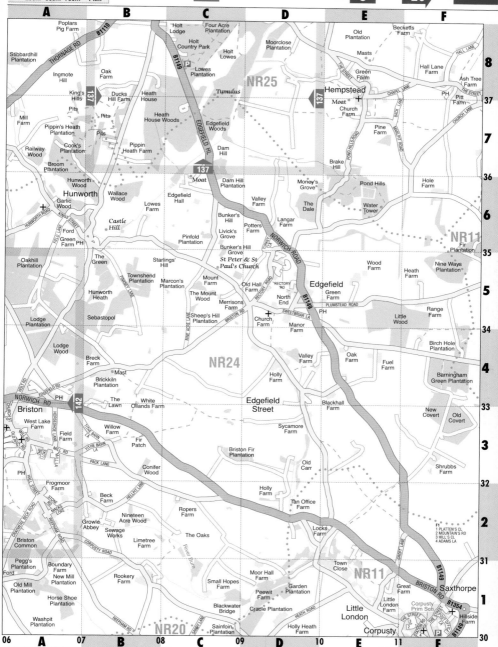

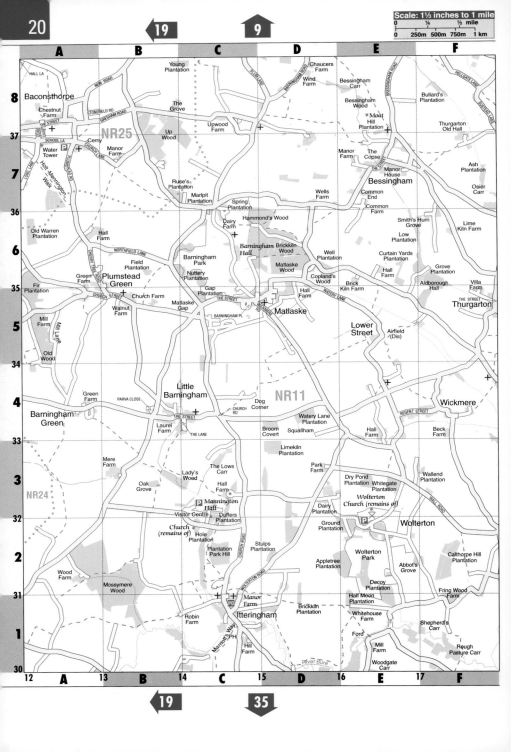

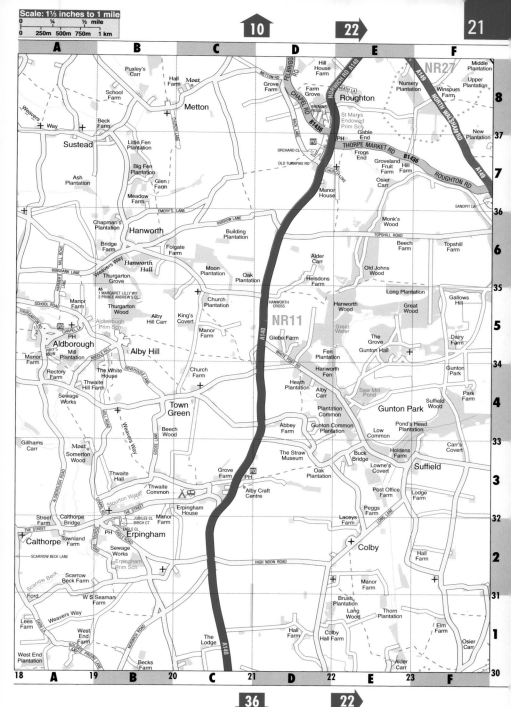

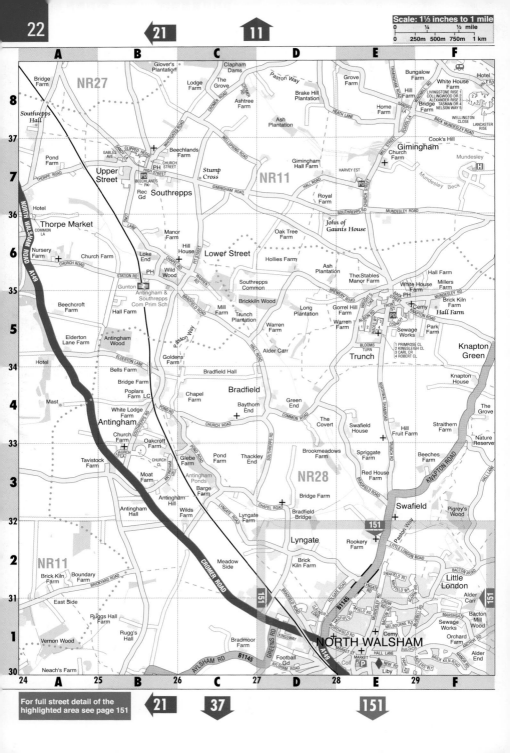

Scale: 1⅓ inches to 1 mile

0   ¼   ½ mile
0   250m 500m 750m   1 km

Cliftonville

Liby

Mundesley Maritime Museum

Mundesley

LINKS ROAD

Water Tower

Hotel

Sch

Stow Mill

Stow Hill Farm

Holiday Centre

Stow Hill

NR11

Paston Way

The Spinney

Paston

Great Barn

Hall Farm

Gas Distribution Station

Mast

Mast

Knapton

Church Farm

Rookery Plantation

Bacton Road

BEACH RD

Bacton Green

Bacton

Watch House Gap

Bromholm Field End

Keswick

Water Tower

Sewage Works

Paston Green

Lowlands Farm

WODEHOUSE RD

Church Farm

PH

ANNE STANNARD WAY

KESWICK RD

Old Hall Street

Parrs Farm

Croft Farm

Hill Farm

Church Farm

NR12

Hall Farm

THE PADDOCKS

Bacton-on-Sea First Sch

Abbey Farm

PRIORY RD

PH

Rudram's Gap

Pollard Street

Grange Farm

Broomholm

Stories Farm

Gap End

ST HELENS RD

HELENA RD

THE CEDARS

POPLAR DR

Dead Man's Grave

Honeytop Farm

The Grove

Edingthorpe

Church Farm

The Grange

Ash Tree Farm

Barchams Farm

Clay Lane Farm

CLAY LANE

NR28

Park Farm

Heath Farm

HENNESSEY'S LOKE

North Plantation

Odessa Farm

Mill Common

Rookery Farm

Edingthorpe Green

Cooper's Covert

Green Farm

Witton Hall

Common Farm

Stonebridge Cottage
Selfs Carr

Bafrington Farm

PH

NORTH WALSHAM RD

Edingthorpe Heath

Church Plantation

Manor Farm

Witton Bridge

Bacton Wood

Road Plantation

Philip's Grove

Verona Plantation

Ivy Farm

MARSH LOKE

Church Farm

South Side

Ridlington

NR12

Spa Common

Muckle Hill Farm

Witton Heath

Old Hall

NORTH WALSHAM ROAD

Hoole House

Primrose Farm

Ridlington Street

Bransmeadow Carr

Heath Farm

Nashs Farm

Ridlington Plantation

OLD LANE

Tumulus

38

24

For full street detail of the highlighted area see page 143

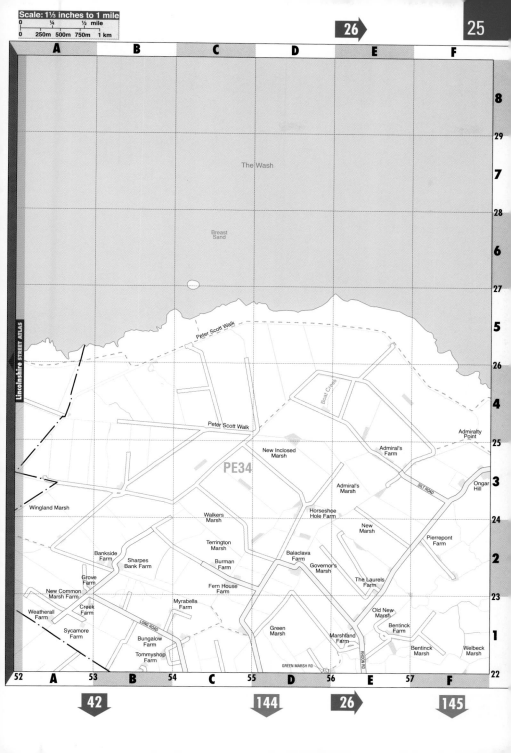

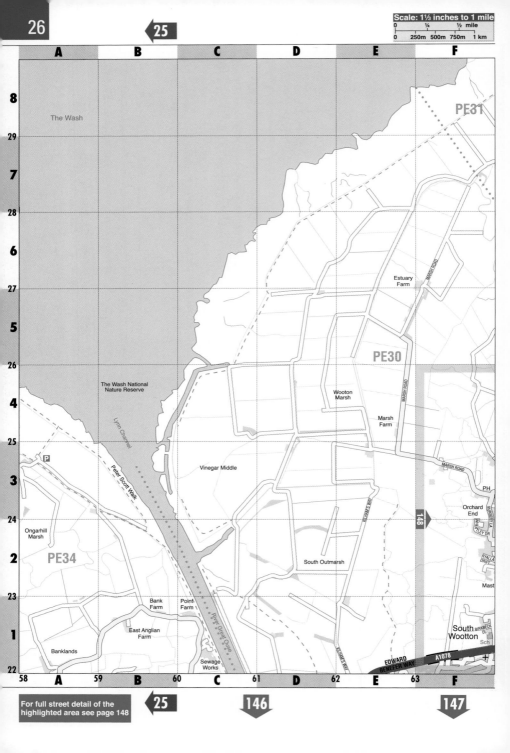

Scale: 1⅓ inches to 1 mile
0   ¼   ½   mile
0   250m 500m 750m 1 km

The Wash

PE31

Estuary Farm

MARSH ROAD

PE30

The Wash National
Nature Reserve

Wooton
Marsh

Marsh
Farm

Lynn Channel

Vinegar Middle

MARSH ROAD

Peter Scott Walk

PH

Orchard
End

148

PE34

Ongarhill
Marsh

KING'S WAY NORTH

South Outmarsh

Mast

Bank
Farm

Point
Farm

River Great Ouse

East Anglian
Farm

Banklands

Sewage
Works

South
Wootton

Sch

EDWARD
BENEFER WAY

A1078

KING'S WAY

For full street detail of the
highlighted area see page 148
25
146
147

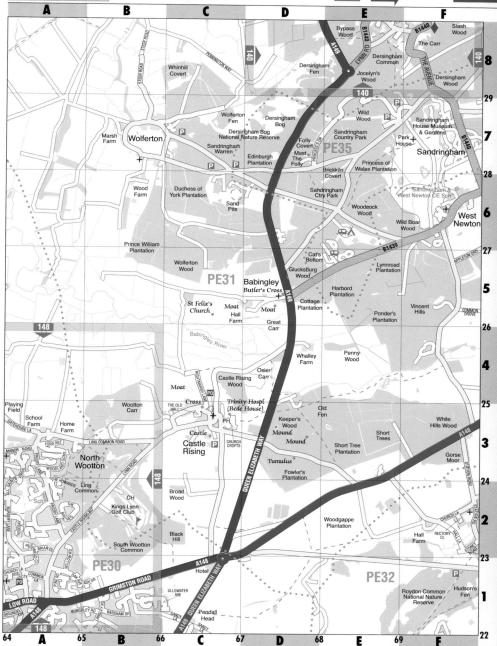

For full street detail of the highlighted area see page 140

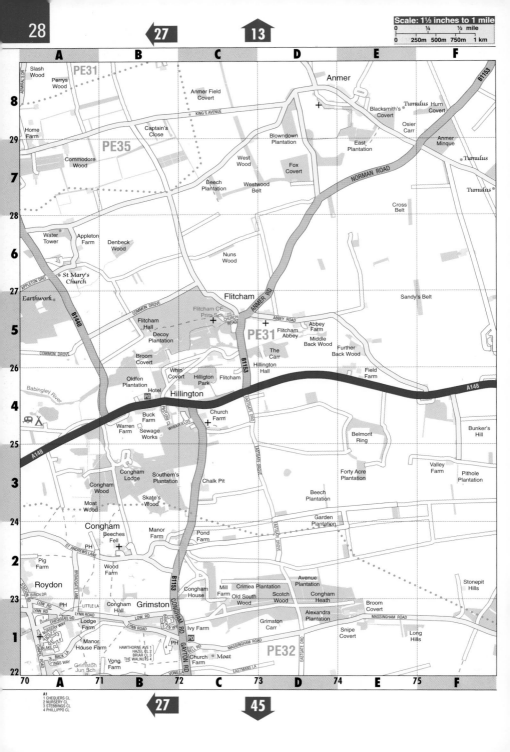

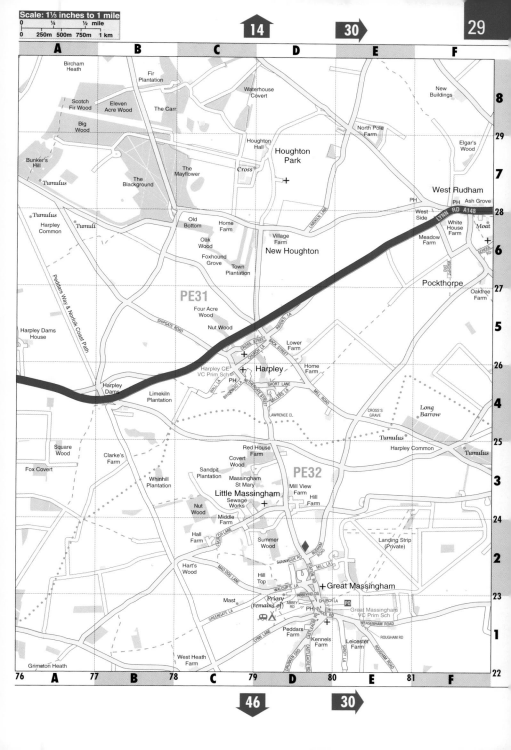

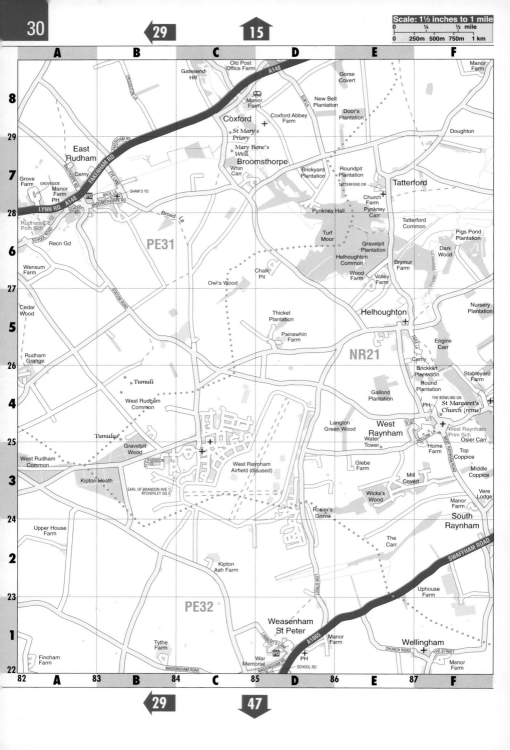

Scale: 1⅓ inches to 1 mile
0   ¼   ½ mile
0 250m 500m 750m 1 km

A   B   C   D   E   F

Manor Farm
Old Post Office Farm
Gatesend Hill
A148
Gorse Covert
New Belt Plantation
Door's Plantation
Doughton

Manor Farm
Coxford
Coxford Abbey Farm

8

St Mary's Priory

29

East Rudham
Mary Bone's Well
Broomsthorpe
Whin Carr
Brickyard Plantation
Roundpit Plantation
TATTERFORD DR
Tatterford

7

Grove Farm
GROVESIDE
Cerny
FAKENHAM RD
EYE LANE
Church Farm
Pynkney Carr

Manor Farm
PH
BACK LA
SHAW'S YD
Pynkney Hall
Tatterford Common

28

LYNN RD A148
SCHOOL RD
BROOMSTHORPE RD
Broad La
Pigs Pond Plantation

Rudham C E Prim Sch
Turf Moor
Gravelpit Plantation
Helhoughton Common
Dark Wood

6

Recn Gd
PE31
Chalk Pit
Wood Farm
Brymur Farm
River Wensum

Wensum Farm
STATION ROAD
Owl's Wood
Valley Farm

27

Cedar Wood
Thicket Plantation
Helhoughton
Nursery Plantation

5

Painswhin Farm
Engine Carr

Rudham Grange
NR21
Cerny

26

Tumuli
Brickkiln Plantation
Round Plantation
Stableyard Farm

West Rudham Common
Gallond Plantation
THE BOWLING GN
PH
St Margaret's Church (rems)

4

Tumulus
Langton Green Wood
West Raynham
West Raynham Prim Sch
Osier Carr

25

West Rudham Common
Gravelpit Wood
A PHENSON CL
West Raynham Airfield (disused)
Water Tower
Home Farm
Top Coppice

Kipton Heath
EARL OF BRANDON AVE 1
ATCHERLEY SQ 2
Glebe Farm
Middle Coppice

3

Wicks's Wood
Mill Covert
Vere Lodge

24

Upper House Farm
Rosier's Grove
Manor Farm
South Raynham

The Carr

2

SWAFFHAM ROAD

Kipton Ash Farm
LOW STREET
Uphouse Farm

23

PE32
A1065

1

Tythe Farm
LAMBERT'S LANE
Manor Farm
Weasenham St Peter
Wellingham
CHURCH ROAD
THE STREET

Fincham Farm
PO
War Memorial
PH
SCHOOL RD
MASSINGHAM RD
Manor Farm

22

MASSINGHAM ROAD

82   A   83   B   84   C   85   D   86   E   87   F

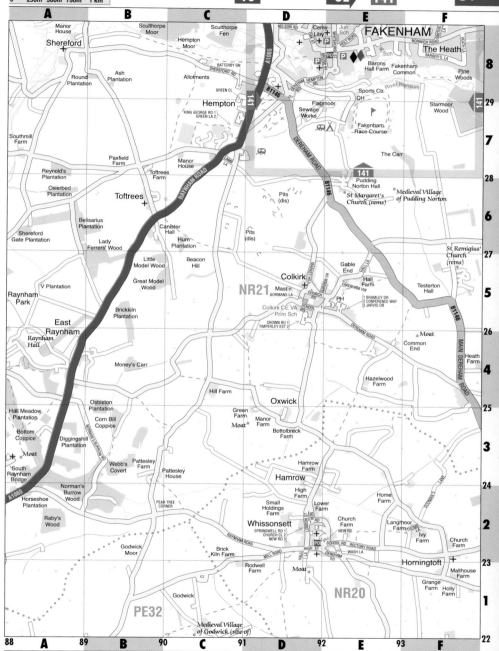

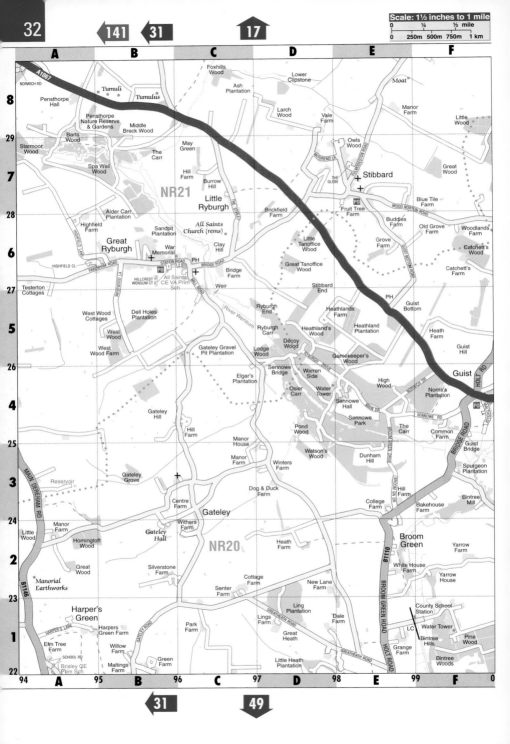

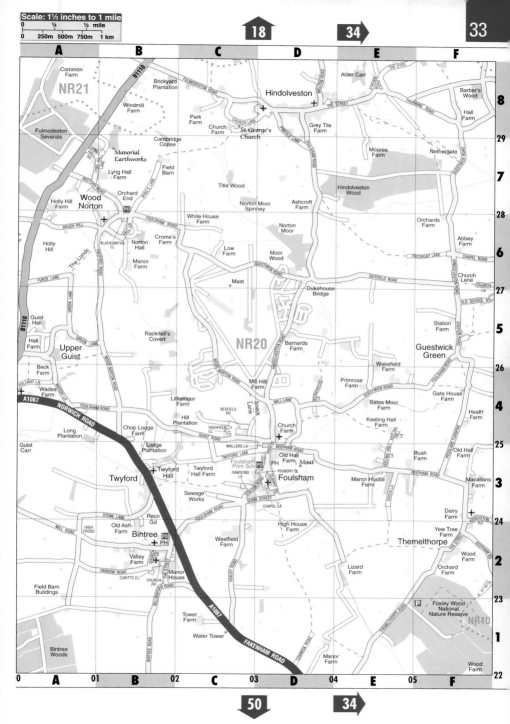

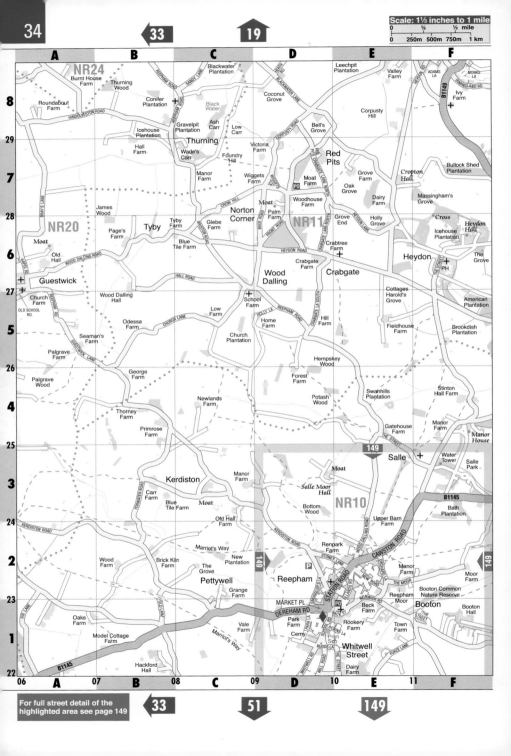

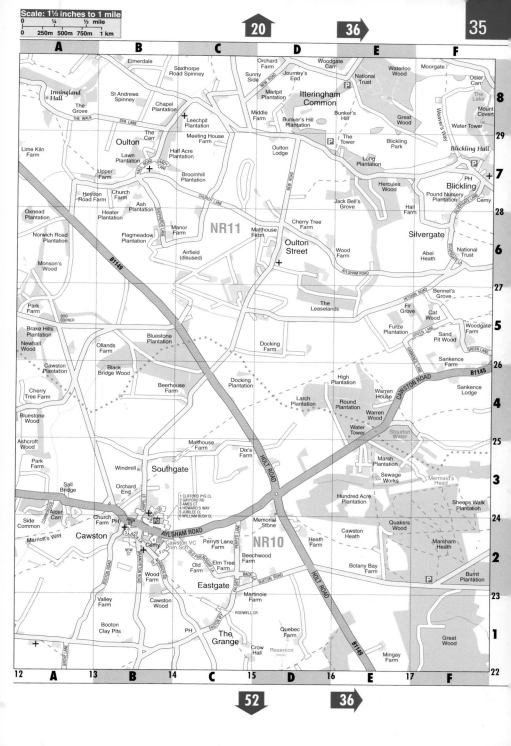

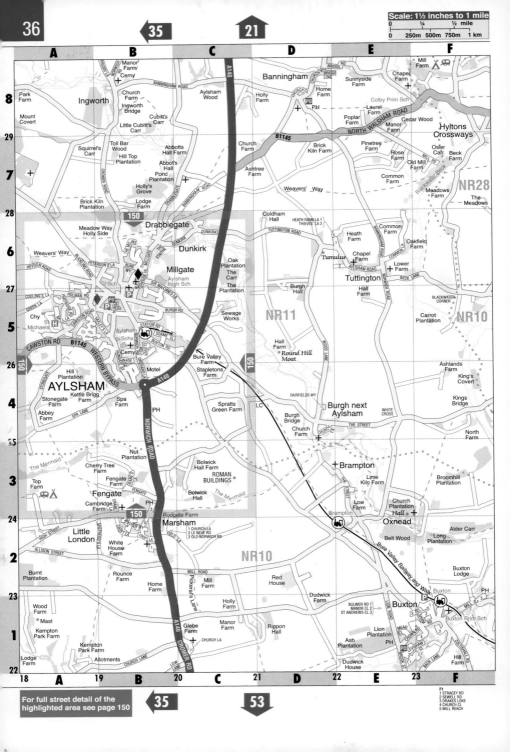

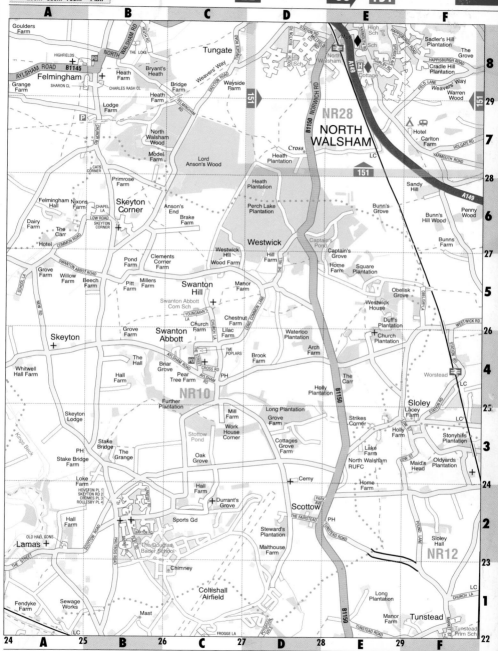

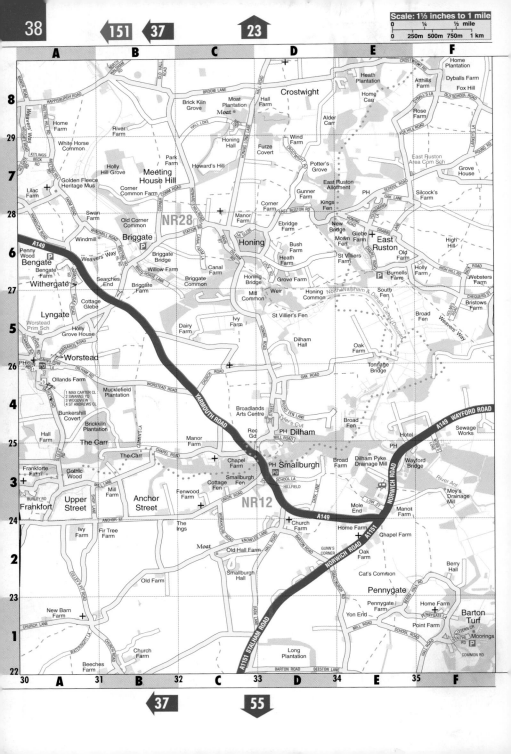

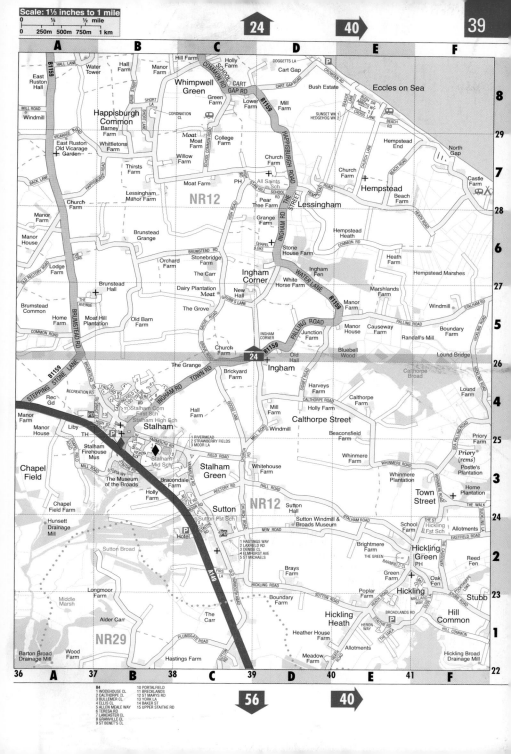

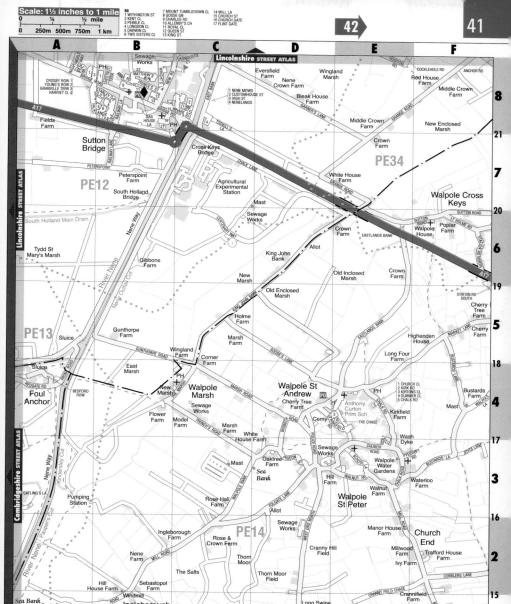

Scale: 1½ inches to 1 mile

0   ¼   ½ mile
0   250m 500m 750m 1 km

B8
1 WITHINGTON ST
2 KENT CL
3 PEBBLE CL
4 LONGDON CL
5 DARWIN CL
6 TWO SISTERS CL

7 MOUNT TUMBLEDOWN CL
8 GOOSE GN
9 CHARLES RD
10 ALLENBY'S CH
11 ROYAL CL
12 QUEEN ST
13 KING ST

14 MILL LA
15 CHURCH ST
16 CHURCH GATE
17 FLINT GATE

42

41

Lincolnshire **STREET ATLAS**

Sewage Works

Eversfield Farm

Nene Crown Farm

Wingland Marsh

Cockiehole Rd

Red House Farm

Anchor Rd

Middle Crown Farm

1 NENE MDWS
2 CUSTOMHOUSE ST
3 HIGH ST
4 NENELANDS

Bleak House Farm

Middle Crown Farm

New Enclosed Marsh

Crosby Row 1
Young's Row 2
Granville Terr 3
Harriet Cl 4

Fields Farm

Sutton Bridge

Cross Keys Bridge

Crown Farm

PE34

Peterspoint Farm

South Holland Bridge

PE12

Agricultural Experimental Station

White House Farm

Walpole Cross Keys

South Holland Main Drain

Mast

Sewage Works

Crown Farm

Walpole House

Poplar Farm

Tydd St Mary's Marsh

Gibbons Farm

King John Bank

Allot

Eastlands Bank

Crown Farm

PE13

Sluice

Gunthorpe Farm

New Marsh

Old Inclosed Marsh

Crown Farm

Cherry Tree Farm

Cherry Tree Farm

East Marsh

Wingland Farm

Holme Farm

Old Enclosed Marsh

Highenden House

Sluice

Corner Farm

Marsh Farm

Long Four Farm

Bustards Farm

Foul Anchor

Bedford Row

New Marsh

Walpole Marsh

Walpole St Andrew

Kirkfield Farm

Mast

Flower Farm

Sewage Works

Cherry Tree Farm

1 CHURCH CL
2 KIRK RD
3 KIRTONS CL
4 SUMMER CL
5 CHALK RD

Model Farm

Marsh Farm

White House Farm

Anthony Curton Prim Sch

Wash Dyke

Mast

Oaktree Farm

Sewage Works

Walpole Water Gardens

Waterloo Farm

Sea Bank

Hill Farm

Walnut Farm

Pumping Station

Rose Hall Farm

Allot

Walpole St Peter

Ingleborough Farm

Rose & Crown Farm

Sewage Works

Manor House Farm

Church End

PE14

Millwood Farm

Trafford House Farm

Nene Farm

Thorn Moor

Cranny Hill Field

Ivy Farm

The Salts

Thorn Moor Field

Cobblers Lane

Hill House Farm

Sebastopol Farm

Cranfield Farm

Sea Bank

Windmill

Ingleborough

Mast

Long Swine Holme Field

Honington House Farm

Grange Farm

The Old Grange Farm

Dixon's Dro

Strattons Farm

Moat

Mill House Peartree Farm

Sewage Works

Five-Alls Rd

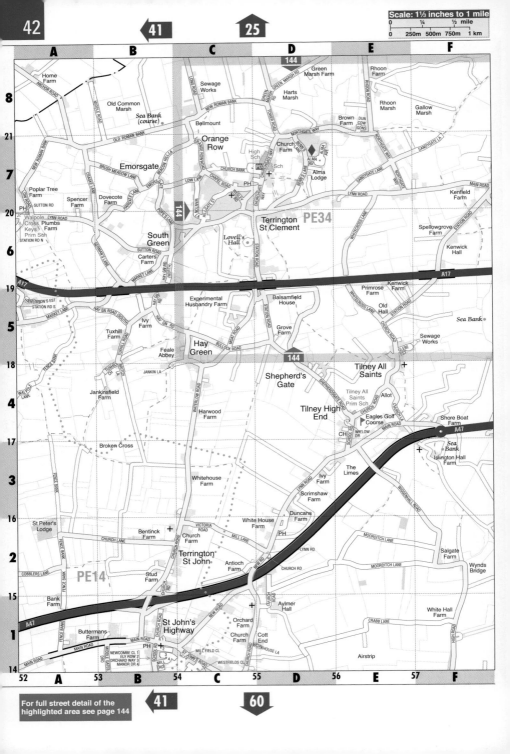

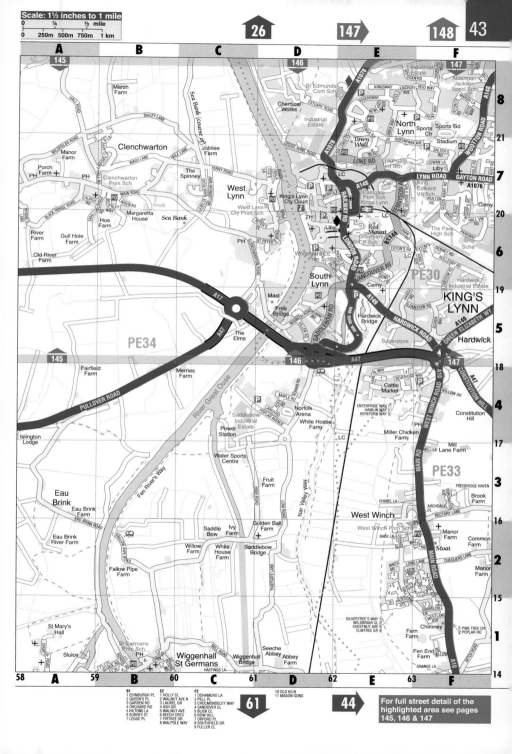

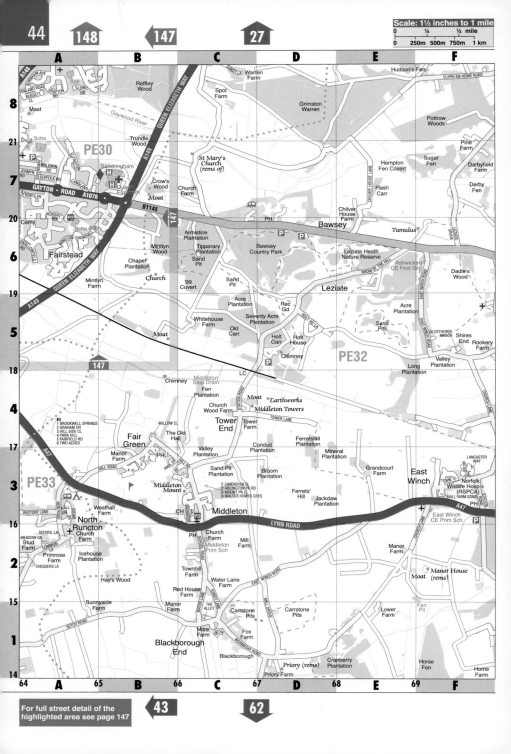

Scale: 1⅓ inches to 1 mile
0   ¼   ½ mile
0   250m 500m 750m 1 km

A   B   C   D   E   F

8
A148
BIRDBEAM AVE
FENLAND ROAD
RUSSELL CL
GRAFTON RD
Sch
C.E.SWDG DR
Reffley Wood
Spot Farm
Warren Farm
SANDY LA
Grimston Warren
Hudson's Fen
CLIFFE-EN-HOWE ROAD
Mast
Gaywood River
Pottrow Woods

21
Schs
Trundle Wood
PE30
St Mary's Church (rems of)
Hempton Fen Covert
Sugar Fen
Pine Farm
Darbyfield Farm

7
JERMYN RD
BALDWIN RD
SUFFOLK RD
ANGLIA RD
Sandringham
H
Queen Elizabeth
Crow's Wood
Church Farm
Flash Carr
CHILVER HOUSE LANE
Derby Fen
GAYTON · ROAD A1076
REGENTS CL
Moat
B1145

20
HICKORY RD
Cemy
WINSTON CHURCHILL
Schs
147
Armistice Plantation
PH
Chilver House Farm
Bawsey
Tumulus
LEZIATE DROVE

6
Fairstead
QUEEN ELIZABETH WAY
Mintlyn Wood
Chapel Plantation
Church
Tipperary Plantation
Sand Pit
Bawsey Country Park
P   P
Leziate Heath Nature Reserve
BROW OF THE HILL
Ashwicken CE First Sch
Dadle's Wood
EAST WINCH ROAD

19
A149
Mintlyn Farm
99 Covert
Sand Pit
Leziate
Acre Plantation
GLOSTHORPE MANOR
+

5
Moat
Whitehouse Farm
Old Carr
Seventy Acre Plantation
Rec Gd
Holt Carr
Holt House
HOLT HO LA
Sand Pits
Shires End
Rookery Farm

18
147
Chimney
Middleton Stop Drain
LC
Chimney
P
PE32
Long Plantation
Valley Plantation
CHURCH LANE

4
A47
Fen Plantation
Church Wood Farm
Moat
Earthworks
Middleton Towers
STATION ROAD

17
B3
1 BROOKWELL SPRINGS
2 GRAHAM DR
3 HILL SIDE CL
4 PARK HILL
5 FAIRFIELD RD
6 TWO ACRES
WILLOW CL
The Old Hall
Tower End
Tower Farm
TOWER LANE
Ferretshill Plantation
Mineral Plantation
LANCASTER WAY
Fair Green
Manor Farm
HILL ROAD
PH
Valley Plantation
Conduit Plantation
Grandcourt Farm
East Winch
TOWN CL
Norfolk Wildlife Hosp (RSPCA)
HALL FARM GDNS
STATION

3
PE33
Westhall Farm
Middleton Mount
Sand Pit Plantation
Broom Plantation
Ferrets' Hill
Jackdaw Plantation
PH
+
1 CAVENDISH CL
2 ARLINGTON PK RD
3 MOUNT PK CL
4 WALTER HOWES CRES

16
RECTORY LANE
NEW HALL
North Runcton
Church Farm
CH
Middleton
LYNN ROAD
East Winch CE Prim Sch
P
A47

2
MEADOW GR
Stud Farm
SCHOOL LA
COMMON LA
Primrose Farm
CHEQUERS LA
Icehouse Plantation
Church Farm
PH
Middleton Prim Sch
Church Farm
Mill Farm
Townhill Farm
EAST WINCH ROAD
Manor Farm
Manor House
Moat (rems)

15
Hay's Wood
Red House Farm
Manor Farm
THE ALLEY
Water Lane Farm
WATER LANE
SANDY LANE
Carrstone Pits
Carrstone Pits
MILL DROVE
Lower Farm
Fen Pit

1
Sunnyside Farm
SETCH ROAD
Mitre Farm
Blackborough End
Fox Farm
Blackborough
Priory (rems)
Priory Farm
Cranberry Plantation
Horse Fen
Home Farm

14
64   A   65   B   66   C   67   D   68   E   69   F

43   62
For full street detail of the highlighted area see page 147

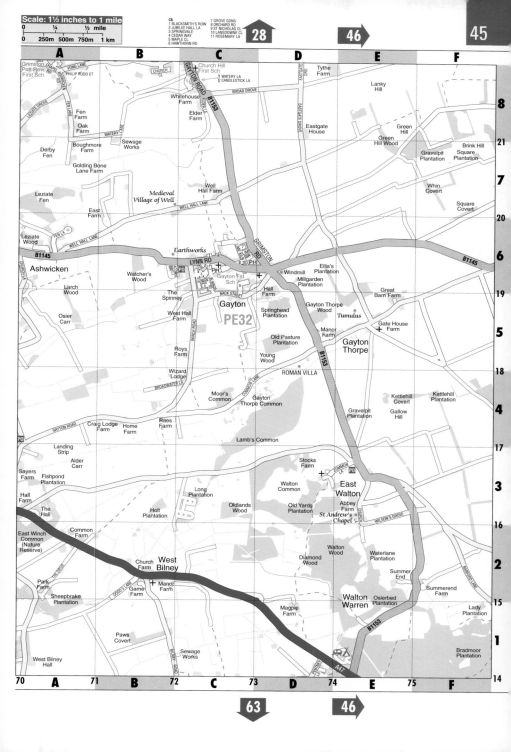

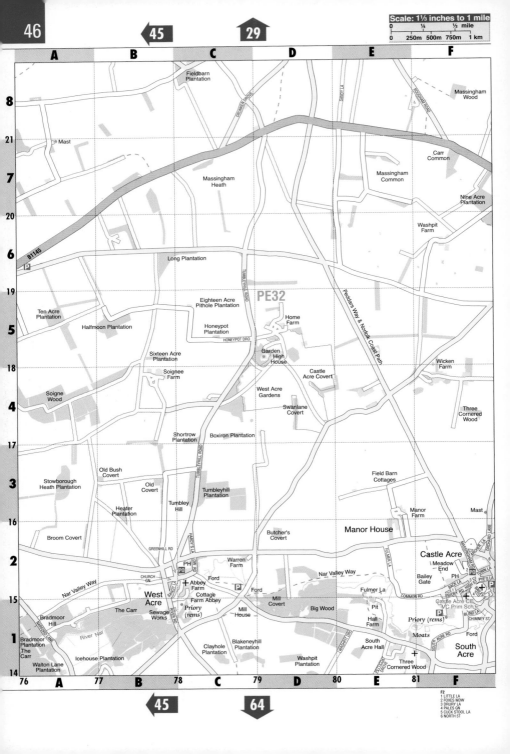

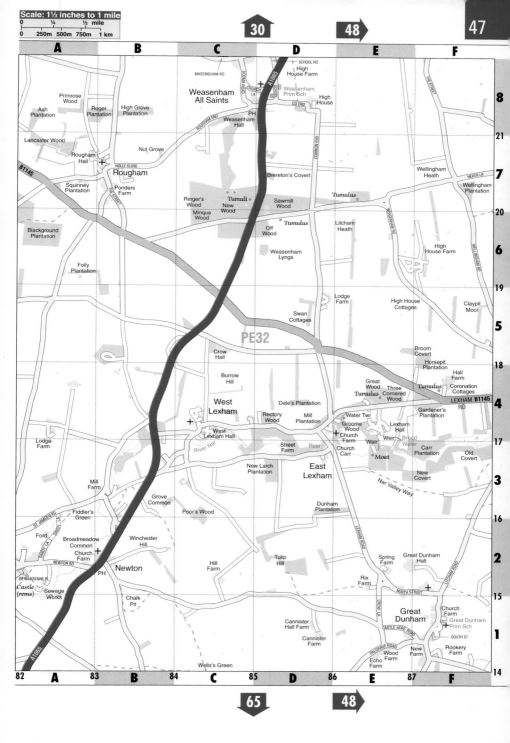

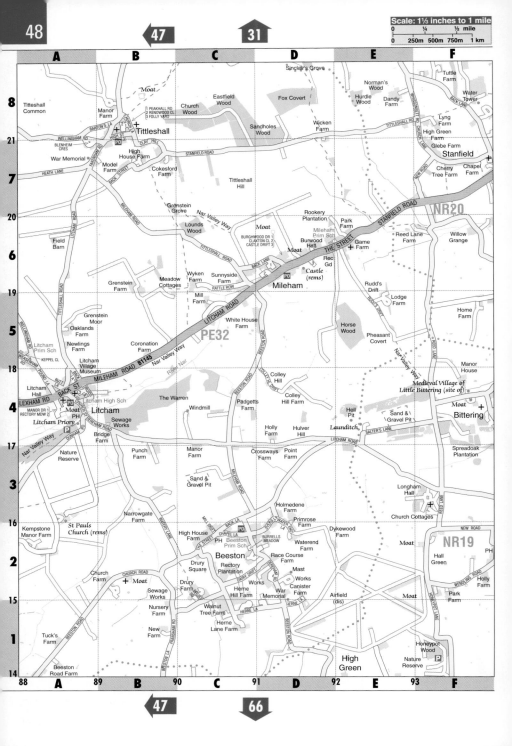

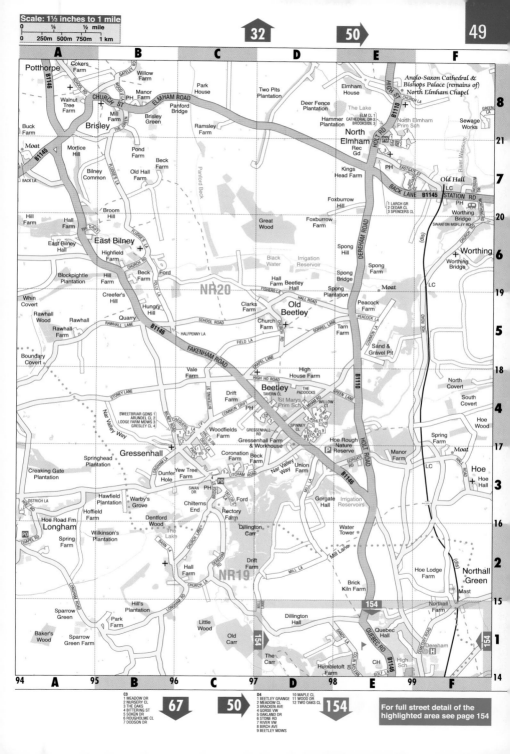

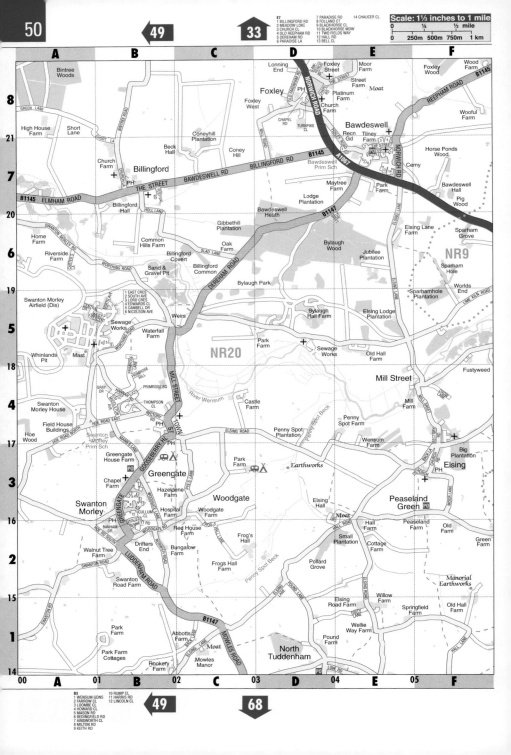

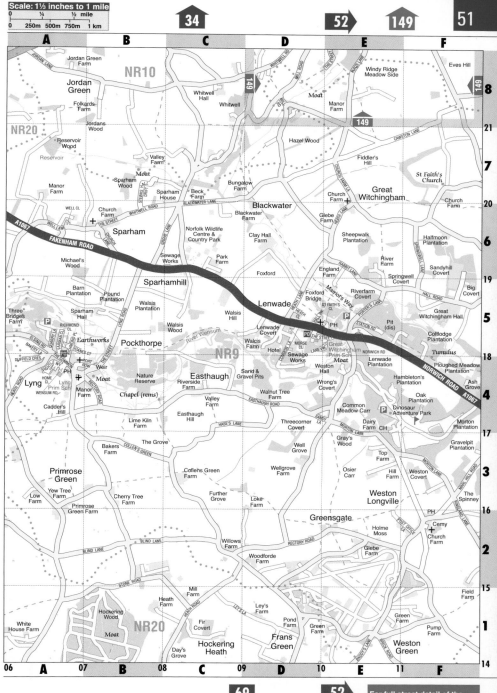

For full street detail of the highlighted area see page 149

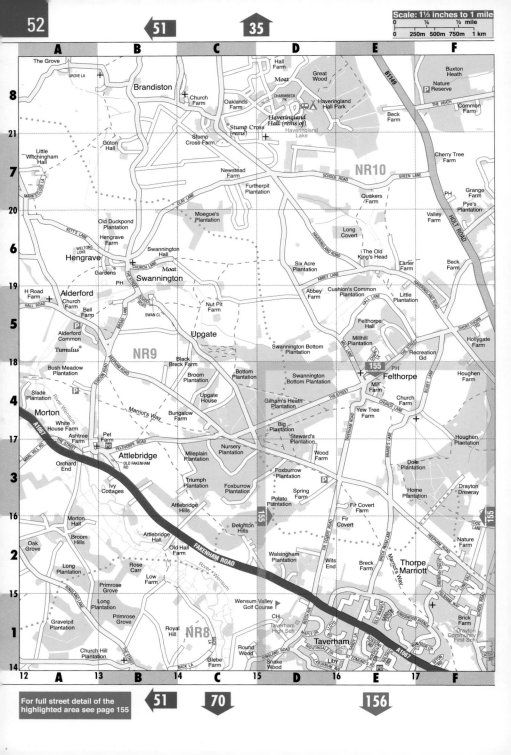

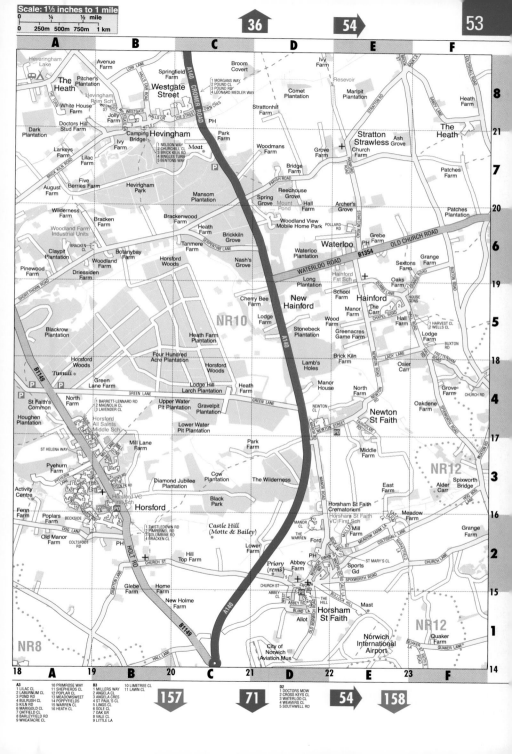

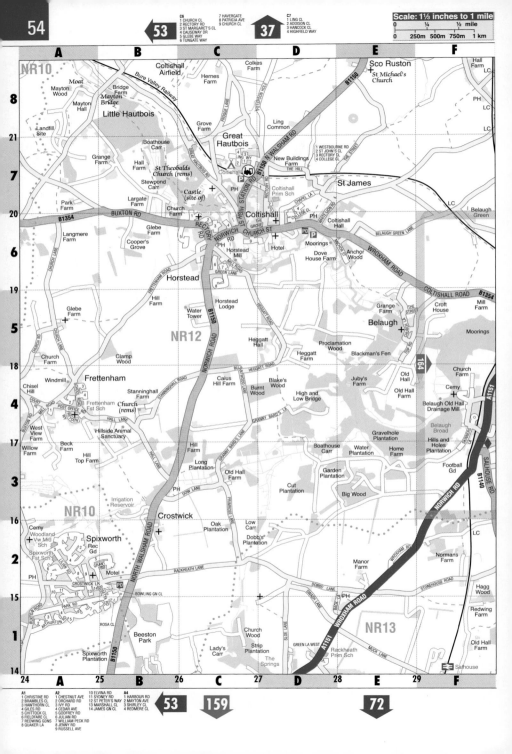

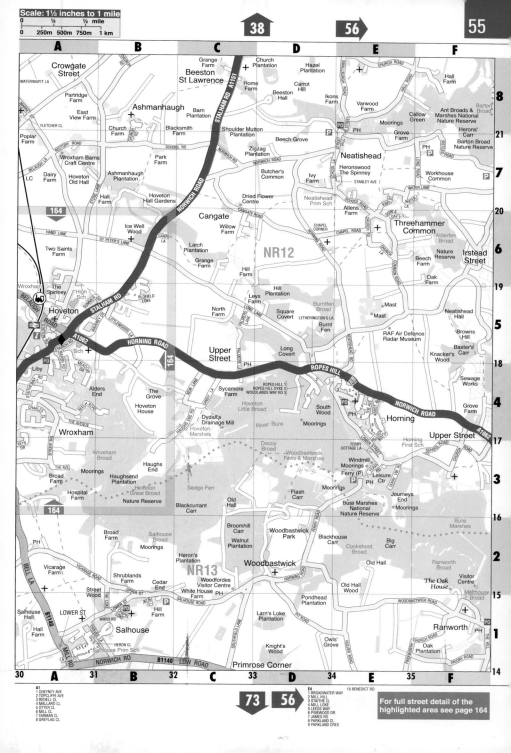

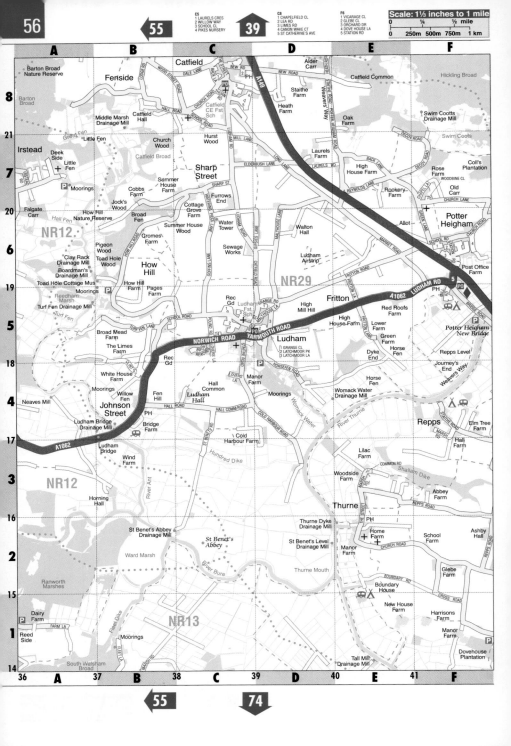

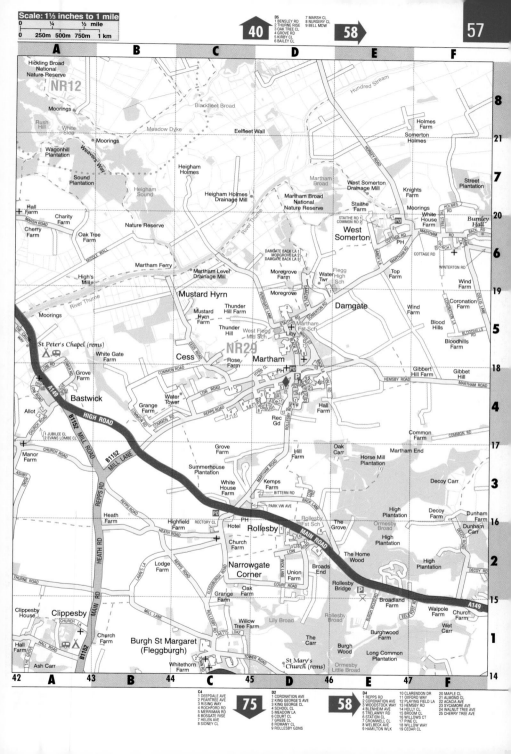

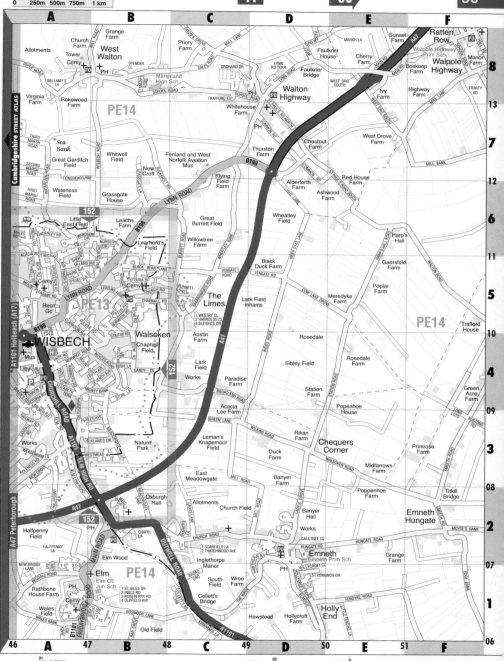

Scale: 1⅓ inches to 1 mile

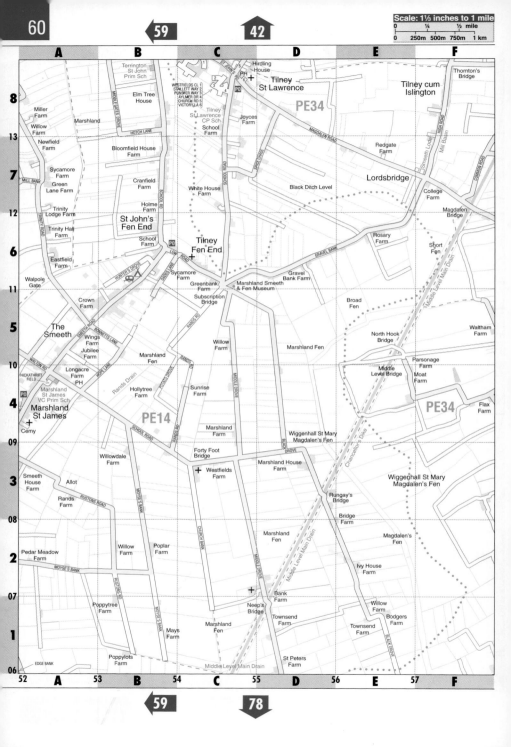

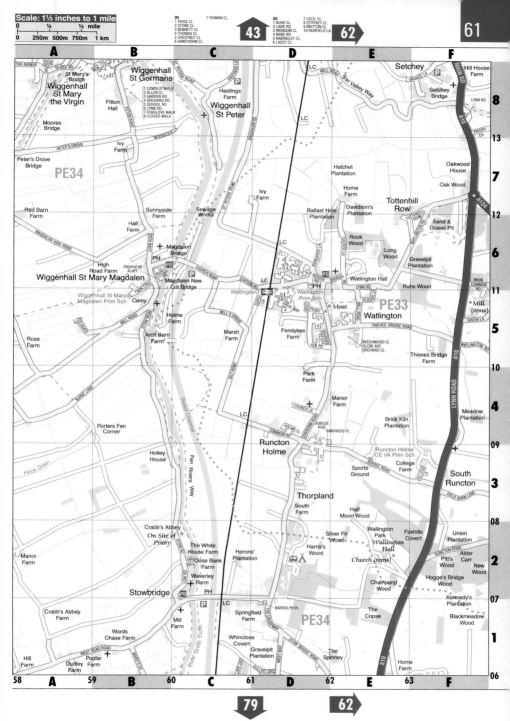

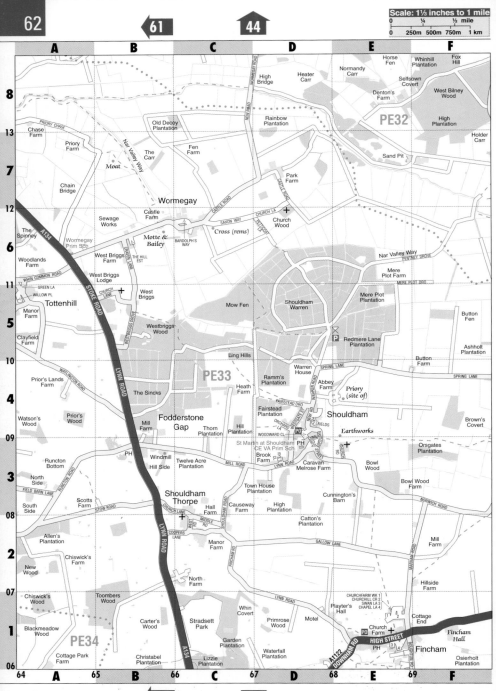

A   B   C   D   E   F

Horse Fen
Whinhill Plantation
Fox Hill

Normandy Carr
Selfsown Covert
West Bilney Wood

High Bridge
Heater Carr
Denton's Farm

PE32

High Plantation

8

Old Decoy Plantation
Rainbow Plantation
Sand Pit
Holder Carr

13

Chase Farm
Priory Farm
The Carr
Fen Farm

PRIORY CHASE
Nar Valley Way
Moat

7

Chain Bridge
Park Farm

Wormegay

CASTLE ROAD
CASTLE ROAD

12

Castle Farm
SAXON WAY
CHURCH LA
Church Wood

The Spinney
Sewage Works
Cross (rems)

A134

6

Wormegay Prim Sch
Motte & Bailey
BARDOLPH'S WAY
Nar Valley Way
FENTNEY DROVE

West Briggs Farm
THE HILL EST
CHURCH LANE

Mere Plot Farm

Woodlands Farm
West Briggs Lodge
Mere Plot Drive
MERE PLOT DRO

11

WHIN COMMON ROAD
GREEN LA
WILLOW PL
CHURCH LANE
West Briggs
Mere Plot Plantation
Button Fen

Tottenhill
STONE ROAD
WESTBRIGGS DRIVE

5

Manor Farm
Westbriggs Wood
Redmere Lane Plantation
Ashholt Plantation

Clayfield Farm
Ling Hills
Button Farm

10

PE33
Warren House
SPRING LANE
SPRING LANE

Prior's Lands Farm
WATLINGTON ROAD
LYNN ROAD
The Sincks
Ramm's Plantation
Abbey Farm
Priory (site of)

4

Heath Farm
FAIRSTEAD DRO

Watson's Wood
Prior's Wood
Mill Farm
Fodderstone Gap
Thorn Plantation
Hill Plantation
Fairstead Plantation
ORCHARD LA
WOODWARD CL
Shouldham
Earthworks
Brown's Covert

09

PH
Windmill Hill Side
Twelve Acre Plantation
St Martin at Shouldham CE VA Prim Sch
Brook Farm
LYNN ROAD
Caravan Melrose Farm
Bowl Wood
Orsgates Plantation

Runcton Bottom
MILL ROAD
Bowl Wood Farm

3

North Side
FIELD BARN LANE
Scotts Farm
STOW ROAD
Shouldham Thorpe
Town House Plantation
Cunnington's Barn
NORWICH ROAD

South Side
Hall Farm
WEST RD
MIDDLE RD
Causeway Farm
High Plantation
Catton's Plantation
Mill Farm

08

CHURCH LANE
COOPERS LANE

Allen's Plantation
Manor Farm
FINCHAM RD
GALLOW LANE
MARSHAM ROAD

2

Chiswick's Farm
North Farm

New Wood

07

Chiswick's Wood
Toombers Wood
Whin Covert
LYNN ROAD
Player's Hall
CHURCHFARM WK 1
CHURCHILL CR 2
SWAN LA 3
CHAPEL LA 4
Cottage End
Hillside Farm

Blackmeadow Wood
Carter's Wood
Stradsett Park
Primrose Wood
Motel
Church Farm
Fincham Hall

PE34
PO
PH
Fincham

1

Cottage Park Farm
Christabel Plantation
Lizzie Plantation
Garden Plantation
Waterfall Plantation
A1122
DOWNHAM RD
HIGH STREET
Osierholt Plantation

06

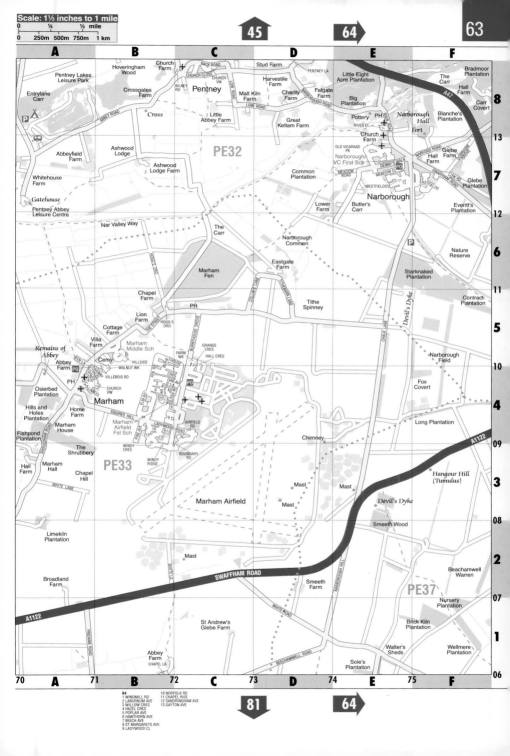

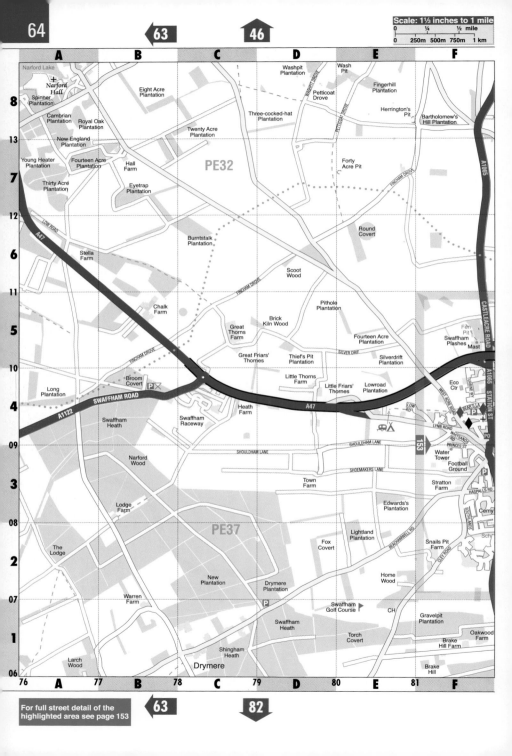

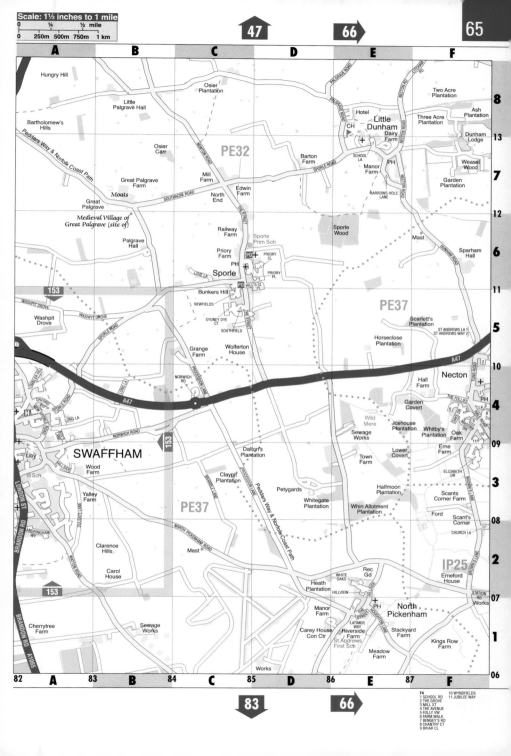

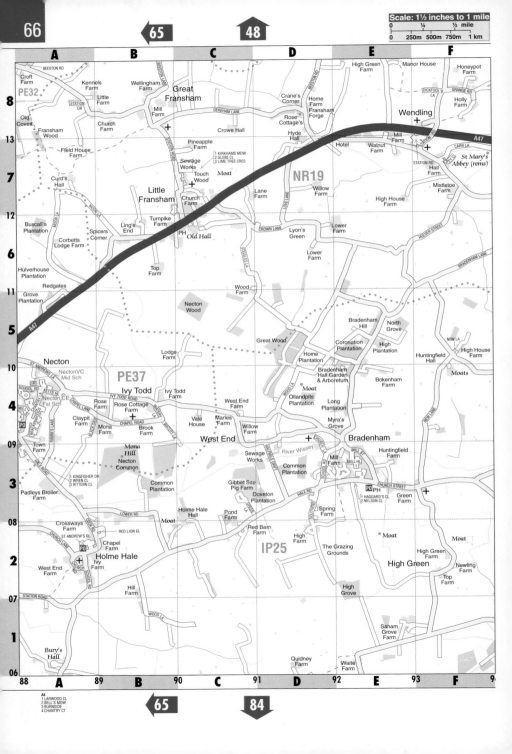

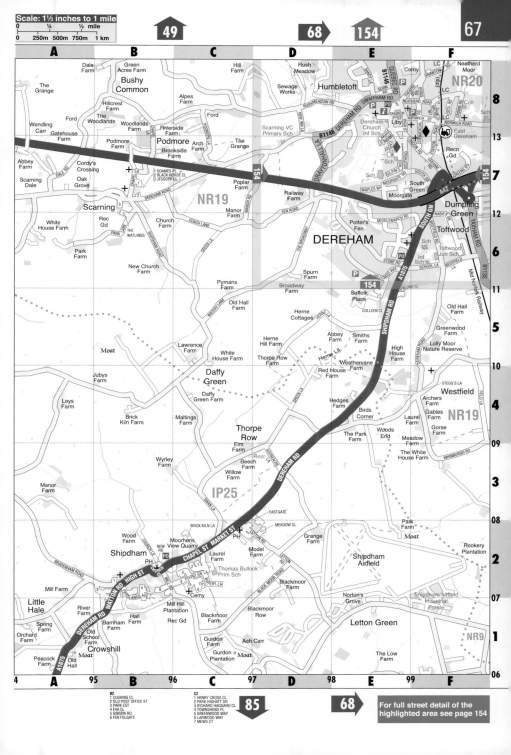

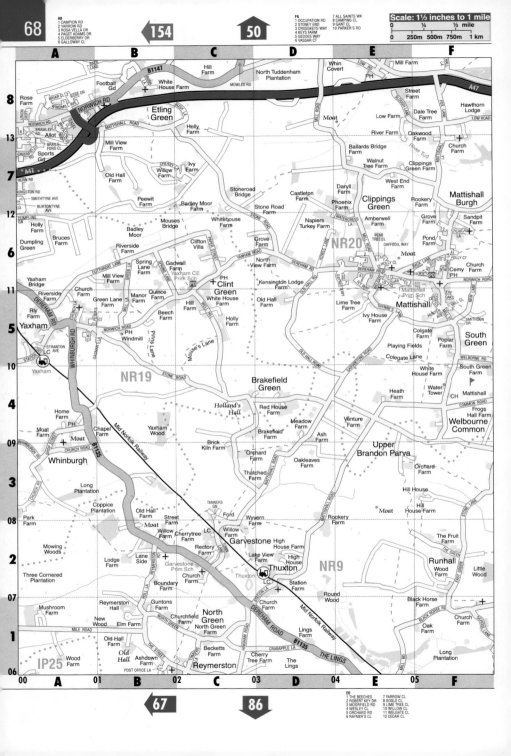

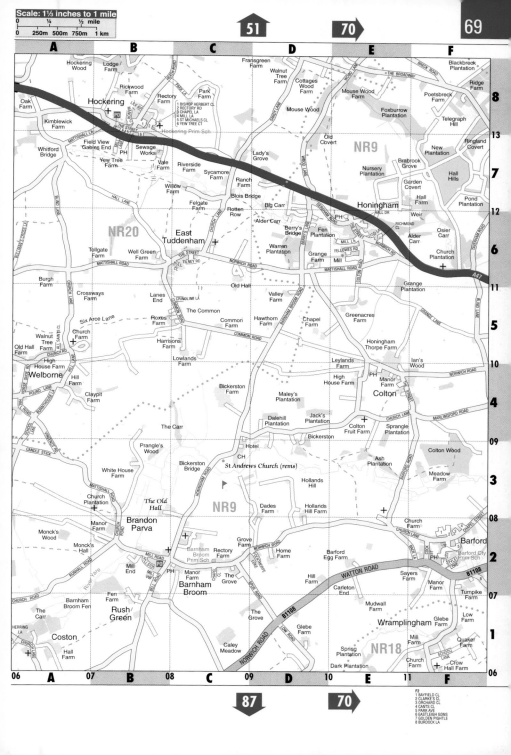

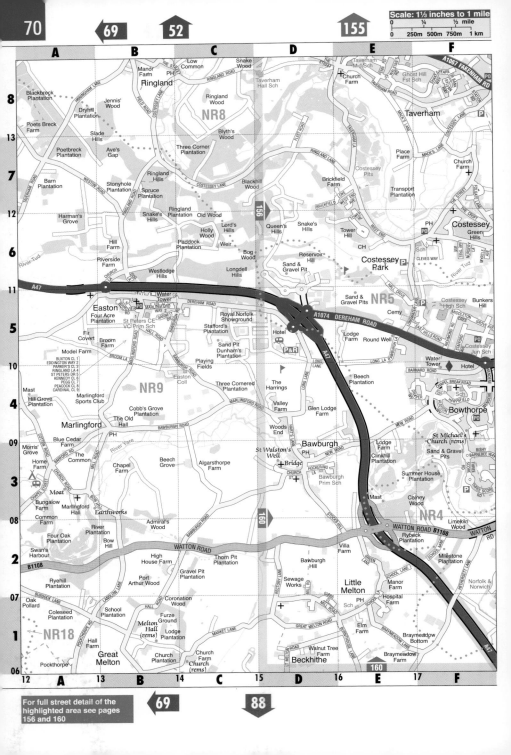

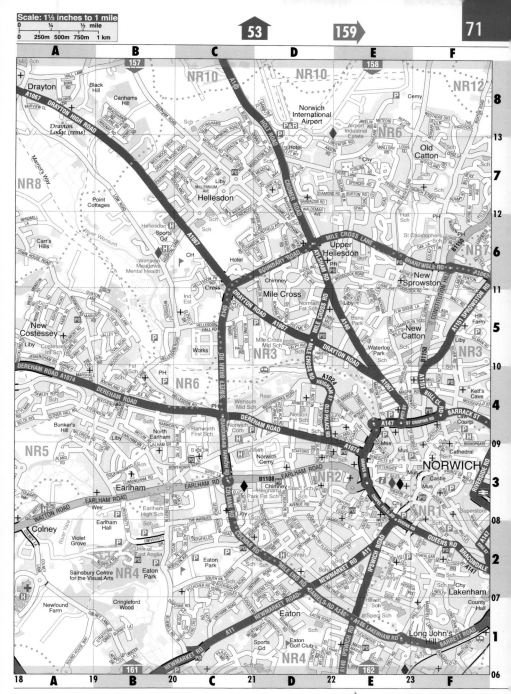

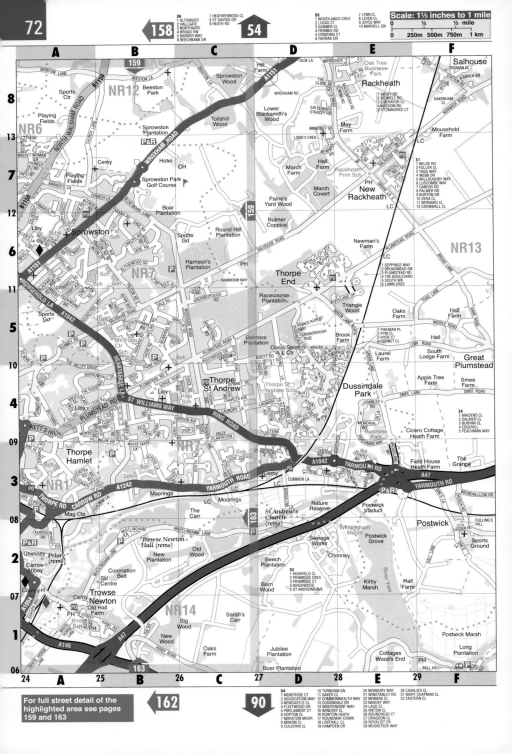

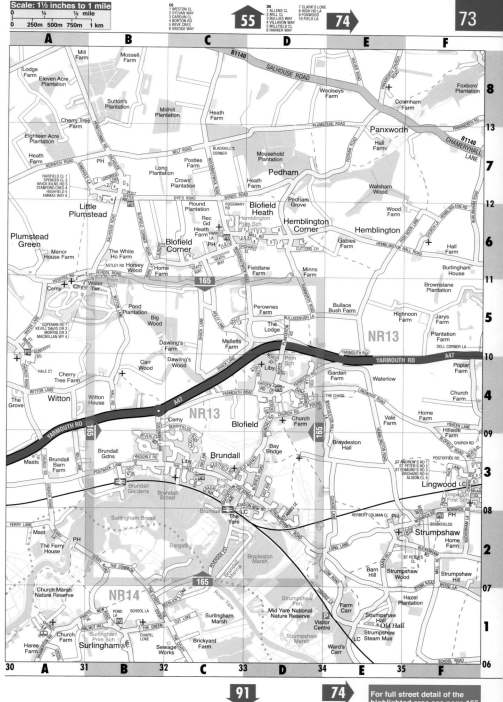

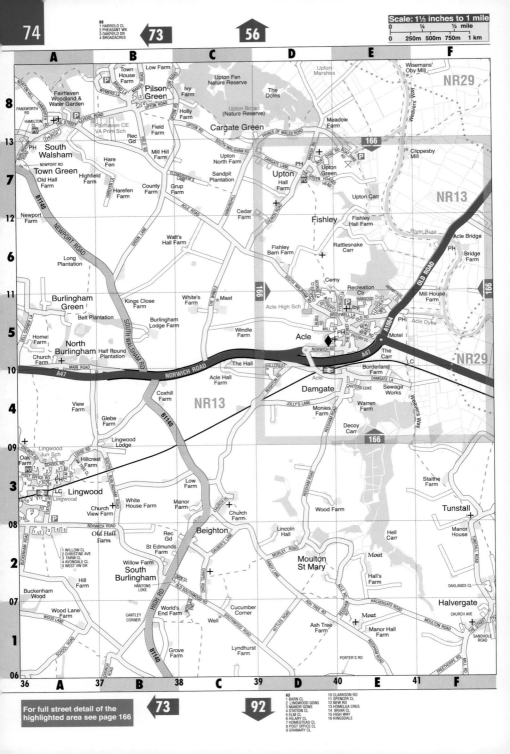

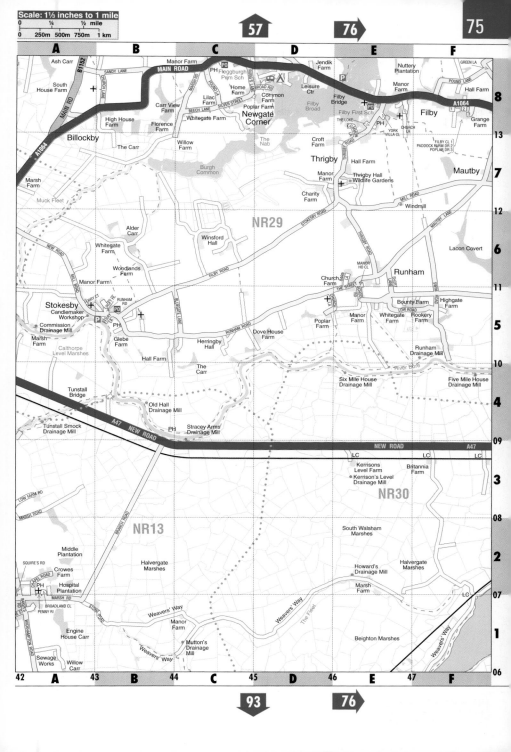

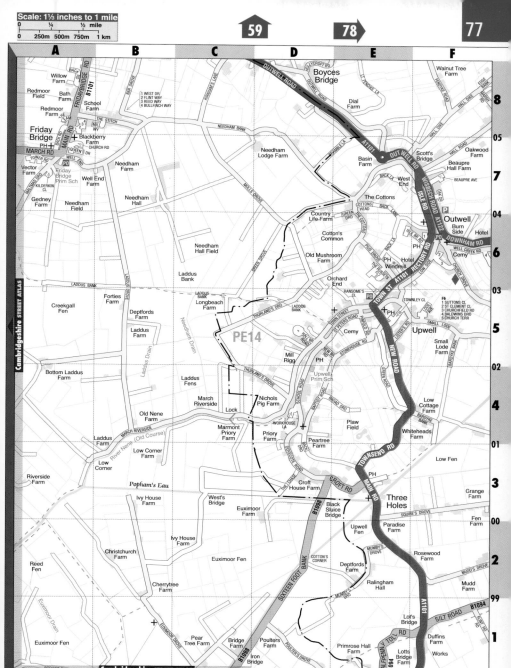

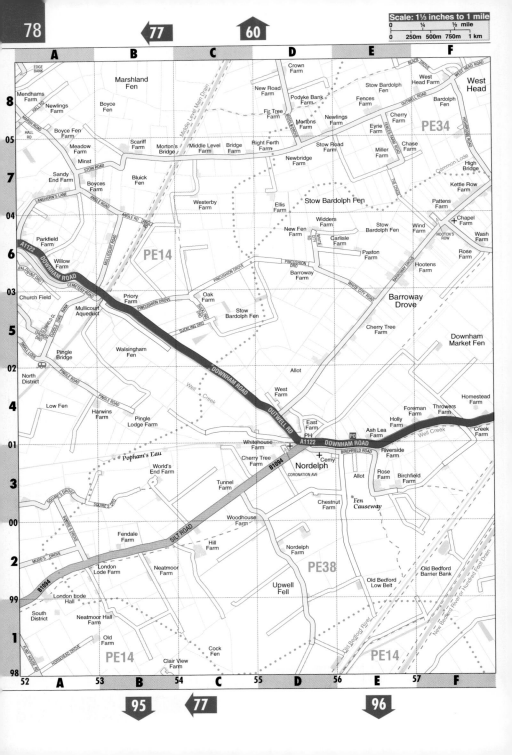

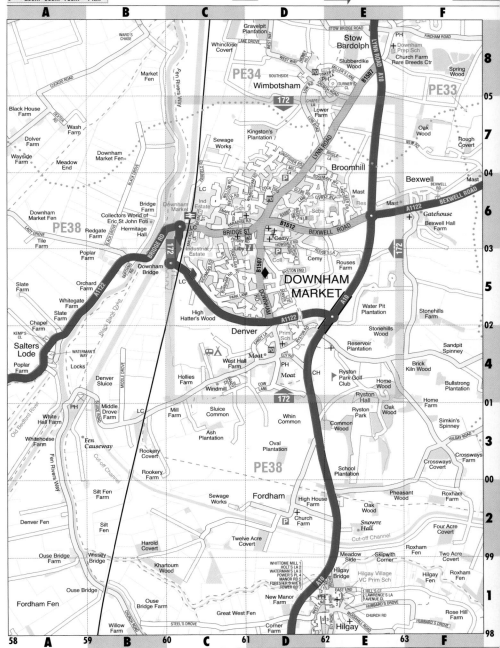

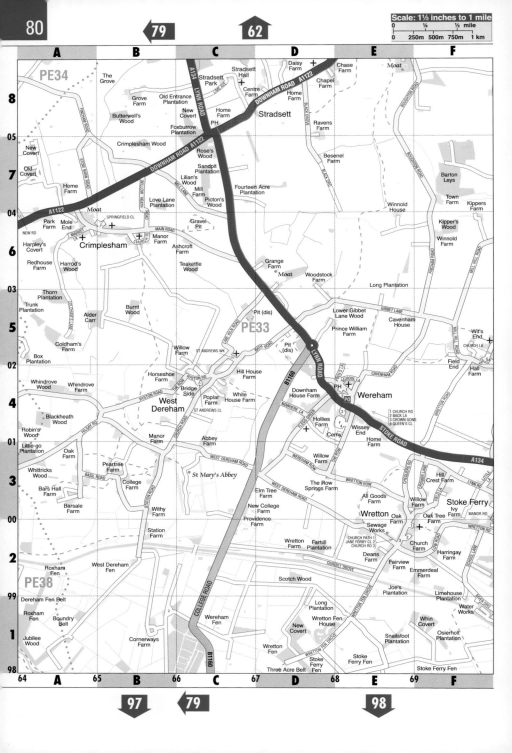

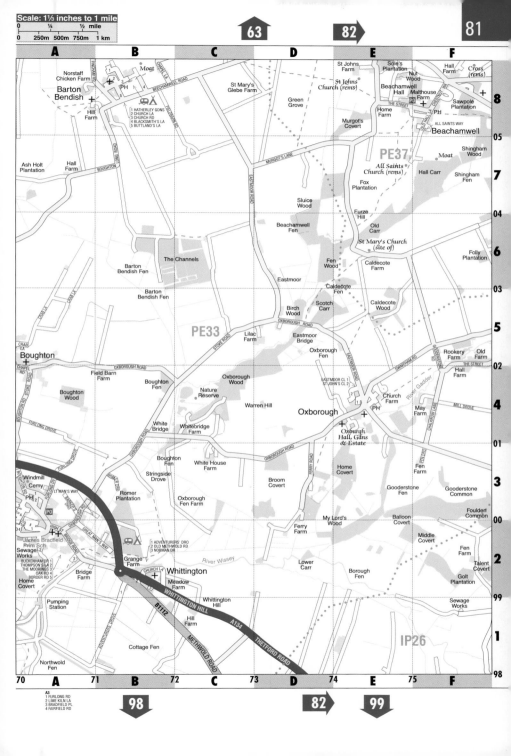

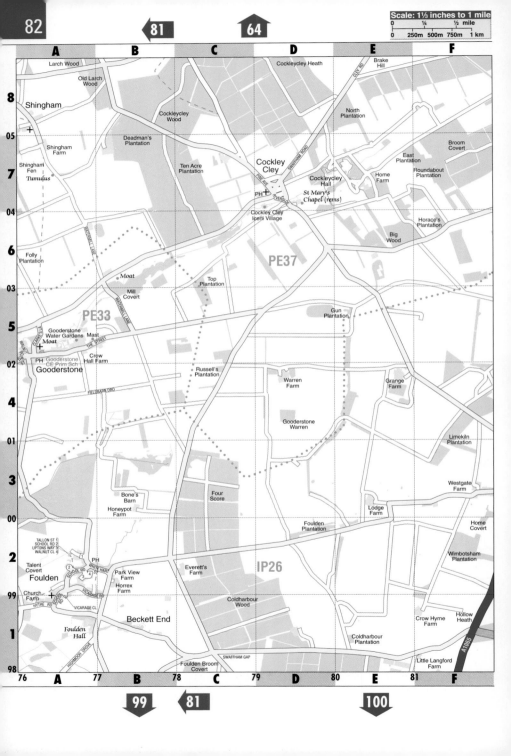

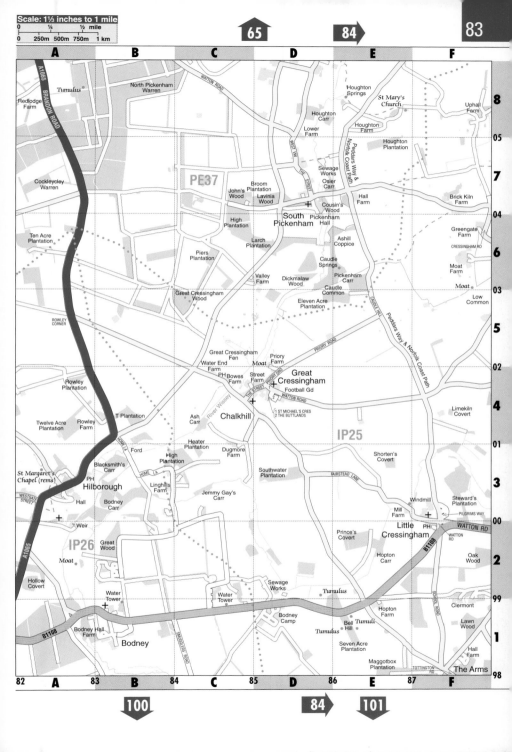

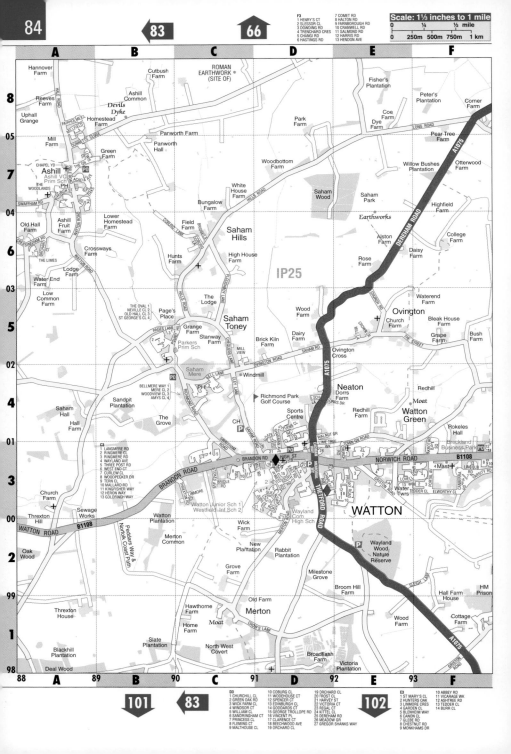

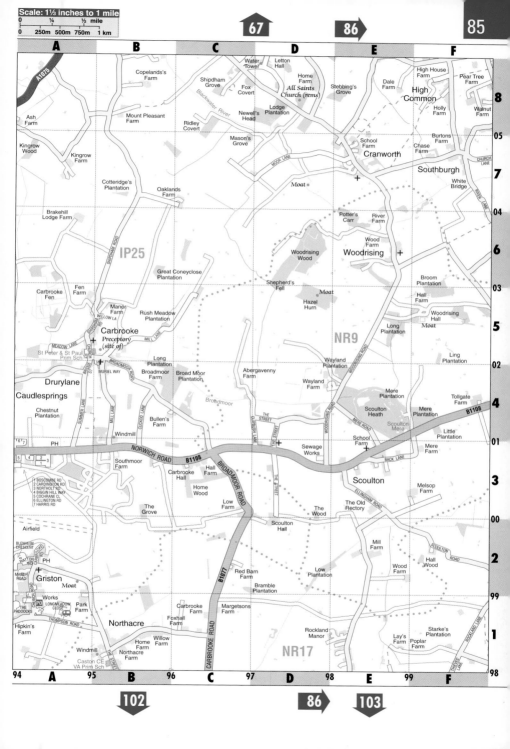

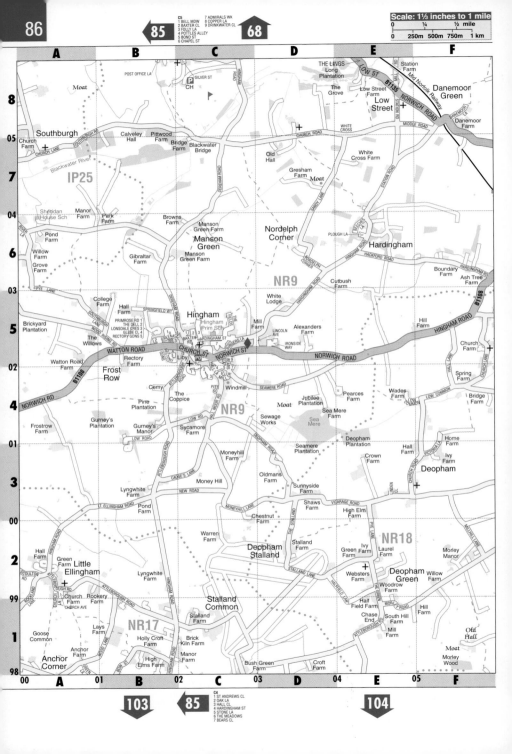

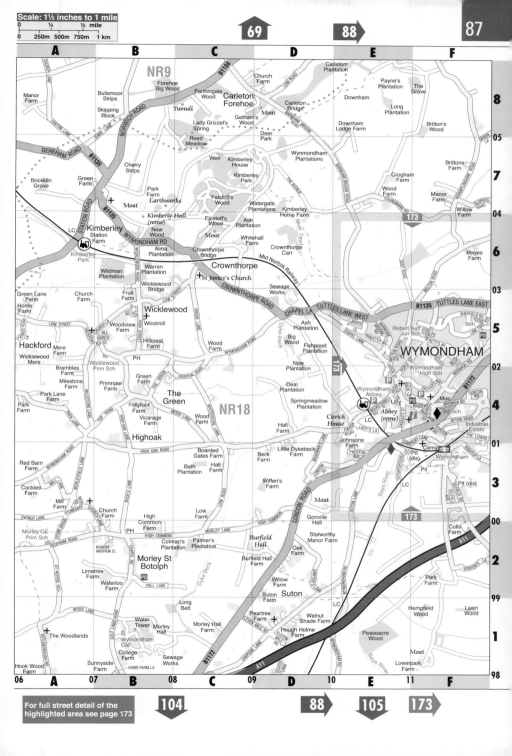

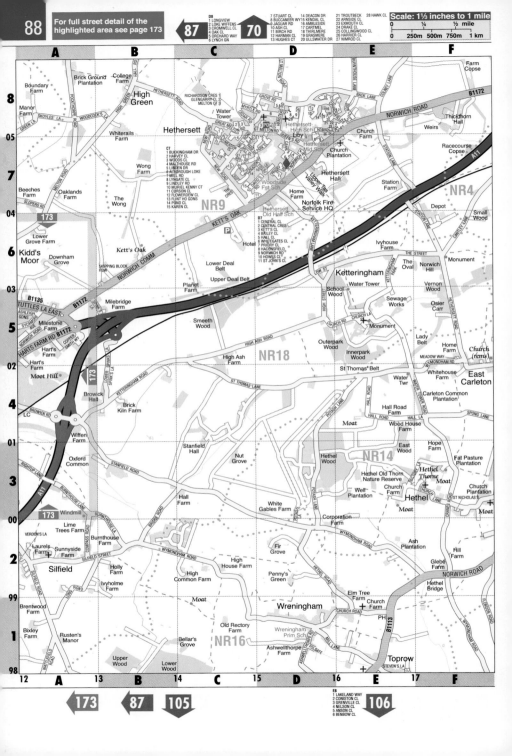

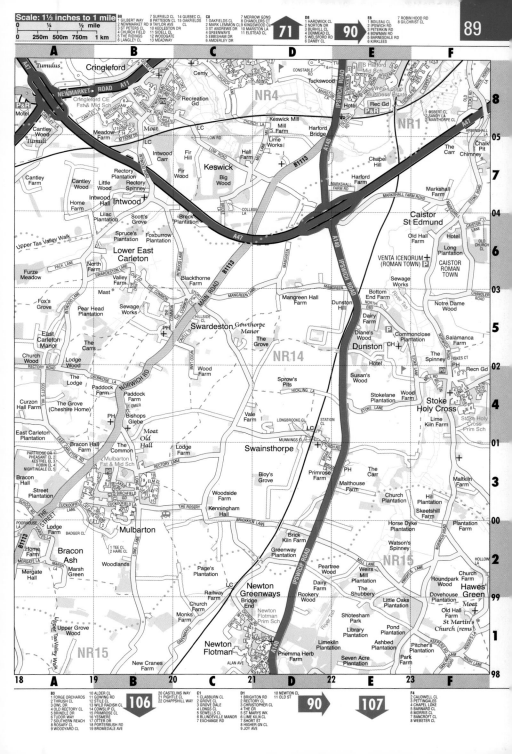

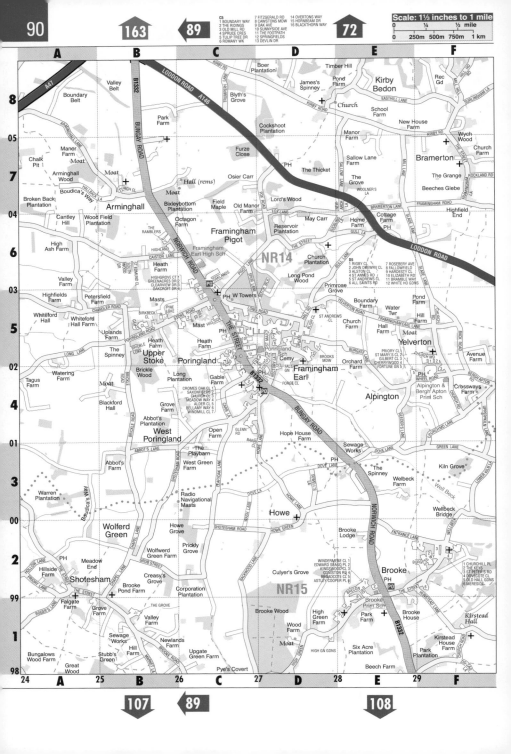

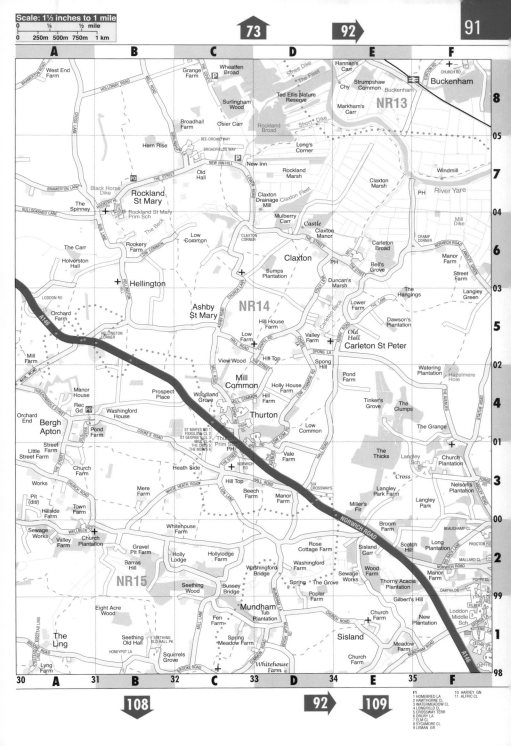

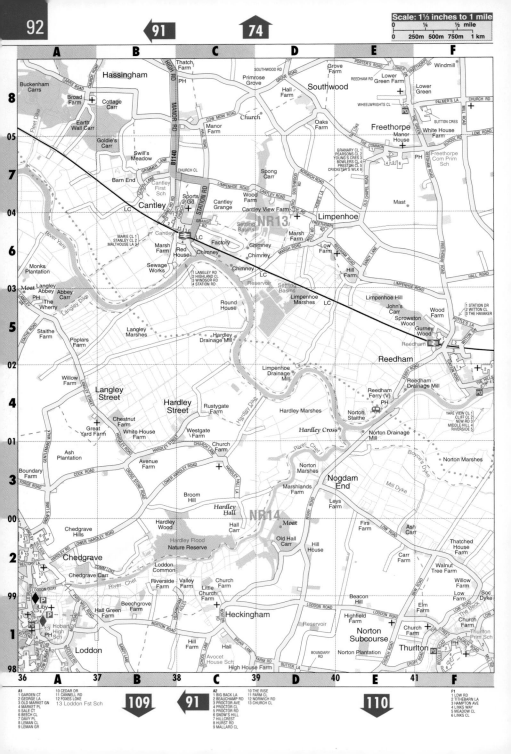

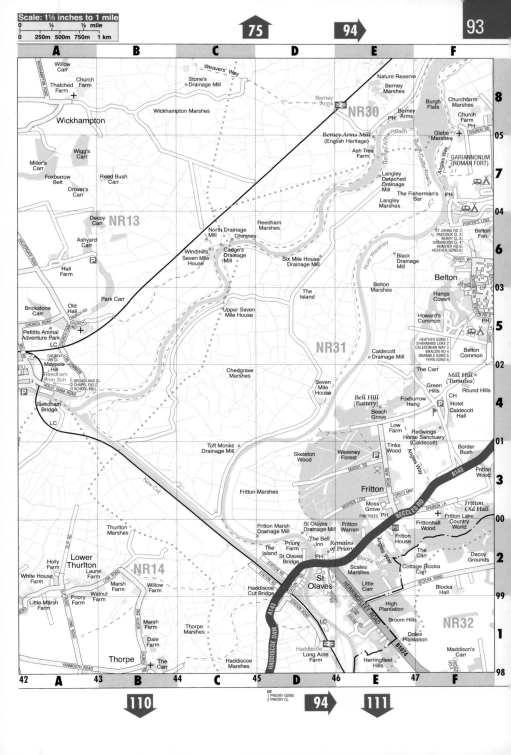

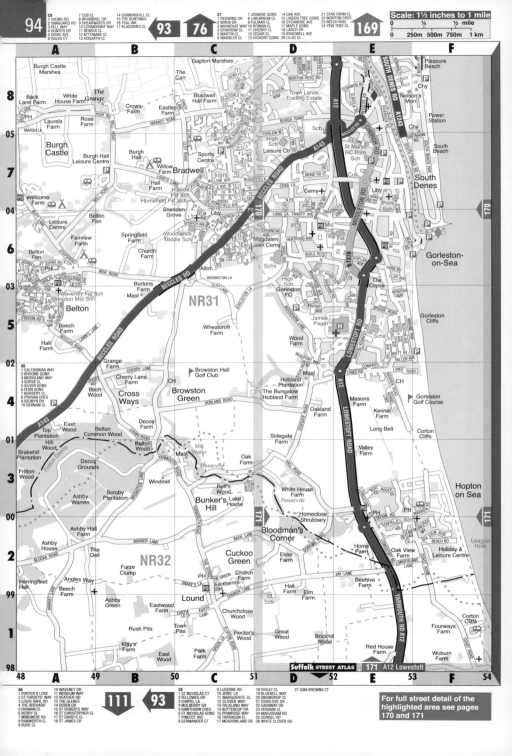

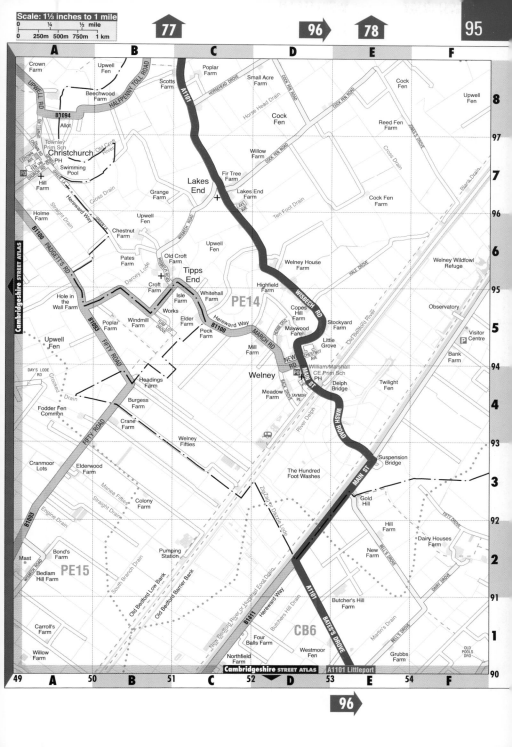

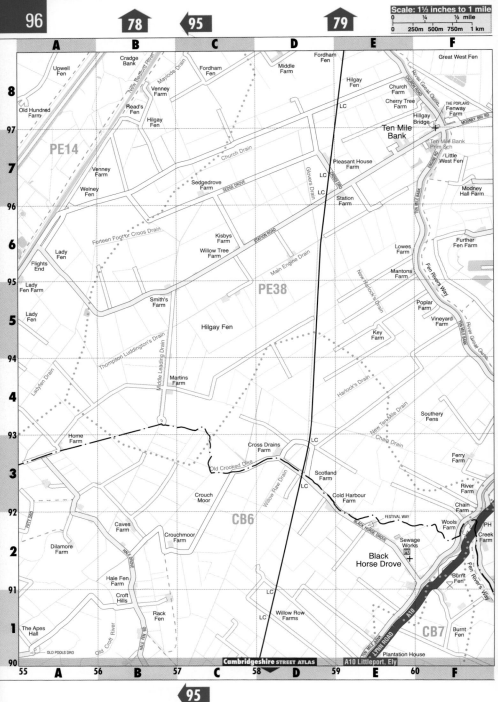

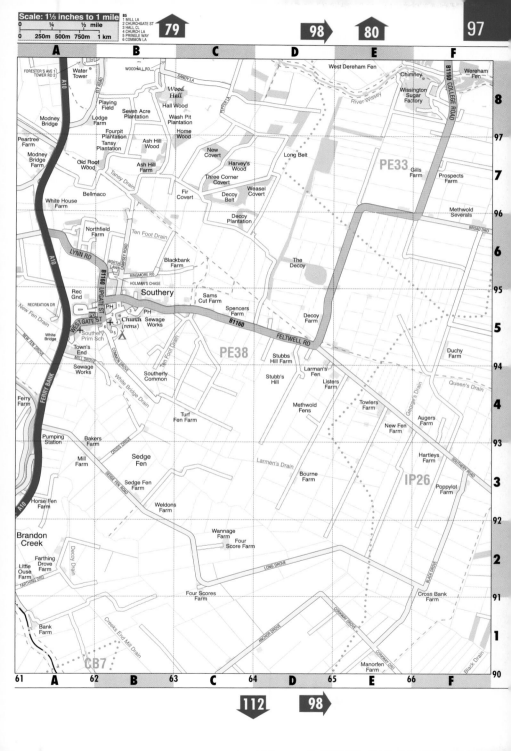

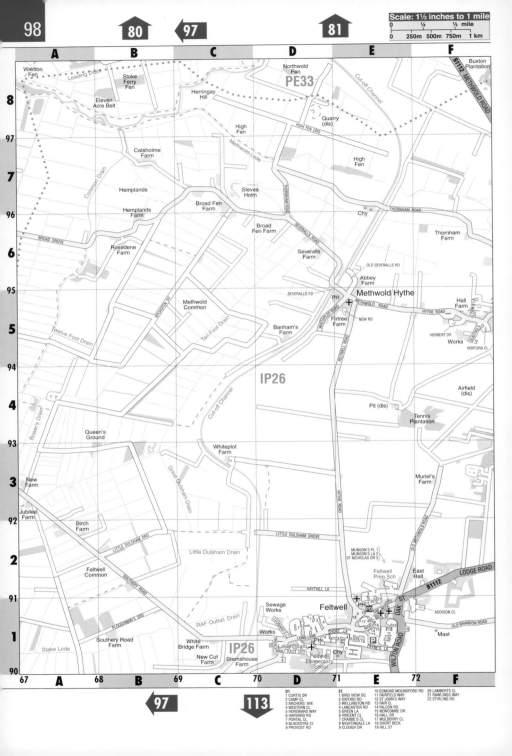

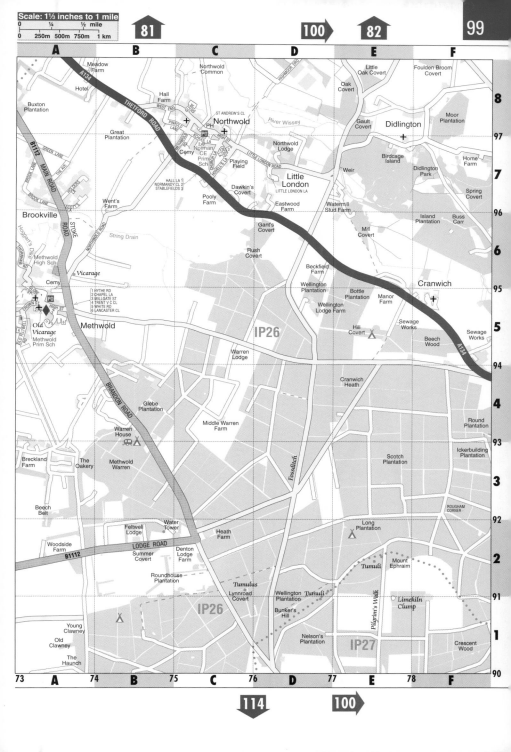

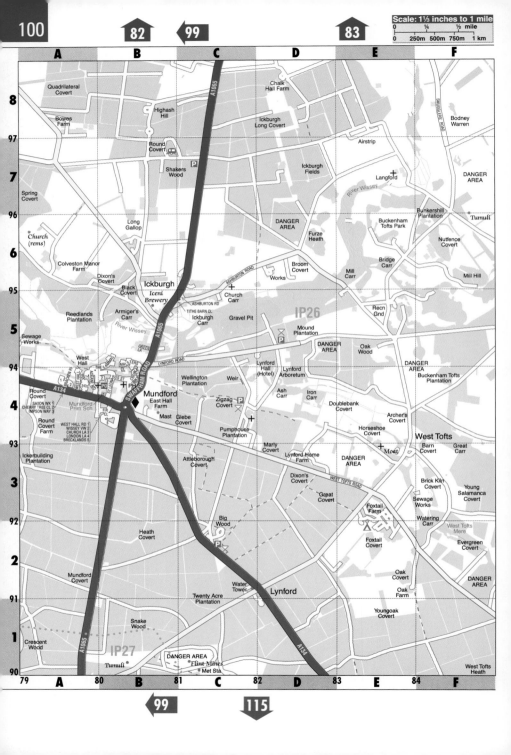

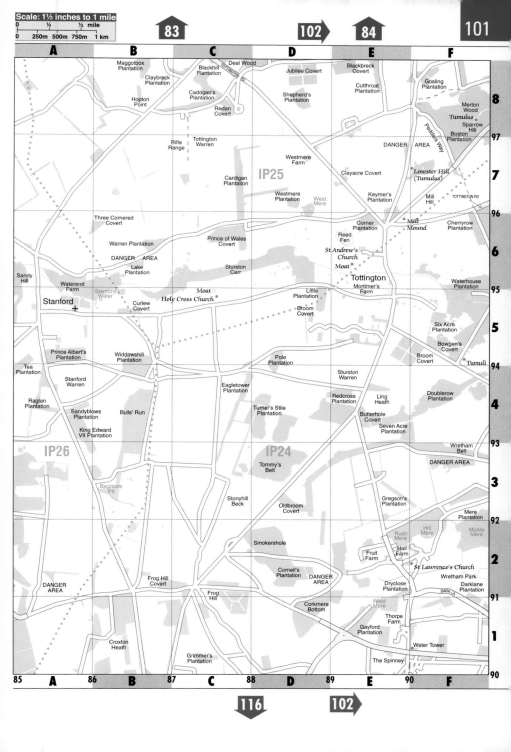

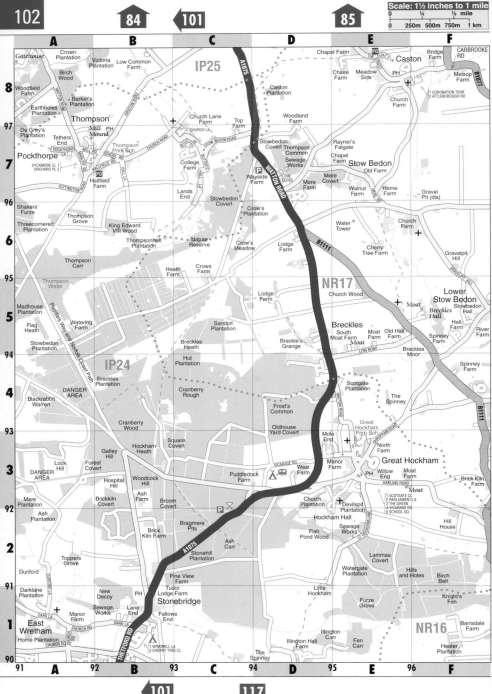

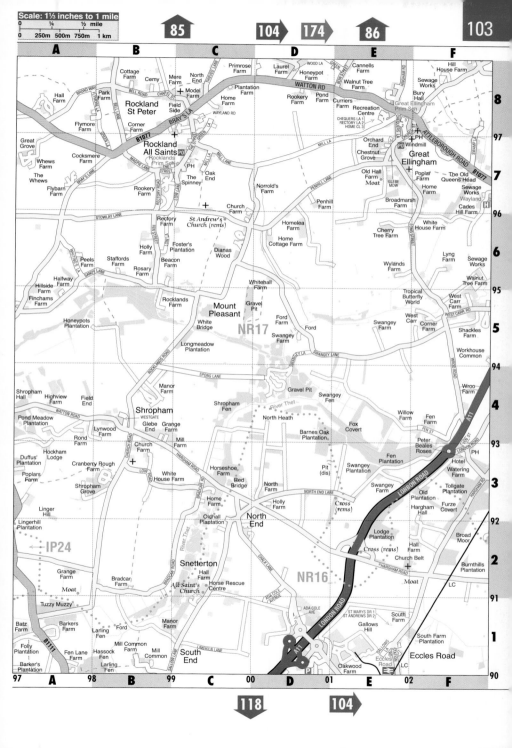

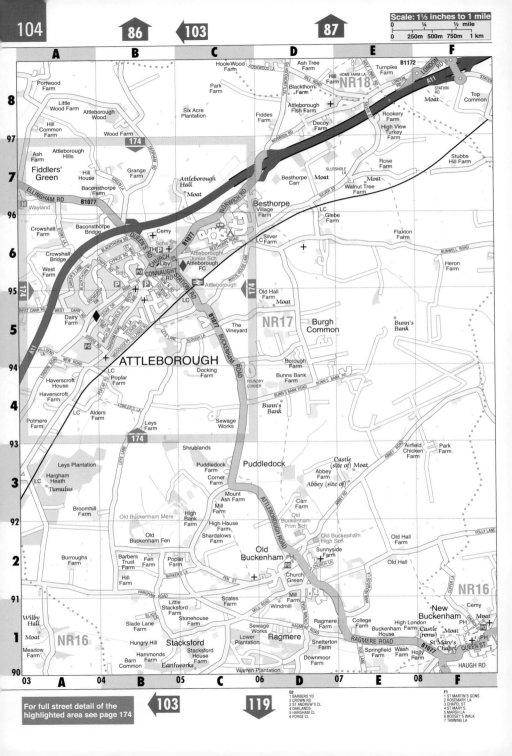

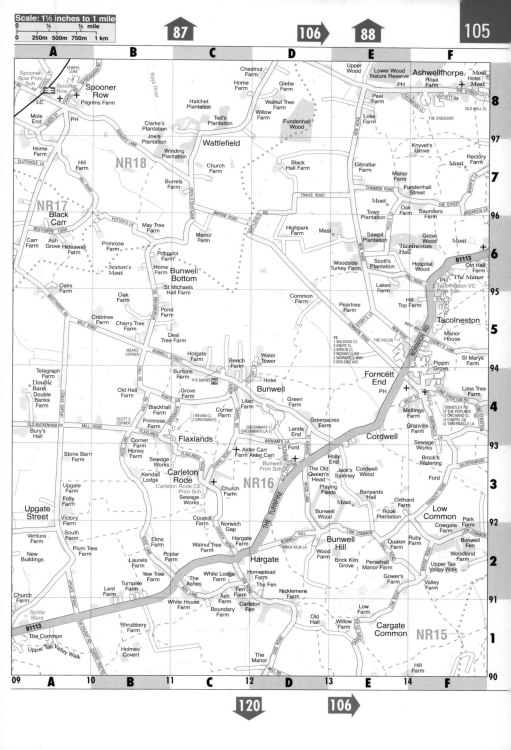

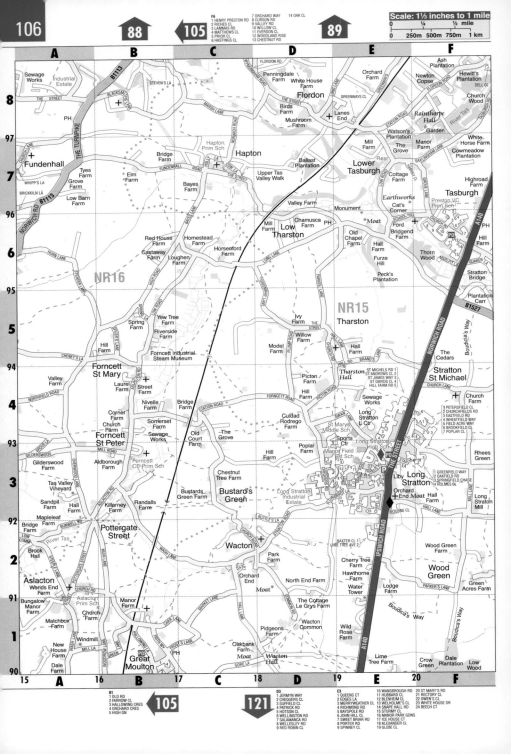

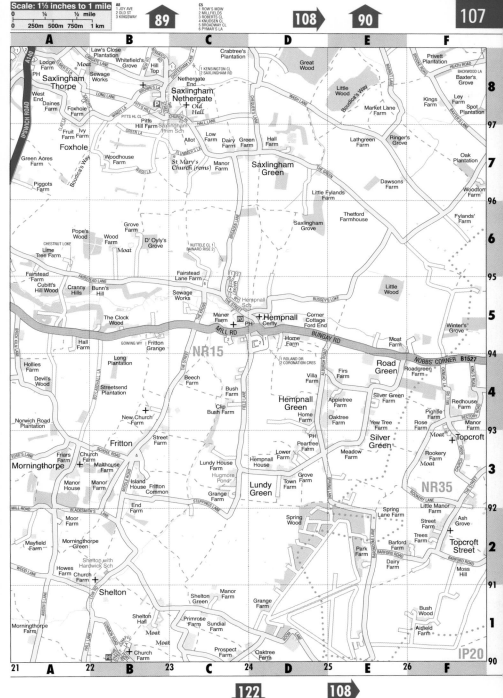

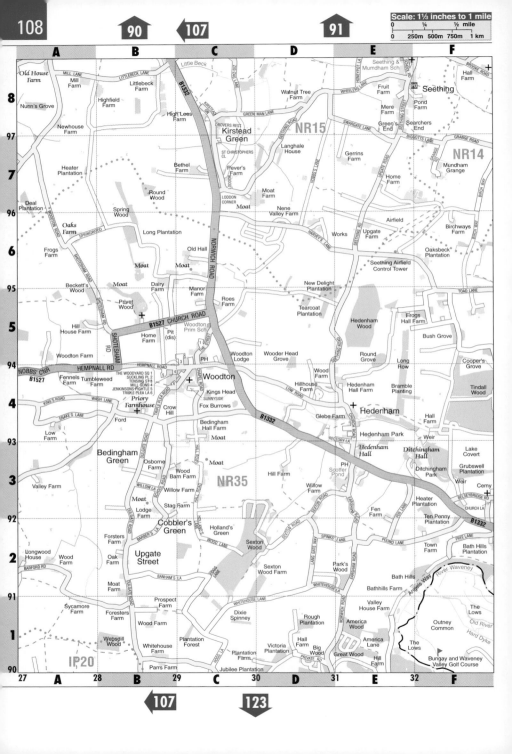

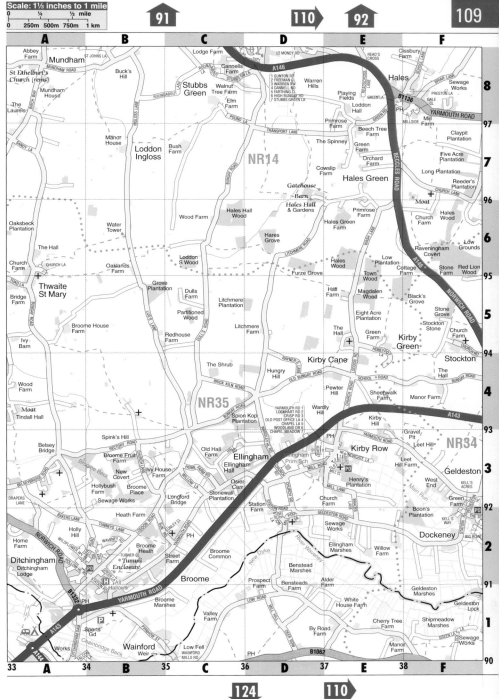

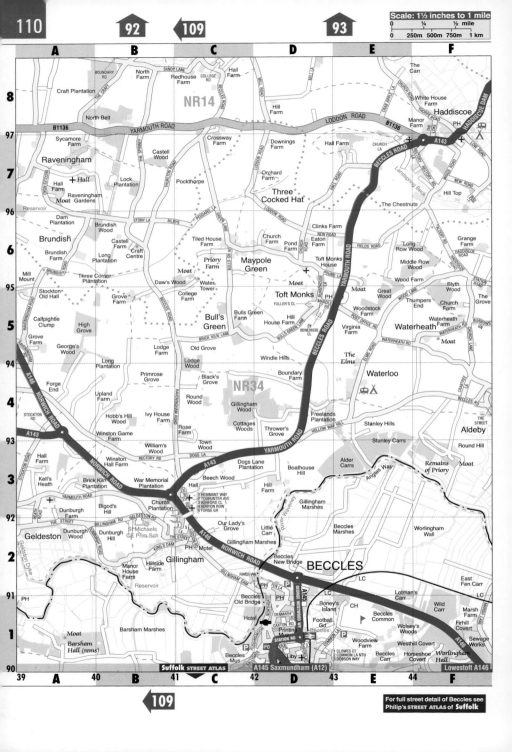

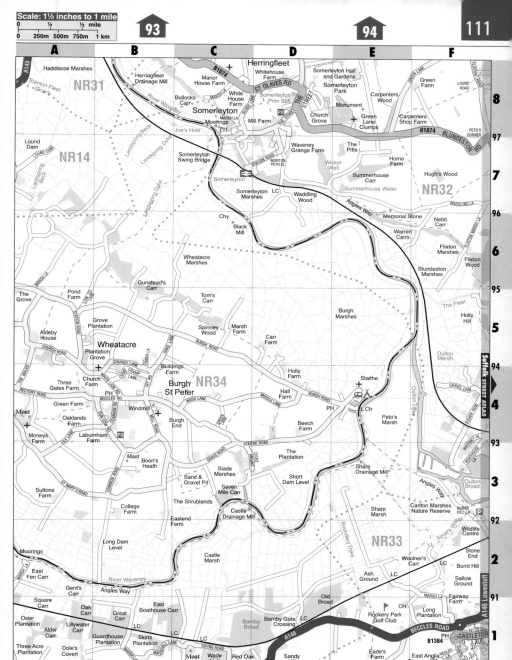

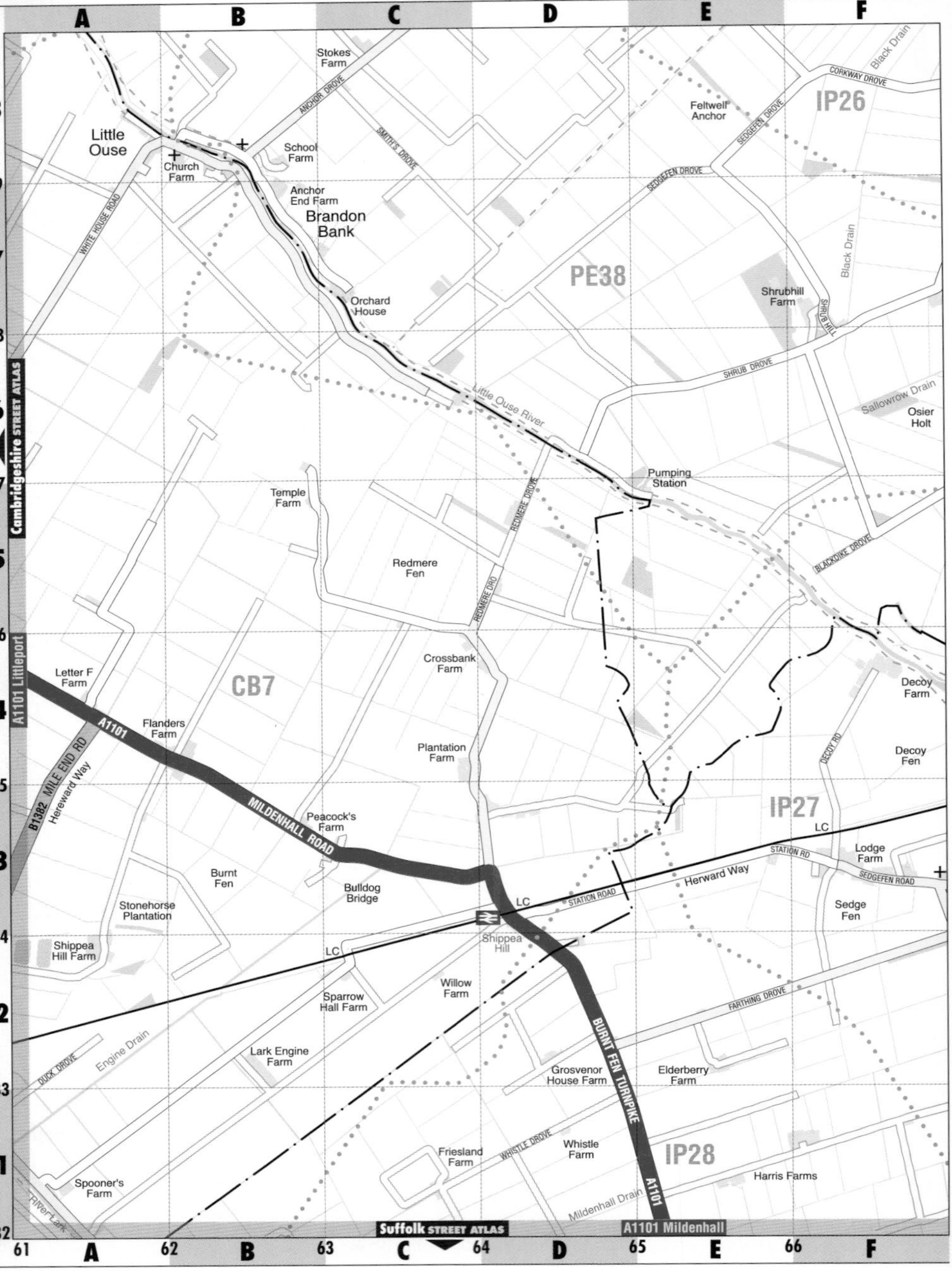

Scale: 1⅓ inches to 1 mile

0   ¼   ½ mile

0   250m 500m 750m 1 km

A B C D E F

8

89

7

88

6

87

5

86

4

85

3

84

2

83

1

82

Cambridgeshire STREET ATLAS

A1101 Littleport

B1382 MILE END RD

Hereward Way

A1101

MILDENHALL ROAD

Little
Ouse

Church
Farm

School
Farm

Stokes
Farm

ANCHOR DROVE

SMITH'S DROVE

Anchor
End Farm

Brandon
Bank

Orchard
House

Little Ouse River

Temple
Farm

REDMERE DROVE

REDMERE DROVE

Redmere
Fen

Crossbank
Farm

CB7

Letter F
Farm

Flanders
Farm

Plantation
Farm

Peacock's
Farm

Burnt
Fen

Bulldog
Bridge

Stonehorse
Plantation

Shippea
Hill Farm

LC

LC

Shippea
Hill

LC

Sparrow
Hall Farm

Willow
Farm

Lark Engine
Farm

DUCK DROVE

Engine Drain

River Lark

Spooner's
Farm

Friesland
Farm

WHISTLE DROVE

Whistle
Farm

BURNT FEN TURNPIKE

Grosvenor
House Farm

Elderberry
Farm

IP28

A1101

Mildenhall Drain

Feltwell
Anchor

CORKWAY DROVE

SEDGEFEN DROVE

IP26

Black Drain

PE38

Shrubhill
Farm

Black Drain

SHRUB DROVE

Sallowrow Drain

Osier
Holt

Pumping
Station

BLACKDIKE DROVE

Decoy
Farm

Decoy
Fen

DECOY RD

IP27

LC

STATION RD

Lodge
Farm

SEDGEFEN ROAD

Herward Way

Sedge
Fen

STATION ROAD

FARTHING DROVE

Harris Farms

A1101 Mildenhall

61   A   62   B   63   C   64   D   65   E   66   F

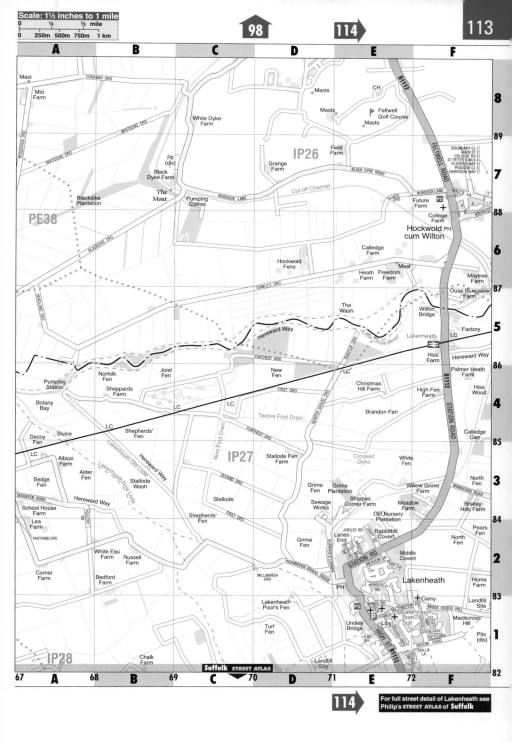

Scale: 1⅓ inches to 1 mile

0   ¼   ½   mile
0   250m 500m 750m 1 km

A   B   C   D   E   F

Mast

Mid
Farm

CORKWAY DRO

WHITEDIKE DRO

WHITEDIKE DRO

RIDDERSMERE DRO

White Dyke
Farm

Pit
(dis)

Black
Dyke Farm

The
Moat

BLACKDIKE DRO

Blackdike
Plantation

BLACKDIKE DRO

PE38

Masts

Masts

CH

Feltwell
Golf Course

Masts

IP26

Field
Farm

Grange
Farm

BURDOCK LANE

Pumping
Station

Cut-off Channel

BLACK DYKE ROAD

BURDOCK LANE

SLUICE
DRO

Future
Farm

College
Farm

Hockwold PH
cum Wilton

FELTWELL ROAD

B1112

BOUNDARY CL 1
MAIN ST 2
COLEGE RD 3
ST PETER'S WLK 4
PLOVERS WAY 5
PEACOCK CL 6
HARRISON WAY 7

MALT'S LA

SOUTH ST

8

89

7

88

6

Calledge
Farm

Hockwold
Fens

COWLES DRO

Heath
Farm

Freedom
Farm

Mast

The
Wash

Little Ouse River

Wilton
Bridge

Ouse Bungalow
Farm

Maytree
Farm

87

Hereward Way

FURTHEST DRO

Norfolk
Fen

Joist
Fen

New
Fen

Lakenheath

LC

Factory

Hiss
Farm

Hereward Way

Palmer Heath
Farm

5

86

Pumping
Station

Sheppards
Farm

Botany
Bay

FIRST DRO

BRIDGE DRO

NEWNES GRAVEL DRO

Christmas
Hill Farm

LC

High Fen
Farm

Hiss
Wood

B1112

STATION ROAD

4

Twelve Foot Drain

LC

LC

Brandon Fen

Calledge
Carr

85

Decoy
Fen

Sluice

LC

Shepherds'
Fen

Lakenheath Old DRO

Hereward Way

Nine Foot Drain

FURTHEST DRO

IP27

Stallode Fen
Farm

Crooked
Dyke

White
Fen

3

LC

Albion
Farm

Alder
Fen

Lakenheath New Lode

SECOND DRO

Stallode
Wash

Stallode

Grime
Fen

Grime
Plantation

Willow Grove
Farm

North
Fen

WANGFORD ROAD

Sedge
Fen

SEDGEFEN ROAD

Hereward Way

POULTRY RD

Shepherds'
Fen

FIRST DRO

Sewage
Works

Sharpes
Corner Farm

Meadow
Farm

Brakey
Hills Farm

84

School House
Farm

Lea
Farm

FARTHING DRO

Grime
Fen

Old Nursery
Plantation

JUBILEE RD

Lanes
End

SHARPES CORNER

Rabbithill
Covert

Poors
Fen

North
Fen

2

White Eau
Farm

Russell
Farm

Corner
Farm

Bedford
Farm

HIGHBRIDGE GRAVEL DROVE

MILLMARSH
DRO

Lakenheath
Poor's Fen

STATION RD

MEADOW DR

WINGFIELD
RD

PH

Middle
Covert

Lakenheath

Cemy

Home
Farm

83

PO

CEMETERY RD

Lakenheath
Prim Sch

MAIDS CROSS HILL

Landfill
Site

Maidscross
Hill

IP28

Chalk
Farm

Turf
Fen

Undely
Bridge

LILAC DR

Liby

HIGH ST B1112

Pits
(dis)

BROOM ROAD

HOLLY LA

1

Landfill
Site

Suffolk STREET ATLAS

82

67   A   68   B   69   C   70   D   71   E   72   F

114 For full street detail of Lakenheath see
Philip's STREET ATLAS of Suffolk

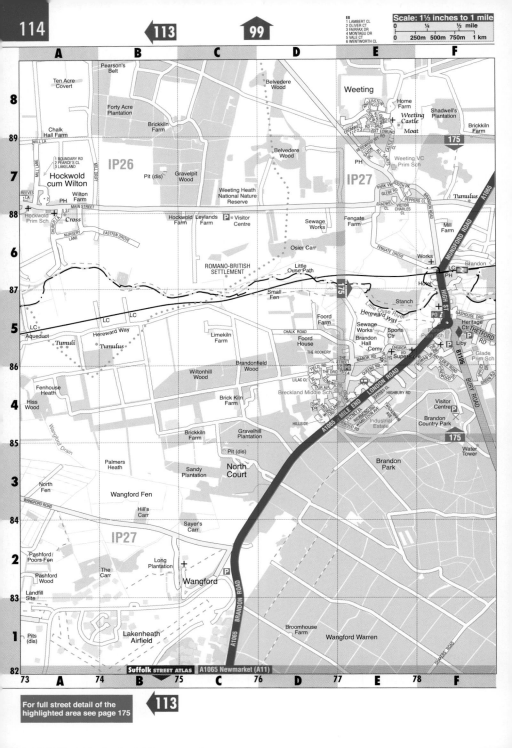

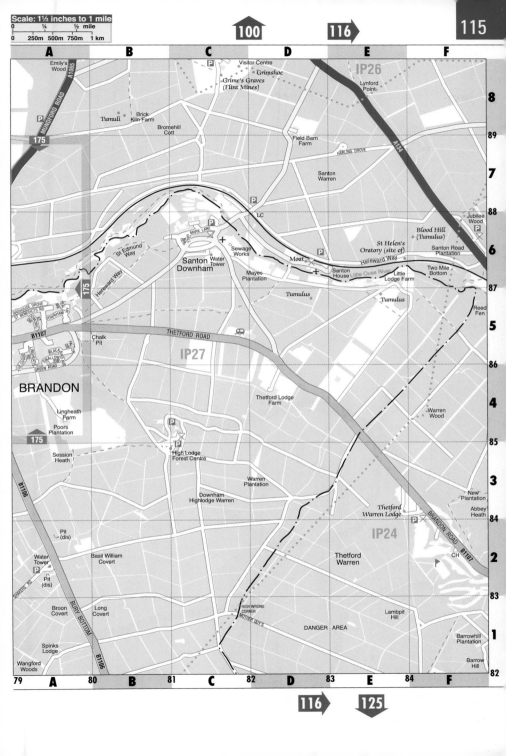

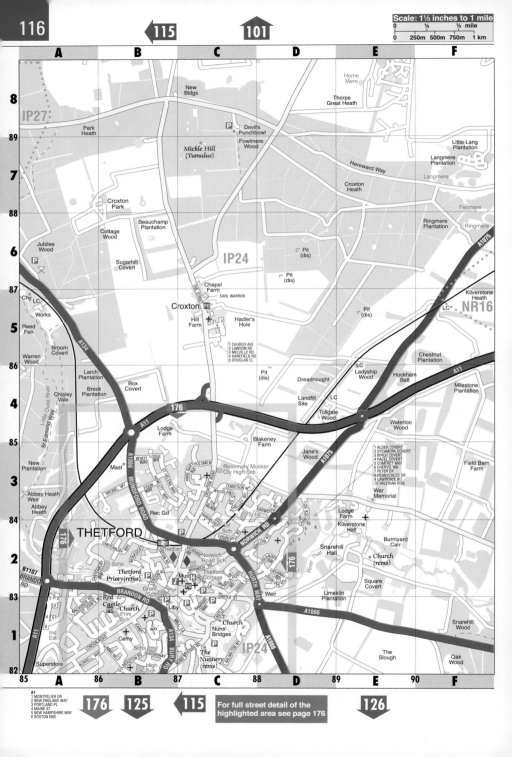

Scale: 1½ inches to 1 mile

0   ¼   ½ mile
0 250m 500m 750m 1 km

A   B   C   D   E   F

8

IP27

New
Bldgs

Home
Mere

Thorpe
Great Heath

89

P

Devil's
Punchbowl

Park
Heath

Mickle Hill
(Tumulus)

Fowlmere
Wood

Little Lang
Plantation

Langmere
Plantation

7

Hereward Way

Croxton
Heath

Langmere

A1075

88

Croxton
Park

Beauchamp
Plantation

Fenmere

Ringmere
Plantation

Ringmere

Cottage
Wood

6

Jubilee
Wood

P

Sugarhill
Covert

IP24

Pit
(dis)

Pit
(dis)

87

Chapel
Farm

EARL WARREN

Kilverstone
Heath

Chy LC

Croxton P.O

Works

Hill
Farm

Hadler's
Hole

Pit
(dis)

LC

NR16

5

Reed
Fen

A134

1 2
J 3

1 CHURCH AVE
2 LAWSON RD
3 MELVILLE RD
4 HAREFIELD RD
5 DOUGLAS CL

Chestnut
Plantation

Warren
Wood

Broom
Covert

Pit
(dis)

Dreadnought

LC
Ladyship
Wood

Hockham
Belt

Milestone
Plantation

86

Chisley
Vale

Larch
Plantation

Breck
Plantation

Box
Covert

Landfill
Site

LC

A11

4

St Edmund's Way

Little Ouse River

176

A11

Tollgate
Wood

Waterloo
Wood

Lodge
Farm

Blakeney
Farm

Jane's
Wood

1 ALDER COVERT
2 SYCAMORE COVERT
3 BIRCH COVERT
4 HAZEL COVERT
5 COMFREY WAY
6 CHERVIL WK
7 PETER DR
8 PENNYCRESS DR
9 LAWRENCE RD
10 VALERIAN RISE

Field Barn
Farm

85

New
Plantation

Mast

WYATT
WAY

LODGE
WY

A1066

Rosemary Musker
Cty High Sch

A1075

War
Memorial

3

Abbey Heath
Weir

Abbey
Heath

BRUNEL WY

PISON WY

ST PETERS WAY

ANNE BARTHOLOMEW

ST FELIX WAY

TENNYSON W

WOODLAND

THE BLADE

HARWOOD

Sch

Lodge
Farm

Kilverstone
Hall

Burntyard
Carr

84

176

THETFORD

Rec Gd

P

CLARKE

Snarehill
Hall

Church
(rems)

Square
Covert

2

B1107
BRANDON
RD

Schs

Thetford
Priory (rems)

MUNFORD ROAD

CANTERBURY

KILVERSTONE
RD

Thetford

NORWICH

Norwich Rd Sch

Thetford
Cottage

MAGDALEN ST

NORWICH RD

MINSTERGATE

GROVE

CHURCH

MARLOW RD

ALEXANDER

CASTLE ST

CARADAM

River Thet

HURTH WAY

176

Snarehill
Wood

Limekiln
Plantation

A1066

83

Mus

Liby

Red
Castle

Church
Prim
Sch

GUILDHALL

CASTLE ST

Weir

IP24

A1068

1

Ind
Est

Cemy

Church
Nuns'
Bridges

The
Slough

Oak
Wood

82

Superstore

High
Sch

BURY RD

A134

BRIDGE RD

QUEENSWAY

The
Nunnery
(rems)

A   B   C   D   E   F

85   86   87   88   89   90

A1
1 MONTPELIER DR
2 NEW ENGLAND WAY
3 PORTLAND PL
4 MAINE ST
5 NEW HAMPSHIRE WAY
6 BOSTON END

176

125

115

For full street detail of the
highlighted area see page 176

126

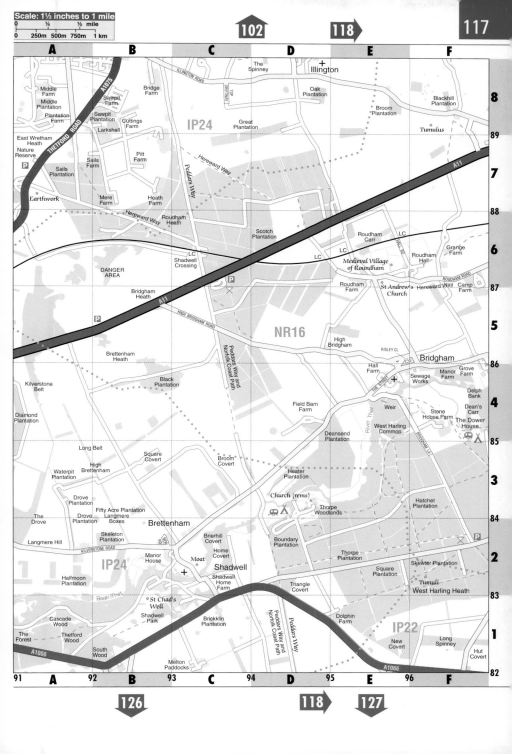

118

117

103

Scale: 1⅓ inches to 1 mile

0   ¼   ½ mile

0   250m   500m   750m   1 km

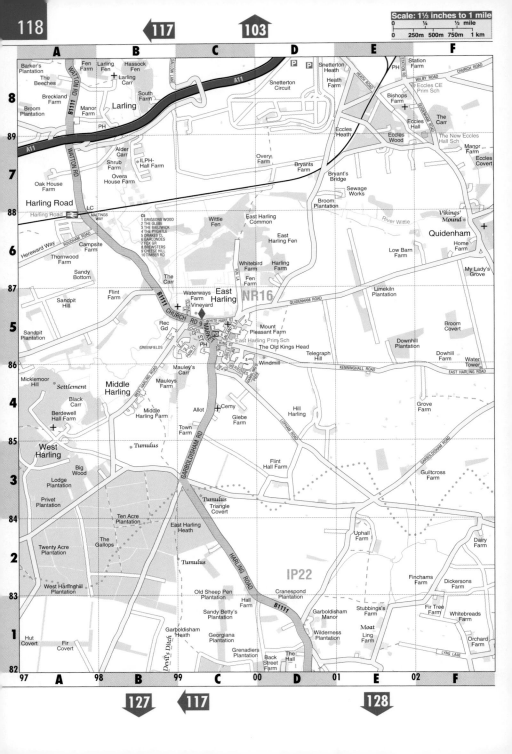

A   **B**   **C**   **D**   **E**   **F**

Barker's Plantation

The Beeches

Breckland Farm

Broom Plantation

WATTON RD

B1111

Fen Farm

Larling Fen

Larling Carr

Hassock Fen

South Farm

Manor Farm

Larling

PH

WATTON RD

A11

Snetterton Heath

Snetterton Circuit

Heath Farm

Eccles Heath

Overy Farm

Bryants Farm

HEATH ROAD

STATION RD

PH

Station Farm

Bishops Farm

Eccles Hall

Eccles Wood

WILBY ROAD

CHURCH ROAD

Eccles CE Prim Sch

The Carr

The New Eccles Hall Sch

Manor Farm

Eccles Covert

8

89

7

Oak House Farm

Harling Road

WATTON RD

Alder Carr

Shrub Farm

Overa House Farm

ILPH-Hall Farm

Bryant's Bridge

Sewage Works

Broom Plantation

Vikings' Mound

River Wittle

Quidenham

88

Harling Road

MALTINGS WAY

LC

C5
1 GRIGSONS WOOD
2 THE GLEBE
3 THE BAILWICK
4 THE PYGHTLE
5 DRAKES CL
6 GARLONDES
7 FOX GR
8 BREWSTERS
9 CHEESE HILL
10 TIMBER RD

Wittle Fen

East Harling Common

East Harling Fen

Low Barn Farm

Home Farm

My Lady's Grove

6

Hereward Way

ROUGHAM ROAD

Campsite Farm

Thornwood Farm

Sandy Bottom

The Carr

Whitebird Farm

Harling Farm

Fen Farm

QUIDENHAM ROAD

Limekiln Plantation

Broom Covert

Downhill Plantation

87

Sandpit Hill

Flint Farm

B1111

CHURCH RD

Waterways Farm Vineyard

East Harling

NR16

Dowhill Farm

Water Tower

5

Sandpit Plantation

Rec Gd

GREENFIELDS

SCHOOL LA

CHURCH RD 9

WHITE HART LA

MARKET ST

KING ST

PH

Mount Pleasant Farm

East Harling Prim Sch

The Old Kings Head

Windmill

Telegraph Hill

KENNINGHALL ROAD

EAST HARLING ROAD

86

Micklemoor Hill

Settlement

Mauley's Carr

Mauleys Farm

WEST HARLING ROAD

Middle Harling

Windmill

Hill Harling

Grove Farm

4

Black Carr

Berdewell Hall Farm

Middle Harling Farm

Allot

Cemy

Glebe Farm

85

West Harling

Big Wood

Tumulus

Town Farm

GARBOLDISHAM RD

Flint Hall Farm

Guiltcross Farm

3

Lodge Plantation

Privet Plantation

Tumulus

Triangle Covert

84

Ten Acre Plantation

East Harling Heath

Uphall Farm

Dairy Farm

2

Twenty Acre Plantation

The Gallops

Tumulus

HARLING ROAD

IP22

Finchams Farm

Dickersons Farm

83

West Harlinghill Plantation

Old Sheep Pen Plantation

Hall Farm

Cranespond Plantation

B1111

Garboldisham Manor

Stubbings's Farm

Fir Tree Farm

Whitebreads Farm

1

Hut Covert

Fir Covert

Garboldisham Heath

Sandy Betty's Plantation

Georgiana Plantation

Grenadiers Plantation

Back Street Farm

The Hall

Wilderness Plantation

Moat

Ling Farm

Orchard Farm

LYNG LANE

Devil's Ditch

82

97   **A**   98   **B**   99   **C**   00   **D**   01   **E**   02   **F**

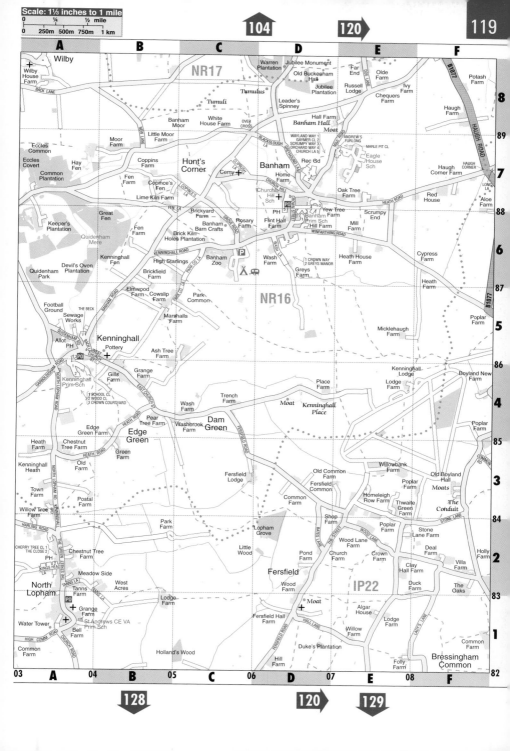

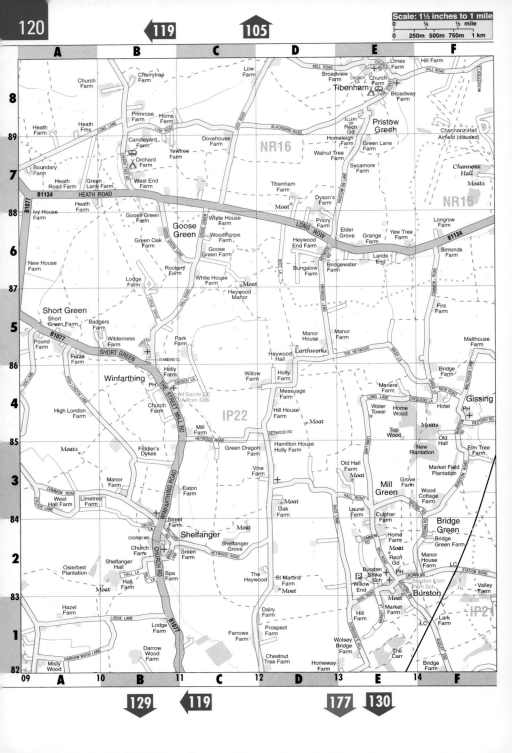

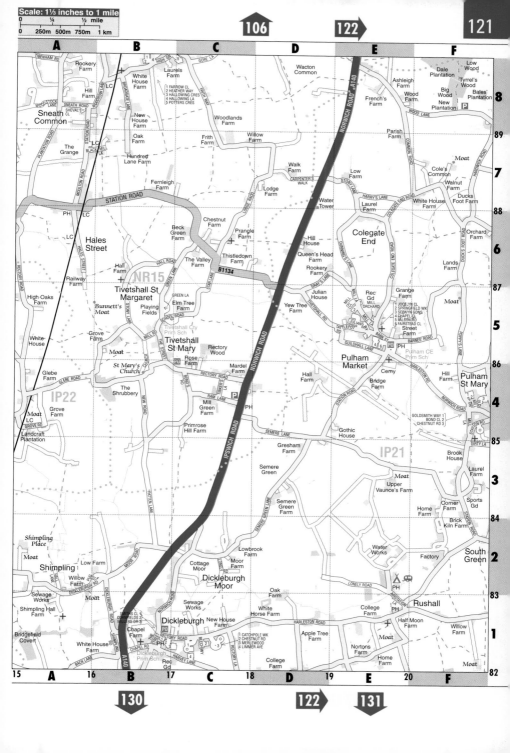

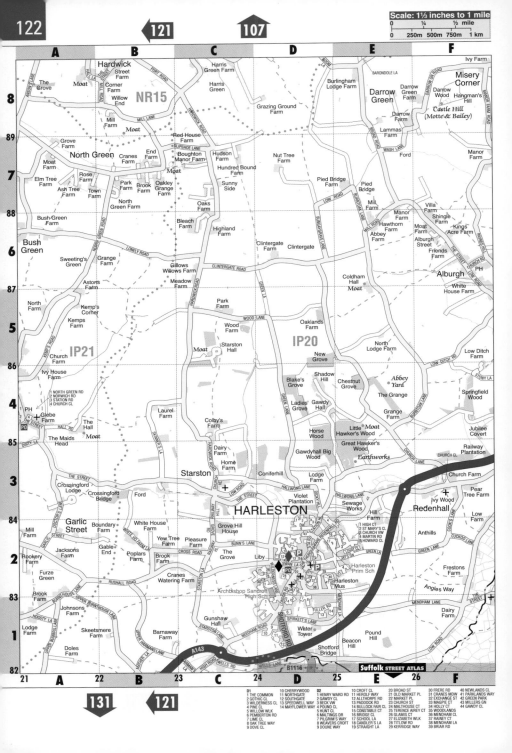

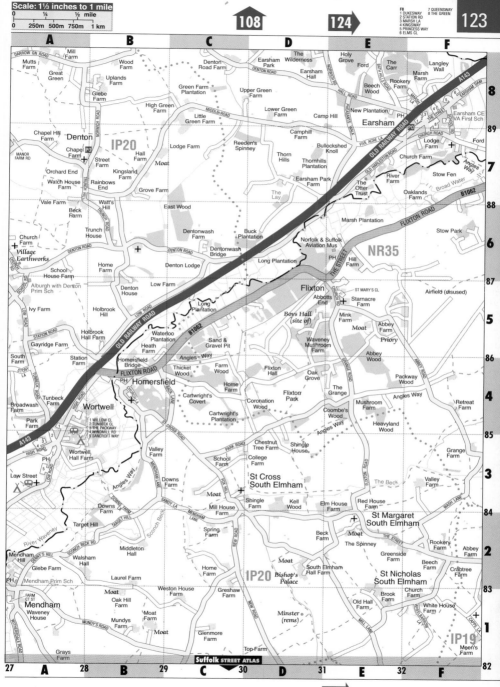

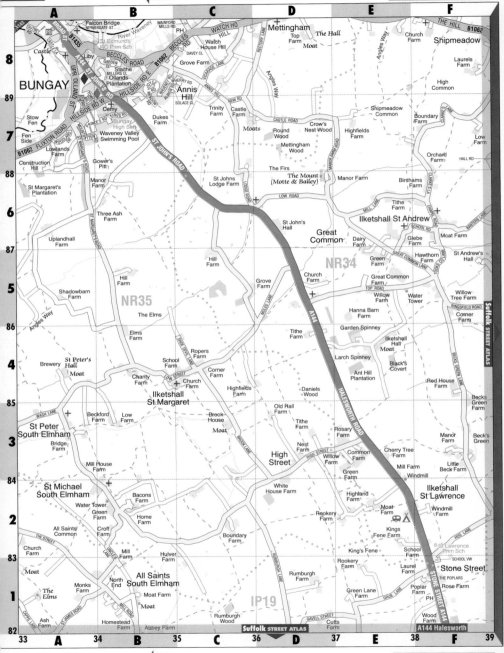

Scale: 1⅓ inches to 1 mile

For full street detail of Bungay see
Philip's STREET ATLAS of Suffolk

Scale: 1⅓ inches to 1 mile

| 0 | ¼ | ½ mile |
| 0 | 250m 500m 750m | 1 km |

115

116 **126**

176

125

F6
1 SALMOND DR
2 ELLINGTON RD
3 NEWALL RD
4 PORTAL CL
5 TEDDER CL
6 EDINBURGH CL

7 WINDSOR CL

A B C D E F

8

81

7

80

6

79

5

78

4

77

3

76

2

75

1

74

Rifle Range

LONDON ROAD
A11

Forest Retail Park

BURRELL WAY

176

Playing Field

A134

176

Olleys Farm

Barnhamcross Common

P

Water Tower

Elveden Gap

St Edmund Way

Nature Reserve

BURY ROAD

Barnham Cross (rems)

Parson's Slip Wood

Milestone Plantation

Boundary Belt

Great Snare Hill

Stonepit Wood

Redneck Farm

LONDON ROAD

Sketchfar Wood

Icknield Way

Aughton Spinney

Elveden

A11

Marmansgrave Wood

Barnham Camp

A11 Newmarket

Millhill Wood

Elveden Hall

Glebe Wood

Gorse Industrial Estate

Water Tower

Pig Farm

Water Tower

Home Wood

Larch Covert

Princess Mary's Plantation

Sewage Works

Thetford Heath

ELVEDEN ROAD

PH

WATER LA 1
ST MARTIN'S LA 2
MILL LA 3
BLACKSMITH LA 4

St Martin's Church (rems)

CHURCH LA

2 3 5
1 4

Barnham

Sandgault Plantation

North Farm

STATION RD

Works

Tumulus

THE STREET

6 7

Basin Wood

IP24

BARROW'S CORNER

Albemarle Plantation

Furze Hill Plantation

Hunwellspring Plantation

Triangle Plantation

Water Tower

A134

Barnham CE Prim Sch

East Farm

Pit (dis)

Summerpit Farm

Old Middlegouch Plantation

Coronation Covert

St Edmund Way

Old Barnham Slip

Works

Little Heath

Cranehill Spinney

Blackbird Spinney

Tumulus

B1106

SUFFOLK STREET ATLAS

Barrow Clump Buildings

Icknield Way Path

Duke's Ride

Bottom Plantation

Ixworth Spinney

Fox Pin

Tumulus

SHELTERHOUSE CORNER

West Calthorpe Heath

Breck Plantation

Monument

Icknield Way Path

West Farm

Icknield Way Path

Four Corners

New Zealand Cotts

D House

Works

Field Barn

IP28

Warren Covert

Pits (dis)

Lodge Farm

Rymer Farm

P

Tumulus

Warren New Covert

Wordwell Barn

Ash Covert

Belchamps Plantation

Rubbinghouse Covert

Culfordheath

IP31

Traveller's Hill (Tumuli)

CHALK LA

Ling Covert

Seven Hills House

Rymer Barn

B1106

Traveller's Hill Plantation

Suffolk STREET ATLAS

A134 Bury St. Edmunds

A134

82 A 83 B 84 C 85 D 86 E 87 F 74

126

For full street detail of the highlighted area see page 176

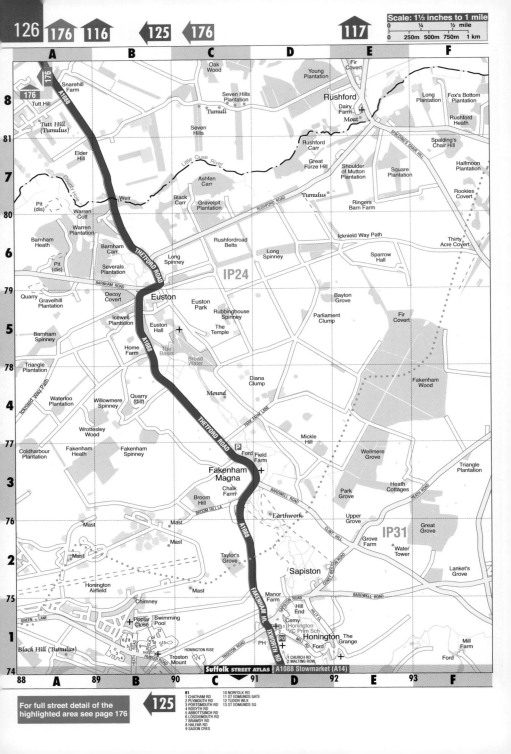

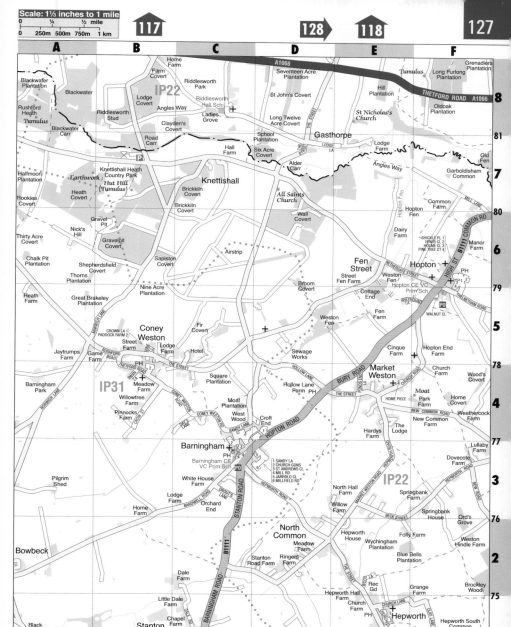

118
127
119

Scale: 1⅓ inches to 1 mile
0 ¼ ½ mile
0 250m 500m 750m 1 km

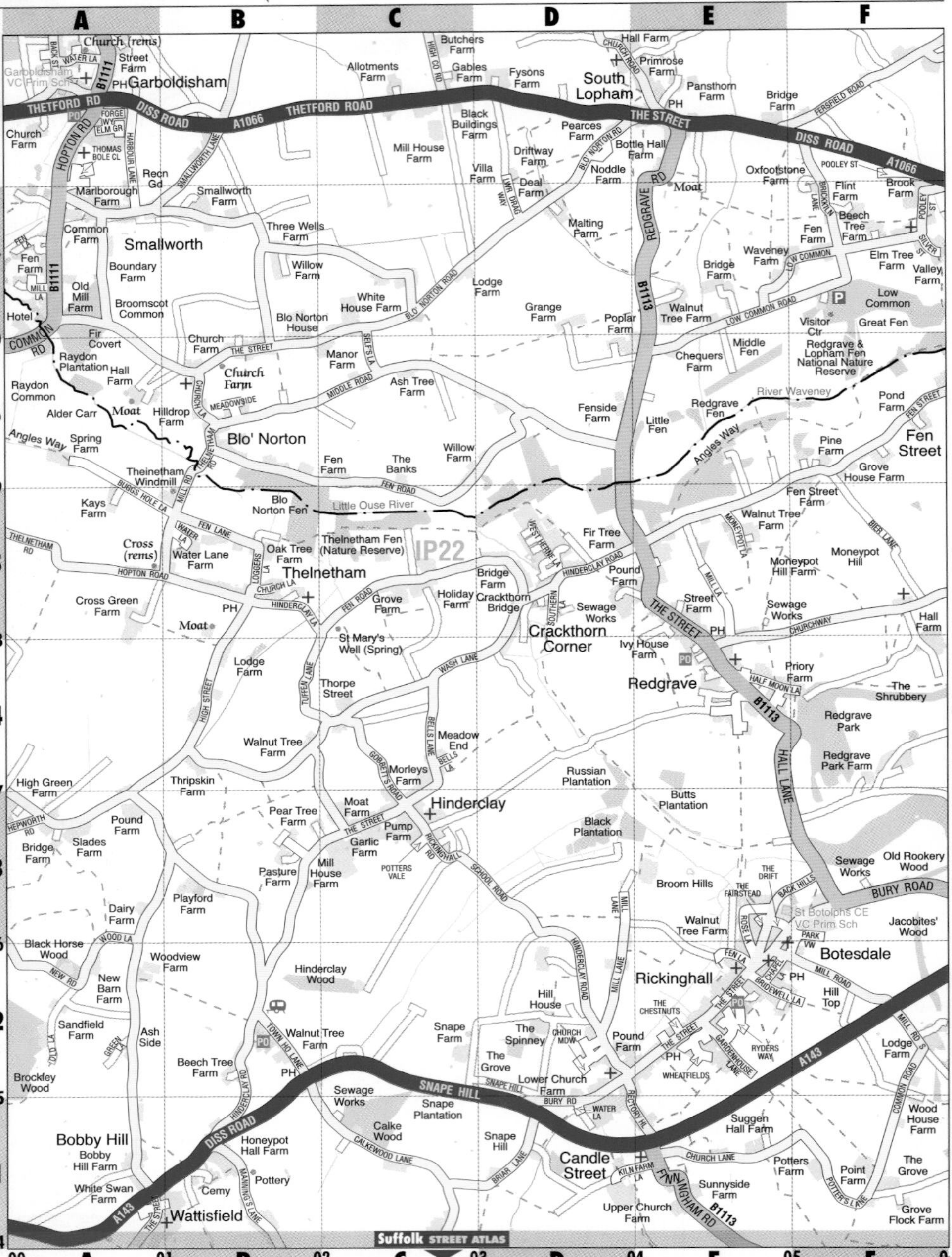
A
B
C
D
E
F
8
81
7
80
6
79
5
78
4
77
3
76
2
75
1
74
00
01
02
03
04
05
Church (rems)
Garboldisham VC Prim Sch
Street Farm
PH
Garboldisham
WATER LA
BACK ST
B1111
THETFORD RD
PO
FORGE WY
ELM GR
DISS ROAD
A1066
THETFORD ROAD
Church Farm
HOPTON RD
THOMAS BOLE CL
HARBOUR LANE
Recn Gd
SMALLWORTH LANE
Marlborough Farm
Smallworth Farm
Common Farm
Smallworth
Three Wells Farm
Willow Farm
Fen Farm
Boundary Farm
Old Mill Farm
MILL LA
Broomscot Common
White House Farm
Hotel
Blo Norton House
COMMON RD
Fir Covert
Church Farm
THE STREET
Raydon Plantation
Hall Farm
Church Farm
Manor Farm
SELFS LA
Raydon Common
Alder Carr
Moat
Hilldrop Farm
CHURCH LA
MEADOWSIDE
MIDDLE ROAD
Ash Tree Farm
Angles Way
Spring Farm
Blo' Norton
Theinetham Windmill
MILL RD
THELNETHAM
Fen Farm
The Banks
Willow Farm
FEN ROAD
BUGGS HOLE LA
Kays Farm
Blo Norton Fen
Little Ouse River
Cross (rems)
WATER LA
FEN LANE
THELNETHAM RD
Water Lane Farm
Oak Tree Farm
Thelnetham Fen (Nature Reserve)
IP22
HOPTON ROAD
LOGGERS LA
CHURCH LA
Thelnetham
Cross Green Farm
PH
HINDERCLAY LA
Moat
FEN ROAD
Grove Farm
St Mary's Well (Spring)
Lodge Farm
TUFFEN LANE
Thorpe Street
WASH LANE
HIGH STREET
Walnut Tree Farm
BELLS LANE
Meadow End
BELLS LA
GORRETT'S ROAD
Morleys Farm
Thripskin Farm
High Green Farm
HEPWORTH RD
Pound Farm
Pear Tree Farm
Moat Farm
THE STREET
Hinderclay
Pump Farm
Garlic Farm
RICKINGHALL RD
POTTERS VALE
Bridge Farm
Slades Farm
Pasture Farm
Mill House Farm
SCHOOL ROAD
Playford Farm
Dairy Farm
WOOD LA
Black Horse Wood
NEW RD
Woodview Farm
Hinderclay Wood
New Barn Farm
Sandfield Farm
GREEN LA
OLD LA
Ash Side
PO
TOWN HO LANE
Walnut Tree Farm
Brockley Wood
Beech Tree Farm
PH
HINDERCLAY RD
DISS ROAD
Bobby Hill
Bobby Hill Farm
Honeypot Hall Farm
MANNING'S LANE
Pottery
Cemy
White Swan Farm
A143
THE STREET
Wattisfield
Butchers Farm
Allotments Farm
HIGH CO RD
Gables Farm
Fysons Farm
Black Buildings Farm
Mill House Farm
Villa Farm
LWR DRAG WAY
Driftway Farm
Deal Farm
BLO' NORTON ROAD
Lodge Farm
Grange Farm
Fen Farm
Hall Farm
CHURCH ROAD
Primrose Farm
South Lopham
Pansthorn Farm
PH
Pearces Farm
Bottle Hall Farm
Noddle Farm
Moat
REDGRAVE RD
Malting Farm
B1113
Poplar Farm
Walnut Tree Farm
Fenside Farm
Little Fen
Redgrave Fen
Fir Tree Farm
WEST HERNE LA
HINDERCLAY ROAD
Pound Farm
Bridge Farm
Holiday Farm
Crackthorn Bridge
SOUTHERN LA
Sewage Works
Crackthorn Corner
THE STREET
Street Farm
PH
Ivy House Farm
PO
Redgrave
B1113
Russian Plantation
Butts Plantation
Black Plantation
Broom Hills
MILL LANE
Walnut Tree Farm
HINDERCLAY ROAD
Hill House
Snape Farm
The Spinney
CHURCH MDW
The Grove
Pound Farm
Rickinghall
THE CHESTNUTS
THE STREET
PH
WHEATFIELDS
GARDENHOUSE LANE
RYDERS WAY
SNAPE HILL
Lower Church Farm
BURY RD
WATER LA
RECTORY HL
Sewage Works
Snape Plantation
Calke Wood
CALKEWOOD LANE
Snape Hill
BRIAR LANE
Candle Street
KILN FARM LA
FINNINGHAM RD
Upper Church Farm
B1113
Bridge Farm
FERSFIELD ROAD
THE STREET
DISS ROAD
A1066
POOLEY ST
Oxfootstone Farm
BRICKKILN LANE
Flint Farm
Brook Farm
Beech Tree Farm
Fen Farm
Waveney Farm
LOW COMMON
Elm Tree Farm
Valley Farm
SILVER ST
POOLEY ST
Bridge Farm
P
Low Common
LOW COMMON ROAD
Visitor Ctr
Great Fen
Middle Fen
Chequers Farm
Redgrave & Lopham Fen National Nature Reserve
River Waveney
Pond Farm
FEN STREET
Pine Farm
Fen Street
Grove House Farm
Angles Way
Fen Street Farm
Walnut Tree Farm
MONEYPOT LA
BIER LANE
Moneypot Hill Farm
Moneypot Hill
MILL LA
Sewage Works
CHURCHWAY
Hall Farm
Priory Farm
HALF MOON LA
The Shrubbery
Redgrave Park
Redgrave Park Farm
HALL LANE
Sewage Works
Old Rookery Wood
BURY ROAD
THE DRIFT
THE FAIRSTEAD
BACK HILLS
St Botolphs CE VC Prim Sch
Jacobites' Wood
ROSE LA
PARK VW
Botesdale
FEN LA
CHAPEL LA
PH
MILL ROAD
PO
BRIDEWELL LA
Hill Top
Lodge Farm
A143
MILL RD
COMMON ROAD
Wood House Farm
Suggen Hall Farm
CHURCH LANE
Potters Farm
Sunnyside Farm
Point Farm
POTTER'S LANE
The Grove
Grove Flock Farm
Suffolk STREET ATLAS

127

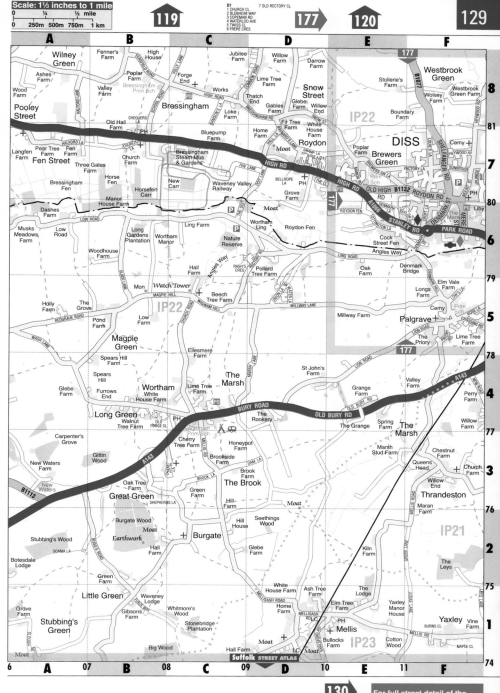

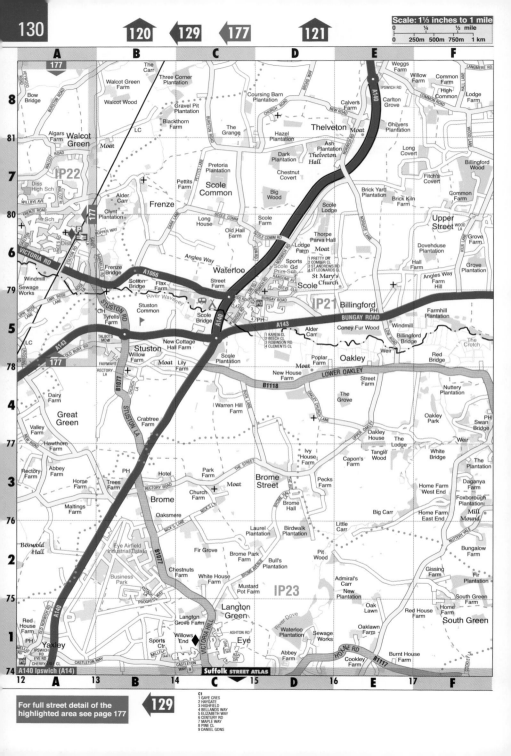

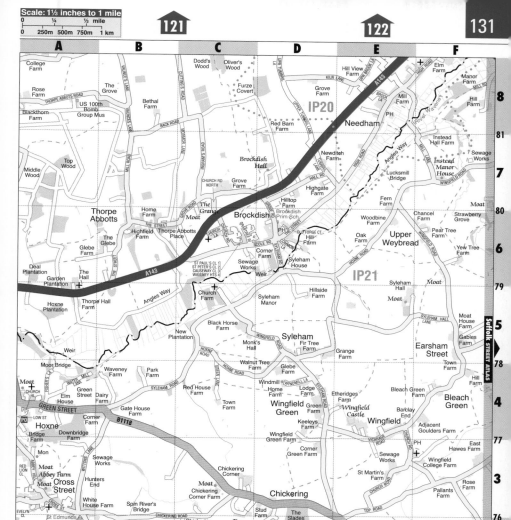

A B C D E F

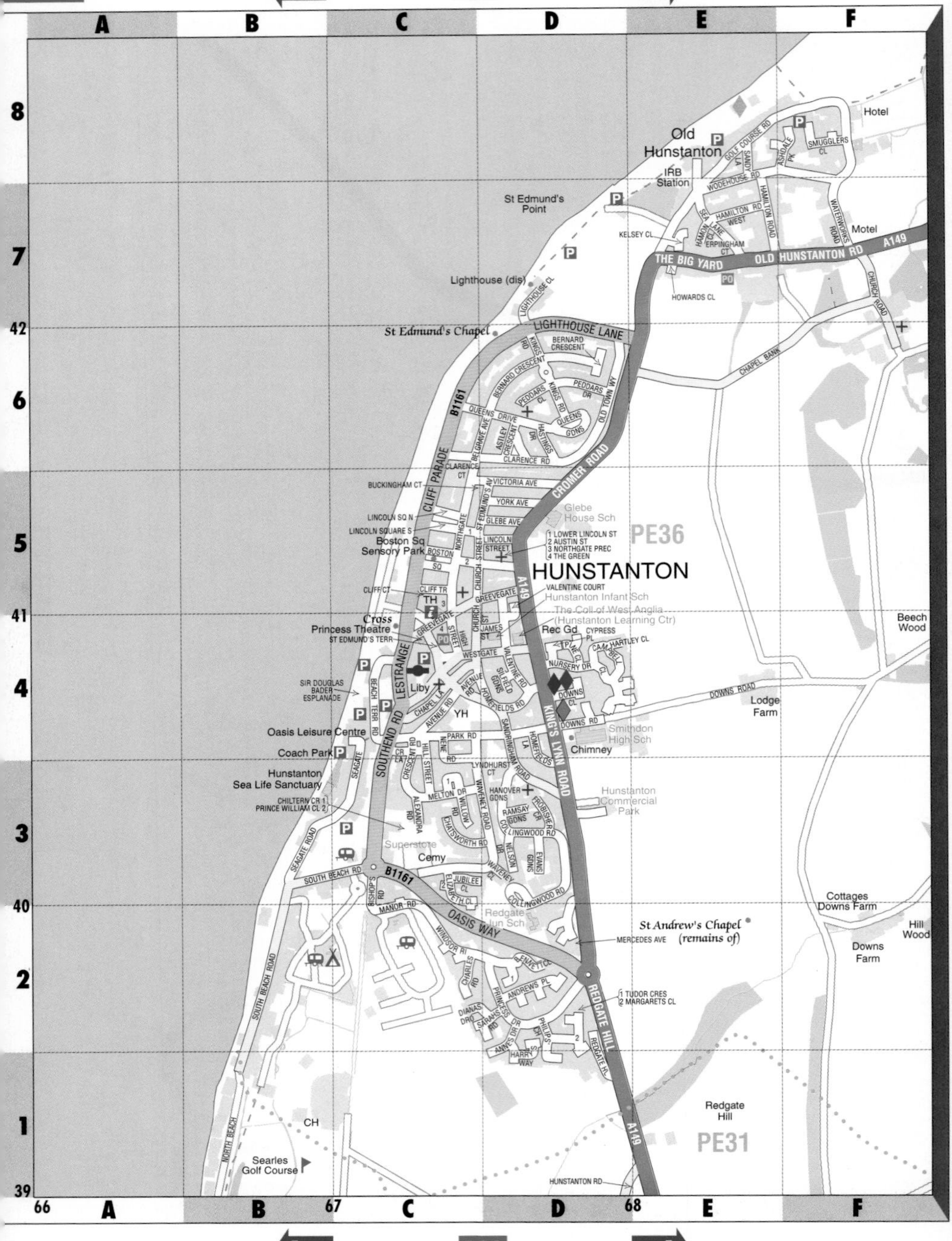

8

Old Hunstanton
Hotel
SMUGGLERS CL
IRB Station
St Edmund's Point
KELSEY CL
Motel
THE BIG YARD   OLD HUNSTANTON RD   A149

7

Lighthouse (dis)
HOWARDS CL
PO
CHAPEL BANK

42

St Edmund's Chapel
LIGHTHOUSE LANE
BERNARD CRESCENT
PEDDARS DR

6

B1161
QUEENS DRIVE
QUEENS
CROMER ROAD

BUCKINGHAM CT
CLIFF PARADE
CLARENCE CT
CLARENCE RD
VICTORIA AVE
YORK AVE
GLEBE AVE

5

LINCOLN SQ N
LINCOLN SQUARE S
Boston Sq
Sensory Park
LINCOLN STREET
1 LOWER LINCOLN ST
2 AUSTIN ST
3 NORTHGATE PREC
4 THE GREEN
Glebe House Sch

PE36

HUNSTANTON

CLIFF TCE
TH
CLIFF TR
GREEVEGATE
VALENTINE COURT
Hunstanton Infant Sch

41

Cross
Princess Theatre
ST EDMUND'S TERR
The Coll of West Anglia
(Hunstanton Learning Ctr)
Rec Gd   CYPRESS
Beech Wood

4

SIR DOUGLAS BADER ESPLANADE
BEACH TCE
Liby
P
WESTGATE
A149
NURSERY DR
Lodge Farm
DOWNS ROAD

YH
PARK RD
KING'S LYNN ROAD
Smithdon High Sch
Chimney

Oasis Leisure Centre
Coach Park
Hunstanton Sea Life Sanctuary
CHILTERN CL 1
PRINCE WILLIAM CL 2
LYNDHURST
MELTON DR
HANOVER GDNS
RAMSAY GDNS
Hunstanton Commercial Park

3

SEAGATE ROAD
ALEXANDRA
Superstore
Cemy
LINGWOOD RD

40

SOUTH BEACH ROAD
MANOR RD
B1161
JUBILEE
Redgate Sch
St Andrew's Chapel
(remains of)
MERCEDES AVE
Cottages
Downs Farm
Hill Wood
Downs Farm

2

OASIS WAY
ANDREWS PL
REDGATE HILL
1 TUDOR CRES
2 MARGARETS CL

NORTH BEACH
DIANES DR
HARRY WAY

1

CH
Searles Golf Course
Redgate Hill
A149
HUNSTANTON RD
PE31

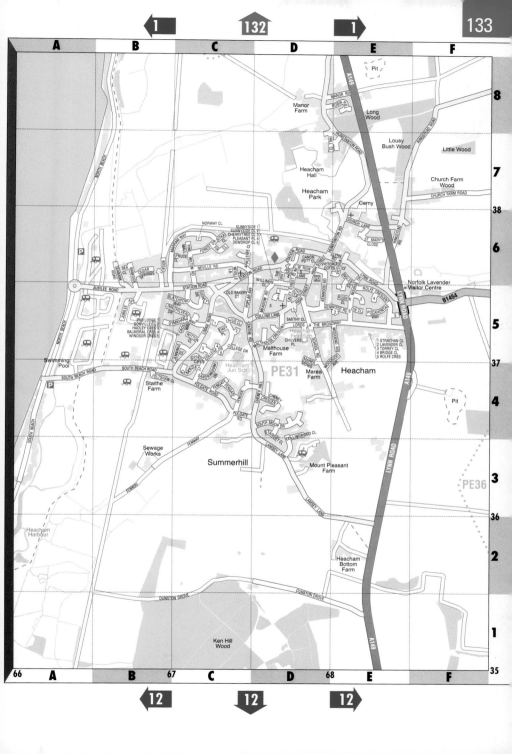

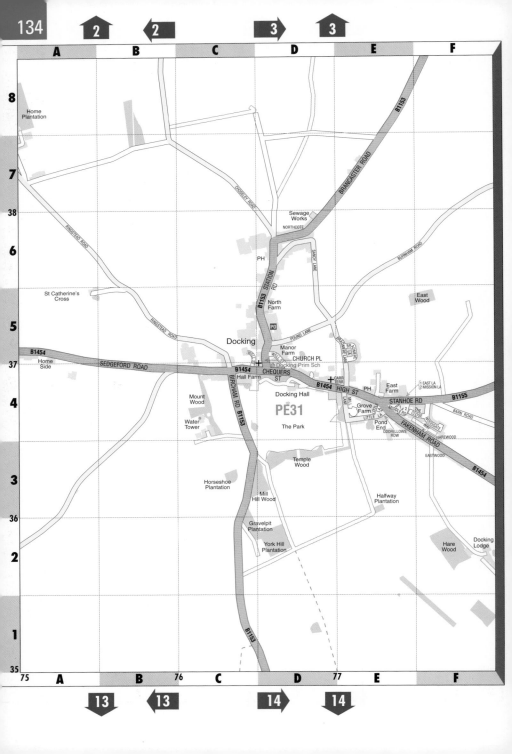

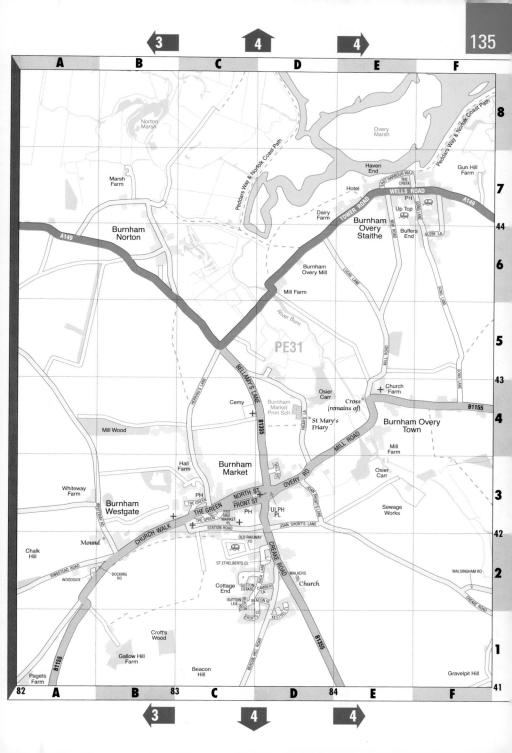

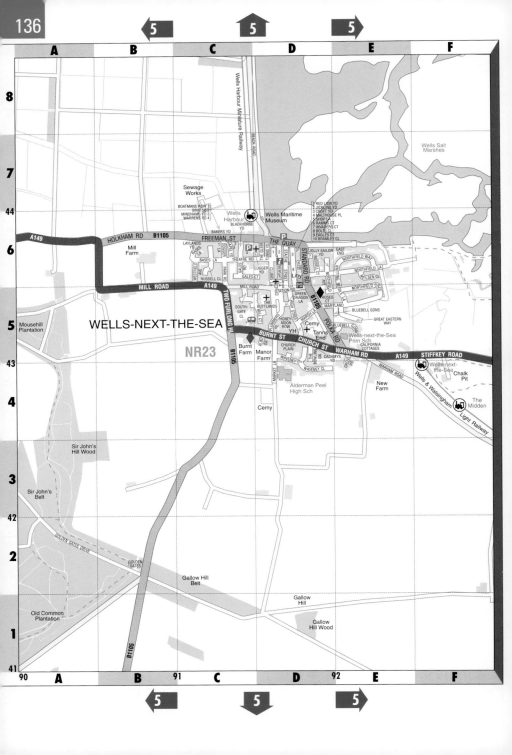

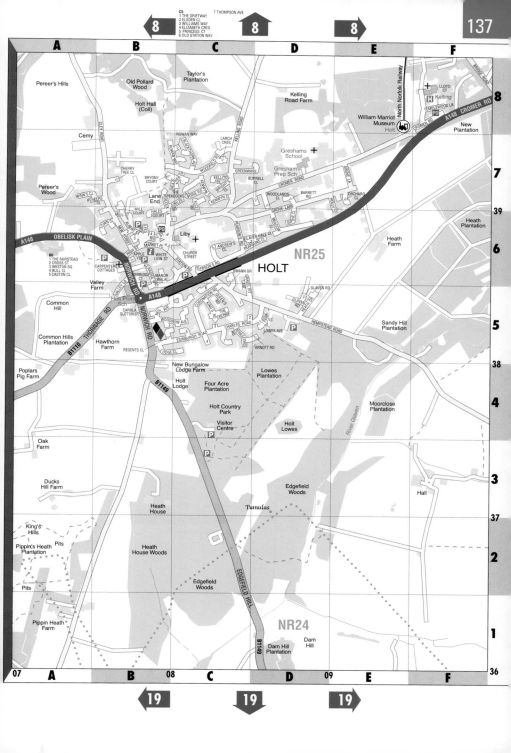

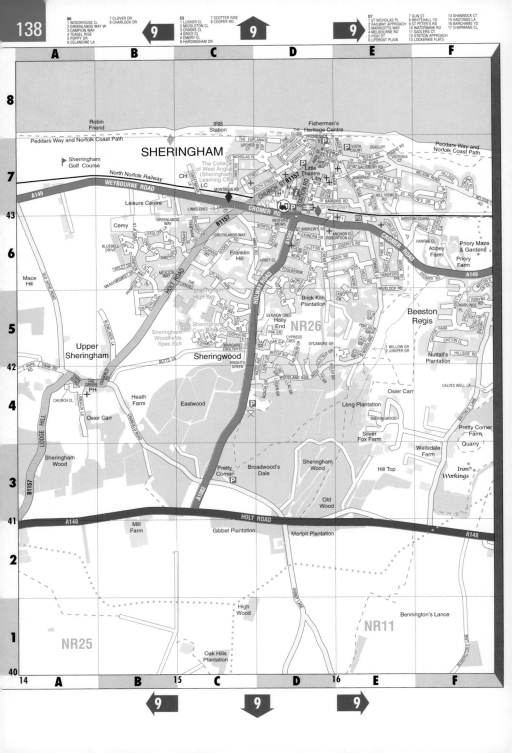

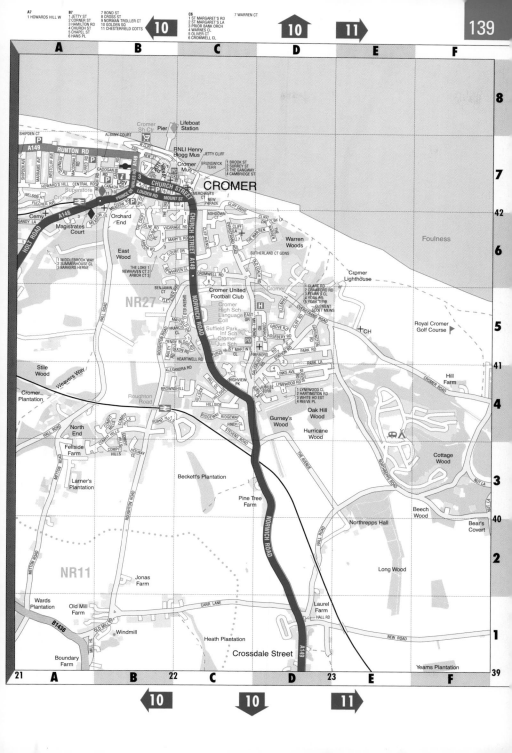

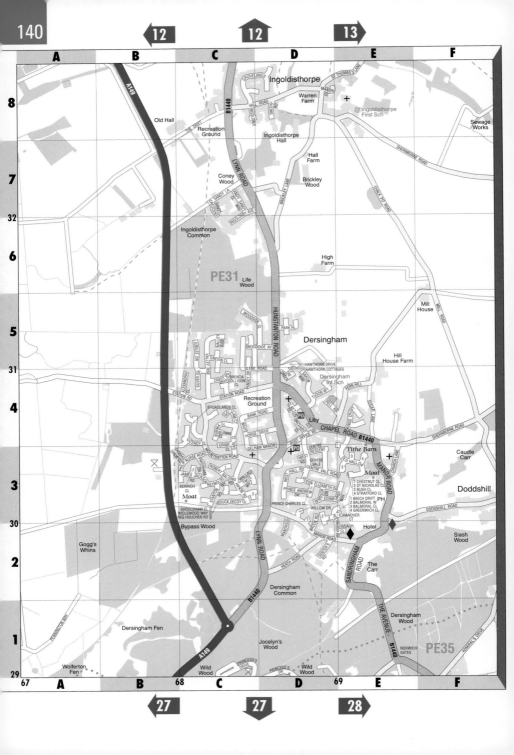

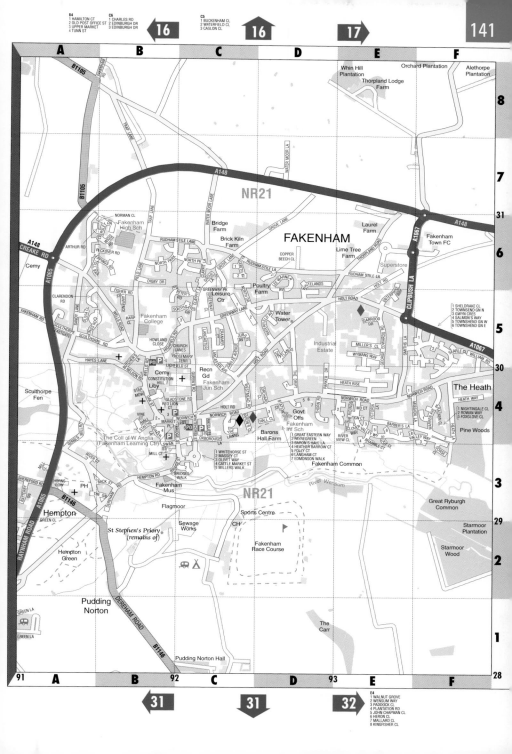

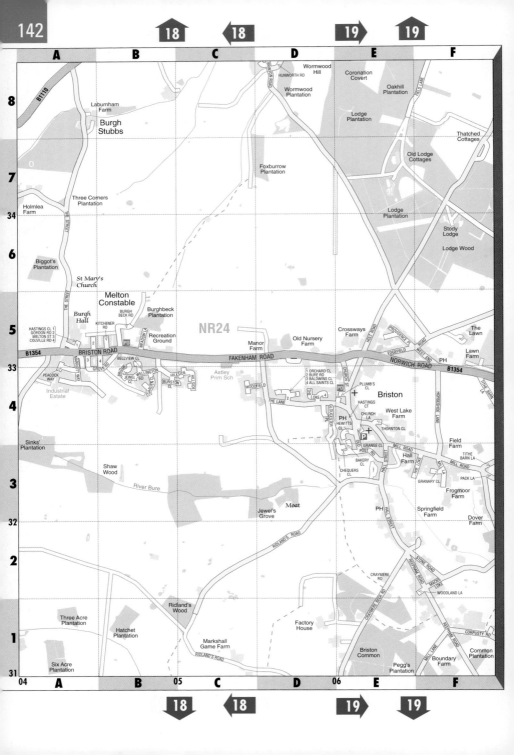

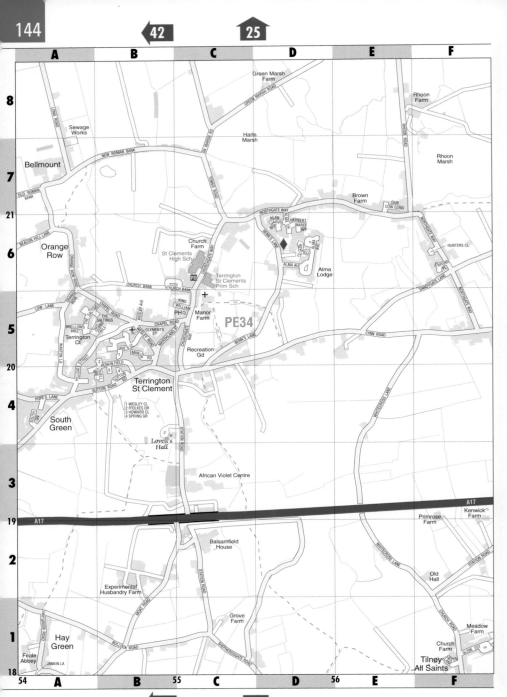

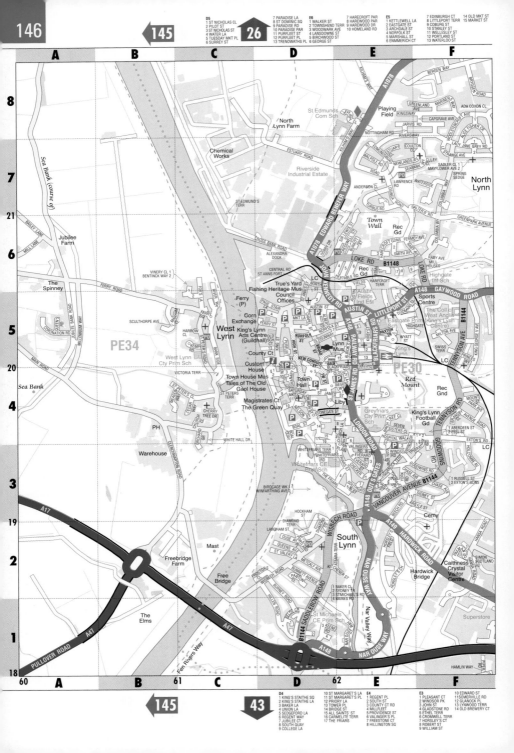

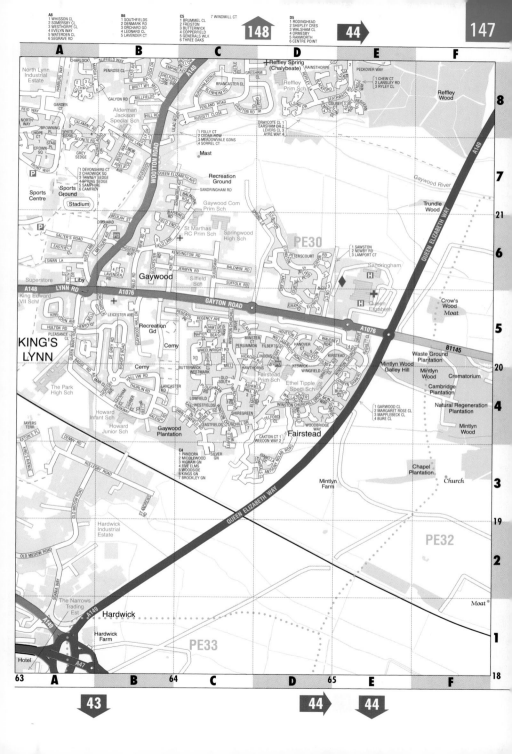

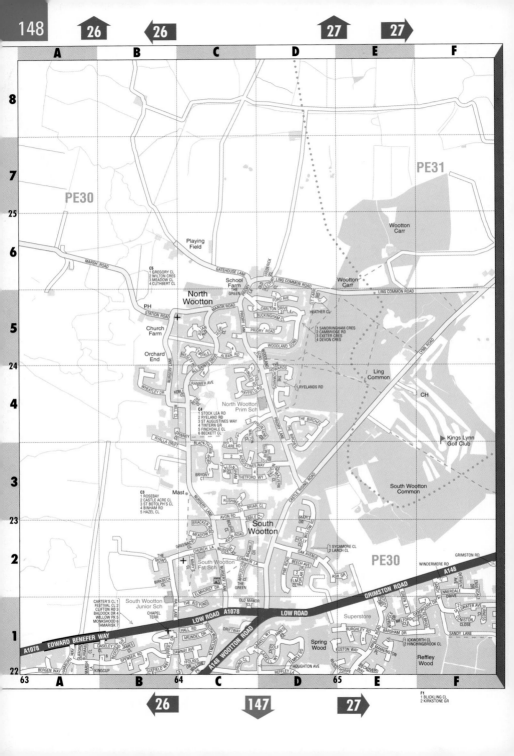

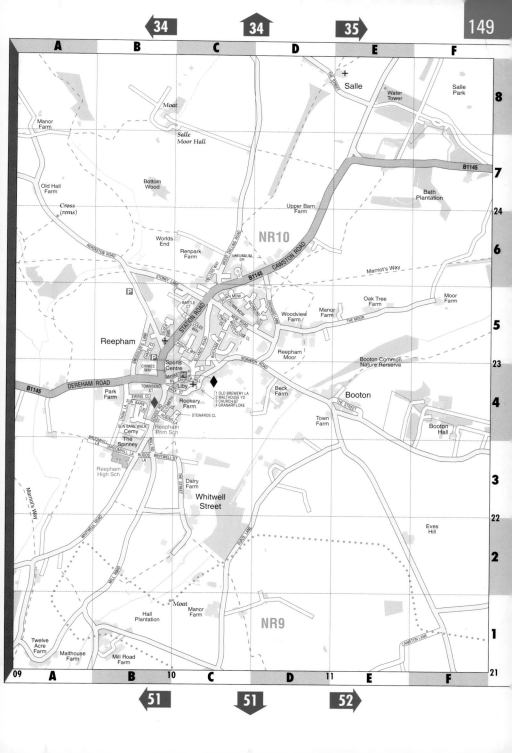

34 34 35

Salle

Salle
Park

Water
Tower

B1145

Bath
Plantation

Manor
Farm

Moat

Salle
Moor Hall

Old Hall
Farm

Bottom
Wood

Cross
(rems)

Upper Barn
Farm

NR10

Marriot's Way

KERDISTON ROAD

Worlds
End

Renpark
Farm

LABURNUM
GR

WOOD DALLING ROAD

B1145

CAWSTON ROAD

Oak Tree
Farm

Moor
Farm

STONEY LANE

CABLES WAY

Woodview
Farm

Manor
Farm

THE MOOR

BATTLE
CT

STATION ROAD

INN MDW

CROWN MDW

WEB MDW

BROADEST LANE

Reepham

SMUGGLERS LANE

SILVER
RD

CHURCH LANE

CYCLES
WAY

DIAL CLO

PRIORY
LANE

WEB LANE

CROWN CLO

BIRCHALL

COLOMBINE CL

NORWICH ROAD

Reepham
Moor

Booton Common
Nature Reserve

DEREHAM ROAD

B1145

CHIMES
WAY

Sports
Centre

MARKET
PL

P

Liby

CHURCH HILL

Booton

Park
Farm

TOWNSEND
CT

EWING CL

SUN BARN
CL

KINGS LA

BACK ST

ST ELIZABETH CT

Rookery
Farm

1 OLD BREWERY LA
2 MALTHOUSE YD
3 CHURCH ST
4 GRANARY LOKE

Beck
Farm

THE STREET

SUN BARN WALK

Cemy

ROBINS

STEWARDS CL

Town
Farm

Booton
Hall

The
Spinney

BROOMHILL

BROOMHILL LA

RUDDS
LA

MILL RD

Reepham
Prim Sch

Reepham
High Sch

WHITWELL ST

Marriot's Way

WHITWELL ROAD

MILL ROAD

THE STREET

Dairy
Farm

Whitwell
Street

Eves
Hill

MILL ROAD

Moat

Manor
Farm

FURZE LANE

NR9

Hall
Plantation

Twelve
Acre
Farm

Malthouse
Farm

Mill Road
Farm

CAWSTON LANE

09

10

11

21

51 51 52

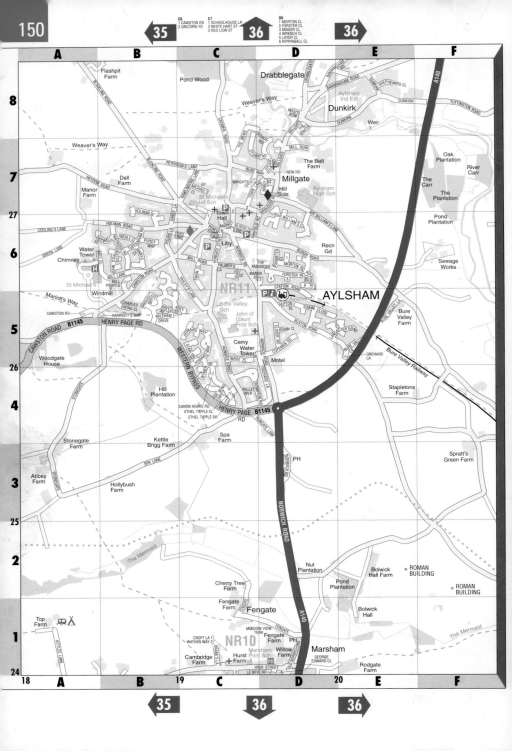

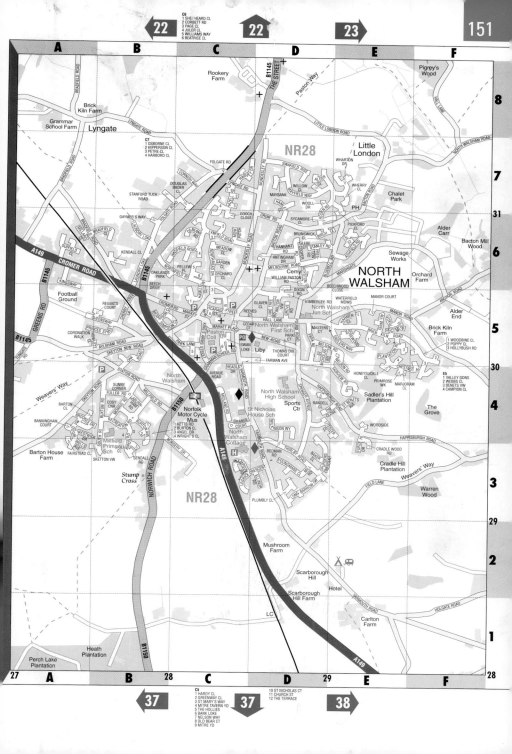

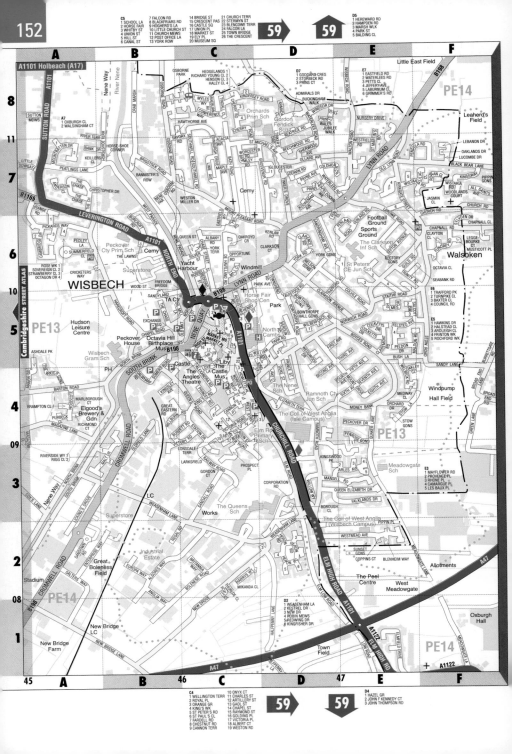

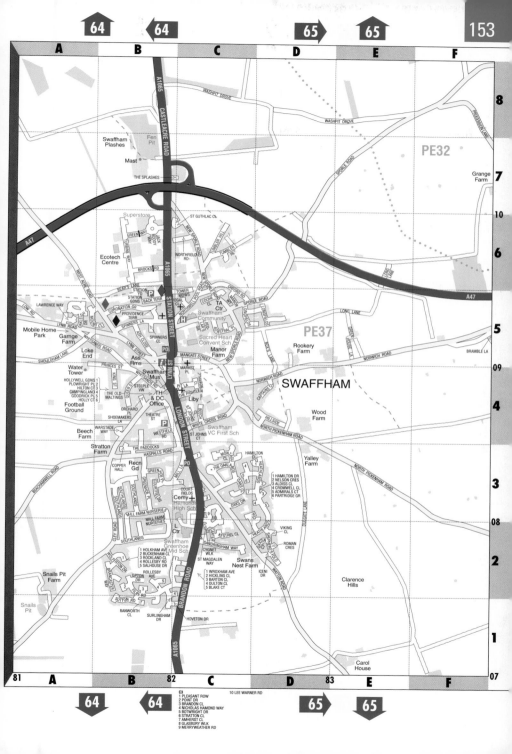

PE32

PE37

SWAFFHAM

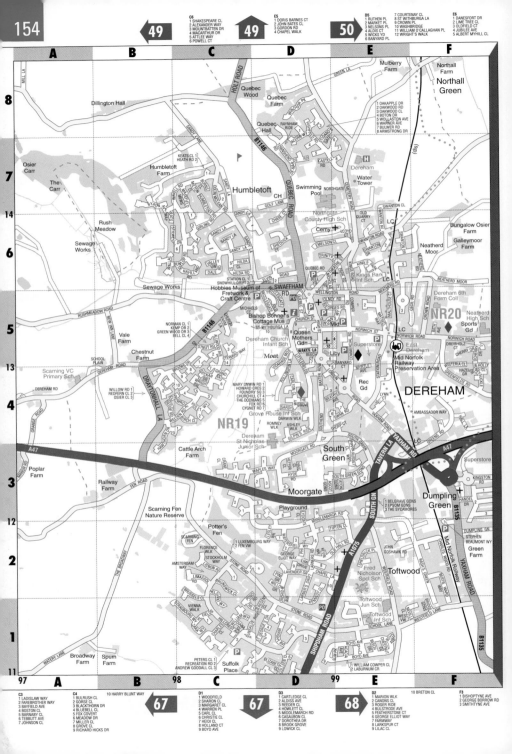

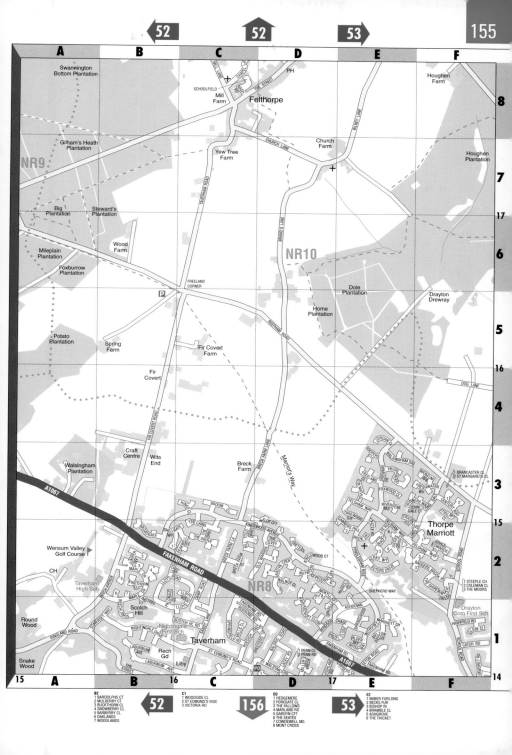

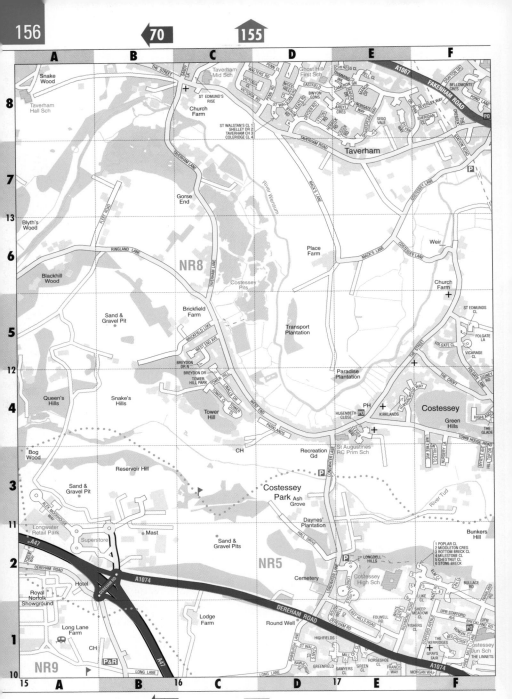

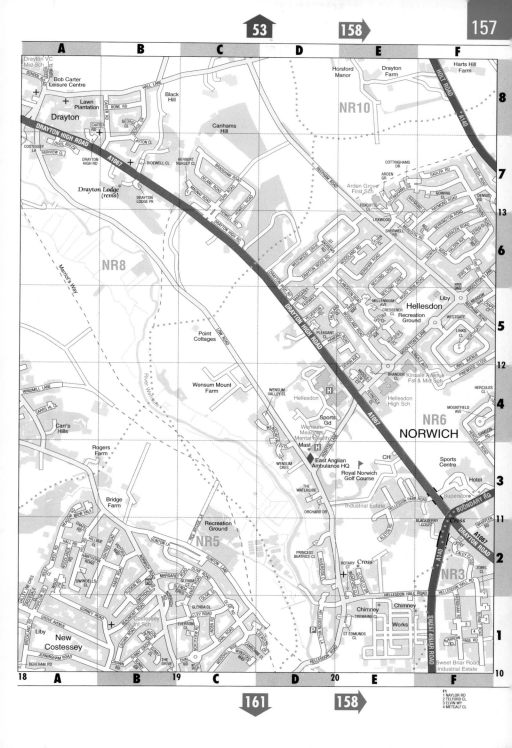

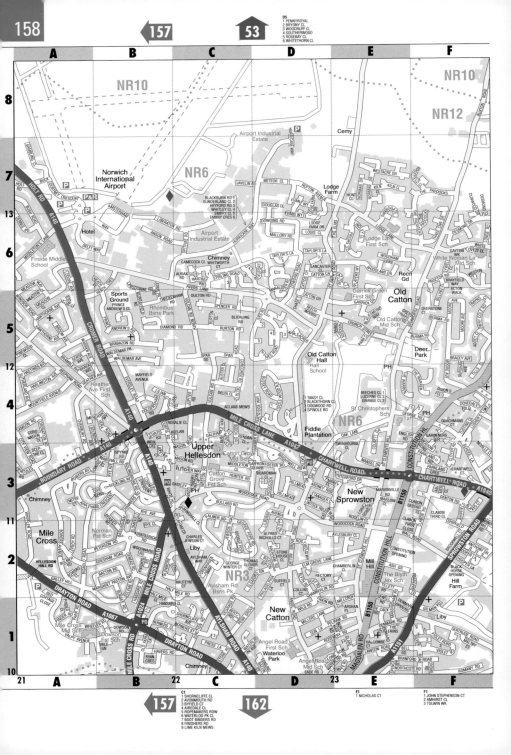

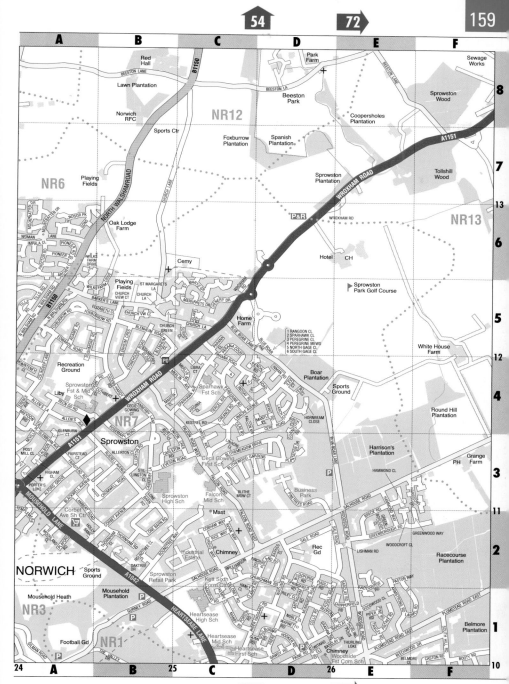

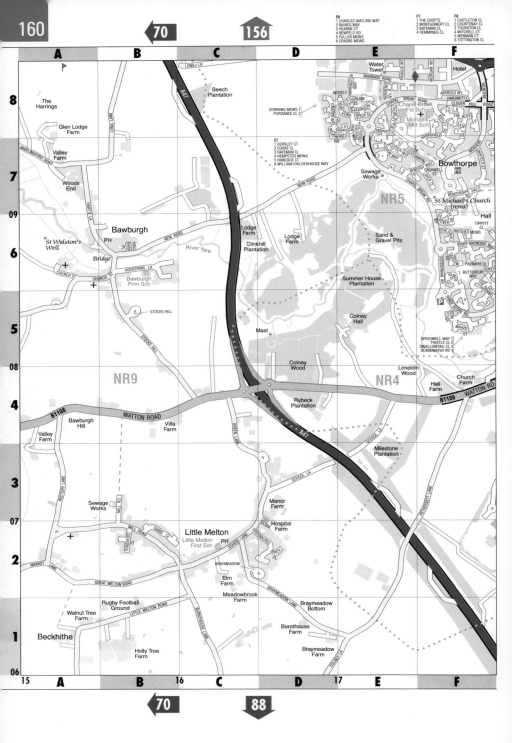

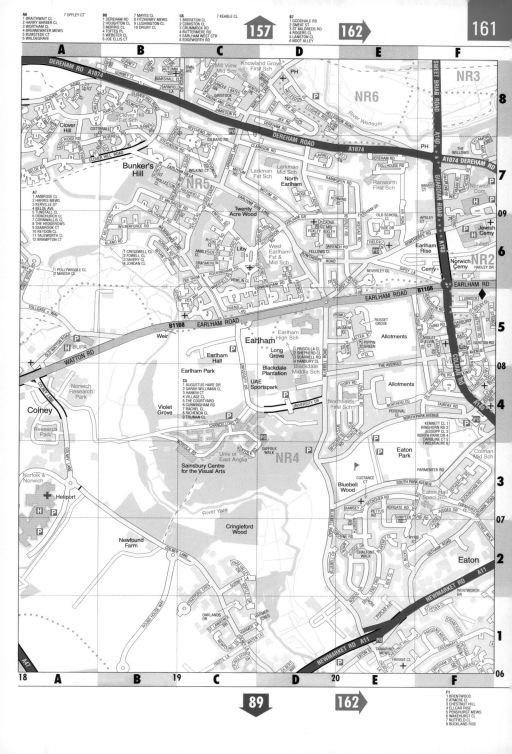

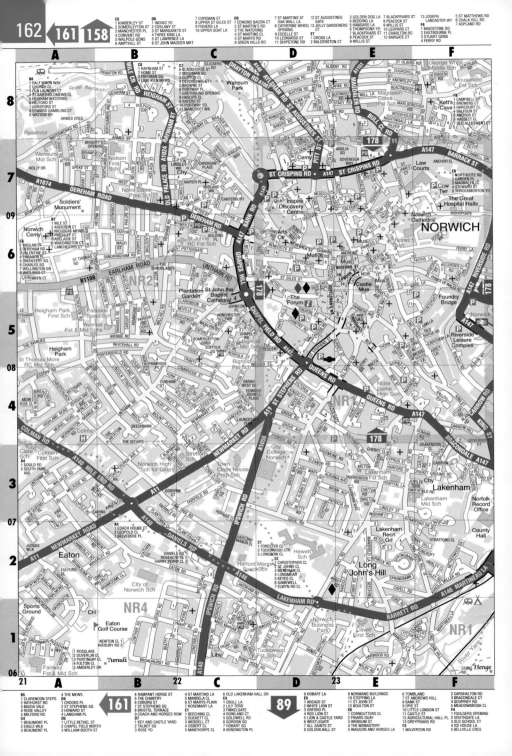

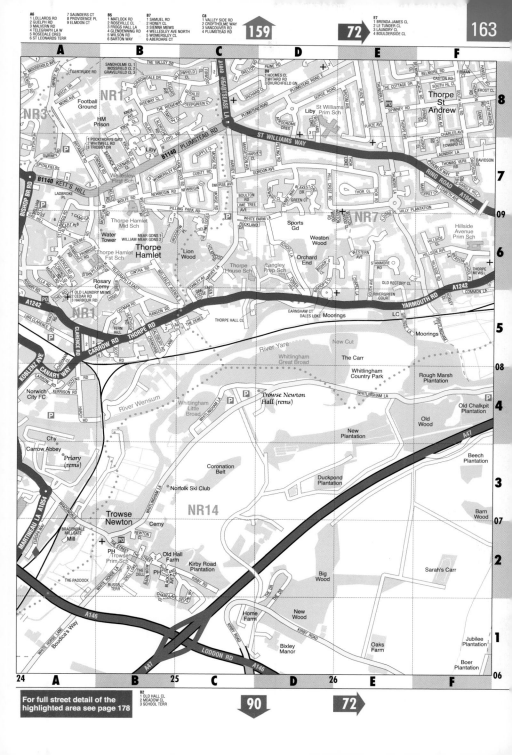

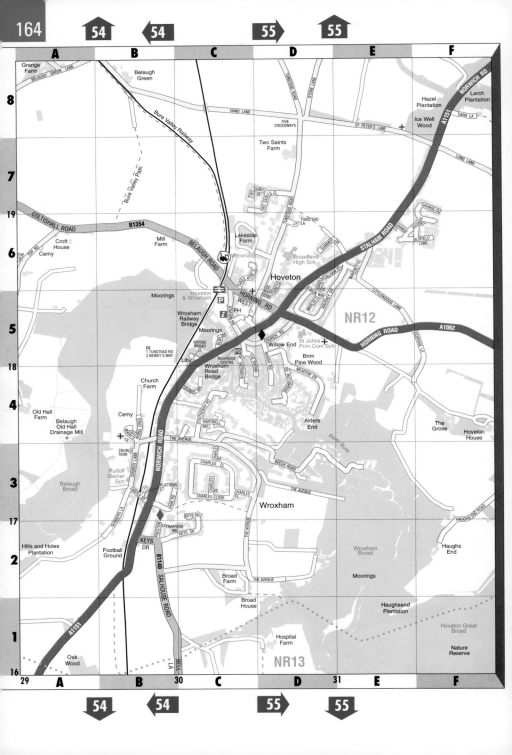

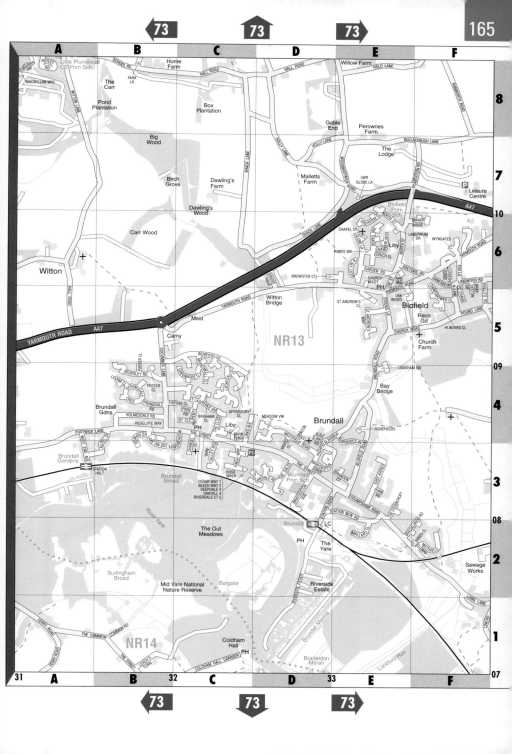

73
73
73
73
73
73

A B C D E F

8
7
10
6
5
09
4
3
08
2
1
07

Little Plumstead
CE/Prim Sch
ASTLEY RD
LANGFORD RD
MACMILLAN WAY
WITTON LANE
SCHOOL RD
PARK LA
Home Farm
HALL ROAD
HALL ROAD
Willow Farm
FIELD LANE
BARMOUTH ROAD

The Carr
Pond Plantation
Big Wood
Box Plantation
HOLLY LANE
HOLLY LANE
Gable End
Perownes Farm
WOODGATE ROAD
BULLACEBUSH LANE
The Lodge
PLANTATION ROAD
P Leisure Centre
A47

Birch Grove
Dawling's Farm
Dawling's Wood
Carr Wood
SHACK LANE
Malletts Farm
LWR GLOBE LA
Blofield Prim
MANOR BRIDGE
CHAPEL CT
NORTH ST
ROPES WK
LABURNUM DR
WYNGATES
YARMOUTH ROAD

Witton
HALL ROAD
Mast
YARMOUTH ROAD
A47
Cemy
Witton Bridge
NR13
BREWSTER CTT
ROPES WK
ST ANDREW'S CL
CHURCH ALLEY
PH
OAK WOOD
POUND LANE
Blofield
Recn Gd
HUNTERS CL

Witton Bridge
DICKHAM LANE
BERRYFIELDS CL
LENACRE
PARKER CL
BEVERLEY RD
LEVINE CL SPRINGDALE RD
FOSTER
CRES
HOLMESDALE RD
Brundall Gdns
POSTWICK LANE
WEST END AVE
Brundall Gardens
STATION HALT
Brundall Broad
River Yare
Surlingham Broad
Mid Yare National Nature Reserve
Bargate

MEDWELL CL
MACKWELL
ST LAURENCE AVE
FIRTREE CL
PAGE RD
BRIGHAM CL
ST CLS
PH
Liby
THE STREET
CHURCH
CEDAR WAY 1
BEECH WAY 2
DEEPDALE 3
OAKHILL 4
RIVERDALE CT 5
MEADOW VW
GROVEBURY CL
BEACON
WESTFIELD RD
OAK
ROSE WALK
ST AVE
ROSEFIELDS
Brundall
CHURCH ROAD
LANGHAM GN
Bay Bridge

Brundall Prim Sch
STRUMPSHAW ROAD
BLOFIELD ROAD
STATION NEW RD
Brundall
LC
PH
The Yare
Riverside Estate
Brundall Marina
Bradeston Marsh
Lockford Run
Sewage Works
LONG LANE

NR14
FERRY ROAD
THE STREET
COMMON RD
THE COMMON
LEACH'S TURN
Coldham Hall
PH
COLDHAM HALL CARNSER

31 A B 32 C D 33 E F

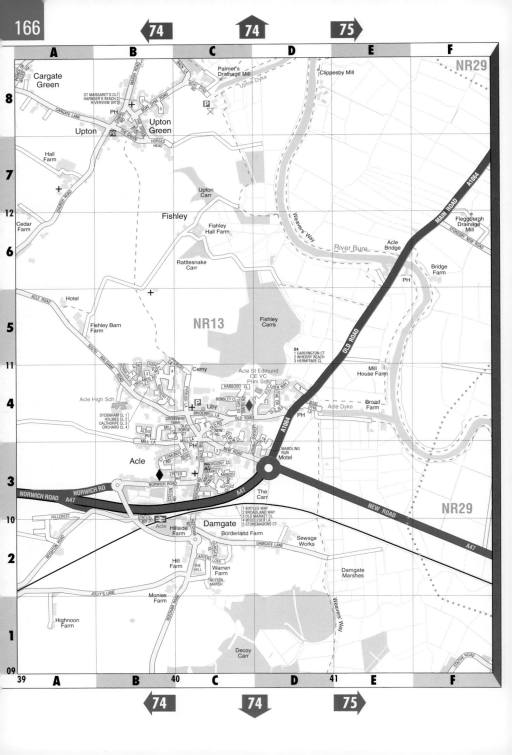

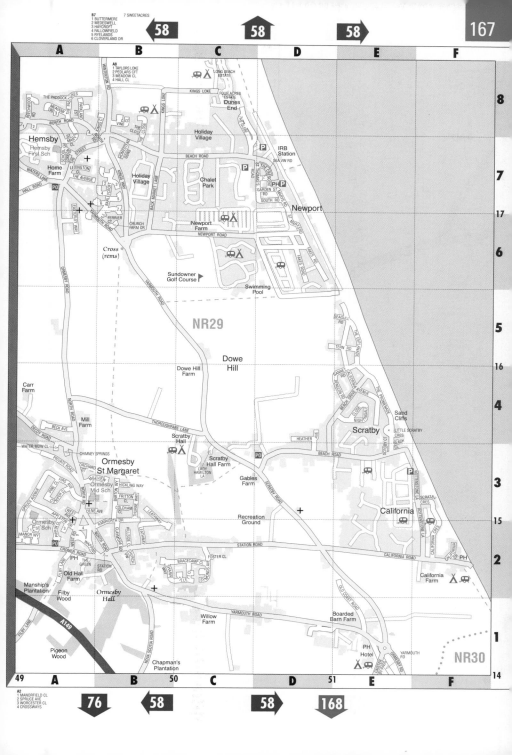

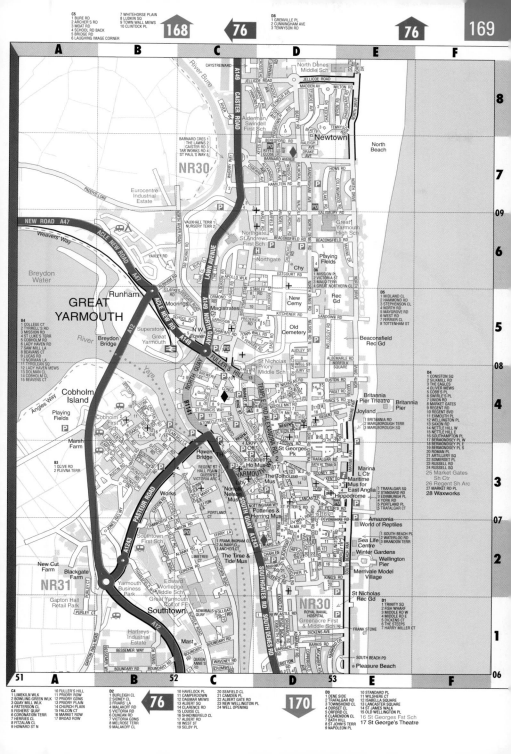

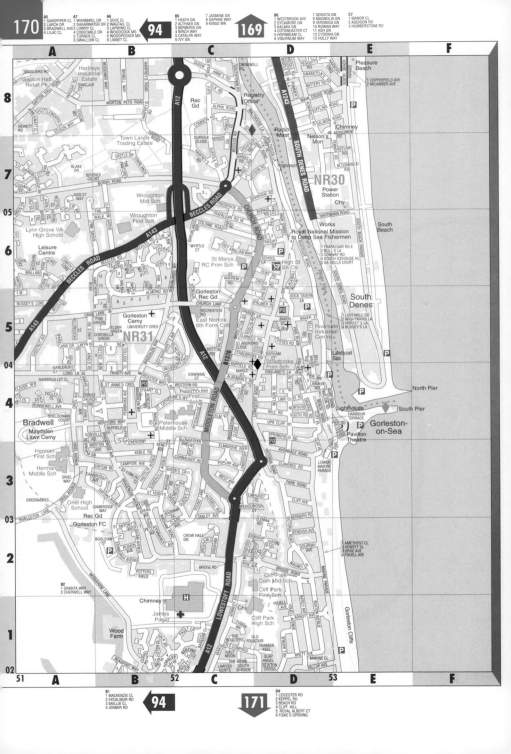

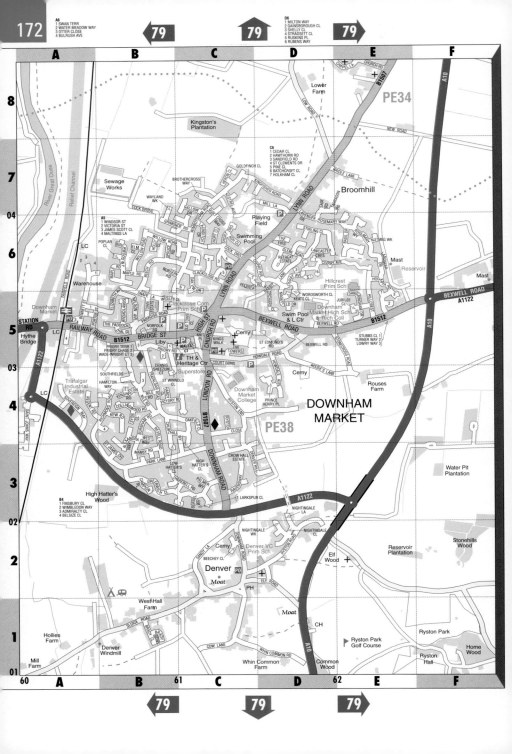

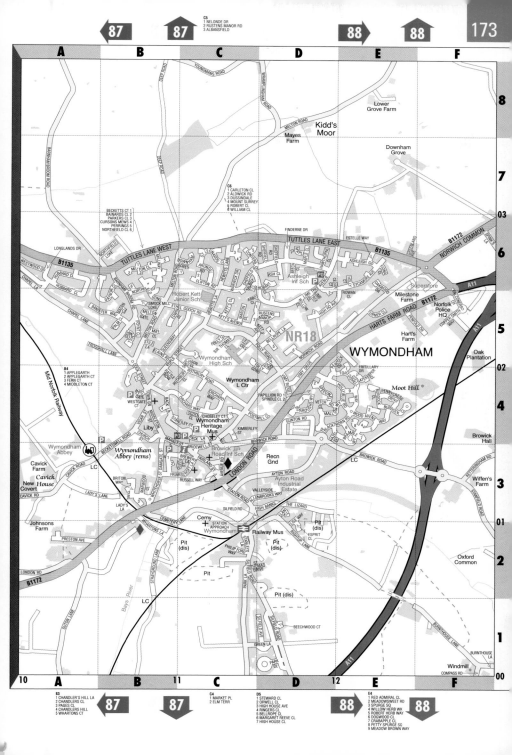

87 87
C5
1 NELONDE DR
2 RUSTENS MANOR RD
3 ALBANSFIELD
88 88
173

A B C D E F

8

Lower
Grove Farm

Kidd's
Moor

Mayes
Farm

Downham
Grove

7

C6
1 CARLETON CL
2 ALDWICK RD
3 DUSSINDALE
4 MOUNT SURREY
6 ROBERT CL
8 WILLIAM CL

03

BECKETTS CT 1
BAINARDS CL 2
PARKERS CL 3
CURSONS MEWS 4
PERRINGS 5
NORTHFIELD CL 6

FINDERNE DR

ESTELLE WAY

NORWICH COMMON

TUTTLES LANE EAST

B1172

6

LONGLANDS DR

TUTTLES LANE WEST

B1135

B1135

A11

Superstore

Ashleigh
Inf Sch

Milestone
Farm

B1172

Norfolk
Police
HQ

Robert Kett
Junior Sch

NR18

Harts Farm Road

Hart's
Farm

5

02

WYMONDHAM

Oak
Plantation

B4
1 APPLEGARTH
2 APPLEGARTH CT
3 FERN CT
4 MIDDLETON CT

Wymondham
High Sch

Moot Hill

Mid Norfolk Railway

Wymondham
L Ctr

4

Browick
Hall

Libv

Wymondham
Heritage
Mus

Wymondham
Abbey

Wymondham
Abbey (rems)

Browick Road

Browick Road

Recn
Gnd

LC

Wiffen's
Farm

3

Cavick
Farm

Cavick
New House
Covert

Ayton Road

Ayton Road
Industrial
Estate

01

Johnsons
Farm

PRESTON AVE

LADY'S LA

Cemy

Wymondham
Railway Mus

Pit
(dis)

Oxford
Common

2

LONDON RD

B1172

Pit
(dis)

Pit
(dis)

Pit

Bays River

LC

Pit (dis)

A11

BEECHWOOD CT

1

GREEN LA

BURNTHOUSE
LA

Windmill

COMPASS RD

00

B3
1 CHANDLER'S HILL LA
2 CHANDLERS CL
3 PAGES CL
4 CHANDLERS HILL
5 WHARTONS CT

C4
1 MARKET PL
2 ELM TERR

D5
1 STEWARD CL
2 ORWELL CL
3 HIGH HOUSE AVE
4 RINGERS CL
5 BELLROPE CL
6 MARGARET REEVE CL
7 HIGH HOUSE CL

E4
1 RED ADMIRAL CL
2 MEADOWSWEET RD
3 SPURGE SQ
4 WILLOW HERB WK
5 ROBERT HERB WAY
6 DOGWOOD CL
7 CRABAPPLE CL
8 PETTY SPURGE SQ
9 MEADOW BROWN WAY

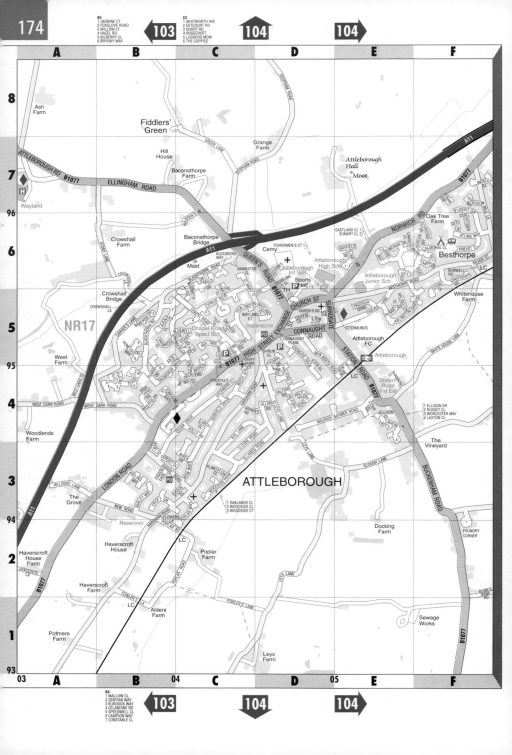

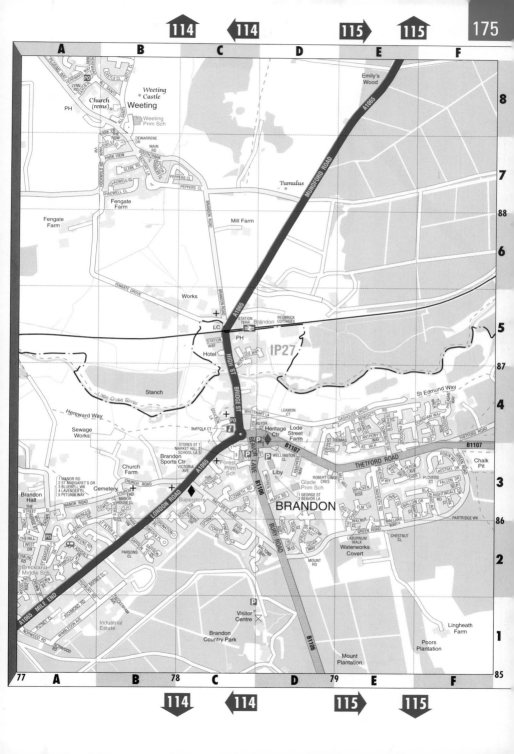

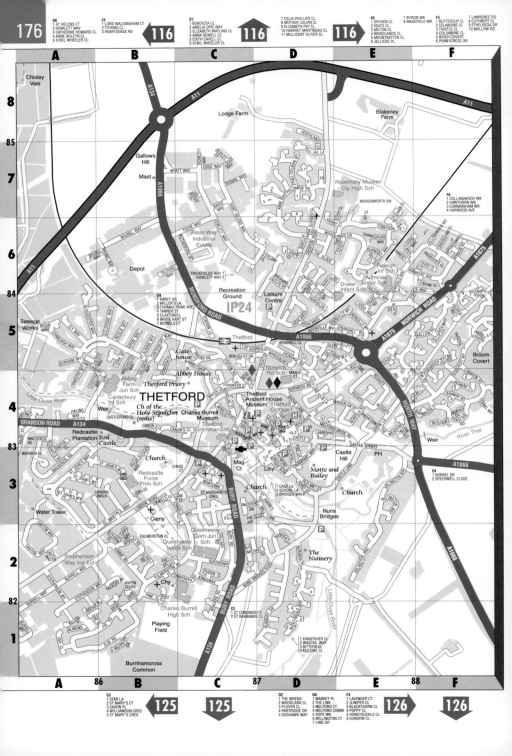

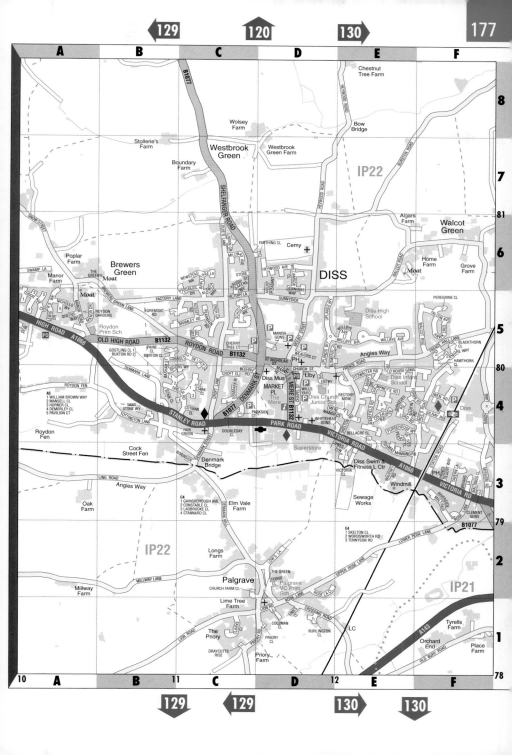

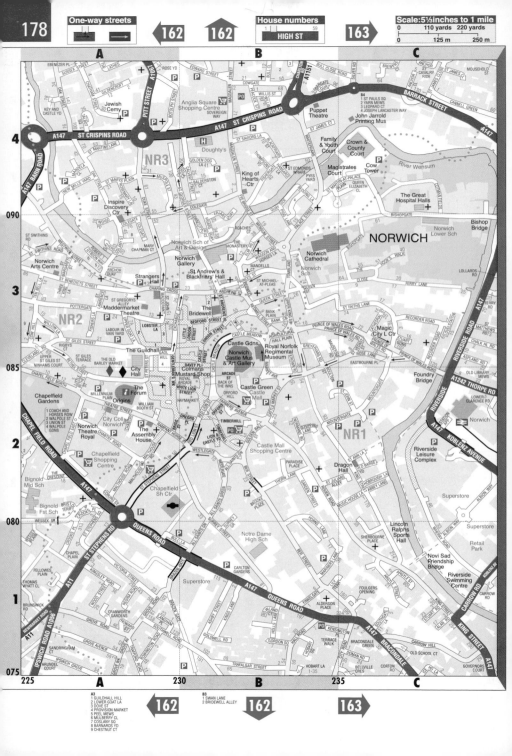

Index

Place name May be abbreviated on the map

Location number Present when a number indicates the place's position in a crowded area of mapping

Locality, town or village Shown when more than one place has the same name

Postcode district District for the indexed place

Page and grid square Page number and grid reference for the standard mapping

Church Rd 6 Beckenham BR2.........**53** C6

Public and commercial buildings are highlighted in magenta   Places of interest are highlighted in blue with a star★

Abbreviations used in the index

Acad	Academy	Comm	Common	Gd	Ground	L	Leisure	Prom	Promenade
App	Approach	Cott	Cottage	Gdn	Garden	La	Lane	Rd	Road
Arc	Arcade	Cres	Crescent	Gn	Green	Liby	Library	Recn	Recreation
Ave	Avenue	Cswy	Causeway	Gr	Grove	Mdw	Meadow	Ret	Retail
Bglw	Bungalow	Ct	Court	H	Hall	Meml	Memorial	Sh	Shopping
Bldg	Building	Ctr	Centre	Ho	House	Mkt	Market	Sq	Square
Bsns, Bus	Business	Ctry	Country	Hospl	Hospital	Mus	Museum	St	Street
Bvd	Boulevard	Cty	County	HQ	Headquarters	Orch	Orchard	Sta	Station
Cath	Cathedral	Dr	Drive	Hts	Heights	Pal	Palace	Terr	Terrace
Cir	Circus	Dro	Drove	Ind	Industrial	Par	Parade	TH	Town Hall
Cl	Close	Ed	Education	Inst	Institute	Pas	Passage	Univ	University
Cnr	Corner	Emb	Embankment	Int	International	Pk	Park	Wk, Wlk	Walk
Coll	College	Est	Estate	Intc	Interchange	Pl	Place	Wr	Water
Com	Community	Ex	Exhibition	Junc	Junction	Prec	Precinct	Yd	Yard

Index of localities, towns and villages

A

Acle.....................166 B3
Alburgh..................122 F6
Alby Hill................21 B5
Aldborough...............21 A5
Aldeby..................110 F4
Alderford................52 A5
All Saints South
Elmham..................124 B1
Alpington................90 E4
Anchor Corner............86 A1
Anchor Street............38 B3
Anmer....................28 E8
Annis Hill..............124 C8
Antingham................22 B4
Arminghall...............90 B7
Ashby St Mary............91 C5
Ashill...................84 A7
Ashmanhaugh..............55 B8
Ashwellthorpe...........105 F8
Ashwicken................45 A6
Aslacton................106 A2
Attleborough............174 D3
Attlebridge..............52 B3
Aylmerton................10 A2
Aylsham.................150 B5

B

Babingley................27 D5
Baconsthorpe.............20 A8
Bacton...................23 E5
Bacton Green.............23 D5
Bagthorpe................14 D3
Bale.....................18 B7
Banham..................119 D7
Banningham...............36 D8
Barford..................69 F2
Barmer...................14 F4
Barney...................17 F3
Barnham.................125 F6
Barnham Broom............69 C2
Barningham..............127 C3
Barningham Green.........20 A4
Barton Bendish...........81 A8
Barton Turf..............38 F1
Bastwick.................57 A4
Battlesea Green.........131 E2
Bawburgh................160 B6
Bawdeswell...............50 E8
Bawsey...................44 D6
Beachamwell..............81 F8
Beccles.................110 D2
Beckett End..............82 B1

Beckhithe...............160 A1
Bedingham Green.........108 B3
Beeston..................48 C2
Beeston Regis...........138 F5
Beeston St Lawrence.....55 C8
Beetley..................49 D4
Beighton.................74 C2
Belaugh..................54 E5
Bellmount...............144 A7
Belton...................93 F6
Bengate..................38 A6
Bergh Apton..............91 A4
Bessingham...............20 E7
Besthorpe...............174 F6
Bexwell..................79 F6
Billingford
Bawdeswell..............50 B7
Diss...................130 E5
Billockby................75 A7
Binham....................6 E2
Bintree..................33 B2
Bircham Newton..........14 A4
Bircham Tofts...........14 B3
Bittering................48 F4
Blackborough End........44 C1
Black Carr..............105 A6
Blackwater...............51 D6
Blakeney..................7 C6
Bleach Green............131 F4
Blenheim Park............15 C3
Blickling................35 F7
Blofield................165 F5
Blofield Corner.........73 C6
Blofield Heath..........73 D6
Blo' Norton............128 B6
Bloodman's Corner.......171 A4
Bobby Hill..............128 A1
Bodham....................9 A3
Bodney...................83 B1
Booton..................149 E4
Botesdale...............128 F2
Boughton.................81 A5
Bowbeck.................127 A2
Bowthorpe...............160 F7
Bracon Ash...............89 A2
Bradenham................66 E4
Bradfield................22 C4
Bradwell.................94 C7
Brakefield Green........68 D4
Bramerton................90 F7
Brampton.................36 E3
Brancaster................3 B6
Brancaster Staithe.......3 C7
Brandiston...............52 B8
Brandon.................175 D3
Brandon Bank...........112 B7
Brandon Creek...........97 A2

Brandon Parva...........69 B2
Breckles................102 E5
Bressingham............129 C8
Bressingham Common.....119 F1
Brettenham.............117 B2
Brewers Green..........177 B6
Bridge Green...........120 F2
Bridgham...............117 F5
Briggate.................38 B6
Briningham...............18 D4
Brinton..................18 D6
Brisley..................49 A8
Briston.................142 E4
Brockdish..............131 C6
Brome...................130 B3
Brome Street...........130 D3
Brooke...................90 E2
Brookville...............99 A6
Broome..................109 C2
Broom Green..............32 E2
Broomhill..............172 E7
Broomholm................23 E4
Broomsthorpe............30 C7
Browston Green...........94 C4
Brundall................165 D4
Brundish...............110 A6
Buckenham................91 F8
Bull's Green...........110 C5
Bumwell Hill...........105 E2
Bungay..................124 A8
Bunker's Hill
Lowestoft...............94 C3
Norwich................161 B7
Bunwell.................105 D4
Bunwell Bottom.........105 C6
Burgate.................129 C2
Burgh Castle............94 A7
Burgh Common...........100 D5
Burgh next Aylsham......36 D4
Burgh St Margaret
(Fleggburgh)............57 C1
Burgh St Peter.........111 C4
Burgh Stubbs...........142 B8
Burlingham Green........74 A5
Burnham Deepdale.........3 E6
Burnham Market.........135 C3
Burnham Norton.........135 B6
Burnham Overy Staithe..135 E6
Burnham Overy Town.....135 E4
Burnham Thorpe...........4 D4
Burnham Westgate.......135 B3
Burston.................120 F2
Bush Green.............122 A6
Bushy Common............67 B8
Bustard's Green........106 C3
Buxton...................36 E1

C

Caister-on-Sea.........168 F6
Caistor St Edmund.......89 F6
California..............167 E3
Calthorpe................21 A2
Calthorpe Street........39 D4
Candle Street..........128 D1
Cangate..................55 C6
Cantley..................92 B7
Carbrooke................85 B5
Cargate Common.........105 E1
Cargate Green..........166 A8
Carleton Forehoe........87 C8
Carleton Rode..........105 C3
Carleton St Peter.......91 E8
Castle Acre..............46 F2
Castle Rising............27 C3
Caston.................102 E8
Catfield.................56 C8
Caudlesprings...........85 A4
Cawston..................35 B2
Cess.....................57 C5
Chalkhill................83 C4
Chapel Field.............39 A3
Chedgrave................92 A2
Chickering.............131 D3
Christchurch.............95 A7
Church End...............41 F2
Claxton..................91 D6
Clenchwarton............145 E5
Cley next the Sea........7 C6
Cliftonville............143 B7
Clint Green..............68 C6
Clippesby................57 A1
Clippings Green..........68 C5
Cobbler's Green........108 B2
Cobholm Island.........169 A4
Cockley Cley.............82 D7
Cockthorpe...............6 E5
Colby....................21 E2
Colegate End...........121 E6
Colkirk..................31 D5
Colney..................161 A4
Coltishall...............54 C6
Colton...................69 E4
Coney Weston...........127 B5
Congham..................28 B2
Copy's Green..............6 A2
Cordwell...............105 E4
Corpusty.................19 E1
Costessey................76 F7
Costessey Park.........156 D3
Coston...................69 A1
Coxford..................30 C8
Crabgate.................34 D6

Crackthorn Corner......128 D5
Cranwich.................99 F6
Cranworth................85 E7
Craymere Beck............18 F1
Crimplesham.............80 B6
Cringleford..............89 B8
Cromer..................139 C7
Crossdale Street.......139 D1
Cross Street...........131 A3
Cross Ways...............94 B4
Crostwick................54 B3
Crostwight...............38 D8
Crowgate Street.........55 A8
Crownthorpe.............87 C6
Crowshill................67 A1
Croxton
Fakenham...............17 E2
Thetford...............116 C5
Cuckoo Green...........171 A4
Culfordheath...........125 D1

D

Daffy Green..............67 C4
Damgate
Acle..................166 C2
Martham................57 E5
Dam Green..............119 C4
Danemoor Green..........86 F8
Darrow Green...........122 E8
Denham..................131 B1
Denton..................123 A7
Denver..................172 C2
Deopham..................86 F3
Deopham Green............86 E2
Deopham Stalland........86 D2
Dereham................154 F4
Dersingham.............140 D5
Dickleburgh............121 C1
Dickleburgh Moor.......121 C2
Didlington...............99 E8
Dilham...................38 D4
Diss...................177 D6
Ditchingham............109 A2
Dockeney...............109 C4
Docking..................134 C5
Doddshill..............140 F3
Dowe Hill..............167 C5
Downham Market.........176 D4
Drabblegate............150 D8
Drayton.................157 A8
Drurylane................85 A4
Drymere..................64 C1
Dumpling Green.........154 F3
Dunkirk................150 E8
Dunston..................89 D5

Dunton 15 F1
Dussindale Park 72 E4

E

Earlham 161 D5
Earsham 123 E8
Earsham Street 131 F5
East Barsham 16 D4
East Bilney 49 B6
East Carleton 88 F4
Eastgate 35 C2
East Harling 118 C5
Easthaugh 51 C4
East Lexham 47 D3
Easton 70 B5
East Raynham 31 A4
East Rudham 30 A7
East Runton 10 B5
East Ruston 38 E6
East Somerton 58 A6
East Tuddenham 69 C6
East Walton 45 E3
East Winch 44 F3
East Wretham 102 A1
Eaton 161 F2
Eau Brink 43 A3
Eccles on Sea 24 E4
Eccles Road 103 F1
Edgefield 19 D5
Edgefield Street 19 D4
Edge Green 119 B4
Edingthorpe 23 C3
Edingthorpe Green 23 A2
Ellingham 109 D3
Elm 59 B1
Elsing 50 F3
Elveden 125 A7
Emneth 59 D2
Emneth Hungate 59 F2
Emorsgate 42 B7
Erpingham 21 B2
Etling Green 68 B8
Euston 126 B5
Eye 130 C1

F

Fair Green 44 B4
Fairstead 147 D4
Fakenham 141 D6
Fakenham Magna 126 C3
Felbrigg 10 C2
Felmingham 37 A8
Felthorpe 155 C8
Feltwell 98 D1
Fengate 150 C1
Fenside 56 B8
Fen Street
  Hopton 127 E6
  Redgrave 128 F6
Fersfield 119 D2
Fiddlers' Green 174 B8
Field Dalling 7 B1
Filby 75 F8
Filby Heath 76 B8
Fincham 62 F1
Fishley 166 C6
Flaxlands 105 C4
Flitcham 28 C5
Flixton 123 D5
Flordon 106 D8
Fodderstone Gap 62 C4
Fordham 79 D2
Forncett End 105 E4
Forncett St Mary 106 B4
Forncett St Peter 106 B4
Foul Anchor 41 A4
Foulden 82 A2
Foulsham 33 D3
Foxhole 107 A7
Foxley 50 D8
Framingham Earl 90 D4
Framingham Pigot 90 C6
Frankfort 38 A3
Frans Green 51 D1
Freethorpe 92 E8
Frenze 130 B7
Frettenham 54 A4
Friday Bridge 77 A7
Fring 13 D5
Fritton
  Great Yarmouth 93 E3
  Long Stratton 107 B3
  Ludham 56 E5
Frogshall 11 B1
Frost Row 86 B4
Fulmodeston 17 F1
Fundenhall 106 A7

G

Garboldisham 128 A8
Garlic Street 122 A2
Garvestone 68 C2
Gasthorpe 127 D7
Gateley 32 C3
Gayton 45 C5
Gayton Thorpe 45 E5
Gaywood 147 B6
Geldeston 109 F3
Gillingham 110 C2
Gimingham 22 E7
Gissing 120 F4
Glandford 7 E4

Gooderstone 82 A4
Goose Green 120 C6
Gorleston-on-Sea 170 E4
Great Barwick 14 E6
Great Bircham 14 B3
Great Common 124 D6
Great Cressingham 83 D4
Great Dunham 47 E1
Great Ellingham 103 E7
Great Fransham 66 B8
Great Green
  Diss 130 A4
  Wortham 129 B3
Great Hautbois 54 C7
Great Hockham 102 E3
Great Massingham 29 D2
Great Melton 70 B1
Great Moulton 106 B1
Great Plumstead 72 F5
Great Ryburgh 32 B6
Great Snoring 17 A5
Great Walsingham 17 A8
Great Witchingham 51 E7
Great Yarmouth 169 A5
Greengate 50 B3
Greensgate 51 E2
Gresham 9 E1
Gressenhall 49 B3
Grimston 28 B1
Griston 85 A2
Guestwick 34 A6
Guestwick Green 33 F5
Guist 32 F4
Gunthorpe 18 B5

H

Hackford 87 A5
Haddiscoe 110 F8
Hainford 53 E5
Hales 109 F8
Hales Green 109 E7
Hales Street 121 A6
Halvergate 74 F1
Hamrow 31 D3
Hanworth 21 B6
Happisburgh 24 C6
Happisburgh Common 24 B4
Hapton 106 C7
Hardingham 86 E6
Hardley Street 92 C4
Hardwick
  King's Lynn 147 B1
  Long Stratton 122 B8
Hargate 105 D2
Harleston 122 D3
Harling Road 118 A7
Harper's Green 32 A1
Harpley 29 D4
Hassingham 92 B8
Hawes' Green 89 F2
Hay Green 144 A1
Heacham 133 E4
Heckfield Green 131 B2
Heckingham 92 C1
Hedenham 108 E4
Helhoughton 30 E5
Hellesdon 157 F5
Hellington 91 B6
Hemblington 73 E6
Hemblington Corner 73 D6
Hempnall 107 D5
Hempnall Green 107 D4
Hempstead
  Holt 19 E8
  Stalham 24 E3
Hempton 141 A3
Hemsby 167 A7
Hengrave 52 A6
Hepworth 127 E1
Herringfleet 111 D8
Hethel 88 F3
Hethersett 88 C8
Hevingham 53 B7
Heydon 34 F6
Hickling 39 E2
Hickling Green 39 F2
Hickling Heath 39 E1
High Common 85 F8
High Green
  Beeston 48 E1
  Bradenham 66 E2
  Hethersett 88 B8
High Kelling 8 E3
Highoak 87 B4
High Street 124 D3
Hilborough 83 A3
Hilgay 79 E1
Hill Common 39 F1
Hillington 28 B4
Hinderclay 128 C3
Hindolveston 33 D8
Hindringham 17 E7
Hingham 86 C5
Hockering 69 B8
Hockering Heath 51 C1
Hockwold cum Wilton 114 A7
Hoe 49 F3
Holkham 5 B6
Holly End 59 D1
Holme Hale 66 B2
Holme next the Sea 2 A6
Holt 137 D6
Homersfield 123 B4
Honing 38 C6
Honingham 69 E7
Honington 126 D1

Hopton 127 F6
Hopton on Sea 171 D6
Horning 55 E4
Horningtoft 31 F1
Horsey 40 D2
Horsey Corner 40 D2
Horsford 53 B3
Horsham St Faith 53 D1
Horstead 54 C6
Houghton St Giles 16 E6
Hoveton 164 D6
Howe 90 D3
How Hill 56 B6
Hoxne 131 A4
Humbletoft 154 C7
Hunstanton 132 D5
Hunt's Corner 119 C7
Hunworth 19 A6
Hyltons Crossways 36 F8

I

Ickburgh 100 B6
Ilketshall St Andrew 124 E6
Ilketshall St Lawrence . . . 124 F2
Ilketshall St Margaret . . . 124 B4
Illington 117 D8
Ingham 39 D4
Ingham Corner 24 D2
Ingleborough 41 B1
Ingoldisthorpe 140 D8
Ingworth 36 B8
Intwood 89 B7
Irstead 56 A7
Irstead Street 55 F6
Itteringham 20 C1
Itteringham Common 35 D8
Ivy Todd 66 B4

J

Johnson Street 56 B4
Jordan Green 51 A8

K

Kelling 8 D5
Kenninghall 119 B5
Kerdiston 34 C3
Keswick
  North Walsham 23 F4
  Norwich 89 C7
Ketteringham 88 E6
Kettlestone 17 C2
Kidd's Moor 173 D8
Kimberley 87 B6
King's Lynn 147 A5
Kirby Bedon 90 E8
Kirby Cane 109 E4
Kirby Green 109 F5
Kirby Row 109 E3
Kirstead Green 108 C8
Knapton 143 B1
Knapton Green 22 F5
Knettishall 127 C7

L

Lakenham 162 F3
Lakenheath 113 E2
Lakes End 95 C7
Lamas 37 A2
Langham 7 B3
Langley Street 92 B4
Langton Green 130 C1
Larling 118 B8
Lenwade 51 D5
Lessingham 24 D3
Letheringsett 8 A1
Letton Green 67 E1
Leziate 44 D6
Limpenhoe 92 D6
Lingwood 73 F3
Litcham 48 A4
Little Barningham 20 C4
Little Barwick 14 E6
Little Cressingham 83 E2
Little Dunham 65 E8
Little Ellingham 86 A2
Little Fransham 66 B7
Little Green 129 B1
Little Hale 67 A1
Little Hautbois 54 B8
Little London
  Aldborough 36 A2
  Corpusty 19 E1
  North Walsham 151 E7
  Northwold 99 D7
Little Marsh 7 A1
Little Massingham 29 C3
Little Melton 160 C2
Little Ouse 112 A8
Little Plumstead 73 B6
Little Ryburgh 32 C7
Little Snoring 17 B3
Little Thornage 7 F3
Little Walsingham 16 F7
Loddon 92 A1
Loddon Ingloss 109 B7
Long Green 129 B4
Longham 49 A2
Long John's Hill 162 E2
Long Stratton 106 E3
Lordsbridge 60 E7

Lound 94 C1
Low Common 105 F3
Lower Bodham 9 A2
Lower East Carleton 89 B6
Lower Gresham 9 F1
Lower Stow Bedon 102 F5
Lower Street
  Southrepps 22 C6
  Wickmere 20 E5
Lower Tasburgh 106 E7
Lower Thurlton 93 A2
Low Street 86 E8
Low Tharston 106 D6
Ludham 56 D5
Lundy Green 107 D3
Lynford 100 D2
Lyng 51 A4
Lyngate
  North Walsham 151 A8
  Worstead 38 A5

M

Magpie Green 129 B5
Manor House 46 E2
Manson Green 86 C6
Marham 63 B4
Market Weston 127 E4
Marlingford 70 A4
Marsham 150 D1
Marshland St James 60 A4
Marsh Side 3 C7
Martham 57 D5
Matlaske 20 D5
Mattishall 68 E5
Mattishall Burgh 68 F7
Mautby 75 F7
Maypole Green 110 C6
Meeting House Hill 38 B7
Mellis 129 E1
Melton Constable 142 B5
Mendham 123 A1
Merton 84 C1
Methwold 99 A5
Methwold Hythe 98 E5
Mettingham 124 E8
Metton 21 C8
Middle Harling 118 B4
Middleton 44 C3
Mile Cross 158 A2
Mileham 48 C6
Mill Common 91 C4
Millgate 150 D7
Mill Green 120 E3
Mill Street 50 E4
Misery Corner 122 F8
Moorgate 154 D3
Morley St Botolph 87 B2
Morningthorpe 107 A3
Morston 7 B6
Morton 52 A4
Moulton St Mary 74 D2
Mount Pleasant 103 C5
Muckleton 3 F2
Mulbarton 89 B3
Mundesley 143 B5
Mundford 100 B4
Mundham 91 C1
Mustard Hyrn 57 C5

N

Narborough 63 E7
Narrowgate Corner 57 C2
Neatishead 55 E7
Neaton 84 E4
Necton 65 F4
Needham 131 D8
New Buckenham 104 F8
New Catton 158 D1
New Costessey 157 A1
Newgate 7 E5
Newgate Corner 75 C8
New Hainford 53 D5
New Holkham 5 A2
New Houghton 29 D6
New Rackheath 72 B4
New Sprowston 158 E3
Newton 47 B2
Newton Flotman 89 C1
Newton Greenways 89 D2
Newton St Faith 53 E4
Newtown 169 D7
Nogdam End 92 D3
Nordelph 78 D3
Nordelph Corner 86 D6
Northacre 85 B1
Northall Green 154 F8
North Barsham 16 D6
North Burlingham 74 A5
North Common 127 D2
North Court 114 C3
North Creake 4 D1
North Denes 168 F4
North Elmham 49 E8
North End 103 C3
North Green
  Harleston 122 A7
  Reymerston 68 C1
North Lopham 119 A2
North Lynn 146 F7
North Pickenham 65 E1
Northrepps 11 A2
North Runcton 44 A2
North Tuddenham 50 D1
North Walsham 151 A6

Northwold 99 C8
North Wootton 148 C5
Norton Corner 34 C7
Norton Subcourse 92 E1
Norwich 178 A3

O

Oakley 130 E5
Old Beetley 49 D5
Old Buckenham 104 D2
Old Catton 158 E5
Old Hall Street 23 A4
Old Hunstanton 132 E8
Orange Row 144 A6
Ormesby St Margaret 167 B3
Ormesby St Michael 58 A1
Ostend 24 A7
Oulton 35 B7
Oulton Street 35 D6
Outwell 77 F6
Overstrand 11 A4
Ovington 84 E5
Oxborough 81 D4
Oxnead 36 E2
Oxwick 31 D4

P

Palgrave 177 C2
Panxworth 73 E7
Paston 143 D2
Paston Green 143 D1
Peaseland Green 50 F3
Pedham 73 D7
Pennygate 38 E2
Pentney 63 C8
Pettywell 34 C2
Pilson Green 74 B8
Plumstead Green
  Great and Little
    Plumstead 73 B6
  Holt 20 B6
Pockthorpe
  Lyng 51 B5
  Watton 102 A7
  West Rudham 29 F6
Podmore 67 B7
Pollard Street 23 D3
Pooley Street 129 A8
Poringland 90 C5
Postwick 72 F2
Pottergate Street 106 B2
Potter Heigham 56 F6
Pottle End 88 A8
Primrose Corner 55 C1
Primrose Green 51 A3
Pristow Green 120 E8
Pudding Norton 141 B1
Puddledock 104 C3
Pulham Market 121 E5
Pulham St Mary 121 F4

Q

Quidenham 118 F6

R

Rackheath 72 E8
Ragmere 104 D1
Ranworth 55 F1
Ratten Row 59 F8
Raveningham 110 A7
Reading Green 131 C1
Redenhall 122 F3
Redgrave 128 E4
Red Pits 34 D7
Reedham 92 E5
Reepham 149 B5
Repps 56 F4
Reymerston 68 C1
Rickinghall 128 E2
Ridlington 23 E1
Ridlington Street 23 E1
Ringland 70 B8
Ringstead 2 A3
Road Green 107 E4
Rockland All Saints 103 B7
Rockland St Mary 91 B7
Rockland St Peter 103 B8
Rollesby 57 D2
Rougham 47 B7
Roughton 21 E8
Roydon
  Diss 129 D7
  King's Lynn 28 A2
Runcton Holme 61 D3
Runhall 68 F2
Runham
  Filby 75 E6
  Great Yarmouth 169 B5
Rushall 121 F1
Rushford 126 E8
Rush Green 69 B1

S

Saham Hills 84 C6
Saham Toney 84 B5
St Cross South Elmham 123 D3
St James 54 E7
St John's Fen End 60 D7

St John's Highway 42 B1
St Margaret South
  Elmham 123 E2
St Michael South
  Elmham 124 A2
St Nicholas South
  Elmham 123 E2
St Olaves 93 D2
St Peter South Elmham 124 A3
Salhouse 55 B1
Salle 149 E8
Salters Lode 79 A4
Salthouse 8 B7
Sandringham 27 F7
Santon Downham 115 C6
Sapiston 126 D2
Saxlingham 7 C2
Saxlingham Green 107 D7
Saxlingham Nethergate 107 C8
Saxlingham Thorpe . . . 107 A8
Saxthorpe 19 F1
Scarning 67 B7
Scole 130 D6
Scole Common 130 C7
Sco Ruston 54 E8
Scottow 37 D2
Sculton 85 E3
Scratby 167 E4
Sculthorpe 16 B2
Sea Palling 40 A6
Sedgeford 13 B7
Seething 108 F8
Setchey 61 E8
Shadwell 117 C2
Sharp Street 56 C7
Sharrington 18 D7
Shelfanger 120 C2
Shelton 107 B1
Shepherd's Gate 42 D4
Shepherd's Port 11 A8
Shereford 31 A8
Sheringham 138 C7
Sheringwood 138 C5
Shernborne 13 B3
Shimpling 121 A2
Shingham 82 A8
Shipdham 67 B2
Shipmeadow 124 F8
Short Green 120 A5
Shotesham 90 A2
Shouldham 62 D4
Shouldham Thorpe 62 C3
Shropham 103 B4
Sidestrand 11 C2
Silfield 88 A2
Silvergate 35 F6
Silver Green 107 E3
Sisland 91 E1
Skeyton 37 A4
Skeyton Corner 37 B6
Sloley 37 F4
Smallburgh 38 D3
Smallworth 128 A7
Sneath Common 121 A8
Snetterton 103 C2
Snettisham 12 E5
Snow Street 129 D8
South Acre 46 F1
Southburgh 85 F7
South Burlingham 74 B2
South Creake 15 C6
South Denes 170 A5
South End 103 C1
Southery 97 B5
Southgate
  Cawston 35 B3
  South Creake 15 E5
South Green
  Aylsham 154 E3

Hoxne 130 F1
Mattishall 68 F5
Pulham St Mary 121 F2
Terrington St Clement 42 B6
South Lopham 128 D8
South Lynn 146 E2
South Pickenham 83 D6
South Raynham 30 F3
Southrepps 22 B7
South Runcton 61 F3
Southtown 169 B1
South Walsham 74 A7
Southwood 92 D8
South Wootton 148 D2
Spa Common 23 A1
Sparham 51 B6
Sparhamhill 51 C5
Spixworth 54 A2
Spooner Row 105 A8
Sporle 65 C6
Sprowston 159 B3
Stacksford 104 C1
Stalham 39 B4
Stalham Green 39 C3
Stalland Common 86 C1
Stanfield 48 F7
Stanford 101 A5
Stanhoe 14 E8
Stanton Chare 127 B1
Starston 122 C3
Stibbard 32 E7
Stiffkey 6 D5
Stockton 109 F4
Stody 18 F6
Stoke Ferry 80 F3
Stoke Holy Cross 89 F4
Stokesby 75 A5
Stonebridge 102 B1
Stone Street 124 F1
Stow Bardolph 79 E8
Stow Bedon 102 E7
Stowbridge 61 B2
Stradbroke 131 E1
Stradsett 80 D8
Stratton St Michael . . 106 F4
Stratton Strawless 53 E7
Strumpshaw 73 F2
Stubb 39 F1
Stubbing's Green 129 A1
Stubbs Green 109 C8
Stuston 130 B5
Suffield 21 F3
Summerfield 2 E1
Summerhill 133 C3
Surlingham 73 B1
Sustead 21 A7
Suton 87 D2
Sutton 39 C3
Sutton Bridge 41 B7
Swaffham 153 D4
Swafield 22 E3
Swainsthorpe 89 D3
Swannington 52 B6
Swanton Abbott 37 C4
Swanton Hill 37 C5
Swanton Morley 50 B3
Swanton Novers 18 B3
Swardeston 89 C5
Syderstone 15 B3
Syleham 131 D5

Ten Mile Bank 96 E7
Terrington St Clement . . 144 B4
Terrington St John 42 C2
Tharston 106 E5
The Arms 83 F1
The Brook 129 C3
The Grange 35 C1
The Green 87 B4
The Heath
  Fakenham 141 F4
  Hevingham 53 A8
  Stratton Strawless . . . 53 F8
The Limes 59 C5
The Ling 91 A1
Thelnetham 128 B5
Thelveton 130 D8
The Marsh
  Thrandeston 129 F3
  Wortham 129 C4
Themelthorpe 33 F2
The Smeeth 60 A5
Thetford 176 B4
Thompson 102 A8
Thornage 18 F7
Thornham 2 D6
Thorpe 93 B1
Thorpe Abbotts 131 B6
Thorpe End 72 D6
Thorpe Hamlet 163 B6
Thorpe Market 22 A6
Thorpe Marriott 155 F2
Thorpe Row 67 C4
Thorpe St Andrew . . . 163 F8
Thorpland 61 D3
Thrandeston 129 F3
Three Cocked Hat . . . 110 D7
Threehammer Common . . 55 E6
Three Holes 77 E3
Thrigby 75 D7
Thurgarton 20 F5
Thurlton 92 F1
Thurne 56 E3
Thurning 34 C7
Thursford 17 E4
Thursford Green 17 D5
Thurton 91 D4
Thuxton 68 D2
Thwaite St Mary 109 A5
Tibenham 120 E8
Tilney All Saints 144 F1
Tilney cum Islington . . 60 F8
Tilney Fen End 60 C6
Tilney High End 42 D4
Tilney St Lawrence . . . 60 D8
Tipps End 95 C6
Titchwell 2 F7
Tittleshall 48 B8
Tivetshall St Margaret . 121 B5
Tivetshall St Mary . . . 121 B5
Toft Monks 110 D5
Toftrees 31 B6
Toftwood 154 E2
Topcroft 107 F3
Topcroft Street 107 F2
Toprow 88 E1
Tottenhill 62 A5
Tottenhill Row 61 E7
Tottington 101 E6
Tower End 44 C4
Town Green
  Aldborough 21 C4
  South Walsham 74 A7
Town Street 39 F3
Trimingham 11 D2
Trowse Newton 163 B3
Trunch 22 E5
Tungate 37 C8
Tunstall 74 F3
Tunstead 37 F1

Tuttington 36 E6
Twyford 33 B3
Tyby 34 B6

U

Upgate 52 C5
Upgate Street
  New Buckenham 105 A3
  Woodton 108 B2
Upper Brandon Parva . . 68 E3
Upper Guist 33 A5
Upper Hellesdon 158 C3
Upper Sheringham . . . 138 A5
Upper Stoke 90 B5
Upper Street
  Horning 55 F4
  Hoveton 55 C5
  Scole 130 F6
  Southrepps 22 B7
  Worstead 38 A3
Upper Weybread 131 E6
Upton 166 A8
Upton Green 166 B8
Upwell 77 F5

W

Wacton 106 C2
Wainford 109 B1
Walcot Green 177 F6
Walcott 24 A7
Walpole Cross Keys . . . 41 F7
Walpole Highway 59 F8
Walpole Marsh 41 C4
Walpole St Andrew . . . 41 D4
Walpole St Peter 41 E3
Walsoken 152 F6
Walton Highway 59 D8
Walton Warren 45 E2
Wangford 114 C2
Warham 6 A4
Waterheath 110 E5
Waterloo 68 C2
Beccles 110 E4
Coltishall 53 E6
Diss 130 C6
Watlington 61 E5
Wattisfield 128 B1
Wattlefield 105 C7
Watton 84 E3
Watton Green 84 E4
Waxham 40 C5
Weasenham All Saints . 47 C8
Weasenham St Peter . . 30 D1
Weeting 175 B8
Welborne 69 A4
Welborne Common . . . 68 F4
Wellingham 30 F1
Wells-Next-The-Sea . . 136 C5
Welney 95 D4
Wendling 66 F8
Wereham 80 E4
West Acre 46 B2
West Barsham 16 C4
West Beckham 9 C2
West Bilney 45 B2
Westbrook Green 177 C7
West Caister 168 C4
West Dereham 80 B4
Westfield
  Necton 66 C4
  West Caister 76 B6
Westfield 67 F4
Westgate 6 D3
Westgate Street 53 B8
West Harling 118 A3

West Head 78 F8
West Lexham 47 C4
West Lynn 146 C5
West Newton 27 F6
Weston Green 51 F1
Weston Longville 51 E3
West Poringland 90 B4
West Raynham 30 E4
West Rudham 29 F7
West Runton 10 A5
West Somerton 57 E6
West Tofts 100 F4
West Walton 59 B8
Westwick 37 D6
West Winch 43 E3
Weybourne 8 F5
Wheatacre 111 B5
Whimpwell Green 24 C4
Whinburgh 68 A3
Whissonsett 31 D2
Whittington 81 B2
Whitwell Street 149 C3
Wicken Green Village . . 15 D2
Wickhampton 93 A8
Wicklewood 87 B5
Wickmere 20 F4
Wiggenhall St Germans . 43 C1
Wiggenhall St Mary
  Magdalen 61 B6
Wiggenhall St Mary the
  Virgin 61 A8
Wiggenhall St Peter . . . 61 C8
Wighton 6 A2
Wilby 119 A8
Wilney Green 129 A8
Wimbotsham 79 D8
Winfarthing 120 B4
Winfield 131 E4
Wingfield Green 131 D4
Winterton-on-Sea 58 C6
Wisbech 152 A6
Withergate 38 A6
Witton 165 A6
Witton Bridge 23 E2
Wiveton 7 F6
Wolferd Green 90 B2
Wolferton 27 B7
Wolterton 20 E2
Woodbastwick 55 D2
Wood Dalling 34 D6
Woodgate 50 C3
Wood Green 106 F2
Wood Norton 33 A7
Woodrising 85 E6
Woodton 108 C4
Wormegay 62 C7
Worstead 38 A5
Wortham 129 B4
Worthing 49 F6
Wortwell 123 B4
Wramplingham 69 E1
Wreningham 88 D1
Wretton 80 E3
Wroxham 164 D3
Wymondham 173 E5

Y

Yaxham 68 A5
Yaxley 130 A1
Yelverton 90 E5

T

Tacolneston 105 F5
Tasburgh 106 F7
Tatterford 30 E7
Tattersett 15 C1
Taverham 155 C1

A

Abbey Cl
Horsham St Faith & Newton St Faith NR10 ...53 D1
Sheringham NR26 ...138 D6
Wendling NR19 ...66 F7
Abbey Farm Mid Sch IP24 ...176 B4
Abbey Gn 1 IP24 ...176 C4
Abbey Hill IP21 ...131 A3
Abbey La
Haveringland NR10 ...52 D6
Norwich NR1 ...178 C2
Abbey Pk NR26 ...138 F5
Abbey Rd
Flitcham with Appleton PE31 ...28 D5
Flixton NR35 ...123 F4
Great Massingham PE32 ...29 D1
Horsham St Faith NR10 ...53 D1
Old Buckenham NR17 ...104 D3
Pentney PE32 ...63 B8
Sheringham NR26 ...138 C6
10 Watton IP25 ...84 E3
Abbey St NR12 ...23 E4
Abbeyfields PE32 ...29 D1
Abbeygate IP24 ...176 C5
Abbot Cl NR18 ...173 C5
Abbot Rd Horning NR12 ...55 E4
Norwich NR1 ...162 D2
Abbot's Cl NR11 ...150 D7
Abbot's La NR14 ...90 B3
Abbots Way NR12 ...24 E4
Abbottsinch Rd 5 IP31 ...126 B1
Aberdare Ct 6 NR1 ...163 B7
Aberdeen St PE30 ...146 F4
Abinger Way NR4 ...89 D8
Abington Gr 4 PE14 ...59 A1
Abyssinia Rd NR30 ...169 D2
Acacia Ave Ashill IP25 ...84 A7
East Dereham NR19 ...154 E1
22 Martham NR29 ...57 D4
Wisbech PE13 ...152 C8
Acacia Gr NR26 ...138 D4
Acacia Rd NR7 ...163 E8
Access Rd NR21 ...15 D2
Acer Rd PE34 ...43 D4
Ackland Cl 7 NR29 ...58 B6
Acland Mews NR6 ...158 C4
Acle High Sch NR13 ...166 B4
Acle New Rd NR30 ...169 B5
Acle Rd Beighton NR13 ...74 E2
South Walsham NR13 ...74 C7
Upton with Fishley NR13 ...166 A5
Acle St Edmund CE VC Prim Sch NR13 ...166 D4
Acle Sta NR13 ...166 B2
Aconite Rd PE30 ...147 B7
Acorn Dr PE32 ...45 B6
Acorn Rd NR28 ...151 D6
Acorn Way NR19 ...154 D7
Acres Way NR8 ...155 E2
Ada Cole Ave NR16 ...103 D1
Ada Coxon Cl PE30 ...146 F8
Adam Cl PE30 ...147 C5
Adams La 4 NR11 ...19 F1
Adams Rd NR7 ...159 A5
Adastral Pl PE37 ...153 C5
Addey Cl NR6 ...158 F5
Addison Cl
2 Coltishall NR12 ...54 C7
Feltwell IP26 ...98 F1
Addison Rd 2 NR31 ...170 C7
Adeane Mdw IP26 ...100 A4
Adelaide Ave PE30 ...147 B7
Adelaide St 5 NR2 ...162 B7
Adey Cl NR11 ...150 B5
Admiral's Dr PE35 ...140 F1
Admirals Cl PE30 ...147 D3
Admirals Ct PE37 ...153 D3
Admirals Dr PE13 ...152 D8
Admirals Jun Sch IP24 ...176 E6
Admirals Quay NR31 ...169 C1
Admirals Way
Hethersett NR9 ...88 D8
Thetford IP24 ...176 E5
Admirals Wlk 7 NR9 ...86 C5
Admiralty Cl 3 PE38 ...172 B4
Admiralty Rd NR30 ...169 D1
Adventurers' Dro PE33 ...81 B1
Aerodrome Cres NR7 ...163 D8
Afghan Pl NR3 ...158 E1
Agricultural Hall Plain NR1 ...178 B3
Ailmar Cl PE30 ...147 A4
Ainsworth Cl 7 NR20 ...50 B3
Airedale Cl 4 NR3 ...158 C1
Airfield Rd PE33 ...63 C4
Airport Ind Est NR6 ...158 C6
Airstation La IP21 ...121 E2
Akrotiri Sq IP25 ...84 F3
Alan Ave NR15 ...89 D1
Alan Jarvis Way PE34 ...144 D6
Alan Rd NR1 ...178 C1
Alban Rd PE30 ...148 C5
Albansfield 3 NR18 ...173 C5
Albany Cl NR31 ...169 C2
Albany Ct NR27 ...139 B7
Albany Rd
Great Yarmouth NR31 ...169 C2
Norwich NR3 ...162 D8
Albany Rd *continued*
Wisbech PE13 ...152 C6
Albemarle Rd
Great Yarmouth NR30 ...169 D5
Norwich NR2 ...162 B3
Albert Ct 18 PE13 ...152 C4
Albert Gate Rd 22 NR30 ...169 D2
Albert Myhill Cl 5 NR20 ...154 E6
Albert Pl NR1 ...163 A6
Albert Rd 17 NR30 ...169 D2
Albert Sq 13 NR30 ...169 D2
Albert St Holt NR25 ...137 B6
King's Lynn PE30 ...146 D5
Albert Terr NR2 ...162 C4
Albion Dr NR7 ...159 A3
Albion Rd Bungay NR35 ...124 B8
Great Yarmouth NR30 ...169 D4
Mundesley NR11 ...143 A7
Trunch NR28 ...22 E5
Albion St PE30 ...146 E5
Albion Way
Norwich NR1 ...178 C1
Wroxham/Hoveton NR12 ...164 D6
Alborough Loke 6 NR9 ...88 C7
Alburgh Rd NR15 ...107 D4
Alburgh with Denton Fst Sch IP20 ...123 A5
Alby Craft Ctr* NR11 ...21 C3
Aldborough Prim Sch NR11 ...21 B5
Aldborough Rd NR11 ...21 A3
Aldeby Rd NR34 ...110 F6
Alder Cl
Great Yarmouth NR31 ...94 C7
10 Mulbarton NR14 ...89 B3
North Walsham NR28 ...151 D7
Poringland NR14 ...90 D4
Alder Covert IP24 ...116 D2
Alder Way NR8 ...155 E1
Alderman Jackson Specl Sch PO30 ...147 B8
Alderman Peel High Sch NR23 ...136 D4
Alderman Swindell Fst Sch NR30 ...169 D8
Alderson Pl NR1 ...178 B1
Alderson Rd NR30 ...169 C5
Aldis Ct NR19 ...154 D5
Aldis Rd NR13 ...166 B4
Aldiss Ave NR19 ...154 D3
Aldiss Cl PE37 ...153 D3
Aldiss Ct PE13 ...154 D6
Aldrich Way IP22 ...177 C5
Aldryche Rd NR1 ...163 B8
Aldwick Rd 2 NR18 ...173 C6
Alex Moorhouse Way NR5 ...156 A3
Alexander Cl
Caister-on-Sea NR30 ...168 C8
18 Long Stratton NR15 ...106 E3
Alexander Rise NR11 ...22 F8
Alexander Way 1 NR19 ...154 C6
Alexandra Ave NR30 ...169 D7
Alexandra Cl PE31 ...140 C4
Alexandra Rd
Cromer NR27 ...139 B4
Great Yarmouth NR30 ...169 D4
Hunstanton PE36 ...132 C3
Mundesley NR11 ...143 A8
Norwich NR2 ...162 B6
Sheringham NR26 ...138 D6
Wisbech PE13 ...152 C5
Alexandra Way
Attleborough NR17 ...174 C6
Downham Market PE38 ...172 B3
Alford Gr NR7 ...159 A3
Alfred Nicholls Ct NR3 ...158 D2
Alfred Rd NR27 ...139 A7
Alfric Cl 11 NR14 ...91 F1
Algores Way PE13 ...152 B2
Alice Fisher Cres PE30 ...146 F7
Alison Cl NR13 ...73 F3
All Hallows' Hospl NR35 ...109 B2
All Saints IP27 ...175 B8
All Saints Ave PE13 ...152 F7
All Saints CE VA Prim Sch
Ryburgh NR21 ...32 C6
Winfarthing IP22 ...120 B4
All Saints Cl
Briston NR24 ...142 D4
Runhall NR20 ...69 A5
2 Weybourne NR25 ...8 F5
Wicklewood NR18 ...87 B5
1 Wisbech PE14 ...59 A1
All Saints Dr PE30 ...148 C4
All Saints Gn NR1 ...178 B1
All Saints Rd 6 NR14 ...90 D5
All Saints Sch NR12 ...24 D3
All Saints' St 15 PE30 ...146 D4
All Saints Way
Beachamwell PE37 ...81 F8
Mundesley NR11 ...143 C6
All Saints Wlk 7 NR20 ...68 F6
Allanadale Rd NR4 ...162 C1
Allen Cl PE34 ...61 B8
Allen Meale Way 5 NR12 ...39 B4
Allen's Ave NR7 ...159 A4
Allen's La NR7 ...159 A4
Allenbrooks Way NR18 ...173 C3
Allenby's Chase 10 PE12 ...41 B8
Allendale Rd NR30 ...168 E5
Allens Cl 1 NR13 ...73 D6
Allens La NR2 ...162 C4
Allerton Cl NR7 ...159 B3
Allerton Rd NR7 ...159 B3
Alley The PE32 ...44 C1
Allison St NR10 ...36 A2
Allotment La NR25 ...9 B3
Allthorpe Rd 12 IP20 ...122 D2
Allwood Ave NR19 ...154 C5
Alma Ave PE34 ...144 D6
Alma Chase PE34 ...144 D6
Alma Rd
Great Yarmouth NR30 ...169 D2
Snettisham PE31 ...12 E5
Alma Terr NR3 ...162 D8
Almond Cl 21 NR29 ...57 D4
Almond Gr IP24 ...176 A1
Almond Rd NR31 ...170 B6
Alpha Rd NR31 ...170 C8
Alpington & Bergh Apton Prim Sch NR14 ...90 F4
Alston Cl 3 NR14 ...90 D5
Alston Rd NR6 ...157 E2
Althaea Gn 2 NR31 ...170 B5
Altongate 1 NR13 ...72 D6
Amazonia World of Reptiles* NR30 ...169 E2
Ambassador Way NR20 ...154 F4
Ambleside
16 Hethersett NR9 ...88 D8
5 Sculthorpe Airfield NR21 ...15 C2
Ambleside Cl NR5 ...161 C6
Ambrose Cl 1 NR5 ...161 A7
Ambrose Rd NR30 ...168 E3
Amderley Dr 6 NR4 ...89 C8
Amelia Opie Way 2 IP24 ...176 D7
Ames Ct NR10 ...35 B2
Amethyst Cl NR31 ...170 D2
Amherst Cl 7 PE37 ...153 C3
Amhirst Cl 2 NR6 ...158 F1
Amhurst Gdns NR31 ...94 A5
Amsterdam NR6 ...158 B6
Amsterdam Way PE13 ...152 C2
Amys Cl IP25 ...84 C4
Anchor Cl Norwich NR3 ...178 C4
Sheringham NR26 ...138 E6
Anchor Ct NR31 ...169 C2
Anchor Dro PE38 ...112 B8
Anchor Quay NR2 ...178 A3
Anchor Rd
North Walsham NR28 ...151 F5
Sutton Bridge PE34 ...41 F8
Anchor St
Coltishall NR12 ...54 D6
5 Norwich NR3 ...162 F8
Norwich NR3 ...178 C4
Tunstead NR12 ...38 B2
Anchor Way 7 NR33 ...111 F1
Anchorage View PE31 ...3 B6
Anderson Cl
King's Lynn PE30 ...146 E7
Wisbech PE13 ...152 A7
Andrew Goodall Cl NR19 ...154 C1
Andrew's Furlong NR16 ...119 E7
Andrews Pl PE36 ...132 D2
Angel Dr NR28 ...151 B4
Angel Rd NR3 ...158 D1
Angel Rd Fst Sch NR3 ...158 D1
Angel Rd Mid Sch NR3 ...158 D1
Angela Cl 2 NR10 ...53 B3
Angela Cres 3 NR10 ...53 B3
Angela Rd NR10 ...53 B3
Angerstein Cl IP27 ...114 E8
Angle Rd PE14 ...78 A7
Anglia Sq NR3 ...178 B4
Anglia Way PE13 ...152 B2
Anglian Way 3 NR31 ...171 D5
Anglo-Saxon Cath & Bishops Pal (remains of)* NR20 ...49 F8
Anmer Cl NR3 ...158 F3
Anmer Rd PE31 ...28 C5
Anna Gurney Cl IP24 ...176 D6
Anna Sewell Cl 4 IP24 ...176 D7
Anne Bartholomew Rd IP24 ...176 D7
Anne Boleyn Cl 4 IP24 ...176 D6
Anne Cl NR7 ...163 F8
Anne Rd PE12 ...41 B8
Anne Stannard Way NR12 ...23 F4
Annes Cl PE30 ...148 D1
Annes Dr PE36 ...132 D1
Annis Hill NR35 ...124 C8
Anson Cl
5 Hethersett NR9 ...88 E8
Mundesley NR11 ...143 A7
Anson Rd
Great Yarmouth NR31 ...169 C2
Norwich NR6 ...158 B6
Anson's La NR15 ...122 A8
Ant Broads & Marshes National Nature Reserve* NR12 ...55 F8
Anthony Curton Prim Sch PE14 ...41 E4
Anthony Dr NR3 ...158 F2
Anthony Nolan Rd PE30 ...147 D3
Antingham & Southrepps Com Prim Sch NR11 ...22 B5
Antingham Dr NR28 ...151 D6
Antingham Hill NR28 ...22 B3
Antingham Rd NR7 ...159 D1
Apeldoorn Wlk PE13 ...152 D7
Apollo Wlk NR30 ...169 C6
Apple Yd NR25 ...137 B6
Appleacres NR6 ...158 D5
Appledore Cl PE30 ...148 C2
Appledore La 4 NR21 ...15 C2
Applegarth 1 NR18 ...173 B4
Applegarth Ct 2 NR18 ...173 B4
Appleton Dr NR29 ...167 A3
Appleton Dro PE31 ...27 F5
Appletree Cl PE31 ...133 C6
Appletree La IP22 ...177 C5
Appleyard Cres NR3 ...158 A3
Apsley Ct NR5 ...161 F6
Apsley Rd NR30 ...169 E3
Arbor Ct NR27 ...139 B6
Arbor Rd NR27 ...139 B6
Arcade St NR1 ...178 B2
Archbishop Sancroft High Sch IP20 ...122 D2
Archdale Cl PE33 ...43 F3
Archdale St 3 PE30 ...146 E5
Archer Cl NR6 ...159 A5
Archer La PE32 ...46 F2
Archer's Rd 2 NR30 ...169 C5
Archers' Ave 3 IP26 ...98 D1
Archibald Rd NR12 ...24 A7
Arden Cl NR27 ...11 A3
Arden Gr NR10 ...157 E7
Arden Gr Fst Sch NR10 ...157 E7
Arderon Ct 2 NR2 ...162 B7
Ardleigh Cl 3 PE13 ...152 E5
Ardney Rise NR3 ...158 D3
Argyle St
King's Lynn PE30 ...146 E3
Norwich NR1 ...178 C1
Argyll Cres NR8 ...156 E8
Arles Ave PE13 ...152 E3
Arlington Cl NR17 ...174 E5
Arlington Gdns NR17 ...174 E5
Arlington La NR2 ...162 C4
Arlington Pk Rd PE32 ...44 C3
Arlington Way IP24 ...176 E3
Armada Cl PE13 ...152 D8
Armes Cres NR2 ...162 A8
Armes St NR2 ...162 B7
Arminghall Cl NR3 ...158 C3
Arminghall La NR14 ...89 F8
Armitage Cl NR4 ...89 B8
Arms Pk Rd NR6 ...158 B6
Armstrong Dr NR19 ...154 E7
Armstrong Rd NR7 ...159 E2
Army Rd NR21 ...15 C2
Arnfield La NR5 ...161 B8
Arnold Ave NR30 ...168 D8
Arnold Miller Rd NR1 ...162 F2
Arnott Ave NR31 ...170 D1
Arnott Rd NR25 ...137 D5
Arnside Cl 22 NR9 ...88 D8
Arthur Ave NR30 ...168 E8
Arthur Rd NR21 ...141 A6
Arthurton Rd NR10 ...54 A1
Artillery Sq 21 NR30 ...169 D4
Artillery St 12 PE13 ...152 C4
Arundel Cl NR20 ...49 C4
Arundel Ct NR2 ...178 A1
Arundel Dr PE30 ...148 C1
Arundel Rd
Great Yarmouth NR30 ...169 D7
Wymondham NR18 ...173 C6
Ascot Gdns NR19 ...154 D3
Ash Cl Brandon IP27 ...175 E3
Downham Market PE38 ...172 C6
10 Hethersett NR9 ...88 D8
Swaffham PE37 ...153 B5
Thetford IP24 ...176 A1
Wymondham NR18 ...173 D6
Ash Dr IP23 ...130 C1
Ash Gn 11 NR31 ...170 B6
Ash Gr King's Lynn PE30 ...148 D2
Norwich NR3 ...158 E2
Sheringham NR26 ...138 E5
4 West Winch PE33 ...43 E2
Ash La NR16 ...105 C2
Ash Rd PE33 ...63 B4
Ash Tree Cl NR17 ...174 C5
Ash Tree Rd NR13 ...74 D1
Ash Yd NR24 ...18 D8
Ashbey Rd PE30 ...147 E8
Ashburton Rd IP26 ...100 C5
Ashby Rd
Ashby St Mary NR14 ...91 C5
Repps with Bastwick NR29 ...57 A3
Thurton NR14 ...91 C4
Ashby St NR1 ...178 B1
Ashdale Pk
Old Hunstanton PE36 ...132 F8
Wisbech PE13 ...152 A5
Ashdown NR8 ...155 E1
Ashdown Ct NR27 ...139 C6
Ashfield Ct PE34 ...144 D6
Ashfield Hill PE30 ...147 C4
Ashfield Rd NR28 ...151 E6
Ashford Cl NR34 ...110 C2
Ashgrove 5 NR8 ...155 E2
Ashill VC Prim Sch IP25 ...84 A7
Ashleigh Gdns NR18 ...173 E6
Ashleigh Inf Sch NR18 ...173 D6
Ashley Rd NR20 ...49 D4
Ashley Wlk PE13 ...154 D4
Ashtree Rd
Norwich NR5 ...157 B2
12 Watton IP25 ...84 E3
Ashwell Ct NR5 ...160 F7
Ashwellthorpe Rd NR16 ...88 D1
Ashwicken CE Fst Sch PE32 ...44 F6
Ashwicken Rd PE32 ...45 A8
Ashwood Cl NR30 ...168 D6
Aslack Way PE36 ...2 A6
Aslacton Prim Sch NR15 ...106 A1
Aslacton Rd NR16 ...106 B3
Aslake Cl NR7 ...159 C5
Aspen Cl IP24 ...176 B2
Aspen Way NR4 ...89 B8
Aspland Rd NR1 ...178 C3
Assembly House The NR2 ...178 A2
Association Way 2 NR7 ...72 D4
Astell Rd NR1 ...89 F8
Astley Cooper Pl NR15 ...90 E1
Astley Cres PE36 ...132 D6
Astley Prim Sch NR24 ...142 C4
Astley Rd
Great & Little Plumstead NR13 ...73 B6
Little Plumpstead NR13 ...165 A8
Norwich NR5 ...160 F8
Astor Ct IP27 ...175 D4
Atbara Terr PE30 ...146 E2
Atcherley Sq PE31 ...30 B3
Atkinson Cl NR5 ...160 E8
Atling Cl NR17 ...174 F6
Atling Way NR17 ...174 F6
Atmere Cl 2 NR4 ...161 F1
Attelsey Way NR5 ...160 E8
Atthill Rd NR2 ...162 A7
Attleborough High Sch NR17 ...174 D6
Attleborough Inf Sch NR17 ...174 D6
Attleborough Jun Sch NR17 ...174 E6
Attleborough Rd
Attleborough NR17 ...174 A7
Caston NR17 ...102 F8
Deopham NR18 ...86 E1
Great Ellingham NR17 ...103 F8
Little Ellingham NR17 ...86 A2
Morley NR18 ...87 A1
Attleborough Sta NR17 ...174 E5
Attlee Way 4 NR19 ...154 C6
Audax Rd NR6 ...158 C6
Audley Ct IP24 ...176 C7
Audley End IP21 ...120 F1
Audley St NR30 ...169 D5
Augusta St NR26 ...138 D7
Augustus Hare Dr 1 NR4 ...161 C5
Aurania Ave NR1 ...162 D3
Auster Cl NR6 ...158 C4
Austin Fields PE30 ...146 E5
Austin Fields Ind Est PE30 ...146 E5
Austin Rd NR31 ...169 B3
Austin St
Hunstanton PE36 ...132 C5
King's Lynn PE30 ...146 D5
Autumn Cl IP24 ...176 E4
Autumn Dr NR5 ...161 B8
Avenue The NR23 ...5 A2
Avebury Rd NR4 ...162 B1
Aveling Way 6 NR33 ...111 F1
Avenue Cl PE38 ...79 E1
Avenue Fst & Mid Schs NR2 ...162 B5
Avenue Rd
Great Yarmouth NR31 ...170 D6
High Kelling NR25 ...8 E2
Hunstanton PE36 ...132 C4
King's Lynn PE30 ...146 F4
North Walsham NR28 ...151 C4
Norwich NR2 ...162 B5
Wymondham NR18 ...173 C3
Avenue S NR26 ...138 E7
Avenue The
Brome & Oakley IP23 ...130 D3
Brookville IP26 ...99 A7
Brumstead NR12 ...24 A1
Dersingham PE35 ...140 E1
Hemsby NR29 ...167 A7
Holkham NR23 ...5 A4
Horning NR12 ...55 E4
4 Necton PE37 ...65 F4
Northrepps NR27 ...139 D3
Sheringham NR26 ...138 E7
Snettisham PE31 ...12 D4
Wiggenhall St Germans PE34 ...61 A8
Wroxham/Hoveton NR12 ...164 B4
Wymondham NR18 ...87 D7
Avenues The
Langley with Hardley NR14 ...91 F4
Norwich NR4 ...161 E4
Thurton NR14 ...91 D3
Avian Way NR7 ...159 C2
Avocet House Sch NR14 ...92 C1
Avon Rd PE30 ...148 C2
Avondale Cl NR13 ...74 A2
Avondale Rd NR31 ...170 D3
Avonmouth Rd 2 NR3 ...158 C1
Aylesbury Cl NR3 ...158 D2
Aylmer Dr PE34 ...60 C8
Aylsham Cres NR3 ...158 C3

Aylsham High Sch
NR11 .... 150 D7
Aylsham Ind Est NR11 .150 E8
Aylsham Rd
Burgh & Tuttington NR11 ...36 E6
Cawston NR10 ....35 B2
Felmingham NR28 ....37 A8
North Walsham NR28 ....22 C1
Norwich NR3 ....158 C1
Oulton NR11 ....35 E6
Swanton Abbott NR10 ....37 C4
Aylsham Rd Bsns Pk
NR6 ....158 C2
Aylsham Sta NR11 ....150 D5
Ayre Way PE30 ....147 D8
Ayton Rd NR18 ....173 D3
Ayton Rd Ind Est
NR18 ....173 D3

B

Babingley Cl 5 PE33 ....61 D6
Bachelor's La NR28 ......23 E2
Back Chapel La NR31 ...170 D6
Back Dro Upwell PE14 ....77 D4
Welney PE14 ....95 D4
Back Hills IP22 ....128 E3
Back La Barford NR9 .....69 F2
Beeston with Bittering
PE32 ....48 C2
Bircham PE31 ....14 B3
Blakeney NR25 ....7 C7
Burgh Castle NR31 ....94 A8
Burnham Market PE31 ...135 D2
Burnham Thorpe PE31 .....4 D4
Buxton with Lammas
NR10 ....53 E8
Castle Acre PE32 ....46 F2
Catfield NR29 ....56 C8
Cawston NR10 ....35 B2
Dereham NR20 ....68 A8
Diss IP22 ....120 D3
East Rudham PE31 ....30 B7
East Ruston NR12 ....24 A3
Elsing NR20 ....50 F3
Happisburgh NR12 ....23 F2
Hempstead NR25 ....19 E7
Hethersett NR9 ....88 E8
Kenninghall NR16 ......119 A5
Litcham PE32 ....48 A4
Lound NR32 ....94 C2
Lyng NR9 ....51 A4
Marthan NR29 ....57 D5
Mattishall NR20 ....68 E6
Mileham PE32 ....48 C6
North Elmham NR20 .....49 E7
Outwell PE14 ....77 E7
Potter Heigham NR29 ....56 E7
Quidenham NR16 ....119 A8
Rackheath NR13 ....54 D1
Ringland NR8 ....52 C1
Rollesby NR29 ....57 D3
Roughton NR11 ....21 D8
Roydon PE32 ....28 A1
St Mary, South Elmham
otherwise Homersfield
IP20 ....123 B4
Scole IP21 ....121 A1
Scoulton NR9 ....85 E3
South Creake NR21 ......15 E6
Stanfield NR20 ....48 F8
Upton with Fishley NR13 .166 C8
Walsingham NR22 ....16 F7
Wereham PE33 ....80 E4
West Beckham NR25 ......9 B3
West Caister NR30 .....168 A4
West Winch PE33 ....43 E2
Wymondham NR18 ......173 C4
Back Mkt La NR29 ......167 B7
Back Mundesley Rd
NR11 ....22 F8
Back of the Inns NR1 ...178 B2
Back Path 1 NR29 ......58 B6
Back Pier Plain NR31 ..170 D4
Back Rd Brockdish IP21 .131 B8
East Ruston NR12 ....38 F6
Elm PE14 ....77 A8
Pentney PE32 ....63 C8
Somerton NR29 ....57 F6
Wisbech PE14 ....77 A7
Wood Dalling NR11 ......34 D6
Yelverton NR14 ....90 F5
Back St Binham NR21 .....6 E2
Fakenham NR21 ....141 B3
Garboldisham IP22 .....128 A8
Gayton PE32 ....45 C5
Harpley PE31 ....29 D5
Horsham St Faith NR10 ..53 D1
Lakenheath IP27 ....113 E1
Litcham PE32 ....48 A4
Mundesley NR11 ....143 C5
Reepham NR10 ....149 B4
South Creake NR21 .....15 D6
Tittleshall PE32 ....48 B7
Trunch NR28 ....22 E5
Back Terr PE37 ....153 B5
Backwood La
Howe NR15 ....90 C2
Shotesham NR15 ....107 F8
Bacon Rd NR4 ....161 F5
Baconsthorpe Castle*
NR25 ....9 A1
Bacton Cl PE30 ....148 D3
Bacton Rd Bacton NR12 ..23 D5
North Walsham NR28 ...151 D6
Norwich NR3 ....158 B2
Paston NR28 ....143 E2

Bacton Rd *continued*
Witton NR28 ....23 C1
Bacton-on-Sea Fst Sch
NR12 ....23 E4
Bader Cl PE30 ....147 D4
Badger Cl NR14 ....89 A2
Badgers Brook Rd
NR8 ....155 F2
Bagge Rd PE30 ....147 A5
Bagthorpe Rd PE31 .....30 A7
Bailey Cl
4 Hethersett NR9 ......88 D7
Marthan NR29 ....57 D5
Bailey La PE34 ....145 E7
Bailey Rd NR27 ....139 B5
Bailey St PE32 ....46 F2
Bailiwick The 3 NR16 ..118 C1
Baillie Cl 3 NR31 ......170 B1
Bainard Rise NR15 ....107 C8
Bainards Cl NR18 ......173 B6
Baines Rd 6 PE30 .....146 D1
Baines Way 2 NR5 .....160 E8
Baird Way PE14 ....176 C7
Baker Cl
King's Lynn PE30 ......146 D1
North Walsham NR28 ...151 D3
Bakers La 5 PE30 .....146 D4
Baker St
Great Yarmouth NR31 ..170 D5
14 Stalham NR12 ....39 B4
Baker's Rd NR13 ....75 A1
Bakers La NR35 ....109 A2
Bakers Rd NR3 ....162 D8
Bakers Yd NR23 ....136 C6
Bakery Cl NR14 ....142 E3
Bakery La NR19 ....51 A5
Balderston Ct NR3 .....178 B4
Baldock Cl 1 NR16 ....105 F5
Baldock Dr PE30 ......147 B8
Baldric Rd NR18 ......155 D1
Baldwin Cl 5 PE13 ....152 D5
Baldwin Rd PE30 ......147 C6
Baldwins Cl NR24 .....142 D4
Baldwins Dro 4 PE14 ...77 F6
Bale Rd Brinton NR24 ...18 C7
Hindringham NR21 ....17 E7
Bamford Rd 4 NR27 ....10 A5
Balfour St 4 NR3 ......162 F8
Baliol Rd NR31 ....170 C5
Ball's La NR21 ....107 D5
Ballygate NR34 ....110 C1
Balmoral Ave NR30 ....169 D7
Balmoral Cl
Attleborough NR17 ....174 F6
Dersingham PE31 ......140 D3
Balmoral Cres PE31 ...133 C5
Balmoral Rd PE30 .....147 C7
Balmoral W PE31 ......140 D3
Bambers La PE14 ....59 C2
Banch Cl 1 NR14 ....89 F4
Banham Barn Craft*
NR16 ....119 C6
Banham Dr NR20 ....50 B2
Banham Prim Sch
NR16 ....119 D6
Banham Rd NR16 .....119 B5
Banham Zoo* NR16 ...119 C6
Banham's La NR35 ....108 B2
Banister Way NR18 ....173 A5
Bank Dr PE13 ....152 A7
Bank Loke 6 NR28 ....151 C5
Bank Plain NR3 ....178 B3
Bank Rd PE31 ....140 C4
Bank Side PE34 ....146 C5
Bank St Norwich NR2 ..178 A3
Pulham Market IP21 ...121 E5
Bankside NR21 ....133 B6
Banningham Ct NR28 ..151 A4
Banningham Rd NR11 ..150 D8
Bannister Cl NR17 .....174 E4
Bannister's Row PE13 .152 B7
Banters La NR14 ....89 A5
Banting Cl NR31 ....170 C1
Banyard Ct PE13 ......154 E5
Banyard Rd PE13 .....154 D5
Banyards Pl PE33 ......61 D4
Baptist Rd PE14 ....77 D4
Bar Dro PE14 ....77 B8
Barber's La
Bedingham NR35 ......108 B2
Fakenham NR21 ....141 E4
Barberry Cl 5 NR6 ....158 E3
Barbers Yd 1 NR17 ...104 D2
Barclay Cl NR7 ....159 B5
Barclay Gn NR7 ....159 D1
Barclay Rd NR7 ....159 C1
Bard Hill NR25 ....8 A1
Bardolph Pl PE34 ......61 D1
Bardolph's Way PE33 ...62 C6
Bardolphs Cl 1 NR8 ...155 B2
Bardwell Rd
Barningham IP31 ......127 C3
Fakenham Magna IP24 ..126 D3
Stanton IP31 ....126 E2
Bardyke Bank PE14 .....77 F4
Barford Cty Prim Sch
NR9 ....69 F2
Barford Rd
Marlingford NR9 ....69 E3
Sheringham NR26 .....138 D7
Topcroft NR35 ....108 A3
Bargate Ct NR3 ....178 B4
Barham Ct NR31 ......170 D5
Barham's La NR16 ....105 D4
Barker Way 5 NR13 ....72 D6
Barker's Dro PE33 ......81 A3

Barker's La
Norwich NR7 ....159 A5
Old Buckenham NR17 ...104 B2
Barkers Herne NR27 ....139 A6
Barkis Rd NR30 ....169 D1
Barley Way
Attleborough NR17 ....174 B3
Thetford IP24 ....176 D6
Barleycroft NR29 ......167 B7
Barleyfield Rd 8 NR10 ..53 A3
Barn Cl
2 Hopton on Sea NR31 .171 E5
1 Lingwood NR13 ....74 A3
Barn Hill NR13 ....73 E2
Barn La
Gressenhall NR19 ......49 B2
Mautby NR29 ....75 E6
Barn Mdw NR14 ....163 B2
Barn Rd Docking PE31 ..134 F4
Norwich NR2 ....178 A4
Barn Terr NR13 ....165 C4
Barnaby Cl 8 NR19 ....154 C3
Barnard Ave NR30 ....169 D7
Barnard Cl
Great Yarmouth NR31 ..170 C1
5 Stoke Holy Cross NR14 .89 F4
Barnard Cres NR30 ...169 C7
Barnard Rd NR5 ......160 E8
Barnards La PE13 ......61 D6
Barnards Rd NR28 ......38 A5
Barnards Yd 8 NR3 ...178 A3
Barnby Rd NR10 ....37 B2
Barnes Cl
Brandon IP27 ....175 A2
Norwich NR7 ....159 D2
Barnes' Rd IP21 ......121 E5
Barnesdale Rd 5 NR4 ...89 E8
Barney Rd NR21 ....17 C5
Barnfield Cl NR12 ......39 E2
Barnham Broom Prim Sch
NR9 ....69 C2
Barnham Broom Rd
East Tuddenham NR20 ..69 D5
Wymondham NR18 .....173 A4
Barnham CE Prim Sch
IP24 ....125 E5
Barnham Rd IP24 .....126 B6
Barningham CE VC Prim Sch
IP31 ....127 C3
Barningham Pl NR11 ...20 C5
Barningham Rd
Gresham NR11 ....20 D8
Stanton IP31 ....127 C1
Barns The NR16 ......105 C4
Barnwell Rd PE30 .....147 B6
Baron's Cl NR21 ......141 C4
Baron's Hall La NR21 ..141 D4
Barondole La
Alburgh IP20 ....122 E8
Topcroft NR35 ....107 E2
Barr Dr IP27 ....113 E2
Barrack Rd
Great Yarmouth NR30 ..169 D1
Norwich NR3 ....163 B7
Barrack St NR3 ....178 C4
Barrett Cl PE30 ....147 E5
Barrett Rd NR25 ......137 D7
Norwich NR1 ....162 E3
Barrett-Lennard Rd
NR10 ....53 A4
Barri Cl NR14 ....90 C3
Barrow Cl NR3 ....157 F1
Barrow's Cnr IP24 ....125 A4
Barroway Dro PE30 ....78 E6
Barrows Hole La PE32 ..65 E7
Barsham Dr PE30 .....148 E1
Barsham Rd NR21 ......17 A5
Bartle Ct NR10 ....149 C5
Barton Broad Nature
Reserve* NR12 ....155 F7
Barton Cl
Great Yarmouth NR30 ..151 A4
Swaffham PE37 ....153 C2
Barton Ct PE30 ....147 D5
Barton Rd
Ashmanhaugh NR12 ....38 D1
Coltishall NR10 ....37 B2
Wisbech PE13 ....152 A4
Barton Way
6 Norwich NR1 ....163 B5
Ormesby St Margaret
NR29 ....167 B3
Barton's La PE32 ....48 A8
Barwell Rd NR18 ......14 E6
Bases La NR23 ....136 C6
Basey Rd NR13 ....72 E8
Basham St PE31 ......177 B4
Basil Dr PE38 ....172 E6
Basil Rd PE33 ....80 A3
Bassingham Rd NR3 ..158 B2
Batchcroft Cl 8 PE28 ..126 C2
Batchelor Dr NR21 ....15 C2
Bately Ave NR31 ......170 D1
Bateman Cl 3 NR5 ....160 E7
Bates Gn NR5 ....161 C8
Bates La IP21 ....119 D2
Bates's Dro CB6 ....95 D1
Bath Hill NR29 ....154 F5
Bath Hill Terr NR30 ..169 D3
Bath Rd NR30 ....169 D3
Bath Rd
West Dereham PE33 ....80 D5
Wisbech PE13 ....152 C7
Bathurst Rd 2 NR2 ...162 C6
Batterby Gn
Fakenham NR21 ....141 A3
Hempton NR21 ....31 C8

Battery Rd NR30 ......170 D8
Battlesea Hill IP21 ....131 E2
Bawburgh Cl NR5 .....156 D1
Bawburgh La NR5 .....156 D1
Bawburgh Prim Sch
NR9 ....160 B6
Bawburgh Rd NR9 .....70 B5
Bawdeswell Prim Sch
NR20 ....50 C7
Bawsey Ctry Pk* PE32 ..44 D6
Baxter Cl 2 Hingham NR9 .86 C5
Long Stratton NR15 ...106 E2
3 Wisbech PE13 ......152 E6
Baxter Ct NR3 ....158 B3
Baxter Rd NR9 ....86 C5
Baxter Row NR19 .....154 D4
Baxter's La NR15 .....107 F8
Bayes La NR16 ....106 C6
Bayfield NR17 ....174 E6
Bayfield Ave 3 NR19 ..154 C3
Bayfield Cl
11 Norwich NR9 ....69 F2
King's Lynn PE30 ......147 D4
Baynard's La IP22 ....129 D7
Bayse's La NR34 ......110 C1
Bayspole Rd 5 NR15 ..106 E3
Beach Cl Hemsby NR29 .167 E3
Mundesley NR11 ....11 A4
Overstrand NR27 ......11 A4
Beach Dr NR29 ....167 E4
Beach Rd NR25 ....8 E6
Beach Rd Bacton NR12 ..23 E5
Caister-on-Sea NR30 ..168 E5
Great Yarmouth NR31 ..94 C8
Cromer NR27 ....139 B7
Eccles on Sea NR12 ....24 E4
3 Great Yarmouth NR31 .170 D4
Happisburgh NR12 .....24 C5
Hemsby NR29 ....167 C7
Holme next the Sea PE36 ..1 F6
Hopton on Sea NR31 ..171 E4
Lessingham NR12 ....24 E3
Mundesley NR11 ......143 C6
Runton NR27 ....10 C5
Salthouse NR25 ....8 C6
Sea Palling NR12 ......40 A6
Sheringham NR26 .....138 E7
Snettisham PE31 ......12 A4
Wells-next-the-Sea
NR23 ....136 C7
Winterton-on-Sea NR29 .58 B6
Beach Terr Rd PE36 ...132 C4
Beachamwell Rd
PE13 ....153 A3
Beacon Hill PE31 .....135 C2
Beacon Hill La PE34 ..144 A6
Beacon Hill Rd PE33 ..135 C1
Beacon Rd NR1 ....11 F1
Beaconsfield Rd
Great Yarmouth NR30 ..169 D6
Norwich NR3 ....162 E8
Bear's La PE37 ....153 B5
Bears Cl 7 NR9 ....86 C4
Bears La NR9 ....86 C5
Bears Rd NR28 ....143 D2
Beatrice Ave NR19 ...154 D4
Beatrice Rd
Norwich NR1 ....163 A6
Wisbech PE13 ....152 D7
Beatty Cl
Great Yarmouth NR30 ..169 D8
Thetford IP24 ....176 E5
Beauchamp Cl
1 Caister-on-Sea NR30 .168 D7
Chedgrave NR14 ....91 F2
Beauchamp Rd 2 NR4 ..92 A2
Beauchamp Rd 2 PE30 .158 D6
Beaufort Way
Great Yarmouth NR31 ..170 B1
Hopton on Sea NR31 ..171 B8
Beaumont Pl 1 NR2 ...162 C4
Beaumont Rd NR5 ....157 B3
Beaumont Way PE30 ..147 C5
Beaupre Ave PE14 .....77 F7
Beavans Cl 3 NR31 ...169 B4
Beavens Ct 15 NR31 ..169 B4
Beavor La IP27 ....175 A2
Beccles Mus* NR34 ...110 C1
Beccles Rd
Aldeby NR34 ....110 F4
Aldeby, Wheatacre,
Burgh St Peter NR34 ..111 B4
Belton with Browston
NR31 ....94 A5
Bungay NR35 ....124 B8
Carlton Colville NR33 ..111 F4
Fritton & St Olaves NR31 .93 E3
Great Yarmouth NR31 ..170 A5
Haddiscoe NR14 ......110 E8
Hales NR14 ....109 E7
Loddon NR14 ....92 A1
Raveningham NR14 ...110 A7
Thurlton NR14 ....92 F1
Beccles Sta NR34 ....110 D1
Beck Ave NR29 ....167 A4
Beck Cl 5 NR25 ....8 F5
Beck La
Burgh & Tuttington NR11 .36 C6
Horsham St Faith &
Newton St Faith NR10 ..53 D2
Beck St IP22 ....127 E3
Bedingham NR35 ......108 D4
11 Bawdeswell NR20 ...50 E2

Beck The *continued*
Kenninghall NR16 .....119 A5
Beck View 3 IP20 .....122 D2
Beck Way NR14 ....91 F1
Becketswell Rd NR18 .173 B3
Beckett Cl 6 PE30 ....148 C4
Becketts Ct NR18 ....173 B6
Beckmeadow Way
NR11 ....143 C5
Becks Fur 2 NR8 .....155 E2
Becks Gn La NR34 ....124 F4
Beckside NR10 ....53 A2
Bedding La NR3 ......178 B4
Bede Cl PE30 ....148 C4
Bedford Dr PE30 .....148 B1
Bedford Mews NR26 .138 D6
Bedford Row PE14 ....41 A4
Bedford St
Norwich NR2 ....178 B3
Wisbech PE13 ....152 C6
Bedingfield Rd 6 NR20 .50 B3
Beech Ave
Attleborough NR17 ...174 C4
King's Lynn PE30 .....148 D3
7 Marham PE33 ....63 E4
Sheringham NR26 ....138 D5
Swaffham PE37 ....153 B5
Beech Cl 1 Gresham NR11 .9 E1
High Kelling NR25 ......8 E2
6 Loddon NR14 ....92 A1
Scole IP21 ....130 C5
Swaffham PE37 ......153 C4
Thetford IP24 ....176 B2
Wymondham NR18 ...173 D6
Beech Cres 6 PE33 ....43 E2
Beech Ct
East Dereham NR19 ..154 E1
North Walsham NR28 ..151 B6
Norwich NR6 ....158 C4
Norwich NR1 ....163 A8
Strumpshaw NR13 .....73 F3
Beech Drift PE31 .....140 D3
Beech La NR20 ....75 C8
Beech Rd Beetley NR20 .49 D4
Downham Market PE38 .172 B6
King's Lynn PE30 .....146 E3
Wroxham/Hoveton
NR12 ....164 D3
Wisbech PE13 ....152 C6
Beech Rise 28 NR31 ...94 C7
Beech Way
Brundall NR13 ....165 D3
Dickleburgh IP21 .....121 C1
Beech Wlk NR14 ....90 D5
Beechamwell Rd PE33 .81 B8
Beechbank NR28 ......151 B6
Beechbank Dr 3 NR13 .72 D6
Beechcroft NR25 ......156 F1
Beeches Cl NR10 .....161 C8
Beeches La NR29 ......86 E6
Beeches The 1 NR20 ...68 E6
Beeches The 3 NR28 ..172 C2
Beechfields IP27 ......175 F4
Beeching Cl 1 NR1 ...162 E1
Beeching Rd NR1 .....162 E2
Beechlands NR8 ....155 D1
Beechlands Pk NR11 ..22 B7
Aylmerton NR11 ....10 A3
18 Watton IP25 ....84 D3
Beechwood Cl
North Walsham NR28 ..151 D6
Watlington PE33 ....61 E5
Beechwood Ct NR18 ..173 D1
Beechwood Dr NR7 ...159 C2
Beechwood Rd
Hemsby NR29 ....167 A8
Wisbech PE13 ....152 C7
Beechwoods NR6 .....158 D5
Beehive Yd IP22 ......177 C4
Beeleigh Way NR30 ..168 C7
Bee-Orchid Way NR14 .91 D4
Beerhills Cl NR14 .....73 B1
Beeston Comm NR26 .138 E6
Beeston Hall Sch NR27 ..9 F5
Beeston La
Barton Turf NR12 ......38 D1
Beeston St Andrew
NR12 ....158 B8
Beeston Prim Sch
PE32 ....48 C2
Beeston Rd
Beeston with Bittering
PE32 ....48 C2
Great Dunham PE32 ...66 A8
Mileham PE32 ....48 D5
Sheringham NR26 ....138 E7
Beetley Grange 1 NR20 .49 D4
Beetley Mdws 9 NR20 .49 D4
Beevor Rd NR30 ......169 D5
Begdale Rd PE14 ....59 A1
Bek Cl NR4 ....161 E2
Belaugh Gn La NR12 ..164 A8
Belaugh La NR12 .....164 A8
Belaugh Rd NR12 ....164 A7
Belgrave Ave PE30 ...148 D6
Belgrave Gdns 3 NR13 .154 E3
15 Bawdeswell NR20 .....50 E2

Bell Cl continued
East Dereham NR19 ......154 C5
Little Snoring NR21 ....17 B3
Norwich NR6 ....157 F6
Taverham NR8 ....156 E8
Bell La Rocklands NR17 ...103 B8
Saham Toney IP25 ....84 C4
Salhouse NR13 ....164 B1
Bell Mdw 1 Hingham NR9 ..86 C5
2 Marthan NR29 ....57 D5
Bell Rd
Barnham Broom NR9 ....69 B2
Grimston PE32 ....28 C1
Norwich NR3 ....158 E1
Rocklands NR17 ....103 B8
Bell St IP26 ....85 C4
Bellacre Cl IP22 ....177 E4
Bellamy Way NR14 ....90 C4
Bellamy's La
Burnham Norton PE31 .....135 C5
West Walton PE14 ....59 A8
Bellands Way 1 IP23 .....130 C1
Bell's Dro Littleport CB6 ...95 E2
Runcton Holme PE33 ....61 C5
Bell's Marsh Rd NR31 ....170 D5
Bellmere Way IP25 ....84 C4
Bellomonte Cres NR8 .....156 F8
Bellrope Cl 5 NR18 ......173 D5
Bellrope La
Roydon IP22 ....129 D7
Wymondham NR18 ....173 D5
Bells La IP22 ....128 C4
Bells Rd NR31 ....170 D4
Bellview Cl NR24 ....142 B4
Bellville Cres NR1 ....178 C1
Belmore Cl NR7 ....159 E1
Belmore Rd NR7 ....163 F8
Beloe Ave 4 NR5 ....161 A7
Beloe Cres PE30 ....146 D1
Belseybridge Rd NR35 ....108 F3
Belsize Cl 1 PE38 ....172 B4
Belsize Rd NR1 ....163 B7
Belstead Ave NR30 ....168 D5
Belt Rd NR13 ....73 C7
Belvedere Pl 1 NR44 .....162 A3
Belvidere Rd NR30 ....169 D5
Belvoir St NR2 ....162 B6
Ben Culey Dr IP24 ....176 C5
Ben's La PE33 ....80 E4
Benbow Cl 6 NR9 ....88 E8
Benbow Rd IP24 ....176 F6
Benchmark La NR31 ......170 D2
Bendish Way NR5 ....160 E7
Benedict Cl PE34 ....145 F5
Benedict Rd 10 NR12 .....55 E4
Benets View 3 NR28 .....151 E5
Bengey's Rd 7 PE37 ......65 F4
Benjamin Ct NR27 ....139 B5
Benn's La PE34 ....144 C5
Bennett Cl
Hunstanton PE36 ....132 D2
3 Watlington PE33 ....61 D5
Bennett Rd NR20 ....50 B2
Bennett St PE38 ....172 A5
Bennington's La
Aylmerton NR11 ....138 F1
East Beckham NR11 ....9 D2
Bensley Cl NR13 ....166 C4
Bensley Rd
1 Marthan NR29 ....57 D5
Norwich NR7 ....162 A4
Bentinck Way 2 PE34 ....146 C5
Bentley Rd NR16 ....105 F4
Bentley Way NR13 ....158 C4
Bentons Way NR10 ....53 B8
Ber St NR1 ....178 B1
Berberis Gn 3 NR31 .....170 B5
Beresford Rd
Caister-on-Sea NR30 ......168 E4
Great Yarmouth NR30 .....169 D7
Holt NR25 ....137 C5
Bergamot Cl IP24 ....176 F4
Bergen Way PE30 ....146 F8
Bergh Apton Rd
Alpington NR14 ....90 F4
Mundham NR14 ....91 D1
Bermondsey Pl H NR30 ...169 D4
Bermondsey Pl S 16
NR30 ....169 D4
Bermondsey Pl W 17
NR30 ....169 D4
Bernard Cl
High Kelling NR25 ....8 E2
11 New Buckenham NR13 ..72 E7
Bernard Cres PE36 ....132 D6
Bernard Rd
Cromer NR27 ....139 A7
11 Watton NR31 ....170 D2
Berners Cl NR3 ....158 B1
Berners St NR3 ....158 B1
Berney Arms Sta NR30 ...93 D8
Berney Arms Windmill*
NR30 ....93 E7
Bernham Rd NR6 ....157 E4
Berrington Rd NR6 ....157 F6
Berry Cl NR31 ....93 F6
Berry Hall Rd NR12 ....38 E1
Berry's La NR9 ....69 D6
Berryfields NR13 ....165 C5
Bertie Rd NR3 ....158 C1
Bertie Ward Way
NR19 ....154 F2
Bessemer Rd NR4 ....162 D1

Bessemer Way NR31 .....169 B1
Besthorpe Carr NR17 .....105 A6
Besthorpe Rd NR17 ......174 E5
Besthorpe Rd NR16 ......105 A5
Bethel St NR2 ....178 A3
Betjeman Cl IP24 ....176 E6
Beulah St PE30 ....147 B6
Bevan Cl
Carleton Rode NR16 ......105 C4
Norwich NR5 ....161 B6
Beveridge Way PE33 ......43 E4
Beverley Cl NR5 ....161 E6
Beverley Rd
Brundall NR13 ....165 B4
Norwich NR5 ....161 E6
Beverley Way
Clenchwarton PE34 ....145 E5
Norwich NR5 ....156 F8
Beverly Cl NR31 ....170 A7
Bevis Way PE30 ....147 B7
Bewfeld Rd 4 NR5 ....160 E8
Bewick Cl
1 Great Yarmouth NR31 ...94 C8
5 Snettisham PE31 ....12 E5
Bewit Rd NR7 ....159 D4
Bexfield Rd NR20 ....33 C4
Bexwell Rd Bexwell PE38 ..79 F6
Downham Market PE38 ...172 D5
Bickley Cl NR17 ....174 F7
Bidewell Cl NR8 ....157 B7
Bidwell Rd NR13 ....72 E8
Bidwells ct IP24 ....176 C4
Bier La IP22 ....128 F5
Big Back La 1 NR14 .....92 A2
Big Row NR34 ....109 F2
Big Yard PE36 ....2 A3
Big Yard The PE36 ....132 E7
Biggin Hill Way IP25 .....85 A3
Biggotts La NR15 ....108 E7
Biggs Rd PE14 ....59 D4
Bignold Fst Sch NR2 .....178 A2
Bignold Mid Sch NR2 ....178 A2
Bignold Rd NR3 ....158 A2
Bilberry Cl 5 NR17 ......174 B5
Bilbys NR14 ....110 B6
Bill Todd Way NR8 ....155 C2
Billing Cl NR6 ....158 F5
Billingford Rd
1 Bawdeswell NR20 ......50 E7
Bintree NR20 ....33 B1
Bilney La NR10 ....155 E8
Bilney Rd Beetley NR20 ...49 B4
East Winch PE32 ....45 B1
Pentney PE32 ....63 C8
Bingles Turn NR10 ....53 B7
Binham Rd
Field Dalling NR25 ....7 A1
Hindringham NR21 ....17 E8
4 King's Lynn PE30 ......148 C3
Langham NR25 ....7 A4
Warham NR23 ....6 A4
Bintree Rd NR20 ....156 D8
Binyon Gdns NR8 ....156 D8
Birbeck Rd NR1 ....162 E2
Birch Ave 8 NR20 ....49 D4
Birch Cl
East Dereham NR19 ......154 C4
Little Melton NR9 ....160 D2
North Walsham NR28 .....151 D6
6 Snettisham PE31 ....12 E4
Birch Covert 5 IP24 .....176 F5
Birch Ct Erpingham NR11 ..21 B2
Norwich NR7 ....159 D4
Birch Dr
Attleborough NR17 ....174 C3
Roydon PE32 ....28 A2
Birch Gr
Sheringham NR26 ....138 D4
West Winch PE33 ....43 E2
Wisbech PE14 ....59 B1
Birch Rd Gayton PE32 ....45 C6
11 Hethersett NR9 ....88 D8
Birch Tree Cl PE30 ......146 E4
Birch Way
4 Great Yarmouth NR31 ..170 B5
Mundham NR14 ....108 F6
Bircham Rd
Docking PE31 ....134 C4
Reepham NR10 ....149 C5
Snettisham PE31 ....13 A4
Stanhoe PE31 ....14 E7
Bircham Windmill*
PE31 ....14 A3
Birches The PE30 ....148 B4
Birchfield Gdns NR14 .....89 B3
Birchfield La NR14 ....89 B3
Birchfield Rd PE38 ....78 E3
Birchgrove Rd PE30 ......147 C4
Birchwood 4 NR7 ....72 D3
Birchwood St 5 PE30 ...146 E6
Bird View Sq 1 IP25 .....98 E1
Birdcage Wlk NR2 ....178 A2
Birds Cnr IP25 ....67 E4
Birds Rd NR28 ....151 B3
Birkbeck Cl
King's Lynn PE30 ....148 B2
Stoke Holy Cross NR14 ...90 B5
Birkbeck Way 1 NR7 ....163 F7
Birkdale NR4 ....162 A2
Birkin Cl 3 NR16 ....105 F5
Birtles Way NR13 ....166 C3
Biscay Gdns NR30 ....168 C6
Bishop Bonner's Cottage
Mus* NR19 ....154 D5
Bishop Bridge Rd
NR1 ....163 A6

Bishop Herbert Cl
NR20 ....69 B8
Bishop Rise 3 NR8 ......155 E2
Bishop's Cl NR7 ....163 D5
Bishop's Rd
Hunstanton PE36 ....132 C2
King's Lynn PE30 ....147 B4
Bishopgate NR1 ....178 C3
Bishops Wlk 5 NR31 ....171 D5
Bishoptyne Ave 1 NR14 .154 F3
Bishy Barnebee Way
NR5 ....160 F6
Bittering St
4 Beetley NR20 ....49 C4
4 Gressenhall NR20 .....49 C3
Bittern Cl Necton PE37 ...66 A3
Thetford IP24 ....176 D1
Bittern Cres NR12 ....38 F1
Bittern Rd NR29 ....57 D3
Bixley Cl NR5 ....161 D6
Black Bear La PE13 ......152 F7
Black Drift PE37 ....66 A4
Black Dro
Downham West PE38 .....79 B6
Feltwell PE38 ....97 F2
Fincham PE33 ....80 D7
Marshland St James
PE14 ....60 D4
Stow Bardolph PE34 ......78 E8
Black Dyke Rd IP26 ......113 C7
Black Horse Cl NR19 .....67 B7
Black Horse Dro CB6 .....96 E2
Black Horse Opening
NR6 ....158 F2
Black Horse Rd
Clenchwarton PE34 ......145 C4
Runhall NR9 ....68 F1
Black Mill La NR15 ....121 A7
Black Moor Rd IP25 ......67 D2
Black St Hemsby NR29 ...58 B6
Marthan NR29 ....57 D5
Melton Constable NR24 ...116 D8
Blackberry Cl NR6 ....157 F2
Blackberry Gr NR27 ......10 C4
Blackberry Hall La
NR11 ....11 D1
Blackbird Ave IP27 ......175 F3
Blackbird Cl 17 NR31 ....94 C8
Blackbird Way 9 IP24 ....98 D1
Blackdale Mid Sch
NR4 ....161 D4
Blackdike Dro IP27 ......112 F5
Blackdyke Cl 8 IP26 .....98 D1
Blackford PE30 ....147 D8
Blackfriars' Rd NR30 ....169 D2
Blackfriars Rd
King's Lynn PE30 ....146 E5
8 Wisbech PE13 ....152 C5
Blackfriars St
King's Lynn PE30 ....146 D4
Norwich NR3 ....178 B4
Blacksmith's Cnr NR13 ...73 C7
Blackhorse Cl 9 NR20 ...50 E7
Blackhorse St 1 NR2 ....162 C7
Blackhorse Yd NR23 .....136 C6
Blackmoor Row 5 IP25 ...67 D2
Blacks Ave NR14 ....163 B2
Blackslough La NR16 ....119 D7
Blacksmith La IP24 ......125 E6
Blacksmith's La
Barton Bendish PE33 .....81 B8
Morning Thorpe NR15 ....107 A2
Blacksmith's Loke
NR32 ....94 C2
Blacksmith's Row 1
PE32 ....45 C6
Blacksmiths CI NR20 .....33 B6
Blacksmiths La
Ashwellthorpe NR16 .....106 B8
Happisburgh NR12 ....24 B6
Hindringham NR21 ....17 E7
Blacksmiths Way NR6 ...158 E5
Blackthorn Ave NR5 .....137 C7
Blackthorn Cl
Diss IP22 ....177 F5
Norwich NR6 ....158 D4
8 Thetford IP24 ....176 F5
Blackthorn Dr 8 NR19 ...154 C4
Blackthorn Rd
Attleborough NR17 ....174 B5
King's Lynn PE30 ....148 C3
Wymondham NR18 ......173 D6
Blackthorn Way 16 NR14 .90 C5
Blackwall Reach
NR31 ....94 C8
Blackwater Cnr NR11 ....36 F5
Blackwater La
Great Witchingham NR9 ...51 C6
Heydon NR11 ....34 D8
Blackwell Ave NR7 ......159 A3
Bladewater Rd NR5 ......160 F5
Blake Cl PE32 ....28 A1
Blake Ct PE13 ....153 C2
Blake Dr NR31 ....170 A7
Blake Rd NR30 ....169 D7
Blakeney CE Prim Sch
NR25 ....7 D6
Blakeney Cl NR4 ....161 C2
Blakeney Long La NR25 ...7 C4
Blakeney Point National
Nature Reserve* NR25 ...7 C8
Blakeney Rd
Binham NR21 ....6 D1
Letheringsett with Glandford
NR25 ....7 F2
Morston NR25 ....7 B6

Blakeney Short La NR25 ..7 C3
Blakes Ct NR3 ....158 F3
Blakestone Dr NR7 ......163 D7
Bland Rd NR5 ....161 B6
Blatchford Way PE31 ....133 B5
Blencowe Terr 25 PE13 .152 C5
Blenheim Ave 4 NR29 ...57 D4
Blenheim Cl
12 Long Stratton NR15 ...106 E3
Norwich NR7 ....159 B5
Blenheim Cres
Beeston with Bittering
PE32 ....48 D2
Griston IP25 ....85 A2
Norwich NR7 ....159 B5
Tittleshall PE32 ....48 A7
Blenheim Dr NR17 ....174 E4
Blenheim Pk Sch NR21 ...15 C3
Blenheim Rd
King's Lynn PE30 ....147 C8
Norwich NR5 ....159 B5
Sculthorpe Airfield NR21 ...15 C3
Blenheim Way
Emneth PE14 ....152 E2
2 Roydon IP22 ....129 D7
5 Watton IP25 ....84 E3
Blick Cl 5 PE33 ....43 F2
Blickling Cl 1 PE30 .....148 F1
Blickling Hall* NR11 .....35 F7
Blickling Rd
Blickling NR11 ....150 A8
Norwich NR5 ....158 C5
Bligh Cl NR14 ....90 D5
Blind Dick's La NR29 .....16 E7
Blind La
Castle Acre PE32 ....46 F1
Hockering NR9 ....51 A2
Honingham NR9 ....69 A7
Horsham St Faith NR10 ...53 D1
Mattishall NR20 ....68 D7
Blithe Mdw Ct NR7 .....159 C3
Blithemeadow Dr
NR7 ....159 C3
Blithewood Gdns NR7 ...159 C3
Blo' Norton Rd IP22 .....128 C2
Blocka Rd NR32 ....93 F2
Blofield Cnr Rd NR13 ....73 B6
Blofield Loke NR12 ......164 E6
Blofield Prim Sch
NR13 ....165 E7
Blofield Rd
Brundall NR13 ....165 B3
Lingwood & Burlingham
NR13 ....73 F3
Blofields Loke NR11 .....150 C6
Blomefield Rd
Diss IP22 ....177 D4
Norwich NR3 ....158 B2
Bloodgate Hill NR21 .....15 C6
Bloodhills Rd NR29 ....57 F5
Bloomfield Rd NR30 .....170 E7
Blooms Turn NR28 ....22 E5
Bloomstile La PE30 ....8 B6
Bloomstiles NR25 ....8 B6
Blowlands La NR26 ......138 B5
Blue Boar La NR7 ....159 D3
Blue Doors Loke NR31 ...94 C3
Blue Sky Cl NR31 ....94 C7
Bluebell Cl
Attleborough NR17 ....174 B5
4 East Dereham NR19 ...154 C4
Thetford IP24 ....176 F4
Bluebell Cres 1 NR61 ....22 D2
Bluebell Dr NR26 ....138 B5
Bluebell Gdns NR25 .....136 E5
Bluebell Rd
Mulbarton NR14 ....89 B3
North Walsham NR28 ....151 D6
Norwich NR4 ....161 D3
Bluebell Way 19 NR61 ...94 C6
Bluebell Wlk IP27 ....175 A2
Bluestone Cres NR11 ....11 C6
Bluestone La NR21 ....15 D7
Blundeston Rd NR32 .....111 F8
Blundeville Manor 6
NR15 ....89 C1
Blunt's Cnr NR23 ....5 B2
Blyth Cres NR26 ....138 D6
Blyth Jex Sch The
NR3 ....158 E2
Blyth Rd NR3 ....158 E2
Boadicea Cl 1 IP24 ......176 D7
Boal Quay PE30 ....146 D4
Boal St PE30 ....146 D4
Boardman Cl NR6 ....158 D3
Boat Dyke La NR13 ......166 D4
Boat Dyke Rd NR13 .....166 D4
Boathouse La NR32 .....111 F3
Boatmans Row NR23 ....136 C6
Bob Carter Leisure Ctr
NR8 ....157 A8
Bodleian Ct NR4 ....161 C6
Boileau Ave 6 NR10 ....105 F5
Boileau Cl 1 NR4 ....89 E8
Boleness Rd PE13 ....152 C2
Bolingbroke Rd NR1 .....162 F3
Boltons The PE37 ....65 C4
Bond Cl 1 IP23 ....136 D6
Bond St 3 Cromer NR27 ..139 B7
5 King's Lynn NR9 ....86 C5
Norwich NR2 ....162 A7
Bond's Rd NR15 ....121 C4
Bond's Rd IP24 ....73 C7
Bone Rd NR8 ....156 E2
Bone's Dro NR23 ....4 F7

Boniface Cl NR4 ....162 C1
Bonnetts La NR14 ....60 B5
Boosey's Wlk 6 NR16 ...104 F1
Boot Binders Rd 7
NR6 ....158 C1
Boot La IP22 ....120 D6
Booton Comm Nature
Reserve* NR10 ....149 E5
Booton Rd NR10 ....35 B2
Booty Rd NR7 ....159 F1
Borage Cl IP24 ....176 F4
Border La NR32 ....94 B2
Border Rd PE33 ....81 A2
Borough Cl PE13 ....152 D3
Borrowdale Dr NR1 .....163 B8
Borrow Rd NR13 ....73 C6
Boscombe Rd IP25 ......85 A3
Bosgate Rise 9 NR29 ...57 C4
Boston Cl 1 NR19 ....154 C3
Boston End 6 IP24 ......116 A1
Boston Sq PE36 ....132 C5
Boston Sq Sensory Pk
PE36 ....132 C5
Boston St 3 NR3 ....158 D2
Botolph St NR3 ....178 A4
Boton Dr NR19 ....154 D7
Bottom Breck Cl NR5 ...156 F2
Botwright Dr 5 PE37 ....153 C3
Boudica's Way NR14 ....163 A1
Boughey Cl PE31 ....3 B6
Boughton Long Rd
PE33 ....81 B7
Boughton Rd
Fincham PE33 ....62 E1
Stoke Ferry PE33 ....81 A3
Boulderside Cl 1 NR7 ...163 E7
Boulevard Rd NR27 .....10 A5
Boulevard The
Sheringham NR26 ....138 D7
Thorpe End NR13 ....72 E6
Boulters The NR31 ......170 C1
Boulton Rd NR7 ....163 C7
Boulton St NR1 ....178 B2
Boundary Ave NR6 ......158 A4
Boundary Cl IP26 ....113 F7
Boundary La
Norwich NR7 ....72 E3
Paston NR28 ....23 B3
Boundary Rd
Ashby with Oby NR29 ....56 E2
Great Yarmouth NR31 ...169 B1
1 Hockwold cum Wilton
PE26 ....114 A7
Marham PE33 ....89 D1
Norton Subcourse NR14 ..92 D1
Norwich NR6 ....157 F3
Raveningham NR14 ......92 D1
Boundary Way 1 NR14 ...90 C5
Bourne Cl
King's Lynn PE30 ....148 C2
Long Stratton NR15 .....106 E3
Bow Hill NR9 ....70 A3
Bow St NR9 ....86 B1
Bowers Ave NR3 ....158 A2
Bowers La NR25 ....158 A2
Bowlers Cl NR13 ....92 E7
Bowling Gn Cl
Attleborough NR17 ....174 D6
Crostwick NR12 ....54 B2
Bowling Gn The
Raynham NR21 ....30 F4
NR23 ....136 D5
Bowling Gn Wlk 2
NR30 ....169 C4
Bowman Rd 4 NR4 ....89 E8
Bowthorpe Hall Gdns*
PE13 ....152 D5
Bowthorpe Hall Rd
NR5 ....160 F7
Bowthorpe Rd
Norwich NR5 ....161 D6
Wisbech PE13 ....152 C5
Box's La PE33 ....153 D5
Boyces Rd PE13 ....152 E5
Boyd Ave 9 NR19 ....154 D1
Boylandhall La NR15 ....107 B4
Brabazon Rd NR6 ....158 B5
Braces La NR35 ....109 E3
Bracey Ave NR6 ....158 F5
Bracken Ave
3 Beetley NR20 ....49 D4
Norwich NR5 ....158 A4
Overstrand NR27 ....11 A3
Bracken Cl
Fakenham NR21 ....141 F4
Horsford NR10 ....53 B2
Stratton Strawless NR10 ..53 A6
Bracken Dr NR17 ....174 B5
Bracken Rd
Thetford IP24 ....148 C2
Thetford IP24 ....176 E4
Bracken Rise
Brandon IP27 ....175 C3
Mundford IP26 ....100 A4
Bracken Way PE32 ......28 B1
Brackenwoods PE37 .....66 A4
Brackon Rd NR13 ....93 F5
Braconash Rd NR14 .....89 D5
Braconbale NR1 ....178 C1
Braconbale Ct 3 NR61 ...162 C1
Braconbale St NR1 ......178 C1
Braconbale Millgate
NR14 ....163 A2
Bradcar Rd NR17 ....103 B2
Braddock Rd NR30 ......168 E5
Bradeham Way NR4 .....162 A1

Bradenham Hall Gdn & Arboretum* IP25 .....66 E4
Bradenham La NR19 ....66 F6
Bradenham Rd IP25 ....67 A2
Bradfield Cl NR28 .....151 A6
Bradfield Pl 3 PE33 ....81 A3
Bradfield Rd
  Antingham NR11 ....22 C5
  North Walsham NR28 ....151 A6
  Swafield NR28 ....22 C5
Bradman's La NR18 ......87 D3
Bradmere La PE31 ......134 E5
Bradshaw Rd NR8 ......157 C7
Bradwell Ave 3 NR31 ...170 A5
Brady Cl PE38 ....172 B1
Brady Gdns PE38 ....172 B1
Braeburn Ave PE13 ....152 C8
Braeford Cl NR5 ....157 E2
Brailsford Cl NR20 .....68 A7
Braithwait Cl 1 NR5 ...161 A8
Brake La NR21 ....16 C4
Bramble Ave NR6 ......158 A5
Bramble Cl
  Mundesley NR11 ....143 D5
  Sculthorpe Airfield NR21 ..15 C2
  4 Taverham NR8 ....155 E2
Bramble Ct NR21 ......148 E4
Bramble Dr PE30 ......148 C2
Bramble Gdns NR31 ....93 F5
Bramble La
  Outwell PE14 ....77 D7
  Swaffham PE37 ....153 F5
Bramble Way
  1 Poringland NR14 .....90 D5
  Wymondham NR18 ....173 E4
Brambles Cl 2 NR10 ...54 A1
Bramerton La
  Framingham Pigot NR14 ...90 E7
  Rockland St Mary NR14 ...91 A7
Bramerton Rd NR14 ....91 A8
Bramfield Cl NR2 .....162 A7
Bramley Cl NR23 .....136 D6
Bramley Dr NR21 ......31 E5
Bramley Rd
  Dereham NR20 ....68 A8
  Diss IP22 ....177 C5
  Wisbech PE13 ....152 C7
Brampton Cl PE13 .....152 A4
Brampton Ct 12 NR5 ...161 A7
Brampton Sta NR10 ....36 D3
Brancaster Cl
  King's Lynn PE30 ......147 C8
  1 Taverham NR8 ......155 F3
Brancaster Rd PE31 ...134 E7
Brancaster Way PE37 ..153 B2
Branch Rd NR13 ....75 B2
Brand's La
  Felthorpe NR10 ....155 D6
  Thorston & Hapton
  NR15 ....106 E5
Brandiston Rd NR10 ....35 B2
Brandon Cl
  Norwich NR6 ....157 E4
  3 Swaffham PE37 .....153 C3
Brandon Ct NR13 ......165 E3
Brandon Her Ctr*
  IP27 ....175 D4
Brandon Rd
  Cockley Cley PE37 .....83 A8
  Methwold IP26 ....99 B4
  Saham Toney IP25 .....84 B3
  Swaffham PE37 ....65 A1
  Thetford IP24 ....176 A4
  Wangford IP27 ....114 C1
  Watton IP25 ....84 C3
  Weeting-with-Broomhill
  IP27 ....175 C5
Brandon Sports Ctr
  IP27 ....175 B3
Brandon Sta IP27 .....175 C5
Brandon Terr NR30 ....169 E2
Brandnvnm (Roman Fort)
  (Branodunum)* PE31 ....3 C6
Branford Rd
  Caister-on-Sea NR30 ...168 D7
  Norwich NR3 ....158 E1
Branksome Cl NR4 .....162 B2
Branksome Rd NR4 ....162 B2
Branodunum PE31 ......3 B7
Bransby Cl PE30 ......146 F4
Brasenose Ave NR31 ...170 B3
Brasier Rd NR3 ....158 B2
Brawdy Rd 7 IP31 ....126 B1
Bray's La
  Guestwick NR20 ....34 A6
  Rocklands NR17 ....103 A7
Braydeston Ave NR13 ..165 D3
Braydeston Cres
  NR13 ....165 D3
Braydeston Dr NR13 ...165 F6
Braydeston Hall La
  NR13 ....73 E4
Brayfield Way NR6 ....158 F6
Braymeadow NR10 ....160 C2
Braymeadow La NR9 ...160 D2
Brazen Gate NR11 .....178 A1
Breck Farm Cl NR8 ...155 C2
Breck Farm La NR8 ...155 C2
Breck Rd Norwich NR7 ..159 E2
  Weston Longville NR9 ...51 E1
Breckland Bsns Pk
  IP25 ....84 F3
Breckland Leisure Ctr &
  Waterworld IP24 .....176 D5
Breckland Mid Sch
  IP27 ....175 A2
Breckland Rd NR5 ....157 A1

Brecklands
  Mundford IP26 ....100 B4
  1 Stalham NR12 ....39 B4
Brecklands Rd NR13 ...165 E2
Brecon Rd NR15 ....90 E2
Breeze Ave NR11 .....150 B5
Brellows Hill PE34 ....144 A5
Brenda Collison Cl
  PE31 ....140 C4
Brenda James Cl 1
  NR7 ....163 E7
Brennewater Mews 4
  NR5 ....161 A8
Brent Ave PE31 ....12 E5
Brenton Rd NR4 ....161 F1
Brereton Cl 1 NR5 ....161 C6
Bressingham Prim Sch
  IP22 ....129 B8
Bressingham Rd
  5 Gresham NR11 ....9 E1
  Roydon IP22 ....129 C8
  Sustead NR11 ....20 E8
Bressingham Steam Mus &
  Gdns* IP22 ....129 C7
Breton Cl 10 NR19 ....154 D2
Brett Ave NR31 ....170 D1
Brett Way PE30 ......147 B8
Brettingham Ave NR4 ..89 B8
Brewers Cl NR3 ....178 C4
Brewers Gn La IP22 ...177 B6
Brewery La NR18 .....173 C3
Brewery Rd NR28 ......22 D5
Brewery St NR30 .....169 C4
Brewster Cl NR13 ....165 D6
Brewsters 8 NR16 ....118 C5
Breydon Dr NR8 ......156 C4
Breydon Dr N NR8 ...156 C5
Breydon Junc NR30 ....92 A5
Breydon Rd
  Great Yarmouth NR31 ..169 B4
  King's Lynn PE30 ....147 D5
  Norwich NR7 ....159 A4
Breydon Way NR30 ...168 D6
Brian Ave NR1 ....162 D3
Briar Ave NR31 ....94 C7
Briar Cl Dereham NR20 ..68 A8
  Grimston PE32 ....28 B1
  King's Lynn PE30 .....148 C3
  14 Lingwood NR13 .....74 A3
  9 Necton PE37 ....65 F4
Briar La
  Heckingham NR14 .....109 F8
  Rickinghall Inferior
  IP22 ....128 D1
  Swainsthorpe NR14 ....89 D3
Briars Ct NR5 ....161 F7
Brick Kiln La
  Ellingham NR35 ......109 C4
  Gillingham NR34 ......110 C5
  Long Stratton NR15 ...107 A5
  Shipdham IP25 ....67 C2
Brick Kiln Rd
  Ellingham NR35 ......109 C4
  Hevingham NR10 ......53 A7
  North Walsham NR28 ..151 E5
  Thursford NR21 ....17 F4
Brick Kilns Rd NR13 ...73 B7
Brick La NR27 ....10 B5
Brickfield Loke NR8 ..156 C5
Brickfields NR13 ....73 F2
Brickfields Way IP24 ..176 C6
Brickkiln La
  Ashwellthorpe NR16 ..105 F7
  Mulbarton NR14 ....89 C2
  South Lopham IP22 ...128 F7
Brickle Loke NR14 ....90 B5
Brickle Rd NR14 ......90 B4
Brickley La PE31 .....140 D7
Brickyard La PE32 .....29 C4
Brickyard Rd NR28 ....22 A2
Bridewell Alley 2 NR2 ..178 B3
Bridewell La
  Acle NR13 ....166 C4
  Botesdale IP22 ....128 E2
Bridewell Mus The*
  NR2 ....178 B3
Bridewell St
  1 Little Walsingham NR22 ..16 F7
  Wymondham NR18 ....173 C3
Bridge Broad Cl NR12 ..164 F5
Bridge Cl
  18 Harleston IP20 ....122 D2
  Pentney PE31 ....133 E5
  Melton Constable NR24 ..142 B4
Bridge Farm La NR4 ..161 C6
Bridge Gdns NR19 ....154 F1
Bridge La IP25 ....84 C6
Bridge Mdw NR26 .....58 A4
Bridge Rd
  Brome & Oakley IP21 ..130 C5
  Bunwell NR16 ....105 F2
  Burston & Shimpling
  IP22 ....120 A3
  Colney NR4 ....161 A8
  Downham West PE38 ...79 B5
  Great Ryburgh NR21 ..32 C6
  Great Yarmouth NR30 ..169 C5
  High Kelling NR25 ....137 F8
  North Elmham NR20 ....32 F3
  Potter Heigham NR29 ..56 F5
  Stoke Ferry PE33 ......81 A2
  Sutton Bridge PE12 ....41 A8
  Upwell PE14 ....77 D7
Bridge St Brandon IP27 ..175 C4
  Carbrooke IP25 ....85 A4
  Downham Market PE38 ..172 B5

Bridge St continued
  Fakenham NR21 ....141 B3
  Gressenhall NR20 .....49 C3
  Hilgay PE38 ....79 E1
  14 King's Lynn PE30 ...146 D4
  Loddon NR14 ....92 A2
  Stiffkey NR23 ....6 D5
  Thetford IP24 ....176 C4
  14 Wisbech PE13 .....152 C5
Bridgecourt NR29 .....58 A4
Bridgefoot La NR25 ....7 F5
Bridges Wlk
  Fakenham NR21 ....141 A3
  Thetford IP24 ....176 D3
Bridgford Cl NR31 ....170 C2
Bridgham La NR16 ....117 F4
Bridle La
  Downham Market PE38 ..172 D7
  Keswick NR4 ....89 C7
Bridle Rd IP25 ....84 C3
Brig Sq NR23 ....136 C6
Brigg St NR1 ....178 A2
Briggs Loke NR11 .....36 D8
Brigham Cl NR13 .....165 C4
Brighton Rd 1 NR15 ...89 C1
Brightwell Rd NR4 ....161 E1
Brighty's Opening
  NR2 ....162 B7
Brigstock Rd PE13 ...152 B7
Brimbelow Rd NR12 ..164 D4
Brindle Dr 5 NR14 ....89 B3
Brinell Way NR31 .....170 B8
Brinton Rd NR24 .....142 D8
Briscoe Way IP27 .....113 E2
Brisley CE Prim Sch
  NR20 ....32 A1
Bristol Terr NR2 .....178 A2
Briston Rd
  Briston NR24 ....142 A5
  Corpusty NR11 ....19 F1
  Edgefield NR24 ....19 C5
  Wood Dalling NR11 ....34 C6
Britannia Pier Theatre
  NR30 ....169 E4
Britannia Rd
  Great Yarmouth NR30 ..169 E4
  Norwich NR1 ....163 A7
Britannia Way PE13 ...152 C2
Briton La PE34 ....42 B4
Briton Way NR18 .....173 B3
Briton's La
  Beeston Regis NR26 ..138 F4
  Sheringham NR26 ......9 F5
Briton's La Cl
  2 Beeston Regis NR27 ...9 F5
  Sheringham NR26 .....138 F5
Britton Cl 3 NR23 ...136 D6
Broad Dro Emneth PE14 ..59 C1
  Grimston PE32 ....28 C4
  Methwold IP26 ....97 F6
  Upwell PE14 ....77 D4
Broad End La PE13 ...152 F4
Broad End Rd PE14 ...152 F4
Broad Fen La NR28 ....38 D4
Broad La Brancaster PE31 ..3 A7
  Great & Little Plumstead
  NR13 ....74 B8
  Swannington NR9 .....52 B5
Broad Rd Alburgh IP20 ..122 E8
  Fleggburgh NR29 ......75 C8
Broad Reaches NR29 ..56 C5
Broad Row NR30 .....169 C4
Broad St Bungay NR35 ..124 A8
  Brundall NR13 ....170 D2
  King's Lynn PE30 ....146 D5
Broad View NR13 ......72 D6
Broad Way
  Dickleburgh & Rushall
  IP21 ....130 D8
  Rocklands NR17 ......103 A8
Broadacres 15 NR13 ...74 B8
Broadcote Cl NR5 .....90 E1
Broaden La NR15 ....107 C6
Broadfen Dro IP26 .....98 B5
Broadfields Way NR14 ..91 C7
Broadgate NR8 ....155 B2
Broadgate Cl NR27 ....11 A2
Broadgate La
  Great Moulton NR15 ..121 B8
  Roydon PE32 ....28 A2
Broadhurst Rd NR4 ...162 B1
Broadland Cl NR13 ....93 A4
Broadland Dr NR13 ....72 D6
Broadland High Sch
  NR12 ....164 D6
Broadland Sports Club
  NR29 ....75 D8
Broadland Way
  Acle NR13 ....166 C3
  Postwick with Witton NR7 ..72 E3
Broadlands 15 NR13 ..74 B8
Broadlands Cl PE31 ..140 C4
Broadlands Dr NR12 ..72 E6
Broadmead Gn NR13 ..72 E6
Broadmoor Rd IP25 ...85 B4
Broadsman Cl NR1 ...163 A4
Broadwater Rd 26 NR29 ..57 D4
Broadwater Way 1 NR12 ..55 E4
Broadway 15 NR15 ...107 C5
Broadway The
  Heacham PE31 ....133 D5
  Honingham NR9 ....69 E8
Broadwood Cl NR11 ...11 E1
Brockdish Prim Sch
  IP21 ....131 D6

Brockley Gn 7 PE30 ...147 C4
Brocks Rd PE37 ......153 B6
Brockwell Ct NR3 ....158 F2
Brome Ave IP23 ......130 C2
Brome Hall La IP23 ...130 D3
Bromedale Ave 19 NR14 ..89 B3
Brook Gr 8 NR19 .....154 D3
Brook La Brookville IP26 ..99 A7
  Burgate IP22 ....129 C3
  Needham IP20 ....131 E8
  St Margaret, Ilketshall
  NR35 ....124 C3
Brook Pl NR1 ....178 B2
Brook Rd
  Dersingham PE31 .....140 D2
  Sheringham NR26 .....138 E6
Brook St
  Buxton with Lammas
  NR10 ....36 E1
  Cromer NR27 ....139 C7
  Lamas NR10 ....53 E8
Brooke Ave NR30 .....168 D5
Brooke Prim Sch NR15 ..90 E1
Brooke Rd
  Kirstead NR15 ....91 A1
  Mundham NR14 ....90 D1
  Seething NR15 ....91 C1
  Shotesham NR15 .....107 F8
Brookes Dr NR28 .....151 A4
Brookfield Cl NR15 ...106 F4
Brooks Dr NR10 ......154 B4
Brooks Mdw NR14 ....90 D5
Brooks Rd NR10 ......53 B3
Brookside NR20 ....49 E8
Brookwell Springs 1
  PE32 ....44 B3
Broom Ave
  Norwich NR5 ....158 A5
  Norwich NR7 ....163 E8
Broom Cl
  18 Marthan NR29 .....57 D4
  Norwich NR5 ....162 F3
  Taverham NR8 ....155 C3
Broom Gn Dr NR20 ....32 E4
Broom Gn Rd NR20 ...32 E4
Broom La Easton NR9 ..70 B5
  Witton NR28 ....38 C8
Brook Rd
  Lakenheath IP27 .....113 F1
  Wymondham NR18 ...105 C6
Broome Gdns 2 NR31 ..94 A5
Broomhill 1 NR27 ....10 B5
Broomhill La NR10 ...149 B3
Broomsthorpe Rd PE31 ..30 A7
Broorscros Way
  PE38 ....172 C7
Brow of the Hill PE32 ..44 E6
Browick Rd NR18 ....173 C4
Browick Rd Inf Sch
  NR18 ....173 C6
Brown's La
  Holme Hale IP25 ......65 F2
  Mautby NR29 ....76 B7
  Necton PE37 ....65 F3
  Saxlingham Nethergate
  NR15 ....107 B8
Browne St 5 NR2 .....162 C7
Browning Pl PE30 ....147 A8
Brownsfield NR11 .....21 D6
Brownshill NR27 .....139 B4
Browston Hall Leisure Ctr
  NR31 ....94 C4
Browston La NR32 ....94 B3
Brummel Cl 8 PE30 ..147 C5
Brumstead Rd
  Brumstead NR12 ......24 A1
  Stalham NR12 ....39 A4
Brundall Gdns Sta
  NR13 ....165 A3
Brundall Low Rd NR13 ..72 F3
Brundall Prim Sch
  NR13 ....165 B8
Brundall Rd NR13 ....165 E4
Brundish Rd NR14 ...110 A6
Brunel Way IP24 .....176 B6
Brunswick Cl
  North Walsham NR28 ..151 D6
Brunswick Rd NR2 ...178 A1
Brunswick Terr NR27 ..139 B7
Brush Hill NR20 ....33 A6
Brush Mdw La PE34 ..42 B7
Brushmakers Way
  IP22 ....177 C6
Brussels Cl NR19 ....154 C2
Bryars La IP22 ......177 F3
Bryggen Rd PE30 ....146 F8
Bryony Cl NR17 ......174 B6
Bryony Cour NR25 ...158 D5
Bryony Cour 4 NR17 ..174 B5
Bryony Ct PE30 ......148 C2
Bryony Way 6 NR17 ..174 B5
Buccaneer Way 8 NR9 ..88 D8
Buck Courtney Cres
  NR6 ....158 A7
Buck La IP21 ....130 C4
Buck's Heath La NR11 ..11 D1
Buck's Hill NR29 ......87 B3
Buckenham Cl
  1 Fakenham NR21 ....141 C5
  Swaffham PE13 ......153 B2
Buckenham Dr PE31 ...81 A2
Buckenham La NR13 ...73 F2
Buckenham Rd
  Attleborough NR17 ...174 F3
  Lingwood and Burlingham
  NR13 ....74 A2

Buckenham Rd continued
  Strumpshaw NR13 .....73 F2
Buckenham Sta NR13 ..91 F8
Bucket Rd NR21 ......15 D2
Buckingham Cl PE30 ..148 C5
Buckingham Ct PE36 ..132 C5
Buckingham Dr 1 NR9 ..88 C7
Buckingham Rd NR4 ..161 F3
Buckingham Wlk
  PE13 ....152 D8
Buckland Rise 8 NR4 ..161 F1
Buckshott Rd PE14 ....59 B7
Buckthorn Cl 3 NR8 ..155 B2
Buddell's La NR23 ......5 F2
Buggs Hole IP22 .....129 B2
Buggs Hole La IP22 ..128 A6
Buildings Rd NR30 ...168 E4
Bull Cl
  East Tuddenham NR20 ..69 C6
  4 Holt NR25 ....137 B6
  Norwich NR3 ....178 B4
Bull Cl La NR21 ....17 B3
Bull Cl Rd NR3 ....178 B4
Bull La NR1 ....178 A1
Bull St NR25 ....137 B6
Bullace Rd NR5 ......156 F2
Bullacebush La NR13 ..165 E7
Bullard Rd NR3 ......158 C3
Bull's La NR31 ....170 D6
Bull's Row NR27 ......11 A2
Bullemer Cl 3 NR12 ..39 B4
Bullfinch Way 4 PE14 ..77 A8
Bullies Way 3 NR13 ..73 D6
Bullman's Cross La
  NR20 ....29 A6
Bullock Fair Cl 14 IP20 ..122 D2
Bullock Hill NR10 ......53 E1
Bullock Rd PE34 ......144 B1
Bullocks Loke NR30 ..168 E4
Bulls Gn La NR34 ....110 D5
Bulls Gn Rd NR34 ....110 C6
Bulmer La NR29 ....58 B6
Bulmer Rd NR3 ......158 A6
Bulrush Ave 4 NR28 ..172 A6
Bulrush Cl
  1 East Dereham NR19 ..154 C4
  4 Horsford NR10 .....53 A3
Bulstrode Ave 4 NR19 ..154 C2
Bultitudes Loke NR30 ..168 E4
Bulwer Rd
  East Dereham NR19 ...154 E7
  Norwich NR1 ....163 B6
Bumstede Ct 5 NR5 ..161 A8
Bungalow La NR7 ....159 D1
Bungay High Sch
  NR35 ....124 A7
Bungay Rd Bixley NR14 ..90 B8
  Dickleburgh & Rushall
  IP21 ....130 E5
  Ellingham NR35 ......109 C4
  Hempnall NR15 ......107 D5
  Loddon NR14 ....109 C7
  Poringland NR14 ......90 D4
  Scole IP21 ....130 D5
  Stockton NR34 ....109 F4
  Thwaite NR35 ....108 E6
Bungaygarae La IP20 ..122 D6
Bunkel Rd NR13 ....72 E8
Bunn's Bank Rd
  Attleborough NR17 ...174 F2
  Old Buckenham NR17 ..104 E4
Bunn's La
  Great Yarmouth NR31 ..169 C3
  Starston IP20 ....122 C2
Bunnett Ave PE30 ....146 D2
Bunnewell Ave NR31 ..170 A4
Bunting's La IP26 .....98 F5
Buntings The 15 NR21 ..18 D3
Bunwell Hill NR16 ...105 D2
Bunwell Prim Sch
  NR16 ....105 D3
Bunwell Rd
  Aslacton NR16 ....106 A2
  Attleborough NR17 ...174 F6
  Besthorpe NR17 ......105 B8
  Bunwell NR16 ....105 B5
Bunwell Cl 8 NR13 ....72 E4
Burch Cl PE30 ....147 E4
Burcroft Rd PE13 ....152 B6
Burdett Rd PE13 .....152 B4
Burdock La NR18 ....173 E4
Burdock Cl
  Hockwold cum Wilton
  IP26 ....113 C7
  8 Wrampingham NR9 ..69 F2
Buttonk Way 3 NR17 ..174 B4
Bure Cl 9 Belton NR31 ..94 A6
  Caister-on-Sea NR30 ..168 D6
  4 Great Yarmouth NR30 ..169 C6
  4 King's Lynn PE33 ...147 E5
  8 Watlington PE33 ....61 C6
  Wroxham/Hoveton
  NR12 ....164 C5
Bure Marshes National
  Nature Reserve*
  NR13 ....55 E3
Bure Rd Briston NR24 ..142 D4
  1 Great Yarmouth NR30 ..169 C5
Bure Valley La NR11 ..150 C5
Bure Valley Sch NR11 ..150 C5
Bure Way NR11 ......150 C5
Burgate La NR14 ......90 C5
Burgess Cl PE30 .....147 C4
Burgess Rd NR3 .....158 B2

Burgess Way NR15 90 E2
Burgh Beck Rd NR24 142 B5
Burgh Hall Leisure Ctr NR31 94 B7
Burgh La NR20 68 F6
Burgh Rd
Aylsham NR11 150 D6
Burgh St Peter NR34 111 C5
Great Yarmouth NR31 170 B7
Burgh Wood Rd NR29 57 E1
Burghley Rd PE30 148 E1
Burghwood Dr PE32 48 D6
Burhill Cl 3 NR4 89 D8
Burkitt St PE30 146 E6
Burleigh Cl 1 NR30 169 D2
Burley Rd NR12 38 A3
Burlingham Dr 2 NR33 111 F1
Burlingham Rd NR13 73 F6
Burlington Cl IP22 177 D1
Burma Cl PE31 140 C4
Burma Rd NR6 158 E5
Burnet Rd
Great Yarmouth NR31 94 C6
Norwich NR3 157 F1
Burney Rd PE30 146 D2
Burnham Ave PE30 147 C8
Burnham Mkt Prim Sch PE31 135 D4
Burnham Rd
Docking PE31 134 E6
Downham Market PE38 172 B4
North Creake NR21 4 D2
Ringstead PE36 2 C3
South Creake NR21 15 D7
Burns Cl
East Dereham NR19 154 C7
Thetford IP24 176 E6
Yaxley IP23 129 F1
Burnside 3 PE37 66 A4
Burnt Fen Turnpike IP28 112 D2
Burnt Hill La NR33 111 F3
Burnt Hills NR27 139 B4
Burnt House Rd NR13 92 B6
Burnt La
Great Yarmouth NR31 170 C7
Wiggenhall St Mary Magdalen PE34 61 A4
Burnt St NR23 136 D5
Burnthouse Cres PE33 63 B4
Burnthouse Dro PE33 63 C5
Burnthouse La
Hethersett NR9 160 C1
Runhall NR20 69 A4
Scole IP20 122 A1
Toft Monks NR34 110 D5
Wymondham NR18 173 F1
Burntoak La IP20 122 E4
Burntwood La NR12 54 C4
Burr Cl 14 IP25 84 E3
Burrell Cl NR25 137 D7
Burrell Way IP24 176 A1
Burrett Gdns PE13 59 C5
Burrett Rd PE13 59 C5
Burrettgate Rd PE13 152 F5
Burroughs Way NR18 173 D4
Burrow Dr IP27 113 E2
Burrows Gn NR34 110 F5
Burston Cl NR24 142 B4
Burston Com Prim Sch IP22 120 E2
Burston Rd
Dickleburgh & Rushall IP21 130 C8
Diss IP22 177 E7
Gissing IP22 120 F3
Burston Strike Sch* IP22 120 E2
Burton Ave NR28 151 B4
Burton Cl
North Walsham NR28 151 B4
Norwich NR6 158 C5
Roydon IP22 177 B5
Burton Dr 9 NR13 72 E7
Burton Rd NR6 158 C5
Burtontyne Ave NR19 68 A7
Bury Bottom IP27 115 A1
Bury Rd Botesdale IP22 128 F3
Brandon IP27 175 D2
Hepworth IP22 127 F1
Market Weston IP22 127 E4
Rickinghall Inferior IP22 128 D1
Thetford IP24 176 C1
Wortham IP22 129 C4
Bury St NR2 162 B4
Bush Cl PE31 140 E3
Bush Dr NR12 24 E4
Bush Est NR12 24 D4
Bush La Dereham NR20 68 B8
Wisbech PE13 152 E5
Bush Rd Hemsby NR29 58 B5
Norwich NR6 157 F7
Bussey Rd NR6 158 D4
Bussey's La NR31 170 D5
Bussey's Loke
Great Yarmouth NR31 170 A5
Hempnall NR15 107 D5
Bustards' La PE14 41 F3
Butcher's La NR21 141 B4
Butchers La PE31 3 B7
Butt La Belton NR31 94 A6
Litcham PE32 48 A4
Butter La NR14 92 D1
Butter's Hall La IP24 102 C7
Buttercup Cl 1 IP24 176 F5
Buttercup Dr 14 NR31 94 C6
Buttercup Way NR5 160 F6
Buttermere 1 NR29 167 B7
Buttermere Rd 4 NR5 161 C6
Butterwick 3 PE30 147 C5
Buttland's La PE33 81 B8
Buttlands Cl NR21 6 E2
Buttlands The
Great Cressingham IP25 83 D4
Wells-next-the-Sea NR23 136 D5
Buttle's La NR15 106 D3
Butts La NR26 138 B5
Butts The NR5 160 F8
Buxton Ave NR31 170 D1
Buxton Cl 4 Cromer NR27 10 B5
Easton NR9 70 B5
Buxton Prim Sch NR10 36 F1
Buxton Rd
Aylsham NR11 150 D5
Cawston NR10 35 D2
Diss IP22 177 B4
Frettenham NR12 53 F3
Hainford NR10 53 F5
Horstead with Stanninghall NR12 54 B6
North Walsham NR28 151 B4
Norwich NR3 162 D8
Spixworth NR10 158 F8
Buxton Sta NR10 36 F2
Byfield Ct 3 NR3 158 C1
Byron Ave PE13 154 B7
Byron Rd
Great Yarmouth NR30 169 E8
Taverham NR8 156 D8
Byron Way NR30 168 D6
Byron Wlk 7 IP24 176 E6

C

Cabbell Rd NR27 139 B7
Cabin Cl 11 NR33 111 F1
Cadamys Yd NR23 136 D5
Cadge Cl NR5 161 D7
Cadge Rd NR5 161 D6
Cadge's La NR9 86 B3
Cadiz Way NR31 171 E4
Cadman Way IP25 84 D3
Cadogan Rd NR27 139 B7
Caernarvon Rd NR2 162 B6
Cage La IP24 176 D3
Cains The NR8 155 C2
Cairns Ct NR4 162 A3
Caister By-pass NR30 168 C4
Caister Castle Car Collection* NR30 168 A5
Caister High Sch NR30 168 E6
Caister on Sea Fst & Mid Schs NR30 168 E5
Caister Rd NR30 169 C7
Caister Sands Ave NR29 168 E8
Caistor La
Caistor St Edmund NR14 89 F6
Poringland NR14 90 B6
Caistor Roman Town* NR14 89 F6
Caithness Crystal Visitor Ctr* PE30 146 F2
Caius Cl PE31 133 C5
Calamint Rd PE30 147 A8
Caledonian Way 1 NR31 94 A5
Caley Cl NR3 157 F2
Caley St PE31 133 D5
Calf La NR10 53 E2
California Ave NR29 167 E4
California Cotts NR23 136 E5
California Cres NR29 167 F2
California Rd NR29 167 E2
Calkewood La IP22 128 C1
Calthorpe Cl
Acle NR13 166 B4
2 Stalham NR12 39 B4
Calthorpe Rd
Ingham NR12 39 D4
Norwich NR5 161 B6
Calvert St NR3 178 B4
Calves Well La
Beeston Regis NR26 138 F4
Sheringham NR27 10 A5
Camargue Pl 4 PE13 152 E3
Cambell Dr NR20 50 B5
Camberley Rd NR4 162 A2
Cambers La PE31 135 D2
Camborne Cl NR5 157 C1
Cambridge Ave NR31 170 A3
Cambridge Dr PE13 152 A6
Cambridge Rd PE30 148 D5
Cambridge St
Cromer NR27 139 C7
Norwich NR2 162 C4
Cambridge Way NR31 170 B3
Camden Pl 21 NR30 169 D2
Camden Rd NR30 169 D2
Camelot Rd NR31 171 B8
Cameron Cl PE31 133 C4
Cameron Cres 4 PE31 12 D4
Cameron Gn NR8 156 E8
Camfrey 6 PE30 147 B7
Camp Cl 2 IP26 98 D1
Camp Gr NR1 163 A6
Camp La NR27 10 A4
Camp Rd NR8 155 C1
Campbell Cl PE36 132 D4
Campbell Ct 1 NR3 162 F8
Camperdown 11 NR30 169 D2
Camping Cl 8 NR20 68 F6
Camping Field La NR12 39 B4
Campingland PE13 153 C4
Campion Ave NR31 170 B3
Campion Cl 4 NR28 151 E5
Campion Pl PE38 172 B3
Campion Rd
1 Dereham NR20 68 A8
Thetford IP24 176 F4
Campion Way
6 Attleborough NR17 174 B4
3 Sheringham NR26 138 B6
Campsey Rd PE38 97 B6
Canada Cl 6 PE31 12 E5
Canada Rd NR27 139 B7
Canal Farm La NR28 38 C6
Canal St 6 PE13 152 C5
Canary Way NR1 163 A4
Canberra Rd IP25 84 F3
Candle Stick NR9 69 A3
Candlemaker Workshop* NR29 75 A5
Candler's La 18 IP20 122 D2
Candlestick La PE32 45 C8
Canfor Rd 7 NR13 72 E7
Cangate Rd NR12 55 C6
Cann's La NR9 88 D7
Cannell Gn NR3 178 C4
Cannell Rd 11 NR14 92 A1
Cannerby La NR7 159 B3
Cannon St PE13 152 C4
Cannon Terr 9 PE13 152 C4
Canon Cl 6 IP25 84 E3
Canon Hoare Rd NR11 150 C4
Canon Pickering VC Jun Sch IP20 122 D2
Canon Pott Cl PE31 133 D6
Canon Wake Ct 4 NR29 56 C8
Canon's Cl IP24 176 B4
Canons Cl 2 NR19 154 D2
Canons Wlk IP24 176 B3
Canterbury Inf Sch IP24 176 B4
Canterbury Pl NR2 162 C7
Canterbury Way IP24 176 B5
Cantley Cnr NR13 74 B1
Cantley Fst Sch NR13 92 B7
Cantley La
Cringleford NR4 89 A8
Ketteringham NR18 88 F6
Cantley Rd NR13 92 D7
Cantley Sta NR13 92 B6
Cants Cl 4 NR9 69 F2
Capgrave Ave PE30 146 F8
Capps La IP19 123 F1
Capstan Way 9 NR33 111 F1
Captains Cl PE13 153 D4
Caraway Dr 22 NR31 94 C6
Caraway Rd IP24 176 F4
Carbrooke Rd
Caston NR17 85 C1
Griston IP25 85 A2
Cardiff Rd NR2 162 B5
Cardigan Pl NR2 162 C7
Cardinal Cl NR9 70 B5
Cardington Ct 1 NR13 166 D4
Cardington Rd IP25 85 A3
Cardun Cl 3 NR13 73 C6
Carey House Con Ctr PE37 65 D1
Cargate Comm Rd NR16 105 E1
Cargate La
Saxlingham Nethergate NR15 107 A8
Upton with Fishley NR13 166 A8
Carl Cl 5 NR19 154 D1
Carl Cres NR28 22 E5
Carleton Cl 1 NR18 173 C6
Carleton Rd NR7 159 B3
Carleton Rode CE Prim Sch NR16 105 C3
Carlton Cl NR19 154 D4
Carlton Dr PE30 148 D5
Carlton Gdns NR1 178 B1
Carlton Marshes Nature Reserve* NR33 111 F3
Carlyle Rd NR1 162 F3
Carmelite Terr 16 PE30 146 D4
Carmen's La NR28 38 B3
Carn Cl NR13 74 B2
Carnoustie NR4 162 A1
Carnoustie Ct PE31 41 C8
Carol Cl NR14 90 B5
Carola Sutton Ct NR25 137 B5
Caroline Ct NR4 161 F4
Carpenter's Wlk NR15 121 D7
Carpenters Cotts NR25 137 B6
Carr La
Great Moulton NR15 106 B1
Hoveton NR12 164 F8
Northrepps NR27 139 C1
Overstrand NR27 11 A3
Poringland NR14 90 C4
Wendling NR19 66 F7
Carr Terr PE31 134 E5
Carrell Rd NR31 170 B1
Carrington Rd NR27 139 D5
Carrow Abbey NR1 163 A3
Carrow Cl NR1 162 F3
Carrow Hill NR1 178 C1
Carrow Rd NR1 178 C1
Carrs Hill Cl NR8 157 A4
Carrs Rd NR13 92 A8
Carshalton Rd 2 NR1 162 F3
Cart Gap Rd NR12 24 C4
Carter Cl
Caister-on-Sea NR30 168 D8
Swaffham PE37 153 C2
Carter Rd NR8 157 A8
Carter's Cl PE30 148 B1
Carter's La NR20 50 A6
Carterford Dr NR6 158 E3
Carters Loke NR13 166 C2
Cartledge Cl 1 NR19 154 D3
Cartmel 17 NR9 88 D8
Carver's La NR17 174 B5
Casaubon Cl 6 NR19 154 D3
Caslon Cl 3 NR21 141 C5
Castelins Way 20 NR14 89 B3
Castell Rd NR19 154 D7
Castle Acre Castle* PE32 47 A2
Castle Acre CE VC Fst Sch PE32 46 F1
Castle Acre Cl 2 PE30 148 C3
Castle Acre Rd PE32 47 E1
Castle Cl 3 Gresham NR11 9 E1
King's Lynn PE30 147 C8
Weeting IP27 175 B8
Castle Drift PE32 48 D6
Castle Gn NR31 170 B7
Castle La Bungay NR35 124 A8
Thetford IP24 176 E3
West Caister NR30 168 B5
Castle Mdw NR1 178 B2
Castle Mkt St NR1 178 B2
Castle Rd
Mettingham NR35 124 D7
Wormegay PE33 62 C6
Castle Rise NR8 155 E3
Castle Rising Castle* PE31 27 C3
Castle Rising Rd PE30 148 D3
Castle Sq 16 PE13 152 C5
Castle St Norwich NR2 178 B3
Thetford IP24 176 D4
Wroxham/Hoveton NR12 164 B3
Castleacre Rd
Great Massingham PE32 29 D1
Swaffham PE37 153 B8
Castleford Cl IP24 176 B4
Castleton Ave NR33 111 F1
Castleton Cl 1 NR5 160 F8
Castleton Way IP23 130 A1
Caston CE VA Prim Sch NR17 85 B1
Caston Cl 5 NR25 137 B6
Caston Rd NR7 163 F8
Catalpa Way 5 NR31 170 B5
Catbridge La NR14 89 A4
Catchpole Wlk IP21 121 C1
Catfield CE Fst Sch NR29 56 C8
Catfield Rd NR29 56 D6
Cathedral Dr NR20 49 E8
Cathedral St NR1 178 C3
Catherine Howard Cl 3 IP24 176 D6
Catherine Wheel Opening 8 NR3 162 D8
Catling's La PE13 41 A3
Catmere Herne NR14 89 A3
Cator Rd NR8 155 F1
Catriona Ct NR25 8 B6
Cats Cnr NR10 37 B7
Cattle Mkt St 4 NR21 141 C4
Catton Chase NR6 158 D5
Catton Ct NR6 158 E6
Catton Gr Fst Sch NR3 158 C3
Catton Gr Mid Sch NR3 158 C3
Catton Gr Rd NR3 158 D2
Catton View Ct NR3 158 D3
Caudle Hill IP25 83 E5
Caudwell Cl 2 NR14 89 F4
Causeway Cl
Brockdish IP21 131 C6
Norwich NR2 162 C8
Causeway Dr 4 NR12 54 C6
Causeway The
Heigham Bridge NR29 57 A5
Hickling NR12 39 F2
Stow Bardolph PE34 61 D1
Cavalier Cl 30 NR7 72 D4
Cave's Cl PE34 144 B5
Cavell Cl NR14 89 C5
Cavell Fst Sch NR1 162 E1
Cavell Rd NR1 162 E2
Cavendish Cl PE32 44 C3
Cavenham Rd PE33 80 E4
Cavick Rd NR18 173 A3
Cawdor Cl NR17 174 E6
Cawston La
Great Witchingham NR9 51 E7
Little Witchingham NR9 149 E1
Cawston Rd
Aylsham NR11 150 A5
Reepham NR10 149 D6
Cawston VC Prim Sch NR10 35 B2
Cawstons Mdw 8 NR14 90 C5
Caxton Cl NR26 138 F5
Caxton Ct PE30 147 D4
Caxton Pk NR26 138 F5
Caxton Rd NR34 110 D1
Caxton Way IP24 176 A2
Caystreward NR30 168 E1
Cecil Cl 7 PE33 61 D6
Cecil Gowing Ct NR7 159 B4
Cecil Gowing Fst Sch NR7 159 C3
Cecil Rd
East Dereham NR20 154 F5
Norwich NR1 162 D3
Cedar Ave 4 NR10 54 A2
Cedar Cl
1 Downham Market PE38 172 C6
12 Great Yarmouth NR31 94 C7
19 Martham NR29 57 D4
12 Mattishall NR20 68 E6
North Elmham NR20 49 E7
Cedar Ct
North Walsham NR28 151 C5
Wymondham NR18 173 D6
Cedar Dr
Attleborough NR17 174 C4
10 Loddon NR14 92 A1
Cedar Gr
North Runcton PE33 44 A3
Sheringham NR26 138 E5
Cedar Rd
Hethersett NR9 88 C8
Marham PE33 63 B4
Norwich NR1 163 A5
Cedar Rise NR20 68 E6
Cedar Row PE30 147 B7
Cedar Springs PE31 133 B6
Cedar Way
Brandon IP27 175 D2
Brundall NR13 165 C3
4 Gayton PE32 45 C6
King's Lynn PE34 146 C4
Cedars The Keswick N12 23 F3
Norwich NR2 162 B4
Shepherd's Port PE31 12 B4
Celandine Cl 2 IP24 176 F5
Celandine La 6 NR26 138 B6
Celandine Rd 4 NR17 174 B4
Celia Phillips Cl 7 IP24 176 D7
Cemetery La NR18 173 B3
Cemetery Rd
East Dereham NR19 154 E7
Lakenheath IP27 113 E1
Outwell PE14 78 A6
Centenary Way PE12 41 C6
Central Ave NR7 72 D3
Central Cl 1 NR9 88 D7
Central Cres 2 NR9 88 D7
Central Dr NR20 50 A5
Central Rd
Cromer NR27 139 A7
King's Lynn PE30 146 D6
Centre Cres PE31 140 D3
Centre Point 6 PE30 147 D5
Centre Vale PE31 140 D3
Centre Vale Rd PE31 140 D3
Century Rd 6 Eye IP23 130 C1
Great Yarmouth NR31 169 B3
Century Way NR8 155 F3
Cere Rd NR7 159 C4
Cess Rd NR29 57 C5
Chadwick Sq 2 PE30 147 A7
Chalfont Wlk NR4 161 E2
Chalk Hill Rd NR1 178 C3
Chalk La Culford IP31 125 C1
Narborough PE32 63 E5
North End NR16 106 D2
Sutton Bridge PE12 41 C7
Chalk Pit Rd PE31 140 E7
Chalk Rd Brandon IP27 114 D5
5 Walpole St Andrew PE14 41 E4
Chalkpit Rd PE31 3 A6
Chalkrow La PE33 81 F4
Chamberlin Cl NR3 158 E2
Chamberlin Ct NR13 165 E6
Chamberlin Rd NR3 158 D1
Chambers Rd NR3 158 B3
Chameryhall La NR13 73 F7
Champney's Rd IP22 177 E4
Chancel Cl NR13 165 C3
Chancellors Dr NR4 161 C4
Chandler Rd NR14 89 F5
Chandler's Hill La 1 NR18 173 B3
Chandlers Cl 2 NR18 173 B3
Chandlers Ct 8 NR4 89 C8
Chandlers Hill 4 NR18 173 B3
Changi Rd 5 IP25 84 F3
Chantry Ct 8 PE37 65 F4
Chantry La PE37 66 A4
Chantry Rd NR2 178 A2
Chantry The NR2 178 A2
Chapel Ave NR15 106 E3
Chapel Bank PE36 132 E6
Chapel Break Fst Sch NR5 160 F8
Chapel Break Rd NR5 160 E7
Chapel Cl
Barnham Broom NR9 69 C2
Pulham Market IP21 121 E5
Reepham NR10 149 B5
Tacolneston NR16 105 F4
Winfarthing IP22 120 B5
Chapel Cnr NR12 55 D6
Chapel Ct Blofield NR13 165 E6
Norwich NR6 157 F5
Chapel Field NR13 93 A4
Chapel Field E NR2 178 A2
Chapel Field N NR2 178 A2
Chapel Field Rd
Norwich NR2 178 A2
Stalham NR12 39 A3
Chapel La
Aldborough NR11 21 A5
Ashby St Mary NR14 91 D5

Chapel La continued
Barton Bendish PE33 ......81 B8
Beeston with Bittering
PE32 ....48 C2
Beetley NR20 ....49 C4
Botesdale IP22 ....128 E2
Burgate IP22 ....129 C3
Coltishall NR12 ....54 D7
East Dereham NR19 ......154 D2
Emneth PE14 ....59 B2
Felthorpe NR10 ....155 C8
Fincham PE33 ....62 E1
Foulsham NR20 ....33 D3
8 Great Yarmouth NR31 ...94 C6
Hempstead NR25 ....19 E8
Hockering NR20 ....69 B8
Hunstanton PE36 ....132 C4
Kirby Row NR35 ....109 E3
Methwold IP26 ....99 A5
Necton PE37 ....66 A4
Norwich NR7 ....163 E6
Potter Heigham NR29 ...56 F7
Ringstead PE36 ....2 A3
Scarning NR19 ....67 B7
Sculthorpe NR21 ....16 B1
Shelton NR15 ....107 B1
Shotesham NR15 ....90 B2
Skeyton NR10 ....37 B6
West Caister NR30 .....168 C4
West Winch PE33 ....43 E3
Wimbotsham PE34 ......172 E8
Wiveton NR25 ....7 E6
Wymondham NR18 ....173 A5
Chapel Loke
Lessingham NR12 ....24 C2
Salhouse NR13 ....55 B1
8 Stoke Holy Cross NR14 ..89 F4
Surlingham NR14 ....73 B1
Wymondham NR18 ....105 A8
Chapel Mdw NR35 ....109 E3
Chapel Rd
Alby with Thwaite NR11 ...21 B3
Ashby St Mary NR14 .....91 D5
Attleborough NR17 .....174 C5
Beighton NR13 ....74 C2
Boughton PE33 ....81 A4
Carleton Rode NR16 ....105 C3
Dersingham PE31 ....140 D4
Dilham NR28 ....38 B3
East Ruston NR12 ....38 E6
Foxley NR20 ....50 D8
Grimston PE32 ....28 A1
Guestwick NR20 ....33 F6
Hainford NR10 ....53 E5
Halvergate NR13 ....75 A2
Lingwood NR13 ....73 F3
Longham NR19 ....49 A2
Lowestoft NR33 ....111 F1
Morley NR18 ....87 B2
Neatishead NR12 ....55 E6
Necton PE37 ....66 B4
Norwich NR5 ....157 A2
Paston NR28 ....143 D1
Roughton NR11 ....21 D8
Royston PE32 ....45 A8
St Andrew, Ilketshall
NR34 ....124 F6
Scole IP21 ....121 B1
Sea Palling NR12 ....40 A6
Southrepps NR11 ....22 B6
Sparfield NR28 ....22 D3
Terrington St Clement
PE34 ....144 B5
Upton with Fishley NR13 .166 B8
Wisbech PE13 ....152 B5
Woodton NR35 ....108 C4
Wymondham NR18 ....105 A8
Chapel Rd Specl Sch
NR17 ....174 C5
Chapel Rise 3 PE33 ...63 B4
Chapel St Barford NR9 ...70 A3
Cawston NR10 ....35 B3
3 Cromer NR27 ....139 B7
Diss IP22 ....177 D4
8 Hingham NR9 ....86 C5
Ixworth NR9 ....69 F2
King's Lynn PE30 ......146 D5
8 Old Buckenham NR16 ..104 F1
Rocklands NR17 ....103 B8
Shipdham IP25 ....67 C2
Warham NR23 ....6 A4
4 Wisbech PE13 ....152 C4
Chapel Terr PE30 ...148 B1
Chapel Wlk 4 NR19 ...154 E5
Chapel Yd Ashill IP25 ..84 A7
Wells-next-the-Sea
NR23 ....136 C6
Chapelfield Cl 1 NR29 ..56 C8
Chapman Ave NR30 ...168 E5
Chapmans Cl 17 NR26 ..138 D7
Chapnall Cl PE13 ....152 F6
Chapnall Rd PE13 ....152 F6
Chappshill Way 22 NR14 ..89 B3
Chare Rd IP31 ....127 B1
Charing Cross NR2 ...178 A3
Charles Ave
Norwich NR7 ....163 F8
Watton IP25 ....84 D3
Charles Burrell High Sch
IP24 ....176 C1
Charles Burrell Mus*
IP24 ....176 C4
Charles Burton Cl 6
NR30 ....168 D7
Charles Cl Acle NR13 ..166 B4
Caister-on-Sea NR30 ...168 E5
Cromer NR27 ....10 C4
Dereham NR19 ....154 C1

Charles Cl continued
Wroxham/Hoveton
NR12 ....164 C3
Charles Ewing Cl
NR11 ....150 B5
Charles Jewson Ct
NR6 ....158 B2
Charles Rash Cl NR28 ...37 B8
Charles Rd
Fakenham NR21 ....141 C6
Holt NR25 ....137 C5
Hunstanton PE36 ....132 C2
8 Sutton Bridge PE12 ....41 B8
Charles Sq 8 NR32 ...162 C6
Charles St
Great Yarmouth NR30 ...169 D2
King's Lynn PE30 ......146 E3
11 Wisbech PE13 ......152 C4
Charles Watling Way 1
NR5 ....160 E8
Charles Wood Rd
NR19 ....154 F2
Charlock PE30 ......147 A8
Charlock Dr 8 NR26 ...138 B6
Charlotte's Cl 1 NR27 ...9 F5
Charlton Rd NR13 ...178 B4
Charmbeck Pk NR10 ...52 D8
Charolais Cl NR14 ....163 B2
Charter Cl NR31 ....170 B4
Chartwell Cl NR7 ....158 F3
Chartwell Rd NR16 ...158 D3
Chase Ave PE30 ....146 E3
Chase Cl NR6 ....158 D5
Chase Ct
East Dereham NR19 ....154 D6
Thetford IP24 ....176 B3
Chase St PE13 ......152 C6
Chase The
Brandon IP27 ....175 E2
Brundall NR13 ....165 F6
Stow Bardolph PE34 ....78 E7
Upwell PE14 ....77 D3
Walpole St Andrew PE14 ..41 A4
Chatham Rd 8 IP31 ...126 B1
Chatham St NR3 .....178 A4
Chatsworth Rd PE36 ...132 C3
Chaucer Cl 14 NR20 ...50 E7
Chaucer Rd NR30 ....169 D8
Checker Hill 8 NR16 ..118 C5
Cheeney Dr NR7 ......159 C5
Cheney Cres PE31 ...133 D4
Cheney Hill PE31 ....133 D4
Cheney's La NR16 ...105 F5
Chepore La NR18 .....87 C1
Chequers Cl
Briston NR24 ....142 E3
2 Long Stratton NR15 ..106 D3
11 Roydon PE32 ....28 A1
Chequers La
Bressingham IP22 .....129 B7
Burston & Shimpling
IP22 ....120 E4
Great Ellingham NR17 ..103 E8
Gressenhall NR20 ....49 B4
North Runcton PE33 ....44 A2
Saham Toney IP25 ......84 C5
West Winch PE33 ....43 F2
Chequers Rd
Roydon PE32 ....28 A1
Tharston & Hapton
NR15 ....106 D3
Wretton PE33 ....80 E3
Chequers St
Docking PE31 ....134 D4
East Ruston NR12 ......38 F5
Gresham NR11 ....9 E1
Cherry Cl
11 Great Yarmouth NR31 ..94 C7
Marham PE33 ....63 A4
Norwich NR1 ....162 E3
Cherry Dr NR19 .....154 F5
Cherry Drift NR19 ...154 E6
Cherry La
Belton with Browston
NR31 ....94 B4
Dereham NR20 ....68 B7
North Lopham IP22 ....119 A2
Cherry Orch NR20 ...154 F5
Cherry Rd
Great Yarmouth NR31 ..170 B6
Wisbech PE13 ....152 C8
Cherry Tree Ave 25 NR29 ..57 D4
Cherry Tree Cl
Holt NR25 ....137 B7
Mundford IP26 ....100 A4
North Lopham IP22 ....119 A2
Watton IP24 ....102 B1
Cherry Tree Cr IP27 ...177 C5
Cherry Tree Dr PE34 ...146 C4
Cherry Tree La NR28 ...151 B5
Cherry Tree Rd
Carleton Rode NR16 ...105 A1
Dereham NR20 ....48 C1
Snettisham PE31 ....12 E5
Tibenham NR16 ....120 B7
Cherrytree Cl PE31 ...133 D6
Cherrywood
Alpington NR14 ....90 F4
10 Redenhall with Harleston
IP20 ....122 D1
Cherrywood Ave NR21 ..15 C2
Cherwell Wlk IP27 ...116 D2
Cherwell Way 2 NR31 ..170 B2
Chester Pl NR2 .....162 C4
Chester St NR2 .....162 C4
Chester Way IP24 ...176 A4

Chesterfield Cotts 11
NR27 ....139 B7
Chestnut Ave
Great Yarmouth NR31 ...170 A5
North Walsham NR28 ...151 E4
Sculthorpe Airfield NR21 ..15 C2
11 Spixworth NR10 ......54 A2
Welney PE14 ....95 D5
West Winch PE33 ......43 E1
Chestnut Cl
Brandon IP27 ....175 E2
Dersingham PE31 ......140 E3
East Dereham NR19 ....154 E1
Norwich NR5 ....156 E2
5 Watlington PE33 .....61 D5
Chestnut Ct 9 NR2 ...178 A3
Chestnut Gr NR26 ...138 D4
Chestnut Hill 3 NR4 ..161 F1
Chestnut Loke NR15 ...107 A6
Chestnut Rd
Dickleburgh IP21 ......121 C1
East Dereham NR19 ....154 C5
Pulham St Mary IP21 ..121 F4
5 Snettisham PE31 .....12 E4
16 Tasburgh NR15 ....106 F6
8 Watton IP25 ....84 E3
8 Wisbech PE13 ....152 C4
Chestnut Terr PE12 ...41 B8
Chestnut Wlk PE37 ...81 F8
Chestnuts The IP22 ...128 E2
Chew Ct PE30 ....147 E8
Cheyham Mount NR4 ..161 F1
Cheyney Ave 1 NR13 ...55 A1
Chickering Rd IP21 ...131 B2
Childs Rd NR9 ....88 C8
Childs Way NR26 .....138 C5
Chiltern Cres PE36 ...132 C3
Chilver House La PE32 ..44 E7
Chilvers Pl PE31 ....133 D5
Chimes Way NR10 ...149 B4
Chimney Springs
NR29 ....167 A3
Chimney St PE12 .....46 F1
Chipperfield Rd NR7 ..159 E1
Chittock Cl 5 NR30 ...54 A1
Cholmondeley Way 8
PE33 ....43 F2
Choseley Cl NR18 ...173 C4
Choseley Rd
Docking PE31 ....134 C7
Thornham PE36 ....2 D6
Christ Church Rd
NR31 ....170 A4
Christchurch Rd NR2 ..162 A4
Christie Cl 8 NR19 ...154 D1
Christine Ave NR13 ...74 A2
Christine Rd 1 NR10 ...54 A1
Christopher
3 Newton Flotman NR15 ..89 D1
1 Norwich NR1 ....162 E3
Christopher Dr NR13 ...152 A7
Church Alley NR13 ...165 B6
Church Ave
Croxton IP24 ....116 C5
Halvergate NR13 ....74 F1
Marlingford NR9 ....86 A1
Norwich NR4 ....162 B3
Church Ave E NR2 ...162 B3
Church Bank
Marshland St James PE14 ..60 C2
Terrington St Clement
PE34 ....144 B6
Church Cl
Antingham NR28 ....22 B3
8 Bawdeswell NR20 .....50 E7
Beeston Regis NR27 .....9 F5
Bixley NR14 ....90 B7
Brandon IP27 ....175 B3
Caister-on-Sea NR30 ...168 D5
Cantley NR13 ....92 C7
Colby NR11 ....36 D8
9 Coltishall NR12 .....54 C6
Grimston PE32 ....45 B8
Hepworth IP22 ....127 E1
17 Horstead with Stanningehall
NR12 ....54 C6
King's Lynn PE34 .....146 C6
Lamas NR10 ....36 F1
Mundford IP26 ....99 F5
Overstrand NR27 ....11 A3
Pentney PE32 ....63 C8
Pulham St Mary IP21 ..122 A4
1 Roydon PE32 ....129 D7
Sea Palling NR12 ....40 B5
Shipdham IP25 ....67 B2
South Walsham NR13 ...74 A8
Upper Sheringham
NR26 ....138 A4
Walpole St Andrew PE14 ..41 A4
Whissonsett NR20 ....31 D2
Wiggenhall St Mary Magdalen
PE34 ....60 A1
Wortwell IP20 ....122 F3
Church Cotts NR19 ...48 E3
Church Crofts PE31 ...27 C3
Church Dam PE33 .....93 A5
Church Dro PE14 .....77 F6
Church End IP27 ....175 B3
Church Farm Cl
Palgrave IP22 ....177 C2
11 Runhall NR20 ....69 A6
Church Farm Cres
NR29 ....167 B6
Church Farm La NR19 ...48 E3
St Mary, South Elmham
otherwise Homersfield
IP20 ....123 B4
Church Farm Rare Breeds
Ctr* PE34 ....79 F8

Church Farm Rd PE31 ..133 F7
Church Field 4 NR4 ...89 B8
Church Gate 16 PE12 ...41 B8
Church Gdns IP31 ...127 C3
Church Gn
Norwich NR7 ....159 B5
West Acre PE32 ....46 B2
Church Hill
Banham NR16 ....119 D7
Beighton NR13 ....74 C3
Hoxne IP21 ....131 A4
Reepham NR10 ....149 C4
Saxlingham Nethergate
NR15 ....107 B8
Starston IP20 ....122 C3
Church Hill Fst Sch
PE32 ....45 C8
Church Hill Sch NR16 ..119 D7
Church La Aldeby NR14 ..174 C5
Aldeby, Wheatacre,
Burgh St Peter NR34 ..111 B5
Antingham NR28 ....22 B3
Ashwellthorpe NR16 ...106 A7
Baconsthorpe NR25 ....19 F7
Bacton NR28 ....23 C3
Banham NR16 ....119 D7
Barnham IP24 ....125 F6
Barton Bendish PE33 ...81 B8
Belaugh NR12 ....54 E5
Belton with Browston
NR31 ....94 A5
Billingford NR20 ......50 B7
Binham NR21 ....33 B2
Bircham PE31 ....14 B3
Blo' Norton IP22 .....128 B6
Boughton PE33 ....80 F5
Bracon Ash NR14 ......88 F3
Bradenham IP25 ....66 D4
Bressingham IP22 .....129 B7
Briston NR24 ....142 E4
Brockdish IP21 ....131 C6
Broome NR35 ....109 B3
Bunwell NR16 ....105 D4
Burgh & Tuttington NR11 ..36 D4
Claxton NR14 ....91 C5
Cley next the Sea NR25 ..7 E6
Corton NR32 ....171 F1
Cranworth IP25 ....85 F7
Deopham NR18 ....86 F4
Dersingham PE31 ......140 E3
Ditchingham NR35 .....108 F3
East Rudham NR21 ......65 C6
East Walton PE32 ......45 E3
East Winch PE32 ....44 F2
Easton NR9 ....70 B6
Felthorpe NR10 ......155 D7
Filby NR29 ....75 E8
Flitcham with Appleton
PE31 ....28 A7
Frettenham NR12 ....54 A7
Fritton & St Olaves NR31 ..93 F3
Great Massingham PE32 ..29 D1
Great Yarmouth NR31 ..170 C5
Gresham NR11 ....9 E1
Gressenhall NR19 ......49 C2
Guestwick NR20 ....33 F6
Haddiscoe NR14 ......110 D7
Hales NR14 ....109 F7
Harpley PE31 ....29 C5
Heacham PE31 ....133 C6
Heckingham NR14 ......92 C1
Hemblington NR13 .....73 F6
Hempton PE31 ....127 E1
Hevingham NR10 ....36 B1
Hindolveston NR20 ....33 A1
Hockwold cum Wilton
IP26 ....114 A6
Holme Hale PE37 ....65 F2
Ixworth NR9 ....69 E2
Ketteringham NR18 .....88 E5
King's Lynn PE30 .....146 E4
Langley with Hardley
NR14 ....92 C3
Lessingham NR12 ....24 C2
Leziate PE32 ....44 F4
Little Ellingham NR17 ..86 A1
Little Massingham PE32 ..29 F2
Long Stratton NR15 ...106 F4
Lound NR32 ....171 A3
Marham PE33 ....63 A4
Marlingford NR9 ....69 E4
Marsham NR10 ....36 B2
Mattishall NR20 ....69 B5
Morley NR18 ....75 D5
Morley NR13 ....87 B2
Mundesley NR11 ....143 C6
Mundford IP26 ....99 F6
Neatishead NR12 ......55 E6
North Lopham IP22 ....119 A2
North Elmham NR20 ....49 E8
Norwich NR7 ....81 B2
Norwich NR9 ....159 C5
Norwich NR14 ....161 C1
Old Buckenham NR17 ...104 D2
Norwich NR1 ....35 C7
Potter Heigham NR29 ...56 F7
Redenhall with Harleston
IP20 ....122 C6
Rockingball Superior
IP20 ....122 C6
Roydon PE32 ....27 F2
Runhall NR20 ....69 A6
Runhall NR14 ....87 A8
St Mary, South Elmham
otherwise Homersfield
IP20 ....123 B4
Sheringham NR26 .....138 F6
Shipdham IP25 ....67 B2

Church La continued
Shouldham Thorpe PE33 ...62 B3
South Creake NR21 .....14 D7
4 Southery PE38 ....97 B5
Sparham NR9 ....51 B6
Spixworth NR10 ....53 F2
Sprowston NR7 ....159 B5
Stanfield NR20 ....48 F8
Stanhoe PE31 ....14 F7
Stuston IP21 ....130 B4
Surlingham NR14 ......73 A1
Sustead NR11 ....21 B8
Swannington NR9 ......59 E8
Swanton Abbott NR10 ..37 C5
Terrington St John PE14 ..42 B2
Thelnetham IP22 .....128 B5
Thompson IP24 ....102 C7
Thwaite NR35 ....109 A6
Tibenham NR16 ....120 B8
Tilney All Saints PE34 ..42 E4
Tittleshall PE32 ......32 A4
Tivetshall St Mary NR15 ..121 B4
Tunstead NR12 ....37 F1
Watlington PE33 ......61 E6
Weasenham All Saints
PE32 ....47 C8
Wicklewood NR18 ......87 B5
Winfarthing IP22 .....120 B4
Wood Dalling NR11 .....34 B5
Wormegay PE33 ....62 D6
Wroxham/Hoveton
NR12 ....164 B3
Yaxham NR19 ....68 A5
Church Lanes NR21 ...141 B5
Church Loke NR11 ....21 D7
Church Marsh Nature
Reserve* NR14 ....73 A1
Church Mdw
Rickinghall Inferior
IP22 ....128 D2
Yelverton NR14 ....90 E5
Church Mdw La NR14 ...90 F4
Church Mews PE13 ...152 C5
Church of the Holy Sepulchre
(rems)* IP24 ....176 B4
Church Path PE33 .....80 E2
Church Pl PE31 .....134 D5
Church Plain
14 Great Yarmouth NR30 ..169 C4
Norwich NR13 ....92 B5
4 Norwich NR9 ....136 D5
Church Rd
Alburgh IP20 ....122 F4
Alpington NR14 ....90 F4
Aslacton NR15 ....106 A2
Aylmerton NR11 ....10 A3
Barford NR9 ....22 D4
Barningham IP31 ......127 C3
Barton Bendish PE33 ...81 B8
Barton Turf NR12 ......55 E8
Beeston with Bittering
PE32 ....48 B2
Beetley NR20 ....49 B6
Bergh Apton NR15 .....91 A3
Bintree NR20 ....33 B2
Brandon IP27 ....175 B3
Bridgham NR16 ....118 B5
Brockdish IP21 ......131 C6
Brundall NR13 ....165 E5
Burgh Castle NR31 .....93 F8
Cantley NR13 ....92 D7
Carleton Rode NR16 ...105 C2
Catfield NR29 ....56 C8
Christchurch PE14 ......95 A7
Clenchwarton PE34 ...145 D5
Colby NR11 ....36 D8
Colkirk NR21 ....31 D5
Crimplesham PE33 .....80 B6
Denham IP21 ....131 A1
Deopham NR18 ....86 E3
Dickleburgh & Rushall
IP21 ....130 D8
Dilham NR28 ....38 C4
Downham Market PE38 ..172 C5
Earsham NR35 ....123 F7
Ellingham NR35 ....109 D3
Elm PE14 ....43 A5
Elsing NR20 ....50 F3
Felmingham NR28 ......37 B5
Flitcham PE31 ....28 C5
Flordon NR15 ....123 E5
Fordham PE38 ....79 B1
Freethorpe NR13 ......92 F8
Frettenham NR10 ....53 F4
Garboldisham IP22 ...128 A8
Gillingham NR34 ......110 C3
Great & Little Plumstead
NR13 ....73 A4
Great Yarmouth NR31 ..170 C7
Griston IP25 ....85 A1
Haddiscoe NR14 ....93 E7
Hardingham NR9 ....86 D7
Hemsby NR29 ....56 C8
Hethersett NR9 ....88 E6
Hingey PE38 ....79 E1
Hingey PE38 ....79 E1
Hoe NR20 ....49 F5
Holme Hale PE37 ....66 A2
Honingham IP31 ....126 D1
Horning NR12 ....55 B2
Hunstanton PE36 .....132 F7
Itteringham NR11 ......20 F4
Ketteringham NR18 .....88 E5
Kirby Cane NR35 ......109 E4
Kirstead NR15 ....90 F1
Leverington PE13 .....152 F7

Church Rd continued
Lingwood & Burlingham
NR13 . . . . .73 F3
Little Barningham NR11 . . .20 C4
Market Weston IP22 . . . .127 E4
Marlingford NR9 . . . . .70 A3
Neatishead NR12 . . . . .55 E6
Newton Flotman NR15 . . . .89 C1
North Lopham IP22 . . . . .119 A1
Norton Subcourse NR14 . . .92 E1
Ovington IP25 . . . . .84 E5
Postwick with Witton
NR13 . . . . .72 F3
Potter Heigham NR29 . . . .56 F6
Quidenham NR16 . . . . . . .118 F8
Reedham NR13 . . . . .93 A5
Repps with Bastwick
NR29 . . . . .57 A4
Runhall NR9 . . . . .69 A1
Sea Palling NR12 . . . . .40 A5
Shelfanger IP22 . . . . .120 B2
Shouldham PE33 . . . . .62 E3
Shropham NR17 . . . . .103 B3
Sisland NR14 . . . . .91 D1
Snettisham PE31 . . . . .12 E5
Somerton NR29 . . . . .57 F6
South Lopham IP22 . . . . .128 D8
Stockton NR34 . . . . .109 F5
Stoke Ferry PE33 . . . . .80 E2
Strumpshaw NR13 . . . . . . .91 F8
Sutton NR12 . . . . .39 C3
Swafield NR28 . . . . .22 C4
Swainsthorpe NR14 . . . . . .89 D4
Tasburgh NR15 . . . . .106 F6
Terrington St John PE14 . .42 B1
Tharston & Hapton
NR15 . . . . .106 D5
Thompson IP24 . . . . .102 B7
Thurlton NR14 . . . . .92 F1
Thurne NR29 . . . . .56 E2
Tibenham NR16 . . . . .120 E8
Tilney All Saints PE34 . . .144 F1
Tilney St Lawrence PE34 . .42 D2
Toft Monks NR34 . . . . . .110 D6
Topcroft NR35 . . . . .106 F2
Tunstead NR12 . . . . .55 B8
Upton with Fishley NR13 .166 A6
Wacton NR15 . . . . .106 C2
Walpole St Andrew PE14 . .41 E3
Walsingham NR22 . . . . . . .16 F8
Watlington PE34 . . . . .61 C6
Watton IP25 . . . . .84 E3
Wellingham PE32 . . . . . . .30 E1
Wereham PE33 . . . . .80 E4
West Beckham NR25 . . . . . .9 C2
West Dereham PE33 . . . . .80 B4
Wheatacre NR34 . . . . . . .111 A5
Whinburgh & Westfield
NR19 . . . . .68 A3
Wiggenhall St Germans
PE34 . . . . .61 A8
Wimbotsham PE34 . . . . .172 E8
Wingfield IP21 . . . . .131 E3
Wormegay PE33 . . . . . . .108 B5
Wortham IP22 . . . . .129 C5
Wreningham NR16 . . . . . . .88 E1
Wroxham/Hoveton
NR12 . . . . .164 D5
Yelverton NR14 . . . . .90 F5
Church Rd N IP21 . . . .131 C7
Church St Ashill IP25 . . .84 A7
Attleborough NR17 . . . . .174 D5
Bawburgh NR9 . . . . .160 A6
Bradenham IP25 . . . . .66 E3
Brisley NR9 . . . . .49 A8
Briston NR24 . . . . .142 E4
Carbrooke IP25 . . . . .85 A5
Coltishall NR12 . . . . .54 C6
Cromer NR27 . . . . .139 C6
Diss IP22 . . . . .177 D4
East Dereham NR19 . . . . .154 D5
Elsing NR20 . . . . .50 F3
Gimingham NR11 . . . . .22 E7
Great Ellingham NR17 . . .103 E7
26 Hardingham IP20 . . . .122 D2
Hingham NR9 . . . . .86 C5
Holt NR25 . . . . .137 C6
Horsford NR10 . . . . .53 B2
Hunstanton PE36 . . . . . . .132 C4
Kenninghall NR16 . . . . . .119 B4
King's Lynn PE30 . . . . . .146 D4
Litcham PE32 . . . . .48 A4
Little Walsingham NR22 . . .16 F7
New Buckenham NR16 . . .104 F1
North Creake NR21 . . . . . .15 D8
11 North Walsham NR28 .151 C5
Northrepps NR27 . . . . .11 A2
Norwich NR6 . . . . .158 E5
Plumstead NR11 . . . . .20 A5
Reepham NR10 . . . . .149 C4
Sheringham NR26 . . . . . .138 D7
Southrepps NR11 . . . . . . .22 B7
Stiffkey NR23 . . . . .6 C6
15 Sutton Bridge PE12 . .41 B8
Thornham PE36 . . . . .2 D6
Trimingham NR11 . . . . . . .11 D1
Wells-next-the-Sea
NR23 . . . . .136 D5
Wymondham NR18 . . . . .173 B4
Church Terr
5 Outwell PE14 . . . . .77 F6
17 Wisbech PE13 . . . . . .152 C5
Wroxham NR12 . . . . .164 B3
Church View
Harleston IP20 . . . . .122 E2

Church View continued
Marham PE33 . . . . .63 B4
Ormesby St Margaret
NR29 . . . . .167 B2
Pentney PE32 . . . . .63 C8
Church View Cl
Norwich NR7 . . . . .159 B5
Reedham NR13 . . . . .93 A5
Church View Ct NR7 . . .159 B5
Church Wlk
Burnham Market PE31 . . .135 B2
Great Yarmouth NR31 . . . .94 C6
Shelfanger IP22 . . . . .120 B2
Churchfarm Wlk PE33 . . .62 E1
Churchfield Cl 3 NR7 . .163 D8
Churchfield Rd 3 PE14 . .77 F6
Churchfields NR9 . . . . . .88 D8
Churchfields Rd NR15 . .106 F4
Churchgate St 2 PE38 . . .97 B5
Churchgate Way PE34 . .144 C5
Churchill Cl
Hingham NR10 . . . . .53 B8
1 Watton IP25 . . . . .84 D3
Churchill Cres
Fincham PE33 . . . . .62 E1
Sheringham NR26 . . . . . .138 B5
Churchill Ct NR19 . . . . .154 D4
Churchill Pl NR15 . . . . . .90 F2
Churchill Rd
Great Yarmouth NR30 . . .169 D6
Norwich NR3 . . . . .162 E8
Thetford IP24 . . . . .176 E5
Wisbech PE13 . . . . .152 D4
Churchill Way PE38 . . . .172 B4
Churchman Rd NR7 . . . .159 C2
Churchway IP22 . . . . . .128 F5
Cider Cl NR17 . . . . .174 E4
Cinder La NR34 . . . . . . .111 B4
Cintra Rd NR1 . . . . .163 B6
Cirrus Way NR7 . . . . . .159 C2
City Coll Norwich
NR2 . . . . .178 A2
City of Norwich Aviation
Mus* NR6 . . . . .53 D1
City of Norwich Sch
NR4 . . . . .162 B2
City View Rd NR6 . . . . .158 A4
Civic Gdns NR3 . . . . . . .158 B3
Civray Ave PE38 . . . . . .172 C6
Clabburn Cl 1 NR15 . . . .89 C1
Clabon Fst Cl NR3 . . . . .158 F2
Clabon Rd NR3 . . . . . . .158 F2
Clabon Second Cl
NR3 . . . . .158 F3
Clabon Third Cl NR3 . . .158 F3
Clackclose Com Prim Sch
PE38 . . . . .172 B5
Clackclose Rd PE38 . . . .172 C6
Clancy Rd NR7 . . . . . . .159 C1
Clapper La PE34 . . . . . .145 E5
Clare Ave NR31 . . . . . .170 B2
Clare Cl NR3 . . . . .158 E1
Clare Rd Cromer NR27 . .139 D5
King's Lynn PE30 . . . . . .148 C3
Sutton Bridge PE34 . . . . .162 A3
Claremont Rd
Norwich NR4 . . . . .162 A2
Wisbech PE13 . . . . .152 E5
Clarence Ct
Hunstanton PE36 . . . . . .132 C6
17 Watton IP25 . . . . .84 D3
Clarence Rd
14 Great Yarmouth NR30 .169 D2
Hunstanton PE36 . . . . . .132 C6
Norwich NR1 . . . . .163 A5
Wisbech PE13 . . . . .152 D6
Clarendon Cl 6 NR30 . . .169 D2
Clarendon Dr 10 NR29 . . .57 D4
Clarendon Rd
Norwich NR2 . . . . .162 C5
Sculthorpe NR21 . . . . . . .141 A5
Clarendon Stps 1 NR2 . .162 B5
Clark Rd NR35 . . . . . . .109 B2
Clark's La NR21 . . . . . . .17 E5
Clark's Loke 7 NR13 . . . .73 D6
Clarke Cl IP22 . . . . .177 C1
Clarke Rd NR3 . . . . . . .162 D8
Clarke's Cl 2 NR9 . . . . . .69 F7
Clarke's La
Barsham NR34 . . . . .124 F7
Gooderstone PE33 . . . . . . .82 A5
Clarke's Rd NR31 . . . . .170 C5
Clarkes Rd NR30 . . . . . .169 B5
Clarkson Ave PE13 . . . .152 D5
Clarkson Ct PE13 . . . . .152 D6
Clarkson Inf Sch The
PE13 . . . . .152 E6
Clarkson Rd
10 Lingwood NR13 . . . . .74 A3
Norwich NR5 . . . . .161 C7
Claxton Cl Mileham PE32 . .48 D6
5 Thetford IP24 . . . . . .176 C4
Claxton Cnr NR14 . . . . . .91 C6
Clay Gully PE32 . . . . .48 B7
Clay La Bacton NR28 . . . .23 B3
Bradwell NR31 . . . . .94 C5
Hepworth IP22 . . . . .127 F1
Saxlingham Nethergate
NR15 . . . . .107 A7
Swannington NR9 . . . . . . .52 C2
Clay Rd NR30 . . . . .168 F5
Claymore Gdns NR29 . . .167 A3
Claypit La NR21 . . . . . .141 C5
Claypit Rd NR20 . . . . . . .33 D3
Clayton Cl
Dersingham PE31 . . . . . .140 D4

Clayton Cl continued
Wisbech PE13 . . . . .152 F6
Clearview Dr NR14 . . . . . .90 C5
Cleaves Dr NR22 . . . . . . .16 F8
Clement Gdns IP22 . . . .177 F3
Clement Scott Mews
NR27 . . . . .139 D5
Clements Cl IP22 . . . . . .130 C5
Clements Ct PE34 . . . . .144 B5
Clenchwarton Prim Sch
PE34 . . . . .145 C5
Clenchwarton Rd
PE34 . . . . .146 B4
Clerc Cl NR13 . . . . .173 C5
Cleveland Rd NR22 . . . .178 A3
Clevey Way NR8 . . . . . .156 E4
Cley La IP25 . . . . .84 C4
Cley Marshes Nature
Reserve* NR25 . . . . .7 F7
Cley Rd Blakeney NR25 . . .7 D6
Bodney IP26 . . . . .82 E8
Cockley Cley PE37 . . . . . . .82 B8
Holt NR25 . . . . .137 B8
Swaffham PE37 . . . . .153 B2
Clickers Rd NR3 . . . . . .162 C8
Cliff Ave Cromer NR27 . .139 C6
Great Yarmouth NR31 . . .170 D3
Cliff Cl NR13 . . . . .92 F4
Cliff Ct PE36 . . . . .132 C6
Cliff Dr NR27 . . . . .139 C7
Cliff Hill 4 NR31 . . . . . .170 D4
Cliff La Cromer NR27 . . .139 C6
Great Yarmouth NR31 . . .171 D8
Cliff Par PE36 . . . . .132 C5
Cliff R Com Mid Sch
NR31 . . . . .170 D2
Cliff Pk Fst Sch NR31 . . .170 D2
Cliff Pk High Sch
NR31 . . . . .170 D1
Cliff Rd Cromer NR27 . . .139 D5
Overstrand NR27 . . . . . . .11 A3
Sheringham NR26 . . . . . .138 E7
Cliff Terr PE36 . . . . .132 C5
Cliffe-en-Howe Rd
PE32 . . . . .44 F8
Clifford Ave NR30 . . . . .168 D5
Clifford Burman Cl
PE30 . . . . .148 A1
Clifford Pye Cl NR10 . . . .35 B2
Clifton Cl 3 NR2 . . . . . .162 C7
Clifton Pk NR27 . . . . . . .10 C5
Clifton Rd
King's Lynn PE30 . . . . . .148 B1
Wymondham NR18 . . . . .173 C6
Clifton St NR2 . . . . .162 B7
Clifton Way NR27 . . . . . .11 B3
Clink Hill NR30 . . . . . . .168 B4
Clink Rd NR12 . . . . .40 A6
Clink Rd IP31 . . . . .126 D2
Clint St NR29 . . . . .56 B5
Clintergate Rd NR20 . . .122 C6
Clintock Pl 10 NR30 . . .169 C5
Clipbush La
Banham NR16 . . . . .119 C2
Fakenham NR21 . . . . . . .141 E5
9 Scottow NR10 . . . . . . .85 C4
Clipped Hedge La NR11 . .22 B7
Clipstreet La NR21 . . . . .18 B8
Close The
Brancaster PE31 . . . . .3 D7
Brundall NR13 . . . . .165 C4
Docking PE31 . . . . .134 E4
Great Yarmouth NR31 . . .170 A5
Hemsby NR29 . . . . .167 B7
Martham NR29 . . . . .137 C5
Little Melton NR9 . . . . . .160 D2
North Lopham IP22 . . . . .119 A2
North Walsham NR28 . . .151 D4
Norwich NR1 . . . . .178 C3
Roydon IP22 . . . . .177 A5
Sheringham NR26 . . . . . .138 D8
Stow Bedon NR17 . . . . . .102 D7
Clough Dr 9 IP26 . . . . . .98 E1
Clough La PE30 . . . . . . .146 D4
Clovelly Dr NR6 . . . . . . .157 E2
Clover Dr 7 NR26 . . . . . .138 B5
Clover Hill Fst Sch
NR5 . . . . .161 B8
Clover Hill Rd NR5 . . . .160 F8
Clover Way
Fakenham NR21 . . . . . . .141 E4
Great Yarmouth NR31 . . .170 A4
Thetford IP24 . . . . .176 D5
Clover Wlk PE34 . . . . . .144 B5
Cloverland Dr 8 NR29 . .167 B7
Clover Rd NR34 . . . . . . .110 D1
Clubbs La NR23 . . . . .6 D4
Clydesdale Rise NR31 . . .94 C8
Coach & Horses Row
NR2 . . . . .178 A2
Coach House Ct 1 NR4 .162 A3
Coach La NR19 . . . . .67 C6
Coachmans Ct NR7 . . . .159 C1
Coalbrookdale PE13 . . . .152 A4
Coast Rd Bacton NR12 . . .23 F4
Cley next the Sea NR25 . . .7 F7
Corton NR32 . . . . .171 F1
Happisburgh NR12 . . . . . .24 E5
Hopton on Sea NR31 . . . .171 D4
Overstrand NR27 . . . . . . .11 B3
Salthouse NR25 . . . . .8 A7
Wiveton NR25 . . . . .7 D6
Coastguard Rd NR30 . . .168 F5

Coates Ct 5 PE14 . . . . . .59 D2
Cob 7 NR31 . . . . .94 C8
Cobb's Pi 5 NR30 . . . . .169 D4
Cobblers La PE14 . . . . . .41 F2
Cobbleways The 9 NR29 .58 B6
Cobbold St IP22 . . . . . . .177 B5
Cobbs Hill PE34 . . . . . . .144 B5
Cobham Way NR7 . . . . .159 C2
Cobholm Cl NR31 . . . . .169 B4
Cobholm Fst Sch
NR31 . . . . .169 B4
Coburg Cl 10 IP25 . . . . . .84 D3
Coburg Rd IP25 . . . . .84 B6
Coburg St
8 King's Lynn PE30 . . . .146 E5
Norwich NR2 . . . . .178 A2
Cochrane Cl IP25 . . . . . . .85 A3
Cock Dro PE38 . . . . .172 B7
Cock Fen Rd PE14 . . . . . .95 D7
Cock Rd NR14 . . . . .92 A3
Cock St Ixworth NR9 . . . .69 F2
Wymondham NR18 . . . . .173 B5
Cocketts Dr PE13 . . . . . .152 E5
Cocklehole Rd PE34 . . . .41 F8
Codling's La NR11 . . . . .150 A6
Coigncroft The NR13 . . .165 E3
Coke Rd NR33 . . . . .170 D4
Coker's Hill NR22 . . . . . .16 F7
Colby Prim Sch NR11 . . .36 E8
Cold Harbour Rd NR29 . .56 D4
Coldershaw Rd NR6 . . . .158 B4
Coldham Cl NR29 . . . . . .167 B3
Coldham Hall Carnser
NR14 . . . . .165 C1
Coldham Rd NR21 . . . . . .17 D7
Coldham's La PE33 . . . . .80 A5
Coldhorn Cres PE13 . . . .152 D7
Coleburn Rd NR1 . . . . . . .89 E8
Colegate NR3 . . . . .178 A3
Colegate End Rd IP21 . .121 E6
Coleman Cl
Palgrave IP22 . . . . .177 D1
Taverham NR8 . . . . .155 F2
Coleridge Cl NR8 . . . . . .156 D8
Coleridge Rd IP22 . . . . .177 E4
Coles Way NR10 . . . . . .149 C5
Colin McLean Rd
NR19 . . . . .154 C7
Colindeep La NR7 . . . . .159 A4
Colkett Dr NR6 . . . . . . .158 E3
Colkirk CE VA Prim Sch
NR21 . . . . .31 D5
Coll of W Anglia (Fakenham
Learning Ctr) The
NR21 . . . . .141 B4
Coll of W Anglia (Hunstanton
Learning Ctr) The
PE36 . . . . .132 D4
Coll of W Anglia (Isle
Campus) The PE13 . . . .152 E2
Coll of W Anglia (King's Lynn
Ctr) The PE30 . . . . . . .146 F5
Coll of W Anglia
(Sheringham Centre) The
NR26 . . . . .138 C7
Coll of W Anglia (Wispech
Campus) The PE13 . . . .152 E2
Collectors World of Eric St
John Foti* PE38 . . . . . .79 B6
Colleen Cl
Dereham NR19 . . . . .67 E5
College Cl NR12 . . . . .54 D7
College Cl 1 NR31 . . . . .169 B4
College Dr PE31 . . . . . . .133 C4
College La Keswick NR4 . .89 C7
9 King's Lynn PE30 . . . .146 D4
Runcton Holme PE33 . . . .61 F3
College Rd
Hockwold cum Wilton
IP26 . . . . .113 F7
Norwich NR2 . . . . .162 A5
Thompson IP24 . . . . .102 C7
Thurlton NR14 . . . . .110 C8
Wereham PE33 . . . . .97 F8
College Sq PE31 . . . . . . .91 B3
Collers Way NR10 . . . . . .149 C6
Collett's Bridge La
PE14 . . . . .59 C1
Colley Hill Drift PE32 . . .48 D4
Collin's La PE33 . . . . . . .63 C5
Collingwood Cl
Heacham PE31 . . . . .133 D3
25 Hethersett NR9 . . . . .88 D7
Collingwood Dr NR11 . . .22 F8
Collingwood Rd
Downham Market PE38 . .172 B4
Great Yarmouth NR30 . . .169 E2
Hunstanton PE36 . . . . . .132 D3
Collingwood Way
IP24 . . . . .176 F6
Collingwood Wlk 1
IP24 . . . . .176 F6
Collins Ct NR6 . . . . .158 D2
Collins La PE31 . . . . . . .133 D5
Collins Way NR29 . . . . . .57 F5
Colls Rd NR7 . . . . .159 C2
Colman Ave 1 NR14 . . . .89 F4
Colman Fst Sch NR4 . . .162 A3
Colman Hospl NR2 . . . . .162 A4
Colman Mid Sch NR4 . . .161 F3
Colman Rd NR4 . . . . . . .161 F3
Colmans Mustard Shop*
NR1 . . . . .178 B2
Colne Pl NR27 . . . . .139 B6
Colne Rd NR27 . . . . .139 B6
Colney La Colney NR4 . . .161 A3

Colney La continued
Hethersett NR9 . . . . .160 D1
Colney Rd PE30 . . . . . . .147 D5
Colomb Rd NR31 . . . . . .170 C6
Coltishall Airfield NR10 . .54 B8
Coltishall La NR10 . . . . . .53 E2
Coltishall Prim Sch
NR12 . . . . .54 D7
Coltishall Rd
Belaugh NR12 . . . . .164 A6
Buxton with Lammas
NR10 . . . . .53 F8
Coltishall Sta NR12 . . . . .54 C7
Coltofts Way NR9 . . . . . .69 E6
Coltsfoot Rd NR10 . . . . . .53 A7
Coltsfoot Way NR24 . . . .176 F5
Columbia Way IP24 . . . .146 F6
Columbine Cl 4 IP24 . . .176 F5
Columbine Rd NR10 . . . . .53 B2
Columbine The NR6 . . . .158 E7
Colvile Rd PE13 . . . . . . .152 E5
Colville Rd NR24 . . . . . .142 B5
Comber Cl IP21 . . . . . . .130 D6
Comet Rd 7 IP25 . . . . . . .84 F3
Comfrey Way NR14 . . . .116 D2
Commercial Rd NR19 . . .154 E5
Common Dr NR20 . . . . . .49 C4
Common Dro
Flitcham with Appleton
PE31 . . . . .27 C5
Southery PE38 . . . . .97 B5
Common End PE32 . . . . . .47 D8
Common La
Beccles NR34 . . . . .110 D1
Beetley NR20 . . . . .49 E5
Brancaster PE31 . . . . .3 D6
Brockdish IP21 . . . . .131 D6
Burgh & Tuttington NR11 . .36 E6
East Walton PE32 . . . . . . .45 E3
Field Dalling NR25 . . . . . . .7 B1
Filby NR29 . . . . .75 E8
Gayton PE32 . . . . .45 C4
Great Witchingham NR9 . .51 D4
King's Lynn PE30 . . . . . .148 C2
North Runcton PE33 . . . . .44 A2
Norwich NR7 . . . . .163 F5
Sheringham NR26 . . . . . .138 E6
6 Southery PE38 . . . . . . .97 B5
Thorpe Market NR11 . . . .22 A6
Common La N NR34 . . . .110 D1
Common Loke NR14 . . . .92 A2
Common Pl 3 NR22 . . . . .16 F7
Common Rd
Aldeby NR34 . . . . .111 B3
Ashwellthorpe NR16 . . . .105 E7
Barton Turf NR12 . . . . . . .38 F1
Botesdale IP22 . . . . .128 F1
Bressingham IP22 . . . . . .129 C8
Brumstead NR12 . . . . . . .24 A1
Burston & Shimpling
IP22 . . . . .120 E2
Castle Acre PE32 . . . . . . .46 F5
East Tuddenham NR20 . . .69 B5
Forncett NR16 . . . . .105 E5
Foxley NR20 . . . . .33 D1
Garvestone NR9 . . . . .68 C3
Great Yarmouth NR31 . . .170 C8
Hemsby NR29 . . . . .57 F4
Hopton IP22 . . . . .127 C4
Lessingham NR12 . . . . . . .24 E2
Martham NR29 . . . . .57 B4
Mundham NR14 . . . . .91 C1
Neatishead NR12 . . . . . . .55 E6
Pulham Market IP21 . . . .121 E7
Runcton Holme PE33 . . . .61 D4
Runhall NR20 . . . . .68 F4
Scole IP21 . . . . .130 F8
Shelfanger IP22 . . . . .119 F3
Shelton NR15 . . . . .107 B1
Skeyton NR10 . . . . .37 A6
Snettisham PE31 . . . . . . .12 D4
Somerton NR29 . . . . .57 E6
Surlingham NR14 . . . . . .165 B1
Swafield NR28 . . . . .22 D4
Thurne NR29 . . . . .56 E2
Wacton NR15 . . . . .106 D2
West Walton PE14 . . . . . .59 D7
Wiggenhall St Germans
PE34 . . . . .60 F7
Common The
Freethorpe NR13 . . . . . . .92 E7
1 Harleston IP20 . . . . . .122 D1
Lyng NR9 . . . . .51 A4
Mundham NR14 . . . . . . .165 A1
Swardeston NR14 . . . . . . .89 B6
Commonside NR10 . . . . . .35 A2
Commonwealth Way 12
NR7 . . . . .72 D4
Compass Rd NR18 . . . . .173 F1
Copal Hills NR27 . . . . . .139 B3
Concorde Rd NR6 . . . . . .158 C5
Conesford Dr NR1 . . . . .162 F3
Coney Weston Rd
Barningham IP31 . . . . . .127 C4
Sapiston IP31 . . . . .126 D2
Conference Way
PE13 . . . . .131 E5
Wisbech PE13 . . . . .152 C8
Conge The NR30 . . . . . .169 C5
Congham Rd PE32 . . . . . .28 B1
Conifer Cl NR29 . . . . . . .167 A3
Coniston Cl
2 Hethersett NR9 . . . . .88 E8
King's Lynn PE30 . . . . . .148 F1
2 Norwich NR5 . . . . . .161 C6
Coniston Rd NR15 . . . . .106 D2
Coniston Sq 1 NR30 . . .169 D4
Connaught Ave NR31 . . .170 C5

Connaught Plain
NR17 ....174 D5
Connaught Rd
Attleborough NR17 .....174 D5
Cromer NR27 ....139 D5
Norwich NR2 ....162 B7
Constable Cl
7 Attleborough NR17 ...174 B4
2 Diss IP22 ....177 C4
Constable Ct 6 IP20 ...122 D2
Constable Dr 4 NR31 ...170 A7
Constable Rd NR4 .....162 C1
Constitution Hill
Fakenham NR21 ....141 B4
North Runcton PE33 ....43 F4
Norwich NR6 ....158 E3
Constitution Opening
NR3 ....158 E2
Convent Rd 4 NR2 ....162 C5
Convy Priors NR30 ...168 C6
Conway Rd
Great Yarmouth NR31 ...170 D6
Sheringham NR26 ......138 F7
Norwich NR6 ....173 C6
Cook Rd IP25 ....66 A3
Cook's La IP20 ......122 F2
Cooke Cl NR15 ......160 E7
Cooke's Rd NR1 ......91 B4
Cookley La IP21 ....130 F1
Cooper La NR1 ....89 F8
Cooper Rd
North Walsham NR28 ...151 D6
8 Sheringham NR26 ...138 C5
Co-operative St NR26 ...138 D7
Coopers Cl NR28 ....155 C3
Coopers La PE33 .....62 B2
Copeman Rd
Aylsham NR11 ....150 D5
Great & Little Plumstead
NR13 ....73 A6
3 Roydon IP22 ....129 D7
Copenhagen Way
NR6 ....158 C2
Copince's La NR16 ...119 C7
Copper Beech Cl
NR21 ....141 D6
Copper Hall PE37 ...153 B3
Copper La 8 NR9 ....86 C5
Copper Smith Way
NR18 ....173 F5
Copperfield Rd NR30 ...147 C5
Copperfield Ave 1
NR30 ....170 D8
Coppice Ave NR6 ...157 E5
Coppice The 6 NR17 ...174 C5
Coppice La NR7 .....152 E2
Corbet Ave NR7 .....59 B2
Corbett Rd 2 NR28 ...151 C6
Corbyn Shaw Rd PE30 ...147 E4
Cordon St PE13 .....152 C4
Coriander Dr IP24 ...176 F4
Corie Rd NR4 ....161 F4
Corkway Dro PE38 ...97 E1
Cormorant Way NR31 ...94 C8
Corncutters Cl NR3 ...178 B3
Corner Comm Rd NR28 ...38 B7
Corner La NR10 .....53 B3
Corner St 2 NR27 ...139 B7
Cornfield The NR25 ...2 A3
Cornfields IP21 ....121 B1
Cornish Ave NR28 ...22 E5
Cornish Way IP24 ...132 D5
Cornwallis Cl 7 NR5 ...161 C7
Coronation Ave
2 Marthan NR29 ......57 D4
Nordelph PE38 ....78 D3
1 Worksop NR29 .....57 D2
West Winch PE33 .....43 F3
Coronation Cl NR6 ...158 A4
Coronation Cotts PE32 ...47 F4
Coronation Cres
NR15 ....107 D5
Coronation Gn NR31 ...169 B3
Coronation Gr NR7 ...153 B5
Coronation La
Blakeney NR25 ....7 D7
Somerton NR29 ......57 F5
Coronation Pl IP27 ...175 B2
Coronation Rd
Clenchwarton PE34 ...146 A5
Great Yarmouth NR31 ...169 B3
Holt NR25 ....137 C5
Norwich NR6 ....158 A4
Coronation Terr
Caston NR17 ....102 F8
6 Great Yarmouth NR30 ...169 C4
Coronation Wlk NR28 ...151 A5
Coronilla Gn NR31 ...170 B5
Corporation Rd PE13 ...152 F3
Corpusty Prim Sch
NR11 ....19 F1
Corpusty Rd
Briston NR24 ....142 F1
Norwich NR19 ....19 B2
Wood Dalling NR11 ...34 D7
Corton Rd NR1 .....178 C1
Coslany Sq NR3 ....178 C4
Coslany St NR3 ....178 A3
Costessey High Sch
NR5 ....156 E2
Costessey Inf Sch
NR5 ....157 B1
Costessey Jun Sch
NR5 ....156 F1
Costessey La
Drayton NR8 ....156 A8
Ringland NR8 ....70 B8
Taverham NR8 ......157 A7

Coston La NR18 .....87 A8
Cosy Cnr NR28 ......151 B4
Cotman Cl IP22 .....177 C4
Cotman Dr NR31 ....170 A7
Cotman Fields NR1 ...178 C4
Cotman Rd NR1 .....163 B5
Cotoneaster Ct 4 NR31 ...170 B6
Cottage Dr The NR7 ...163 E8
Cottage Farm Abbey
PE32 ....46 C2
Cottage Rd NR29 ...57 E6
Cotterall Ct NR5 ...161 A8
Cottinghams Dr NR10 ...157 E7
Cotton Rd NR9 .....70 A4
Cotton's Cnr PE14 ...77 D2
Cottons Head PE14 ...77 E7
Cotts La PE34 ......144 F1
Coughtrey Cl NR7 ...159 B5
Coulson Cl NR7 ....153 C5
Coulson La IP20 ...175 C4
Coulton Cl PE30 ...146 E7
Council Rd 4 PE13 ...152 E6
County Ct Rd 3 PE30 ...146 E4
Court Cl 8 NR29 ...57 D2
Court Dr NR27 .....139 B6
Court Gdns PE38 ...172 C5
Court Hill NR12 ...54 A4
Court Rd
Great Snoring NR21 ...17 B5
Rollesby NR29 ......57 D2
Courtenay Cl
4 East Dereham NR19 ...154 D5
2 Norwich NR5 .....160 F8
Courtfields PE37 ...153 B3
Courtnell Pl PE30 ...147 D5
Courtyard The 8 NR4 ...161 C5
Courtyard 7 NR19 ...154 D5
Covent Gdn Rd NR13 ...168 C7
Coventry St 2 NR21 ...15 C2
Coventry Way IP24 ...176 A4
Covert Sycamore
IP24 ....176 A4
Covert The NR24 ...176 E6
Covey The
Surlingham NR14 ....91 C8
Taverham NR8 ......155 D2
Covey Way IP27 ...113 F1
Cow Hill NR2 ......178 A3
Cow La Denver NR18 ...172 C1
Tharston & Hapton
NR15 ....106 C7
Cow Lake Dro PE14 ...59 D5
Cow Mdw Rd NR13 ...92 C8
Cow Tro NR29 ......57 D3
Cow Twr* NR1 .....178 C3
Cowdewell Mews 7
NR8 ....155 D1
Cowgate NR3 ......178 B4
Cowle's Dro IP26 ...113 D5
Cowper Cl NR11 ...143 C5
Cowper Rd NR19 ...154 E5
Cowslip Cl 14 NR14 ...89 B3
Cowslip La NR26 ...138 B6
Cowslip Wlk PE34 ...61 B5
Cox's La PE13 .....152 A3
Coxswain Read Way
NR30 ....168 D4
Cozens Rd NR1 ....163 A4
Cozens-Hardy Rd NR7 ...159 B4
Crab Apple La NR14 ...110 E8
Crab La Boughton PE33 ...81 A5
Great Yarmouth NR31 ...170 A5
Crab Marsh PE13 ...152 B8
Crabapple Cl 7 NR18 ...173 E4
Crabapple La NR9 ...68 D1
Crabb La PE34 .....42 E1
Crabb's Abbey PE34 ...6 A2
Crabbe's Cl IP26 ...98 E1
Crabgate La N NR11 ...34 D6
Crabgate La S NR11 ...34 D5
Crabtree La NR34 ...110 D1
Crabtree Rise IP22 ...131 C6
Cradle Wood Rd NR28 ...151 E3
Cradock Ave NR30 ...169 D8
Craft La NR27 .....11 A1
Craft The
Raveningham NR14 ...110 B8
Winterton-on-Sea NR29 ...58 B6
Cramp Cnr NR14 ...91 F6
Cranage Rd NR1 ...162 E1
Crane Cl NR19 ....154 C3
Crane's La NR10 ...150 C1
Cranes Mdw 31 IP20 ...122 D2
Cranes Rd NR14 ...88 F3
Cranfield Rd NR26 ...138 A4
Cranleigh Rise NR4 ...161 F1
Cranley Rd NR7 ....72 E4
Cranmer Ave PE30 ...148 C4
Cranmer Cl NR21 ...141 C5
Cranny Field Chase
PE14 ....41 E1
Cranwell Rd 10 IP25 ...84 F3
Cranworth Gdns NR11 ...178 A1
Craske Cl NR28 ...138 C5
Craske Dr NR12 ...72 E7
Craske La PE34 ...42 A7
Craske Mews NR11 ...160 E8
Craven La PE33 ...62 B6
Crawford Rd NR17 ...139 D5
Craymere Beck Rd
NR24 ....142 E1
Craymere Rd NR24 ...142 E2
Creake Rd
Burnham Market PE31 ...135 D2
Sculthorpe NR21 ....141 A6
Sculthorpe Airfield PE31 ...15 B3
Creance Rd NR7 ...159 C4

Crecen La PE36 ....132 C4
Creek The PE31 ...135 E7
Cremer Cl 14 PE31 ...12 E4
Cremer Rd NR26 ...138 D7
Cremer's Drift NR26 ...138 D6
Cremorne La NR1 ...163 B5
Crescent Pas PE13 ...152 C5
Crescent Cl PE36 ...132 C3
Crescent The
Ashwellthorpe NR16 ...105 F8
Bacton/Walcott NR12 ...24 A7
East Dereham NR19 ...154 C1
East Harling NR16 ...118 C4
Hemsby NR29 ......167 D7
Hethersett NR9 .....88 C7
4 Newton Flotman NR15 ...89 D1
Norwich NR8 ....178 A2
Taverham NR8 .....156 F8
Thurton NR14 ....91 C4
Wisbech PE13 ......152 C4
Cressener Cl NR6 ...157 E5
Cressingham Rd IP25 ...83 F6
Cresswell Cl NR5 ...161 B6
Cresswell St PE30 ...146 E6
Crest Rd PE31 ....140 C4
Crick's Wlk IP22 ...177 A5
Cricket Cl NR5 ...155 E3
Cricket Gd Rd NR1 ...162 E3
Cricket Pasture The
PE31 ....3 E7
Cricketer's Wlk NR13 ...92 E7
Cricketers Way PE13 ...152 A6
Crimp Cramp La NR34 ...111 B4
Cringleford CE Fst & Mid Sch
NR4 ....89 B8
Cringleford Chase
NR4 ....161 C1
Crinoline La NR20 ...69 C5
Crisp Cl PE31 ....140 C3
Crisp Rd NR35 ...109 C3
Critten's Rd NR31 ...169 B4
Croft Cl Diss IP22 ...177 C4
10 Harleston IP20 ...122 D2
Croft Gn NR17 ...174 B3
Croft Hill NR29 ...75 B5
Croft La Corpusty NR11 ...19 F7
Diss IP22 ....177 C4
Marsham NR10 ....150 C1
Croft Rd
Caister-on-Sea NR30 ...168 E5
Norton Subcourse NR14 ...92 E1
Upwell PE14 ....77 D3
Croft The
Costessey NR8 .....156 F4
Cromer NR27 ......139 B6
Little Snoring NR21 ...17 C3
Swanton Novers NR24 ...18 A3
Croft Yd NR23 ...136 D6
Croftholme Way 1 NR7 ...163 C8
Crofts Cl NR11 ...160 F6
Crofts The 1 NR5 ...160 F7
Cromarty Way NR30 ...168 D5
Crome Cl IP22 ...177 B4
Crome Rd NR3 ...162 E8
Cromer High Sch Language
Coll NR27 ....139 C5
Cromer Hospl NR27 ...139 D6
Cromer Jun Sch NR27 ...139 C5
Cromer La NR23 ...36 E3
Cromer Mus* NR27 ...139 C7
Cromer Rd
Aylsham NR11 .....150 C8
Blickling NR11 .....36 B7
Holt NR25 ....137 D7
Hunstanton PE36 ...132 E6
Mundesley NR11 ...143 B7
North Walsham NR28 ...151 C6
Norwich NR6 ....158 A5
Ormesby St Margaret
with Scratby NR29 ...167 A2
Overstrand NR27 ...139 F4
Runton NR27 ......10 C6
Sheringham NR26 ...138 E6
Southrepps NR11 ...22 C1
Trimingham NR11 ...11 A2
Cromer Sta NR27 ...139 A7
Cromes Oak Cl NR14 ...90 C4
Cromes Pl NR7 ...37 B2
Crompton Rd NR11 ...150 C4
Cromwell Cl
5 Cromer NR27 ....139 C6
8 Hethersett NR9 ...88 D8
4 Marthan NR29 ...57 D4
Swaffham PE37 ....153 D3
Cromwell Rd
Cromer NR27 ......139 C6
Great Yarmouth NR30 ...169 C1
Norwich NR18 .....173 C6
Weeting-with-Broomhill
IP27 ....114 E8
Wisbech PE13 ......152 C3
Cromwell Terr 6 PE30 ...146 E3
Crooks Pl NR2 ...162 C3
Crosby Row PE12 ...41 A8
Cross Dro Hilgay PE38 ...96 D7
Southery PE38 .....97 B3
Cross Keys Cl 2 NR10 ...53 D2
Cross La Brancaster PE31 ...3 C7
Easton NR9 ....70 C4
Fleggburgh NR29 ...57 C2
Northwold IP26 ...99 C7
Norwich NR3 ......178 A4
Runton NR27 ......10 A6
Stanhoe PE31 .....14 E7
Surlingham NR14 ...91 A8
Cross Rd
Ashby with Oby NR29 ...56 F1

Cross Rd *continued*
Great Yarmouth NR31 ...170 D6
Starston IP20 ......122 C2
Cross St 6 Cromer NR27 ...139 B6
Harpley PE31 ......29 C5
2 Holt NR25 ....137 B6
Hoxne IP21 ....131 A3
Salthouse NR25 ....137 C8
Cross Stone Rd NR14 ...92 B3
Cross Way PE31 ...133 C5
Cross's Grave PE31 ...29 E4
Crossing Rd
Great Green IP21 ...130 A5
Palgrave IP22 .....177 D1
Crosskeys Way 3 NR20 ...68 F6
Crossroad NR10 ...37 C4
Crosstead NR30 ...169 D8
Crossway Terr
Acle NR13 ....166 B4
5 Loddon NR14 ....91 F1
Crossways 4 NR29 ...167 A2
Crostwick La NR10 ...54 A2
Crostwight Rd NR28 ...38 D7
Croughton La PE31 ...30 B8
Crow Hall Est PE38 ...172 C3
Crow La NR17 ....170 C2
Crow Hill NR11 ...34 C7
Crow La Bircham PE31 ...14 A2
Elsing NR20 ....50 F4
Great Dunham PE32 ...47 E1
Crow Rd NR28 ....151 D6
Crow St PE31 ....127 B4
Crow's La IP25 ...84 C1
Crowden Rd NR12 ...24 D4
Crowes Loke NR13 ...73 B7
Crown Ave PE14 ...95 A7
Crown Cres IP25 ...84 E5
Crown Ctyd NR14 ...119 A4
Crown Gdns PE33 ...80 E4
Crown Gn PE22 ...120 E2
Crown La
Coney Weston IP31 ...127 B4
Fransham NR19 ...66 D6
Crown Mdw NR10 ...149 C5
Crown Pl NR19 ...154 D6
Crown Rd
Christchurch PE14 ...95 A7
Colkirk NR21 ....31 D5
East Dereham NR20 ...154 F5
Great Yarmouth NR30 ...169 D3
Horsham St Faith NR10 ...53 D2
Lamas NR10 ....36 E1
Mundford PE26 ....100 B4
Norwich NR1 ......178 B3
2 Old Buckenham NR17 ...104 D2
Crown Sq PE30 ...147 A7
Crown St
Banham NR16 .....119 D7
Brandon IP27 ......175 A2
Methwold IP26 ....99 A5
Crown Way NR16 ...119 D6
Crownthorpe Rd NR18 ...87 C6
Crowshall La PE13 ...174 B5
Croxton Rd
Fulmodeston NR21 ...17 E2
Thetford IP24 ......176 D4
Crummock Rd 3 NR5 ...161 C6
Cubitt Rd NR1 ...163 C7
Cubitts Cl NR20 ...33 B2
Cuck Stool La 5 PE32 ...46 F2
Cuckoo Hill Rd PE31 ...14 B3
Cuckoo La
Brundall NR13 .....73 E3
Carbrooke IP25 ....85 B4
Redenhall with Harleston
IP20 ....122 F2
Cuckoo Rd PE34 ...79 A8
Cuckoo's La PE34 ...43 E7
Cucumber La NR13 ...165 B5
Cuddle Dike Bank PE14 ...78 A5
Cuffer La NR16 ...104 F2
Culey Cl NR30 ...146 F7
Culley's Pit Rd NR12 ...38 A2
Culling's Hill NR13 ...72 F2
Cullum Cl NR20 ...50 B3
Culverin Cl 3 NR7 ...72 D4
Cumming's Bvd NR21 ...15 C2
Cunningham Ave 2
NR30 ....169 D8
Cunningham Cl IP24 ...176 F6
Cunningham Rd 6 NR5 ...161 C5
Cunningham Wlk 3
IP24 ....176 F6
Curd's Hall NR19 ...66 A7
Curie Dr NR1 ....170 B1
Curlew Cl 7 IP25 ...84 C1
Curlew Way NR10 ...146 A6
Curson Cl 11 NR9 ...88 C7
Curson Rd NR18 ...173 B6
Cursons Mews NR18 ...173 B6
Curtis Dr 1 IP26 ...98 D1
Curtis La NR26 ...138 D4
Curtis Rd NR13 ...158 B4
Cushing Cl 1 IP27 ...67 B2
Cushing La NR35 ...123 B3
Custance Ct NR4 ...162 A2
Customhouse St PE12 ...41 C8
Cut Loke NR14 ...90 C5
Cuthbert Cl
4 King's Lynn PE30 ...148 C5
Norwich NR7 ......159 D1
7 Thetford IP24 ...176 F5
Cutler Way
Bowthorpe NR5 ...160 F6
Norwich NR5 ......160 E8
Cutthroat La NR19 ...68 A8
Cutting's Rd IP21 ...131 C8
Cuttons Cnr NR13 ...73 D6

Cydonia Gn 12 NR31 ...170 B6
Cygnet Cl NR17 ...174 F6
Cygnet Rd NR19 ...154 E4
Cygnet Wlk PE13 ...153 C2
Cypress Cl NR6 ...158 E8
Cypress Cres NR26 ...138 D5
Cypress Pl PE36 ...132 D4
Cypress Rd NR17 ...174 C5
Cyprus St NR1 ...162 E3
Cyril Rd NR7 ...163 F7

D

Da Volls Ct NR31 ...170 D6
Dacre Cl NR4 ....161 E1
Dades La PE14 ...60 B6
Daffodil Way NR20 ...68 E6
Dagmar Mews 12 NR30 ...169 D2
Dairy Drift PE32 ...48 C2
Dairy Dro CB6 ...95 F2
Dairy Farm Cl NR21 ...141 C6
Dairy Farm Ct NR17 ...174 C5
Dairy La NR11 ...9 E1
Dakenham Cl NR13 ...72 F8
Dakin Rd NR3 ...158 D1
Dalbier Cl 2 NR13 ...72 E4
Dale End PE31 ...3 D7
Dale La NR29 ...56 C8
Dales Cl 8 NR31 ...94 C8
Dales Loke NR14 ...163 D5
Dales The NR13 ...163 D5
Dalrymple Way NR3 ...158 C4
Dam La IP22 ...129 D3
Damgate Back La NR29 ...57 D6
Damgate Cl NR13 ...166 C2
Damgate La Acle NR13 ...166 D2
Marthan NR29 ....57 D6
Damgate St NR13 ...173 B3
Danby Cl 3 NR4 ...89 D8
Danby Rd NR13 ...170 C6
Dane Cl IP24 ...176 B3
Danemoor La NR9 ...86 F8
Danesbower Cl NR13 ...165 F6
Danesfort Dr NR13 ...165 E6
Danesfort Dr NR19 ...154 E6
Daniels Rd NR4 ...162 A3
Danish House Gdns
NR27 ....11 A4
Daphne Way 8 NR31 ...170 B5
Dark La
Ashmanhaugh NR12 ...38 C1
Dickleburgh & Rushall
IP21 ....130 B6
Erpingham NR11 ...21 A1
Kimberley NR18 ...87 B7
Smallburgh NR12 ...38 D3
Somerton NR29 ...57 F6
Wretham IP24 .....132 D3
Darrell Pl NR5 ...161 D7
Darrow Gn Rd IP20 ...122 F8
Darrow Wood* IP22 ...122 F8
Darrow Wood La IP22 ...120 A1
Darwin Cl 5 PE12 ...41 B8
Daseley's Cl NR4 ...158 A8
Dashwood Cl NR31 ...93 F6
Dauber's La NR13 ...74 C2
Davey Cl NR35 ...124 C8
Davey Pl NR2 ...178 B3
Davidson Cl NR17 ...163 F7
Davidson Rd NR7 ...72 D4
Davy Pl Heacham PE31 ...133 C5
7 Loddon NR14 ...92 A1
Dawber Cl PE30 ...147 B4
Dawes La 2 PE31 ...12 E4
Dawnay Ave PE30 ...148 B1
Dawsons La NR20 ...33 C3
Day's La IP31 ...127 C4
Day's Lode Rd PE14 ...95 A4
De Caux Rd NR3 ...158 E2
De Grey Rd PE30 ...147 B5
De Hague Rd NR4 ...162 B1
De Havilland Rd
Dereham NR19 ...154 C6
Wisbech PE13 ......152 C6
De Lucy Cl 2 IP22 ...177 C5
De Morley Cl 4 IP22 ...177 A5
De Morley Garth
NR26 ....138 C6
De Warrenne Pl NR2 ...47 A2
Deacon Cl NR13 ...165 D4
Deacon Dr NR8 ...88 D8
Deben Dr 4 NR31 ...94 A6
Debenne Rd NR28 ...151 D5
Deborah Rd NR11 ...94 A5
De-Carle Smith Rd
NR13 ....166 C4
Decoy Rd
Lakenheath IP27 ...112 F4
Ormesby St Margaret
with Scratby NR29 ...167 A4
Ormesby St Michael NR29 ...57 F2
Deep Rd NR18 ...173 B8
Deepdale NR13 ...165 D3
Deepdale Ave 1 NR29 ...57 C4
Deer Row NR35 ...124 C8
Delane Rd NR17 ...157 C2
Delft Way NR6 ...158 A6

Delgate La PE31 ....3 E7
Dell Cl NR15 ....106 F8
Dell Cnr La NR13 ....73 F5
Dell Cres NR5 ....161 D7
Dell Loke NR14 ....163 B2
Dell The Bodham NR25 ....9 A3
　Hingham NR9 ....86 B5
　Mundesley NR11 ....143 D5
　Trowse Newton NR14 ...163 B2
Deloney Rd NR7 ....159 C2
Delta Cl NR6 ....158 C4
De-Narde Rd NR19 .....154 D7
Denbigh Rd NR2 ......162 B5
Dene Ave NR29 ....167 A3
Dene Side 1 NR30 .....169 D3
Denes The NR1 ....163 C5
Denham Low Rd NR21 ..131 A1
Denham Rd NR21 .....131 B2
Denmark Hill IP22 ....177 C3
Denmark La IP22 .....177 B4
Denmark Opening
　NR3 ....158 E1
Denmark Rd
　Beccles NR34 ....110 D1
　2 King's Lynn PE30 ..147 B6
　Norwich NR3 ....158 E1
Denmark Rise IP22 ...177 C4
Denmark St IP22 .....177 C3
Denmead Cl 4 NR4 ....89 D8
Dennis Rd NR6 ....157 F7
Dennis Sneezum Ct
　PE38 ....172 B4
Denny Rd PE30 ....147 A4
Denny's Hill IP20 ....123 A2
Denny's Wlk PE32 ....63 E7
Denton Rd
　Denton IP20 ....123 C6
　Norwich NR3 ....158 F3
Denver Hill PE38 .....172 C3
Denver VC Prim Sch
　PE38 ....172 D2
Denver Windmill*
　PE38 ....172 B1
Deopham Rd
　Attleborough NR17 ...174 C7
　Hingham NR9 ....86 C4
　Morley NR18 ....87 A2
Derby St NR2 ....162 C7
Dereham 6th Form Coll
　NR20 ....154 F5
Dereham Church Inf Sch
　NR19 ....154 D5
Dereham Hospl NR19 ..154 E7
Dereham La NR19 ......66 C8
Dereham Rd
　5 Bawdeswell NR20 ...50 E7
　Beeston with Bittering
　PE32 ....48 D2
　Briningham NR24 .....18 D5
　Bylaugh NR20 ....50 C5
　Colkirk NR21 ....31 E5
　Costessey NR5 ....156 D1
　East Dereham NR19 ...56 A8
　Easton NR9 ....70 C5
　Garvestone NR9 ....68 C1
　Gressenhall NR19 .....49 C2
　Hempton NR21 ....141 B2
　Hingham NR9 ....86 B5
　Honingham NR9 ....69 D7
　Kimberley NR18 ....87 A7
　Litcham PE32 ....48 A4
　Mattishall NR20 ......68 D6
　North Elmham NR20 ...49 E6
　1 Norwich NR5 ....161 B8
　Ovington IP25 ....84 E6
　Pudding Norton NR21 ..141 B1
　Reepham NR10 ....149 A4
　Scarning NR19 ....154 A4
　Shipdham IP25 ....67 A1
　28 Watton IP25 ....84 D3
　Whinburgh & Westfield
　NR19 ....67 F5
　Whissonsett NR20 .....31 E2
　Yaxham NR19 ....68 A8
Dereham St Nicholas Jun Sch
　NR19 ....154 D4
Dersingham Bog National
　Nature Reserve*
　PE31 ....27 D7
Dersingham Inf Sch
　PE31 ....140 D4
Dersley Ct NR5 ....160 E7
Derwent Ave PE30 ....148 F2
Desborough Way NR13 ..72 D4
Desmond Dr NR6 .....158 F6
Devlin Dr 18 NR14 ....90 C5
Devon Ave NR6 ....162 C4
Devon Cres PE30 .....148 D5
Devon Way NR14 .....163 C1
Devonshire Cl 7 IP30 ..147 A7
Devonshire Rd NR30 ..169 D2
Devonshire St 4 NR2 ..162 C7
Devwarrene Dr IP27 ..175 B7
Dewdrop Cl PE31 .....140 C6
Dewing Rd NR13 ......72 E8
Dexter Rd PE34 ....79 A7
Dial Cl PE38 ....172 B5
Diamond Cl IP22 .....120 B5
Diamond Rd NR6 ......158 D7
Diamond Sq NR1 .....146 D2
Diamond Terr PE30 ...146 D2
Dian Rd NR13 ....165 E3
Diana Cl NR19 ......154 C1
Diana Way NR30 .....168 C6

Dianas Dro PE36 .....132 C2
Dibden Rd NR3 ......162 F8
Dickens Ave NR30 ...169 D1
Dickens Ct 5 NR30 ...169 D1
Dickfool's La NR19 ....64 C8
Dickleburgh Prim Sch
　IP21 ....121 B1
Dickleburgh Rd IP21 ..121 A1
Dicks Mount NR34 ...111 D3
Dicky Hill IP20 ....122 D3
Digby Dr NR21 ....141 B6
Dilham Arts Ctr* NR28 ..38 C6
Dilham Rd Honing NR28 ..38 C6
　Worstead NR28 ....38 A4
Dilldash La NR21 ....17 A5
Dinosaur Adventure Pk*
　NR9 ....51 E4
Dirty La
　North Tuddenham NR20 ..50 E1
　Pulham St Mary IP21 ...121 F3
Diss Church Jun Sch
　IP22 ....177 D4
Diss High Sch IP22 ...177 E5
Diss Inf Sch IP22 .....177 E4
Diss Mus* IP22 ......177 D4
Diss Rd
　Burston & Shimpling
　IP22 ....120 E1
　Garboldisham IP22 ....128 A8
　Scole IP21 ....130 C5
　South Lopham IP22 ....128 F8
　Tibenham NR16 ....120 C8
　Wattisfield IP22 ......128 B1
　Diss Sta IP22 ....177 F4
Diss Swimming & Fitness Ctr
　IP22 ....177 E3
Distillery Sq 5 NR2 ...162 C6
Ditchingham Dam
　NR35 ....109 A1
Dix Cl PE31 ....133 E5
Dixon Rd Cromer NR27 ..139 B5
　North Walsham NR28 ..151 D5
　Norwich NR7 ....159 A4
Dixon's Dro PE14 .....59 C8
Dixon's Fold NR6 ....158 F4
Dobbs' La NR13 ....54 D2
Dobby Dr PE30 ....146 D6
Dobson Way NR34 ...110 D1
Dock Tavern La NR1 ..170 D5
Docking Prim Sch
　PE31 ....134 D4
Docking Rd
　Burnham Westgate
　PE31 ....135 B2
　Ringstead PE36 ....2 B2
　Sedgeford PE36 ....13 B7
　Stanhoe PE31 ....14 D7
　Syderstone PE31 ....15 A3
Doctor's La IP31 .....122 A2
Doctors Mdw 11 NR10 ..53 D2
Doctors Rd NR15 .....155 E6
Dodd Cl NR30 ....168 D7
Dodd's La PE32 ....45 B2
Dodderman Way NR5 ..160 F6
Dodds Cl NR17 ....174 B3
Dodds La NR17 ....174 B3
Dodds Rd NR17 ......174 B3
Doddshill Rd PE31 ...140 F3
Dodgers La NR15 ......91 A3
Dodma Rd PE32 ....47 C8
Dodman's La NR20 ....31 F2
Dodmans Cl PE30 .....146 E5
Dodmans The NR19 ..154 D4
Dodson Dr
　7 Beetley NR19 ....49 C3
　1 Gressenhall NR20 ...49 C3
Doe La Banham NR16 ..119 E8
　Old Buckenham NR17 ..104 E1
Dog Cnr NR11 ....35 A5
Dog La Easton NR9 ....70 B6
　Horsford NR10 ....155 F4
　Shelfanger IP22 ......120 A4
Dogger La NR23 .....136 C6
Doggetts La NR12 .....24 D4
Dogs La NR34 ....110 C3
Dogwood Cl 6 NR18 ..173 E4
Dogwood Rd NR6 ....158 D4
Dohamero La 1 PE38 ..43 F2
Doit La IP22 ....129 D7
Doit The IP22 ....129 C6
Dolman Cl 18 NR31 ...169 B4
Dolphin Gr NR2 ......162 B8
Doman Rd NR1 ......178 C1
Donchurch Cl 8 NR5 ..161 A7
Doris Barnes Ct 1
　NR19 ....154 E5
Doris Rd NR2 ....162 B5
Dorking Rd NR31 ....171 B4
Dorothea Dr 7 NR19 ..154 D3
Dorothy Ave NR31 ....94 C7
Dorrs Dr IP25 ....84 D4
Dorset Cl
　Attleborough NR17 ...174 B3
　4 Great Yarmouth NR30 ..169 D3
Doubleday Cl IP22 ...177 C4
Doughty's Hospl NR3 ..178 B4
Douglas Bader Cl
　NR28 ....151 C7
Douglas Bader Sch The
　NR10 ....37 B2
Douglas Cl
　Croxton IP24 ....116 C5
　Norwich NR6 ....158 D7
Douglas Haig Rd NR31 ..94 C8
Doune Way IP20 .....122 D2
Douro Pl NR2 ....162 C6
Dove Cl
　1 Great Yarmouth NR31 ..170 A6

Dove Cl continued
　8 Harleston IP20 .....122 D1
Dove House La 4 NR29 ..56 F6
Dove La NR15 ....90 C3
Dove St 3 NR2 ....178 A3
Dovecote Cl NR15 ....90 F2
Dovecote Rd PE14 ....77 D3
Dovedale Rd NR16 ...105 F5
Dovedales Fold NR7 ..158 F4
Dovehouse La NR11 ...21 B4
Dover Cl NR30 ......168 C5
Dover St NR2 ....162 B5
Dow Cl NR5 ....160 F5
Dow La NR12 ....54 C3
Dowding Rd
　Norwich NR6 ....158 D6
　3 Watton IP25 ....84 F3
Downham Cres NR18 ..173 B6
Downham Dro PE32 ..63 C7
Downham Mkt Coll
　PE38 ....172 C4
Downham Mkt High Sch &
　Tech Coll PE38 ......172 D5
Downham Mkt Sta
　PE38 ....172 A5
Downham Prep Sch
　PE34 ....79 B8
Downham Rd
　Crimplesham PE33 ....80 B7
　Denver PE38 ....172 C2
　Fincham PE33 ....62 E1
　Nordelph PE38 ....78 D3
　Outwell PE14 ....77 F6
　Runcton Holme PE33 ..61 D4
　Stradsett PE33 ....80 D8
Downham Way IP27 ..175 F4
Downing Ct NR31 ....170 C4
Downing Mews NR5 ..160 D8
Downing Rd NR31 ....170 C4
Downs Ct PE36 ....132 D4
Downs Farm La IP20 ..123 B3
Downs Rd PE36 ......132 D4
Downside Ct 5 NR13 ..72 D5
Dowson Fst Sch NR3 ..158 A1
Dowson Rd NR3 .....158 B1
Drabblegate NR11 ....150 D8
Drabbs La NR12 ......38 E6
Dragon Hall* NR1 ...178 C2
Dragoon Ct 27 NR27 ..72 D4
Drake Ave NR30 .....169 D7
Drake Inf Sch PE14 ..176 E6
Drake Rd IP24 ......176 E6
Drakes Cl 5 NR16 ...118 C5
Drakes Loke NR10 ....36 F1
Draper Way NR5 .....160 D8
Drapers La NR35 ....109 A3
Draycote Cl PE30 ...147 D8
Draycotts Rise IP22 ..177 C1
Drayton Com Fst Sch
　NR8 ....155 F1
Drayton Gr NR8 .....158 C8
Drayton High Rd NR8 ..157 A8
Drayton La NR10 .....53 B1
Drayton Lodge Pk
　NR8 ....157 B7
Drayton Rd NR3 .....157 F2
Drayton Wood Rd
　NR6 ....157 D6
Draytonhall La NR19 ..154 B3
Dreibholz Ct NR20 ...154 F5
Drewray Dr NR8 .....155 E3
Dried Flower Ctr*
　NR12 ....55 C7
Drift La NR20 ....49 C3
Drift Rd
　Caister-on-Sea NR30 ..168 C7
　Lakenheath IP27 ......113 E2
Drift The
　Bawdeswell NR20 ......50 E6
　Beetley NR20 ....49 A6
　Botesdale IP22 ....128 E3
　Fakenham NR21 ....141 D4
　Fulmodeston NR21 ....17 F3
　Heacham PE31 ....133 D6
　Ingoldisthorpe PE31 ..140 C8
　Swardeston NR14 ....89 B5
Driftlands NR21 .....141 D5
Driftway PE30 ....148 C1
Driftway The
　1 Holt NR25 ....137 C5
　Sheringham NR26 ....138 D8
Drift St NR21 ....133 C5
Drinkwater Cl 9 NR9 ..86 C5
Drive The Acle NR13 ..166 D4
　East Winch PE32 ......45 A2
　Norwich NR5 ....161 B8
　Trowse with Newton
　NR14 ....163 D1
Drout's La IP31 .....127 C3
Drove The
　Brandon IP27 ....114 D4
　Raynham NR21 ....30 E4
　Taverham NR8 ....155 C2
Drovers Rest NR15 ..108 C8
Drudge Rd NR31 ......94 C8
Druids La Litcham PE32 ..48 A4
　Shelfanger IP22 ......120 B2
Druids' La IP22 ......120 A3
Drunken Dro PE32 ...46 C8
Drury Cl IP20 ....161 B8
Drury La
　5 Castle Acre PE32 ...46 F2
　6 Loddon NR14 ......91 F1

Duck's Foot Rd IP21 ..121 F6
Duckett Cl 2 NR1 ....162 E1
Duff Rd NR3 ....158 D2
Duffield Cres NR9 ....51 A4
Dugard Ave NR1 .....163 B8
Duke Rd NR31 ......170 D6
Duke St Norwich NR3 ..178 A4
　Wisbech PE13 ....152 D4
Duke's La NR17 .....102 E8
Dukesway 1 NR35 ...123 F8
Dulgate La PE37 ....153 D2
Dulgate Rd NR35 ....108 B3
Dull's Rd NR35 .....109 C5
Dumbs La NR10 ......53 E5
Dumpling Gn
　Dereham NR19 ....68 A6
　East Dereham NR19 ..154 F2
Dun Cow Gdns PE34 ..144 E7
Dun Cow Rd NR34 ...111 B4
Dunburgh Rd NR34 ..110 A2
Dunbury Cl PE33 ....79 A4
Duncan Cl 6 NR30 ...169 D2
Duncan Rd IP24 .....102 A2
Dunford La IP24 ....102 A2
Dunhill La IP22 ....127 F1
Dunkirk NR11 ....150 D8
Dunlop Rd NR19 ....154 B6
Dunnett Cl NR17 ...174 E5
Dunnetts Cl IP25 ....84 A7
Dunning's La IP21 ..121 E6
Dunns La NR21 ....4 D1
Dunsmore Dr PE30 ..133 B1
Dunwood Dr NR6 ...158 D7
Durbidge's Hill IP22 ..120 E1
Durham Ave NR31 ...170 B2
Durham Rd NR31 ...170 B2
Durham St NR2 .....162 B4
Durham Way IP24 ...176 A5
Dussindale 8 NR18 ..173 C6
Dussindale Dr 18 NR7 ..72 D4
Duverlin Cl 2 NR8 ...162 A1
Dyball's La NR12 .....38 F8
Dye's Rd NR13 ....73 C7
Dyers Rd NR13 ......73 A3
Dyers Yd NR3 ....178 A3
Dyes The NR20 ....33 E8

E

Eade Rd NR3 ....162 D8
Eagle Cl NR11 ....21 B2
Eagle House Sch
　NR16 ....119 E7
Eagle Rd NR11 ....21 B2
Eagle Wlk 2 NR2 ....162 C4
Eagles Ct NR23 .....136 E6
Eagles The 3 NR30 ..169 D4
Earl Cl PE31 ....140 C3
Earl of Brandon Ave
　PE31 ....30 B3
Earl Rd NR13 ....72 E8
Earl Warren IP24 ....116 C5
Earlham Gr NR5 .....161 B7
Earlham High Sch
　NR4 ....161 D5
Earlham Rd NR4 ....161 C5
Earlham W Ctr 5 NR5 ..161 C6
Earls' St IP24 ......176 D4
Earlsford Rd IP23 ...129 D1
Earnshaw Ct NR1 ...163 D5
Earsham CE VA Fst Sch
　NR35 ....123 F8
Earsham Dr PE30 ...147 D8
Earsham Rd NR35 ...108 E2
Earth La NR32 ....94 C1
East Anglia Transport Mus*
　NR33 ....111 F1
East Anglian Way
　NR31 ....170 C6
East Ave NR13 ......165 E3
East Bank PE12 ......41 C8
East Bilney Hall NR20 ..49 A6
East Carleton Rd NR14 ..89 A4
East Cres NR30 ....50 B5
East Dereham Sta
　NR20 ....154 E5
East End Cl NR30 ...168 C8
East End Rd NR30 ..168 E8
East Farm La NR10 ..53 E3
East Gn NR9 ....68 F2
East Gr NR27 ....139 C5
East Harbour Way
　PE31 ....135 E7
East Harling Prim Sch
　NR16 ....118 C5
East Harling Rd NR16 ..118 F4
East Hills Rd NR5 ...156 E1
East La PE31 ....14 D8
East Norfolk 6th Form Coll
　NR31 ....170 C5
East Rd
　Great Yarmouth NR30 ..169 D5
　Watton IP25 ....84 E6
East Ruston Area Com Sch
　NR12 ....38 F7
East Ruston Old Vicarage
　Gdn* NR12 ....24 A3
East Ruston Rd NR28 ..38 D5
East Winch CE Prim Sch
　PE32 ....44 F3
East Winch Rd
　Leziate PE32 ....44 F5
　Middleton PE32 ....44 E5
East Winchcommon (Nature
　Reserve)* PE32 ....45 A2

Eastbourne Pl NR1 ....178 C3
Easterley Way NR29 ..167 A7
Eastern Ave
　Caister-on-Sea NR30 ..168 E6
　Norwich NR7 ....72 D4
Eastern Cl
　Caister-on-Sea NR30 ..168 C5
　82 Norwich NR7 ......72 D4
　Norwich NR7 ....72 D4
Eastern Rd NR7 ......72 D4
Eastfen Dro IP26 ....114 B6
Eastfield NR8 ....156 D8
Eastfield Cl PE30 ....147 A6
Eastfield Rd
　Hickling NR12 ....39 F2
　Long Stratton NR15 ..106 F4
　1 Wisbech PE13 .....152 E7
Eastfield Way PE13 ..152 C6
Eastfields
　King's Lynn PE30 ....147 C4
　Roughton PE32 ....63 C7
Eastgate IP25 ....67 D3
Eastgate Dro
　Congham PE31 ....28 D2
　Grimston PE32 ....45 D8
　Hillington PE31 ....28 C3
Eastgate Prim Sch
　NR30 ....146 E5
Eastgate Rd PE36 ....2 A6
Eastgate St
　2 King's Lynn PE30 ..146 E5
　North Elmham NR20 ..49 E7
　Shouldham PE33 ......62 D4
Easthaugh Rd NR9 ...51 D4
Easthill La NR14 .....90 E8
Eastland Cl NR17 ...174 F6
Eastlands Bank PE14 ..41 E5
Eastleigh Gdns 6 NR9 ..69 F2
Eastmans La NR9 ....28 C1
Eastmoor Cl PE33 ...81 E4
Eastmoor Rd PE33 ...81 C7
Easton Coll NR9 .....70 C4
Easton Way NR10 ....35 C1
Eastwood PE31 .....134 F3
Eaton Chase NR4 ...161 E2
Eaton Dro
　Sedgeford PE36 ....13 A7
　Snettisham PE31 ......12 F5
Eaton Gdns NR19 ...154 E3
Eaton Hall Specl Sch
　NR4 ....161 F3
Eaton Rd NR4 ....162 B2
Eaton St Cringleford NR4 ..89 B8
　Norwich NR4 ....72 D4
Eau Brink Rd PE34 ..43 A2
Ebbisham Dr NR4 ...161 F1
Ebble Cl PE30 ......148 C2
Ebenezer Pl NR3 ...178 A4
Eccles CE Prim Sch
　NR16 ....118 F8
Eccles Rd NR25 .....137 C7
Eccles Rd Sta NR16 ..103 E1
Ecclestone Cl NR31 ..170 A4
Eckersley Dr NR21 ..141 A6
Ecotech Ctr* PE37 ..153 B6
Edderthorpe St NR1 ..178 C4
Ecton Wlk 6 PE14 ...59 A1
Eddington Way NR9 ..70 B5
Eden Cl
　Bacton/Walcott NR12 ..23 A4
　Norwich NR7 ....163 C6
Eden La NR17 ....174 D5
Edenside Dr NR17 ...174 D5
Edge Bank PE14 ......77 F8
Edge's La NR15 .....107 A3
Edgebrook NR26 ....138 D6
Edgefield Cl NR6 ...158 F7
Edgefield Hill NR25 ..137 C2
Edgefield Rd NR24 ..142 E5
Edgehill 4 NR7 ....72 D4
Edges La 2 NR15 ...106 E3
Edgeworth Rd 6 NR5 ..161 C6
Edinburgh Ave
　Great Yarmouth NR30 ..170 B2
　King's Lynn PE30 ....147 C7
Edinburgh Cl
　6 Barnham IP24 .....125 F6
　Caister-on-Sea NR30 ..168 E5
　18 Wisbech IP25 .....84 D3
Edinburgh Ct 7 PE30 ..146 E5
Edinburgh Dr
　Fakenham NR21 ......141 C6
　1 Wisbech PE13 .....152 C8
Edinburgh Pl
　Great Yarmouth NR30 ..169 B3
　1 Wiggenhall St Germans
　PE34 ....43 B1
Edinburgh Rd
　Holt NR25 ....137 C5
Edinburgh Way
　Dersingham PE31 ....140 D3
　Thetford IP24 ....176 A5
Edison Way NR31 ...170 A8
Edith Cavell Cl 5 IP24 ..176 C7
Edma St PE31 ....146 E6
Edmondson Wlk NR11 ..21 A4
Edmund Bacon Ct 1
　NR3 ....162 D8
Edmund Rd IP27 ....175 A2
Edrich Cl NR13 .....165 E6
Edrich Way NR5 ....160 F7
Edward Benefer Way
　King's Lynn PE30 ....146 D6
　North Wootton PE30 ..26 E1

Edward Gambling Ct 8
NR2 . . . . .162 B8
Edward Rd NR29 . . . . .58 B5
Edward Sago Pl NR15 . .90 E2
Edward St
10 King's Lynn PE30 . . . .146 E3
Norwich NR3 . . . . .178 B4
Edward Worlledge Mid Sch
NR31 . . . . .169 C2
Edwards Cl NR20 . . . . .50 B5
Edwards Rd NR7 . . . . . . .159 A5
Edwin Cl NR18 . . . . .173 B5
Eels Foot Rd NR29 . . . . . . .57 E1
Egmere Medieval Village of*
NR22 . . . . .16 B8
Egmere Rd NR22 . . . . .16 F8
Egremont Rd IP22 . . . . .177 B5
Eighth Ave PE13 . . . . .152 E4
El Alamein Way NR31 . . .94 C8
Elan Cl NR18 . . . . .173 D3
Elden's La IP26 . . . . .98 F5
Elder Gn NR31 . . . . .170 B5
Elder La PE13 . . . . .45 C8
Elderberry Dr 5 NR20 . . . .68 A8
Elderbush La NR29 . . . . . .56 C7
Elders The IP27 . . . . .113 F1
Elderton La NR28 . . . . .22 B5
Eleanor Rd NR1 . . . . .162 D3
Eleven Mile Rd NR18 . . . .87 C1
Elgin IP24 . . . . .176 A5
Elgood's Brewery & Gdn*
PE13 . . . . .152 A4
Eliot Cl IP24 . . . . .176 E6
Elise Way NR18 . . . . .173 D2
Elizabeth Ave
Downham Market PE38 . . .172 B5
Fakenham NR21 . . . . .141 C6
Norwich NR7 . . . . .163 F7
Elizabeth Cl
Attleborough NR17 . . . . . .174 C6
East Dereham NR19 . . . . . .154 D1
Hunstanton PE36 . . . . .132 C3
Norwich NR7 . . . . .159 A5
Reepham NR10 . . . . .149 B4
Elizabeth Cres
Caister-on-Sea NR30 . . . . .168 E6
4 Holt NR25 . . . . .137 C5
Elizabeth Dr NR7 . . . . . . .65 F3
Elizabeth Fry Cl 9
IP24 . . . . .176 D7
Elizabeth Fry Rd NR2 . .161 F4
Elizabeth Rd
Brandon IP27 . . . . .175 C3
10 Poringland NR14 . . . . . .90 D5
Elizabeth Terr PE13 . . . .152 D4
Elizabeth Watling Cl 3
IP24 . . . . .176 D7
Elizabeth Way 5 IP23 . .130 C1
Elizabeth Wlk 27 IP20 . .122 D2
Elizabethan House Mus*
NR30 . . . . .169 C3
Elkins Rd NR18 . . . . .173 B5
Ella Rd NR1 . . . . .163 A6
Ellcar Rise 4 NR4 . . . . . .161 F1
Ellenhill NR27 . . . . .139 D5
Eller Dr PE33 . . . . .43 E2
Ellingham Prim Sch
NR35 . . . . .109 D3
Ellingham Rd
Attleborough NR17 . . . . . .174 B7
Scoulton NR9 . . . . .85 E3
Ellinor Rd NR28 . . . . .151 D3
Ellis Cl 24 NR12 . . . . .39 B4
Ellison Cl NR17 . . . . .174 E4
Ellison Dr NR17 . . . . .174 E4
Elm Ave NR31 . . . . .170 C4
Elm CE Jun Sch PE14 . . .59 B1
Elm Cl Acle NR13 . . . . . . .166 C4
Brandon IP27 . . . . .175 E3
Downham Market PE38 . . .172 B6
King's Lynn PE30 . . . . .148 D2
5 Lingwood NR13 . . . . . . .74 A3
7 Loddon NR14 . . . . .91 F1
Mulbarton NR14 . . . . .89 B3
North Elmham NR20 . . . . . .49 E8
Norwich NR5 . . . . .156 F2
Yaxham NR19 . . . . .68 A5
Elm Gr
Garboldisham IP22 . . . . . .128 A8
Sheringham NR26 . . . . .138 E5
Elm Gr La NR3 . . . . .158 D2
Elm High Rd PE14 . . . . . .152 E1
Elm Hill NR3 . . . . .178 B3
Elm La NR13 . . . . .30 D8
Elm Low Rd PE14 . . . . . .152 D2
Elm Pk NR19 . . . . .154 C1
Elm Rd
Caister-on-Sea NR30 . . . . .168 E4
Lingwood NR13 . . . . .74 A3
Marham PE33 . . . . .63 B4
Thetford IP24 . . . . .176 B1
Wisbech PE13 . . . . .152 D3
Elm Rd Prim Sch
PE13 . . . . .152 D4
Elm Terr 2 NR18 . . . . . . .173 C4
Elmdon Ct 9 NR1 . . . . . .163 A6
Elmer's La NR15 . . . . . . .107 A8
Elmfield Dr PE14 . . . . .59 B1
Elmgrove Rd NR31 . . . . .170 C3
Elmham Rd
Beetley NR20 . . . . .49 D4
North Elmham NR20 . . . . . .50 A7
Elmhurst Cl NR31 . . . . . .170 C3
Elmhurst Dr PE30 . . . . . .148 C2

Elms Cl 6 NR35 . . . . .123 F8
Elms Rd NR34 . . . . .110 E5
Elms The
Hindringham NR21 . . . . . . .17 E6
Norwich NR6 . . . . .158 E6
Elmside PE14 . . . . .59 D1
Elmstead Rd PE30 . . . . . .147 C4
Elmtree Gr PE33 . . . . .43 E1
Elsden Cl 2 NR25 . . . . . .137 C5
Elsie Rd NR31 . . . . .169 B3
Elsing Dr PE30 . . . . .147 D8
Elsing La
Bawdeswell NR20 . . . . .50 E6
Dereham NR20 . . . . .50 C1
Elsing Rd Lyng NR9 . . . . .51 A5
North Tuddenham NR20 . . .50 E2
Swanton Morley NR20 . . . . .50 C4
Elstead Cl 11 NR4 . . . . . . .89 C8
Elveden Cl NR4 . . . . .161 F1
Elveden Rd IP24 . . . . .125 D6
Elvin Rd NR19 . . . . .154 D6
Elvin Way 3 NR3 . . . . . . .157 F1
Elvina Rd NR10 . . . . .54 A2
Elvington PE30 . . . . .147 D5
Elworthy Cl IP25 . . . . .84 F3
Elwyn Rd 7 NR1 . . . . . . .162 E2
Ely Cl 7 PE13 . . . . .152 C5
Ely Rd Denver PE38 . . . . .172 D2
Hilgay PE38 . . . . .97 B8
Ely Row PE14 . . . . .42 B1
Ely St NR2 . . . . .162 C7
Ely Way IP24 . . . . .176 A5
Embry Cl NR6 . . . . .158 D6
Embry Cres NR6 . . . . .158 C6
Emelson Cl NR19 . . . . . . .154 D6
Emery Cl 1 NR30 . . . . . . .168 D5
Emery's La NR11 . . . . .21 B6
Emmanuel Ave NR31 . . .170 B2
Emmas Way NR13 . . . . . . .73 B6
Emmerich Ct 6 PE30 . . .146 E5
Emms's La NR21 . . . . .17 A1
Enneth Prim Sch PE14 . . .59 D2
Emorsgate PE34 . . . . .42 B7
Empire Ave PE30 . . . . . . .147 B8
Empress Rd NR31 . . . . . .169 B3
Empsons Loke NR29 . . . .58 B6
End Lodge PE31 . . . . .133 C5
Enfield Rd NR5 . . . . .161 C6
Engine Rd Hilgay PE38 . . .96 F7
Sculthorpe Airfield NR21 . .15 D2
England's La NR31 . . . . . .170 C4
Englands Rd NR13 . . . . . .166 B4
English Rd NR6 . . . . .158 C5
Ennerdale Rd PE30 . . . . .148 F2
Enterprise Way
Fakenham NR21 . . . . .141 C5
King's Lynn PE33 . . . . .43 E4
Wisbech PE13 . . . . .152 A2
Entrance La NR15 . . . . . . .90 E2
Enue 10 PE33 . . . . .63 B4
Eppingham Cl IP24 . . . . .176 F6
Epsom Gdns NR19 . . . . . .154 E3
Erica Way NR31 . . . . .170 B6
Erins The 1 NR6 . . . . .158 E1
Eriswell Dr IP27 . . . . .113 E1
Erpingham Ct PE36 . . . . .132 D7
Erpingham Prim Sch
NR11 . . . . .21 B2
Estelle St 9 NR31 . . . . . .162 D8
Esplanade NR27 . . . . .139 B7
Esplanade The
Hemsby NR29 . . . . .167 E5
Sheringham NR26 . . . . .138 C7
Esprit Cl NR18 . . . . .173 D2
Essex St NR2 . . . . .162 C5
Estcourt Rd
2 Attleborough NR17 . . . .174 C5
Great Yarmouth NR30 . . . .169 D6
Estelle Way NR18 . . . . . .173 E6
Estuary Cl PE30 . . . . .146 E7
Estuary Rd PE30 . . . . . . .146 D7
Ethel Colman Way
IP24 . . . . .176 D7
Ethel Gooch Rd NR18 . .173 B5
Ethel Rd NR1 . . . . .163 A5
Ethel Terr 5 PE30 . . . . . .146 E3
Ethel Tipple Cl NR11 . . .150 C4
Ethel Tipple Dr NR11 . . .150 C4
Ethel Tipple Specl Sch
PO30 . . . . .147 D4
Eurocentre Ind Est
NR30 . . . . .169 B4
Europa Way
Norwich NR1 . . . . .163 A2
Wisbech PE13 . . . . .152 B2
Euston Hall * IP24 . . . . .126 B5
Euston Rd NR30 . . . . .169 D4
Euston Way PE30 . . . . . . .148 D1
Euximoor Dro PE14 . . . . .77 B1
Eva Cl 4 IP25 . . . . .67 B2
Eva Rd NR13 . . . . .72 E7
Evans Gdns PE36 . . . . . . .132 D3
Evans Lombe Cl NR29 . . .57 A4
Evans Way NR6 . . . . .158 D6
Evelyn Cl IP21 . . . . .131 A3
Evelyn Way 4 NR30 . . . .147 A8
Eversley Rd NR6 . . . . .158 B4
Everson Cl
Norwich NR5 . . . . .157 C1
1 Tasburgh NR15 . . . . . .106 F6
Ewing Cl NR10 . . . . .149 B4
Excalibur Rd 2 NR31 . . .170 B1
Exchange Rd 7 NR15 . . .89 C1
Exchange Sq PE13 . . . . . .152 B5
Exchange St
Attleborough NR17 . . . . . .174 D5
32 Harleston IP20 . . . . . .122 D2

Exchange St continued
Norwich NR2 . . . . .178 A3
Exeter Cres PE30 . . . . . . .148 D5
Exeter Rd NR31 . . . . .170 B4
Exeter St NR2 . . . . .162 C7
Exeter Way 2 IP24 . . . . .176 F5
Exmouth Cl 2 NR9 . . . . . .88 D8
Exmouth Pl 11 NR30 . . .169 D4
Exmouth Rd NR30 . . . . . .169 D1
Exton's Gdns PE30 . . . . .146 F3
Exton's Pl PE30 . . . . .147 A3
Exton's Rd PE30 . . . . .146 F4
Eye Airfield Ind Est
IP23 . . . . .130 B2
Eye La PE31 . . . . .30 B7
Eye Rd IP23 . . . . .130 A1

F

Factory La IP22 . . . . .177 B5
Factory Rd NR30 . . . . . . .169 D5
Faeroes Dr NR30 . . . . . . .168 C6
Fair Cl Beccles NR34 . . . .110 D1
18 Feltwell IP26 . . . . .98 E1
Fair Gn IP22 . . . . .177 C4
Fairfax Dr 6 Norwich NR7 .72 D4
3 Weeting IP27 . . . . .114 E1
Fairfax Rd NR4 . . . . .161 F4
Fairfield Cl
Great & Little Plumstead
NR13 . . . . .73 B7
Mundesley NR11 . . . . .143 C6
Fairfield Dr NR17 . . . . . .174 C4
Fairfield Rd
Downham Market PE38 . . .172 A5
5 Middleton PE32 . . . . . . .44 B3
1 Stoke Ferry PE33 . . . . .81 A3
Fairfield Way 11 IP26 . . . .98 E1
Fairfields Cawston NR10 . .35 D2
Thetford IP24 . . . . .176 D5
Fairfields Way NR11 . . . .36 D4
Fairhaven CE VA Prim Sch
NR13 . . . . .74 B8
Fairhaven Ct NR2 . . . . . .162 A6
Fairhaven Woodland & Water
Gdns* NR13 . . . . .74 A8
Fairhill Dro PE33 . . . . .80 E2
Fairholme Cl IP25 . . . . . . .84 A8
Fairholme Rd NR30 . . . . .53 E4
Fairisle Dr NR30 . . . . . . .168 C5
Fairland St NR18 . . . . . . .173 C3
Fairmile Cl NR2 . . . . .162 B3
Fairstead Cl
North Walsham NR28 . . . .151 A3
Pulham Market IP21 . . . . .121 E5
Fairstead Ct NR7 . . . . . . .159 A3
Fairstead Dro NR30 . . . . .62 D4
Fairstead La
Hempnall NR15 . . . . .107 A5
Little Cressingham IP25 . . .83 D3
Fairstead Prim Sch
PE30 . . . . .147 D4
Fairstead Rd NR7 . . . . . .159 A3
Fairstead The
Botesdale IP22 . . . . .128 E3
2 Cley next the Sea NR25 . . .7 E6
Fairview Rd NR28 . . . . . .151 D6
Scottow NR10 . . . . .37 B6
Fairview Cl NR1 . . . . .157 A7
Fairview Dr NR21 . . . . . . .31 E5
Fairview Rd NR28 . . . . . .151 E4
Fairway NR30 . . . . .168 E3
Fairway Fst Sch NR4 . . . . .162 A1
Fairway Mid Sch NR4 . . . .162 A1
Fairway The NR31 . . . . . .171 D8
Fairways Norwich NR6 . .157 F5
Stuston IP21 . . . . .130 B5
Fakenham Coll NR21 . . .141 B6
Fakenham High Sch
NR21 . . . . .141 B6
Fakenham Hill IP31 . . . .126 C2
Fakenham Jun Sch
NR21 . . . . .141 C4
Fakenham Mus*
NR21 . . . . .141 B3
Fakenham Race Course
NR21 . . . . .141 D2
Fakenham Rd
Attlebridge NR9 . . . . .52 C2
Beetley NR20 . . . . .49 C5
Briston NR24 . . . . .142 C5
Docking PE31 . . . . .134 E4
East Rudham PE31 . . . . .30 A7
Foxley NR20 . . . . .33 C1
Great Snoring NR21 . . . . . .17 A5
Ryburgh NR21 . . . . .32 A6
Sculthorpe NR21 . . . . .141 A5
South Creake NR21 . . . . . . .15 C6
Sparham NR9 . . . . .51 A6
Taverham NR8 . . . . .155 B2
Tittleshall PE32 . . . . .48 C7
Fakenham View NR21 . . .31 E5
Fakes Rd NR29 . . . . .167 D6
Falcon Ave PE30 . . . . . . .177 F5
Falcon Cl 18 NR30 . . . . . .169 C4
Falcon La Bungay NR35 . .124 B7
20 Wisbech PE13 . . . . . .152 C5
Falcon Mews NR7 . . . . . .159 C3
Falcon Mid Sch NR7 . . .159 C3
Falcon Rd 14 Feltwell IP26 .98 E1
Norwich NR7 . . . . .159 C3
Pulham Market IP21 . . . . .121 C6
17 Wisbech PE13 . . . . . .152 C5
Falcon Rd E NR7 . . . . . . .159 C2

Falcon Rd W NR7 . . . . . .159 C4
Falconers Chase NR18 . .173 F5
Falgate NR10 . . . . .35 C2
Falkland Cl NR6 . . . . .157 D5
Falkland Way 15 NR31 . . .94 C6
Falklands Dr PE13 . . . . . .152 E3
Falklands Rd PE12 . . . . . .41 A8
Fall Gn NR14 . . . . .90 D4
Fallow Pipe Rd PE34 . . . .43 B2
Fallowfield
4 Hemsby NR29 . . . . . . .167 B7
8 Poringland NR14 . . . . . .90 C5
Fallowfield Cl NR1 . . . . .163 B8
Fallows The 3 NR8 . . . . .155 D2
Faraday Pl IP24 . . . . .176 B2
Faraday Rd NR31 . . . . . . .170 A8
Fardell Rd 7 PE13 . . . . . .152 E4
Fareborther Way 2
NR19 . . . . .154 C3
Farm Cl Lingwood NR13 . .74 A2
11 Loddon NR14 . . . . .92 A2
Farm Ct St PE20 . . . . .123 A1
Farm La NR13 . . . . .56 A1
Farm Rd
Heckingham NR14 . . . . .92 D1
Worstead NR28 . . . . .38 A7
Farm View NR28 . . . . . . .151 E5
Farm Wlk Marham PE33 . .63 C5
6 Necton PE37 . . . . .65 F4
Farman Ct NR28 . . . . .151 D5
Farman Cl 5 Belton NR31 .94 A6
Lyng NR9 . . . . .51 A3
7 Salhouse NR13 . . . . . . .55 A1
Farmers Ave NR1 . . . . . .178 B2
Farmland Rd NR5 . . . . . .156 F1
Farmway 7 NR19 . . . . . . .154 D2
Farnborough Rd 9 IP25 .84 F3
Farrow Cl
2 Great Moulton NR15 . .106 B1
2 Mattishall NR20 . . . . . .68 E6
2 Swanton Morley NR20 . .50 B3
Farthing Cl Diss IP22 . . .177 D6
Loddon NR14 . . . . .109 D8
Farthing Dro
Beck Row, Holywell
Row & Kenny Hill IP27 . . .112 E2
Lakenheath IP27 . . . . .113 A2
Southery PE38 . . . . .97 A2
Farthing Rd PE38 . . . . . . .79 B5
Farthing Way 1 NR30 . . .168 C6
Fastolf Cl NR6 . . . . .157 E5
Fastolff Ave NR30 . . . . . .170 B3
Fayers Terr PE30 . . . . . . .147 A4
Fayregreen NR21 . . . . . . .141 D4
Feale Abbey PE34 . . . . . .144 A1
Fearn's Cl NR27 . . . . .139 D5
Featherstone Ct 5
NR10 . . . . .149 B4
Felbrigg Cl PE30 . . . . . . .148 F1
Felbrigg Hall Garden &
Park* NR11 . . . . .10 B2
Felbrigg Rd
Downham Market PE38 . . .172 C6
Norwich NR11 . . . . .21 D8
Fell Way 9 NR31 . . . . .94 C8
Fellowes Dr 2 NR31 . . . . .94 C6
Fellowes Rd NR9 . . . . .69 E6
Fellows Cl NR5 . . . . .161 D6
Felmingham Rd NR28 . . .37 C7
Felsham Way NR8 . . . . . .155 E2
Feltham Cl PE13 . . . . .152 E5
Felthorpe Rd NR9 . . . . . . .52 B3
Feltwell Elementary Sch
IP26 . . . . .98 D1
Feltwell Prim Sch IP26 . .98 E2
Feltwell Rd
Hockwold cum Wilton
IP26 . . . . .113 F7
Methwold IP26 . . . . .99 B8
Southery PE38 . . . . .97 D5
Fen Cl PE13 . . . . .152 E6
Fen Dro PE33 . . . . .81 F3
Fen Folgate 6 IP25 . . . . . .67 B2
Fen La Banham NR16 . . . .118 B8
Beccles NR34 . . . . .110 D2
Ditchingham NR35 . . . . . .108 E3
Garboldisham IP22 . . . . . .128 A7
Grimston PE32 . . . . .45 A7
Harling NR16 . . . . .118 C6
Leziate PE32 . . . . .45 A6
Fen St
Attleborough NR17 . . . . . .103 F3
Old Buckenham NR17 . . . .104 C2
Redgrave IP22 . . . . .128 E5
Rocklands NR17 . . . . .103 B6
Fen View
Christchurch PE14 . . . . . . .95 A7
East Dereham NR19 . . . . . .154 A7
Fen Way 2 PE14 . . . . .59 E1
Fence Bank PE14 . . . . .78 E6
Fendyke Rd PE14 . . . . .59 A1
Fengate Heacham PE31 . .133 C4
Marsham NR10 . . . . .150 D1
Fengate Dro IP27 . . . . . . .175 B6
Fengate Rd PE30 . . . . . . .147 B7

Fenland Rd
King's Lynn PE30 . . . . .147 C8
Wisbech PE13 . . . . .152 E6
Fenn Cres NR3 . . . . .158 B1
Fennel Way IP24 . . . . .176 F4
Fenner Rd NR30 . . . . .170 E7
Fenside PE31 . . . . .133 C4
Fenway PE31 . . . . .133 B3
Ferguson Way NR17 . . . .174 F7
Fermoy Ave PE30 . . . . . . .147 B5
Fern Cct 13 NR13 . . . . . . .173 B4
Fern Dr NR28 . . . . .151 E5
Fern Gdns NR31 . . . . .93 F5
Fern Hill
Dersingham PE31 . . . . .140 E4
Norwich NR3 . . . . .163 B5
Ferndale Cl NR6 . . . . .157 E4
Fernlea Rd PE33 . . . . .147 C4
Ferrier Cl 7 NR30 . . . . . .169 D5
Ferrier Rd NR30 . . . . .169 C5
Ferry Bank PE38 . . . . .97 A4
Ferry Farm NR29 . . . . .75 A5
Ferry Hill NR31 . . . . .170 D7
Ferry La
Great Yarmouth NR31 . . . .169 C2
Norwich NR1 . . . . .178 C3
Postwick with Witton
NR13 . . . . .73 A2
Stokesby with Herringby
NR29 . . . . .75 B5
Ferry Rd
Carleton St Peter NR14 . . .91 E5
Clenchwarton PE34 . . . . . .145 F5
Horning NR12 . . . . .55 E3
King's Lynn PE34 . . . . .146 B6
Norton Subcourse NR14 . . .92 D2
Norwich NR1 . . . . .81 D3
Oxborough PE33 . . . . .81 D3
Reedham NR13 . . . . .92 E4
Surlingham NR14 . . . . .165 A1
Woodbastwick NR13 . . . . .55 D2
Ferry Sq PE34 . . . . .146 C5
Ferry St PE30 . . . . .146 D5
Ferry View Rd NR12 . . . . .55 E3
Ferryboat La NR31 . . . . . .170 D7
Ferrygate La NR29 . . . . . .57 D5
Fersfield Rd
Bressingham IP22 . . . . . . .129 B8
Kenninghall NR16 . . . . . . .119 C4
South Lopham IP22 . . . . . .128 F8
Festival Cl PE30 . . . . .50 B7
Festival Rd NR30 . . . . . . .169 C5
Festival Way CB6 . . . . . . .96 E2
Ffolkes Dr
King's Lynn PE30 . . . . .148 C1
Terrington St Clement
PE34 . . . . .144 B5
Ffolkes Pl 1 PE33 . . . . . . .61 D4
Fiddle Wood Rd NR6 . . . .158 D4
Field Barn Cotts PE32 . . .46 E3
Field Barn La PE33 . . . . . .61 F3
Field Dalling Rd
Gunthorpe NR21 . . . . .18 B8
Field End Cl PE30 . . . . . . .147 B6
Field House Gdns
IP22 . . . . .177 E5
Field La Beetley NR20 . . .49 C5
10 Blofield NR13 . . . . . . .73 D6
Blofield NR13 . . . . .165 E8
Fakenham NR21 . . . . .141 B6
Hempnall NR15 . . . . .107 C4
King's Lynn PE30 . . . . .147 B6
Marsham NR10 . . . . .36 B2
North Walsham NR28 . . . .151 E3
Stody NR24 . . . . .142 F8
Whinburgh & Westfield
NR19 . . . . .67 F4
Wretton PE33 . . . . .80 F3
Field Rd Brandon IP27 . . .114 D4
King's Lynn PE30 . . . . .147 B5
Ringland NR8 . . . . .70 B8
South Walsham NR13 . . . .74 B8
Stalham NR12 . . . . .39 C3
Fieldbarn Dro PE33 . . . . . .82 A4
Fieldbarn Rd PE33 . . . . . .81 B8
Fieldfare Cl 3 NR12 . . . . . .39 C3
Fields Rd NR34 . . . . .110 E6
Fields The
Forncett NR16 . . . . .105 E5
Hingham NR9 . . . . .86 C5
Fieldview NR5 . . . . .161 E6
Fiennes Rd 4 NR7 . . . . . . .72 D5
Fifth Ave PE13 . . . . .152 E4
Fifty Dro CB6 . . . . .95 F3
Fifty Rd PE14 . . . . .95 A5
Filbert Rd NR14 . . . . .91 F1
Filby Cl PE30 . . . . .147 D5
Filby Cl NR29 . . . . .75 F8
Filby Fst Sch NR29 . . . . . .75 F8
Filby La NR29 . . . . .167 A1
Filby Rd Coltishall NR10 . .37 B2
Stokesby with Herringby
NR29 . . . . .75 C6
Finch Cl Cromer NR27 . . .139 B6
Finch Way NR10 . . . . .159 D2
Norwich NR7 . . . . .159 D2
Fincham Dro PE32 . . . . . . .64 B5
Fincham Rd
Barton Bendish PE33 . . . . .81 A8
Crimplesham PE33 . . . . . . .80 A8

Fincham Rd continued
Fincham PE33 ....63 A1
Shouldham Thorpe PE33 ...62 C2
Stow Bardolph PE34 ......79 F8
Wereham PE33 ....80 F6
Finchdale Cl 5 PE30 ..148 C4
Finchley Ct 4 NR2 .....162 B7
Finderne Dr NR18 .....173 D6
Finishers Rd 8 NR6 ....158 C1
Finisterre Rise 2 NR30 .168 C6
Finkelgate NR1 ....178 B1
Finningham Rd IP22 ...128 E1
Finsbury Cl 1 PE38 ...172 B4
Fiona Cl NR18 ....173 E6
Fir Cl Heacham PE31 ....133 C6
Mundford IP26 ....100 B4
Fir Covert Rd
Carleton Rode NR16 ....105 A1
Taverham NR10 ....155 B4
Fir Gr NR26 ....138 D4
Fir La NR10 ....34 A1
Fir Pk IP25 ....84 A7
Fir Rd IP24 ....176 B1
Fir Tree Dr 7 PE33 ....43 E2
Firethorn Cl NR8 ......155 B2
Firman Ct NR7 ....163 F8
Firs Ave NR29 ....167 A3
Firs La NR12 ....39 C2
Firs Rd Hethersett NR9 ...88 D7
Norwich NR6 ....157 F6
Firs The
Downham Market PE38 ..172 D6
Lakenheath IP27 ....113 F1
Firs Way IP27 ....175 C2
Firside Mid Sch NR6 ...158 A6
First Ave PE13 ....152 D5
First Dro IP27 ....113 C3
First Marsh Rd PE13 ...59 A6
Firtree Cl NR13 ....165 B4
Firtree Rd NR7 ....159 E1
Firwood Cl NR1 ....163 C8
Fish Wharf 2 NR30 ...169 D1
Fisher Ave NR30 ......169 D8
Fisher Rd Diss IP22 ...177 E4
Fakenham NR21 ....141 B5
Fisher Row NR32 ......111 F4
Fisher Way IP24 ......176 E5
Fisher's La IP21 ......131 A4
Fishergate NR3 ....178 B4
Fisherman's Her Ctr*
NR26 ....138 D8
Fishermen's Ct NR17 ..174 D6
Fishers Cl NR5 ....156 E1
Fishers La Beetley NR20 ..49 D6
Norwich NR2 ....178 A3
Fishers' Quay 5 NR30 .169 C4
Fishley View NR13 ....166 B4
Fiske's Opening 6
NR31 ....170 D4
Fiskes Ct NR14 ....89 F5
Fison Way IP24 ....176 C6
Fison Way Ind Est
IP24 ....176 C6
Fitton Rd PE34 ....61 B8
Fitzalan Cl 8 NR30 ...169 C4
Fitzgerald Rd
Norwich NR1 ....162 E1
7 Poringland NR14 ....90 C5
Fitzhenry Mews 5 NR5 .161 B8
Fitzwalter Rd IP22 ....177 E4
Five Acre La NR35 ....123 E7
Five Acres NR14 ......89 F4
Five Alls Rd PE14 .....41 F1
Five Crossways NR12 ..164 D8
Five Elms 4 PE30 ....147 C4
Flag St NR21 ....15 C2
Flaxlands NR16 ....105 B4
Flaxlands Rd NR16 ....105 C3
Fleet La NR13 ....56 B1
Fleet Rd NR8 ....156 B6
Fleetwood Dr 4 NR13 ..72 D4
Flegg Gn PE33 ....80 D8
Flegg High Sch NR29 ..57 E6
Fleggburgh Prim Sch
NR29 ....75 C8
Fleggburgh Rd NR29 ..57 C2
Fleming Ct 3 IP25 ....84 D3
Fletcher Cl NR12 .....55 A8
Fletcher Way
Acle NR13 ....166 D4
Cromer NR27 ....139 B5
Norwich NR3 ....158 C3
Flint Dr NR23 ....136 D5
Flint Gate 6 PE12 ....41 B8
Flint House Gdns 8 NR9 .88 C7
Flint House Rd PE14 ...77 F1
Flint Way 2 PE14 .....77 A8
Flitcham Abbey PE31 ..28 D5
Flitcham CE Prim Sch
PE31 ....28 C5
Flixton Marsh La
NR32 ....111 F6
Flixton Rd
Bungay NR35 ....124 A7
Flixton NR35 ....123 E6
Lound NR32 ....94 C1
St Margaret, South Elmham
IP20 ....123 E3
Somerleyton, Ashby &
Herringfleet NR32 ....111 F8
Flordon Rd
Bracon Ash NR14 ......88 F1
Flordon NR15 ....106 D8
Florence Barclay Cl
IP24 ....176 D6

Florence Rd NR1 ......163 A6
Florence Wlk NR19 ...154 C2
Florida Bvd NR21 .....15 C2
Flowerday Cl NR31 ...171 D5
Flowerdew Cl 12 NR9 ..88 C7
Flowerdew's La NR13 ..74 B7
Flowerpot La NR15 ...106 D3
Flowers La NR17 .....174 B3
Fludge's La NR20 .....49 B6
Flymore La NR17 .....103 A8
Fodderfen Dro PE38 ..113 A7
Foldgate La PE34 .....61 A5
Folgate NR16 ....88 D1
Folgate Cl
Costessey NR8 ....156 F5
Thornham PE36 ....2 D6
Folgate La
Costessey NR8 ....156 F4
Walpole PE14 ....41 D3
Folgate Rd
Heacham PE31 ....133 C4
North Walsham NR28 ..151 B6
Folland Ct 3 NR20 ...50 E7
Follies The PE37 ......65 F4
Folly Cl NR18 ....173 C5
Folly Ct
Fakenham NR21 ......141 D4
King's Lynn PE30 .....147 B7
Mattishall NR20 ......68 F6
Folly Gdns NR18 .....173 C5
Folly Gr PE30 ....147 B7
Folly La Beetley NR20 ..49 B6
Bressingham IP22 ....129 C8
Claxton NR14 ....91 D5
3 Hingham NR9 ......86 C5
Old Buckenham NR17 ..104 F2
Folly Rd NR18 ....173 C5
Folly View 5 PE37 ....65 F4
Folly Yd PE32 ....87 B3
Folwell Rd NR5 ......156 E1
Fonnereau The 11 NR14 ..90 C5
Ford Ave PE30 ....148 D5
Ford St IP24 ....176 D3
Foregate Cl 2 NR8 ...155 D2
Forge Cl IP27 ....175 C2
Forest Dr NR31 ......170 A3
Forest Mount NR31 ...93 E3
Forest Prim Sch IP27 .175 C3
Forest Ret Pk IP27 ...125 D8
Forester Cl 1 NR4 ...162 C1
Forester's Ave PE38 ..97 A8
Forge Cl
Old Buckenham NR17 ..104 D2
Palgrave IP22 ....177 D2
Poringland NR14 .....90 D4
Forge Gr NR34 ......110 C2
Forge Orchards 1 NR14 ..89 B3
Forge La NR14 ....91 F3
Forge Way IP22 ......128 A8
Forget-Me-Not Rd 3
PE31 ....12 D4
Forncett CE Prim Sch
NR16 ....106 B3
Forncett Ind Steam Mus*
NR16 ....106 B5
Forncett Rd
Bunwell NR16 ....105 F3
Tharston & Hapton
NR15 ....106 D4
Forster Cl 2 NR11 ...150 D6
Forster Way NR11 ....150 D6
Forsythia Rd NR31 ...170 B5
Forth Cl NR30 ....168 C5
Forties Cl 5 NR30 ...168 C6
Fortune Gn NR14 ....90 E4
Forum The* NR2 .....178 A2
Forwater Rd NR10 ....34 B3
Foster Cl Brundall NR13 .165 B4
Ormesby St Margaret
NR29 ....167 C2
Foster Rd NR3 ....158 D3
Foulgers Opening
NR1 ....178 C1
Foulsham Prim Sch
NR20 ....33 D3
Foulsham Rd
Bintree NR20 ....33 C2
Guestwick NR20 ......33 F4
Guist NR20 ....33 A4
Hindolveston NR20 ...33 D7
Wood Norton NR20 ...33 B6
Foundry Cl
Foulsham NR20 ......33 D3
Northrepps NR27 .....11 A2
Sculthorpe NR21 .....16 C2
Foundry La NR19 ....154 D4
Foundry Sq NR19 ....154 D4
Fountaine Gr PE30 ...148 C4
Fountains Rd NR4 ....89 E8
Four Acres Est NR29 .167 C8
Fourth Ave PE13 .....152 E4
Fowell Cl NR5 ....161 B6
Fowler's La NR17 ....174 B2
Fox Covert 3 NR14 ...88 C5
Fox Gr 7 NR6 ....118 C5
Fox Hill IP20 ....123 C3
Fox Hill Rd NR12 .....38 E7
Fox La Brundall NR13 ..165 F6
Framingham Pigot NR14 ..90 D6
North Tuddenham NR20 ..68 F8
Fox Rd Dereham NR19 ..154 D4
Framingham Pigot NR14 ..90 D7
Fox's La PE14 ....146 C6
Foxburrow Rd NR7 ...159 A5
Foxcotte Cl NR6 .....157 E7
Foxes Loke 12 NR14 ..92 A1
Foxes Mdw 2 PE32 ...46 F2

Foxglove Cl
Fakenham NR21 ......141 F4
North Walsham NR28 ..151 E5
Thurton NR14 ....91 C4
Foxglove Dr 21 NR31 ..94 C6
Foxglove La NR26 ....138 B6
Foxglove Rd
2 Attleborough NR17 ..174 B5
Thetford IP24 ....176 F4
Foxglove Wlk PE34 ...61 B8
Foxley Cl NR5 ....161 D6
Foxley Rd
Bawdeswell NR20 .....50 D8
Foulsham NR20 ......33 C2
Foxley Wood National Nature
Reserve* NR10 ......33 F1
Foxs Loke NR11 ......150 B6
Foxwood 9 NR13 .....73 D6
Foxwood Cl NR8 .....155 E3
Framingham Earl High Sch
NR14 ....90 C6
Framingham Earl La
NR14 ....90 E5
Framingham La NR14 ..90 F7
Framingham Rd NR14 ..90 F7
Framlingham Ct NR3 ..178 A4
Francis Cl NR27 ......139 C5
Francis La NR13 .....73 C6
Francis Rd NR15 .....106 E3
Francis Stone Ct NR7 ..72 D3
Francis Way NR5 .....160 E8
Frank Stone Ct NR30 .169 E1
Franklin Cl PE14 .....145 E6
Fransham Forge*
NR19 ....66 D8
Fransham Rd PE32 ...48 B1
Frazer Cres NR11 ....143 A7
Fred Nicholson Specl Sch
NR19 ....154 E2
Frederick Cl PE30 ....148 D6
Frederick Rd NR30 ...169 C5
Free La NR35 ....108 F2
Freebridge Haven PE33 ..43 A4
Freedom Bridge PE13 .152 B6
Freeland Cl NR8 .....155 E3
Freeland Cnr NR10 ...155 C6
Freeman Cl NR14 ....109 D8
Freeman Sq NR22 ...162 C8
Freeman St NR23 ....136 C6
Freestone Ct 7 PE30 ..148 C4
Freethorpe Com Prim Sch
NR13 ....92 F7
Freethorpe Rd
Cantley NR13 ....92 D6
Freethorpe NR13 .....74 F1
Freiston 2 PE30 .....147 C5
Fremantle Rd NR30 ..168 E1
French's Rd PE14 ....41 C6
Frensham Rd NR3 ...157 F2
Frenze Hall La IP22 ..177 E6
Frenze Rd IP22 ......177 E4
Frere Cnr 6 IP22 .....129 D7
Frere Rd
20 Harleston IP20 ....122 D2
Norwich NR1 ....159 D1
Fresher Mews NR5 ...160 F6
Freshfield Cl NR5 ....161 C7
Freshgap La NR20 ...33 E6
Freshwater Way NR8 .155 F3
Frettenham Fst Sch
NR12 ....54 A4
Frettenham Rd
Hainford NR10 ....53 F5
Horstead with Stanninghall
NR12 ....54 B5
Freyden Way NR12 ...54 A4
Friar Tuck Rd NR4 ...162 C1
Friar's La PE31 ......135 D4
Friars Ct NR13 ....169 D2
Friars' Quay NR3 ....178 B3
Friars St NR30 ....146 E3
Friars The 17 PE30 ..146 D4
Friarscroft La NR18 ..173 B3
Friday Bridge Prim Sch
PE14 ....77 A7
Friday Mkt 4 NR22 ..16 F7
Fridaybridge Rd
Elm PE14 ....77 A8
Wisbech PE14 ....59 A1
Friends Cl NR5 ......161 D6
Friends Rd NR4 ......161 C5
Fring Rd Bircham PE31 ..14 A3
Snettisham PE31 .....13 A5
Frinton Way 4 PE13 .152 E5
Frith Way NR15 .....106 B1
Fritillary Dr NR18 ...173 E4
Fritton La IP20 ......167 B3
Fritton La NR29 .....56 E6
Fritton Lake Cntry World*
NR31 ....93 F2
Fritton Rd NR31 .....93 E3
Frobisher Cl IP24 ....176 F6
Frobisher Cres PE36 .132 D3
Frog's Hall La NR20 .50 C2
Frogge Hall
Coltishall NR12 ......54 C8
Scottow NR10 ....37 C1
Frogs Hall La 3 NR1 .163 B5
Frogs Hole
Blofield NR13 ....165 D6
Somerleyton, Ashby &
Herringfleet NR32 ....93 F1
Frogshall La NR28 ...120 B3
Front Rd
Tydd St Giles PE13 ...41 A4
Wood Dalling NR11 ...34 D6
Front St Binham NR21 ..6 E2
Burnham Market PE31 .135 C3

Front St continued
Trunch NR28 ....22 E5
Front Way PE30 .....147 A7
Frost Cl Norwich NR7 .163 F8
20 Watton IP25 ....84 D3
Frost's La NR15 ......106 B1
Fugill Rd NR7 ....159 D1
Fulcher Ave NR27 ...139 A7
Fulford Cl NR4 ......162 A2
Fuller Cl
2 Rackheath NR13 ...72 E7
8 West Winch PE33 ..43 F2
Fuller Mews 5 NR5 ..160 E8
Fuller Rd
North Walsham NR28 ..151 B4
Redenhall with Harleston
IP20 ....122 D1
Fuller's Cl NR34 .....110 D5
Fuller's Hill 10 NR30 .169 C4
Fullmer Cl 9 NR31 ...94 C7
Fulmer La PE32 ......46 E2
Fulmerston Rd IP24 ..176 B2
Fulmodeston Rd
Fulmodeston NR21 ....18 B1
Fulmodeston NR20 ...33 C8
Stibbard NR21 ....32 E7
Fulton Cl 4 NR4 .....162 A1
Fundenhall Rd NR15 .106 B7
Fundrey Rd PE13 ....152 F6
Furlong Dro PE33 ....81 A3
Furlong Rd 8 PE33 ...81 A3
Furness Cl PE30 .....148 F1
Furthest Dro IP27 ...113 C4
Furze Ave NR7 ......163 E8
Furze Hill NR28 .....139 C5
Furze Hill Dr NR28 ..151 E3
Furze La
Great Witchingham NR9 .149 C2
Guist NR20 ....33 A6
Furze Rd NR7 ....163 E8
Furze Way IP22 .....129 B1
Fye Bridge St NR3 ...178 B4

G

Gablehurst Ct NR31 ..170 A4
Gables Ave NR11 ....22 B7
Gage Rd NR7 ....159 C4
Gagman's La NR19 ...68 A5
Gainsborough Ave
1 Diss IP22 ....177 C4
Great Yarmouth NR31 .170 A7
Gainsborough Cl 2
PE38 ....172 D6
Gale Cl NR14 ....109 F8
Gales Ct NR23 ......136 D6
Gales Rd NR23 ......136 C6
Gallant's La NR16 ...118 C5
Galley Cl 8 NR33 ....111 F1
Galley Hill NR3 ......158 A2
Gallow Dr PE38 .....172 C7
Gallow Hill (Tumulus)*
NR3 ....8 B5
Gallow La NR13 .....62 D2
Galloway Cl NR20 ...68 A8
Gallowhill La NR24 ..18 C3
Gallows La NR16 ....103 E1
Galyon Rd PE30 .....147 B8
Gambling Cl NR6 ....158 A7
Gamecock Cl NR6 ...158 C6
Gamewell Cl 8 NR6 ..162 E3
Gangway The NR27 ..139 C7
Ganners Hill NR8 ....155 E3
Gannet Rd NR29 ....167 E4
Gant Cl 9 NR30 .....68 F6
Gaol St NR3 ....178 B3
Gapton Hall Ind Est
NR31 ....170 A8
Gapton Hall Rd NR31 .170 A8
Gapton Hall Ret Pk
NR31 ....169 A1
Garboldisham Rd
Harling NR16 ....118 C3
Kenninghall NR16 ...118 F3
Garboldisham VC Prim Sch
IP22 ....128 A8
Garden Cl Briston NR24 .142 A4
Bungay NR35 ....124 B8
North Walsham NR28 ..151 C6
4 Watton IP25 ......84 E3
Garden Ct
King's Lynn PE30 .....147 A8
11 Loddon NR14 .....92 A1
Garden La NR25 .....8 F5
Garden Pl 2 NR3 ....162 E8
Garden Rd
Brundall NR13 ....165 E6
Hemsby NR29 ....167 D7
Sheringham NR26 ...138 D6
PE34 ....45 C3
Garden Row PE30 ...146 E3
Garden St
Cromer NR27 ....139 B7
Norwich NR1 ....178 B2
Gardeners Terr NR7 .159 D1
Gardenhouse La IP22 .128 E2
Gardyn Croft 8 NR8 .155 D2
Garfield Rd NR30 ...169 D4
Garfield Terr NR30 ..169 D4
Gargle Hill NR7 .....158 B2
Gariannonum (Roman Fort)*
NR31 ....93 F7
Garlic St IP21 ....122 A2
Garlondes 6 NR16 ...118 C5

Garner's La PE34 .....41 D8
Garnham Rd NR31 ...170 C7
Garrett Cl NR3 ......158 F1
Garrick Gn NR6 .....158 C5
Garrick Gn Fst Sch
NR6 ....158 E5
Garrison Rd NR30 ...169 C5
Garrood Dr NR21 ....141 E5
Garvestone Prim Sch
NR9 ....68 C2
Garvestone Rd NR20 .68 E4
Garwood Cl PE30 ...147 E4
Gas Hill NR1 ....163 A6
Gas House La PE12 ..41 B8
Gashouse Dro IP27 ..175 C4
Gashouse Hill NR11 .150 D6
Gaskell Way PE30 ...148 C1
Gatacre Rd NR31 ....169 B3
Gate House La NR24 ..16 C6
Gatekeeper Cl NR18 .173 E4
Gateley Gdns NR3 ...158 B3
Gateley Rd NR20 ....49 B8
Gaultree Sq PE14 ...59 D2
Gavell St IP19 ......124 D1
Gawdy Cl 2 IP20 ....122 D2
Gawdy Rd NR1 ......159 D1
Gaye Cres 1 IP23 ...130 C1
Gaymer Cl NR16 ....119 D7
Gaymer's Way NR28 .151 B6
Gaynor Cl NR18 .....173 B5
Gayton Fst Sch PE32 .45 C6
Gayton Rd
East Winch PE32 .....45 A4
Grimston PE32 ......45 C8
King's Lynn PE30 ....147 C5
Gayton Wlk NR6 ....158 F6
Gaywood Cl NR30 ...168 D5
Gaywood Com Prim Sch
PE30 ....147 C7
Gaywood Hall Dr
PE30 ....147 B5
Gaywood Rd PE30 ...146 F5
Geddes Way 8 NR20 .68 F6
Gedge Rd NR30 .....168 E6
Geldeston Hill NR34 .109 F2
Geldeston Rd
Ellingham NR35 .....109 D2
Geldeston NR34 .....110 B2
Gelham Manor NR3 ..32 A4
Generals Wlk 8 PE30 .147 C5
Geneva Gdns NR31 ..171 E4
Genista Gn 7 NR31 ..170 B6
Gentian Way 2 NR17 .174 B4
Gentleman's Wlk NR2 .178 A3
Gentry Pl NR5 ....161 C8
Geoffrey Rd 4 NR1 ..162 F3
George Beck Rd 8 NR29 .58 B6
George Borrow Rd
2 East Dereham NR19 .154 F3
Norwich NR4 ....161 E5
George Cl NR8 ......157 B8
George Dance Pl NR5 .161 C7
George Dr NR9 ....71 A6
George Edwards Rd
NR21 ....141 E5
George Elliot Way 6
NR19 ....154 F3
George Fox Way NR5 .161 B5
George Hill
Norwich NR6 ....158 E4
Stanton IP31 ....127 C1
George La Acle NR13 ..166 B4
2 Loddon NR14 ......92 A1
George Pope Cl NR3 .158 C2
George Pope Rd NR3 .158 C2
George Rd IP24 .....176 F5
George St
Brandon IP27 ....175 D3
Great Yarmouth NR30 .169 C4
6 King's Lynn PE30 ..146 E6
Sheringham NR26 ....138 C6
George Trollope Rd 15
IP25 ....84 D3
George Westwood Way
NR34 ....110 D2
George White Mid Sch
NR3 ....162 F8
George Winter Ct
NR33 ....111 F1
Georges Rd NR19 ...154 D5
Georgia Rd NR21 ....15 C2
Gerald Cl NR1 ......163 C8
German's La PE34 ...42 A6
Germander Ct 8 NR31 .94 C6
Gertrude Rd NR3 ....158 F1
Ghost Hill Fst Sch
NR8 ....156 D8
Gibbet La
East Beckham NR11 ..138 D2
Wereham PE33 ....80 E5
Gibbs Cl NR9 ....160 B2
Gibson Rd 5 IP25 ...67 B2
Gidney Dr PE33 .....43 E3
Giggle Cl NR28 .....151 B3
Gigli Cl NR28 ....151 E3
Gilbert Cl NR5 ......161 C7
Gilbert Rd PE14 .....90 F4
Gilchrist Cl 8 NR14 ..89 E8
Gildencroft NR3 ....178 A4
Gildenswood NR16 ..105 A1
Giles Rd NR10 ......54 A1
Gillingham Rd NR34 .110 A2
Gillingham Dam NR34 .110 C2
Gilman Rd NR3 .....158 F3
Gilpin's Ride NR19 ..154 D4

Gilray Rd IP22 177 F4
Gimingham Rd
Mundesley NR11 143 A6
Southrepps NR11 22 C7
Gipsies' La NR25 9 A3
Gipsies La NR29 56 D6
Gipsy Cl NR5 161 D6
Gipsy La Norwich NR5 161 E5
Watlington PE33 61 D5
Girling Rd NR19 154 C6
Girlings La NR7 163 E5
Girton Rd
Great Yarmouth NR31 170 A3
Norwich NR2 162 B4
Gissing Rd IP22 120 F2
Glade Prim Sch IP27 175 D3
Glade The
Costessey NR8 156 F4
Overstrand NR27 11 A3
Thetford IP24 176 D6
Gladstone Rd
Fakenham NR21 141 B4
4 King's Lynn PE30 146 E3
Gladstone St NR2 162 B6
Glamis Ct 26 IP20 122 D2
Glandford Rd NR25 7 E5
Glasbury Wlk PE13 153 C3
Glaven PE30 147 C5
Glaven Cl NR28 151 D5
Glaven Hale Cl NR25 137 C6
Glaven Rd NR25 137 D5
Glebe Ave
Hunstanton PE36 132 D5
Watlington PE33 61 E5
Glebe Cl Fransham NR19 66 C7
Hingham NR9 86 B5
19 Long Stratton NR15 106 E3
Northwold IP26 99 C8
2 Potter Heigham NR29 56 F6
Taverham NR8 155 F1
Thetford IP24 176 D5
Glebe Ct NR28 151 D6
Glebe Est PE34 144 F1
Glebe House Sch
PE36 132 D5
Glebe La PE31 135 F6
Glebe Mdw NR17 103 E7
Glebe Rd Acle NR13 166 C3
Dersingham PE31 140 C4
Downham Market PE38 172 D6
Gissing IP21 121 A4
Norwich NR2 162 A4
7 Watton IP25 84 E3
Weeting IP27 175 B7
Glebe The
2 Harling NR16 118 C5
Hemsby NR29 167 C8
Honing NR28 38 C6
Stibbard NR21 32 E7
Wells-next-the-Sea
NR23 136 D6
Glebe Way 5 NR12 54 C6
Glebes The 13 NR31 94 A5
Glenalmond NR4 162 A1
Glenburn Ave NR7 159 A3
Glenburn Ct NR7 159 A3
Glenda Cl NR5 157 C1
Glenda Cres NR5 157 B2
Glenda Ct NR5 157 B1
Glenda Rd NR5 157 C1
Glendenning Rd 4 NR1 163 B5
Glenfield Cl PE14 78 A5
Glengarry Cl NR9 88 C8
Glenham Ct PE31 140 C4
Glenmore Ave NR30 168 D7
Glenmore Gdns NR3 158 B2
Glenn Rd NR14 90 C4
Globe La NR13 165 E6
Globe Pl NR2 162 C5
Globe St IP26 99 A5
Glosthorpe Manor
PE32 44 F5
Gloucester Ave NR31 170 C4
Gloucester Ct PE13 152 D7
Gloucester Pl NR24 142 D4
Gloucester Rd PE30 147 B6
Gloucester St NR2 162 C4
Gloucester Way IP24 176 A5
Gobbett's Rd IP22 128 C4
Goddard Cres 1 PE13 152 D7
Goddards Ct 14 IP25 84 D3
Godfrey Rd 5 NR10 54 A2
Godric Pl NR2 161 F6
Godwick Medieval Village
of* PE32 31 C1
Godwin Rd PE13 152 D7
Goffe Cl IP25 84 D4
Goffins La NR29 56 C6
Gogg's Mill Rd NR21 141 A3
Goggles La NR19 66 C6
Gogle Cl 8 NR20 68 E6
Golden Ball St NR1 178 B2
Golden Dog La NR3 178 B4
Golden Fleece Heritage
Mus* NR28 38 A7
Golden Gates NR23 136 B2
Golden Gates Dr
NR23 136 A2
Golden Pightle 7 NR9 69 F2
Golden Sq 10 NR27 139 B7
Goldfinch Cl PE38 172 C7
Goldfinch Way 13 IP25 84 C3
Golding Pl
Norwich NR2 162 C6
16 Wisbech PE13 152 C4
Golds Pightle PE36 2 B3
Goldsmith St NR2 162 C7
Goldsmith Way IP21 121 F4
Goldwell Rd NR1 178 B1
Golf Cl King's Lynn PE30 148 D1
Runton NR27 10 A5
Golf Course Rd PE36 132 E8
Golf La NR19 154 D7
Golf Links Rd
Brundall NR13 165 D4
Wymondham College
NR18 104 E8
Gong La PE31 135 F6
Gonville Cl PE31 133 C5
Gonville Rd NR31 170 A4
Gooch Cl NR28 151 C6
Gooderstone CE Prim Sch
PE33 82 A5
Gooderstone Rd PE33 81 F5
Gooderstone Water Gdns*
PE33 82 A5
Goodhale Rd 1 NR5 161 B7
Goodman Sq 2 NR2 162 C7
Goodminns PE36 13 A7
Goodrick Pl PE13 153 C4
Goodwin Rd NR11 143 C6
Goodwins Rd PE30 146 E3
Goodwood Cl NR7 159 E1
Goosander Cl 4 PE31 12 E5
Goose Gn
8 Sutton Bridge PE12 41 B8
Winfarthing IP22 120 C6
Goose Gn La IP22 120 B6
Goose Gn Rd PE31 12 E4
Goose La
Alby with Thwaite NR11 21 B3
Stalham NR12 39 C4
Gooseacre La IP25 67 D3
Goose's La PE14 41 D5
Gooseberry Hill NR20 50 B3
Gordon Ave NR7 163 C7
Gordon Ct PE13 152 C3
Gordon Fendick Sch
PE13 152 D8
Gordon Godfrey Way
NR10 53 A3
Gordon Rd
Briston NR24 142 A5
3 East Dereham NR20 154 E5
Great Yarmouth NR31 169 C2
Gordon Sq NR1 178 B1
Gordon Terr NR11 143 B4
Gore La NR15 121 C8
Gorgate Rd NR20 49 E3
Gorleston La NR31 170 A2
Gormans La NR21 31 D5
Gorse Ave NR6 158 A5
Gorse Cl 4 Belton NR31 94 A5
2 East Dereham NR19 154 C4
Fakenham NR21 141 F3
Mundesley NR11 143 B5
Gorse Ind Est IP24 125 C6
Gorse Rd NR7 163 D8
Gorse View 4 NR20 49 D4
Gorse Vw 4 NR20 49 D4
Goshawk Way 5 IP24 176 D2
Gosmoor La PE14 59 B1
Gostling Cl IP22 177 B4
Gothic Cl 2 IP20 122 D1
Goulburn Rd NR7 159 D1
Gould Rd 1 NR2 162 A4
Gournay Ave NR31 170 D2
Governors Ct NR1 178 C1
Gowing Cl NR6 157 F7
Gowing Ct NR3 158 B3
Gowing Rd
11 Mulbarton NR14 89 B3
Norwich NR6 157 F6
Gowing Way NR15 107 B5
Grace Edwards Cl
NR8 155 F2
Grafton Cl PE30 147 C8
Grafton Rd PE30 147 C8
Graham Dr 2 PE32 44 B3
Graham Sq NR7 159 D1
Graham St PE30 146 E3
Grammar Sch Rd
NR28 151 C4
Granary Cl
Briston NR24 142 F3
Freethorpe NR13 92 E7
9 Lingwood NR13 74 A3
Granary Ct PE30 146 D4
Granary Loke NR10 149 C4
Granary Rd NR17 174 C4
Grand Cl NR19 154 C4
Grange Ave NR27 11 B3
Grange Cl Briston NR24 142 E3
Ludham NR29 56 D5
Norwich NR6 158 E4
10 Snettisham PE31 12 E4
Wroxham/Hoveton
NR12 164 E6
Grange Cres PE33 63 C5
Grange Ct NR28 151 C4
Grange La
Honingham NR9 69 F5
West Winch PE33 61 E8
Grange Rd
Caister-on-Sea NR30 168 D5
Cantley NR13 92 C6
Flixton NR35 123 E4
Hainford NR10 53 F5
Ludham NR29 56 D5
Mundham NR14 108 F7
Norwich NR2 162 A4
Scarning NR19 154 A4
Sutton Bridge PE34 41 E8
Wendling NR19 66 F8
Wisbech PE13 152 A7
Grange Wlk NR12 164 C4
Granny Bard's La NR12 54 C3
Grant Rd NR10 54 A2
Grant St NR2 162 A7
Granta Way 1 NR31 170 B2
Grantly Ct PE30 147 D5
Granville Cl 8 NR12 39 B4
Granville Rd NR31 169 B4
Granville Terr PE12 41 A8
Grapes Hill NR2 162 C6
Grasmere 19 NR9 88 D8
Grasmere Cl NR5 161 C6
Grassgate La PE14 59 B7
Gravel Bank PE14 60 D6
Gravel Dam NR32 111 F4
Gravel Hill NR14 89 F4
Gravel Pit La NR25 137 C5
Gravelfield Cl NR1 163 B8
Gravelhill La PE33 43 F1
Gravelpit Hill NR17 102 F6
Gray Dr NR20 50 B4
Gray's La Barsham NR22 16 E6
Pulham Market IP21 121 D5
Grays Fair NR5 156 F1
Grays La PE14 59 C2
Grays Rd NR34 111 C3
Great Barn Rd NR23 5 A4
Great Barwick Medieval
Village of* PE31 14 E6
Great Cl NR30 168 F5
Great Comm La NR34 124 E5
Great Dunham Prim Sch
PE32 47 F1
Great Eastern Rd
PE13 152 B4
Great Eastern Way
Fakenham NR21 141 D4
Wells-next-the-Sea
NR23 136 E5
Great Ellingham Prim Sch
NR17 103 E8
Great Hautbois Rd
NR12 54 C7
Great Hockham Prim Sch
IP24 102 E4
Great Hospl NR1 178 C4
Great Man's Way PE33 81 A2
Great Massingham VC Prim
Sch PE32 29 E1
Great Melton Rd
Hethersett NR9 88 C8
Little Melton NR9 160 A2
Great Northern Cl
NR30 169 D6
Great Palgrave Medieval
Village of* PE32 65 B6
Great Snoring Rd NR21 17 D6
Great Witchingham Prim Sch
NR9 51 E5
Great Yarmouth Coll
NR31 169 C1
Great Yarmouth High Sch
NR30 169 E6
Great Yarmouth Race Course
NR30 168 F2
Great Yarmouth Sea Life
Ctr* NR30 169 E2
Great Yarmouth Sta
NR30 169 B5
Greatheath Rd NR20 32 D1
Grebe Cl
Great Yarmouth NR31 170 A7
7 Rollesby NR29 57 D2
Green Bank PE36 2 A5
Green Cl
Hempton NR21 141 A2
Norwich NR5 156 E1
Green Comm La PE31 3 C6
Green Ct
Fakenham NR21 141 E4
Norwich NR7 163 D7
Green Dragon La
NR23 136 D5
Green Dro PE14 77 D6
Green Gr PE33 81 D8
Green Hill La PE31 14 B3
Green Hills Cl NR8 156 F3
Green Hills Rd 6 NR3 162 D8
Green House La PE37 153 E5
Green La Alpington NR14 90 F3
Attleborough NR17 174 C7
Aylsham NR11 150 A6
Bawburgh NR9 160 C4
Beetley NR20 49 D4
Billingford NR20 49 F8
Burgh St Peter NR34 111 C4
Burnham Thorpe PE31 4 D3
Caister-on-Sea NR30 168 E4
Christchurch PE14 95 A7
Coltishall NR12 54 C6
Dereham NR19 154 E8
Ditchingham NR35 109 B2
Earsham NR35 108 E2
5 Feltwell IP26 98 E1
Filby NR29 75 F8
Foulsham NR20 33 E3
Great & Little Plumstead
NR13 72 E5
Great Ellingham NR17 103 E8
Great Moulton NR15 106 B1
Great Yarmouth NR31 94 C6
Guist NR20 33 A5
Hales NR14 109 E8
Haveringland NR10 52 E7
Horsford NR10 53 B4
King's Lynn PE30 148 E2
Little Ellingham NR17 86 A1
Methwold IP26 99 A7
Mundford IP26 100 B5
Green La *continued*
Postwick with Witton NR7 72 E4
Potter Heigham NR29 56 F6
Pudding Norton NR21 141 A1
Redenhall with Harleston
IP20 122 E2
Rocklands NR17 103 C7
Saxlingham Nethergate
NR15 107 B7
Shipdham IP25 67 D4
Shipmeadow NR34 109 F1
Somerleyton, Ashby &
Herringfleet NR32 111 E8
South Walsham NR13 74 B6
Starston IP20 122 D4
Stow Bedon NR17 103 B8
Syleham IP21 131 C4
Thelnetham IP22 128 A2
Thetford IP24 176 E4
Thornham PE36 2 D6
Thrandeston IP21 129 F2
Tivetshall St Margaret
NR15 121 B5
Toft Monks NR34 110 C6
Tottenhill PE33 61 F5
Troston IP31 126 A1
Upwell PE14 95 B6
Walsoken PE14 152 F4
Wicklewood NR18 87 C5
Wramplingham NR18 87 F7
Wymondham NR18 173 D1
Yaxham NR19 68 B6
Green La E NR13 72 E7
Green La N NR13 72 D5
Green La W
Horsham St Faith NR13 53 D1
Rackheath NR13 72 D8
Green Man La NR15 108 C8
Green Marsh Rd PE34 144 C7
Green Oak Rd 2 IP25 84 D3
Green Pk 42 IP20 122 D2
Green Pk Rd NR10 53 B3
Green Quay The*
PE30 146 D4
Green Rd Brandon IP27 175 E2
Hales NR14 109 E8
Upwell PE14 77 E4
Green St IP21 131 A4
Green The Ashill IP25 84 A7
Belton with Browston
NR31 94 A5
Boughton PE33 80 F4
Brisley NR20 49 B8
Burnham Market PE31 135 C3
Deopham NR18 86 E2
Dersingham PE31 140 D4
Diss IP22 177 A6
8 Earsham NR35 123 F8
Fakenham NR21 141 A3
Freethorpe NR13 92 E8
Hickling NR12 39 E2
Hockham IP24 102 E3
Hunstanton PE36 132 C4
Lound NR32 94 C2
North Lopham IP22 119 A2
North Wootton PE30 148 C5
Norwich NR2 178 D2
Ormesby St Margaret
NR29 167 A2
Runhall NR9 68 F2
Saxlingham Nethergate
NR15 107 D7
South Wootton PE30 149 C2
Surlingham NR14 73 B1
Thornham PE36 2 D6
Upton with Fishley NR13 166 B8
Wicklewood NR18 87 B4
Green Way
Barsham NR22 16 C6
Stiffkey NR23 6 C6
Swaffham PE37 153 B6
Green Wood Dr NR19 154 C5
Greenacre Cl
Brundall NR13 165 C4
King's Lynn PE30 148 B2
Greenacre Fst & Mid Sch
NR30 169 D1
Greenacre Rd NR9 86 B5
Greenacres
Bradwell NR31 170 A3
Little Melton NR9 160 C2
Greenacres Dr NR14 90 C5
Green's La NR27 10 C4
Greenborough Cl NR7 159 E2
Greenborough Rd
NR7 159 E2
Greencourts 10 NR29 58 B6
Greenfield NR5 156 D1
Greenfield Cl NR27 139 C5
Greenfields NR16 118 B5
Greenfields Rd NR20 154 F4
Greengate NR20 50 B2
Greengate La
Bircham PE31 13 F4
Great Massingham PE32 29 C1
Greenhill Ave NR30 168 D8
Greenhill Rd PE32 46 B2
Greenhoe Pl PE37 153 B3
Greenland Ave
King's Lynn PE30 146 E8
Wymondham NR18 173 E6
Greenlands Way NR26 138 C6
Greenlands Way W 2
NR26 138 B6
Greenpark Ave PE30 146 F6
Greens Rd
East Dereham NR20 154 F3
North Walsham NR28 151 A5
Greenway Cl
Fakenham NR21 141 C5
2 North Walsham NR28 151 C5
Greenway La
Fakenham NR21 141 C5
Tharston & Hapton
NR15 106 D6
Greenway Pk NR21 141 C6
Greenways
Bunwell NR16 105 D4
Flordon NR15 106 E8
Holt NR25 137 C7
Newton Flotman NR15 89 C1
Norwich NR4 161 F1
Greenways Cl NR15 106 E8
Greenways La
Bunwell NR16 105 D4
Carleton Rode NR16 105 B4
Greenwich Cl
Dersingham PE31 140 E3
Downham Market PE38 172 B3
Greenwood Cl NR16 105 E8
Greenwood Rd NR4 162 C1
Greenwood Way
5 Shipdham IP25 67 C2
Thorpe St Andrew NR7 159 F2
Greevegate PE36 132 C4
Gregor Shanks Way 27
IP25 84 D3
Gregory Cl 1 PE30 148 C5
Gregs Cl NR20 68 F5
Grenville Cl 3 NR9 88 E8
Grenville Pl 1 NR30 169 D8
Grenville Way IP24 176 D5
Gresham Cl
Great Yarmouth NR31 170 C2
King's Lynn PE30 147 C8
Gresham Rd
Baconsthorpe NR25 20 B8
Norwich NR3 158 B2
Gresham Village Sch
NR11 9 E1
Greshams Prep Sch
NR25 137 D7
Greshams Sch NR25 137 D7
Gresley Cl NR20 49 C4
Gressenhall Farm &
Workhouse* NR20 49 D4
Gressenhall Rd NR20 49 D4
Grey Sedge PE30 147 A7
Greyfriars Cl NR6 158 E5
Greyfriars Cty Prim Sch
PE30 146 E4
Greyfriars Rd NR1 178 B3
Greyfriars Way NR30 169 C3
Greyhound La
Banham NR16 119 D7
Hopton IP22 127 E5
Greyhound Opening 7
NR2 162 C7
Greylag Cl 8 NR13 55 A1
Greys Manor NR16 119 D6
Grice Cl 4 NR26 138 C5
Griffin La
Attleborough NR17 174 D5
Thorpe St Andrew NR7 72 D3
Grigsons Wood 1
NR16 118 C5
Grime's Graves* IP27 115 C8
Grimmer La NR13 92 B7
Grimmer's Rd 6 PE13 152 E7
Grimshoe Rd PE38 172 B6
Grimston Jun Sch PE32 28 B1
Grimston Pott Row Fst Sch
PE32 45 A8
Grimston Rd
Gayton PE32 45 C6
King's Lynn PE30 148 E1
Gristock Pl NR5 161 C8
Griston Rd
Thompson IP24 102 B8
Watton IP25 84 E3
Groomes Cl 4 NR31 171 D5
Grosvenor Rd
Norwich NR2 162 B5
Wisbech PE13 152 D7
Grouts La NR25 8 B6
Grove Ave
Norwich NR5 157 A1
Norwich NR1 178 A1
Grove Cl
8 East Dereham NR19 154 C4
Holt NR25 137 D6
2 Newton Flotman NR15 89 C1
Grove Dale 3 NR15 89 C1
Grove End IP21 131 F1
Grove Gdns 7 PE32 45 C6
Grove House Inf Sch
NR19 154 D4
Grove La Booton NR10 52 A8
Fakenham NR21 141 C6
Forncett NR16 106 A3
Holt NR25 137 D6
Sparham NR9 51 B6
Tasburgh NR15 106 F7
Thetford IP24 176 D4
Grove Rd
Banham NR16 119 C6
Barsham NR21 16 C4
Brockdish IP21 131 C6
Cantley NR13 92 D8
Cromer NR27 139 D5
Gissing IP21 121 A4
Hethersett NR9 88 D8
Ingham NR12 24 C1

Grove Rd *continued*
4 Marthan NR29 57 D5
Melton Constable NR24 142 A4
North Walsham NR28 151 D5
Norwich NR1 178 A1
Repps with Bastwick NR29 57 A4
Starston IP20 122 C2
Wells-next-the-Sea NR23 136 E4
Grove The
Coltishall NR12 54 D6
East Dereham NR19 154 D4
Fleggburgh NR29 57 A1
2 Necton PE37 65 F4
Roydon PE32 28 A1
Shotesham NR15 90 B1
Grove Way NR15 89 C1
Grove Wlk NR1 178 A1
Grovebury Cl NR13 165 C4
Grovedale Cl NR5 157 A1
Grovelands PE31 140 D8
Groveside PE31 30 A7
Growle Abbey NR24 19 B2
Grub La IP19 124 E1
Grub St
Happisburgh NR12 24 B4
Shotesham NR15 90 B2
Grubb's La NR12 24 C1
Guanock Pl 12 PE30 146 E3
Guanock Terr PE30 146 E3
Guardian Rd NR5 161 F7
Guelph Rd 2 NR1 163 A6
Guernsey Rd NR3 162 E8
Guestwick Rd
Foulsham NR20 33 E4
Hindolveston NR20 33 F7
Wood Norton NR20 33 C6
Guild Rd PE13 152 E6
Guild St NR22 16 F8
Guildford Way IP24 176 B5
Guildhall Hill 1 NR2 178 A3
Guildhall La IP21 121 E5
Guildhall St IP24 176 D3
Guiler's La NR18 105 B8
Guilt Cross Way PE38 172 C6
Guist Bottom Rd NR21 32 E6
Guist Rd NR20 33 C4
Gulgate La NR11 21 A1
Gull La NR14 90 E6
Gullpit Dro PE34 61 D1
Gun St 7 NR26 138 D7
Gunn Rd NR7 159 D1
Gunn St NR20 33 C3
Gunn's Cnr NR12 38 D2
Gunner Cl 3 NR7 72 D5
Gunthorpe Rd PE14 41 B5
Gunton La NR5 157 B2
Gunton Rd
Loddon NR14 109 C8
Norwich NR2 161 F5
Wymondham NR18 173 D4
Gunton Sta NR11 22 B6
Gurney Cl NR5 161 B8
Gurney Ct NR5 161 B8
Gurney Dr NR7 159 D3
Gurney La NR4 161 C2
Gurney Rd
Norwich NR5 157 A1
Norwich NR1 163 A7
Gwyn Cres NR21 141 F5
Gymkhana Way PE31 133 B5

H

Habgood Cl NR13 166 C4
Hackford Rd
Hardingham NR9 86 E6
Wicklewood NR18 87 A5
Haconsfield 8 NR9 88 D7
Haddiscoe Dam NR14 110 F8
Haddiscoe Rd NR34 110 F6
Haddiscoe Sta NR31 93 D1
Hadfield Rd NR28 151 B6
Hadley Cres PE31 133 C5
Hadley Dr NR2 161 F6
Hadley Rd NR26 138 E6
Hagbech Hall Cl 2 PE14 59 D2
Haggard's Cl IP25 66 E3
Haig Cl NR19 154 D3
Hainford Fst Sch NR10 53 E6
Hainford Rd NR10 53 E7
Halcombe Ct NR3 158 E1
Halden Ave NR6 157 F6
Hale Ct NR13 73 A4
Hale Dro Littleport CB6 96 B2
Welney PE14 95 E6
Hale Fen Rd CB6 96 B1
Hale Rd Ashill IP25 84 A7
Bradenham IP25 66 D3
Necton PE37 65 F4
Hales Cl NR30 168 D5
Hales Ct NR25 137 B6
Hales Hall & Gdns* NR14 109 D6
Hales St NR15 121 A6
Halesworth Rd NR34 124 E4
Haley Cl 4 PE13 152 C8
Half Acre Cl NR27 10 B4
Half Mile Cl NR3 158 B2
Half Mile Rd NR3 158 B2
Half Moon NR31 170 C1
Half Moon La IP22 128 E4
Half Moon Way 1 NR2 162 B8
Half Year Cl 7 NR27 10 B5
Halfar Rd 8 IP31 126 B1
Halffield La NR18 86 D2
Halfmile Drift IP25 66 D3
Halford Cl NR17 174 D4
Halford La IP22 129 A7
Halford Pl NR17 174 D4
Halford Rd NR17 174 D4
Halfpenny La
Beetley NR20 49 C5
Elm PE14 59 A2
Wisbech PE14 152 D1
Halfpenny Toll Rd PE14 95 B8
Halifax Cres NR21 15 C3
Haling Way IP24 176 A4
Hall Bridge Rd PE14 77 D5
Hall Cl Fakenham NR21 141 D4
Heacham PE31 133 D7
4 Hemsby NR29 167 A7
5 Hethersett NR9 88 D7
3 Hingham NR9 86 C4
3 Southery PE38 97 B5
Hall Comm Rd NR29 56 C4
Hall Cres PE33 63 C5
Hall Dike PE14 77 F7
Hall Dr Costessey NR5 156 D2
16 Feltwell IP26 98 E1
Honingham NR9 69 E6
North Runcton PE33 44 A3
Santon Downham IP27 115 C6
Hall Farm Gdns PE32 44 F3
Hall Farm Pl NR9 160 B6
Hall Hills IP22 177 C5
Hall La
Baconsthorpe NR25 19 F8
Bressingham IP22 119 D1
Burston & Shimpling IP21 121 A2
Colkirk NR21 31 E5
Deopham NR18 86 F4
East Carleton NR14 88 E4
East Dereham NR20 154 F4
East Ruston NR12 24 A4
East Tuddenham NR20 69 B6
Felthorpe NR10 52 E5
Frettenham NR12 54 B3
Gunthorpe NR24 18 A5
Hingham NR9 86 C5
Horsford NR10 53 B1
King's Lynn PE30 148 B1
Knapton NR28 143 B1
Long Stratton NR15 106 F3
Morley NR18 87 B2
North Tuddenham NR20 68 F8
North Walsham NR28 151 D5
Northwold IP26 99 C7
Postwick with Witton NR13 72 F2
Redgrave IP22 128 E4
Ringstead PE36 2 A3
Roydon IP22 129 D7
Saxlingham Nethergate NR15 107 C7
Scole IP21 130 F8
Shelfanger IP22 120 B2
Shelton NR15 122 A8
Taverham NR8 157 B8
Tharston & Hapton NR15 106 D5
Thompson IP24 102 B7
Thornham PE36 2 D6
Thursford NR21 17 F5
Wacton NR15 106 C1
West Winch PE33 43 E2
Whissonsett NR20 31 D2
Wiveton NR25 7 D6
Wood Norton NR20 33 B6
Hall Loke NR28 38 C8
Hall Moor Rd NR9 86 C4
Hall Orchards PE32 44 C3
Hall Plain NR30 169 C3
Hall Rd Alderford NR9 52 A5
Barsham NR34 124 F7
Barton Turf NR12 55 E8
12 Bawdeswell NR20 50 E7
Bedingham NR35 108 C3
Beetley NR20 49 D5
Blofield NR13 165 C8
Bracon Ash NR14 88 E4
Brockdish IP21 131 D7
Bunwell NR16 105 E2
Burston & Shimpling IP22 120 E3
Cantley NR13 92 C8
Carleton Rode NR16 105 B4
Catfield NR29 56 B8
Clenchwarton PE34 145 D6
Cromer NR27 139 B5
Earsham NR35 123 E8
Easton NR9 70 B5
Ellingham NR35 109 C3
Elsing NR20 50 D2
Felbrigg NR27 139 A4
Fleggburgh NR29 57 A1
Framingham Earl NR14 90 D5
Gimingham NR11 22 D7
Great Melton NR9 88 B8
Great Witchingham NR9 51 F5
Hainford NR10 53 E5
Hemsby NR29 167 A7
Hoe NR20 49 F3
Honing NR28 38 D8
Hopton on Sea NR31 171 B6
King's Lynn PE30 148 C1
Ludham NR29 56 B4
Martham NR29 57 D4
Mautby NR29 76 A6
Northrepps NR27 139 D2
Hall Rd *continued*
Norwich NR5 157 A2
Norwich NR1 178 B1
Oulton NR11 35 B7
Outwell PE14 77 F7
Postwick with Witton NR13 165 A5
Pulham St Mary IP21 122 A4
Reedham NR13 92 F6
Roudham NR16 117 E6
Runhall NR20 69 A4
Smallburgh NR12 38 D2
9 Snettisham PE31 12 E5
Sutton NR12 39 D3
Swafield NR28 22 C5
Tacolneston NR16 105 E6
Tharston & Hapton NR15 106 E5
Thurton NR14 91 C3
Tivetshall St Margaret NR15 121 B6
Toft Monks NR14 110 D7
Walpole Highway PE14 59 F8
Winfarthing IP22 120 C5
Wood Dalling NR11 34 C6
Hall Sch NR6 158 D5
Hall St NR24 142 E3
Hall Staithe NR21 141 B4
Hall View Rd PE30 147 B4
Hall Wlk NR9 51 D5
Hall's Dr NR20 49 C4
Hallback La NR14 90 A7
Hallfield Rd IP24 102 A7
Hallfields PE33 62 D4
Hallgate 2 NR13 72 D6
Hallowing Cres 3 NR15 106 B1
Hallowing La NR15 121 B8
Halls Cnr NR10 53 B8
Halls Cnr Rd NR10 53 B8
Hallwong La IP20 122 D3
Halstead Cl 2 PE13 152 E5
Halt Rd NR30 168 D7
Halton Rd 8 IP25 84 F3
Halvergate Rd
Beighton NR13 74 E1
Reedham NR13 93 A6
Hambling's Piece NR16 118 C4
Hamburg Way PE30 147 A8
Hamilton Cl
North Walsham NR28 151 C5
South Walsham NR13 74 A8
Hamilton Ct 1 NR21 141 B4
Hamilton Dr PE37 153 D3
Hamilton Rd
3 Cromer NR27 139 B7
Great Yarmouth NR30 169 D7
Old Hunstanton PE36 132 E7
Hamilton Rd W PE36 132 E7
Hamilton Way PE38 172 B5
Hamilton Wlk 9 NR29 57 D4
Hamlet Cl NR28 151 D7
Hamlin Way PE30 146 F1
Hammond Cl NR7 159 E3
Hammond Rd 2 NR30 169 D5
Hammond Way NR7 159 E3
Hamon Cl PE36 132 E7
Hamond Rd NR6 157 D5
Hamonds High Sch PE37 153 C3
Hampden Dr 19 NR7 72 D4
Hampden Rd 2 PE13 152 D5
Hampton Ave 3 NR14 92 F1
Hampton Cl NR30 168 C5
Hanbury Cl 4 NR5 161 D5
Hancock Cl 3 NR12 54 C7
Hancock Ct NR5 160 E7
Hand La Barsham NR21 16 C5
Hoveton NR12 164 C8
Handel Dr NR19 154 F3
Handford Dr NR26 138 E6
Hanginghill NR13 74 C6
Hankin Ct 3 NR4 161 C5
Hankinson's Est PE34 42 A5
Hanly Cl NR7 159 C2
Hanly Ct NR30 168 D6
Hannah Cl NR26 138 C6
Hannah Rd NR20 50 B4
Hannant Rd NR28 151 D6
Hanover Ct
Dersingham PE31 140 E3
King's Lynn PE30 147 D5
Hanover Gdns PE36 132 D3
Hanover Rd NR2 162 C4
Hanrae Cl NR26 138 F6
Hans Pl 4 NR27 139 B7
Hansa Rd PE30 146 F2
Hansard Cl NR3 158 B1
Hansard La NR3 178 B4
Hansard Rd NR3 158 B1
Hansell Rd NR7 163 F8
Hantons Loke NR13 74 B2
Hanworth Cross NR11 21 D5
Happisburgh Fst Sch NR12 24 C5
Happisburgh Rd
East Ruston NR12 24 A3
Lessingham NR12 24 D4
North Walsham NR28 151 D4
Witton NR28 23 E2
Hapton Prim Sch NR15 106 C7
Harbord Cl 4 NR28 151 C7
Harbord Cres NR30 170 D8
Harbord Rd
Cromer NR27 139 C5
Norwich NR4 161 F5
Overstrand NR27 11 A3
Harbour La IP22 128 A7
Harbour Rd
1 Frettenham NR12 54 A4
Norwich NR1 163 A5
Harbour Terr NR31 170 E4
Harcourt Cl 3 NR3 162 F8
Hardesty Cl 9 NR14 90 D5
Hardingham Dr 6 NR26 138 C5
Hardingham Rd NR9 86 D5
Hardingham St 4 NR9 86 C4
Hardley Cross* NR14 92 E4
Hardley Hall La NR14 92 C3
Hardley Rd NR14 92 A2
Hardley St NR14 92 B3
Hardwick Cl 1 NR4 89 D8
Hardwick Ind Est PE30 147 B2
Hardwick Rd
King's Lynn PE30 146 E2
Pulham Market IP21 121 F7
Shelton NR15 122 C8
Hardy Cl
Downham Market PE38 172 B4
1 North Walsham NR28 151 C5
Thetford IP24 176 D6
Hardy Rd NR1 163 A4
Hardy's La PE32 46 C2
Hare Cl 2 NR14 89 B2
Hare Rd NR13 72 F5
Harebell Rd PE38 172 B3
Harecroft Gdns PE30 146 E6
Harecroft Par 7 PE30 146 E6
Harecroft Rd PE13 152 B5
Harecroft Terr PE30 146 E6
Harefen La NR13 74 B7
Harefield Rd IP24 116 C5
Hares Cl NR21 17 C3
Harewood PE31 134 F4
Harewood Dr
9 King's Lynn PE30 146 E6
Taverham NR8 155 E3
Harewood Par 8 PE30 146 E6
Harford Manor Cl NR2 162 C2
Harford Manor Specl Sch NR4 162 C2
Harford St NR1 162 E3
Harfrey's Rd NR31 170 B8
Harfreys Ind Est
Gorleston-on-Sea NR31 170 A8
Great Yarmouth NR31 169 B1
Hargate La PE34 42 B7
Hargham Cl 5 NR17 104 D2
Hargham Rd
Attleborough NR17 174 B2
Old Buckenham NR17 104 B2
Shropham NR17 103 C3
Harker Way 6 NR13 73 D6
Harleston Mus* IP20 122 D2
Harleston Prim Sch IP20 122 E2
Harleston Rd
Pulham Market IP21 121 E4
Scole IP21 121 D1
Harley Rd NR30 169 D6
Harling Dro IP27 115 E7
Harling Rd
Garboldisham IP22 118 C2
Hockham IP24 102 E3
North Lopham IP22 119 A2
Harling Rd Sta NR16 118 A6
Harlington Ave NR6 158 A4
Harlingwood La NR17 104 E1
Harman Cl 12 NR9 88 D8
Harman's La IP20 122 C1
Harmer Cl NR28 151 E5
Harmer Cres NR4 161 C1
Harmer La NR4 161 C1
Harmer Rd NR3 158 D3
Harmer's La NR11 21 A5
Harnser's Reach NR13 166 B8
Harp Cl NR21 141 B5
Harp's Hall Rd PE14 59 E5
Harper's La NR20 32 A1
Harpley CE VC Prim Sch PE31 29 C4
Harpsfield NR5 160 E8
Harrier Cl 26 NR9 88 D8
Harriet Cl PE12 41 A8
Harriet Martineau Cl 10 IP24 176 D7
Harriott's Way NR11 150 B5
Harris Mews 2 NR5 161 A7
Harris Rd
11 Swanton Morley NR20 50 B3
12 Watton IP25 84 F3
Harrisons Dr NR7 159 E3
Harrold Cl
1 South Walsham NR13 74 B8
Taverham NR8 155 E2
Harrolds Cl PE13 59 C5
Harrow Cl PE34 146 C5
Harry Barber Cl 2 NR5 161 A8
Harry Blunt Way 10 NR19 154 C4
Harry Miller Ct 7 NR30 169 D1
Harry Perry Cl NR4 162 C2
Harry Watson Ct NR6 158 C3
Harry's La IP21 121 E7
Harrys Way
Hunstanton PE36 132 D1
Wisbech PE13 152 C2
Harsnett Cl NR5 160 F8
Hart La NR25 9 A2
Hart's La NR9 160 A7
Hartbee Rd NR6 158 C6
Hartington Rd NR27 139 D4
Hartley Cl PE36 132 D4
Hartmann Rd NR30 170 E6
Harts Farm Rd NR18 173 E5
Harts La NR4 161 C1
Hartwell Rd NR12 164 C4
Harvard Rd 6 IP26 98 D1
Harvest Cl 1 NR10 53 E5
Harvest La NR21 17 D6
Harvey Cl
2 Hethersett NR9 88 C7
Norwich NR7 163 C7
Tasburgh NR15 106 E7
Harvey Dr NR28 151 C7
Harvey Est NR11 22 E7
Harvey Gn 10 NR14 91 F1
Harvey La
Caister-on-Sea NR30 168 E4
Dickleburgh IP21 121 C1
Norwich NR7 163 C6
Harvey St 21 IP25 84 D3
Harvey's La NR15 108 D6
Harwood Ave 4 IP24 176 E6
Harwood Rd NR1 162 E1
Hase's La NR9 51 C4
Haslips Cl 8 NR2 162 C7
Haspalls Rd PE37 153 B3
Hassett Cl 6 NR3 162 F8
Hastings Ave NR6 158 A4
Hastings Cl
Briston NR24 142 A5
6 Tasburgh NR15 106 F6
Hastings Ct NR24 142 E4
Hastings Dr PE36 132 D6
Hastings La
15 Sheringham NR26 138 D7
Wiggenhall St Germans PE34 61 C8
Hastings Rd 6 IP25 84 F3
Hastings Way NR12 39 C3
Hatherley Gdns PE33 81 B8
Hatton Rd NR1 162 E3
Haugh Cnr NR16 119 F7
Haugh Rd NR16 119 F8
Haughs End Rd NR12 164 F2
Hautbois Rd NR10 37 B2
Hauteyn Ct NR6 158 C2
Havaker The NR13 92 F5
Havant Cl NR4 161 E1
Havelock Pl 10 NR30 169 D2
Havelock Rd
Great Yarmouth NR30 169 D2
Norwich NR2 162 B6
Sheringham NR26 138 E5
Havergate 7 NR12 54 C6
Haveringland Rd NR10 52 E6
Havers Rd NR3 158 B1
Haverscroft Cl NR8 155 D2
Hawk Cres IP22 177 F5
Hawkes La NR14 89 A2
Hawkins Ave NR30 169 C8
Hawkins Cl NR30 169 C8
Hawkins Dr 1 PE13 152 E5
Hawthorn Ave 6 PE33 63 B4
Hawthorn Cl Diss IP22 177 F5
3 Spixworth NR10 54 A1
6 Watlington PE33 61 D5
Hawthorn Cotts PE31 140 D4
Hawthorn Cres NR31 94 C6
Hawthorn Dr
Dersingham PE31 140 D5
East Dereham NR19 154 B3
Hawthorn Rd
2 Downham Market PE38 172 C6
Emneth PE14 59 D1
6 Gayton PE32 45 C5
Great Yarmouth NR31 170 B6
Norwich NR5 157 A2
Hawthorn Rise NR11 143 B5
Hawthorn Way IP24 176 E6
Hawthorn Wlk 2 IP24 176 F6
Hawthorne Ave
Grimston PE32 28 B1
Hellesdon NR6 158 A5
Wisbech PE13 152 C8
Hawthorne Cl
2 Loddon NR14 91 F1
Wymondham NR18 173 D6
Hawthorns PE30 147 C4
Hay Gn Rd PE34 144 A1
Hay Gn Rd N PE34 42 B6
Hay Gn Rd S PE34 42 A5
Haycroft 3 NR29 167 B7
Hayes La NR21 141 A5
Hayfield Rd PE30 148 C4
Haygate 2 IP23 130 C1
Haylett Cl NR30 168 E5
Haymarket NR2 178 B2
Haythill La IP26 98 D2
Hayward Cl 3 NR25 7 C6
Haywood End IP22 120 D6
Hazel Ave NR26 138 D4
Hazel Cl Grimston PE32 28 B1
5 King's Lynn PE30 148 C3
Taverham NR8 155 D1
West Winch PE33 43 E1
Wymondham NR18 173 D4
Hazel Covert IP24 176 F5
Hazel Cres 4 PE33 63 B4
Hazel Gdns 1 PE13 152 D4
Hazel Gr NR19 154 F4
Hazel Rd
4 Attleborough NR17 174 B5
Norwich NR5 156 F1
Hazel Way NR31 170 B6
Hazell Rd NR28 151 C7
Heacham Fst Sch PE31 133 D5

Heacham Jun Sch
PE31 . . . . .133 C4
Heacham Rd PE36 . . . . .13 A7
Headington Cl NR31 . . .170 A5
Headland Dro IP26 . . . .113 A5
Headley Dr NR28 . . . . .151 C4
Hearne Cl **3** NR5 . . . . .160 E8
Heartsease Fst & Mid Sch
NR7 . . . . .159 C1
Heartsease High Sch
NR7 . . . . .159 C1
Heartsease La NR7 . . . .159 B1
Heartsease Mid Sch
NR7 . . . . .159 C1
Heartsease Rd **3** IP24 . .176 E5
Heartwell Rd NR27 . . . .139 C5
Heater La NR13 . . . . . . .73 F4
Heath Cl **11** Horsford NR10 .53 A3
  Lenwade NR9 . . . . .51 D5
  Norwich NR6 . . . . . . .158 A6
Heath Cres NR6 . . . . . .158 B5
Heath Dr NR25 . . . . .8 A5
Heath Farm La NR11 . . .36 E6
Heath Gn **1** NR31 . . . . .170 B5
Heath La
  Fakenham NR21 . . . . .141 F4
  Gimingham NR11 . . . . .22 D8
  Great Witchingham NR9 . .51 E6
  Gunthorpe NR24 . . . . . .18 B5
  Lenwade NR9 . . . . .51 D5
  Mundesley NR11 . . . . .143 B5
  Roughton NR11 . . . . . . .21 E8
  Thursford NR21 . . . . . .17 E4
  Tittleshall PE32 . . . . . . .47 F7
Heath Rd
  Ashby with Oby NR29 . . . .57 B2
  Banham NR16 . . . . . . .119 C7
  Brandon IP27 . . . . . . .175 D3
  Catfield NR29 . . . . .56 D8
  Corpusty NR11 . . . . . . .19 D1
  Dersingham PE31 . . . . .140 D2
  East Dereham NR19 . . .154 C7
  Felmingham NR28 . . . . .37 B8
  Fritton & St Olaves NR31 . .93 E1
  Geldeston NR34 . . . . . .110 A3
  Gunthorpe NR24 . . . . . .18 B5
  Heydon NR11 . . . . .34 D8
  Hickling NR12 . . . . .39 E1
  Hockering NR20 . . . . . .69 B8
  Honing NR28 . . . . .23 E1
  Kenninghall NR16 . . . . .119 A3
  Lessingham NR12 . . . . .24 F2
  Lyng NR9 . . . . .51 A4
  Norwich NR3 . . . . .162 D8
  Quidenham NR16 . . . . .118 E8
  Rollesby NR29 . . . . .57 B2
  Sapiston IP31 . . . . .126 E3
  Sheringham NR26 . . . . .138 D6
  Shotesham NR15 . . . . .107 F8
  9 Thorpe End NR13 . . . . .72 D6
  Troston IP31 . . . . .126 B1
  Winfarthing IP22 . . . . .120 A7
Heath Rise
  Fakenham NR21 . . . . . .141 E4
  Sculthorpe Airfield PE31 . .15 B3
Heath The NR10 . . . . . .52 F8
Heath Way Blofield NR13 .73 C6
  Fakenham NR21 . . . . . .141 F4
Heather Ave
  Hemsby NR29 . . . . . . .167 D4
  Norwich NR6 . . . . .158 A4
Heather Ave Fst Sch
NR6 . . . . .158 B4
Heather Barrow Ct
NR21 . . . . .141 D4
Heather Cl PE30 . . . . . .148 D5
Heather Dr NR25 . . . . .137 B7
Heather Gdns NR31 . . . .93 F6
Heather Rd **17** NR31 . . . .94 A6
Heather Way
  Brandon IP27 . . . . .175 E3
  Great Moulton NR15 . . .121 B8
Heatherwood Cl **7** NR13 .72 D6
Heathfield Cl NR25 . . . . .8 E3
Heathfield Rd NR25 . . . . .8 E3
Heathgate NR1 . . . . . . .163 A8
Heathlands PE37 . . . . .153 D2
Heathlands Dr IP24 . . . .176 D8
Heathside Rd NR1 . . . . .163 B5
Hebrides Way NR30 . . . .168 C6
Heckingham Holes
NR14 . . . . .92 B1
Hedgehog Wlk NR12 . . . .24 E4
Hedgelands **1** PE13 . . . .152 C8
Hedgemere **1** NR8 . . . .155 D2
Hedgerows The **8** NR5 . .161 A7
Hedley La NR33 . . . . . . .111 F1
Heffer Cl NR19 . . . . . . .154 D3
Heggatt Rd NR12 . . . . . .54 C5
Heidi Cl **1** NR19 . . . . . .154 D1
Heigham Gr NR2 . . . . . .162 A5
Heigham Pk Fst Sch
NR2 . . . . .162 A5
Heigham Rd NR2 . . . . .162 B6
Heigham St NR2 . . . . . .162 B8
Heigham Watering **5**
NR2 . . . . .162 A5
Helen Ave **7** NR29 . . . . .57 C4
Helena Rd
  Norwich NR2 . . . . .162 B6
  Witton NR12 . . . . .23 F3
Helford St **8** NR2 . . . . .162 B8
Hellesdon Cl NR5 . . . . .161 D8
Hellesdon Hall Rd
NR6 . . . . .157 E1
Hellesdon High Sch
NR6 . . . . .157 E4
Hellesdon Hospl NR6 . . .157 D4

Hellesdon Mill La
NR6 . . . . .157 D1
Hellesdon Pk Rd NR6 . .157 E3
Hellesdon Rd NR6 . . . . .161 D8
Hellgate La NR11 . . . . . .20 F8
Hellington Cnr NR14 . . . .91 B5
Hellington Hill NR14 . . . .91 B6
Hellpit La NR24 . . . . . . .19 B2
Helsinki Way NR14 . . . .154 C2
Helska Leisure Ctr
NR12 . . . . .55 E3
Hemblington Hall Rd
NR13 . . . . .73 E6
Hemblington Prim Sch
NR13 . . . . .73 C6
Hemblington Rd NR13 . . .73 E4
Hemington Cl PE30 . . . .147 E8
Hemlin Cl NR5 . . . . . . .161 C6
Hemmant Way NR34 . . .110 B3
Hemmings Cl **4** NR5 . . .160 F7
Hempnall Rd NR35 . . . .108 A4
Hempnall Sch NR15 . . . .107 C5
Hempstead Rd
  Holt NR25 . . . . .137 D5
  Lessingham NR12 . . . . .24 D3
Hempstead Mews NR5 . .160 E7
Hempton Rd NR21 . . . . .141 B3
Hemsby Fst Sch NR29 . .167 A7
Hemsby Rd
  15 Marthan NR29 . . . . . . .57 D4
  Winterton-on-Sea NR29 . .58 B5
Henby Way NR7 . . . . . .163 D7
Henderson Rd NR4 . . . .161 F5
Hendon Ave **18** IP25 . . . .84 F3
Hendon Cl NR5 . . . . . . .157 B1
Hendrie Rd NR25 . . . . .137 C7
Henley Rd NR2 . . . . . . .162 A4
Hennessey's Loke NR28 . .23 A3
Henry Bell Cl PE30 . . . .147 A5
Henry Blogg Rd NR27 . .139 B5
Henry Cross Cl **11** IP25 . . .67 C2
Henry Page Rd NR11 . . .150 B5
Henry Preston Rd **1**
NR15 . . . . .106 F6
Henry Ward Rd **1** IP20 .122 D2
Henry's Ct **1** IP25 . . . . .84 F3
Henson Cl **3** PE13 . . . .152 C8
Henstead Rd NR9 . . . . . .88 D8
Hepworth Rd IP31 . . . . .127 D3
Herbert Colman Cl
NR13 . . . . .73 E2
Herbert Dr IP26 . . . . . . .98 F5
Herbert Nursey Cl
NR8 . . . . .157 C2
Herbert Ward Way
PE34 . . . . .144 D6
Hercules Cl NR4 . . . . . .161 F4
Hercules Rd NR6 . . . . .157 F4
Hereford Way PE33 . . . . .43 E4
Hereward Rd **1** PE13 . .152 D5
Hereward Way
  5 Feltwell IP26 . . . . .98 D1
  Weeting IP27 . . . . .175 A8
  Weeting-with-Broomhill
  IP27 . . . . .114 E8
Herman Rd NR31 . . . . .170 A3
Herman Mid Sch
NR31 . . . . .170 A3
Hermanus Leisure Ctr
NR29 . . . . .58 B6
Hermitage Cl **3** NR13 . .166 D4
Herne Cotts NR19 . . . . .67 D5
Herne Dro NR19 . . . . . .95 D8
Herne La
  Beeston with Bittering
  PE32 . . . . .48 C1
  Shipdham NR19 . . . . . . .67 D5
Herolf Way **11** IP20 . . . .122 D2
Heron Ave IP27 . . . . . .175 E3
Heron Cl
  Downham Market PE38 . .172 C7
  6 Fakenham NR21 . . . . .141 E4
  Great Yarmouth NR31 . . .170 A7
  Salhouse NR13 . . . . . . .55 B1
Heron Gdns NR12 . . . . . .39 B3
Heron Rd PE13 . . . . . . .152 D2
Heron Way
  Hickling NR12 . . . . .39 E1
  12 Watton IP25 . . . . . . .84 C3
Herrick Rd NR8 . . . . . . .156 E8
Herries Cl **7** NR30 . . . .169 C4
Herring La NR9 . . . . .69 A1
Herring's La PE31 . . . . .135 C4
Herringfleet Rd NR31 . . .93 F2
Hertford Way NR31 . . . .170 B4
Hethel Old Thorn Nature
  Reserve* NR14 . . . . . . .88 E3
Hethel Rd NR14 . . . . . . .88 D2
Hethersett High Sch
NR9 . . . . .88 D7
Hethersett La NR4 . . . .160 F3
Hethersett Old Hall Sch
NR9 . . . . .88 D7
Hethersett Rd
  East Carleton NR14 . . . . .88 F5
  Great Melton NR9 . . . . . .88 B8
Hevingham Prim Sch
NR10 . . . . .53 D3
Hewett Cl NR31 . . . . . .170 D2
Hewett Rd NR31 . . . . . .170 A8
Hewett Sch NR1 . . . . . .162 D2
Hewitts Cl NR24 . . . . . .142 E4
Hewitts La NR18 . . . . . .173 C5
Hextable Rd PE30 . . . . .146 E6
Heydon Hall* NR11 . . . . .34 F6

Heydon La NR11 . . . . . . .34 E7
Heydon Rd
  Aylsham NR11 . . . . . . .150 A7
  Corpusty NR11 . . . . .34 F8
  Wood Dalling NR11 . . . . .34 D6
Heyford Rd NR6 . . . . . .158 C6
Heywood Ave NR16 . . . .177 D6
Heywood Rd Diss IP22 . .177 E8
  Shelfanger IP22 . . . . . .120 C2
  Tibenham NR16 . . . . . .120 D6
Heywood The IP22 . . . .120 E5
Hickathrift Field PE14 . . .61 A4
Hickling Broad National
  Nature Reserve*
  NR12 . . . . .57 A8
Hickling Broad Visitor Ctr*
  NR12 . . . . .40 A1
Hickling Cl PE37 . . . . . .153 C2
Hickling Cl Sch NR12 . . .39 F2
Hickling La NR14 . . . . . .89 D7
Hickling Rd
  Sea Palling NR12 . . . . . .24 F1
  Sutton NR12 . . . . .39 C2
Hickling Way NR29 . . . .167 B3
Hickling Wlk **11** IP25 . . . .84 F3
Hickory Rd PE30 . . . . . .147 C5
High Ash Rd NR18 . . . . .88 C5
High Banks NR18 . . . . .173 C3
High Bridgham Rd
  NR16 . . . . .117 C5
High Bungay Rd NR14 . .109 D8
High Comm NR18 . . . . .173 D2
High Comm Rd NR18 . . .173 D3
High Comm Rd IP22 . . .128 C8
High Cross NR20 . . . . . .33 A2
High Ct IP20 . . . . .122 E2
High Fen Dro IP26 . . . . .98 D8
High Gn Brooke NR15 . . .90 D1
  5 Great Melton NR9 . . . . .88 B8
  Great Moulton NR15 . . .121 B8
  Norwich NR1 . . . . .163 B5
High Gn Gdns NR15 . . . .90 D1
High Hill Rd NR12 . . . . .38 F6
High House Ave
  2 Wymondham NR18 . . .173 D5
  3 Wymondham NR18 . . .173 D5
High House Cotts PE32 . .47 E5
High House La **8** NR11 . .73 D6
High House Rd NR20 . . . .49 C4
High Lodge Forest Ctr*
  IP27 . . . . .115 C3
High London La IP22 . . .120 A4
High Mill Rd NR31 . . . . .169 B3
High Noon La NR13 . . . . .73 E6
High Noon Rd NR13 . . . .21 D2
High Oak La NR18 . . . . . .87 B4
High Oak Rd NR18 . . . . .87 B3
High Rd Beighton NR13 . .74 B1
  Bressingham IP22 . . . . .129 C8
  Burgh Castle NR31 . . . . .94 B8
  Cantley NR13 . . . . .92 B8
  Forncett NR16 . . . . . . .106 B6
  Great Yarmouth NR31 . .170 D7
  Lessingham NR12 . . . . . .24 C2
  Needham IP20 . . . . . . .131 E2
  Repps with Bastwick
  NR29 . . . . .57 A4
  Roydon IP22 . . . . .177 A5
  Tilney St Lawrence PE34 . .60 F8
  Wiggenhall St Germans
  PE34 . . . . .42 F1
  Wortwell IP20 . . . . . . .123 A3
High St
  Attleborough NR17 . . . .174 D5
  Blakeney NR25 . . . . .7 C6
  Brandon IP27 . . . . .175 C5
  Caister-on-Sea NR30 . . .168 E5
  Castle Acre PE32 . . . . . .46 F2
  Cawston NR10 . . . . .35 B3
  Cley next the Sea NR25 . . .7 E6
  Coltishall NR12 . . . . . . .54 C7
  Cromer NR27 . . . . .139 B7
  Docking PE31 . . . . .134 E4
  Downham Market PE38 . .172 C5
  East Dereham NR19 . . .154 D5
  Feltwell IP26 . . . . .98 E1
  Fincham PE33 . . . . .62 E1
  Foulsham NR20 . . . . . . .33 D3
  Great Yarmouth NR31 . .170 D6
  Hemsby NR29 . . . . . . .167 D4
  Hethersett NR9 . . . . . . .88 D7
  Hilgay PE38 . . . . .79 E1
  Holt NR25 . . . . .137 B6
  Hopton IP22 . . . . .127 F6
  Hunstanton PE36 . . . . .132 C4
  Ketteringham NR18 . . . .88 D5
  King's Lynn PE30 . . . . .146 D5
  Lakenheath IP27 . . . . . .113 E1
  Loddon NR14 . . . . .92 A1
  Ludham NR29 . . . . .56 C5
  Marsham NR10 . . . . . . .150 C5
  Methwold IP26 . . . . .99 A5
  Mundesley NR11 . . . . .143 C5
  North Elmham NR20 . . . .49 E8
  Northwold IP26 . . . . . . .99 C7
  Overstrand NR27 . . . . . .11 A3
  St Margaret, Ilketshall
  NR35 . . . . .124 D3
  5 Sheringham NR26 . . . .138 D7
  Shipdham IP25 . . . . .67 B2
  Southtown NR31 . . . . . .169 C2
  Stalham NR12 . . . . .39 B4
  Stoke Ferry PE33 . . . . . .81 A2
  Sutton Bridge PE12 . . . .41 C8
  Thelnetham IP22 . . . . .128 B4
  Thornham PE36 . . . . .2 D6

High St continued
  Thursford NR21 . . . . . . .17 D5
  Tittleshall PE32 . . . . . . .48 B8
  Walsingham NR22 . . . . .16 F7
  Watton IP25 . . . . .84 D3
  Wells-next-the-Sea
  NR23 . . . . .136 D5
  Whissonsett NR20 . . . . .31 D2
  Wicklewood NR18 . . . . .87 B5
  Wighton NR23 . . . . .5 F2
  Wisbech PE13 . . . . . . .152 C5
High View Dr NR17 . . . .174 B4
High Way **15** NR13 . . . . .74 A3
High Wrong Cnr NR14 . .115 C1
Higham Cl NR27 . . . . . .159 A3
Higham Gn **3** PE30 . . .147 C4
Highbridge Gravel Dro
  IP27 . . . . .113 D2
Highbridge Rd PE34 . . . .78 F8
Highbury Rd IP27 . . . . .175 A2
Highfield Gn **7** NR15 . . .89 D1
Highfield **3** Eye IP23 . .130 C1
  Field Dalling NR25 . . . . . .7 B2
  Great & Little Plumstead
  NR13 . . . . .73 B7
  King's Lynn PE30 . . . . .147 C5
Highfield Ave NR13 . . . .165 D3
Highfield Cl
  Foulsham NR20 . . . . . . .33 C4
  Ryburgh NR21 . . . . .32 A6
Highfield La NR21 . . . . . .32 A6
Highfield Rd
  East Dereham NR19 . . .141 B5
  Fakenham NR21 . . . . . .141 B5
  Great Yarmouth NR31 . .170 C7
  Taverham NR8 . . . . . . .155 F1
Highfield Way **4** NR12 . .54 C7
Highfields
  Felmingham NR28 . . . . .37 A8
  Lakenheath IP27 . . . . . .113 F1
  Norwich NR5 . . . . .156 D1
Highgate PE30 . . . . . . .146 F6
Highgate Inf Sch
  PO30 . . . . .146 F6
Highgrove Ct NR14 . . . . .90 C6
Highland NR18 . . . . .90 B6
Highland Ave NR22 . . . .162 A4
Highland Cl NR13 . . . . . .92 C6
Highland Cres NR14 . . . .54 C7
Highland Rd
  Norwich NR8 . . . . .162 A4
  Taverham NR8 . . . . . . .155 D1
Highlands
  Costessey NR8 . . . . . . .156 F4
  Thetford IP24 . . . . .176 D5
Highlow Rd NR5 . . . . . .157 A1
Highmoor Dro IP26 . . . . .99 D8
Highview Rd NR13 . . . .165 E6
Highview Pk NR22 . . . . .16 F7
Hilary Ave NR1 . . . . . . .163 B8
Hilary Cl **6** NR19 . . . . . .154 C1
Hilda Rd NR11 . . . . . . .143 C6
Hilgay Rd Ryston PE38 . . .79 F3
  West Dereham PE33 . . . .80 A4
Hilgay Village Prim Sch
  PE38 . . . . .170 E1
Hill Ave NR31 . . . . .170 D1
Hill Cl NR12 . . . . .39 F1
Hill Comm NR12 . . . . . .39 F1
Hill Crest Rd NR7 . . . . .163 D7
Hill Est The PE33 . . . . . .62 B6
Hill Fields NR19 . . . . . .154 C1
Hill Fort Cl IP24 . . . . . .176 C7
Hill House Ave
  Bramerton NR14 . . . . . .90 F8
  Norwich NR1 . . . . .163 A5
Hill House Rd
  6 La Runhall NR20 . . . . . .69 A8
  Sculthorpe Airfield NR21 . .15 C2
Hill Rd
  Ingoldisthorpe PE31 . . .140 C8
  King's Lynn PE30 . . . . .147 B8
  Middleton PE33 . . . . . . .44 B3
  Morley NR18 . . . . .104 D8
  Norwich NR5 . . . . .157 A2
  Tibenham NR16 . . . . . .120 F8
  Wymondham NR18 . . . .105 A7
Hill Side Cl **3** PE32 . . . .44 B3
Hill St **11** Feltwell IP26 . .98 E1
  Hunstanton PE36 . . . . .132 C4
  Norwich NR2 . . . . .162 C4
  5 Wisbech PE13 . . . . . .152 C4
Hill Top
  Cley next the Sea NR25 . . .7 E7
  Stanton IP31 . . . . .127 C1
Hill Top Dr NR8 . . . . . . .156 F7
Hill View Rd NR25 . . . . .137 B5
Hillary Rd IP24 . . . . . . .176 C2
Hill's Cl PE38 . . . . .79 D7
Hill's Ct **3** Corpusty NR11 .19 F1
  Sporle PE32 . . . . .65 C6
Hillburn Dr NR13 . . . . .152 B4
Hillcourt PE14 . . . . .59 A1
Hillcrest Acle NR13 . . . . .166 C4
  Downham Market PE38 . .172 E5
  Great Ryburgh NR21 . . . .32 B6
Hillcrest Ave NR19 . . . .154 C1

Hillcrest Prim Sch
  PE38 . . . . .172 E6
Hillen Rd PE30 . . . . . . .146 D2
Hillfield NR12 . . . . .38 D3
Hillgate St PE34 . . . . . .144 A4
Hillingdon Pk NR27 . . . . .11 A4
Hillings Way PE32 . . . . .28 A1
Hillington Sq PE30 . . . .146 E4
Hillmead NR3 . . . . .158 D3
Hills Rd IP25 . . . . .84 C5
Hills The NR13 . . . . .92 F4
Hillsend La NR17 . . . . . .174 A3
Hillside
  Barnham Broom NR9 . . . .69 B2
  Barsham NR21 . . . . .16 D5
  Brandon IP27 . . . . .114 D4
  Briston NR24 . . . . .142 B4
  Cromer NR27 . . . . .139 C4
  Loddon NR14 . . . . .92 A2
  Marham PE33 . . . . .63 B5
  Mundesley NR11 . . . . .143 D5
  North Pickenham PE37 . . .65 E2
  Poringland NR14 . . . . . .90 C5
  Roughton NR11 . . . . . . .10 D1
  Sheringham NR26 . . . . .138 D6
  Swaffham PE37 . . . . . .153 D4
Hillside Animal Sanctuary*
  NR12 . . . . .54 B4
Hillside Ave NR7 . . . . . .163 F6
Hillside Ave Prim Sch
  NR7 . . . . .163 F6
Hillside Cl
  Norwich NR7 . . . . .163 F6
  Ormesby St Margaret
  NR29 . . . . .167 B2
  Swardeston NR14 . . . . .89 C5
Hillside Cres NR18 . . . . .87 B5
Hillside Fst Sch NR31 . . .94 C7
Hillside Rd
  Horning NR12 . . . . .55 E3
  Norwich NR7 . . . . .163 F6
  Sheringham NR26 . . . . .138 F5
Hilltop Rd W NR35 . . . .124 A7
Hilltop Way NR7 . . . . . .127 C1
Hillview NR7 . . . . .165 E2
Hillview Dr NR29 . . . . . .58 B6
Hillvue Cl NR5 . . . . . . .157 A2
Hilly Plantation NR7 . . .163 D7
Hilton Cl IP27 . . . . .153 C4
Hilton Ct PE13 . . . . . . .153 D4
Hiltons La **5** PE34 . . . . .43 B1
Hinchingbrook Cl
  PE30 . . . . .148 E1
Hinderclay La IP22 . . . .128 B5
Hinderclay Rd
  Redgrave IP22 . . . . . . .128 D5
  Rickinghall Inferior
  IP22 . . . . .128 D3
  Wattisfield IP22 . . . . . .128 D3
Hindolveston Rd
  Foulsham NR20 . . . . . . .33 D4
  Fulmodeston NR21 . . . . .17 F1
  Guestwick NR20 . . . . . .33 F6
  Thurning NR20 . . . . . . .34 A8
Hindringham Prim Sch
  NR21 . . . . .17 A8
Hindringham Rd
  Binham NR21 . . . . .6 E2
  Gunthorpe NR21 . . . . . .18 A7
  Hindringham NR21 . . . . .17 F7
  Walsingham NR22 . . . . .17 A8
Hingham Prim Sch
  NR9 . . . . .86 C5
Hingham Rd
  Deopham NR18 . . . . . . .86 F5
  Garvestone NR9 . . . . . .86 E8
  Great Ellingham NR17 . .103 E8
  Hardingham NR9 . . . . . .86 E6
  Little Ellingham NR17 . . .86 A2
  Hingley Cl NR31 . . . . . .170 C8
  Hinks Cl NR13 . . . . . . .155 C3
Hinshalwood Way
  NR8 . . . . .156 E4
Hipkin Rd PE31 . . . . . .140 C3
Hipperson Cl **2** NR28 . .151 C7
Hippodrome* NR30 . . . .169 C3
Hobart Cl NR18 . . . . . .173 C6
Hobart High Sch NR14 . .92 A1
Hobart La NR12 . . . . . .178 B1
Hobart Sq NR1 . . . . . . .178 B1
Hobb's La NR13 . . . . . . .92 D7
Hobbies Mus of Fretwork &
  Craft Ctr* NR19 . . . . .154 C5
Hobbs's La NR15 . . . . .108 D7
Hobland Rd
  Belton with Browston
  NR31 . . . . .94 C4
  Bradwell NR31 . . . . . . .171 A7
Hobrough La NR14 . . . .178 C2
Hockering La NR9 . . . . .160 B6
Hockering Prim Sch
  NR20 . . . . .69 B8
Hockham St PE30 . . . . .146 D5
Hockwold Prim Sch
  IP26 . . . . .114 A6
Hockwold Rd IP27 . . . . .175 B7
Hodgson Rd NR4 . . . . . .161 F5
Hoe Hall NR20 . . . . .50 E6
Hoe Rd NR20 . . . . .49 F5
  Longham NR19 . . . . . . .49 A3
Hoe Rd N NR20 . . . . . . .50 A3
Hoe Rd S NR20 . . . . . . .50 A4

Hoe Rough Nature Reserve*
NR20 ....49 E4
Hog Bog La NR10 ....53 F3
Hog La NR34 ....124 F2
Hogarth Cl 15 NR31 ...94 C8
Hogarth Rd PE38 ....172 E6
Hogg La NR35 ....108 C1
Hogg's Dro PE33 ......63 B5
Hogherd's La 5 PE13 .152 C5
Hogsty La IP21 .....122 A1
Holbrigg La NR21 ....17 C1
Holcombe Ave PE30 .146 F3
Holders La IP26 .....99 A7
Holgate Hill NR25 .....8 D4
Holgate La 5 NR27 ..10 B5
Holgate Rd
North Walsham NR28 ...151 F1
South Creake NR21 ....15 C7
Holkham Ave PE37 ..153 B2
Holkham Cl 7 PE38 .172 C6
Holkham Hall & Bygones,
Mus* NR23 ....5 A5
Holkham National Nature
Reserve* NR23 ......5 B8
Holkham Rd NR23 ...136 B6
Holl La Billingford NR20 ..50 F7
Garvestone NR9 ......68 B1
Holl Rd NR11 ....21 B4
Holland Ct 8 NR19 ..154 D1
Holland's La NR35 ..108 C3
Holley Wlk NR11 ....150 C4
Hollies The
Clenchwarton PE34 ...145 D5
8 North Walsham NR28 .151 C5
Hollow Hill Rd NR35 ..109 A2
Hollow La
Barningham IP31 ....127 D4
4 Langham NR25 ......7 A4
Raynham NR21 ....30 F3
Shotesham NR15 .....89 F2
Hollow Way Hill NR14 .110 D4
Holloway Rd NR14 ....91 B8
Holls La NR21 ....178 B1
Hollway La NR20 .....33 A4
Holly Ave NR31 ......94 C7
Holly Bank NR2 .....159 A2
Holly Blue Rd NR18 .173 E4
Holly Cl Dereham NR19 ..154 F4
Downham Market PE38 ..172 B6
Holt NR25 ....137 D7
King's Lynn PE30 ...148 D2
12 Marthan NR29 .....57 D4
Mattishall NR20 .....68 E6
Rougham PE32 ....47 B7
1 West Winch PE33 ...43 E2
Holly Ct
34 Harleston IP20 ...122 D2
5 Sheringham PE13 ..153 C4
Wymondham NR18 ...173 E6
Holly Dr NR2 ....162 A7
Holly Farm Rd NR13 ..93 A4
Holly Gr NR26 ......138 D5
Holly La Blofield NR13 ..165 D7
Lackenheath IP27 ...113 E1
13 Tharston & Hapton
NR15 ....106 D3
Wood Dalling NR11 ..34 C5
Holly Rd NR17 ....174 C4
Holly Way 13 NR31 ..170 B6
Hollybush Rd NR28 ..151 F5
Hollycroft Cl PE14 ...59 D1
Hollycroft Rd PE14 ...77 D8
Hollywell Gdns PE13 .153 B4
Holman Cl NR11 ....150 B7
Holman Rd NR11 ....150 B6
Holman's Chase PE38 ..97 B6
Holme Cl Hopton IP22 ..127 F6
Runcton Holme PE33 ....61 D4
Holme Dunes National
Nature Reserve* PE36 ..2 A8
Holme Rd PE36 ......2 A4
Holmes Cl Acle NR13 ..166 B4
Norwich NR7 ....163 D8
Holmes Dr PE13 ....152 E5
Holmes Rd
East Ruston NR12 .....38 F5
Somerton NR29 ......57 F7
Holmesdale Rd NR13 ..165 B4
Holmwood Rise NR7 ..163 C6
Holt Ct PE14 ....41 E3
Holt Ctry Pk* NR25 ..137 C4
Holt House La PE27 ..24 D7
Holt Prim Sch NR25 .137 B5
Holt Rd Aylmerton NR11 ...9 D8
Briston NR24 ....142 E5
Cawston NR10 ....35 D2
Cley next the Sea NR25 ..7 E6
Cromer NR27 ....139 A6
Fakenham NR21 .....141 C4
Felthorpe NR10 ......52 F6
Field Dalling NR25 ....7 B2
Gresham NR11 ....9 E1
Guist NR20 ....32 F4
Hoe NR19 ....154 C8
Langham NR25 ....7 A4
Letheringsett with Glandford
NR25 ....8 A1
Little Snoring NR21 ..17 C3
North Elmham NR20 ..49 E7
Norwich NR10 ......157 F8
Sheringham NR26 ...138 B5
Thornage NR25 ......18 F7
Upper Sheringham
NR26 ....138 C3
Walsingham NR22 ...16 F7

Holt Rd *continued*
Weybourne NR25 ....8 E5
Holt Sta NR25 ....137 E8
Holt's La PE38 ....79 D1
Holway Cl NR27 .....139 B3
Holway Rd NR26 ....138 D5
Holway The NR29 ....58 B6
Holworthy Rd NR5 ..161 B8
Holy Rd NR24 ....18 D5
Holyrood Dr PE31 ..140 D3
Home Cl
Great Ellingham NR17 ..103 E8
Lyng NR9 ....51 A4
5 Sheringham NR27 ..10 A5
Home Farm La NR18 ..104 E8
Home Farm Rd NR15 ..109 C3
Home Farm Rise NR25 ..8 E6
Home La
Hilborough IP25 ......83 B4
Hindringham NR21 ....17 F7
Home Piece IP22 ....127 E4
Home St NR2 ....162 C2
Homebred La 1 NR14 ..91 F1
Homefield Ave NR31 ..94 C7
Homefield Fst Sch
NR31 ....94 C7
Homefields La PE36 ..132 D4
Homeland Rd 10 PE36 ..146 E6
Homelea Cres 15 NR13 ..74 A3
Homestead Cl 7 NR13 ..74 A3
Homestead Gdns
NR29 ....167 B7
Honey Cl 2 NR1 ....163 B7
Honey Dro PE33 .....80 B1
Honey Hill IP34 .....79 D8
Honey Hills PE31 ....14 A5
Honeycombe Rd NR13 ..73 B8
Honeymoon Loke
NR30 ....168 F4
Honeymoon Row
NR23 ....136 D5
Honeypot Dro PE32 ..46 C5
Honeypot La
Kirby Cane NR35 ....109 E5
Longham NR19 ......48 F2
Seething NR15 ......108 E8
Honeysuckle Cl
North Walsham NR28 ..151 E4
5 Thetford IP24 .....176 F4
Honeysuckle Dr NR20 ..154 F4
Honeysuckle Way
NR17 ....174 B5
Honing Long La NR28 ..38 C7
Honing Rd NR28 .....38 D5
Honing Row NR28 ...38 A5
Honingham La NR8 ...70 A8
Honington Airfield
IP31 ....126 A2
Honington Rise IP31 .126 C1
Honington VC Prim Sch
IP31 ....126 D1
Hood Way IP24 .....176 E5
Hook's Wlk NR1 ....178 C3
Hooker Rd NR7 .....159 D1
Hooks Hill Rd NR26 .138 C6
Hookwood La NR18 ..104 C8
Hooper La NR3 .....158 F2
Hooton's Row PE38 ..78 F6
Hope Ct PE30 ......147 A8
Hope La PE14 ....60 A4
Hopton CE VC Prim Sch
IP22 ....127 F5
Hopton Cl 6 NR7 ....72 D4
Hopton Gdns NR31 ..171 D5
Hopton Rd
Barningham IP31 ....127 D4
Garboldisham IP22 ..128 A8
Thelnetham IP22 ....128 A5
Horizon Views NR12 ..24 A7
Hornbeam Cl
5 Great Yarmouth NR31 ..170 B6
Norwich NR7 ....159 D4
Hornbeam Dr 15 NR14 ..90 C5
Horner Cl 3 IP22 ...177 A5
Horning Cl NR5 ....161 D7
Horning Fst Sch NR12 ..55 F3
Horning Rd
Hoveton NR12 ......164 E5
Neatishead NR12 ....55 D6
Woodbastwick NR13 ..55 D2
Horning Rd W NR12 .164 C5
Hornor Cl NR2 .....162 C3
Horns La NR1 ......178 B2
Horns Row NR11 ...141 A3
Horsbeck Way NR10 ..53 A3
Horse Fair 2 PE13 ..152 C5
Horse Rescue Ctr*
NR16 ....103 C2
Horsefen Rd NR29 ...56 D4
Horsehead Dro PE14 ..95 C8
Horses Head NR13 ..166 B7
Horseshoe Cl NR5 ..156 E1
Horse-Shoe Cnr PE13 ..152 B7
Horseshoe La NR24 ..142 F4
Horseshoe Terr PE13 ..152 B7
Horsey Rd NR29 .....57 E7
Horsey Windpump*
NR29 ....40 D1
Horsey's La NR13 ..170 D5
Horsford All Saints Mid Sch
NR10 ....53 B4
Horsford St 7 NR2 ..162 B8
Horsford VC Fst Sch
NR10 ....53 B3

Horsham St Faith VC Fst Sch
NR10 ....53 E2
Horsley Dr
Great Yarmouth NR31 ..170 B1
Hopton on Sea NR31 ..171 D4
Horsley's Chase PE30 ..146 E2
Horsley's Ct 7 PE30 ..146 E3
Horsley's Field PE30 ..146 E2
Horton Rd PE30 ....147 D6
Hospital La
Hellesdon NR6 ......157 D3
Norwich NR1 ....162 E3
Hospital Rd
Great & Little Plumstead
NR13 ....73 A5
Sutton Bridge PE12 ..41 E8
Wicklewood NR18 ....87 C4
Hospital Wlk PE30 ..146 E4
Hotblack Rd NR2 ...162 A8
Hotch La PE14 ....60 B8
Hotson Cl 5 NR15 ..106 D3
Houghton Ave PE30 ..148 D1
Houghton Cl 3 NR5 ..160 F8
Houghton Hall* PE31 ..29 C7
Houghton La PE37 ...65 E1
House Gdns NR10 ...53 E5
Hovell's La IP26 .....99 C7
Hoveton & Wroxham Sta
NR12 ....164 C5
Hoveton Cl PE30 ...147 D5
Hoveton Hall Gdns*
NR12 ....55 B7
Hoveton Pl NR10 ....37 B2
How Hill Nature Reserve*
NR29 ....56 A6
How Hill Rd NR29 ...56 B6
Howard Cl
Harleston IP20 .....122 E2
Norwich NR7 ....153 E4
4 Swanton Morley NR20 ..50 B3
Terrington St Clement
PE34 ....144 B4
Howard Cres NR19 ..154 D4
Howard Inf Sch PE30 ..147 B4
Howard Jun Sch PE30 ..147 B4
Howard Mews NR3 ..158 E1
Howard St NR1 .....178 A1
Howard St NR1 .....178 A2
Howard St S NR30 ..169 C4
Howard Way NR11 ..150 C5
Howard's Hill NR27 ..139 A7
Howard's Hill Rd NR28 ..38 C7
Howard's Way NR10 ..35 B2
Howards Cl PE36 ...132 E7
Howards Hill Cl NR27 ..10 C5
Howards Hill W 1
NR27 ....139 A7
Howards The PE30 ..148 D4
Howdale Rd PE38 ...172 C5
Howe Gn NR15 ......90 D2
Howe La NR15 ....90 D3
Howe Rd NR30 .....169 D7
Howell Rd NR8 .....157 C6
Howes Cl 10 NR9 ....88 D7
Howes La NR20 .....68 D6
Howes Yd 8 NR25 ...7 E6
Howland Cl NR21 ..141 B5
Howlett Cl
4 East Dereham NR19 ..154 D2
North Walsham NR28 ..151 A5
Howlett Way 2 IP24 ..176 D6
Howletts Hill PE13 ..152 C4
Hoxne Rd Denham IP21 ..131 B1
Eye IP23 ....130 E1
Syleham IP21 ....131 C4
Upper Weybread IP21 ..131 E6
Hubbard Cl
11 Long Stratton NR15 ..106 E3
Wymondham NR18 ...173 A6
Hubbard's Dro PE38 ..79 E1
Hudson Leisure Ctr
PE13 ....152 A5
Hudson Way NR5 ...160 E7
Hugh Cl PE30 ......148 C5
Hugh Rd NR1 ......162 E8
Hughes Cl 25 NR9 ...88 D8
Hulton Rd PE30 ....147 A5
Hulver Rd NR13 .....73 E8
Hulver St NR19 ......66 F6
Humber Cl NR30 ...168 C5
Humber Keel NR31 ..170 D1
Humberstone Rd 3
NR31 ....170 C7
Humbleyard NR5 ...161 A7
Hungate La NR11 ...150 C4
Hungate Rd PE14 ....59 E2
Hungate St NR11 ...150 C4
Hungry Hill NR27 ....11 B7
Hunstanton Commercial Pk
PE36 ....132 D3
Hunstanton Inf Sch
PE36 ....132 D5
Hunstanton Rd
Dersingham PE31 ....140 D5
Heacham PE31 ......132 D1
Hunstanton Sea Life
Sanctuary* PE36 ...132 B3
Hunstead La NR15 ...90 F2
Hunt Cl Old Catton NR6 ..158 E7
5 Redenhall with Harleston
IP20 ....122 D2
Hunter Ave NR20 ....68 F5
Hunter Dr 4 NR31 ...94 C8

Hunter Rd
Norwich NR3 ....158 C3
Troston IP31 ....126 B1
Hunter's Dro PE14 ...60 B6
Hunters Cl
Brundall NR13 .....165 F5
Terrington St Clement
PE34 ....144 F6
Hunters Oak 2 IP25 ..84 E3
Huntley Cres NR25 .138 E6
Hunts Gn NR16 ....105 B4
Hunworth Rd NR24 .142 D8
Hurd Rd NR4 ....161 E3
Hurdle La NR25 ......7 E4
Hurn La NR16 ......106 A6
Hurn Rd Dereham NR20 ..68 A7
Taverham NR8 ......157 E7
Hurrell Rd NR30 ...168 D6
Hurricane Way NR6 ..158 C6
Hurst Rd 8 NR14 ....92 A2
Hurth Way NR14 ...176 E4
Husenbeth Cl NR8 ..156 D4
Hutchinson Rd NR5 ..161 D6
Huxley Cl NR1 ......162 F2
Huxley Rd NR1 .....162 F2
Hyde Cl PE31 ....14 D4
Hyde Cl NR13 ....72 E5
Hyde Rd NR19 ......154 D3
Hydrographic La NR17 ..174 A2
Hyrn Cl NR29 ....57 D4
Hythe Rd Feltwell IP26 ..98 E3
Foulden IP26 ....82 A1
Methwold IP26 ......98 F5

I

Ice House Ct 17 NR15 ..106 E3
Ice House La NR1 ...178 C1
Iceni Dr PE37 ......153 D2
Icknield Cl IP24 ....176 B3
Icknield Way IP24 ..176 B3
Ickworth Cl PE30 ..148 E1
Ilex Ct NR7 ....159 D4
Illington Rd IP24 ..122 C8
ILPH Hall Farm*
NR16 ....118 B7
Impala Cl NR6 .....159 A6
Imperial Mews NR31 ..171 C4
Impson Way IP26 ...99 C6
Incleborough Cl 2 NR27 ..10 B5
Independent Way 14
NR7 ....72 D4
Indigo Yd NR3 .....178 A3
Ingham Cnr NR12 ...24 D1
Ingham Rd
Lessingham NR12 ....24 D2
Stalham NR12 ......39 B4
Ingle Rd PE14 ....59 B1
Ingleby Cl
Feakenham PE31 ...133 E6
King's Lynn PE30 ..147 B4
Ingloss La NR14 ...109 B7
Ingoldale PE31 .....144 C6
Ingoldisthorpe Fst Sch
PE31 ....140 E8
Ingoldsby Ave PE31 ..140 D6
Ingolside PE31 ......12 D4
Ingram Ct NR1 ....162 E3
Ingram's Rd IP21 ..131 C7
Inman Rd NR7 .....159 D3
Inspire Discovery Ctr*
NR3 ....178 A4
Intwood La
East Carleton NR14 ..89 A5
Swardeston NR14 ....89 C6
Intwood Rd NR4 ....89 B8
Invaders Ct NR23 ..136 D6
Ipswich Gr NR2 ....178 A1
Ipswich Rd
2 Norwich NR2 .....89 E8
Norwich NR2 ....178 A1
Pulham Market NR15 ..121 E8
Saxlingham Nethergate
NR15 ....107 A7
Scole IP21 ....130 D5
Yaxley IP23 ....130 A1
Ireton Cl 25 NR7 ....72 D4
Iris Cl NR17 ....174 B5
Irmingland Rd NR11 ..34 F8
Ironside Way NR9 ...86 D5
Irstead Rd
Barton Turf NR12 ....55 F7
Irstead NR12 ......56 A7
Irving Rd NR4 .....161 E6
Irwin Cl NR10 ......149 D4
Isaac's Rd NR31 ...169 B4
Isabella Cl PE30 ...147 D3
Isabella Sq 12 NR30 ..169 D3
Isbets Dale NR8 ....155 D2
Isis Cl NR31 ....170 B3
Isle Bridge Rd PE14 ..77 E6
Isle Rd PE14 ....77 F7
Iveagh Cl PE12 ....140 E2
Ives Cl IP22 ....177 E4
Ives Rd NR6 ....158 E5
Ivory Rd NR4 ......161 E4
Ivy Gn NR30 ....170 A5
Ivy Rd 1 Earlham NR5 ..161 E7
8 Spixworth NR10 ...54 A2
Ivy Todd Rd PE37 ...66 A4
Ivy Way NR20 ......68 E6
Ixworth Rd IP31 ...126 D1

J

Jack Plummer Way
NR30 ....168 C7
Jaguar Rd 9 NR9 ....88 D8
James Bradfield Prim Sch
PE33 ....81 A2
James Carter Rd NR19 ..154 C4
James Cl PE30 .....148 B1
James Gn Cl 10 NR20 ..54 A2
James Jackson Rd
PE31 ....140 C3
James Paget Hospl
NR31 ....170 B1
James Rd 7 NR31 ...55 E4
James Scott Cl 3 PE38 ..172 A5
James St PE36 ......132 D4
James Watt Cl 11 NR31 ..170 A8
Jamieson Pl NR5 ...161 C8
Jane Forby Cl PE33 ..80 E2
Jankin La PE34 .....144 A1
Jannys Cl NR11 ....150 B6
Jarrold Ct IP31 .....127 D3
Jarrold Way NR5 ..160 F8
Jarvie Cl PE36 ....13 A7
Jarvis Dr NR21 ......31 E5
Jarvis Rd PE30 ....146 E8
Jasmin Cl PE13 ...152 F7
Jasmine Cl
Earlham NR4 ....161 E5
Thetford IP24 ......176 F4
Jasmine Cl 1 NR17 ..174 B5
Jasmine Gdns 7 NR31 ..94 C7
Jasmine Gn 8 NR31 ..170 B5
Javelin Rd NR6 ....158 C7
Jay Gdns NR5 ......160 F8
Jay La NR32 ....171 C3
Jay's Gn IP20 ......122 E2
Jefferey Ave 4 PE13 ..152 E7
Jeffery Cl PE30 ....146 E8
Jegon Cl NR11 .....150 D5
Jellicoe PI 11 PE13 ..152 E7
Jellicoe Rd PE30 ..169 C8
Jenkinsons Pightle
NR35 ....108 B4
Jenner Rd 4 NR31 .170 B1
Jennings Cl PE31 ..133 C5
Jennings Way IP22 ..177 D5
Jenny Rd 8 NR10 ...54 A2
Jermyn Rd PE30 ...147 C6
Jermyn Way 1 NR15 ..106 D3
Jerningham Rd NR5 ..157 A1
Jessopp Cl
Norwich NR2 ......161 F4
Scarning NR19 .....67 B7
Jessopp Rd NR4 ...161 F4
Jetty Cl NR27 ......139 B7
Jetty Cliff NR27 ....139 C7
Jetty St 2 NR27 ....139 C7
Jewel Cl NR24 .....142 C6
Jews' La 10 NR31 ...94 C6
Jewson Rd NR3 ....158 C2
Jex Ave NR5 ....161 C8
Jex La NR5 ....161 D8
Jex Rd NR5 ....161 D8
Jickling Yd NR23 ...136 D6
Joan Short's La PE31 ..133 D3
Jodrell Cl 3 NR21 ..121 E5
Joe Ellis Ct 6 NR5 ..161 B8
John Bates Cl 2 NR19 ..154 E5
John Chapman Cl 5
NR21 ....141 E4
John Davis Way PE13 ..61 D5
John Drewry Cl 2 NR14 ..90 D5
John F Kennedy Cl 2
PE13 ....152 D4
John Gale Ct NR8 ..155 E3
John Goshawk Rd
NR19 ....154 E2
John Grant Specl Sch
NR30 ....168 D6
John Hill Cl 8 NR15 ..106 E3
John Jarrold Printing Mus*
NR1 ....178 C4
John Kennedy Rd
PE30 ....146 D6
John of Gaunt Fst Sch
NR11 ....150 C5
John O'Gaunt Cl NR11 ..150 B6
John Rd
Caister-on-Sea NR30 ..168 E7
Great Yarmouth NR31 ..170 D5
John St 3 PE30 ....146 E3
John Stephenson Ct 1
NR6 ....158 F1
John Thompson Rd 3
PE13 ....152 D4
John Woodhouse Dr
NR28 ....151 D5
Johnson Cl 7 NR19 ..154 C3
Johnson Cres PE31 ..133 C4
Johnson Pl NR2 ...162 C3
Jolly Gardeners Ct 13
PE30 ....146 E3
Jolly Sailor Yd NR23 ..136 D6
Jolly's La NR13 ....166 C3
Jones (GC) Way NR31 ..169 B2
Jones's Dro PE14 ....95 E8
Jordan Cl Norwich NR8 ..155 E4
Jordan La NR10 ....149 D4
Jordan Rd NR30 ...168 E6
Jose Neville Cl 2 NR8 ..168 D7
Joseph Lancaster Way 4
NR3 ....178 B4
Josephine Cl NR1 ..162 D3
Joshua Ct NR1 .....171 D8
Joy Ave 1 NR15 ...107 A8

Joyce La
Heacham PE31 . . . . .133 D5
Walpole PE14 . . . . .41 F3
Joyce Rd NR35 . . . . .124 B8
Joyce Way 🟥 NR7 . . . . . . .72 D5
Joyland* NR30 . . . . .169 E4
Jubilee Ave
🟦 East Dereham NR20 . . .154 E6
East Harling NR16 . . . . . .118 C5
Fakenham NR21 . . . . .141 C4
Heacham PE31 . . . . .133 B5
Jubilee Bank Rd PE34 . . .146 A5
Jubilee Cl Cawston NR10 . .35 B2
Downham Market PE38 . . .172 E5
Erpingham NR11 . . . . .21 B2
Hunstanton PE36 . . . . . . .132 C3
Repps with Bastwick
NR29 . . . . .57 A4
Thetford IP24 . . . . .176 B3
Weeting IP27 . . . . .175 B7
Jubilee Ct 🟥 PE30 . . . . . .146 D4
Jubilee Dr
Dersingham PE31 . . . . . . .140 C5
Sheringham NR26 . . . . . . .138 E6
Jubilee Gdns 🟥 PE31 . . . .12 E4
Jubilee Hall La 🟥 PE32 . . .45 C6
Jubilee La NR27 . . . . .139 C4
Jubilee Rd
Heacham PE31 . . . . .133 A5
Holt NR25 . . . . .137 B6
Lackenheath IP27 . . . . . . .113 E2
Watton IP25 . . . . .84 D3
Jubilee Rise PE33 . . . . . . .61 D3
Jubilee Terr
Caister-on-Sea NR30 . . . .168 E4
Cromer NR27 . . . . .139 D4
Norwich NR1 . . . . .162 F3
Jubilee Way 🟥🟥 PE32 . . . .65 F4
Jubilee Wlk PE13 . . . . . .152 D8
Judas La IP23 . . . .
Judges Dr NR4 . . . . .161 F2
Judges Gdns NR8 . . . . . .155 E2
Judges Wlk NR4 . . . . . . .161 F2
Juler Cl 🟦 NR28 . . . . . . .151 C6
Julian Hospl NR2 . . . . . . .161 F6
Julian Rd
King's Lynn PE30 . . . . . . .148 C5
🟦 Spixworth NR10 . . . . . .54 A2
Julian Way NR31 . . . . . . .171 D5
Julians Way IP21 . . . . . . .121 E5
Junction Rd NR3 . . . . . . .158 C1
Juniper Cl 🟦 IP24 . . . . . .176 F4
Juniper Gr NR26 . . . . . . .138 E5
Juniper Way NR8 . . . . . . .155 E2
Jupiter Rd NR6 . . . . .158 C4
Jury St NR30 . . . . .169 D4

K

Kabin Rd NR5 . . . . .157 B2
Kalmia Gn 🟦 NR31 . . . . . .170 B6
Karen Cl
🟦 Hethersett NR9 . . . . . . .88 C7
Scole IP21 . . . . .130 C5
Keable Cl 🟥 NR5 . . . . . . .161 C6
Keats Cl
Downham Market PE38 . . .172 D5
East Dereham NR19 . . . . .154 C7
🟦 Thetford IP24 . . . . . . .176 E6
Keats Rd NR8 . . . . .156 D8
Keble Cl PE30 . . . . .148 B4
Keble Rd NR31 . . . . .170 B3
Kedleston Dr 🟥🟥 NR4 . . . .89 B8
Keel Cl 🟥🟥 NR30 . . . . . . .111 F1
Keelan Cl NR6 . . . . .158 B4
Keeling Hall La NR20 . . . .33 E3
Keeling Way NR17 . . . . . .174 B3
Keene Rd PE30 . . . . .146 D1
Keepers Rd NR15 . . . . . . .89 F3
Keepham Rd NR20 . . . . . . .33 F2
Keillers Cl PE13 . . . . . . .152 A7
Keith Rd 🟦 NR20 . . . . . . .50 B3
Kelling Cl NR25 . . . . .137 C7
Kell's Way NR34 . . . . . . .109 F3
Kell's Way NR34 . . . . . . .109 F2
Kelling Cl NR25 . . . . .137 C7
Kelling Heath Pk Sta
NR25 . . . . .8 E4
Kelling Hospl NR25 . . . . .137 F8
Kelling Prim Sch NR25 . . .8 D6
Kelling Rd NR25 . . . . . . .137 C7
Kelsey Cl PE36 . . . . .132 D7
Kelvin Pl IP24 . . . . .174 A4
Kemp Dr NR19 . . . . .154 C5
Kemp's Cl PE38 . . . . .79 A4
Kemp's Rd IP21 . . . . .122 A5
Kempe Cl NR7 . . . . .159 C1
Kempe Rd NR14 . . . . . . .146 C5
Ken Dur NR17 . . . . .174 F7
Kendal Cl 🟦 NR9 . . . . . . .88 D8
Kendall Cl NR28 . . . . . . .151 B6
Kendle Way PE30 . . . . . . .147 E8
Kenhill Cl 🟥 PE31 . . . . . . .12 E5
Kenlan Rd IP25 . . . . .152 D6
Kennedy Ave NR31 . . . . .170 C1
Kennedy Cl
East Dereham NR19 . . . . .154 D1
Easton NR9 . . . . .70 B5
Kennel Loke NR31 . . . . . .171 D8
Kennett Cl NR1 . . . . .161 F4
Kenninghall Prim Sch
NR16 . . . . .119 A4
Kenninghall Rd
🟦 Banham NR16 . . . . . . .119 B6
Harling NR16 . . . . .118 E4
Kenninghall NR16 . . . . . .119 A3
Kenside Rd 🟥 PE31 . . . . .12 E5
Kensington Cl NR15 . . . . .107 C8

Kensington Pl NR1 . . . .178 B1
Kensington Rd
Downham Market PE38 . . .172 B4
King's Lynn PE30 . . . . . . .147 B6
Kent Ave NR31 . . . . .170 C3
Kent Cl
Attleborough NR17 . . . . . .174 B3
🟦 Sutton Bridge PE12 . . .41 B8
Kent Rd PE30 . . . . .147 B6
Kent Sq NR30 . . . . .169 D3
Kenwood Rd PE31 . . . . . .133 D5
Kenwood Rd S PE31 . . . .133 D5
Kenwyn Cl NR25 . . . . . . .137 C7
Kenyon Row NR34 . . . . . .110 C2
Keppel Cl PE32 . . . . .48 A5
Keppel Rd 🟦 NR31 . . . . .170 D4
Kerdiston Rd
Reepham NR10 . . . . .149 A6
Themelthorpe NR20 . . . . .33 F2
Kered Cl NR5 . . . . .160 E8
Kered Rd NR6 . . . . .157 F6
Kerrich Cl PE13 . . . . .140 C3
Kerridge Ct NR25 . . . . . .137 B6
Kerridge Way
🟦 Harleston IP20 . . . . . .122 D2
Holt NR25 . . . . .137 B6
Kerridges NR16 . . . . .118 C4
Kerridges The NR5 . . . . .156 F1
Kerville St 🟥 NR5 . . . . . .161 A7
Kestrel Ave PE38 . . . . . . .172 C7
Kestrel Cl
Burnham Market PE31 . . .135 D1
Great Yarmouth NR31 . . .170 A7
Mulbarton NR14 . . . . .89 A3
Swaffham PE37 . . . . .153 C2
Thetford IP24 . . . . .176 D1
Kestrel Dr
Brandon IP27 . . . . .175 F3
🟦 Wisbech PE14 . . . . . . .152 D2
Kestrel Rd NR7 . . . . .159 C4
Keswick PE30 . . . . .147 D5
Keswick Cl NR4 . . . . .89 B8
Keswick Rd Bacton NR12 . .23 F4
Cringleford NR4 . . . . .89 B8
Kerk Sixth Form Ctr
NR7 . . . . .159 C2
Kett's Ave NR18 . . . . .173 C5
Kett's Cl
🟦 Hethersett NR9 . . . . . . .88 D7
Wymondham NR18 . . . . . .173 C5
Kett's Hill NR1 . . . . .163 A7
Kett's La NR9 . . . . .52 A6
Kett's Oak NR9 . . . . .88 C6
Ketteringham La NR18 . . . .88 E6
Ketteringham Pk NR18 . . .88 E6
Ketteringham Rd
NR18 . . . . .173 F3
Ketterstone Rd NR21 . . . .17 B3
Kettlewell La 🟦 PE30 . . . .146 E5
Ketts Rd NR28 . . . . .151 B4
Kevill Davis Dr NR13 . . . . .73 A5
Kevin Wlk NR19 . . . . .154 D2
Key & Castle Yd NR3 . . . .178 A4
Keyes Ave NR30 . . . . .169 D7
Keyes Cl 🟥 NR1 . . . . .162 E2
Keyes Rd NR1 . . . . .162 E2
Keys Dr NR12 . . . . .164 B2
Keys Farm 🟦 NR20 . . . . . .68 F6
Keys The NR15 . . . . .90 F2
Kilderkin Cl PE14 . . . . . . .77 A7
Kilham's Way
King's Lynn PE30 . . . . . . .146 E2
North Wootton PE30 . . . . .26 E1
Kiln Cl NR6 . . . . .158 E7
Kiln Farm La IP22 . . . . . .128 C1
Kiln La
Dickleburgh & Rushall
IP21 . . . . .130 F6
Needham IP20 . . . . .131 D8
Kiln Rd 🟦 NR10 . . . . .53 A3
Kilverstone Rd IP24 . . . . .117 A2
Kimberley Pk Sta NR18 . .87 A6
Kimberley Rd NR28 . . . . .151 D5
Kimberley St
🟦 Wymondham NR18 . . . .162 C5
Wymondham NR18 . . . . . .173 C4
Kimberley Terr NR30 . . . .169 E2
Kimms Belt IP24 . . . . . . .176 B2
Kinderley Rd PE13 . . . . . .152 C8
King Edward VII Sch
PE30 . . . . .147 A5
King George Cl 🟥 NR20 . .57 D2
King George Rd NR21 . . . .31 C7
King George V Ave
PE30 . . . . .146 F5
King George VI Sch
PE30 . . . . .14 A3
King George's Ave 🟥 . . . .
🟦 NR20 . . . . .57 D2
King John Ave PE30 . . . . .147 A5
King John Bank PE14 . . . .41 C5
King of Hearts Ctr*
NR1 . . . . .178 B4
King St
East Harling NR16 . . . . . .118 C5
Great Yarmouth NR30 . . .169 C4
King's Lynn PE30 . . . . . . .146 D5
Neatishead NR12 . . . . . . .55 E7
Norwich NR1 . . . . .178 C1
🟥 Sutton Bridge PE12 . . .41 B8
Swaffham PE37 . . . . .153 B4
Thetford IP24 . . . . .176 C4
Winterton-on-Sea NR29 . .58 B6
Wisbech PE13 . . . . .152 C5
King William Cl PE34 . . . .144 C5

Kingcup PE30 . . . . .148 A1
Kingfisher Cl
🟦 Fakenham NR21 . . . . .141 E4
🟥 Fakenham NR21 . . . . .141 E4
Great Yarmouth NR30 . . .169 C6
Thetford IP24 . . . . .176 D1
Kingfisher Dr
Brandon IP27 . . . . .175 E3
Necton PE37 . . . . .66 A3
🟥 Wisbech PE14 . . . . . . .152 D2
Kingfisher Rd
Attleborough NR17 . . . . . .174 F6
Downham Market PE38 . . .172 C7
Kingfisher Way 🟥 IP25 . . .84 C3
Kinghorn Rd NR2 . . . . . . .161 F4
King's Arms St NR28 . . . .151 C5
King's Ave Anmer PE31 . . .28 C8
King's Dro NR15 . . . . . . .147 A3
Kings Croft PE31 . . . . . . .140 E4
Kings Ct NR29 . . . . .167 A8
King's Dam NR34 . . . . . . .110 B2
Kings Gn 🟥 PE30 . . . . . . .147 C4
Kings Head La
Deopham NR18 . . . . .87 A5
North Lopham IP22 . . . . .119 A2
Kings La NR1 . . . . .178 B1
Kings Loke NR29 . . . . . . .167 B8
King's Lynn Arts Ctr
(Guildhall)* PE30 . . . . . .146 D5
King's Lynn Rd PE36 . . . .132 D4
King's Lynn Sports Ctr
PE30 . . . . .146 F5
King's Pk Fst Sch . . . .
King's Rd Bungay NR35 . .124 B7
East Dereham NR19 . . . . .154 D6
Fakenham NR21 . . . . .141 A5
King's Rd
Great Yarmouth NR30 . . .169 D2
Holt NR25 . . . . .137 C5
Kings Rd PE36 . . . . .132 D6
King's Rd NR35 . . . . .108 A4
Kings Rd PE30 . . . . .147 A5
Kings St NR24 . . . . .19 A6
King's Staithe La 🟥 . . . .
PE30 . . . . .146 D4
Kings Way NR19 . . . . . . .167 B2
Kings Way 🟥 PE13 . . . . . .152 C4
Kings Wlk
Downham Market PE38 . . .172 C5
🟥 Great Yarmouth NR31 . .170 B5
Kingsdale IP26 🟥 NR13 . . .74 A3
Kingsleigh Cl NR28 . . . . . .22 E5
Kingsley Ave PE13 . . . . . .152 B4
Kingston Ave NR30 . . . . .168 E5
Kingston Rd NR19 . . . . . .154 F3
Kingston Sq NR4 . . . . . . .162 A3
Kingsway Blakeney NR25 . .7 C6
🟦 Earsham NR35 . . . . . .123 F8
King's Lynn PE30 . . . . . . .146 E8
🟥 Newton Flotman NR15 .107 A8
North Walsham NR28 . . . .151 A6
Norwich NR2 . . . . .162 B6
Thetford IP24 . . . . .176 C2
Kirkgate La NR23 . . . . .6 A2
Kirkgate St
Holme next the Sea PE36 . .2 A6
Wisbech PE13 . . . . .152 E7
Kirkham's La PE14 . . . . . .77 C8
Kirkhams Mdw NR19 . . . .66 C7
Kirklands NR13 . . . . .156 E4
Kirklees 🟥 NR4 . . . . .89 E8
Kirkpatrick Rd NR3 . . . . .158 B1
Kirkstone Gr 🟥 PE30 . . . .148 F1
Kirstead PE30 . . . . .147 D5
Kirstead Gn NR15 . . . . . .108 C8
Kirstead Ling NR15 . . . . . .91 A1
🟥 Kitchener Cl PE14 . . . . .41 E4
Kitchener Rd
Great Yarmouth NR30 . . .169 D5
Melton Constable NR24 . .142 A5
Kitlings Beck Rd NR28 . . .38 A7
Kittel Cl 🟦 NR25 . . . . .84 D3
Kittens La NR14 . . . . .90 C8
Kittiwake Cl 🟥 NR31 . . . . .94 C8
Kittles La NR10 . . . . .150 A1
Kittles Rd NR13 . . . . .74 D1
Knappers Way IP27 . . . . .175 D3
Knapton Rd
Knapton NR28 . . . . .22 F3
Mundesley NR11 . . . . .22 F5
Knevet Cl NR17 . . . . .174 F6
Knight St NR22 . . . . .16 F7
Knight's La NR15 . . . . . . .89 E2

Knights Gn NR26 . . . . . . .138 C5
Knights Rd NR3 . . . . .158 B2
Knipe Cl 🟥 NR16 . . . . . . .105 F5
Knitting Needle La
NR23 . . . . .136 E6
Knowland Gr NR5 . . . . . .161 C8
Knowland Gr Fst Sch
NR5 . . . . .161 C8
Knowle Cres NR26 . . . . . .138 E5
Knowle Rd NR26 . . . . . . .138 E5
Knowles' La NR12 . . . . . . .38 C2
Knowsley Rd NR3 . . . . . .162 E8
Knox Ave NR1 . . . . .163 B8
Knox Cl NR1 . . . . .163 B8
Knox Rd NR1 . . . . .163 B7
Knudsen Cl 🟥 NR25 . . . . .107 C5
Knyvett Gn NR16 . . . . . . .105 F8
Koblenz Ave NR1 . . . . . . .178 C1
Kooreman Ave PE13 . . . . .152 D7
Krons The NR15 . . . . .107 C5

L

Laburnham Rd NR28 . . . .151 B4
Laburnum Ave
🟦 Marham PE33 . . . . .63 B4
🟦 Great Yarmouth NR31 . . .94 C7
🟦 Horsford NR10 . . . . . . .53 A3
🟥 Wisbech PE13 . . . . . . .152 E7
Laburnum Cres NR19 . . . .154 E1
Laburnum Dr NR13 . . . . .165 F6
Laburnum Gr
Reepham NR10 . . . . .149 C6
Sheringham NR26 . . . . . . .138 C4
Thetford IP24 . . . . .176 B1
Laburnum Wlk IP27 . . . . .175 E2
Lacey Cl 🟦 PE13 . . . . .61 D6
Lacey Rd NR5 . . . . .155 D1
Lackford Cl NR13 . . . . . .165 C6
Lacon Rd NR30 . . . . .168 E5
Ladbroke Pl NR1 . . . . . . .163 A7
Ladbrooke Cl 🟥 IP22 . . . .177 C4
Laddus Bank PE14 . . . . . . .77 A6
Laddus Dro PE14 . . . . .77 B6
Ladislaw Way 🟥 NR19 . . .154 C3
Lady Ann's Rd NR23 . . . . . .5 B7
Lady Betty Rd NR1 . . . . . .162 D3
Lady Dro NR28 . . . . .79 A6
Lady Hamilton La
NR29 . . . . .167 C6
Lady Haven Mews 🟥 . . . .
NR31 . . . . .169 C6
Lady Haven Rd 🟥 NR31 . .169 B4
Lady Jane Grey Rd
NR30 . . . . .146 F7
Lady La NR10 . . . . .53 E5
Lady Margaret's Ave
NR30 . . . . .170 B4
Lady Mary Rd NR1 . . . . . .162 D3
Lady's Dro 🟥 PE14 . . . . . .59 D2
Lady's La
Bressingham IP22 . . . . . .119 F1
Wymondham NR18 . . . . . .173 A3
Ladywood Cl PE33 . . . . . . .63 B4
Ladywood Rd PE33 . . . . . .63 B4
Lake Ave PE14 . . . . .95 C7
Lake Ct PE13 . . . . .152 D4
Lake View Cl NR19 . . . . . .51 D5
Lake View Dr NR6 . . . . . .158 C3
Lakeland 🟦 IP26 . . . . . . .114 A7
Lakeland Way 🟦 NR9 . . . .88 E8
Lakenfields NR1 . . . . .162 F2
Lakenham Fst Sch . . . .
NR1 . . . . .162 E3
Lakenham Mid Sch
NR1 . . . . .162 F3
Lakenham Rd NR4 . . . . . .162 C2
Lakenham Way NR1 . . . . .162 D2
Lakenheath Airfield
IP27 . . . . .114 B1
Lakenheath Prim Sch
IP27 . . . . .113 E1
Lakenham Sta 🟦 IP27 . . . .113 F5
Lakesend NR1 . . . . .162 D3
Lakes Ave NR14 . . . . .73 C2
Lamb La NR21 . . . . .31 C7
Lambert Cl 🟥 NR7 . . . . . .159 A3
Lambert Rd NR7 . . . . . . .159 A3
Lambert's La PE32 . . . . . . .30 D1
Lamberts Cl 🟦 IP26 . . . . . .98 E1
Lambert Rd 🟥 NR7 . . . . . .98 E1
Lammas Terr PE36 . . . . . .100 A4
Lamport Ct 🟥 PE30 . . . . .147 D6
Lamsey La PE31 . . . . .133 D3
Lancaster Ave NR21 . . . . .141 C5
Lancaster Cl . . . .
Fakenham NR21 . . . . .141 C5
Methwold IP26 . . . . .99 A5
Norwich NR6 . . . . .158 D6
🟥 Stalham NR12 . . . . .39 B4
Lancaster Cres 🟥 NR28 . .22 E6
Lancaster Gdns NR11 . . . .150 D5
Lancaster Rd
🟦 Fakenham NR21 . . . . . .98 E1
Great Yarmouth NR31 . . .169 D3
King's Lynn PE30 . . . . . . .147 B4
Lancaster Rise 🟥 NR28 . .22 E6
Lancaster Sq 🟥🟥 NR30 . .169 D3
Lancaster Way 🟦 NR23 . . .162 E7
Lanchester Ct 🟥 NR3 . . . .162 E8
Lane The Briston NR24 . . .142 D4
Carleton St Peter NR14 . . .91 E5

Joy - Law 197

Lane The continued
Little Barningham NR11 . . .20 C4
Winterton-on-Sea NR29 . . .58 B6
Lang Gate Way NR35 . . .108 D2
Langham Ct
Fakenham NR21 . . . . .141 D4
Sheringham NR26 . . . . . . .138 C7
Langham Glass & Rural
Crafts* NR23 . . . . .7 D3
Langham Gn NR13 . . . . . .165 E4
Langham La NR25 . . . . . . .7 C3
Langham Pl NR1 . . . . . . .178 A1
Langham Rd
Binham NR21 . . . . .6 E2
Blakeney NR25 . . . . .7 C6
Field Dalling NR25 . . . . . . .7 A2
Morston NR25 . . . . .7 A6
Langham St PE30 . . . . . . .146 D2
Langland PE30 . . . . .147 D6
Langley Abbey NR14 . . . . .92 A6
Langley Cl 🟦 NR4 . . . . . . .89 B8
Langley Gn NR14 . . . . .91 F6
Langley Prep Sch
NR14 . . . . .163 D6
Langley Rd
Cantley NR13 . . . . .92 C6
Chedgrave NR14 . . . . .91 F3
King's Lynn PE30 . . . . . . .147 E8
Loddon NR14 . . . . .92 A2
Langley Sch NR14 . . . . . . .91 F3
🟥 Langley St NR14 . . . . . .92 A4
Langley Wlk NR1 . . . . . . .162 C2
Langmere Rd
Scole IP21 . . . . .130 F8
🟥 Watton IP25 . . . . .84 C3
Langton Cl 🟥 NR5 . . . . . .161 B7
Lansdowne Cl 🟥🟥 PE32 . .165 B6
Lansdowne St 🟥 PE32 . . .146 E6
Lantern La NR12 . . . . .24 B5
Lapwing Cl 🟥 NR31 . . . . .170 A6
Larch Cl
Attleborough NR17 . . . . . .174 C4
King's Lynn PE30 . . . . . . .148 D2
Norwich NR7 . . . . .159 D4
Larch Cres NR25 . . . . . . .137 C7
Larch Dr
🟦 Great Yarmouth NR31 . . .94 C7
🟦 Great Yarmouth NR31 . .171 A4
Larch Gr NR20 . . . . .49 E7
Larch Rd NR26 . . . . .43 D4
Lark Cl IP27 . . . . .175 F3
Lark Rd 🟥 PE33 . . . . .61 D6
Lark Rise NR4 . . . . .89 A3
Lark St NR30 . . . . .94 C7
Larkey's La NR12 . . . . .38 F7
Larkman Fst Sch NR5 . . . .161 C7
Larkman La NR5 . . . . . . .161 C7
Larkman Mid Sch
NR5 . . . . .161 D7
Larksfield PE13 . . . . .152 C3
Larkspur Cl PE38 . . . . . . .172 C3
Larkspur Ct 🟥 NR19 . . . .154 D1
Larner's Drift NR19 . . . . .154 D2
Larwood Cl 🟥 PE37 . . . . . .66 A4
Larwood Way 🟥 IP25 . . . . .67 C2
Lathes The NR3 . . . . .178 A4
Latchmoor Pk NR29 . . . . .56 D7
Latchmoor Pk NR29 . . . . .56 D7
Lathes The NR3 . . . . .178 A4
Latimer Cl 🟥 NR19 . . . . . .68 A4
Latimer Way PE37 . . . . . . .65 E1
Laud Cl 🟦 NR7 . . . . .72 D4
Laughing Image Cnr 🟥
NR30 . . . . .169 C5
Laundtich Cres PE38 . . . .172 C6
Laundry Cl 🟦 NR7 . . . . . .163 C2
Laundry La 🟥 Blofield NR13 . .73 B6
Norwich NR7 . . . . .163 F7
Laundry Loke NR28 . . . . .151 B6
Laurel Dr
Brundall NR13 . . . . .165 B3
Great Yarmouth NR31 . . . .94 C7
🟦 Snettisham PE31 . . . . . .12 E5
Laurel Rd NR7 . . . . .159 E1
Laurels Cres 🟥 NR29 . . . .56 C5
Laurels The NR31 . . . . . .171 D5
Lavender Cl
Attleborough NR17 . . . . . .174 B5
🟦 Brandon IP27 . . . . .175 E3
Heacham PE31 . . . . .133 E5
Horsford NR10 . . . . .53 A4
Lavender Ct
🟥🟥 Hemsby NR29 . . . . . .58 B6
🟥 King's Lynn PE30 . . . . .147 B6
🟥 Thetford IP24 . . . . . . .176 F4
Lavender Dr PE38 . . . . . .172 C6
Lavender Rd 🟦 NR14 . . . .154 D2
Lavengro Rd 🟥 NR3 . . . . .163 A8
Lawn Ave NR30 . . . . .169 C6
Lawn Cl 🟥 Horsford NR10 . .53 A4
🟦 Poringland NR14 . . . . . .90 C5
Lawn Cres 🟥 NR13 . . . . . .72 E6
Lawn's La
Belton with Browston
NR31 . . . . .94 A5
🟦 Raphoe NR29 . . . . .57 B6
Lawns The
Cromer NR27 . . . . .141 C4
Great Yarmouth NR30 . . .169 C5
Wisbech PE13 . . . . .152 B6
Lawnswood Dr NR30 . . . .168 C6

Lawrence Cl
Fakenham NR21 ....141 B5
Harpley PE31 ....29 D4
Lawrence Pl NR20 ....50 D8
Lawrence Rd
King's Lynn PE30 ......146 E7
7 Thetford IP24 ....176 F5
Lawrence Way PE27 .153 A5
Lawrence's La PE38 ...79 E1
Lawson Rd
Croxton IP24 ....116 C5
Norwich NR3 ....158 E1
Lawson Way NR26 ....138 F7
Lawyer Corys NR31 ..170 C1
Laxfield Rd NR12 ......39 C3
Laxton Cl NR17 ....174 E4
Layer Cl
5 Aylsham NR11 ......150 D6
Norwich NR5 ....160 F7
Laylands Yd NR23 ....136 C6
Layton Cl NR8 ....157 B7
Le Neve Rd NR10 .....150 D1
Le Strange Ave PE30 .146 F7
Le Strange Cl NR2 ....161 F5
Le Tunder Cl **2** NR7 ..163 E7
Lea Rd **3** NR29 ....56 C8
Lea The NR30 ....169 C6
Lea Way PE30 ....147 B8
Leach Cl
Great Yarmouth NR31 .170 A4
Wisbech PE13 ....152 C2
Leach's Turn NR14 ...165 B1
Leafield Rd PE30 ......147 C3
Leafyoak La NR14 .....90 C3
Leamon Ct IP27 ....175 D4
Leaside PE31 ....133 B6
Leatherpool La NR25 ..7 E6
Leathway NR29 ....167 B2
Lebanon Dr PE13 ......152 F7
Lee Warner Ave NR21 .141 D6
Lee Warner Rd **10** PE13 153 C3
Leeder Hill NR13 ....72 F2
Leeds Way **5** NR12 ....55 E4
Lees Yd NR25 ....137 B6
Leete Way PE33 ....43 E2
Leewood Cres NR5 ...157 C1
Lefevre Way NR31 ....94 C8
Lefroy Rd NR3 ....158 A2
Legge Pl **7** PE34 ......43 B1
Legge-Bourke Ct
PE13 ....152 F6
Legrice Cres NR28 ...151 C3
Leicester Ave PE30 ..147 B5
Leicester Rd **1** NR31 .170 D4
Leicester St NR2 ......162 C4
Leigh Cl NR17 ....174 C5
Leman Cl **8** NR14 .....92 A1
Leman Gr **6** NR14 ....91 F1
Leman Rd NR31 ....170 D2
Leng Cres NR4 ....161 E2
Lenthall Cl **18** NR7 ...72 D4
Leonard Cl **4** PE30 ..147 B6
Leonard Medler Way
NR10 ....53 B8
Leonard's La IP26 ....98 D1
Leonards St **16** NR3 ..162 D8
Leopard Cl **3** NR3 ....178 B4
Leopold Cl **2** NR4 ....162 A3
Leopold Rd NR4 ....162 A3
Lerowe Rd PE13 ......152 E7
Les Baux Pl **5** PE13 ..152 E3
Lesley Wlk NR19 ......154 D2
Lestrange PE36 ....132 D4
Letheringsett Rd NR25 .18 F7
Letherington's La NR12 .55 D5
Letton Rd IP25 ....67 C2
Leven Cl **8** NR7 ....72 D5
Leverington Rd PE13 .152 A6
Levers Cl PE10 ....147 D8
Leveson Rd NR7 ......159 B3
Levine Cl NR13 ....165 B4
Levishaw Cl NR10 ....36 E1
Lewis Cl Ashill IP25 ..84 A7
Hopton IP22 ....127 F6
Lewis Dr Roydon IP22 .177 A5
Wiggenhall St Germans
PE34 ....61 A8
Lexham Rd
Great Dunham PE32 ..47 E2
King's Lynn PE30 .....147 E8
Litcham PE32 ....47 F4
Lexington Ct NR29 ...167 A7
Ley's La NR20 ....51 C1
Leyland Cl IP24 ....176 D6
Leys Cl NR31 ....169 C1
Leys La
Attleborough NR17 ...174 D2
Old Buckenham NR17 .104 B3
Yaxley IP23 ....129 F1
Leziate Dro
Grimston PE32 ....45 A8
Leziate PE32 ....44 F6
Leziate Heath Nature
Reserve* PE32 ....44 E6
Liberator Cl NR13 ....72 E8
Liberator Rd NR6 ....158 B6
Libra Ct NR7 ....159 C4
Lichfield Rd NR3 .....169 B3
Lichfield St NR21 ....141 B4
Licking's Dro PE13 ..152 C4
Lifeboat Plain **6** NR26 .138 D7
Light La PE14 ....59 D6
Lighthouse Cl
Happisburgh NR12 ...24 C5
Hunstanton PE36 .....132 D7

Lighthouse La PE36 ..132 D6
Lilac Cl Brandon IP27 .114 D4
9 East Dereham NR19 .154 D2
20 Great Yarmouth NR31 .94 C7
4 Great Yarmouth NR31 .170 A5
1 Horsford NR10 ......53 A3
Mundesley PE13 ....152 F7
Lilac Dr IP27 ....113 E1
Lilac Gr NR26 ....138 D4
Lilac Wood PE30 .....147 B8
Lilburne Ave NR13 ...158 D2
Lilian Cl NR6 ....158 B4
Lilian Rd NR10 ....54 A2
Lily Ave NR20 ....69 B8
Lily La NR34 ....111 A3
Lily Terr NR1 ....178 B1
Limasol Rd NR19 .....154 C2
Lime Ave Stradsett PE33 .80 C8
Wisbech PE13 ....152 C7
Lime Cl
7 Harleston IP20 .....122 D1
Marham PE33 ....63 A4
Lime Dr NR19 ....154 D2
Lime Gr Gayton PE32 .45 C6
Sheringham NR26 .....138 D4
7 Thetford IP24 ......176 D4
Lime Kiln Cl
5 Cley next the Sea NR25 ..7 E6
6 Newton Flotman NR15 .89 D1
Lime Kiln La
2 Stoke Ferry PE33 ...81 A3
Thetford IP24 ....176 D4
Lime Kiln Mews
9 New Catton NR3 ...158 C1
Norwich NR3 ....162 C8
Lime Kiln Rd
Gayton PE32 ....45 C6
Sparham NR9 ....50 F5
West Dereham PE33 .80 C5
Lime St PE12 ....41 C8
Lime Tree Ave
Costessey NR8 ....156 F4
Long Stratton NR15 ..106 E2
Norwich NR7 ....163 C7
Wymondham NR18 ..173 D6
Lime Tree Cl
2 East Dereham NR19 .154 E6
3 Mattishall NR20 ...68 E6
Wymondham NR18 ..173 D5
Lime Tree Cres NR19 .66 C7
Lime Tree Rd
North Walsham NR28 .151 D5
Norwich NR2 ....162 B3
Lime Tree Wlk IP25 ..84 D3
Lime Way NR31 ....170 B5
Limekiln La
Houghton PE31 ....29 D6
South End NR16 ......106 C1
Upper Sheringham
NR26 ....138 A4
Limekiln Wlk **1** NR30 .169 C4
Limes Ave PE14 ....59 A1
Limes Cl IP22 ....177 D1
Limes Rd **3** NR29 ....56 C8
Limes The IP25 ....84 A6
Limetree Cl **10** NR10 .53 B3
Limetree Ct
Great Yarmouth NR31 .169 C2
Taverham NR8 ....155 B2
Limmer Ave IP21 .....121 C1
Limmer Rd NR13 .....73 C6
Limpenhoe Rd
Cantley NR13 ....92 C7
Reedham NR13 ....92 E6
Linacre Ave NR7 .....159 C4
Linacre Cl NR7 ....159 C3
Linalls Dr NR8 ....156 C4
Lincoln Ave
Great Yarmouth NR31 .170 C3
Hingham NR9 ....86 D5
Lincoln Cl **12** NR20 ..50 B3
Lincoln Ralphs Sports Hall
NR1 ....178 C2
Lincoln Rd IP25 ......84 F3
Lincoln Sq N NR26 ..132 C5
Lincoln Sq S NR26 ..132 C5
Lincoln St
Hunstanton PE36 ....132 D5
Norwich NR2 ....162 B5
Lincoln Way IP24 ....176 B5
Linden Cl NR18 ....86 E3
Linden Dr **5** NR9 .....88 C7
Linden Gr Diss IP22 .177 C6
Sheringham NR26 ...138 D4
Linden Rd
Clenchwarton PE34 ..145 E5
Norwich NR5 ....157 C1
Linden Tree Gdns 15
NR11 ....94 C7
Lindford Dr NR4 ......89 C8
Lindley Cl NR6 ....158 E6
Lindley Rd **8** NR9 ....88 C7
Lindley St NR1 ....162 E3
Lindsay Rd NR7 ......159 C4
Linford PE34 ....145 D6
Linford Clapper La
PE34 ....145 E6
Linford Est **1** PE34 ..54 C7
Ling Comm Rd PE30 .148 D6
Ling House Rd PE31 ..15 F1
Ling IP22 ....177 B3
Ling Way NR12 ....40 A7
Lingheath Rd IP27 ...175 E3
Lings Cl **6** NR13 .....74 A3
Lings The NR9 ....86 D8
Lingwood Fst Sch NR13 .73 F4
Lingwood Gdns **2** NR13 .74 A3

Lingwood Jun Sch
NR13 ....74 A3
Lingwood Rd
Blofield NR13 ....73 E4
Brundall NR13 ....165 F6
Lingwood Sta NR13 ..74 A3
Link The **2** IP24 ......176 D4
Links Ave
Brundall NR13 ....165 C4
Cromer NR27 ....139 D4
Norwich NR6 ....157 F4
Links Cl
Caister-on-Sea NR30 .168 E4
Norwich NR6 ....157 F5
6 Thurlton NR14 ......92 F1
Links Cres NR26 .....138 C7
Links Rd
Great Yarmouth NR31 .171 D8
Mundesley NR11 ......143 B6
Sheringham NR26 ....138 C7
Links Way
Sheringham NR27 .....10 A5
8 Thurlton NR14 ......92 F1
Linmore Cres **8** IP25 .84 E3
Linmore Ct IP25 ......84 C3
Linn Chilvers Dr PE31 .133 B5
Linnet Cl **8** NR31 ....170 A6
Linnet Cres IP27 .....175 E3
Linnets The NR5 .....156 F1
Lintock Rd NR13 .....158 D3
Linton Cl NR7 ....159 B3
Linton Cres NR7 .....159 B4
Lion & Castle Yd NR1 .178 B2
Lion La NR14 ....91 C3
Lion Rd
Buxton with Lammas
NR10 ....36 E1
Palgrave IP22 ....177 C1
Lion Wood Rd NR1 ..163 B7
Lion's Mouth NR11 ...10 A3
Lisbon Rd NR19 ......154 C2
Lisbon Rd NR7 ....159 E2
Lisle Rd NR5 ....160 B1
Lister Cl NR31 ....170 B1
Lister's Rd IP14 ......77 E5
Litcham Hall PE32 ...48 A4
Litcham High Sch PE32 .48 A4
Litcham Prim Sch PE32 .48 A5
Litcham Rd
Beeston with Bittering
PE32 ....48 D4
Great Dunham PE32 .47 F2
Gressenhall NR20 ....49 C3
Little Dunham PE32 ..65 F8
Mileham PE32 ....48 C5
Tittleshall PE32 ......48 A4
Litcham Village Mus*
PE32 ....48 A4
Litchmere Rd NR14 .109 D6
Litester Cl NR28 .....151 D4
Little Armes St NR2 .162 A8
Little Barney La NR21 .17 F3
Little Bethel St NR2 .178 A2
Little Bittering Medieval
Village of* NR19 ....48 F4
Little Carr Rd PE30 ..148 D5
Little Church St PE13 .152 C5
Little Dowgate PE13 .152 A7
Little Ellingham Rd
NR9 ....86 A3
Little Fendike La PE14 .77 E8
Little Hockham La
IP24 ....102 E2
Little Holme Rd PE34 .41 F6
Little John Rd NR4 ..162 C1
Little La
1 Castle Acre PE32 ..46 F2
Docking PE31 ....134 E4
9 Horsford NR10 .....53 B3
Roydon PE32 ....28 A1
Stoke Ferry PE33 .....80 F3
Little London Rd
North Walsham NR28 .151 C6
Northwold IP26 ....99 C7
Little London St NR2 .178 B3
Little Man's Way PE33 .81 A3
Little Melton Fst Sch
NR9 ....160 C2
Little Melton Rd NR9 .160 B1
Little Money Rd NR14 .109 D8
Little Oulsham Dro
IP26 ....98 B2
Little Plumstead CE Prim Sch
NR13 ....165 A8
Little Scratby Cres
NR29 ....167 E4
Little Snoring Prim Sch
...........................17 B3
Little Snoring Rd NR21 .17 B3
Little Walsingham Cl
PE30 ....148 C3
Littlebeck La NR15 ..108 B8
Littlefields NR19 .....154 D5
Littleport St PE30 ...146 E5
Littleport Terr **8** PE30 .146 E5
Littlewoods La NR17 .174 C3
Livingstone Rise NR11 .22 F8
Livingstone St NR2 ..162 A7
Lizard The NR18 ......173 D3
Lloyd Cl NR25 ....137 F8
Lloyd Rd Norwich NR1 .162 F4
Taverham NR8 ....155 B2
Loanin The NR11 ....143 C3
Lobster La NR1 ....178 A3
Loch La IP25 ....84 D4
Lock Rd NR28 ....38 D6
Lock's La NR34 ......109 F1

Lockerbie Flats 18
NR26 ....138 D7
Lockhart Rd NR35 ...109 D3
Locksley Rd NR4 ....89 E8
Loddon Nr15 ....108 C7
Loddon Cnr NR15 ...108 C7
Loddon Fst Sch **13** NR14 .92 A1
Loddon Mid Sch NR14 .91 F1
Loddon Rd
Ditchingham NR35 ...109 B2
Gillingham NR34 .....110 C2
Haddiscoe NR14 .....110 D8
Heckingham NR14 ...92 D1
Holverston NR14 ....91 A5
Kirby Cane NR35 ....109 E4
Norton Subcourse NR14 .92 E1
Toft Monks NR34 ....110 D7
Trowse with Newton
NR14 ....163 C1
Yelverton NR14 ......90 E6
Lode Ave PE14 ....77 F5
Lode St IP27 ....175 C4
Lodge Breck NR28 ...157 A7
Lodge Cl NR25 ....137 B5
Lodge Dr IP22 ....120 B5
Lodge Farm Dr NR6 .158 D6
Lodge Farm Mdws
NR20 ....49 C6
Lodge Hill NR26 .....138 A3
Lodge La Norwich NR6 .158 E6
Riddlesworth IP22 ...127 D7
Shelfanger IP22 ......120 B1
18 Snettisham PE31 .12 E4
Lodge La Fst Sch NR6 .158 E6
Lodge Pl NR7 ....159 A5
Lodge Rd Catfield NR29 .56 B8
Feltwell IP26 ....98 E2
Heacham PE31 ....133 C5
Lingwood & Burlingham
NR13 ....74 A3
St John, Ilketshall
NR34 ....124 C6
Tivetshall St Margaret
NR15 ....121 C6
Lodge Way IP24 .....176 C7
Lodore Ave NR6 .....158 A6
Loggers La IP22 .....128 B5
Loke Rd PE30 ....146 E6
Loke The
Belton with Browston
NR31 ....93 F6
Briston NR24 ....142 D4
Brumstead NR12 ....24 A2
Cringleford NR4 .....89 C8
Cromer NR27 ....139 B6
East Beckham NR11 ..9 D2
Felmingham NR28 ...37 B8
Filby NR29 ....75 E8
Freethorpe NR13 ....92 E7
2 Gresham NR11 ....9 E1
Haddiscoe NR14 .....110 F8
Marlingford NR9 .....58 B6
Salhouse NR13 ......55 B2
Strumpshaw NR13 ..73 F4
London St
Brancaster PE31 .....3 B7
Norwich NR2 ....178 B3
Swaffham PE37 ......153 C4
Whissonsett NR20 ..31 D2
Londs The NR27 .....11 A3
Lone Barn Rd NR7 ..159 B2
Lonely Rd
Pulham St Mary PE21 .122 B6
Scole IP21 ....121 C2
Long Barrow Dr NR28 .151 D3
Long John Hill NR1 .162 E2
Long La
Baconsthorpe NR25 ..20 A7
Bawburgh NR9 ....160 B8
Burston & Shimpling
IP22 ....120 D4
Catfield NR29 ....56 D7
Feltwell IP26 ....98 D1
Flordon NR15 ....106 E8
Great Yarmouth NR31 .170 A4
Hoveton NR12 ....164 D2
Mulbarton NR14 ....89 B2
Saxlingham Nethergate
NR15 ....107 B8
Southrepps NR11 ...22 A6
Stoke Holy Cross NR14 .89 F4
Strumpshaw NR13 ..165 F5
Swaffham PE37 .....153 E5

Long La *continued*
Tharston & Hapton
NR15 ....106 D6
West Winch PE33 ...43 E2
Winfarthing IP22 ....119 F7
Long Lots PE14 ....59 F3
Long Rd
Barton Turf NR12 ....55 F7
Poringland NR14 ....90 C5
Saham Toney IP25 ..84 F8
Terrington St Clement
PE34 ....144 A8
Thurlton NR14 ....93 A1
Wymondham NR18 ..88 A1
Long Row Norwich NR3 .158 D1
Tibenham NR16 .....120 D6
Tivetshall NR15 ......103 E6
Long Stratton Mill*
NR15 ....106 F3
Long Stratton High Sch
NR15 ....106 E4
Long Stratton Ind Est
NR15 ....106 D3
Long Stratton Leisure Ctr
NR15 ....106 E4
Long Stratton Rd
NR16 ....105 F4
Long's Cres NR13 ...72 D7
Longbow Cl **8** NR4 ..162 C1
Longbrooke Cl NR14 .89 C4
Longdell Hills NR5 ..156 E2
Longdon Cl **4** PE12 ..41 B8
Longe Rd NR6 ....158 F6
Longfellow Rd NR30 .168 D5
Longfield Cl **2** NR14 .91 F1
Longfields PE37 .....153 C5
Longfields Rd NR7 ..72 C5
Longfulans La NR31 .171 D3
Longham La NR20 ...49 B3
Longham Rd NR19 ..49 A2
Longhead La PE14 ..59 A4
Longlands Dr NR18 ..62 A3
Longmead **4** NR1 ...162 E2
Longmeadow NR13 .165 B3
Longmeadow Cl IP25 .85 A1
Longs Cl NR15 ....89 C1
Longview **1** NR7 .....88 D8
Longview Cl **4** PE31 ..12 E4
Longwater La NR8 ..156 D3
Longwater Ret Pk
NR5 ....156 A2

Lonsdale Cres NR9 ..86 B5
Lonsdale Rd NR13 ..72 C4
Lonsdale Terr PE13 .152 C3
Loombe Cl **8** NR20 ..50 B3
Lopham Rd NR16 ....11 D1
Lord Cres NR20 .....50 B5
Lord Rd IP22 ....177 E4
Lord Walsingham Ct 1
PE34 ....176 E5
Lord's La NR31 ......94 B7
Lords La PE31 ....133 C5
Lorraine Gdns NR3 ..158 E3
Losinga Cres NR3 ..158 B3
Losinga Rd PE30 ....146 D7
Lossiemouth Rd 6
NR31 ....126 B1
Lothian St NR2 ......162 C6
Lothingland Mid Sch
NR32 ....171 A3
Louden Rd NR27 ....139 B7
Louie's La IP22 ......177 C6
Louis Cl NR6 ....158 D6
Louis Dahl Rd **3** NR31 .94 A6
Louise Cl **15** NR30 ..169 D2
Lound Dam NR14 ...111 A7
Lound Rd
Belton with Browston
NR31 ....94 B4
Norwich NR4 ....161 F5
Somerleyton, Ashby &
Herringfleet NR32 ..111 F8
Lovat Cl IP20 ....122 C2
Love La Fransham NR19 .66 D7
Sporle with Palgrave
PE32 ....65 C6
Wisbech PE13 ....152 C4
Lovelace Rd NR14 ..161 E4
Lovell Gdns IP25 ...84 E3
Lovell Way PE34 ....144 B4
Lovells The **6** PE14 ..59 D2
Lovelstaithe NR1 ...178 C3
Lovers' La NR29 ....56 C4
Lovett Cl NR1 ....158 F6
Lovewell Rd NR31 ..170 A5
Low Bungay Rd NR14 .92 A1
Low Comm
Aslacton NR16 ....106 A2
Bunwell NR16 ....105 E2
Deopham NR18 .....86 E4
Hethersett NR9 .....88 C2
Hingham NR9 ....86 C3
South Lopham IP22 .128 F7
Swardeston NR14 ..89 B6
Low Comm La NR14 .89 A5
Low Comm Rd
South Lopham IP22 .128 E7
Thurlton NR14 ....91 D3
Low Ditch Rd IP22 ..122 C4
Low Farm Rd NR13 ..75 A3
Low Hatter's Cl PE38 .172 B3
Low La Hevingham NR10 .53 B8
Rocklands NR17 ....103 B6
Low Rd Alburgh IP20 .122 F6
Bunwell NR16 ....105 E1

Low Rd *continued*
Denton IP20 ....123 B5
Dickleburgh & Rushall IP21 ....130 E5
Forncett NR16 ....106 B5
Freethorpe NR13 ....92 F7
Great & Little Plumstead NR13 ....72 E5
Grimston PE32 ....28 B1
Haddiscoe NR14 ....110 F7
Hedenham NR35 ....108 D4
Hellesdon NR6 ....157 C5
Hingham NR9 ....86 B4
Keswick NR4 ....89 C7
Kimberley NR9 ....87 D8
King's Lynn PE30 ....148 C1
Mautby NR29 ....75 E5
Mettingham NR35 ....109 D1
Narborough PE32 ....63 F7
North Tuddenham NR20 ....68 E8
Norton Subcourse NR14 ....92 E2
Pentney PE32 ....63 C8
Redenhall with Harleston IP20 ....122 F1
Repps with Bastwick NR29 ....57 A4
Rollesby NR29 ....57 D2
Roydon PE32 ....28 A1
St John, Iketshall NR34 ....124 D6
St John's Fen End PE14 ....60 B6
Scole IP21 ....130 C5
Shelton NR15 ....107 B1
Shropham NR17 ....103 B3
Skeyton Corner NR10 ....37 B6
South Walsham NR13 ....74 B8
Starston IP20 ....123 C2
Stoke Ferry PE33 ....80 F2
Stow Bardolph PE34 ....61 C2
Stow Bedon NR17 ....102 E5
Strumpshaw NR13 ....165 F1
Swaffham PE37 ....153 A5
Tasburgh NR15 ....106 E7
1 Thurlton NR14 ....92 F1
Thurlton NR14 ....93 B2
Tibenham NR16 ....120 B8
Walpole Cross Keys PE34 ....42 A7
West Acre PE32 ....46 C2
West Caister NR30 ....168 A3
Wicklewood NR18 ....87 C3
Wimbotsham St Germans PE34 ....43 D3
Wimbotsham PE34 ....172 D8
Winterton-on-Sea NR29 ....58 B6
Wisbech PE14 ....152 E1
Woodbastwick NR13 ....55 C1
Wortwell IP20 ....123 A3
Low Side PE14 ....77 F6
Low St Hardingham NR9 ....86 E8
Hoxne IP21 ....131 A4
Ketteringham NR18 ....88 D6
St Margaret, Iketshall NR35 ....124 B4
Sloley NR12 ....37 C3
Smallburgh NR12 ....38 E3
Weasenham St Peter PE32 ....30 D2
Wicklewood NR18 ....87 A5
Low Wr La IP22 ....129 D5
Low's La IP22 ....177 D2
Lowe's La PE11 ....4 D4
Lower Clarence Rd NR1 ....178 C2
Lower Cliff Rd NR31 ....170 D4
Lower Drag Way IP22 ....128 E8
Lower Espl NR31 ....170 D3
Lower Globe La NR13 ....165 E7
Lower Goat La 2 NR2 ....178 A3
Lower Hall La NR24 ....18 D7
Lower Hardley Rd NR14 ....92 A2
Lower Kiln La NR15 ....90 F3
Lower Lincoln St PE36 ....132 C5
Lower Marine Par NR31 ....170 D3
Lower Oakley IP21 ....130 D4
Lower Rd Holme Hale IP25 ....66 B3
Rockland St Mary NR14 ....91 C7
Lower Rose La IP21 ....177 E2
Lower Spink's La NR18 ....88 B4
Lower St Horning NR12 ....55 E4
Salhouse NR13 ....55 A1
Lower Wood Nature Reserve* NR15 ....105 E8
Lowes Ave NR25 ....137 D5
Lowes View IP22 ....177 E3
Lowestoft Rd NR31 ....170 C1
Lowfield PE30 ....147 C4
Lowick Cl 9 NR19 ....154 D3
Lowry Cl 3 NR31 ....170 A7
Lowry Cole Rd NR6 ....158 F5
Lowry Way PE38 ....172 E6
Lowther Rd NR4 ....162 B1
Loxwood NR6 ....157 E6
Lubbock Cl NR2 ....161 F5
Lucas Ct 2 NR7 ....72 D5
Lucas Rd 4 NR5 ....161 B4
Lucerne Cl NR16 ....158 F4
Lucerne Rd 9 NR18 ....94 C6
Lucombe Dr PE13 ....152 F7
Luddenham NR20 ....50 B2
Ludham Airstrip NR29 ....56 D6
Ludham Fst Sch NR29 ....56 C5

Ludham Rd
Catfield NR29 ....56 C6
Potter Heigham NR29 ....56 F5
Ludkin Sq 8 NR30 ....169 C5
Lug's La NR35 ....109 B5
Lugger Yd NR23 ....136 D6
Luke Cl NR5 ....156 F2
Luscombe Way 6 NR13 ....72 E7
Lusher Cl 1 NR26 ....138 C5
Lusher Rise NR5 ....161 D8
Lusher's Loke NR7 ....158 F4
Lushers Mdw 5 NR17 ....174 C5
Lushington Cl 7 NR5 ....161 B8
Luxembourg Way NR19 ....154 C2
Lydgate Cl NR19 ....154 D3
Lyhart Rd NR4 ....162 B1
Lynch Gn 8 NR9 ....88 D8
Lyndford Rd NR12 ....39 B4
Lyndhurst Ct PE36 ....132 D3
Lynewood Cl NR27 ....139 D4
Lynewood Rd NR27 ....139 D4
Lynfield Rd NR28 ....151 C6
Lynford Rd IP26 ....100 B5
Lyng Hall La NR20 ....33 A3
Lyng Hall Rd NR20 ....33 A7
Lyng La IP22 ....118 F1
Lyng Prim Sch NR9 ....51 A4
Lyng Rd NR9 ....51 B5
Lyngate Cl 1 NR9 ....88 C7
Lyngate Rd NR28 ....151 B8
Lynn Cl 7 NR7 ....72 D5
Lynn Ct NR19 ....154 E4
Lynn Gr NR31 ....170 A6
Lynn Gr High Sch NR31 ....170 A6
Lynn La PE32 ....29 D1
Lynn Mus* PE30 ....146 E5
Lynn Rd
Castle Rising PE30 ....148 F5
Clenchwarton PE34 ....144 E5
Dersingham PE31 ....140 C2
Downham Market PE38 ....172 C6
East Rudham PE31 ....30 A7
Gayton PE32 ....45 C6
Grimston PE32 ....28 B1
Heacham PE31 ....133 E3
Ingoldisthorpe PE31 ....140 C7
King's Lynn PE30 ....147 A5
Littleport CB7 ....96 E1
Middleton PE34 ....144 D2
Roydon PE32 ....28 A1
Runcton Holme PE33 ....61 F4
Shouldham PE33 ....62 D3
Shouldham Thorpe PE33 ....62 B2
Southery PE38 ....97 A6
Stow Bardolph PE34 ....79 E8
Swaffham PE37 ....153 A5
Terrington St Clement PE34 ....42 A6
Tilney St Lawrence PE34 ....42 D2
Walpole Cross Keys PE34 ....41 F6
Walsingham PE31 ....59 B6
Watlington PE33 ....61 E6
Wereham PE33 ....80 D5
West Rudham PE31 ....29 F6
West Walton PE14 ....59 D8
West Winch PE33 ....61 F8
Wiggenhall St Mary Magdalen PE34 ....61 C7
Wisbech PE13 ....152 C6
Wretton PE33 ....80 F3
Lynn Rd Terr PE14 ....59 D8
Lynn St PE37 ....153 B4
Lynton Rd NR12 ....24 A7
Lynwood Terr 13 PE30 ....146 E5
Lytton Rd NR8 ....156 D8

M

MacArthur Dr 3 NR19 ....154 C4
MacDonald Rd NR7 ....139 A7
Mack's La NR10 ....156 D7
MacKenzie Cl 1 NR11 ....170 B1
MacKenzie Rd IP24 ....176 A3
Mackintosh Rd NR13 ....72 E8
Macks Loke NR24 ....142 F2
Macmillan Way NR13 ....165 A8
Mad Dog La PE32 ....29 C6
Madden Ave NR30 ....169 D8
Maddermarket Theatre NR2 ....178 A3
Maden Cl NR18 ....173 B5
Magazine Cl PE13 ....152 A4
Magazine La PE13 ....152 A4
Magdalen Cl 3 NR31 ....162 E8
Magdalen Gates Fst Sch NR3 ....162 E8
Magdalen High Rd PE34 ....61 A6
Magdalen Rd
Norwich NR3 ....162 E8
Tilney St Lawrence PE34 ....60 D8
Wiggenhall St Germans PE34 ....61 C7
Magdalen St
Norwich NR3 ....178 B4
Thetford IP24 ....176 D4
Magdalen Way NR31 ....170 B8
Magic City Leisure Ctr NR1 ....178 C3
Magnay Rd NR8 ....157 C7
Magnolia Cl NR10 ....53 A4
Magnolia Gn 8 NR31 ....170 B6

Magpie Ct 33 IP20 ....122 D2
Magpie Hill IP22 ....129 B5
Magpie La NR17 ....103 B7
Magpie Rd NR3 ....162 D8
Maid Marian Rd NR4 ....162 C1
Maida Vale 3 NR2 ....162 B5
Maidens Cl 1 NR13 ....72 E4
Maids Cross Hill IP27 ....113 F1
Maidstone Rd NR1 ....178 B3
Main Cross Rd NR30 ....170 D8
Main Dereham Rd NR21 ....31 F4
Main Dr NR20 ....32 E4
Main Rd
Clenchwarton PE34 ....145 B5
Crimplesham PE33 ....80 B6
Filby NR29 ....76 A8
Fleggburgh NR13 ....166 F6
Holme next the Sea PE36 ....2 A5
Lingwood & Burlingham NR13 ....74 A5
Methwold IP26 ....99 A7
Narborough PE32 ....63 E8
Ormesby St Michael NR29 ....58 A1
Rollesby NR29 ....57 D2
Swardeston NR14 ....89 C5
Tilney All Saints PE34 ....42 E4
Upwell PE14 ....77 E3
Walpole Highway PE14 ....59 E8
Weeting IP27 ....175 E8
West Caister NR30 ....168 A6
West Winch PE33 ....61 F8
Main St
Hockwold cum Wilton IP26 ....113 F7
Honing NR28 ....38 C6
Hopton on Sea NR31 ....171 D4
Maine Sch
4 Thetford IP24 ....116 A1
Thetford IP24 ....176 A4
Malakoff Cl 9 NR30 ....169 D2
Malakoff Rd 4 NR30 ....169 D2
Malborough Gn Cres NR29 ....57 D4
Malbrook Rd NR5 ....161 B7
Maldon Rd PE13 ....152 E5
Malin Ct 7 NR30 ....168 C6
Mallard Cl
Brundall NR13 ....165 E2
Chedgrave NR14 ....91 F7
2 Fakenham NR21 ....141 E4
4 Loddon NR14 ....92 A2
4 Salhouse NR13 ....55 A1
1 Snettisham PE31 ....12 E4
Mallard Rd 10 IP25 ....84 C3
Mallard Way
Brandon IP27 ....175 E2
Great Yarmouth NR31 ....170 A6
Hickling NR12 ....39 F1
Mallory Rd NR6 ....158 D6
Mallow Cl 1 NR17 ....174 B4
Mallow Rd 10 IP24 ....176 F5
Malt Dr PE13 ....152 B3
Malt's La PE26 ....113 F7
Malthouse Cl 9 IP25 ....84 D2
Malthouse Cres PE31 ....133 D5
Malthouse Ct
East Dereham NR20 ....154 E5
8 Redenhall with Harleston IP20 ....122 D2
Thornham PE36 ....2 D6
Malthouse La
Cantley NR13 ....92 A6
Gissing IP22 ....120 F4
Great Yarmouth NR31 ....170 C4
Guist NR20 ....32 F4
Malthouse Pl NR23 ....136 D6
Malthouse Rd
4 Hethersett NR9 ....88 C7
Norwich NR2 ....178 A2
Maltings Yd NR10 ....149 C4
Maltings Cl 6 IP20 ....122 D2
Maltings La 4 PE33 ....172 A5
Maltings Way NR16 ....119 B6
Maltmas Dro PE14 ....77 A7
Malvern Cl PE30 ....148 D3
Malvern Rd 3 NR1 ....163 A6
Manby Rd
Downham Market PE38 ....172 B3
Great Yarmouth NR30 ....169 D4
Norwich NR7 ....159 C1
Mancetter Cl 5 NR2 ....162 C2
Mancroft Wlk 8 NR2 ....162 C7
Mandela Ct NR13 ....92 B6
Mandells Ct NR3 ....178 B4
Mangate St PE37 ....153 C5
Mangreen NR14 ....89 D6
Mangreen La NR14 ....89 C5
Mann's La NR20 ....32 D1
Manning's La IP22 ....128 B1
Mannington Hall* NR11 ....20 C3
Mannington Pl NR18 ....148 E1
Manor Chase NR8 ....156 E8
Manor Cl
1 Aylsham NR11 ....150 D6
2 Downham Market PE38 ....172 A5
Hockering NR20 ....69 C6
Horsham St Faith & Newton St Faith NR10 ....53 D2
Ingoldisthorpe PE31 ....140 D8

Manor Cl *continued*
Lamas NR10 ....36 E1
4 Little Snoring NR21 ....17 B3
Tunstead NR12 ....37 F1
Manor Ct
Aylsham NR11 ....150 C6
North Walsham NR28 ....151 E5
Manor Dr Litcham PE32 ....48 A4
Roydon IP22 ....177 A5
Terrington St John PE14 ....42 E1
Manor Farm Cl NR8 ....157 A8
Manor Farm Rd
Denton IP20 ....122 F8
St John, Iketshall NR34 ....124 D7
Somerton NR29 ....58 A6
Manor Field Fst Sch NR15 ....106 E3
Manor Gdns Diss IP22 ....177 D5
Hopton on Sea NR31 ....171 D4
3 Lingwood NR13 ....74 A3
Wisbech PE13 ....152 A4
Manor House Cl
Brandon IP27 ....175 B3
Mautby NR29 ....75 E6
Manor Pk NR14 ....89 C5
Manor Pk Gdns 18 NR15 ....106 E3
Manor Rd
Brandon IP27 ....175 A3
Caister-on-Sea NR30 ....168 F5
Cantley NR13 ....92 B8
Dersingham PE31 ....140 D2
Great Yarmouth NR31 ....170 C2
Griston IP25 ....85 A2
Heacham PE31 ....133 D8
Hilgay PE38 ....79 D1
Hopton on Sea NR31 ....171 D4
Horsham St Faith & Newton St Faith NR10 ....53 D3
Hunstanton PE36 ....132 C2
King's Lynn PE30 ....148 C5
Long Stratton NR15 ....106 E3
Mundesley NR11 ....143 C6
Newton St Faith NR10 ....53 D4
North Walsham NR28 ....151 E5
Roydon IP22 ....177 A5
Scarning NR19 ....154 A3
Stoke Ferry PE33 ....80 F2
Terrington St Clement PE34 ....144 B5
Manor Ridge NR15 ....165 E6
Manor Way
Ormesby St Margaret NR29 ....167 A2
Swaffham PE37 ....153 C5
Manor Wlk NR25 ....137 B6
Manorfield Cl 1 NR29 ....167 A2
Manorfield Rd NR14 ....92 A2
Manse Ct IP24 ....176 D4
Mansel Dr NR6 ....158 E3
Mansell Cl 2 IP22 ....177 A5
Mansell Rd PE13 ....152 E3
Mansfield La NR1 ....162 E1
Manthorpe Cl 5 NR1 ....162 E1
Mantle Cl NR7 ....159 C4
Maple Ave PE13 ....152 C3
Maple Cl 10 Beetley NR20 ....49 D4
5 Gayton PE32 ....45 C6
20 Martham NR29 ....57 D4
Wymondham NR18 ....173 D6
Yaxley IP23 ....129 F1
Maple Dr
King's Lynn PE30 ....148 D3
Norwich NR7 ....161 F7
Sculthorpe Airfield NR21 ....15 C3
Taverham NR8 ....155 B1
Wisbech PE13 ....152 C5
Maple Gdns 17 NR31 ....94 C7
Maple Rd
Downham Market PE38 ....172 B6
King's Lynn PE34 ....43 D4
Maple Way 8 Eye IP23 ....130 C1
Great Yarmouth NR31 ....170 B6
Mapplebeck Cl NR30 ....167 A4
Marauder Rd NR6 ....158 D6
March Cl PE14 ....59 E8
March Rd Elm PE14 ....77 A7
Welney PE14 ....95 C5
March Riverside PE14 ....77 B4
Mardle Rd NR34 ....110 D5
Mardle St NR5 ....160 F5
Mardling Run NR13 ....166 D3
Mares Cl NR11 ....150 B3
Margaret Cl PE34 ....146 A5
Margaret Cres NR7 ....163 F7
Margaret English Cl NR26 ....138 C5
Margaret Lilly Way 1 NR11 ....21 A5
Margaret Paston Ave NR3 ....158 A2
Margaret Reeve Cl 8 NR18 ....173 D5
Margaret Rose Cl PE30 ....148 C2
Margarets Cl PE36 ....132 D2
Margetson Ave NR7 ....163 C7
Marguerite Cl 11 NR31 ....94 C6
Marham Airfield PE33 ....63 B5
Marham Cl 1 PE34 ....146 A5
Marham Fst Sch PE33 ....63 B5
Marham Mid Sch PE33 ....63 B5

Marham Rd PE33 ....62 E2
Marie Cl NR13 ....92 B6
Marigold Cl 6 NR10 ....53 A3
Marina Leisure Ctr NR30 ....169 E3
Marina Rd NR11 ....143 C6
Marine Cl NR31 ....170 D1
Marine Cres
Great Yarmouth NR30 ....169 E6
5 Hemsby NR29 ....58 B6
Marine Dr NR30 ....168 E8
Marine Par NR31 ....170 D2
Mariner's Cl NR31 ....171 D8
Mariner's Compass NR31 ....171 C8
Mariners La NR1 ....178 B1
Mariners Pk Cl NR31 ....171 D5
Mariners' Rd NR30 ....169 D2
Mariners Way PE30 ....146 F8
Marion Cl NR18 ....173 C5
Marion Rd NR1 ....163 A6
Marion Wlk 1 NR19 ....154 D2
Marionville Rd NR1 ....163 A6
Maritime Mus for E Anglia* NR30 ....169 E3
Marjoram Cl 2 NR28 ....151 E4
Marjoram Rd 2 NR31 ....94 C6
Mark La IP27 ....115 C6
Mark Lemmon Cl 2 NR4 ....89 C8
Mark's Cl La NR9 ....52 A7
Markant Ave NR1 ....178 B3
Market Gates 8 NR30 ....169 D4
Market Hill
Brandon IP27 ....175 C3
Colkirk NR21 ....31 D5
Diss IP22 ....177 D4
Market La
Blundeston NR32 ....171 D1
Brancaster PE31 ....3 B6
Burston & Shimpling IP22 ....120 E1
Crimplesham PE33 ....80 A6
Filby NR29 ....76 B7
Great Moulton NR15 ....70 C1
King's Lynn PE30 ....146 D5
Little Melton NR9 ....160 A2
Salthouse NR25 ....8 B6
Shotesham NR15 ....107 E8
Somerleyton, Ashby & Herringfleet NR32 ....94 A1
Terrington St Clement PE34 ....42 B6
Walpole Cross Keys PE14 ....41 F5
Wells-next-the-Sea NR23 ....136 D4
Market Manor NR13 ....166 C3
Market Mews PE13 ....152 C3
Market Pl
Aylsham NR11 ....150 C6
Burnham Westgate PE31 ....135 C3
Diss IP22 ....177 D4
Downham Market PE38 ....172 C5
2 East Dereham NR19 ....154 D5
Fakenham NR21 ....141 B4
Great Yarmouth NR30 ....169 C4
22 Harleston IP20 ....122 D2
Holt NR25 ....137 B6
4 Loddon NR14 ....92 A1
North Walsham NR28 ....151 C5
Reepham NR10 ....149 B4
Swaffham PE13 ....153 C4
14 Winterton-on-Sea NR39 ....58 B6
Wisbech PE13 ....152 C5
Market Rd NR13 ....173 C4
Market St
East Harling NR16 ....118 C5
16 King's Lynn PE30 ....146 D5
North Walsham NR28 ....151 C5
Shipdham IP25 ....67 C2
Tunstead NR12 ....37 F1
18 Wisbech PE13 ....152 C5
Wymondham NR18 ....173 B4
Market Weston Rd IP22 ....127 A1
Marketfield La NR10 ....53 E2
Markshall Farm Rd NR14 ....89 E7
Marl Hill Rd NR9 ....51 A3
Marl Pit La NR5 ....161 C8
Marland Rd 4 PE30 ....147 D5
Marlborough Ct PE13 ....152 A4
Marlborough La NR14 ....89 F7
Marlborough Rd
Great Yarmouth NR30 ....169 E4
Norwich NR3 ....178 C4
Marlborough Sq NR30 ....169 E4
Marlborough Terr NR30 ....169 E5
Marle Cl NR31 ....170 C4
Marle Pit Cl NR14 ....92 B6
Marlingford Rd
Easton NR9 ....160 A2
Marlingford NR9 ....70 B4
Marlingford Sports Club NR9 ....70 B4
Marlingford Way NR9 ....70 B4
Marlow Cl NR3 ....158 E3
Marlpit La NR15 ....106 F6

Marlpit Rd
Hempstead NR25 ....19 E7
Thompson IP24 ....102 A7
Marram Dr NR30 ....168 E8
Marram Way PE31 .....133 B6
Marrams Ave NR27 ....139 A7
Marriot Cl NR22 ....162 C7
Marriott Chase NR8 ....155 E1
Marriott Way NR24 ....142 A5
Marriotts Way 3 NR26 .138 D7
Marryat Rd NR7 ....159 C1
Marryats Loke 3 NR25 ...7 A4
Marsh Cl 7 NR26 ....57 D5
Marsh La Aldeby NR34 .111 A6
Bracon Ash NR14 ....89 A2
Burgh Castle NR31 ......94 A8
Carlton Colville NR33 ...111 F2
3 Earsham NR35 ....123 F8
King's Lynn PE30 ....148 A1
5 New Buckenham NR16 .104 F1
North Cove NR34 ....111 B1
Somerleyton, Ashby &
Herringfleet NR32 .....111 C8
Tharston & Hapton
NR15 ....106 C8
Wells-next-the-Sea
NR23 ....136 D5
Wiveton NR25 ....7 E6
Worlingham NR34 ......110 F1
Wortham IP22 ....129 D4
Marsh Loke NR28 ....23 D1
Marsh Rd Cantley NR13 ..92 D6
Fleggburgh NR29 ....75 C8
Fritton & St Olaves NR31 ..93 E3
Great Yarmouth NR31 ..169 B3
Halvergate NR13 ....75 A1
North Wootton PE30 ...148 A6
Outwell PE14 ....77 F8
Potter Heigham NR29 ...57 A6
Repps with Bastwick
NR29 ....56 F4
South Walsham NR13 ...74 B8
Thurne NR29 ....56 E3
Upton with Fishley NR13 .166 B8
Walpole PE14 ....41 C4
Wroxham/Hoveton
NR12 ....164 D5
Marsh Side PE31 ....3 B7
Marsh The PE14 ....41 C4
Marsh Wlk PE13 ....152 D5
Marshall Cl
Norwich NR5 ....161 B8
10 Spixworth NR10 .....54 A2
Marshall Rd NR3 ......158 B3
Marshall St 5 PE30 ...146 E5
Marsham Prim Sch
NR10 ....150 C1
Marshgate NR28 ....113 E6
Marshland High Sch
PE14 ....59 B8
Marshland Smeeth & Fen
Mus* PE14 ....60 C6
Marshland St 4 NR34 .144 B5
Marshland St James VC Prim
Sch PE14 ....60 A4
Marston La 10 NR4 .....89 C8
Marston Moor 7 NR7 ...72 D4
Martham Broad National
Nature Resrve* NR29 ..57 D7
Martham Fst Sch NR29 ..57 D5
Martham Rd
Martham NR29 ....57 F4
Rollesby NR29 ....57 D3
Somerton NR29 ....57 E6
Martin Cl Brandon IP27 .175 E3
5 Great Yarmouth NR31 .94 C7
Norwich NR7 ....159 B4
3 Weybourne NR25 ......8 F5
Martin Rd Diss IP22 ...177 E4
Harleston IP20 ....122 E2
Martineau La NR1 .....162 F1
Marvell Gn 10 NR7 ......72 D5
Marwood Cl NR18 .....173 B3
Mary Chapman Cl 8
NR7 ....72 D4
Mary Chapman Ct
NR3 ....178 A3
Mary Unwin Rd NR19 .154 D4
Maryland NR23 ....136 D5
Masefield Dr PE38 ....172 D5
Masefield Mews NR19 .154 C2
Masefield Rd IP22 ....177 E4
Masefield Wlk 8 IP24 .176 E6
Mashs Row NR11 ....3 A3
Mason Gdns 11 PE33 ...43 F2
Mason Rd Norwich NR6 .158 B3
5 Swanton Morley NR20 .50 B3
Masons Dr PE37 ....65 F4
Masquers Cl NR1 .....170 C2
Massey Cl 2 NR21 ....141 C3
Massingham Rd
Castle Acre PE32 ....46 F2
Grimston PE31 ....28 C1
Norwich NR3 ....158 C1
Weasenham All Saints
PE32
Mast Cl 13 NR33 ......111 F1
Masters Ct PE28 .....151 D5
Mather La IP20 ....122 B1
Matlock Rd 1 NR1 ....163 B5
Matsell Way NR19 ....154 E5
Matthews Ct 4 NR15 ..106 F6
Mattishall La
Hockering NR20 ....69 A7
Mattishall NR20 ......68 F7

Mattishall Prim Sch
NR20 ....68 F5
Mattishall Rd
Dereham NR20 ....68 B8
East Tuddenham NR20 ..69 B6
Garvestone NR9 ....68 D2
Honingham NR9 ....69 D6
Runhall NR9 ....69 A3
Maud St NR2 ....162 B6
Maurice Gaymer Rd
NR17 ....174 D4
Mautby La NR29 ....75 F6
Mavish Cl NR5 ....161 A6
Max Carter Cl NR28 ...38 A4
May Cl NR18 ....173 B5
Maybank NR28 ....151 D7
Mayes Cl 3 NR5 ......161 B8
Mayfield Ave NR6 .....158 B4
Mayfield Dr NR27 ....139 B5
Mayfield Rd NR28 ....151 D7
Mayflower Ave PE30 ..146 F7
Mayflower Cl 9 PE13 .152 E3
Mayflower Way 14 IP20 .122 D1
Maygrove Rd 5 NR30 .169 D5
Mayton Ave 2 NR12 ...54 A4
Mdws The 2 PE31 ......12 C4
Mead Cl NR10 ....36 E1
Meadow Way PE34 ...146 B4
Meadow Brown Way 9
NR18 ....173 E4
Meadow Cl
2 Beetley NR20 ....49 D4
Cromer NR27 ....139 A6
3 Hemsby NR29 ....167 A8
Hethersett NR9 ....87 D6
Holt NR25 ....137 D6
3 King's Lynn PE30 ...148 C5
Mundesley NR11 ......143 C5
Narborough PE32 ......63 E7
North Walsham NR28 ..151 C6
Norwich NR14 ....163 B2
Shipdham IP25 ....67 D2
5 Thurlton NR14 ......92 F1
Meadow Cotts PE32 ...48 B6
Meadow Ct
Fakenham NR21 ....141 E4
Great Yarmouth NR31 .171 C8
Meadow Dr
1 Beetley NR19 ....49 C3
6 East Dereham NR19 .154 C4
1 Gressenhall NR20 ...49 C3
Lackenheath IP27 .....113 E2
Mundesley NR11 ......143 C5
Wroxham/Hoveton
NR12 ....164 D4
Meadow Farm Dr NR4 .89 B7
Meadow Farm La NR10 .53 E2
Meadow Gdns NR6 ...158 F4
Meadow Gr
North Runcton PE33 ...44 A2
20 Watton IP25 ....84 D3
Meadow La
Briston NR24 ....142 B5
Carbrooke IP25 ....85 A5
Kelling NR25 ....8 B5
Norwich NR7 ....163 F6
5 Rollesby NR29 ....57 D2
Meadow Loke 2 NR20 ..50 E7
Meadow Patch NR28 ..151 C6
Meadow Rd
Bungay NR35 ....124 B8
Cromer NR27 ....139 B6
Heacham PE31 ....133 D5
4 King's Lynn PE30 ..148 C2
Narborough PE32 ......63 E7
Norwich NR5 ....157 A2
Meadow Rise NR29 ...167 A8
Meadow Rise Ave
NR2 ....162 A4
Meadow Rise Cl NR2 .162 A4
Meadow Rise Rd NR2 .162 A4
Meadow Vale NR5 ....157 A3
Meadow View NR13 ...165 D4
Meadow View Terr
NR11 ....150 B5
Meadow Way
Attleborough NR17 ...174 C3
East Carleton NR14 ...88 F5
Horsford NR10 ....53 B3
Norwich NR6 ....157 F5
Poringland NR14 ....90 C4
Sheringham NR26 .....138 B6
Meadowbrook Cl 6
NR11 ....162 F3
Meadowcroft NR20 ...168 C8
Meadowgate La PE14 .152 E2
Meadowgate Sch
PE13 ....152 E2
Meadowland Dr 17 NR31 .94 C6
Meadowrun NR21 ......15 C6
Meadows The
Aylsham NR11 ....150 C7
6 Hingham NR9 ....86 C4
South Wootton PE30 ..148 B2
Thetford IP24 ....176 B4
Thurton NR14 ....91 D4
Meadowside IP22 ....128 B6
Meadowsweet 18 NR10 .53 A3
Meadowsweet Dr
NR26 ....138 B6
Meadowsweet Rd 2
NR18 ....173 E4
Meadowvale Gdns
NR30 ....147 B7
Meadway 8 NR4 ......89 B8
Mear Gdns NR13 ......163 B6
Mears Cnr NR16 ......105 B5

Medeswell 2 NR29 ...167 B7
Medwell Cl NR13 .....165 C5
Medway Cl PE14 ......152 E4
Meer Dyke La PE14 ....59 D5
Meeting Hill Rd NR28 ..38 A7
Meeting House Hill Rd
NR28 ....38 B6
Melbourne Rd
North Walsham NR28 .151 D6
4 Sheringham NR26 ..138 D7
Melford Bride Rd
IP24 ....176 D4
Melford Cl PE30 ......148 E1
Melford Comm 4 IP24 .176 D4
Melford Ct 3 IP24 ....176 D4
Mellis Rd
Thrandeston IP21 .....129 F2
Wortham IP22 ....129 C3
Yaxley IP23 ....130 A1
Mellisash Rd IP23 ....129 D1
Melrose Dr NR11 ......10 A2
Melrose Rd IP24 .....162 A3
Melrose Terr 13 NR30 .169 D2
Melton Cl NR18 ......173 B6
Melton Constable Hall*
.......................18 D2
Melton Ct NR9 ....88 C8
Melton Dr
Hunstanton PE36 .....132 C3
Taverham NR8 ....155 E1
Melton Gate NR18 ...173 B5
Melton Rd
Hindolveston NR20 ....33 D8
Wymondham NR18 ...173 B5
2 Melton St NR24 ....142 A5
Melville Rd IP24 .....116 C5
Memorial Way
Thorpe St Andrew NR7 .72 E4
Watton IP25 ....84 D4
Mendham Cl
3B Harleston IP20 ....122 D2
3 Norwich NR1 ....162 E2
Mendham La
3B Harleston IP20 ....122 D2
St Mary, South Elmham
otherwise Homersfield
IP20 ....123 B3
Mendham Prim Sch
IP20 ....123 A2
Mercedes Ave NR1 ...162 D2
Merchant Way NR6 ..158 A4
Merchants Ct NR27 ..139 C7
Mere Cl IP25 ....84 C4
Mere Manor Ct 2 NR27 .177 D4
Mere Plot Dro PE33 ...62 E5
Mere Rd Scoulton NR9 .85 E4
Stow Bedon NR17 .....102 E7
Meredith Rd NR6 .....157 E6
Mereside NR5 ....90 F2
Mergate La NR14 ......89 A2
Meridian Way NR7 ....72 E3
Merlewood IP21 .....121 C1
Merlin Ave NR7 ......159 B4
Merlin Cl NR12 ......164 D5
Merlin Mews NR7 ....159 B4
Merriman Rd 5 NR29 ..57 C4
Merrivale Model Village*
NR30 ....89 C8
Merrow Gdns 4 NR4 ..89 C8
Merryweather Cl 8
NR15 ....106 E3
Merryweather Rd 9
NR15 ....153 C3
Merton Ave NR3 .....170 A3
Merton Rd
Norwich NR2 ....162 A7
Watton IP25 ....84 D2
Metcalf Ave NR30 ....146 D2
Metcalf Cl 4 NR3 ....157 F1
Meteor Cl NR6 ....158 D7
Methuen Ave PE30 ...147 B6
Methwold High Sch
IP26 ....99 A6
Methwold Rd
IP26 ....99 A5
Methwold Rd
Northwold IP26 ....98 E5
Northwold IP26 ....99 C7
Metton Rd
Felbrigg NR11 ....139 A2
Roughton NR11 ....21 D8
Mews Ct 7 IP25 ....67 C2
Mews The
Great Yarmouth NR31 .170 C1
4 Norwich NR2 ......162 C4
Micawber Ave 2 NR30 .170 B8
Michaels Ct NR19 ....154 C5
Mid Norfolk Rly*
NR19 ....154 E5
Mid Yare National Nature
Reserve* NR13 ......165 D1
Midden Sta The NR23 .136 F4
Middle Dro Denver PE38 .79 B4
Marshland St James PE14 .60 C2
Stow Bardolph PE14 ...61 A4
Middle Gates Dro PE14 .60 B8
Middle Hill
Alby with Thwaite NR11 .21 A5
Reedham NR13 ....92 F4
Middle La NR14 ....90 F4
Middle Mkt Rd NR30 .169 D4
Middle Rd
Blo' Norton IP22 .....128 C6
Earsham NR35 ....123 D8
Earsham IP20 ....123 C8
Great & Little Plumstead
NR13 ....72 F5

Middle Rd continued
Hardingham NR9 ......86 E8
Morning Thorpe NR15 .107 B3
Shouldham Thorpe NR31 .62 C2
Terrington St Clement
PE34 ....42 B8
Middle Rd E 8 NR30 .169 D1
Middle Rd W 3 NR30 .169 D1
Middle Rd NR11 ....11 E1
Middle Rigg NR19 ....57 A6
Middle Wall NR29 ....57 A6
Middlebrook Way
Cromer NR27 ....139 A6
Runton NR27 ....10 C4
Middlegate NR30 .....169 D2
Middlemarch Rd 5
NR19 ....154 D3
Middlesex La NR13 ..166 D3
Middlestone Cl NR31 ..170 C4
Middleton Ave NR20 ...50 B4
Middleton Cl
Norwich NR3 ....158 C3
2 Sheringham NR26 ..138 C5
Middleton Cres NR5 .156 E2
Middleton Cl NR31 ...170 C4
Middleton Gdns NR31 ..170 C5
Middleton Prim Sch
PE32 ....44 C2
Middleton Rd NR31 ..170 C4
Middleton St NR18 ...173 B4
Middleton's Cl NR6 ..157 E4
Middleton's La NR6 ..157 F5
Middlewood 2 PE30 ..147 C4
Midland Cl
Caister-on-Sea NR30 .168 F5
18 Great Yarmouth NR30 .169 D5
Midland Rd NR28 ....151 C4
Midland St NR2 ......162 C7
Midland Wlk NR2 ....162 C7
Mikanda Cl PE14 .....152 C2
Mildenhall Rd CB7 ...112 B3
Mile Cross La NR6 ...158 C4
Mile Cross Mid Sch
NR3 ....158 B1
Mile Cross Rd NR3 ..162 B8
Mile End IP27 ....175 A1
Mile End Cl NR4 .....162 A3
Mile End Rd
Littleport CB7 ....112 A3
Norwich NR4 ....162 A3
Mile Rd
Carleton Rode NR16 ...105 A5
Garvestone NR9 ......68 A1
Mileham Prim Sch
NR13 ....48 D6
Mileham Rd
Beeston with Bittering
PE32 ....48 C3
Litcham PE32 ....48 A4
Milestone Cl NR5 ....156 F2
Milestone La NR18 ...87 A4
Milford Rd 8 NR12 ..162 B5
Mill Bank PE14 ....59 F7
Mill Cl Aylsham NR11 .150 A6
2 Blofield Heath NR13 .73 D6
Hempton NR21 ....141 A3
Hethersett NR9 ....88 C7
Hickling NR12 ....39 F2
Kirby Row NR35 ......109 E3
Mattishall NR20 ......162 D3
Norwich NR1 ....162 E3
Poringland NR14 ......90 C5
Pulham Market IP21 .121 E5
6 Salhouse NR13 .....55 A1
Thurton NR14 ....91 C4
Wisbech PE13 ....152 C6
Mill Comm NR14 .....91 C4
Mill Comm Rd NR28 ...23 E2
Mill Cres NR13 ......166 B4
Mill Croft NR5 ....156 E1
Mill Ct Fakenham NR21 .141 B3
Holt NR25 ....137 B6
Wells-next-the-Sea
NR23 ....136 D5
Mill Drift
Beeston with Bittering
PE32 ....48 C3
Hockwold cum Wilton
IP26 ....114 A7
Mill Dro
Gooderstone PE33 .....81 F4
Middleton PE32 ....44 D2
Southery PE38 ....97 A5
Mill Farm Nurseries
NR7 ....153 B2
Mill Field Cl 7 IP24 ...42 C1
Mill Gdns
Bedingham NR35 ....108 B4
Horsford NR10 ....53 B3
Mill Gn
Burnham Market PE31 .135 D3
Stoke Holy Cross NR14 .89 F4
Mill Hill Bradenham IP25 .66 E3
Bramerton NR14 ......90 F8
Brancaster PE31 ....3 B6
Brandon IP27 ....175 E3
2 Horning NR12 ......55 E4
Mettingham NR35 ...109 D1
Norwich NR3 ....158 E2
Roughton NR11 ......139 A1
Salhouse NR13 ....55 A2
Strumpshaw NR13 .....73 F2
Mill Hill Rd
Boughton PE33 ....80 F5
Norwich NR2 ....162 B5
Mill Houses PE30 ...146 F6
Mill La Acle NR13 ...166 C3

Mill La continued
All Saints & St
Nicholas, South Elmham
IP20 ....123 E1
Aslacton NR15 ....106 A1
Attleborough NR17 ...174 F7
Aylsham NR11 ....150 B6
Bacton/Walcott NR12 ..23 E4
Barnham PE32 ....125 E6
Bircham PE31 ....33 E1
Blackborough End PE32 .44 C1
Briston NR24 ....142 F3
Brooke NR15 ....108 A8
Burnham Thorpe PE31 ..4 D4
Caistor PE25 ....85 A4
Catfield NR29 ....56 C7
Claxton NR14 ....91 E6
Clenchwarton PE34 ..145 F6
Crimplesham PE33 ....80 B7
Cromer NR27 ....10 B5
Dereham NR19 ....154 A8
Docking PE31 ....134 E4
Downham Market PE38 .172 D7
Ellingham NR35 ......109 E3
Felthorpe NR10 ......155 C8
Fleggburgh NR29 .....57 B1
Foulsham NR20 ....33 D4
Garboldisham IP22 ...103 B3
Great Ellingham NR17 .103 D7
Great Massingham PE32 .29 D2
Great Yarmouth NR31 ..94 C7
Haddiscoe NR14 .....110 D8
Hindringham NR21 ....17 E8
Hockering NR20 ....69 B7
Hockwold cum Wilton
IP26 ....114 A7
Hoe NR20 ....49 D3
Honingham NR9 ......69 E6
Hopton IP22 ....127 F7
Horsford NR10 ....53 B3
Horsham St Faith &
Newton St Faith NR10 ..53 E2
Keswick NR4 ....89 D7
King's Lynn PE30 ....147 B8
Kirby Bedon NR14 .....90 E7
Long Stratton NR15 ..106 F3
Morley NR18 ....87 A3
Newton Flotman NR15 ..89 E2
Norwich NR3 ....162 A3
Ormesby St Margaret
with Scratby NR29 ....58 A1
Ovington IP25 ....84 E5
Postwick with Witton
NR13 ....73 A3
Pulham Market IP21 .121 E5
Redgrave IP22 ....128 E5
Repps with Bastwick
NR29 ....57 B3
Rickinghall Inferior
IP22 ....128 D2
Rocklands NR17 .....103 C7
St John, Ilketshall
NR34 ....124 E6
Seething NR15 ....91 C1
Shelton NR15 ....122 B8
1 Southery PE38 ......97 B5
14 Sutton Bridge PE12 ..41 B8
Swaffham PE37 ......153 C3
Syderstone PE31 ......15 E3
Thetford IP24 ....176 D3
Tilney St Lawrence PE34 .42 C2
Tunstead NR12 ....38 A3
Walpole Highway PE14 ..59 F7
Walsingham NR22 .....16 F8
West Walton PE14 ....59 C8
Weybread IP21 ......131 F7
Wreningham NR16 ....88 D1
Mill Loke 4 NR12 ....55 E4
Mill Orch IP21 ......121 E5
Mill Pightle NR11 ...150 B6
Mill Pool La NR35 ...109 D2
Mill Rd Alburgh IP20 .122 E6
Aldborough NR11 ......21 A6
All Saints South Elmham
IP19 ....124 B1
Ashby St Mary NR14 ..91 C4
Banham NR11 ....150 C6
Bacton NR28 ....23 A1
Barnham NR11 ....119 D7
Barnham Broom NR9 ..69 B2
Barningham IP31 .....127 C3
Barton Turf NR12 .....38 E1
Bergh Apton NR14 ....91 A4
Bintree NR20 ....33 A2
Blofield Heath NR13 ..73 D6
Botesdale IP22 ......128 F2
Brancaster PE31 ....3 B6
Briston NR24 ....142 F3
Brockdish IP21 ......131 B7
Burgh St Peter NR34 .111 B4
Burnham Market PE31 .135 C6
Burston & Shimpling
IP22 ....120 E2
Carleton Rode NR16 ..105 A4
Colby NR11 ....36 F7
Cromer NR27 ....139 C5
Dersingham PE31 ....140 F5
Dilham NR28 ....23 A4
East Ruston NR12 .....24 A4
Emneth PE14 ....59 D2
Forncett NR16 ....106 B3
Foxley NR20 ....50 B6
Freethorpe NR13 ......92 F8
Fretenham NR12 ......54 A4
Great Yarmouth NR31 .169 B3

Mill Rd continued
Gresham NR11 ....9 D1
Halvergate NR13 ....74 F1
Hardingham NR9 ....86 E8
Harpley PE31 ....29 D4
Hempnall NR15 ....107 C5
Hemsby NR29 ....58 A4
Hethersett NR9 ....88 C7
Honington IP31 ....126 D1
Kirby Row NR35 ....109 D3
Lakenheath IP27 ......113 E1
Little Melton NR9 ......160 B2
Loddon NR14 ....92 A1
Long Stratton NR15 ...107 A2
Marlingford NR9 ....70 A3
Marsham NR10 ....36 C2
Mattishall NR20 ....68 E6
Mautby NR29 ....75 E7
North Walsham NR28 .151 D3
Old Buckenham NR17 .104 C1
Potter Heigham NR29 ..56 F5
Reedham NR13 ....93 A5
Reepham NR10 ....149 B2
Repps with Bastwick
NR29 ....57 A4
Ryburgh NR21 ....32 C6
Salhouse NR13 ....55 A1
Shelton NR15 ....122 B8
Shipdham IP25 ....67 B2
Shouldham Thorpe PE33 .62 C3
Stalham NR12 ....39 A3
Stoke Holy Cross NR14 .89 F4
Stokesby with Herringby
NR29 ....75 A6
Surlingham NR14 ......91 B8
Sutton NR12 ....39 C3
Terrington St John PE14 .42 B1
Thelnetham IP22 .....128 B5
Thompson IP24 ......102 A7
Thurlton NR14 ....110 D8
Tibenham NR16 ......120 D8
Tivetshall St Mary NR15 121 B5
Topcroft NR35 ....107 F4
Walpole St Andrew PE14 .41 E3
Watlington PE34 ......61 D8
Watton IP25 ....84 D3
Wells-next-the-Sea
NR23 ....136 B5
West Walton PE14 .....59 B8
Weybread IP21 ....131 F8
Whissonsett NR20 .....31 D2
Wiggenhall St Germans
PE34 ....43 C1
Wiggenhall St Mary Magdalen
PE34 ....61 B5
Winfarthing IP22 .....120 B4
Mill Rd S IP22 ......128 F2
Mill Reach NR10 ....36 F1
Mill Row NR11 ......150 D7
Mill St Bradenham IP25 .66 E3
Elsing PE20 ....50 F4
Gimingham NR11 ......22 E7
Holt NR25 ....137 B6
Horsham St Faith NR10 .53 E2
Lamas NR10 ....36 F1
Mattishall NR20 ....68 F5
Necton NR27 ....65 F4
Swanton Morley NR20 .50 B4
Mill View
Barnham Broom NR9 ..69 B2
Saham Toney IP25 .....84 C5
Sedgeford PE36 ....13 A7
Mill View Cl NR11 ..143 D5
Mill View Mid Sch
NR5 ....161 C8
Mill Way PE14 ......77 B8
Millard Cl NR28 ....151 A6
Millcroft NR3 ......158 E1
Millennium Plain NR2 .178 A2
Millennium Way PE34 .146 A5
Miller Cl NR19 .....154 C4
Miller's Breck NR8 .155 F2
Miller's La
Thetford IP24 ....176 C4
Wimbotsham PE34 .....79 E8
Millers Cl NR35 ....124 B8
Millers Dr IP21 .....92 F4
Millers Gn IP20 ...122 D2
Millers La Harpley PE31 ..29 D4
Norwich NR3 ....158 D1
Millers Sq NR17 ...174 C5
Millers Way NR11 ...53 B3
Millers Wlk NR21 ..141 C3
Millfield Ashill IP25 ..84 A8
Eye IP23 ....130 B1
Millfield Cl NR13 ...73 D6
Millfield La PE33 ...43 F3
Millfield Prim Sch
NR28 ....151 B3
Millfield Rd
Barningham IP31 .....127 D3
North Walsham NR28 .151 B4
Millfields NR15 ....107 C5
Millfleet PE30 .....146 E4
Millgate NR11 ......150 D7
Millgate St IP26 ...109 A5
Millhill La NR18 ....86 F2
Millicent Oliver Cl
IP24 ....176 D7
Millington Ct IP24 ..176 D4
Millmarsh Dro IP27 .113 D2
Mills Cl NR18 ......155 C1
Millside Hales NR14 .109 F8
Stalham NR12 ....39 B3
Millview NR29 .....167 A3
Millway NR18 ......173 B6
Millway Ave IP27 ..177 C6

Millway La
Palgrave IP22 ....177 B2
Wortham IP22 ....129 D5
Milner Rd PE13 ....152 C4
Milnes Way NR33 ..111 F1
Milton Ave PE30 ...146 F5
Milton Cl
East Dereham NR19 ..154 C4
Norwich NR1 ....162 E3
Thetford IP24 ....176 E6
Milton Rd
Great Yarmouth NR30 .169 D8
Swanton Morley NR20 .50 B3
Milton Way PE38 ...172 D6
Milverton Rd NR1 ..162 F3
Mindhams Yd NR23 .136 C6
Mingay Rd IP24 ....176 B2
Minion Cl NR7 .....72 D4
Minsmere Rd NR31 ..94 A6
Minster Ct IP24 ...147 C5
Minstergate IP24 ..176 C4
Miriam Cl NR29 ....168 E8
Misburgh Way NR31 .171 E4
Mission La
Docking PE31 ....134 E4
Fakenham NR21 ......141 C4
Mission Pl NR30 ...169 D6
Mission Rd Diss IP22 .177 F3
Great Yarmouth NR31 .169 B4
Rackheath NR13 ......72 E8
Mitchell Ct NR5 ...160 F8
Mitre Ct NR3 ......158 A3
Mitre Tavern Yd
NR28 ....151 C5
Mitre Yd NR28 ....151 C5
Moat Rd
Great Yarmouth NR30 .169 C5
Terrington St Clement
PE34 ....144 B1
Modney Bridge Rd
PE38 ....96 F8
Mokyll Croft NR8 ..155 D2
Moles La NR34 ....124 D5
Molls Dro PE14 ....77 C7
Monastery The NR3 .178 B3
Money Bank NR1 ..152 E4
Moneyhill La NR9 ..86 C3
Moneypot La IP22 .128 E5
Monkhams Dr IP25 .84 C3
Monks Cl NR31 ....14 D5
Monksgate IP24 ..176 B4
Mons Ave NR1 ....163 A8
Mont Cross NR8 ..155 D2
Montagu Cl PE37 ..153 C3
Montagu Dr IP27 ..127 C4
Montague Rd NR26 .138 C7
Montcalm Rd NR1 .163 B6
Montgomery Cl NR5 .160 F7
Montgomery Way
PE30 ....147 D4
Montpelier Dr NR1 .116 A1
Montrose Ct NR7 ..72 D4
Monument Rd NR20 .170 E7
Moor La Cranworth IP25 .85 D7
Elsing NR20 ....50 F3
Fransham NR19 ....50 F3
Sculthorpe NR21 .....16 B2
Stalham NR12 ....39 C3
Moor Rd
Burston & Shimpling
IP21 ....121 B2
Stalham NR12 ....39 C3
Moor The NR10 ...149 E5
Moorditch La PE34 .42 E2
Moore Ave NR1 ...158 F5
Moorend La NR21 ..32 D7
Moorfield Rd NR20 .68 A8
Moorgate Rd
East Dereham NR19 ..154 D3
Hindringham NR21 ....17 E8
Moorhouse Cl NR10 .149 C5
Moorings The PE33 .81 A2
Moorland Cl NR29 ..168 E8
Moorland Way NR31 .94 A5
Moors The NR8 ...155 F2
Morar Dr NR27 ....174 E6
Morello Cl NR4 ....161 E5
Morgan Way NR5 ..160 F8
Morgans Way NR10 .53 C8
Morgrove La NR20 .57 D6
Morley CE Prim Sch
NR18 ....87 A2
Morley La NR18 ....87 C2
Morley Rd
Beighton NR13 ....74 D2
Deopham NR18 ......86 E1
Sheringham NR26 ...138 D6
Morley Rd N NR26 .138 D6
Morley St NR18 ...162 F8
Morleyfield La NR18 .87 A3
Mornington La NR21 .131 C8
Mornington Rd NR2 .162 A4
Morris Cl
Norwich NR5 ....161 B8
Stoke Holy Cross NR14 .89 F4
Morris Dr NR13 ....165 B3
Morris Rd NR28 ...151 B4
Morrison Cl NR18 .138 D7
Morrison Rd NR31 .171 B5
Morse Ave NR1 ...163 A8
Morse Cl
Brundall NR13 ....165 D3
Great Witchingham NR9 ..51 D5
Morse Rd NR30 ...170 C6
Morston Chase NR25 ..6 F4
Morston Rd
Blakeney NR25 ....7 C6

Morston Rd continued
Stiffkey NR23 ....6 D6
Mortimer Cl NR17 ..174 F6
Morton Cl NR11 ...150 D6
Morton Cres NR31 ..94 C7
Morton La NR9 ....51 F3
Morton Peto Cl NR32 .111 D7
Morton Peto Rd NR31 .170 B8
Morton Rd NR11 ..150 D6
Mosely Ct NR5 ....160 E8
Mossfield Cl NR1 ..163 B8
Mother Julian Cl
IP24 ....176 D7
Mother Quy's IP24 .115 C1
Mottram Cl NR5 ...161 D6
Motum Rd NR5 ....161 C7
Moulton Rd
Halvergate NR13 ......74 F1
Tivetshall St Margaret
NR15 ....121 A7
Mount Cl Brandon IP27 .175 D2
Swaffham PE37 ......153 A5
Mount Dr PE13 ....152 C4
Mount Pk Cl PE32 .44 C3
Mount Pleasant
Diss IP22 ....177 D5
Little Walsingham NR22 ..16 F8
Norwich NR2 ....162 C5
Mount Pleasant Rd
PE13 ....152 C7
Mount Rd IP27 ....175 D2
Mount St Cromer NR27 .139 B7
Diss IP22 ....177 D5
King's Lynn PE30 ....146 F4
Mount Surrey NR18 .173 E3
Mount Tumbledown Cl
PE12 ....41 B8
Mountain's Rd NR11 ..19 F1
Mountbatten Cl IP24 .176 E6
Mountbatten Dr
East Dereham NR19 ..154 C6
Old Catton NR6 ......159 A6
Wisbech PE13 ....152 A7
Mountbatten Rd
Bungay NR35 ....124 A7
Dersingham PE31 ...140 C3
Mountbatten Way
NR30 ....168 D6
Monteneey Cl NR7 .159 A4
Mountergate NR1 .178 B2
Mountfield Ave
Hellesdon NR6 ......157 F4
Norwich NR6 ....158 A4
South Wootton NR3 ..163 A8
Mousehold Fst Sch
NR3 ....162 F8
Mousehold La NR7 .159 A3
Mousehold St NR3 .178 C4
Mowles Rd NR20 ..146 B8
Moyse's Bank
Emneth Hungate PE14 .59 F2
Marshland St James PE14 .60 A2
Muck La NR13 .....72 F8
Muckleburgh Collection
The* NR25 ....8 E6
Mud Rd NR21 .....15 D2
Mudd's Dro PE14 ..77 C7
Mudge La NR15 ...106 B2
Muir La NR31 .....106 B2
Mulbarton Fst Sch
NR14 ....89 B3
Mulbarton Mid Sch
NR14 ....89 B3
Mulberry Cl
Feltwell IP26 ....98 E1
Norwich NR3 ....178 A3
Mulberry Ct NR8 ..155 B2
Mulberry Gr NR31 ..94 C6
Mulberry La NR15 .107 A3
Mulberry Rd PE30 ..147 D4
Mullicourt Rd PE14 .78 B6
Mumby's Dro PE14 .77 E1
Mumford Prim Sch
PE36 ....100 B4
Mumford Rd
Thetford IP24 ....176 C6
Weeting-with-Broomhill
IP27 ....175 D7
Mundham La NR14 .91 D2
Mundham Rd
Loddon NR14 ....91 E1
Mundham NR14 ......109 A8
Mundy's Rd IP20 ..123 A1
Munhaven Cl NR11 .143 C5
Munnings Cl NR14 ..89 B3
Munnings Rd NR7 ..159 D1
Munson's Cl IP26 ..98 E2
Munson's Pl IP26 ..98 E2
Murgot's La PE33 ..80 D7
Muriel Kenny Ct NR9 .88 C7
Muriel Rd NR2 ....162 A4
Muriel Way IP25 ...85 A3
Murrayfield Rd NR6 .158 B5
Mus of the Broads The*
NR12 ....39 B3
Museum Sq NR15 .152 C5
Music House La NR1 .178 B2

Musketeer Way NR7 ..72 D4
Muspole St NR3 ...178 A4
Musticott Pl PE13 ..152 F6
Myles Way PE13 ...152 C8
Myrtle Ave
Costessey NR8 ......156 F3
East Dereham NR19 ..154 E4
Myrtle Cl NR31 .....170 C6
Myrtle Rd NR9 .....88 C8

N

Naber Furlong NR8 .155 E2
Napier Cl PE30 ....147 C5
Napier Pl Norwich NR2 .162 C7
Thetford IP24 ....176 A1
Naples Cl NR31 ...171 E4
Napoleon Pl NR30 .169 D3
Narborough Hill PE33 .63 E2
Narborough Rd PE32 ..63 D8
Narborough VC Fst Sch
PE32 ....63 E7
Narford La PE32 ...45 F2
Narford Rd PE32 ...63 F7
Narrows Trading Est The
PE30 ....147 A1
Naseby Way NR7 ..72 D4
Nash Rd NR10 ....155 C8
Nash's La NR20 ...32 C8
Nasmith Rd NR4 ..161 E3
Naylor Rd NR3 ....157 F1
Neale Cl NR11 ....150 B6
Neatherd High Sch
NR20 ....154 F5
Neatherd Moor NR20 .154 F6
Neatherd Rd NR20 .154 E5
Neatishead Prim Sch
NR12 ....55 D7
Neatishead Rd NR12 ..55 E5
Necton CE Fst Sch
PE37 ....66 A4
Necton Mid Sch PE37 ..66 A4
Necton Rd PE32 ...65 E7
Needham Bank PE14 .77 C8
Needham Rd IP20 ..122 C1
Neil Ave NR25 ....137 B5
Nelonde Dr NR18 .173 C5
Nelson Ave PE38 ..172 B5
Nelson Cl
Bradenham IP25 .....66 E3
Hethersett NR9 ......88 E8
Nelson Cres PE37 ..153 D3
Nelson Ct IP25 ....84 D4
Nelson Dr PE13 ...152 D3
Nelson Fst Sch NR2 .162 B7
Nelson Gdns PE13 ..152 D6
Nelson Hts NR27 ..139 A7
Nelson Pl NR19 ...154 C5
Nelson Rd NR3 ...169 D3
Nelson Rd N NR30 .169 D5
Nelson Rd S NR30 .169 D2
Nelson St
King's Lynn PE30 ....146 D4
Norwich NR2 ....162 B7
Nelson Way
Hevingham NR10 ....53 B8
Mundesley NR11 ....143 A7
North Walsham NR28 .151 C5
Nene Mdws PE12 ..41 C8
Nene Par PE13 ....152 B6
Nene Quay PE13 ..152 C5
Nene Rd
Hunstanton PE36 ...132 C4
Wisbech PE13 ....152 D6
Nene Sch The PE13 .152 D4
Nenelands PE12 ...41 C8
Nether Row NR12 .176 D3
Nethergate St
Ditchingham NR35 ..124 A8
Harpley PE31 ....29 D4
Hopton IP22 ....127 E6
Netherwood Gn NR1 .162 F2
Nettle Hill E NR30 .169 D4
Nettle Hill W NR30 .169 D4
Neve's Cl NR13 ...73 F3
Neville Cl
East Dereham NR19 ..154 C1
Norwich NR7 ....158 F3
Neville La PE31 ...38 B5
Neville Rd
Heacham PE31 ......133 C6
Norwich NR7 ....159 A3
Stalham NR12 ....39 A3
Neville St NR2 ....162 C5
New Bridge La
Elm PE14 ....59 A1
Wisbech PE14 ....152 A1
New Bridge Rd PE14 .59 A1
New Buckenham Cl
NR1 ....163 C3
New Coll Cl NR31 .170 B5
New Comm Rd IP27 .113 E5
New Conduit St PE30 .146 D5
New Cut PE13 .....152 D2
New Eccles Hall Sch The
NR16 ....105 B8
New England Way
IP24 ....116 A1
New Fen Dro PE38 .97 A5

New Hampshire Way
IP24 ....116 A1
New Inn Hill NR14 .91 C7
New Inn La NR19 ..154 B5
New La Banham NR16 ..119 B8
Bradenham IP25 .....66 F4
Hoveton NR12 ....55 C4
Mattishall NR20 .....68 F5
New Mills Yd NR3 .178 A4
New N Rd NR17 ..174 D5
New Par NR27 ....139 C7
New Rd Acle NR13 .166 C3
Attleborough NR17 ..174 B3
Aylsham NR11 ....150 D7
Baconsthorpe NR25 ..20 A8
Bawburgh NR9 ......160 B6
Belton NR31 ....94 A5
Blakeney NR25 ......7 C6
Bodham NR25 ......9 B1
Brettenham IP24 ...117 B2
Brinton NR24 ....18 D8
Burnham Overy Staithe
PE31 ....135 E7
Catfield NR29 ......56 C8
Crimplesham PE33 ..80 A6
Dickleburgh & Rushall
IP21 ....130 D8
Dunton NR11 ....16 A2
Fritton & St Olaves NR31 .93 E3
Gissing IP22 ....120 F4
Great Yarmouth NR30 .169 A6
Haddiscoe NR14 ....110 F7
Halvergate NR13 ....89 C7
Hethersett NR9 .....88 C3
Hingham NR9 ....86 C3
Itteringham NR11 ...35 D8
King's Lynn PE30 ...147 B6
Lingwood NR13 .....74 A3
Longham NR19 .....48 F2
Methwold IP26 .....98 E5
Mettingham NR35 ..124 C7
Morley NR18 ....87 A3
North Runcton PE33 ..44 A3
North Walsham NR28 .151 D5
Northrepps NR27 ...139 E1
Norton Subcourse NR14 .92 E1
Oulton NR11 ....35 C2
Outwell PE14 ....77 E5
Palgrave IP22 ....129 F4
Reedham NR13 .....92 F4
Reepham NR10 .....149 C3
St Cross, South Elmham
IP20 ....123 D1
Saxlingham Nethergate
NR15 ....107 B8
Sculthorpe NR21 ...16 A3
Sheringham NR26 ..138 C4
Shipdham IP25 .....67 B2
Stibbard NR21 .....32 D4
South Creake NR21 .15 D7
Stanfield NR20 .....48 F7
Stokesby with Herringby
NR29 ....75 A6
Surlingham NR14 ...73 B1
Sutton NR12 ....39 D2
Sutton Bridge PE12 ..41 A8
Tacolneston NR16 ..105 E5
Thelnetham IP22 ...127 F3
Thetford IP24 ......176 C4
.Thrandeston IP21 ..130 A4
Tilney St Lawrence PE34 .42 C1
Tivetshall St Mary NR15 .121 B4
Tilt Monks NR34 ...110 C6
Welney PE14 ....95 D5
Whissonsett NR20 ..31 D2
Wimbotsham PE34 ..172 E8
Wiveton NR25 ....7 E6
Wormegay PE33 ....44 B7
New Roman Bank
PE34 ....144 B7
New Row NR11 ...133 D6
New Sporle Rd PE37 .153 C5
New St Cawston NR10 ..35 B2
Cromer NR27 ......139 B7
Holt NR25 ....137 B6
Sheringham NR26 ..138 C7
New Wellington Pl
NR30 ....169 D2
Newall Rd IP24 ...125 F6
Newarch La NR14 .90 E7
Newark Cl NR7 ...72 D4
Neway Way NR10 .163 D8
Newbegin Cl NR1 .163 C7
Newbegin Rd NR11 .36 E5
Newbury Rd NR7 ..72 D4
Newby Rd NR7 ...72 D4
Newcastle Cl NR7 ..72 D4
Newcombe Cl IP24 .42 E1
Newcombe Dr IP26 .98 E1
Newell Crescent NR27 .12 B4
Newey's Way NR12 .164 C5
Newfen Gravel Dro
IP27 ....113 D4
Newfield Cl NR28 ..151 D6
Newfound Dr NR4 .161 C1
Newgate NR35 ....109 E3
Newgate La
Kirby Cane NR35 ...109 E3
Wells-next-the-Sea
NR23 ....136 C5
Newhaven Cl NR27 .139 B6
Newhaven Ct NR27 .139 B6

Newlands Ave PE30 ....146 E7
Newlands Cl 10 IP20 ....122 D2
Newman Rd NR13 ....72 D7
Newmarket Rd
2 Cringleford NR4 ....89 B8
Norwich NR2 ....178 A1
Newmarket St NR2 .....162 C4
Newnham Gn NR31 .....170 A4
Newport NR29 ....167 D6
Newport Rd
Hemsby NR29 ....167 C6
South Walsham NR13 ....74 A6
Newstead Wlk IP22 ....177 C6
Newstead's La NR27 .....10 C4
Newton Cl
Horsham St Faith &
Newton St Faith NR10 ......53 D4
10 Newton Flotman NR15 ...89 D1
Norwich NR4 ....162 B1
Newton Cross NR31 ....170 D1
Newton Flotman Prim Sch
NR15 ....89 D1
Newton Rd
Hainford NR10 ....53 E5
Newton by Castle Acre
PE32 ....47 A2
Sporle with Palgrave
PE32 ....65 C7
Newton St NR10 ....53 D4
Newtown IP24 ....176 C3
Neylond Cres NR6 ......157 E6
Nicholas Ave PE34 .....145 E6
Nicholas Hamond Way 4
PE37 ....153 C3
Nicholas Mews 3 NR2 ..162 B7
Nicholls Way IP22 .....177 A5
Nick's La IP23 ....130 B2
Nicolson Ave NR20 ......50 B5
Nightingale Cl
Denver PE38 ....172 D2
Fakenham NR21 ....141 F4
Hemsby NR29 ....167 E4
Mulbarton NR14 ....89 A3
Nightingale Dr NR8 ....155 B1
Nightingale Fst Sch
NR8 ....155 B1
Nightingale La
Denver PE38 ....172 D3
8 Feltwell IP26 ....98 E1
3 Feltwell IP26 ....98 E1
Norwich NR3 ....162 E8
Nightingale Rd IP27 ...175 F3
Nightingale Way IP24 ..176 D1
Nightingale Wlk PE38 ..172 C2
Nightmarsh La PE31 .....27 C4
Nile Rd
Downham Market PE38 ...172 B4
Great Yarmouth NR31 .....170 D4
Nile St 1 NR2 ....162 B7
Nimrod Cl 27 NR9 ....88 D8
Nine Acre La NR24 ......19 C4
Ninham St NR1 ....162 E3
Ninhams Ct NR2 ....178 A3
Nobb's Loke NR12 ....38 F4
Nobbs' Cnr NR35 ....108 A4
Nobel Cres NR12 ....164 B4
Noble Cl NR7 ....159 D1
Noel Cl NR31 ....171 C5
Noot Alley 6 NR5 ......161 B7
Nordelph Cnr NR9 ....86 D6
Norfolk & Norwich Univ
Hospl NR4 ....161 A3
Norfolk & Suffolk Aviation
Mus* NR35 ....123 D6
Norfolk Arena PE34 ....168 F2
Norfolk Dr NR17 ....174 C6
Norfolk Lavender Visitor
Ctr* PE31 ....133 E6
Norfolk Motor Cycle Mus*
NR28 ....151 C4
Norfolk Nelson Mus*
NR30 ....169 C3
Norfolk Rd
10 Honington IP31 ....126 B1
10 Marham PE33 ....63 B4
Norwich NR4 ....161 B3
Sheringham NR26 ....138 D6
Thetford IP24 ....176 E4
Norfolk Record Office
NR1 ....162 F3
Norfolk Shire Horse Ctr*
NR27 ....9 F5
Norfolk Sq
Downham Market PE38 ...172 B5
Great Yarmouth NR30 .....169 E5
Norfolk St
4 King's Lynn PE30 ......146 E5
Norwich NR2 ....162 C5
Wisbech PE13 ....152 C4
Norfolk Wildlife Ctr &
Country Pk* NR9 ....51 C6
Norfolk Wildlife Hospl
(RSPCA)* PE32 ....44 F3
Norgate La IP21 ....130 E6
Norgate Rd NR4 ....161 E3
Norgate Way NR8 ....156 E8
Norman CE Prim Sch
IP26 ....99 C7
Norman Cl
East Dereham NR19 ......154 C5
Fakenham NR21 ....141 B6
Norman Dr
Northwold PE33 ....81 B2
Norwich NR6 ....158 E7
Norman Fst Sch NR3 ...158 B2
Norman La 10 NR31 .....169 B4
Norman Rd
Flitcham with Appleton
PE31 ....28 E7
Norwich NR3 ....158 E1
Norman Troller Ct 9
NR27 ....139 B7
Norman Way PE31 ....15 B3
Norman's Burrow Rd
NR21 ....31 B3
Normandy Cl IP26 ....99 C7
Normans Bldgs NR1 ....178 B2
Normans La NR21 ....4 D1
North Ave NR20 ....50 B5
North Beach PE36 ......132 B1
North Brink PE13 ......152 A4
North Cambridgeshire Hospl
PE13 ....152 D5
North Denes Airfield
NR30 ....168 D2
North Denes Mid Sch
NR30 ....169 D8
North Denes Rd NR30 ..169 D6
North Dr
Fakenham NR21 ....141 C5
Great Yarmouth NR30 .....169 E4
North Elmham Chapel*
NR20 ....49 F8
North Elmham Prim Sch
NR20 ....49 E8
North End
Haddiscoe NR14 ....93 B1
Stoke Holy Cross NR14 ....89 E5
Wisbech PE13 ....152 B6
North End La NR16 .....106 D3
North Everard St
PE30 ....146 E3
North Gage Cl NR7 .....159 C4
North Gn NR9 ....68 B1
North Gn Rd IP21 ......122 A4
North La NR21 ....17 E5
North Lawn PE38 ....97 B6
North Lopham Rd
NR16 ....119 A3
North Lynn Ind Est
PE30 ....147 A8
North Mkt Rd
7 Great Yarmouth NR30 ..169 D4
Winterton-on-Sea NR29 ....58 B6
North Norfolk Rly*
NR26 ....9 B6
North Pickenham Rd
PE37 ....153 D4
North Pk NR21 ....141 B6
North Pk Ave NR4 ......161 E4
North Pk Dr NR4 ....161 F4
North Quay NR30 ....169 C4
North Rd Bunwell NR16 ..105 C4
4 Great Yarmouth NR30 ..169 D5
Great Yarmouth NR31 .....170 D4
Hemsby NR29 ....167 A7
Ormesby St Margaret
with Scratby NR29 ....167 A4
Watton IP25 ....84 D3
North River Rd NR30 ...169 C6
North St Brundall NR13 ..165 E6
Burnham Market PE31 ....135 C3
6 Castle Acre PE32 ....46 F2
Great Dunham PE32 ....47 E2
King's Lynn PE30 ....146 D6
Langham NR25 ....7 A4
North Walsham NR28 .....151 C5
Sheringham NR26 ....138 C7
Wisbech PE13 ....152 C5
North View NR21 ....17 F3
North Walsham Cottage
Hospl NR28 ....151 C4
North Walsham Fst Sch
NR28 ....151 D5
North Walsham High Sch
NR28 ....151 D4
North Walsham Jun Sch
NR28 ....151 D5
North Walsham Rd
Bacton NR28 ....23 C3
Coltishall NR12 ....54 D7
Crostwick NR12 ....54 B2
Felmingham NR28 ....37 B8
Happisburgh NR12 ....23 F2
Northrepps NR27 ....10 E1
Norwich NR6 ....159 A5
Paston NR28 ....151 F7
Sprowston NR6 ....159 B6
Swafield NR28 ....22 E4
Thorpe Market NR11 ....22 A7
Witton NR28 ....38 B8
North Walsham Sta
NR28 ....151 C4
North Way PE30 ....147 A8
North Wootton Prim Sch
PE30 ....148 D4
Northcote PE31 ....134 D6
Northcote Rd 1 NR3 ....162 E8
Northern Cl NR30 ......168 F5
Northfield Ave NR23 ...136 D6
Northfield Cl NR18 ....173 B6
Northfield Cres NR23 ..136 E5
Northfield Gdns NR18 ..173 B5
Northfield La
Plumstead NR11 ....20 B6
Wells-next-the-Sea
NR23 ....136 E6
Northfield Loke NR18 ..173 B6
Northfield Rd
Forncett NR16 ....106 A4
Mundesley NR11 ....143 C5
North Walsham NR28 .....151 B6
Swaffham PE37 ....153 C6
Northfield Way NR23 ...136 E6
Northfields NR4 ....161 E4
Northfields Fst Sch
NR4 ....161 E4
Northgate
Beccles NR34 ....110 D1
Dereham NR19 ....154 C7
11 Harleston IP20 ....122 D1
Hunstanton PE36 ....132 C5
Norwich NR6 ....157 F5
3 Thorpe End NR13 ....72 D6
Northgate Cty High Sch
NR19 ....154 D6
Northgate Hospl
NR30 ....169 D6
Northgate Prec PE36 ...132 C6
Northgate St NR30 .....169 C5
Northgate St Andrews Fst
Sch NR30 ....169 C6
Northgate Way PE34 ....144 D6
Northmead Dr NR28 .....151 C6
Northolt Rd IP25 ....85 A3
Northrepps Prim Sch
NR27 ....11 A2
Northrepps Rd NR27 ...139 E3
Northside NR7 ....72 E3
Northumberland St
NR2 ....162 B7
Northview Rd NR5 .....157 C1
Northwell Pool Rd
PE37 ....153 C5
North-West Twr*
NR30 ....169 C5
Northwold Rd IP26 ......99 A6
Norton Dr 2 Norwich NR4 .89 D8
Norwich NR4 ....162 A1
Norton Hill NR13 ....74 A8
Norton Rd NR14 ....92 B1
Nortridge Rd NR5 ......161 A7
Norvic Dr NR4 ....161 E1
Norway Cl PE31 ....133 C6
Norwich Arts Ctr*
NR2 ....178 A3
Norwich Bsns Pk NR4 ..162 D1
Norwich Castle Mus & Art
Gall* NR1 ....178 B3
Norwich Cath* NR1 ....178 B3
Norwich City FC NR1 ...163 A4
Norwich Com Hospl
NR2 ....161 F7
Norwich Comm NR18 ...173 F6
Norwich Dr NR20 ....32 E4
Norwich Gall* NR1 .....178 B3
Norwich Gates PE35 ....140 E1
Norwich High Sch for Girls
NR2 ....162 B3
Norwich Int Airport
NR6 ....158 B7
Norwich La IP31 ....127 A4
Norwich Lower Sch
NR1 ....178 C3
Norwich Puppet Theatre
NR1 ....178 B4
Norwich Rd Acle NR13 ..166 A3
Ashmanhaugh NR12 ....55 C7
Attleborough NR17 ......174 E6
Aylsham NR11 ....150 C6
Barnham Broom NR9 ....69 D2
Bawdeswell NR20 ....50 E7
Bracon Ash NR14 ....88 F2
Briston NR24 ....142 E5
Brooke NR15 ....90 E3
Burgh & Tuttington NR11 ....36 E6
Caister-on-Sea NR30 .....168 C5
Cantley NR13 ....92 D7
Carbrooke IP25 ....85 B3
Cawston NR10 ....35 B2
Chedgrave NR14 ....91 F2
Cromer NR27 ....139 C5
Denton IP20 ....123 B7
Dickleburgh & Rushall
IP21 ....130 D6
Ditchingham NR35 ....109 A2
Earsham NR35 ....108 E1
East Dereham NR20 ......154 F5
East Tuddenham NR20 .....69 C6
Edgefield NR24 ....19 D6
Fakenham NR21 ....141 C4
Foxley NR20 ....50 D8
Gillingham NR34 ....110 C2
Great & Little Plumstead
NR13 ....73 A7
Guist NR20 ....33 A4
Hardingham NR9 ....86 E8
9 Hethersett NR9 ....88 D7
Hingham NR9 ....86 D5
Holt NR25 ....137 B5
Horning NR12 ....55 E4
Horsham St Faith NR10 ....53 D2
Horstead with Stanninghall
NR12 ....54 C4
Ingworth NR11 ....36 B8
Kimberley NR18 ....87 B7
Langley with Hardley
NR14 ....91 F6
Lingwood & Burlingham
NR13 ....74 A2
12 Loddon NR14 ....92 A2
Long Stratton NR15 .....106 F5
Ludham NR29 ....56 C5
Marlingford NR9 ....69 F4
Mattishall NR20 ....68 F6
Mulbarton NR14 ....89 B4
Neatishead NR12 ....164 F8
North Walsham NR28 .....151 B3
Norwich NR5 ....157 B2
Poringland NR14 ....90 B6
Pulham St Mary IP21 .....121 F4
Norwich Rd *continued*
Rackheath NR13 ....72 F8
Reepham NR10 ....149 C5
Roughton NR11 ....21 D8
Salhouse NR13 ....55 B1
Saxlingham Nethergate
NR15 ....107 B8
Scole IP21 ....121 B1
Shotesham NR15 ....89 F2
Shouldham PE33 ....62 F3
Smallburgh NR12 ....38 D2
Stockton NR34 ....109 F5
Strumpshaw NR13 ....73 F2
Swaffham PE37 ....153 D4
Swanton Morley NR20 ......50 B2
4 Tacolneston NR16 .....105 F5
Tacolneston NR16 ....106 A6
Tharston & Hapton
NR15 ....106 C7
Thetford IP24 ....176 D4
Thurton NR14 ....91 C3
Tivetshall St Mary NR15 ...121 D4
West Caister NR30 ......168 B6
Weston Longville NR9 .....51 E5
Wisbech PE13 ....152 E5
Woodton NR35 ....108 C6
Wroxham/Hoveton
NR12 ....164 B3
Wymondham NR18 ....173 D5
Yaxham NR19 ....68 B5
Norwich Rd Sch IP24 ..176 D4
Norwich Research Pk
NR4 ....161 A4
Norwich Riverside
NR1 ....178 C2
Norwich Sch NR1 ......178 B3
Norwich Sch of Art & Design
NR3 ....178 B3
Norwich St
East Dereham NR19 ......154 E5
Fakenham NR21 ....141 B4
Hingham NR9 ....86 C5
Mundesley NR11 ....143 A7
Norwich Sta NR1 ......178 C2
Norwich Theatre Royal
NR2 ....178 A2
Norwood Rd IP27 ....175 A1
Notre Dame High Sch
NR1 ....178 B1
Notre Dame Prep Sch
NR2 ....162 B7
Nottingham Rd PE30 ...146 E8
Nottingham Way
NR30 ....169 C3
Notykin St NR5 ....161 A8
Nourse Dr PE31 ....133 E5
Nova Scotia Rd
Filby NR30 ....168 A7
Ormesby St Margaret
with Scratby NR29 ....167 B1
Nowhere La PE33 ....80 D4
Nuffield Cl NR31 ......170 B4
Nuffield Cres NR31 ....170 B4
Nunn's Way NR19 ....154 D5
Nunnery Dr IP24 ....176 D1
Nunnery Pl IP24 ....176 D2
Nunnery The* IP24 .....176 D2
Nuns' Bridges Rd
IP24 ....176 C2
Nunsgate IP24 ....176 D2
Nurseries Ave NR13 ....165 E4
Nursery Cl Acle NR13 ...166 B4
2 Beetley NR19 ....49 C3
7 Belton NR31 ....94 A5
2 Gressenhall NR20 ....49 C3
King's Lynn PE30 ....148 C2
8 Martham NR29 ....57 D5
Norwich NR6 ....157 E5
2 Roydon PE32 ....28 A1
Nursery Dr
Hunstanton PE36 ....132 D4
North Walsham NR28 .....151 B3
Wisbech PE13 ....152 E8
Nursery Gdns NR13 ....165 F6
Nursery La
Brancaster PE31 ....3 E6
Costessey NR8 ....156 F3
Hockwold cum Wilton
IP26 ....114 A6
King's Lynn PE30 ....148 C3
Nursery Rd PE38 ....172 C6
Nursery Terr NR30 .....169 C6
Nursery Way PE32 ....28 A1
Nursey Cl NR35 ....109 D3
Nut La NR27 ....139 F3
Nutfield Cl 7 NR4 .....161 F1
Nuthall Cres PE30 .....147 A8
Nutmeg Wlk PE38 ......172 E6
Nuttele Cl NR15 ....107 C6
Nuttery Vale IP23 .....130 F2
Nutwood Cl NR8 ....155 D2

O

Oak Ave
14 Great Yarmouth NR31 ...94 C7
King's Lynn PE30 ....148 D2
Marham PE33 ....63 B4
North Elmham NR20 ....49 E7
Norwich NR7 ....163 F8
9 Poringland NR14 ....90 C5
West Winch PE33 ....43 F2
Oak Cl 4 Hethersett NR9 ..88 D8
Norwich NR5 ....156 F2
14 Tasburgh NR15 ....106 F6
Thetford IP24 ....176 A1
Oak Cres IP23 ....130 C1
Oak Dr PE14 ....77 F7
Oak Gr 7 Horsford NR10 ..53 B3
Sheringham NR26 ....138 D5
Oak La East Ruston NR12 ..38 E7
2 Hingham NR9 ....86 C4
Norwich NR3 ....158 D3
Oak Lodge NR7 ....163 C5
Oak Rd Dilham NR28 ......38 D4
Great Yarmouth NR31 .....170 B6
North Walsham NR28 .....151 B4
Stoke Ferry PE33 ....81 A2
Oak St Fakenham NR21 ...141 B4
Feltwell IP26 ....98 E1
Norwich NR3 ....178 A4
Oak Tree Bsns Pk NR13 ..72 E8
Oak Tree Cl 3 NR29 .....57 D5
Oak Tree Way 8 IP20 ...122 D1
Oak View Dr PE38 ......172 C6
Oak Wood NR13 ....165 E5
Oakapple Dr NR19 .....154 D8
Oak's La NR13 ....72 F2
Oakcroft Dr NR14 ....90 C5
Oakdale Rd NR13 ......165 D3
Oakdene NR21 ....15 C2
Oakfield Cl PE38 ......172 C4
Oakfield Dr 3 NR13 ......74 B8
Oakfield Rd
Aylsham NR11 ....150 C6
Long Stratton NR15 .....106 F3
Oakfields NR14 ....91 F2
Oakfields Cl 1 NR4 ......89 C8
Oakfields Rd NR4 ....89 B8
Oakhill NR13 ....165 D3
Oakland Dr 5 NR20 ......49 D4
Oaklands
Little Snoring NR21 ....17 C3
4 Old Buckenham NR17 ..104 D2
Poringland NR14 ....90 C6
6 Taverham NR8 ....155 B2
Oaklands Cl
Attleborough NR17 ......174 C3
Halvergate NR13 ....74 F2
Oaklands Dr
Brandon IP27 ....114 D4
Cringleford NR4 ....161 C1
Walsoken PE13 ....152 F7
Oaklands La 2 PE33 .....61 D3
Oaklands Pk NR28 ......151 B6
Oaklands The PE37 .....153 C3
Oakleigh Dr PE13 ......153 A5
Oakley Church La
IP21 ....130 D4
Oakley Cl PE13 ....152 E4
Oakroyd Cres PE13 .....152 C6
Oaks Cl PE37 ....153 C3
Oaks Dr Necton PE37 .....65 F4
Swaffham PE37 ....153 C3
Oaks La NR34 ....111 B5
Oaks The Ashill IP25 ....84 A7
3 Beetley NR19 ....49 C3
3 Gressenhall NR20 ....49 C3
Mattishall NR20 ....68 F5
Oaktree Dr NR7 ....159 B2
Oakwood Cl NR19 ....154 D8
Oakwood Dr NR18 ....173 E6
Oakwood Rd NR19 ....154 D8
Oasis Leisure Ctr
PE36 ....132 C4
Oasis Sport & Leisure Ctr
NR7 ....72 D5
Oasis Way PE36 ....132 C2
Oatfield Cl 7 NR10 ......53 A3
Obelisk La NR28 ....37 F5
Obelisk Plain NR25 ....137 A6
Occupation Rd 1 NR20 ...68 F6
Octagon Dr 4 PE13 .....152 A6
Octavia Cl PE13 ....152 F6
Octavia Hill Birthplace Mus*
PE13 ....152 C5
Oddfellows Field 4 NR25 ..7 C6
Oddfellows Row PE31 ...134 E4
Offley Ct 7 NR5 ....161 A8
Ogden Cl NR18 ....173 C4
Oil Mill La PE13 ......152 B5
Old Allotment Ct 7
NR3 ....162 F8
Old Bakery Ct PE31 ....133 C5
Old Barge Yd NR1 .....178 C2
Old Barley Mkt The
NR2 ....178 A3
Old Bear Ct NR28 ......151 C5
Old Becclesgate NR19 ..154 D5
Old Brandon Rd IP26 ....98 F1
Old Brewery Ct 14 PE30 .146 E3
Old Brewery La NR10 ...149 C4
Old Buckenham High Sch
NR17 ....104 D2
Old Buckenham Prim Sch
NR17 ....104 D3
Old Buckenham Rd
NR16 ....105 A4
Old Bungay Rd NR35 ...109 D4
Old Bury Rd
Palgrave IP22 ....129 E4
Stuston IP21 ....177 F1
Thetford IP24 ....176 C4
Wortham IP22 ....129 D4
Old Catton Mid Sch
NR6 ....158 E5
Old Chapel Rd
Cantley NR13 ....92 E7
2 Hemsby NR29 ....58 B6
Old Chapel Way NR7 .....72 E3
Old Church Cl NR14 .....89 F6
Old Church Rd
Hainford NR10 ....53 E6
Hopton on Sea NR31 .....171 D4
Snettisham PE31 ....12 E5

Old - Pec 203

Old Coach Rd NR27 ....139 C6
Old Coast Rd NR29 ....167 E2
Old Fakenham Rd
Attlebridge NR9 ....52 B3
Foxley NR20 ....50 D8
Old Farm La NR3 ....158 B1
Old Feltwell Rd IP26 ....99 A5
Old Forge Cl IP22 ....129 B4
Old Forge Ct
Acle NR13 ....166 C4
Brockdish IP21 ....131 D6
Old Fountain NR31 ....170 C1
Old Friendship La
NR10 ....35 C2
Old Gr Ct NR3 ....158 D2
Old Hall Cl
Ashwellthorpe NR16 ....105 F8
1 Norwich NR14 ....163 B2
Saham Toney IP25 ....84 B5
Old Hall Dr PE31 ....140 E3
Old Hall Gdns
Brooke NR15 ....90 F2
Buxton with Lammas
NR10 ....37 A2
Caister-on-Sea NR30 ....168 E5
Old Hall La PE37 ....81 F8
Old Hall Rd
East Dereham NR19 ....154 D2
Mattishall NR20 ....68 D5
Witton NR28 ....38 B8
Old Hall The PE31 ....27 C3
Old Harleston Rd
NR35 ....123 E7
Old High Rd IP22 ....177 A5
Old Hithe Rd NR26 ....138 A6
Old Hunstanton Rd
PE36 ....132 E7
Old Kiln 10 PE33 ....43 F2
Old La East Ruston NR12 ....24 A5
Happisburgh NR12 ....23 F1
Reepham NR10 ....34 B1
Thelnetham IP22 ....128 A2
Old Lakenham Hall Dr 6
NR1 ....162 E1
Old Laundry Ct 3 NR2 ....162 B8
Old Laundry Mews
NR1 ....163 A5
Old Liby Mews NR1 ....178 C2
Old Lynn Rd PE13 ....152 E7
Old Maltings The
PE13 ....153 B4
Old Manor Cl PE30 ....148 C1
Old Methwold Rd
Feltwell IP26 ....98 E2
Northwold PE33 ....81 B2
Old Mill Dr IP21 ....121 F4
Old Mill Rd
Caister-on-Sea NR30 ....168 F5
3 Poringland NR14 ....90 C5
Roughton NR11 ....139 B1
Old Mkt PE13 ....152 C5
Old Mkt Cl NR13 ....166 C3
Old Mkt Gn 3 NR14 ....92 A1
Old Mkt Pl 21 IP20 ....122 D2
Old Mkt St
14 King's Lynn PE30 ....146 E5
Thetford IP24 ....176 D3
Old Mkt Way NR15 ....107 C5
Old Norwich Rd
Horsham St Faith &
Newton St Faith NR10 ....53 D1
Yaxley IP23 ....130 A1
Old Pal Rd NR2 ....162 B7
Old Pools Dro CB6 ....95 F1
Old Post Office La
NR35 ....109 E3
Old Post Office St
2 Fakenham NR21 ....141 B4
2 Shipdham IP25 ....67 B2
Old Post Rd NR24 ....142 E4
Old Quarry Ct NR19 ....154 E6
Old Rd Acle NR13 ....166 E5
1 Great Moulton NR15 ....106 B1
Old Rectory Cl
King's Lynn PE30 ....148 D5
4 Mulbarton NR14 ....89 B3
Norwich NR7 ....163 E6
7 Roydon IP22 ....129 D7
South Wootton PE30 ....148 B1
Old Rectory Rd NR12 ....24 A1
Old Reepham Rd 4
NR20 ....50 E7
Old Rly Rd IP20 ....123 B5
Old Rly Yd PE31 ....135 C2
Old Roman Bank
PE34 ....144 A7
Old Sch Cl NR5 ....161 E5
Old Sch Ct NR1 ....178 C1
Old Sch Rd
East Ruston NR12 ....38 F8
Guestwick NR20 ....33 F5
Old Severalls Rd IP26 ....98 E6
Old South PE30 ....147 C4
Old Southwood Rd
NR13 ....74 B2
Old St 2 NR15 ....107 A8
Old Sta La NR35 ....109 D2
Old Sta Way 6 NR25 ....137 C5
Old Stoke Rd NR14 ....89 F8
Old Town Way PE36 ....132 D6
Old Turnpike Rd NR11 ....21 D7
Old Vicarage Pk PE32 ....63 E7
Old Warren NR8 ....155 D2
Old Watton Rd NR4 ....161 A5
Old Wellington Pl 15
NR30 ....169 D3
Old Wells Rd
Sculthorpe NR21 ....16 A2
Old Wells Rd *continued*
Walsingham NR22 ....16 E8
Old Woman's La NR25 ....7 F6
Old Yarmouth Rd NR12 ....39 C2
Oldfield Ave PE14 ....59 B1
Oldfield Ct 3 NR19 ....154 E6
Oldfield La PE13 ....152 B3
Oldhall La NR16 ....118 C5
Oldhall Rd NR4 ....89 E8
Oldmedow Rd PE30 ....147 A2
Oldsunway PE30 ....146 D5
Oldwash La NR16 ....105 D3
Olive Ave NR15 ....89 D1
Olive Cl NR5 ....157 C1
Olive Cres NR10 ....53 A4
Olive Rd
Great Yarmouth NR31 ....169 B3
Norwich NR5 ....157 C1
Oliver Ct
5 Cromer NR27 ....139 C6
2 Weeting IP27 ....114 E1
Oliver Mews 4 NR30 ....169 D4
Olivet Way NR21 ....141 C3
Olivia Cl NR21 ....141 A5
Ollands Rd
Attleborough NR17 ....174 C3
Reepham NR10 ....149 C4
Ollard Ave PE13 ....152 D7
Olley Rd 1 NR27 ....10 A5
Olney Rd NR19 ....154 D5
Onedin Cl PE31 ....140 C5
Onley St NR2 ....162 B4
Onslow Ave NR30 ....169 D7
Onyx Ct 10 PE13 ....152 C4
Opie St NR2 ....178 B3
Opportune Rd PE13 ....152 C6
Orange Gr 3 PE13 ....152 C4
Orange Row PE34 ....144 A5
Orange Row Rd PE34 ....144 A6
Orchard Bank NR8 ....156 E8
Orchard Cl Acle NR13 ....166 B4
Ashill IP25 ....84 A6
Attleborough NR17 ....174 C5
Blofield Heath NR13 ....73 C6
Brancaster Staithe PE31 ....3 D7
Briston NR24 ....142 D4
Caister-on-Sea NR30 ....168 E4
Dersingham PE31 ....140 D4
Downham Market PE38 ....172 D5
Fakenham NR21 ....141 D4
Holt NR25 ....137 E7
3 Ixworth NR9 ....69 F2
Mundesley NR11 ....143 B7
North Elmham NR20 ....49 E7
North Walsham NR28 ....151 C6
Norwich NR7 ....163 C8
Roughton NR11 ....21 D7
Sheringham NR26 ....138 C6
Tacolneston NR16 ....105 F4
Watlington PE33 ....61 E5
19 Watton IP25 ....84 D3
8 Wisbech PE14 ....59 A1
Orchard Cres 4 NR15 ....106 B1
Orchard Ct
King's Lynn PE30 ....147 B6
Ormesby St Margaret
NR29 ....167 A3
Orchard Dr
Hellesdon NR6 ....157 D3
3 Potter Heigham NR29 ....56 F6
West Walton PE14 ....59 C8
Wisbech PE13 ....152 E4
Orchard Gdns 3 PE30 ....147 B6
Orchard Gr Diss IP22 ....177 C5
Kettlestone NR21 ....17 C2
King's Lynn PE34 ....146 C3
Orchard La
Aylsham NR11 ....150 D4
Castle Acre PE32 ....46 F2
King's Lynn PE30 ....147 B5
Reepham NR10 ....149 D5
Shouldham PE33 ....62 D4
Orchard Pl
Swaffham PE37 ....153 B4
Thompson IP24 ....102 A7
Orchard Rd
8 Gayton PE32 ....45 C6
Lingwood NR13 ....73 F3
5 Mattishall NR20 ....68 E6
2 Spixworth NR10 ....54 A2
4 Wiggenhall St Germans
PE34 ....43 B1
Orchard St NR2 ....162 C7
Orchard The
4 Belton NR31 ....94 A6
Brandon IP27 ....175 C3
Orchard Way
Banham NR16 ....119 D7
4 Burgh St Margaret
(Fleggburgh) NR29 ....57 C1
5 Hethersett NR9 ....88 D8
7 Tasburgh NR15 ....106 F6
Terrington St John PE14 ....42 B1
Thetford IP24 ....176 D5
Wymondham NR18 ....173 C4
Orchards Prim Ssh
PE13 ....152 D8
Orchid Ave NR19 ....154 D1
Orde Ave NR31 ....170 C2
Ordnance Rd NR30 ....169 D1
Orford Cl 5 NR30 ....169 D3
Orford Hill NR1 ....178 B2
Orford Pl Norwich NR1 ....178 B2
7 West Winch PE33 ....43 F2
Orford Rd PE37 ....153 C6
Orford St NR1 ....178 B2
Orhard Gr PE33 ....43 E2
Oriel Ave NR31 ....170 A3
Oriel High Sch NR31 ....170 A3
Origins* NR2 ....178 A2
Ormesby 4 PE30 ....147 D5
Ormesby Fst Sch
NR29 ....167 A2
Ormesby La NR29 ....76 A8
Ormesby Mid Sch
NR29 ....167 A3
Ormesby Rd
Caister-on-Sea NR30 ....168 D7
Hemsby NR29 ....167 A6
Ormesby St Margaret
with Scratby NR29 ....168 C8
Scottow NR10 ....37 B2
Ormond Rd NR30 ....169 C5
Orwell Cl
King's Lynn PE30 ....147 D4
2 Wymondham NR18 ....173 D5
Orwell Cres NR31 ....94 A6
Orwell Rd NR2 ....162 C3
Osbert Cl 4 NR1 ....162 E1
Osborne Ave NR30 ....169 C7
Osborne Cl 1 NR28 ....151 C7
Osborne Ct NR4 ....162 B3
Osborne Pk PE13 ....152 C8
Osborne Rd
Norwich NR4 ....161 D2
Wisbech PE13 ....152 B7
Osier Cl NR19 ....154 B4
Osier La NR25 ....9 C1
Osprey Cl NR12 ....164 D5
Ostend Gap NR12 ....24 A7
Ostend Pl NR12 ....24 A7
Ostend Rd NR12 ....24 A6
Ostrich La NR19 ....49 A3
Otter Cl
3 Downham Market
PE38 ....172 A6
5 Salhouse NR13 ....55 A1
Otter Dr 17 NR14 ....89 B3
Otter Trust The*
NR35 ....123 E7
Oulton Cl PE37 ....153 C2
Oulton Rd NR6 ....158 C5
Ouse Ave PE30 ....146 D2
Ouse Ave The IP24 ....176 C3
Ouse La NR12 ....39 F1
Out S Gates PE30 ....146 E3
Outney Rd NR35 ....124 A8
Outwell Rd Emneth PE14 ....59 B2
Stow Bardolph PE34 ....78 E8
Oval Ave NR5 ....161 C8
Oval Rd NR5 ....157 C1
Oval The IP25 ....84 B5
Over Cross NR16 ....119 C8
Overbury Rd NR6 ....158 A4
Overstone Ct NR6 ....158 F5
Overstrand Belfry VA Prim
Sch NR27 ....11 A3
Overstrand Rd NR27 ....139 C6
Overstrand Sports Club
NR27 ....11 A3
Overtons Way 14 NR14 ....90 C5
Overwood La NR16 ....106 A3
Overy Rd PE31 ....135 D3
Ovington Rd IP25 ....84 C4
Owen Rd Diss IP22 ....177 F4
Great Yarmouth NR31 ....169 B1
Owen's Cl 22 NR15 ....106 E3
Owl Dr 3 NR14 ....89 B3
Oxborough Dr PE30 ....148 E1
Oxborough La NR21 ....141 C4
Oxborough Rd
Oxborough PE33 ....81 D3
Stoke Ferry PE33 ....81 A2
Oxburgh Cl 1 PE13 ....152 A7
Oxburgh Hall Gdns & Estate*
PE33 ....81 E4
Oxcroft NR13 ....166 C4
Oxford Ave NR31 ....170 B3
Oxford Pl PE34 ....144 F6
Oxford Rd 2 Feltwell IP26 ....98 E1
2 Feltwell IP26 ....98 E1
Oxford St NR2 ....162 C5
Oxford Way 11 NR29 ....57 D4
Oxnead Dr NR30 ....168 C7
Oxnead La NR35 ....107 F4
Oxnead Rd NR3 ....158 B2

P

Pack La Briston NR24 ....142 F3
East Carleton NR14 ....89 A6
Strumpshaw NR13 ....73 F3
Packway The IP20 ....123 A3
Paddock Cl Belton NR31 ....93 F6
3 Fakenham NR21 ....141 E4
Paddock Farm IP31 ....127 B4
Paddock Farm Dr NR29 ....75 F8
Paddock Gdns NR17 ....174 E5
Paddock Rd 13 IP20 ....122 D2
Paddock St NR2 ....162 C8
Paddock The
3 Cromer NR27 ....10 B5
Hemsby NR29 ....167 A8
Trowse with Newton
NR14 ....163 A2
Paddocks The
Aylsham NR11 ....150 C6
Bacton/Walcott NR12 ....23 E4
Beetley NR20 ....49 D4
Brandon IP27 ....175 E4
Downham Market PE38 ....172 B5
Griston IP25 ....85 A1
Norwich NR6 ....158 F6
Swaffham PE37 ....153 B3
Paddy's La NR9 ....51 E1
Paddys Loke NR30 ....169 A7
Padgate NR13 ....72 D6
Padgett's Rd PE14 ....95 A6
Page Cl
3 North Walsham NR28 ....151 C6
Poringland NR14 ....90 C5
Page Rd Brundall NR13 ....165 C4
Norwich NR3 ....157 F1
Page Stair La PE30 ....146 D5
Pages Cl 3 NR18 ....173 B3
Pages La IP25 ....84 B5
Paget Adams Dr 4 NR20 ....68 A8
Paget Cres NR31 ....170 C1
Paget Rd NR30 ....169 D4
Paige Cl 1 PE33 ....61 D5
Paine Cl IP22 ....177 B5
Paine Rd NR7 ....163 D8
Painter St IP24 ....176 C4
Pakenham Dr PE31 ....140 C3
Palace St NR1 ....178 B3
Pales Gn 4 PE32 ....46 F2
Palgrave Cl NR8 ....155 B1
Palgrave Rd
Great Dunham PE32 ....47 E1
Great Yarmouth NR30 ....169 C5
Little Dunham PE32 ....65 D8
Palgrave VC Prim Sch
IP22 ....177 D2
Palling Rd NR12 ....24 D1
Palm Cl NR18 ....173 B5
Palmer Rd
Great Yarmouth NR31 ....170 D5
8 New Rackheath NR13 ....72 E7
Norwich NR3 ....158 C3
Palmer Way PE38 ....172 C3
Palmer's La
Aylsham NR11 ....150 C6
Freethorpe NR13 ....92 F8
Palmers La NR12 ....55 C5
Pandora 1 PE30 ....147 C4
Pansey Dr PE31 ....140 C4
Panton Cl PE30 ....146 D2
Panxworth Church Rd
NR13 ....73 E8
Panxworth Rd NR13 ....73 F7
Paper St NR19 ....68 C6
Papillion Rd NR18 ....173 D4
Paradise La
6 Bawdeswell NR20 ....50 E7
7 King's Lynn PE30 ....146 D5
Paradise Par 10 PE30 ....146 D5
Paradise Pl NR1 ....178 B2
Paradise Rd
7 Bawdeswell NR20 ....50 E7
Downham Market PE38 ....172 B5
9 King's Lynn PE30 ....146 D5
Paragon Pl 4 NR2 ....162 C6
Parana Cl NR7 ....159 C5
Parana Ct NR7 ....159 C5
Parana Rd NR7 ....159 C5
Parish Rd NR10 ....53 D7
Park Ave 5 Barford NR9 ....69 F2
King's Lynn PE30 ....146 F4
North Walsham NR28 ....151 D5
Scottow NR10 ....37 D2
Wisbech PE13 ....152 C6
Park Cl Hethersett NR9 ....88 D7
Holt NR25 ....137 D5
Norwich NR6 ....158 E5
Thurton NR14 ....91 C4
Wymondham NR18 ....173 D1
Park Comm La NR16 ....119 B5
Park Cres PE34 ....61 B5
Park Ct Harling NR16 ....118 C5
North Walsham NR28 ....151 D5
Park Dr NR9 ....88 C7
Park Est 3 IP25 ....67 B2
Park Farm La
Euston IP24 ....126 C4
Hoxne IP21 ....131 C2
Park High Sch PE30 ....147 A4
Park Highatt Dr 2 IP25 ....67 C2
Park Hill PE31 ....140 D5
Park La Blofield NR13 ....165 B8
Cromer NR27 ....139 D4
Deopham NR18 ....87 A4
Downham Market PE38 ....172 B3
Helhoughton NR21 ....30 E5
Hockering NR20 ....69 C8
North Walsham NR28 ....151 C5
Norwich NR2 ....162 B5
Reepham NR10 ....149 B4
Scarning NR19 ....67 B6
Snettisham PE31 ....12 E4
Wymondham NR18 ....173 C2
Park Rd Cromer NR27 ....139 D5
Diss IP22 ....177 D4
East Dereham NR19 ....154 E6
Great Yarmouth NR31 ....170 D3
Gressenhall NR20 ....49 C3
Hunstanton PE36 ....132 C4
St Cross, South Elmham
IP20 ....123 C3
Spixworth NR10 ....54 A1
Upper Sheringham
NR26 ....138 A4
Warham NR23 ....6 A4
Wells-next-the-Sea
NR23 ....136 C6
Wisbech PE13 ....152 D5
Wroxham/Hoveton
NR12 ....164 B3
Park St 4 PE13 ....152 D5
Park The NR16 ....118 B5
Park View
Botesdale IP22 ....128 F3
Brandon IP27 ....175 B2
Weeting IP27 ....175 A7
Park View Ave NR29 ....57 D3
Park Way NR6 ....157 E5
Parker Cl NR13 ....165 B4
Parker Dr NR21 ....141 D4
Parker Rd NR2 ....162 B5
Parker's La NR15 ....106 F2
Parker's Rd 10 NR20 ....68 F6
Parker's Cl NR9 ....70 C5
Parkers Cl NR18 ....173 B6
Parkers Prim Sch IP25 ....84 C5
Parkes La NR15 ....106 D6
Parkhill 4 PE32 ....44 B3
Parkland Cl 8 NR12 ....55 E4
Parkland Cres
9 Horning NR12 ....55 E4
Norwich NR6 ....158 F3
Parkland Dr NR31 ....170 A5
Parkland Est NR29 ....167 A8
Parkland Rd NR6 ....158 F3
Parklands NR8 ....156 D4
Parklands Ave IP25 ....67 B2
Parklands Way 41 IP20 ....122 D2
Parkside PE36 ....13 A7
Parkside Ct IP22 ....177 C4
Parkside Dr NR6 ....158 E5
Parkside Specl Sch
NR2 ....162 A5
Parkview IP24 ....176 E4
Parkway PE30 ....147 B4
Parliament Ct 5 NR7 ....72 D4
Parliament La IP24 ....102 E3
Parmenter Rd NR4 ....161 F3
Parmeter Cl NR11 ....150 D6
Parr Rd NR3 ....158 A1
Parrow La NR11 ....21 C6
Parsons Cl IP27 ....175 B2
Parsons La PE31 ....14 D8
Parsons Mead NR4 ....161 F1
Partridge Dr
Mulbarton NR14 ....89 A3
4 Thetford IP24 ....176 D2
Partridge Gr PE37 ....153 D3
Partridge Rd NR11 ....150 B6
Partridge Way NR6 ....158 D4
Partridge Wlk IP27 ....175 F3
Parva Cl NR11 ....20 B4
Pasteur Rd NR31 ....169 B2
Paston Cl 4 NR11 ....9 E1
Paston Coll NR28 ....151 C5
Paston Dr NR30 ....168 C8
Paston Great Barn*
NR28 ....143 E2
Paston Rd
Great Yarmouth NR31 ....170 C5
Mundesley NR11 ....143 D5
Paston Way NR7 ....159 E2
Pasture Cl PE31 ....28 B4
Pastures The
5 Blakeney NR25 ....7 C6
Great Yarmouth NR31 ....170 B7
Hemsby NR29 ....167 A8
Little Snoring NR21 ....17 B3
Patricia Ave NR12 ....54 C6
Patricia Rd NR1 ....162 D3
Patrick Rd 4 NR15 ....106 D3
Patten La NR15 ....121 B3
Patterson Cl 4 NR30 ....169 C4
Patteson Cl 8 NR4 ....89 B8
Patteson Rd NR3 ....162 D8
Paul Dr PE32 ....44 B3
Pauls La NR27 ....11 A3
Pavilion Ct 5 IP22 ....177 A5
Pavilion Rd NR31 ....170 D4
Pavilion Theatre NR31 ....170 E4
Paxman Rd PE30 ....146 F2
Paxton Terr PE30 ....146 E5
Payne Ave PE13 ....152 D7
Payne's La IP26 ....98 E1
Paynes Hill IP20 ....122 F6
Peachman Way 5 NR7 ....72 E4
Peachtree St 6 NR21 ....15 C2
Peacock Chase NR18 ....173 D4
Peacock Cl Easton NR9 ....70 B5
Hockwold cum Wilton
IP26 ....113 F6
Peacock La
Beetley NR20 ....49 E5
Holt NR25 ....137 B7
Peacock St NR3 ....178 B4
Peacock Way NR24 ....142 A4
Peacocks The NR25 ....137 C7
Peakhall Rd PE32 ....48 B8
Peakwell Cl NR8 ....155 C2
Pear Tree Cl NR20 ....68 E6
Pear Tree Cnr NR21 ....31 C2
Pearce Rd IP22 ....177 E4
Pearce's Cl 2 IP26 ....114 A7
Pearcefield NR3 ....158 E2
Pearmain Rd IP22 ....177 C5
Pearson's Rd NR25 ....137 C6
Pearsons Cl
Freethorpe NR13 ....92 E7
Holt NR25 ....137 C6
Peartree Ave 2 NR29 ....57 C4
Peartree Way 9 PE14 ....59 A1
Peatlings La PE13 ....152 A7
Pebble Cl 3 PE12 ....41 B8
Pebble View Wlk
NR31 ....171 E4
Peck Cl NR5 ....160 E8
Peckover Cty Prim Sch
PE13 ....152 B6
Peckover Dr PE13 ....152 E4
Peckover House*
PE13 ....152 B5

Peckover Rd
Fakenham NR21 ....141 A6
Norwich NR4 ....161 E3
Peckover Way PE30 ....147 E8
Peddars Cl PE36 ....132 D6
Peddars Dr PE36 ....132 D6
Peddars' La NR34 ....110 C6
Peddars Way NR8 ....155 D2
Peddars Way N PE36 ....2 A4
Peddlars Turnpike
NR20 ....33 F3
Pedham Rd NR13 ....73 E7
Pedlar's Gr PE37 ....153 C5
Pedlar's La NR21 ....17 F1
Pedlars Croft 2 NR29 ....167 A8
Pedley La PE13 ....152 A6
Peel Mews 8 NR3 ....178 A3
Peel St PE30 ....146 F4
Pegasus Cl NR30 ....168 D7
Pegg Cl NR9 ....70 B5
Pegg Rd NR26 ....138 C5
Pegg's La NR16 ....105 E6
Peggotty Rd NR30 ....170 D8
Peldon Dr PE13 ....152 E5
Pelham Rd NR3 ....158 D1
Pell Pl 2 PE33 ....43 F2
Pell Rd PE31 ....140 D4
Pellew Pl NR28 ....151 C6
Pemberton Rd 6 NR20 ....22 C6
Pembrey Cl NR3 ....158 D3
Pembroke Ave NR31 ....170 B4
Pembroke Rd NR2 ....162 B5
Pendlesham Rise NR8 ....155 E2
Pendula Rd PE13 ....152 E7
Penfold Dr NR18 ....38 F1
Penfold St NR11 ....150 C6
Penguin Rd NR29 ....167 D4
Penhill La NR17 ....103 D7
Penn Cl NR8 ....156 D8
Penn Gr NR3 ....158 C1
Penn Rd NR8 ....156 D8
Pennington Way PE31 ....140 A1
Penny Croft 3 NR21 ....15 C2
Pennycress Dr
6 Thetford IP24 ....176 F5
Wymondham NR18 ....173 E4
Pennygate La NR12 ....38 F1
Pennyroyal 1 NR6 ....158 D5
Penrose Cl PE30 ....147 B8
Penrose Gdns PE13 ....152 E4
Penryn Cl NR4 ....161 E5
Penshurst Mews 5
NR4 ....161 F1
**Pensthorpe Nature Reserve &
Gdns*** NR21 ....32 B8
Pentney Abbey Leisure Ctr
PE32 ....63 A7
Pentney Dro PE33 ....62 E6
Pentney La PE32 ....63 D8
Pepper La PE38 ....77 C8
Pepper's Gn PE30 ....148 B1
Peppers Cl IP27 ....175 B7
Percival Cl NR4 ....161 E4
Perebrown Ave NR30 ....169 D7
Pereers Cl NR25 ....137 A2
Peregrine Cl Diss IP22 ....177 F5
Norwich NR7 ....159 C4
Peregrine Mews NR7 ....159 C4
Peregrine Rd NR7 ....159 C4
Perkin Field PE34 ....144 B4
Perrings NR18 ....173 B6
Perrys La NR10 ....35 C2
Persimmon PE30 ....147 C5
Peter Ave NR13 ....166 B3
Peter Beales Roses*
NR17 ....103 F3
Peter Cl NR29 ....168 D8
Peter Dr IP24 ....176 F5
Peter's Dro PE34 ....61 A7
Peterhouse Ave NR31 ....170 C4
Peterhouse Fst Sch
NR31 ....170 C4
Peterhouse Mid Sch
NR31 ....170 B4
Peterkin Rd 3 NR4 ....89 E8
Peters Cl NR19 ....154 C1
Peterscourt PE30 ....147 D6
Petersfield Cl NR15 ....106 F4
Peterson Rd NR3 ....158 A2
Peterson's La NR11 ....150 B7
Peterspoint PE12 ....41 A7
Peto Ct NR5 ....161 C7
Peto's Cnr PE32 ....111 F8
Peter Cl NR28 ....151 C7
Petticoat Dro PE32 ....64 E8
Petticoat La PE33 ....62 D6
Pettingales 3 NR14 ....89 F4
Pettits La IP21 ....130 C7
Pettitts Animal Adventure*
NR14 ....93 A1 5
Petts Cl 3 PE13 ....152 E7
Pettus Rd NR4 ....161 E3
Petunia Way IP27 ....175 A2
Peverell Rd NR5 ....161 B7
Pheasant Cl NR14 ....89 A3
Pheasant Way IP27 ....175 F4
Pheasant Wlk 2 NR13 ....72 D8
Pheasants Wlk NR35 ....123 E8
Phelps Rd NR7 ....163 F7
Philadelphia La NR3 ....158 D2
Philip Ford Way NR18 ....173 C2
Philip Nurse Rd PE31 ....140 B3
Philip Rd NR19 ....154 D2
Philip Rudd Ct PE32 ....45 A8
Philips' Chase PE36 ....132 D2

Phillippo Cl 4 PE32 ....28 A1
Pickards Way PE13 ....152 A6
Pickford Cl NR28 ....151 E6
Picton Rd NR15 ....106 D4
Pier Gdns NR31 ....170 E4
Pier Pl NR30 ....169 D2
Pier Plain NR31 ....170 D5
Pier Rd NR31 ....170 E4
Pier Wlk NR31 ....170 D4
Pigeon St PE14 ....41 D3
Pigg La NR3 ....178 B4
Pightle Cl 2 NR14 ....89 B3
Pightle The PE37 ....153 C4
Pightle Way Lyng NR9 ....51 A4
Reepham NR10 ....149 C5
Pigot La NR14 ....90 C6
Pike La IP24 ....176 D3
Pikeman Pl NR13 ....72 E5
Pikes Nursery 4 NR29 ....56 C5
Pilgrim's Way 7 NR20 ....122 D2
Pilgrims Way
Little Cressingham IP25 ....83 F3
Weeting IP27 ....175 A8
Pilling Pk Rd NR1 ....163 B7
Pilling Rd NR7 ....163 D7
Pilot St 2 PE30 ....146 D6
Pimpernel Rd NR10 ....53 B2
Pincushion Dro PE14 ....78 B5
Pinder Cl NR3 ....158 A1
Pinder Rd NR3 ....158 A1
Pine Ave
Cockley Cley PE37 ....82 D7
Marham PE33 ....63 B4
Pine Cl
5 Downham Market
PE38 ....172 C6
8 Eye IP23 ....130 C1
4 Harleston IP20 ....122 D1
Hunstanton PE36 ....132 D4
17 Marthan NR29 ....57 D4
Norwich NR4 ....162 A3
Ormesby St Margaret
NR29 ....167 A3
3 Snettisham PE31 ....12 E4
Thetford IP24 ....176 B1
Pine Coombe 1 NR21 ....15 C2
Pine Ct NR17 ....174 D4
Pine Gn NR31 ....170 B5
Pine Gr
East Dereham NR19 ....154 D2
Sheringham NR26 ....138 E6
Pine Loke NR14 ....90 B5
Pine Mall PE31 ....133 C6
Pine Rd
King's Lynn PE30 ....148 D2
Norwich NR7 ....159 E1
Pine Tree Chase PE33 ....43 F1
Pine Tree Ct IP22 ....127 F5
Pine Trees Bsns Pk
NR7 ....159 D3
Pine Wlk 6 NR25 ....8 F5
Pinecot Ave 7 NR31 ....94 C6
Pineheath Rd NR25 ....8 E3
Pinelodges The NR7 ....163 C6
Pinetrees NR3 ....163 C3
Pinetrees Rd NR7 ....159 D3
Pinewood Cl NR6 ....157 F4
Pinewood Dr
Brandon IP27 ....175 C2
8 Horning NR12 ....55 E4
Pinewood Leisure Ctr
NR25 ....9 B3
Pinfold La
Hindolveston NR20 ....33 D8
Northwold IP26 ....99 B8
Pinfold Rd PE14 ....77 E5
Pingle Rd PE14 ....78 A4
Pingles Rd PE30 ....148 C4
Pinkney La NR24 ....19 B5
Pintail Dr 2 Blakeney NR25 ....7 C6
Great Yarmouth NR31 ....170 A6
Pioneer Rd NR6 ....159 A6
Piper Rd
King's Lynn PE30 ....146 F1
Norwich NR7 ....159 E1
Pipit's Mdw NR11 ....21 A5
Pippin Cl
Dereham NR19 ....154 E3
Ormesby St Margaret
NR29 ....167 A2
Pippin Gdns PE13 ....152 F7
Pippin Gn NR4 ....161 E5
Pippin Pl PE13 ....152 E2
Pirnhow St NR35 ....109 B1
Pishmire Cl NR5 ....160 F6
Pit La PE37 ....153 C4
Pit Rd
Aldeby, Wheatacre,
Burgh St Peter NR34 ....111 B4
Hemsby NR29 ....167 A7
Northrepps NR27 ....11 A1
Woodbastwick NR13 ....55 D1
Pit St NR11 ....22 C6
Pitchford Rd NR5 ....161 C6
Pitt Sq NR9 ....86 C4
Pitt St NR3 ....178 A4
Pitt's Hill NR15 ....107 B8
Pitts Hill Cl NR15 ....107 B8
Pius Dro PE14 ....77 E6
Plaford Rd NR7 ....159 D2
Plane Rd NR31 ....170 B6
Plantation Cl NR7 ....174 C3
Plantation Dr NR7 ....159 D3
Plantation Gdn The*
NR2 ....162 C5
Plantation Rd
Aslacton NR15 ....121 A7
Blofield NR13 ....165 F7

Plantation Rd continued
4 Fakenham NR21 ....141 E4
North Walsham NR28 ....151 E5
Norwich NR6 ....157 E6
Plantation The NR2 ....162 B4
Plantsman Cl NR2 ....162 B3
Plasset Dr NR17 ....174 F7
Platten's Cl 1 NR11 ....19 F1
Plattens Ct NR12 ....164 B3
Playbarn The* NR15 ....90 C3
Players Way NR6 ....158 E6
Playing Field La 2 NR29 ....57 D4
Pleasance Cl PE30 ....147 A5
Pleasant Cl NR6 ....157 D5
Pleasant Ct 1 PE30 ....146 E3
Pleasant Pl PE31 ....133 D6
Pleasant Row 1 PE37 ....153 C3
Pleasure Beach*
NR30 ....169 C1
Plevna Terr NR31 ....169 B3
Plough La
Hardingham NR9 ....86 D6
Watlington PE33 ....61 E5
Ploughboy La IP25 ....84 C6
Ploughman Rd PE20 ....147 C4
Ploughman's Dro IP26 ....98 B1
Ploughman's La PE33 ....61 E7
Ploughman's Piece PE36 ....2 E6
Plover Cl
Great Yarmouth NR31 ....170 A7
3 Thetford IP24 ....176 D2
Plovers Cl IP27 ....175 F3
Plovers Way IP26 ....113 F7
Plowright Pl PE13 ....153 B4
Plum La NR11 ....20 C8
Plumb's Cl NR24 ....142 E4
Plumbly Cl NR28 ....151 D3
Plummer's La NR15 ....107 C7
Plummers Hill NR23 ....136 D5
Plump Rd NR15 ....106 D5
Plumsgate Rd NR12 ....39 C1
Plumstead Rd NR17 ....174 E6
Plumstead Rd
Baconsthorpe NR25 ....20 A7
Edgefield NR24 ....19 E5
Great & Little Plumstead
NR13 ....72 E6
6 Norwich NR1 ....163 C8
Thorpe End NR13 ....72 E6
Woodbastwick NR13 ....73 D7
Plumstead Rd E NR7 ....163 D8
Plymouth Cl 3 NR30 ....168 C6
Plymouth Rd 2 IP31 ....126 B1
Pocahontas Way PE31 ....133 E5
Pockthorpe La IP24 ....102 A7
Pockthorpe Loke
Barnham Broom NR9 ....69 D2
Hickling NR12 ....39 F2
Pockthorpe Rd NR9 ....88 A8
Podmore La NR19 ....67 C8
Point Dr 2 PE37 ....153 C3
Police Rd PE14 ....41 D4
Polka Rd NR13 ....165 D3
Pollard Rd NR10 ....53 E6
Pollywiggle Cl NR5 ....161 A6
Pommer's La NR30 ....170 D8
Pond Cl NR9 ....88 C7
Pond Hills Rd NR25 ....19 E7
Pond La Brandon IP27 ....175 A2
Knapton NR28 ....143 B2
Surlingham NR14 ....73 C1
Taverham NR8 ....156 F8
Pond Rd
Antingham NR28 ....22 B4
Hevingham NR10 ....54 C2
3 Horsford NR10 ....53 A3
Swafield NR28 ....22 C3
Ponds End La IP22 ....127 E4
Pooley St IP22 ....128 F7
Poorhouse La NR14 ....89 A2
Pope's La PE34 ....144 A4
Poplar Ave
Great Yarmouth NR31 ....170 C3
Heacham PE31 ....133 C5
5 Marham PE33 ....63 B4
Norwich NR4 ....161 E1
Poplar Cl
Downham Market PE38 ....172 B6
Hunstanton IP31 ....126 B1
12 Horsford NR10 ....53 A3
Long Stratton NR15 ....106 F4
Norwich NR5 ....156 F2
Poplar Dr Filby NR29 ....75 F8
Norwich NR4 ....161 E1
Happisburgh NR12 ....23 F3
5 Hethersett NR9 ....88 D8
Poplar Gr NR26 ....138 E5
Poplar Rd
Attleborough NR17 ....174 B2
West Winch PE33 ....43 F1
Poplar Way NR17 ....174 C2
Poplars The Hilgay PE38 ....96 F8
Spexhall IP19 ....124 F1
Swanton Abbott NR10 ....37 C4
Tacolneston NR16 ....105 F4
Pople St NR18 ....173 B4
Poppy Cl
Chedgrave NR14 ....91 F2
North Walsham NR28 ....151 F5
4 Thetford IP24 ....176 F5
Poppy Dr 3 NR26 ....138 B6
Poppy's La PE21 ....121 F5
Poppyfields NR17 ....53 A3
Poringland Prim Sch
NR14 ....90 D5
Poringland Rd NR14 ....90 B5
Porson Rd NR7 ....159 C1

Port Rd NR15 ....122 B8
Port Row NR9 ....51 B4
Portal Ave IP25 ....84 F3
Portal Cl
4 Barnham IP24 ....125 F6
3 Feltwell IP26 ....98 D1
Portafield Ln NR12 ....39 B4
Porter Rd 8 NR15 ....106 E3
Porter St PE38 ....172 A5
Porter's La NR9 ....51 E5
Porter's Loke
1 Belton NR31 ....94 A6
Burgh Castle NR31 ....93 F6
Norwich NR7 ....159 A3
Porter's Rd
Beighton NR13 ....74 E1
Freethorpe NR13 ....92 E8
Porterbush Rd 18 NR14 ....89 B3
Portersfield Rd NR2 ....162 B5
Porthole Cl NR10 ....111 F1
Portland Ct NR11 ....169 C3
Portland Pl
Great Yarmouth NR30 ....169 C3
King's Lynn PE30 ....146 D2
3 Thetford IP24 ....116 A1
Portland St
12 King's Lynn PE30 ....146 E5
Norwich NR2 ....162 B5
Portman Rd 3 NR11 ....150 B7
Portway Pl 6 NR2 ....162 C7
Portway Sq NR2 ....162 C7
Portway's Rd NR10 ....147 C5
Post Mill PE30 ....147 C5
Post Mill Cl NR7 ....159 A3
Post Office Cl 8 NR13 ....74 A3
Post Office La
Corpusty NR11 ....34 F8
Garvestone NR9 ....86 B8
Guestwick-Gwilde NR9 ....51 E2
3 Wisbech PE13 ....152 C5
Post Office Rd
Dersingham PE31 ....140 D3
Frettenham NR12 ....54 A4
Great & Little Plumstead
NR13 ....73 B7
Lingwood NR13 ....74 A3
Lingwood & Burlingham
NR13 ....73 F3
Toft Monks NR34 ....110 E5
Postmill Cl NR18 ....173 C4
Postwick La NR13 ....165 A4
Postwick Sta NR7 ....72 E3
Potash La
Bracon Ash NR16 ....88 D2
Eye IP23 ....130 B2
Potato Dro PE14 ....60 B4
Potspoon Hole
Lingwood NR13 ....54 D8
Tunstead NR12 ....37 D1
Potter Heigham Rd
NR29 ....56 D8
Potter's La
Rickinghall Superior
IP22 ....128 F1
Wymondham NR18 ....105 B6
Pottergate NR2 ....178 A3
Pottergate St NR15 ....106 A2
Potters Cres NR15 ....121 C8
Potters Dr NR31 ....171 D5
Potters Vale IP22 ....128 C3
Pottle's La NR13 ....92 F5
Pottles Alley 8 NR9 ....86 C5
Poulter's Dro PE14 ....77 D1
Poultry Rd IP27 ....113 A3
Pound Cl
4 Harleston IP20 ....122 D2
Hevingham NR10 ....53 C8
Pound Gn La IP25 ....67 C2
Pound Hill IP25 ....84 B5
Pound La
Aylsham NR11 ....150 B6
Brundall NR13 ....165 F5
Burgh St Margaret (Fleggburgh)
NR29 ....75 C8
Ditchingham NR35 ....108 E2
Docking PE31 ....134 D5
Filby NR29 ....75 F8
Great Yarmouth NR31 ....170 C3
Heacham PE31 ....133 D6
Litcham PE32 ....48 A4
Loddon NR14 ....109 C8
North Tuddenham NR20 ....50 D2
Norwich NR7 ....159 A3
Runhall NR20 ....69 A4
Sloley NR12 ....37 F2
Toft Monks NR34 ....110 D6
Pound Rd
East Ruston NR12 ....38 F7
Hevingham NR10 ....53 C8
Ludham NR29 ....56 C5
Powell Ct 5 NR19 ....154 C6
Power's Pl PE38 ....79 D1
Poynt Ct NR18 ....173 B5
Pratts Hill NR14 ....73 A1
Press La NR3 ....158 C1
Preston Ave NR18 ....173 A2
Preston Cl
Freethorpe NR13 ....92 E7
Wroxham/Hoveton
NR12 ....164 B2
Preston La NR18 ....173 A2
Preston VC Prim Sch
NR15 ....106 F7
Pretty Dr IP25 ....130 D6
Pride Way NR13 ....72 E5
Primrose Cl
Attleborough NR17 ....174 B5

Primrose Cl continued
East Dereham NR19 ....154 B4
15 Mulbarton NR14 ....89 B3
Mundesley NR11 ....143 B5
Thetford IP24 ....176 F4
Trunch NR28 ....22 E5
Primrose Cres 2 NR7 ....72 D3
Primrose Ct 3 NR7 ....72 D3
Primrose Dr IP27 ....175 A2
Primrose Hill NR20 ....50 B4
Primrose La
Crostwick NR12 ....54 C3
Sheringham NR26 ....138 B5
Swanton Morley NR20 ....50 B4
Primrose Pl NR2 ....162 B5
Primrose Rd
Hingham NR9 ....86 B5
Norwich NR1 ....163 A6
Primrose Sq NR20 ....50 B4
Primrose Wlk NR31 ....94 C6
Primula Dr NR4 ....161 D5
Prince Andrew Dr
PE31 ....140 D3
Prince Andrew's Cl
2 Aldborough NR11 ....21 A5
Norwich NR6 ....158 B5
Prince Andrew's Rd
NR1 ....158 B5
Prince Charles Cl
PE31 ....140 D3
Prince Edward Cl NR13 ....163 F7
Prince Henry Pl PE38 ....172 D4
Prince of Wales Cl
PE13 ....152 D8
Prince of Wales Rd
Caister-on-Sea NR30 ....168 C6
Cromer NR27 ....139 B7
Norwich NR1 ....178 B3
Upton with Fishley NR13 ....166 A8
Prince Regent Way
PE32 ....177 F3
Prince Rupert Way
NR13 ....72 D5
Prince St PE13 ....152 D5
Prince William Cl
PE36 ....132 C3
Prince's Rd
Bungay NR35 ....124 A7
Great Yarmouth NR30 ....169 D4
Prince's St PE12 ....41 B8
Princes Cl IP27 ....175 A2
Princes Rd NR13 ....152 C4
Princes St
North Walsham NR28 ....151 A5
Norwich NR3 ....178 B3
Swaffham PE37 ....153 B4
Princes Way PE30 ....146 F5
Princess Beatrice Cl
NR6 ....157 D2
Princess Cl 7 IP25 ....84 D3
Princess Ct NR25 ....137 C5
Princess Dr PE36 ....132 D2
Princess Theatre
PE36 ....132 C4
Princess Way 5 NR35 ....123 F8
Princess's Dr
Dersingham PE35 ....140 C1
Sandringham PE35 ....27 D7
Pringle Way 5 PE38 ....97 B5
Prins Ave PE13 ....152 D7
Prins Ct 3 PE13 ....152 D7
Printing Mus* NR34 ....110 D1
Prior Bank Orch 3
NR27 ....139 C6
Prior Cl 5 NR15 ....106 F6
Prior Rd NR7 ....72 D5
Prior Stephen Way
IP24 ....176 B3
Priors Dr NR6 ....158 E6
Priorswood NR8 ....155 E3
Priory Chase
Downham Market PE38 ....172 B5
Wormegay PE33 ....61 F8
Priory Cl Acle NR13 ....166 C3
Alpington NR14 ....90 F5
Caister-on-Sea NR30 ....168 C4
2 Fritton & St Olaves
NR31 ....93 D2
7 Hethersett NR9 ....88 D7
Palgrave IP22 ....177 D1
Sheringham NR26 ....138 F5
Sporle with Palgrave
PE32 ....65 D6
Priory Cres NR21 ....6 E2
Priory Dro IP25 ....83 D4
Priory Gdns
4 Fritton & St Olaves
NR31 ....93 D2
12 Great Yarmouth NR30 ....169 D4
Priory La Ingworth NR11 ....21 A1
12 King's Lynn PE30 ....146 D4
Shotesham NR15 ....90 A2
Priory Maze & Gdns*
NR26 ....138 F6
Priory Pk IP24 ....176 C5
Priory Pl IP22 ....177 C1
Priory Plain 18 NR30 ....169 C4
Priory Rd Bacton NR12 ....23 E4
Castle Acre PE32 ....46 F1
Downham Market PE38 ....172 B5
Fritton & St Olaves NR31 ....93 D2
Great Cressingham IP25 ....83 D5
Hethersett NR9 ....88 D7
King's Lynn PE30 ....148 C5
Palgrave IP22 ....177 C1

Priory Rd continued
Sheringham NR26 . . . .**138** E7
Watton IP25 . . . .**84** E3
Woodbastwick NR13 . . . .**55** F1
Priory Row 🔟 NR30 . . . . .**169** C4
Priory St NR31 . . . .**170** D6
Priory Terr PE38 . . . .**172** B5
Priscilla Cl 🔟 NR5 . . . . . .**161** D5
Pristow Gn La NR16 . . . . . .**120** E7
Private Rd
Earsham NR35 . . . .**123** D8
Ormesby St Margaret
NR29 . . . .**167** A3
Procession La PE32 . . . . .**153** F8
Proctor Ave 🔟 NR14 . . . . .**92** A2
Proctor Cl 🔟 NR14 . . . . . .**92** A2
Proctor Rd
Chedgrave NR14 . . . .**91** F2
🔟 Loddon NR14 . . . .**92** A2
Norwich NR6 . . . .**158** F6
Proctors Cl PE30 . . . .**146** C2
Progress Way IP23 . . . . . .**130** B1
Prom The NR29 . . . .**167** E4
Promenade
Overstrand NR27 . . . .**11** A4
Sheringham NR26 . . . .**138** D7
Prophets Alley PE34 . . . . .**61** B6
Prospect Pl PE13 . . . .**152** C3
Proudfoot Way NR14 . . . . .**89** C8
Provan Cres 🔟 NR31 . . . . .**94** A5
Provence Pl 🔟 PE13 . . . . .**152** C3
Providence Pl
Briston NR24 . . . .**142** E5
🔟 Thorpe Hamlet NR1 . . . .**163** A6
Providence St 🔟 PE30 . . . .**146** E4
Providence Terr PE13 . . . .**153** A5
Provision Mkt NR2 . . . . . .**178** A3
Provost Rd IP26 . . . .**98** D1
Pudding Norton Medieval
Village of* NR21 . . . .**31** E6
Puddingmoor NR34 . . . . . .**110** C1
Pug St IP21 . . . .**121** B2
Pulham CE Prim Sch
IP21 . . . .**121** E5
Pullover Rd PE34 . . . .**146** A1
Pump La NR30 . . . .**168** D3
Punsfer Way PE34 . . . .**60** C8
Purbeck Cl PE13 . . . .**152** A4
Purdance Cl NR5 . . . .**160** D8
Purdy St NR25 . . . .**8** B6
Purdy Way NR11 . . . .**150** B6
Purfleet PE30 . . . .**146** D5
Purfleet St
🔟 King's Lynn PE30 . . . . . .**146** D5
🔟 King's Lynn PE30 . . . . . .**146** D5
Purland Rd NR7 . . . .**159** D2
Purley Ct NR31 . . . .**169** A1
Pursehouse Way PE30 . . . .**177** E4
Purtingay Cl 🔟 NR4 . . . . .**162** A1
Putney Cl IP27 . . . .**175** A1
Pye La Cranworth IP25 . . . .**86** A6
Deopham NR18 . . . .**86** E2
Pye's La Castle Acre PE32 . .**46** F2
Swanton Morley NR20 . . . . . .**50** C3
Pyebush La NR13 . . . .**166** B5
Pyecroft Rd PE14 . . . .**41** E3
Pyehurn La NR10 . . . .**53** A3
Pyehurn Mews NR8 . . . . . .**155** E3
Pyes Cl 🔟 NR25 . . . .**7** C6
Pyes Mill Rd NR14 . . . .**92** A1
Pyghtle The 🔟 NR16 . . . . .**118** C5
Pyke Ct NR30 . . . .**168** D7
Pym Cl NR13 . . . .**72** E5
Pymar's La 🔟 NR15 . . . . . .**107** C5
Pyrford Dr NR4 . . . .**161** F1

Q

Quaker La
Fakenham NR21 . . . .**141** B4
Norwich NR6 . . . .**53** E1
🔟 Spixworth NR12 . . . .**54** A1
Tasburgh NR15 . . . .**106** F6
Wisbech PE13 . . . .**152** E3
Quarry La NR9 . . . .**51** A5
Quay Angel NR31 . . . .**7** D1
Quay La NR25 . . . .**7** A7
Quay Mill Wlk 🔟 NR30 . . . .**169** C4
Quay Ostend NR31 . . . .**171** C8
Quay Rd NR31 . . . .**170** D4
Quay Side NR3 . . . .**178** B4
Quay The Blakeney NR25 . . .**7** C6
Wells-next-the-Sea
NR23 . . . .**136** D6
Wiveton NR25 . . . .**7** E7
Quebec Cl 🔟 NR4 . . . .**89** B8
Quebec Rd
Dereham NR19 . . . .**154** D7
Norwich NR1 . . . .**163** A4
Quebec St NR19 . . . .**154** D5
Queen Anne's Rd
NR1 . . . .**170** C8
Queen Elizabeth Ave
PE30 . . . .**147** B7
Queen Elizabeth Cl
NR3 . . . .**178** C4
Queen Elizabeth Dr
Dersingham PE31 . . . .**140** D3
Wisbech PE13 . . . .**152** D2
Queen Elizabeth Hospl
PE30 . . . .**147** C5
Queen Elizabeth Way
Bawsey PE30 . . . .**147** F6
Castle Rising PE30 . . . .**27** C1
Queen Mary Rd PE30 . . . . .**147** A5

Queen St
Great Yarmouth NR30 . . . . .**169** C3
King's Lynn PE30 . . . .**146** D5
New Buckenham NR16 . . . . .**104** F1
Norwich NR1 . . . .**178** B3
Stradbroke IP21 . . . .**131** E1
🔟 Sutton Bridge PE12 . . . . .**41** B8
Swaffham PE37 . . . .**153** B4
Wisbech PE13 . . . .**152** C6
Wymondham NR18 . . . .**173** C3
Queen's Cl PE33 . . . .**80** E4
Queen's Cres
Bircham PE31 . . . .**14** A3
Great Yarmouth NR31 . . . . .**170** B3
Queen's Ct NR17 . . . .**174** D6
Queen's Dr PE14 . . . .**77** A7
Queen's Pl 🔟 PE34 . . . .**43** B1
Queen's Rd
Attleborough NR17 . . . .**174** C6
Clenchwarton PE34 . . . .**146** A5
Fakenham NR21 . . . .**141** C4
Great Yarmouth NR30 . . . . .**169** D2
Hethersett NR9 . . . .**88** D8
Holt NR25 . . . .**137** C5
Queen's Sq NR17 . . . .**174** D5
Queens Ave NR30 . . . .**146** D2
Queens Cl
🔟 Blakeney NR25 . . . .**7** C6
Norwich NR4 . . . .**162** A3
Queens Ct 🔟 NR15 . . . . . .**106** E3
Queens Dr PE36 . . . .**132** C6
Queens Gdns PE36 . . . .**132** D6
Queens Rd
Brandon IP27 . . . .**175** A2
Cromer NR27 . . . .**139** D4
Norwich NR1 . . . .**178** A1
Wisbech PE13 . . . .**152** C4
Queens Sch The PE13 . . . . . .**152** D3
Queensway
Caister-on-Sea NR30 . . . . . .**168** E4
🔟 Fakenham NR21 . . . .**123** F8
King's Lynn PE30 . . . .**147** C6
North Walsham NR28 . . . . . .**151** A5
Roydon IP22 . . . .**177** A5
Thetford IP24 . . . .**176** C2
Watton IP25 . . . .**84** D3
Wymondham NR18 . . . .**173** B5
Queensway Com Jun Sch
IP24 . . . .**176** C2
Queensway Inf Sch
IP24 . . . .**176** C2
Quidenham Rd
Harling NR16 . . . .**118** D5
Kenninghall NR16 . . . .**119** A5
Quidenham NR16 . . . .**118** F8

R

Rabbit La
Downham Market PE38 . . . . .**172** D6
Great Witchingham NR9 . . . . .**51** E6
Raby Ave PE30 . . . .**146** E6
Racecourse Rd NR7 . . . . . .**159** E1
Raceys Cl NR4 . . . .**59** D2
Rachel Cl 🔟 NR5 . . . .**161** C5
Rackham Cl NR31 . . . .**171** C5
Rackham Rd NR3 . . . .**158** D2
Rackheath Prim Sch
NR13 . . . .**54** D1
Radcliffe Rd NR4 . . . .**161** E5
RAF Air Defence Radar Mus*
NR12 . . . .**55** E5
Rafeman Cl NR5 . . . .**160** E7
Raglan St 🔟 NR2 . . . .**162** C6
Ragmere Rd NR17 . . . .**104** D1
Railway App 🔟 NR26 . . . . .**138** D7
Railway Hill IP20 . . . .**122** C2
Railway La PE12 . . . .**41** B7
Railway Rd
Downham Market PE38 . . . . .**172** A5
King's Lynn PE30 . . . .**146** E5
Wisbech PE13 . . . .**152** C3
Rainey Ct 🔟 PE20 . . . .**122** D2
Rainsborough Rise
NR13 . . . .**72** D5
Rainthorpe Hall*
NR15 . . . .**106** F8
Raleigh Ave NR30 . . . .**169** D7
Raleigh Inf Sch IP24 . . . . .**176** E6
Raleigh Rd PE30 . . . .**147** B4
Raleigh Way IP24 . . . .**176** E6
Ram La NR15 . . . .**121** C4
Ramblers The NR14 . . . . . .**90** B6
Rambouillet Cl NR13 . . . . . .**72** D5
Ramm's La PE37 . . . .**65** A4
Ramms Ct NR23 . . . .**136** D6
Ramnoth Cty Jun Sch
PE13 . . . .**152** D4
Ramnoth Rd PE13 . . . .**152** D4
Rampant Horse St
NR2 . . . .**178** A2
Rampart Rd NR30 . . . .**169** C5
Rampart Way IP24 . . . .**176** D3
Ramsay Gdns PE36 . . . .**132** D3
Ramsey Cl
Norwich NR4 . . . .**161** E3
🔟 Thetford IP24 . . . .**176** D3
Randall Cl 🔟 NR1 . . . .**171** D5
Randall Rd NR28 . . . .**151** D4
Randle Gn NR5 . . . .**161** C8
Randolf Rd NR1 . . . .**162** E2
Rands Rd PE14 . . . .**60** C5
Rangoon Cl NR7 . . . .**159** C4
Ransome Ave IP21 . . . .**130** C5

Ransome's Cl PE14 . . . .**77** E5
Ranson Rd NR1 . . . .**163** B5
Ranworth 🔟 PE30 . . . .**147** D5
Ranworth Cl
🔟 Belton NR31 . . . .**94** A6
Swaffham PE37 . . . .**153** B1
Ranworth Dr NR29 . . . .**167** B2
Ranworth Fst Sch
NR5 . . . .**161** E7
Ranworth Rd
Blofield NR13 . . . .**165** F8
Norwich NR5 . . . .**161** D7
South Walsham NR13 . . . . . .**74** A8
Rash's Cres IP22 . . . .**129** C6
Rash's Gn NR19 . . . .**154** F2
Ratcliffe Rd NR21 . . . .**141** C4
Rattle Row
Mileham PE32 . . . .**48** C6
Wymondham NR18 . . . .**173** B4
Rattler's Rd IP27 . . . .**175** C3
Rattlerow Hill IP21 . . . .**131** F2
Raven Cl NR31 . . . .**170** A7
Raven's La PE31 . . . .**29** D5
Raveningham Gdns*
NR14 . . . .**110** A7
Raveningham Rd
Gillingham NR34 . . . .**110** C4
Stockton NR34 . . . .**110** A5
Ravensway PE38 . . . .**172** C3
Ravine Rd NR31 . . . .**93** E1
Rawhall La NR20 . . . .**49** B5
Rawley Rd NR5 . . . .**161** B8
Rawlings Way 🔟 IP26 . . . . .**98** E1
Rawlinsons La NR11 . . . . . .**150** C7
Ray Bond Way NR11 . . . . . .**150** C4
Raymond Cl NR6 . . . .**158** C5
Raymond Rd NR6 . . . .**157** F7
Raymond St
Thetford IP24 . . . .**176** D3
🔟 Wisbech PE13 . . . .**152** C4
Rayner's Cl NR20 . . . .**68** E6
Rayner's La NR35 . . . .**109** D4
Rayner's Way NR20 . . . . . .**68** E6
Raynham Rd
Dunton NR21 . . . .**31** C6
Hempton NR21 . . . .**141** A2
Whissonsett NR20 . . . .**31** C2
Raynham Ride NR19 . . . . . .**154** D7
Rayns Cl NR6 . . . .**158** F5
Read's Cross NR14 . . . .**109** E8
Readscross La NR14 . . . . . .**109** E8
Recorder Rd NR1 . . . .**178** C3
Recreation Dr PE38 . . . .**97** A5
Recreation Gd Rd
NR7 . . . .**159** A4
Recreation Rd
East Dereham NR19 . . . .**154** C1
Great Yarmouth NR31 . . . . .**170** C5
Hethersett NR9 . . . .**88** C7
North Walsham NR28 . . . . . .**151** B4
Norwich NR2 . . . .**162** A5
Stalham NR12 . . . .**39** A4
Rectory Cl
Caister-on-Sea NR30 . . . . . .**168** E5
Coltishall NR12 . . . .**54** D7
🔟 Long Stratton NR15 . . . .**106** E3
🔟 Newton Flotman NR15 . . .**89** F1
Rollesby NR29 . . . .**57** C2
Roydon IP22 . . . .**27** F2
Rectory Ct NR3 . . . .**158** D2
Rectory Dr PE34 . . . .**145** E5
Rectory Gdns
Hingham NR9 . . . .**86** B5
Wisbech PE13 . . . .**152** E6
Rectory Hill IP22 . . . .**128** D2
Rectory La
Bracon Ash NR14 . . . .**88** E3
Bunwell NR16 . . . .**105** C4
Great Ellingham NR17 . . . . .**103** E8
Haddiscoe PE14 . . . .**110** F7
Hedenham NR35 . . . .**108** D4
Little Melton NR9 . . . .**160** A3
Loddon NR14 . . . .**92** A2
Mettingham NR35 . . . .**124** A7
Mulbarton NR14 . . . .**89** B3
Poringland NR14 . . . .**90** D5
Scole IP21 . . . .**121** C1
Stuston IP21 . . . .**130** B4
Watlington PE33 . . . .**61** D5
Weeting IP27 . . . .**175** B7
West Winch PE33 . . . .**43** F3
Rectory Mdw
Diss IP22 . . . .**177** E4
Litcham PE32 . . . .**48** A4

Rectory Rd continued
Rocklands NR17 . . . .**103** B7
Shelfanger IP22 . . . .**120** B2
Sutton NR12 . . . .**39** C3
Swanton Morley NR20 . . . . . .**50** B4
Tivetshall St Mary NR15 . . . .**121** C4
Topcroft NR35 . . . .**107** F4
Weston Longville NR9 . . . . . .**51** D2
Whissonsett NR20 . . . .**31** E2
Wood Norton NR20 . . . .**33** A7
Wortham IP22 . . . .**129** D6
Red Admiral Cl 🔟 NR18 . . .**173** E4
Red Barn La NR11 . . . .**9** D1
Red Bridge La NR5 . . . .**157** C2
Red Cottage Cl NR3 . . . . . .**158** A2
Red Lion Cl
Holme Hale IP25 . . . .**66** B2
Hoxne IP21 . . . .**131** A3
Red Lion St
🔟 Aylsham NR11 . . . .**150** C7
Norwich NR1 . . . .**178** B2
Red Lion Yd NR23 . . . .**136** D6
Red Robin Cl 🔟 NR15 . . . .**106** D3
Redbrick Cotts IP27 . . . . . .**175** D5
Redcastle Furze Prim Sch
IP24 . . . .**176** B3
Redcastle Rd IP24 . . . .**176** A4
Redcliffe Way NR13 . . . . . .**165** B4
Redell Cl 🔟 NR13 . . . .**55** A1
Redenhall Rd IP20 . . . .**122** D2
Redfern Cl
East Dereham NR19 . . . .**154** B4
King's Lynn PE30 . . . .**147** E8
Redfern Rd NR7 . . . .**159** D1
Redgate IP20 . . . .**176** E4
Redgate Hill PE36 . . . .**132** D2
Redgate Jun Sch
PE36 . . . .**132** D2
Redgate Rd PE13 . . . .**41** A4
Redgrave & Lopham Fen
National Nature Reserve*
IP22 . . . .**128** F6
Redgrave Rd
South Lopham IP22 . . . .**128** E7
Wortham IP22 . . . .**129** A5
Redman Rd NR28 . . . .**151** D3
Redmere Cl 🔟 NR12 . . . . . .**54** A4
Redmere Dro CB7 . . . .**112** D5
Redwell St NR2 . . . .**178** B3
Redwing Dr
🔟 Great Yarmouth NR31 . . .**94** C7
🔟 Wisbech PE14 . . . .**152** D2
Redwing Gdns 🔟 NR14 . . . .**54** A1
Redwings Horse Sanctuary
(Caldecott)* NR31 . . . .**93** F4
Reed La NR19 . . . .**48** F3
Reed Way 🔟 PE14 . . . .**77** A8
Reeder's Rd NR14 . . . .**154** D3
Reeder's La NR14 . . . .**90** E4
Reedham Prim Sch
NR13 . . . .**93** A4
Reedham Rd
Acle NR13 . . . .**166** B1
Beighton NR13 . . . .**74** E1
Reedham Sta NR13 . . . .**92** F5
Reepham High Sch
NR10 . . . .**149** B3
Reepham Rd
Bawdeswell NR20 . . . .**50** F8
Briston NR24 . . . .**142** E2
Felthorpe NR10 . . . .**155** D5
Foulsham NR20 . . . .**33** D3
Guestwick NR10 . . . .**34** A5
Horsford NR10 . . . .**157** D7
Norwich NR6 . . . .**157** E2
Swannington NR9 . . . .**52** B5
Thurning NR20 . . . .**34** B8
Wood Dalling NR11 . . . .**34** D5
Reeve Cl IP21 . . . .**130** D6
Reeve Pl NR27 . . . .**139** D4
Reeves Ave PE30 . . . .**147** B8
Reeves Cl PE30 . . . .**151** C5
Reeves La PE26 . . . .**114** A7
Reffley Prim Sch
PE30 . . . .**147** D8
Reg Houchen Rd
PE31 . . . .**140** C3
Regal Cl PE32 . . . .**84** D3
Regal Rd PE13 . . . .**152** B2
Regency Ave PE30 . . . .**147** C5
Regent Bvd 🔟 NR30 . . . . . .**169** D4
Regent Rd NR19 . . . .**154** D1
Regent Pl 🔟 PE30 . . . .**146** D4
Regent St
Great Yarmouth NR30 . . . . .**169** D4
Wickmere NR11 . . . .**20** E4
Regent Way 🔟 PE30 . . . . . .**146** D4
Regents Cl NR25 . . . .**137** B5
Regents Ct NR3 . . . .**158** B5
Regents Pk NR30 . . . .**168** C2
Regina Rd NR1 . . . .**178** A3
Regis Ave 🔟 NR27 . . . .**9** F5
Regis Pl NR25 . . . .**138** C7
Reid Way PE30 . . . .**147** A8
Renowood Cl PE32 . . . .**48** B8
Renson Cl NR3 . . . .**158** C4
Renwick Pk E NR27 . . . .**10** A4
Renwick Pk W NR27 . . . . . .**10** A4
Repps Rd
Ashby with Oby NR29 . . . . . .**57** B3
🔟 Martham NR29 . . . .**57** D4

Repps Rd continued
Thurne NR29 . . . .**56** E3
Repton Ave NR6 . . . .**158** D7
Repton Cl NR11 . . . .**159** C5
Retreat Est PE38 . . . .**172** D6
Reve Cres 🔟 NR13 . . . .**73** C6
Revell Rd PE38 . . . .**172** B4
Reydon Cl 🔟 NR5 . . . .**161** A7
Reymerston Rd NR9 . . . . . .**68** B2
Reynolds Ave NR30 . . . .**168** C8
Reynolds La NR5 . . . .**56** E7
Reynolds Way PE21 . . . .**140** C3
Rhombus Bsns Pk
NR6 . . . .**158** B5
Rhond The NR12 . . . .**164** C5
Rhone Pl 🔟 PE13 . . . .**152** E3
Rhoon Rd PE34 . . . .**144** E8
Rice Way NR7 . . . .**159** C2
Richard Easter Rd
IP24 . . . .**176** D6
Richard Haggard Cl 🔟
IP25 . . . .**67** C2
Richard Hicks Dr 🔟
NR19 . . . .**154** C4
Richard Young Cl 🔟
PE13 . . . .**152** C8
Richards Rd NR21 . . . .**15** D2
Richardson Cres NR9 . . . . . .**88** C8
Richenda Cl 🔟 NR5 . . . . . .**161** C5
Riches Cl 🔟 NR15 . . . .**106** F6
Richmond Cl
Honingham NR9 . . . .**69** E6
Lyng NR9 . . . .**51** A5
Richmond Ct PE13 . . . .**152** A4
Richmond Pk NR17 . . . .**174** F6
Richmond Rd
Brandon IP27 . . . .**175** A1
Downham Market PE38 . . . . .**172** B4
🔟 Long Stratton NR15 . . . .**106** E3
Norwich NR5 . . . .**156** E1
Saham Toney IP25 . . . .**84** C4
Richmond Rise NR10 . . . . . .**149** C5
Rickinghall Rd IP22 . . . .**128** C3
Riddlesworth Hall Sch
IP22 . . . .**127** C2
Rider Haggard Rd
NR7 . . . .**159** D1
Ridgeway
Caister-on-Sea NR30 . . . . . .**168** D5
Cromer NR27 . . . .**139** C4
Ridgeway The NR1 . . . .**163** B8
Ridings The
🔟 Cringleford NR4 . . . .**89** B8
Fakenham NR21 . . . .**141** E4
Poringland NR14 . . . .**90** C5
Ridland's Rd PE34 . . . .**142** C1
Rigby Cl 🔟 NR14 . . . .**90** D5
Rigbys Ct NR2 . . . .**178** A3
Rigg Cl 🔟 PE13 . . . .**152** B3
Rightup Dro IP27 . . . .**113** C5
Rightup La NR18 . . . .**173** D2
Riley Cl NR7 . . . .**159** D1
Rill Cl PE30 . . . .**148** B4
Rimer Cl NR5 . . . .**160** F6
Ring Rd NR7 . . . .**163** F7
Ringbank La NR11 . . . .**21** A6
Ringers Cl 🔟 NR18 . . . .**173** D5
Ringers La NR9 . . . .**86** C5
Ringland La
Costessey NR8 . . . .**156** A6
Easton NR9 . . . .**70** B5
Morton on the Hill NR9 . . . . .**52** A2
Weston Longville NR9 . . . . . .**51** F3
Ringland Rd NR5 . . . .**155** A1
Ringmere Cl 🔟 IP25 . . . . . .**84** C3
Ringmere Rd 🔟 IP25 . . . . . .**84** C3
Ringmore Rd PE38 . . . .**97** B6
Ringsfield Rd NR34 . . . .**124** F5
Ringstead Downs Nature
Reserve* PE36 . . . .**1** F2
Ringstead Rd
Burnham Market PE31 . . . . .**135** A2
Docking PE31 . . . .**134** A6
Heacham PE31 . . . .**133** E6
Ringstead PE36 . . . .**2** A2
Sedgeford PE36 . . . .**13** B8
Thornham PE36 . . . .**2** D6
Ringwood Cl NR9 . . . .**160** B2
Ripley Cl NR2 . . . .**161** F5
Ripon Way IP24 . . . .**176** B5
Rippingall Cl 🔟 NR11 . . . . .**150** D6
Rippingall Rd NR11 . . . .**150** D6
Rise The 🔟 Loddon NR14 . . .**92** A2
Sheringham NR26 . . . .**138** C6
Rising Way NR19 . . . .**57** C4
Risley Cl NR16 . . . .**117** E5
River Cl PE21 . . . .**141** A3
River Ct NR21 . . . .**141** A3
River Dro PE33 . . . .**80** F2
River La Cranworth IP25 . . . .**86** A6
King's Lynn PE30 . . . .**147** A6
River Nst West Acre PE32 . . .**46** B1
River Terr PE13 . . . .**152** A8
River View
Beccles NR34 . . . .**110** C2
🔟 Beetley NR20 . . . .**49** D4
River View Cl NR11 . . . .**141** E4
River Vw NR12 . . . .**49** D4
River Way NR31 . . . .**93** F6
River Wlk
Great Yarmouth NR30 . . . . .**169** C8
King's Lynn PE34 . . . .**146** C6

Riverdale Ct NR13 ......165 D3
Riverdene Mews NR8 ...155 E3
Rivergreen Ct NR1 ......163 E6
Rivermead NR12 ....39 B3
Riverside
  Cockley Cley PE37 ....82 D7
  Diss IP22 ....177 B3
  King's Lynn PE30 ....147 B7
  Norwich NR1 ....178 C2
  Reedham NR13 ....92 F4
Riverside Cl NR6 ....157 D2
Riverside Ctr NR12 .....164 C5
Riverside Est NR13 .....165 D1
Riverside Ind Ctr
  NR31 ....170 D5
Riverside Ind Est
  PE30 ....146 D7
Riverside Maltings
  IP22 ....177 F3
Riverside Rd
  Great Yarmouth NR31 ....170 D6
  Holt NR25 ....8 A1
  Norwich NR1 ....178 C3
  Wroxham/Hoveton
  NR12 ....164 C4
Riverside Swimming Ctr
  NR1 ....178 C1
Riverside Way
  Brandon IP27 ....175 C5
  Wisbech PE13 ....152 B3
Riverside Wlk IP24 .....176 C4
Riversway PE30 ....146 E7
Riverview Dr NR13 ......165 C3
RNLI Henry Blogg Mus*
  NR27 ....139 B7
Roaches Ct NR3 ....178 B3
Robberds Way NR5 ....160 E8
Robert Andrew Cl
  NR18 ....87 B2
Robert Balding Rd
  PE31 ....140 C3
Robert Cl Trunch NR28 ...22 E5
  Wymondham NR18 .....173 C6
Robert Gybson Way
  NR2 ....178 A3
Robert Herb Way 5
  NR18 ....173 E4
Robert Kett Jun Sch
  NR18 ....173 C5
Robert Key Dr 2 NR20 ...68 E6
Robert Linge Cres
  IP27 ....175 D3
Robert St 8 PE30 ....146 E3
Roberts Cl 3 NR15 .....107 C5
Robertson Cl NR26 .....138 E6
Robin Cl
  Great Yarmouth NR31 ....170 A5
  Mulbarton NR14 ....89 A3
Robin Hill PE31 ....133 D8
Robin Hood Rd NR4 ....162 C1
Robin Kerkham Way
  PE34 ....145 E6
Robin Mews 4 PE14 ....152 D2
Robin Wlk IP27 ....175 F3
Robins La NR10 ....149 B4
Robinson Rd IP21 ......130 C5
Robson Rd NR5 ....161 B6
Robyns Rd
  5 Sheringham NR26 ....9 F5
  Sheringham NR26 ....138 F5
Rocelin Cl NR3 ....158 E3
Rochford Cl 4 NR29 .....57 C4
Rochford Wlk 5 PE13 ..152 E5
Rockall Way 6 NR30 ...168 C6
Rockingham Rd NR5 ...161 C6
Rockland Cl PE13 ....53 B2
Rockland Dr NR7 ....163 C6
Rockland La NR17 ....85 F1
Rockland NR14 ....90 F7
Rockland St Mary Prim Sch
  NR14 ....91 B6
Rocklands Prim Sch
  NR17 ....103 B7
Rocklands Rd NR17 ....103 B4
Rode La NR16 ....105 B3
Rodham Rd PE15 ....77 A1
Rodinghead 1 PE30 ....147 D5
Rodney Rd NR30 ....169 D3
Rodwell Cnr NR10 ......35 C1
Roe Dr NR5 ....161 E5
Roedich Dr NR8 ....155 C1
Roger Ride 3 NR19 ....154 D2
Roger's Cl NR31 ....171 D5
Roger's La NR15 ....89 F1
Rogers Cl 4 NR5 ......161 B7
Roland Dr NR15 ....107 D5
Rolfe Cres PE31 ....133 E5
Rollesby Ave PE13 .....153 B2
Rollesby Fst Sch NR29 ...57 D3
Rollesby Gdns 9 NR29 ...57 D2
Rollesby Pl NR10 ....37 B2
Rollesby Rd
  Fleggburgh NR29 ....57 C1
  King's Lynn PE30 ....147 A3
  Martham NR29 ....57 D4
  Swaffham PE37 ....153 B2
Rolleston Cl NR5 ....161 B7
Rollington La NR19 ....154 D4
Roman Cres PE37 ......153 D2
Roman Dr NR13 ....165 B3
Roman Pl 20 NR30 .....169 D4
Roman Way
  Brancaster PE31 ....3 B7
  Caister-on-Sea NR30 ...168 D5
  Thetford IP24 ....176 C7

Romany Cl 8 NR29 .....57 D2
Romany Rd NR3 ....158 F1
Romany Wlk 6 NR14 ...90 C5
Romer Dro PE33 ....81 B3
Romney Wlk NR19 .....154 D4
Rook Dr NR8 ....155 E2
Rookery Cl PE34 ....145 E5
Rookery Farm Rd NR28 ..23 F2
Rookery Hill NR14 .....91 B7
Rookery La NR35 ......107 F3
Rookery Rd PE34 ......145 E4
Room La NR15 ....122 D8
Rope Wlk 5 NR24 .....176 D4
Ropemakers Row 6
  NR3 ....158 C1
Ropes Hill NR12 ....55 D4
Ropes Hill Dyke NR12 ..55 D4
Ropes Wlk NR13 ....165 E6
Rosa Cl NR12 ....54 D4
Rosa Vella Dr 3 NR20 ..68 A8
Rosalie Cl NR6 ....158 B4
Rosary Cl 8 NR14 ......89 B3
Rosary Rd NR1 ....163 A6
Rose Ave IP22 ....129 D7
Rose Cottage's NR19 ...66 D8
Rose Dr NR20 ....68 A8
Rose La Botesdale IP22 ..128 E3
  Diss IP22 ....177 F3
  Norwich NR1 ....178 C3
  3 Elm PE14 ....59 A1
  Palgrave IP22 ....177 D1
Rose La 2 IP22 ....177 D2
Rose Valley 4 NR2 ....162 B5
Rose Wlk
  Brundall NR13 ....165 C3
  Sculthorpe Airfield NR21 ..15 C2
  3 Wisbech PE13 ....152 A6
Rose Yd NR3 ....178 A4
Roseacre Cl NR2 ......162 C2
Roseacre Est NR25 .....9 A2
Rosebay 1 PE30 ....148 C3
Rosebay Cl 5 NR6 ....158 D5
Roseberry Ave
  King's Lynn PE30 ......147 B6
  7 Poringland NR14 ....90 D5
Rosebery Rd
  Cromer NR27 ....139 D5
  Great & Little Plumstead
  NR13 ....73 A4
  Norwich NR3 ....158 D1
  8 Sheringham NR27 ....10 A5
Rosecroft 4 NR17 .....174 C5
Rosecroft Way IP24 ...176 F4
Rosedale Cres 5 NR1 ..163 A6
Rosedale Gdns NR31 ...94 A5
Rosefields NR13 ....165 E4
Rosemary La
  1 Gayton PE32 ....45 C6
  2 New Buckenham NR16 ..104 F1
  Norwich NR3 ....178 A4
Rosemary Musker Cty High
  PE37 IP24 ....176 E7
Rosemary Rd
  Blofield NR13 ....73 C6
  Norwich NR7 ....159 B4
Rosemary Terr NR21 ..141 B5
Rosemary Way PE38 ..172 D6
Rosery The NR14 ......89 C3
Roses Ct NR23 ....136 D5
Rosetta Rd NR10 ....54 A2
Roseville Cl 2 NR1 ....163 B5
Rosewood NR28 ....151 E5
Roslyn Rd NR31 ......170 C5
Rosslare 1 NR4 ....162 A1
Rossons Rd NR8 ......155 C1
Rostwold Way NR8 ....158 D2
Rosyth Rd 4 IP31 ......126 B1
Rothbury Cl NR18 ....173 B4
Rothbury Rd NR18 ...173 C4
Rotten Marsh NR13 ...166 C2
Rottenstone La NR19 ..167 F3
Roudham Rd NR16 ....117 F6
Rouen Rd NR1 ....178 B2
Rougham Cnr IP26 ....99 F3
Rougham End PE32 ....47 C8
Rougham Hall PE32 ...47 A7
Rougham Rd PE32 .....29 E1
Roughlands IP27 ......113 E1
Roughsome Cl
  Belney NR19 ....49 C3
  6 Gressenhall NR20 ...49 C3
Rought Ave IP27 ....175 D2
Roughton Cl NR11 ...139 B2
Thorpe Market NR11 ...21 F7
Roughton Rd Sta
  NR27 ....139 B4
Round House Way
  NR4 ....161 B1
Round Well Rd NR5 ...156 D1
Roundabout La NR14 ..109 B8
Roundham Medieval Village
  of* NR16 ....117 E6
Roundtree Ct 28 NR7 ...27 D4
Roundtree Cl NR7 .....159 B2
Roundtree Way NR7 ...159 B2
Roundway Down 17 NR7 ..72 D4
Rouse's La PE38 ......172 D4
Row Hill PE13 ....43 F2
Row The Weeting IP27 ..175 A7
  Wereham PE33 ....80 D3
  West Dereham PE33 ....80 B4
Rowan Cl
  10 Great Yarmouth NR31 ..94 C7
  Thetford IP24 ....176 B1
  7 Watlington PE33 .....61 D5

Rowan Cl continued
  Wisbech PE13 ....152 F7
Rowan Ct NR5 ....156 F1
Rowan Dr
  Brandon IP27 ....175 C3
  Gayton PE32 ....45 C6
Rowan Rd
  King's Lynn PE34 ....43 D4
  Marthan NR29 ....57 D4
Rowan Way
  Fakenham NR21 ....141 F4
  10 Great Yarmouth NR31 ..170 B6
  Holt NR25 ....137 B7
Row's Mdw 1 NR15 ...107 D5
Rowington Rd NR1 ....178 A1
Rowland Ct NR1 ....178 B1
Rowley Cnr IP26 ....43 A1
Rowton Heath 16 NR7 ...72 D4
Roxley Cl NR7 ....163 F5
Royal Albert Ct 6 NR31 ..170 D4
Royal Arcade NR2 ....178 B3
Royal Ave NR30 ....169 D7
Royal Cl NR13 ....165 D3
Royal Norfolk Regimental
  Mus* NR1 ....178 B3
Royal Pl 2 PE13 ....152 C4
Royal Thames Rd
  NR30 ....168 D7
Royalist Dr 2 NR7 .....72 D4
Royden Way 3 NR29 ...57 C1
Roydon Comm National
  Nature Reserve*
  PE32 ....27 F1
Roydon Fen IP22 ......177 A4
Roydon Gdns IP22 ....177 A5
Roydon Prim Sch
  IP22 ....177 B5
Roydon Rd IP22 ....177 C5
Roydon Gn NR28 .....151 D6
Rubens Way 8 NR30 ..168 C6
Rudd's Drift PE32 ......48 E5
Rudds La NR10 ....149 B3
Rudham CE Prim Sch
  PE31 ....30 A6
Rudham Rd
  Great Massingham PE32 ..29 D2
  Syderstone PE31 ....15 A3
Rudham Stile La NR21 ..141 B6
Rudolf Steiner Sch
  NR12 ....164 B3
Rugg's La NR29 ....75 C8
Rugge Dr NR4 ....161 E2
Ruin Rd NR28 ....38 A5
Rumburgh La NR35 ...124 D2
Rump Cl 10 NR20 ......50 B3
Run La NR14 ....91 B6
Runcton Cl NR5 ....161 B7
Runcton Holme CE VA Prim
  Sch PE33 ....61 E3
Runcton Rd PE33 ......61 F2
Runhall Rd NR9 ....69 A2
Runham Rd
  Great Yarmouth NR30 ..169 B5
  Stokesby NR29 ....75 E8
Runnel The NR5 ......160 F6
Runton House Cl NR27 ..10 A5
Runton Rd NR27 ......139 A7
Rupert St NR2 ....162 C4
Rushall Rd IP20 ......122 B2
Rushford Rd
  Coney Weston IP31 ....127 B5
  Thetford IP24 ....126 D7
Rushmead Cl PE30 ...148 C3
Rushmeadow Rd
  NR19 ....154 A5
Rushmer Way NR26 ..138 C5
Rushmore Rd NR7 ...159 A4
Ruskin Ave NR31 ......170 B2
Ruskin Cl PE31 ....133 E3
Ruskin Pl 8 PE38 .....172 D6
Ruskin Rd NR4 ....161 E4
Russell Ave
  Caister-on-Sea NR30 ..168 E5
  Great Yarmouth NR30 ..170 C3
  Norwich NR7 ....159 B3
  9 Spixworth NR10 .....54 A2
Russell Cl NR23 ......136 C6
Russell Ct NR23 ......136 C6
Russell Rd NR30 .....169 D4
Russell St NR2 ....162 C6
Russell St
  King's Lynn PE30 .....146 F3
  Norwich NR2 ....162 C7
  Wisbech PE13 ....152 C6
Russell Terr
  Mundesley NR11 ......143 C6
  Trowse Newton NR14 ..163 B2
Russell Way NR18 ....173 C3
Russet Cl NR17 ....174 E4
Russet Gr NR4 ....161 E2
Russet Rd NR7 ....177 C5
Russet Way NR19 ....154 E3
Russets The PE14 .....77 E6
Russett Cl NR8 ....155 E2
Russia La NR31 ....94 C8
Rustens Manor Rd 2
  NR18 ....173 C5
Ruston Rd NR14 ......59 F3
Ruthen Pl 1 NR19 ....154 D5
Rutherford Way IP24 ..176 A2
Rutland St NR2 ....162 C4
Ryalla Drift PE30 .....148 B4
Ryburgh Dr NR20 ......32 D5
Rydal Cl NR5 ....161 B8
Ryders Way IP22 ......128 E2
Rye Ave NR23 ....158 B3
Rye Cl
  North Walsham NR28 ..151 E6
  Norwich NR2 ....158 B2

Rye La NR17 ....174 C4
Rye's Cl PE33 ....62 D3
Ryeland Rd 2 PE30 ...148 C4
Ryelands 5 NR29 ......167 B7
Ryelands Rd PE30 ....148 D4
Ryley Cl PE30 ....147 E8
Ryrie Cr NR4 ....161 E2
Ryston Cl PE38 ....172 C4
Ryston End PE38 .....172 C4
Ryston Pk PE38 ......172 F1
Ryston Rd Denver PE38 ..172 D2
  West Dereham PE33 ...80 B4

S

Sackville Cl 4 NR30 ...169 C3
Sacred Heart Convent Sch
  PE37 ....153 C5
Saddlebow Ind Est
  PE34 ....43 C4
Saddlebow Rd PE30 ..146 D1
Sadler Cl PE30 ....146 F7
Sadler Rd NR6 ....157 F7
Sadlers Cl NR14 ......163 A6
Sadlers Ct 11 NR26 ...138 D7
Sadlers Way NR28 ....151 E5
Saffron Cl IP27 ....175 B2
Saffron Sq NR6 ....158 B2
Sage Rd PE38 ....172 D7
Saham Rd IP25 ....84 C4
Sainsbury Ctr for the Visual
  Arts* NR4 ....161 C2
St Albans Way IP24 ..176 B5
St Andrew Cl 1 NR31 ..171 E5
St Andrew's & Blackfriars
  Halls* NR3 ....178 B3
St Andrew's Cl
  Blofield NR13 ....165 E5
  Caister-on-Sea NR30 ..168 D7
  Holme Hale IP25 ....66 A2
  Holt NR25 ....137 C6
  Northwold IP26 ....99 C8
  3 Old Buckenham NR17 ..104 D2
St Andrew's Rd
  2 Norwich NR31 ......170 C6
  Lingwood NR13 ....73 F3
  Sheringham NR26 .....138 D6
St Andrew's Way
  NR13 ....165 E5
St Andrews Ave 5 NR7 ..72 D3
St Andrews CE VA Prim Sch
  IP22 ....119 A1
St Andrews Cl
  Barningham IP31 ....127 C3
  Buxton with Lammas
  Great Yarmouth NR30 ..170 C5
  Norwich NR7 ....36 E1
  Framingham Earl NR14 ..90 D5
  11 Hingham NR9 ....86 C4
  Long Stratton NR15 ...106 E4
  Poringland NR14 ....90 D5
  West Dereham PE33 ....80 C4
  Worstead NR28 ....38 A4
St Andrews Dr
  8 Norwich NR4 ....89 C8
  Quidenham NR16 ......103 E1
St Andrews Drift 2 NR25 ..7 A4
St Andrews La
  Necton PE37 ....65 F5
  Norwich NR2 ....28 A2
St Andrews Rd
  North Runcton PE30 ..147 B3
  Norwich NR6 ....157 D6
  Scole IP21 ....119 D2
  St Andrews Sch NR27 ..10 B5
  St Andrews St NR2 ....178 B3
  St Andrews Way PE37 ..65 F5
  St Andrews Wlk PE33 ..80 C5
  St Ann La NR1 ....178 C2
  St Ann's St PE30 .....146 D5
  St Anne's Cres
  Clenchwarton PE34 ...145 D6
  Great Yarmouth NR31 ..170 A3
  St Annes Rd 4 NR14 ..90 D5
  St Annes Fort PE30 ..146 D6
  St Anthony's Way IP27 ..175 E4
  St Audreys Cl IP24 ...176 D3
  St Augustines Gate 12
  NR3 ....162 D8
  St Augustines RC Prim Sch
  NR8 ....156 E3
  St Augustines Rd
  PE13 ....152 C5
  St Augustines St 3 ...162 D8
  St Austin's Gr NR26 ..138 E7
  St Barnabas Cl 2 IP24 ..176 C1
  St Bartholomews Cl 4
  NR7 ....163 D8
  St Benedicts Cl NR34 ..110 D5
  St Benedicts Rd IP27 ..175 E4
  St Benedicts St NR2 ..178 A3
  St Benet's Abbey*
  NR12 ....56 C2
  St Benet's Cl 2 NR12 ..39 B4
  St Benet's Rd
  Great Yarmouth NR31 ..170 D8
  Norwich NR7 ....39 B4
  St Benets Ave PE30 ..151 E4
  St Benets Rd NR29 ....56 C3
  St Botolph's Cl 3 PE33 ..148 C3

Rye La NR17 ....174 C4
St Botolphs CE VC Prim Sch
  IP22 ....128 F3
St Catherine's Ave 5
  NR29 ....56 C8
St Catherine's Way
  NR31 ....170 B4
St Catherines Rd NR7 ..163 F8
St Christopher Cl
  PE30 ....94 A4
  6 Caister-on-Sea NR30 ..168 D7
St Christophers Cl
  NR15 ....108 C7
St Christophers Sch
  NR6 ....158 E4
St Clare Ct 6 NR31 ...171 E5
St Clement Cl 2 PE14 ..77 F6
St Clement Mews 7
  NR31 ....171 D5
St Clements Dr 4 PE38 ..172 C6
St Clements High Sch
  PE34 ....144 C6
St Clements Hill NR3 ..158 E2
St Clements Way
  NR13 ....165 C4
St Crispins Rd NR3 ...178 A4
St Cross Rd IP20 .....123 B4
St David's Cl 17 NR31 ..94 A6
St David's Rd NR9 ....88 C7
St Davids Cl
  Brandon IP27 ....175 D3
  Long Stratton NR15 ..106 E4
St Davids Dr 8 NR31 ..72 D6
St Dominic Sch 2 PE33 ..148 C3
St Domonic's Dr IP27 ..175 E4
St Edmund Cl
  Attleborough NR17 ....174 C5
  Great Yarmouth NR31 ..170 B3
  Poringland NR14 ....90 B6
St Edmund Rd IP27 ..114 E8
St Edmund's Ave
  PE36 ....132 D5
St Edmund's Rd
  Downham Market PE38 ..172 D5
  Lingwood NR13 ....73 F3
  Taverham NR8 ....155 C1
St Edmund's Rise 2
  NR8 ....155 C1
St Edmund's Terr
  Hunstanton PE36 .....132 C4
  King's Lynn PE30 .....146 C5
St Edmunds Ave NR17 ..174 E5
St Edmunds Cl
  Costessey NR8 ....157 A6
  Norwich NR6 ....157 E1
St Edmunds Com Sch
  PE30 ....146 E8
St Edmunds Cl 1 IP24 ..176 C1
St Edmunds Dr PE14 ..59 D1
St Edmunds Gate
  Attleborough NR17 ...174 E4
  11 Honington IP31 ....126 B1
St Edmunds Prim Sch
  IP21 ....131 A2
St Edmunds RC Prim Sch
  NR35 ....124 B8
St Edmunds Rd NR13 ..166 B3
St Edmunds Sq 16 IP31 ..126 B1
St Edmunds Wharf
  NR30 ....146 D7
St Edmundsbury Rd
  PE30 ....146 E7
St Ethelberts Cl PE31 ..135 C2
St Faith's Church*
  NR9 ....51 F7
St Faith's Cl NR9 .....51 E5
St Faith's Dr NR30 ..147 A6
St Faith's Rd NR6 ....158 D6
St Faiths La NR1 .....178 C3
St Francis Cl IP27 ....175 E4
St Francis Way NR30 ..170 C4
St Fursey's Way 2 NR31 ..94 A6
St George's Cl
  Saham Toney IP25 .....84 B5
  Thurton NR14 ....91 C4
St George's Dr
  Caister-on-Sea NR30 ..168 D7
  East Dereham NR19 ...154 D1
St George's Rd NR30 ..169 D3
St George's Theatre 16
  NR30 ....169 D3
St Georges Fst Sch 16
  NR30 ....169 D3
St Georges Mid Sch
  PE31 ....13 A1
St Georges St NR3 ....178 A4
St Georges St NR3 ....178 A4
St Germans Prim Sch
  PE34 ....43 B1
St Giles Cl PE14 ......59 B1
St Giles' La NR24 ....176 D4
St Giles Rd NR24 .....18 B2
St Giles St NR2 ....178 A3
St Giles Terr NR2 ....178 A3
St Gregorys Alley NR2 ..178 A3
St Guthlac Cl PE37 ..153 C6
St Helena Way NR10 ..35 C1
St Helens Cl 1 IP24 ..176 D6
St Helens Rd NR12 ...164 C3
St Helens Way IP24 ..154 C6
St Hilda Cl NR19 ....154 C6
St Hilda Rd
  Caister-on-Sea NR30 ..168 D6
  East Dereham NR19 ...154 C6
St Hild's Cres NR31 ..170 B5
St Hugh's Gn NR31 ...170 C4
St Hughs Way NR31 ..170 C4
St James Cl NR3 ....178 A4
St James Cres 18 NR31 ..94 A6
St James Ct NR3 .....178 A4

St James Dr PE38 ....172 B4
St James Rd IP19 ....124 A1
St James' Rd PE30 ....146 E4
St James St PE30 ....146 D4
St James Way NR15 ....106 E4
St James Wlk 14 NR30 ....169 D3
St James's Rd PE32 ....47 A2
St John Maddermarket
 NR2 ....178 A3
St John St NR1 ....178 C2
St John the Baptist Cath*
 NR2 ....162 C5
St John's Ave NR31 ....170 A4
St John's Cl
 Coltishall NR12 ....54 D7
 1 Hethersett NR9 ....88 D7
 Oxborough PE33 ....81 E4
St John's Rd
 Bungay NR35 ....124 A8
 Terrington St John PE34 ....60 C8
St John's Terr
 8 Great Yarmouth NR30 ....169 D3
 King's Lynn PE30 ....146 E4
St John's Way 12 IP26 ....98 E1
St Johns Cl
 2 Norwich NR1 ....162 E2
 Swaffham PE37 ....153 C4
St Johns Ct PE13 ....153 C4
St Johns La NR14 ....109 A8
St Johns Prim Sch
 NR12 ....164 D5
St Johns RC Fst Sch
 NR2 ....162 C6
St Johns Rd Belton NR31 ....93 F6
 Stalham NR12 ....39 B4
St Johns Way NR28 ....172 A4
St Joseph's Rd NR26 ....138 D6
St Julian Rd NR30 ....168 E4
St Julians Alley NR1 ....178 B2
St Laurence Ave NR13 ....165 C4
St Lawrence Dr NR4 ....161 C1
St Lawrence La NR18 ....178 A3
St Lawrence Prim Sch
 NR34 ....124 F2
St Leger NR15 ....106 E3
St Leonards Cl
 Scole IP21 ....130 D5
 Wymondham NR18 ....173 C6
St Leonards Rd NR1 ....163 A6
St Leonards St IP26 ....100 B4
St Leonards Terr 6
 NR1 ....163 A6
St Luke's Terr 4 NR31 ....169 B4
St Magdalen Way
 PE13 ....153 C2
St Margaret's Cl
 8 Coltishall NR12 ....54 C6
 Upton with Fishley NR13 ....166 B8
St Margaret's Cres
 IP24 ....175 C3
St Margaret's Dr IP27 ....175 A2
St Margaret's La
 2 Cromer NR27 ....139 C6
 10 King's Lynn PE30 ....146 D4
St Margaret's Pl 11
 PE30 ....146 D4
St Margaret's Rd
 Bungay NR35 ....124 A6
 2 Cromer NR27 ....139 C6
St Margaret's Way
 1 Burgh St Margaret
  (Fleggburgh) NR29 ....57 C1
 2 Hopton on Sea NR31 ....171 D5
St Margarets Ave 8
 PE33 ....63 B4
St Margarets Cl 2
 NR10 ....155 F3
St Margarets Dr NR7 ....159 C5
St Margarets Gdns
 NR12 ....164 D6
St Margarets La NR7 ....159 B5
St Margarets Mdw
 PE34 ....145 E5
St Margarets Pl NR12 ....40 A5
St Margarets St NR2 ....178 A3
St Marthas RC Prim Sch
 PE30 ....147 C6
St Martin's Cl PE30 ....147 C6
St Martin's Gdns 1
 NR16 ....104 F1
St Martin's La IP24 ....125 E6
St Martin's Rd
 2 Norwich NR3 ....162 D8
 Wisbech PE13 ....152 E7
St Martin's Way IP24 ....176 B2
St Martin-at-Palace Plain
 NR3 ....178 B4
St Martins at Oak Wall La 7
 NR3 ....162 D8
St Martins Cl 4 NR3 ....162 D8
St Martins La NR3 ....178 A4
St Mary Cl NR17 ....174 C6
St Mary's 4 NR16 ....104 F1
St Mary's Cl
 Alpington NR14 ....90 F5
 Flixton NR35 ....123 E5
 Harleston IP20 ....122 E2
 Heacham PE31 ....133 E6
 Horsham St Faith &
 Newton St Faith NR10 ....53 E2
 King's Lynn PE30 ....148 C2
 Newton Flotman NR15 ....89 C1
 1 Watton IP25 ....84 E3
 Wroxham/Hoveton
 NR12 ....164 B4
St Mary's Cres 5 IP24 ....176 C3

St Mary's Ct 2 IP24 ....176 C3
St Mary's Dr IP22 ....177 E4
St Mary's La NR31 ....169 C3
St Mary's Rd
 Aldeby NR34 ....111 A3
 Cromer NR27 ....139 B6
 20 Long Stratton NR15 ....106 E3
 Poringland NR14 ....90 D5
 West Walton PE14 ....59 B8
St Mary's Way 3 NR28 ....151 C5
St Marys Cl NR13 ....73 A5
St Marys Dr NR16 ....103 E1
St Marys Endowed Prim Sch
 NR11 ....21 E8
St Marys Gr NR2 ....159 C5
St Marys La 1 NR25 ....7 A4
St Marys Mid Sch
 NR15 ....106 E4
St Marys Plain NR3 ....178 A4
St Marys Prim Sch
 NR20 ....49 D4
St Marys RC Prim Sch
 NR31 ....170 C6
St Marys Rd
 Ashby St Mary NR14 ....91 C4
 Hemsby NR29 ....167 D6
 6 Norwich NR3 ....162 D8
 12 Stalham NR12 ....39 B4
St Marys Wlk 5 NR15 ....89 D1
St Matthew's Dr PE12 ....41 B8
St Matthews Ave NR1 ....178 C3
St Michael's Ave PE13 ....152 C7
St Michael's Cl
 Aylsham NR11 ....150 C7
 Thetford IP24 ....176 C2
St Michael's Cres IP25 ....83 D4
St Michael's Hospl
 NR11 ....150 A6
St Michael's Rd NR30 ....146 D1
St Michael-at-Pleas
 NR3 ....178 B3
St Michaels NR12 ....39 C2
St Michaels CE Prim Sch
 Gillingham NR34 ....110 B8
 King's Lynn PE30 ....146 D1
St Michaels Cl NR20 ....69 B7
St Michaels Inf Sch
 NR11 ....150 B7
St Michaels Mid Sch
 NR5 ....160 F8
St Michels Way NR15 ....106 E4
St Mildreds Rd 8 NR5 ....161 B7
St Nicholas Cl
 Dersingham PE31 ....140 E3
 9 Gayton PE32 ....45 C6
 King's Lynn PE30 ....146 D5
St Nicholas Ct
 1 Great Yarmouth NR31 ....94 C6
 10 North Walsham NR28 ....151 C5
St Nicholas Dr
 Caister-on-Sea NR30 ....168 D6
 Feltwell IP26 ....98 E2
St Nicholas Gdns 6
 NR31 ....94 C6
St Nicholas House Sch
 NR28 ....151 D4
St Nicholas Pl 1 NR26 ....138 D7
St Nicholas Priory Mid Sch
 NR30 ....169 D5
St Nicholas Rd
 Great Yarmouth NR30 ....169 D4
 North Walsham NR28 ....151 D5
St Nicholas St
 Diss IP22 ....177 D5
 East Dereham NR19 ....154 D6
 8 King's Lynn PE30 ....146 D5
 Thetford IP24 ....176 C2
St Nicholas Wlk IP27 ....175 E4
St Nicholas's NR14 ....88 F3
St Olaves Rd
 Herringfleet NR32 ....111 D8
 Norwich NR3 ....162 E8
St Omer Cl NR14 ....89 B4
St Paul's Cl
 Brockdish IP21 ....131 C6
 4 Horsford NR10 ....53 B3
 6 Wisbech PE13 ....152 C4
St Paul's Rd N PE14 ....59 D7
St Paul's Rd S PE14 ....59 E7
St Paul's Way NR30 ....169 C7
St Pauls Cl NR6 ....158 A5
St Pauls Sq 1 NR3 ....178 B4
St Peter & St Paul Prim Sch
 IP25 ....85 A5
St Peter's App IP27 ....175 B3
St Peter's Cl
 Brockdish IP21 ....131 C6
 King's Lynn PE34 ....146 B4
 Strumpshaw NR13 ....73 F2
 Yaxham NR19 ....68 A5
St Peter's La NR14 ....164 E8
St Peter's Pl IP27 ....175 B2
St Peter's Rd
 Brooke NR15 ....90 F1
 Fakenham NR21 ....141 B6
 Great Yarmouth NR30 ....169 D3
 King's Lynn PE34 ....146 C5
 Lingwood NR13 ....73 F3
 8 Sheringham NR26 ....138 D7
 Wisbech PE13 ....152 C4
St Peter's Way 12 NR30 ....54 A2
St Peter's Wlk IP20 ....113 F7
St Peters Ave NR31 ....170 B2
St Peters CE Jun Sch
 PE13 ....152 C4
St Peters CE VC Prim Sch
 NR9 ....70 B5

St Peters Cl 3 NR4 ....89 B8
St Peters Dr NR9 ....70 B5
St Peters Hill NR18 ....87 A2
St Peter's Plain NR30 ....169 D3
St Peters Rd
 Outwell PE14 ....77 E5
 Watlington PE34 ....61 C7
 Wiggenhall St Germans
 PE34 ....61 B8
St Peters St NR2 ....178 A2
St Peters Terr PE34 ....146 C4
St Philips Rd NR2 ....162 B6
St Roberts Way 14 NR31 ....94 A6
St Saviors La NR3 ....178 B4
St Stephen's Cres
 IP27 ....175 A2
St Stephens Rd NR1 ....178 A1
St Stephens Sq NR1 ....178 A2
St Stephens St NR1 ....178 A2
St Swithins Rd NR1 ....178 A3
St Thomas Cl IP27 ....175 E4
St Thomas Dr NR18 ....173 C2
St Thomas' La NR18 ....88 C4
St Thomas More RC Mid Sch
 NR2 ....162 A5
St Thomas Rd NR2 ....162 A5
St Thomas's La
 Ingoldisthorpe PE31 ....140 D8
 Snettisham PE31 ....12 F4
St Thomas's Rd NR29 ....167 C7
St Valery La PE30 ....146 D2
St Vedast St NR1 ....178 C3
St Walstan's Cl
 Norwich NR5 ....156 D1
 Taverham NR8 ....156 D8
St Walstan's Rd NR8 ....156 D8
St Williams Prim Sch
 NR7 ....163 D8
St Williams Way NR7 ....163 C7
St Winnold Cl NR18 ....172 B4
St Withburga La 8
 NR19 ....154 D5
Saker Cl 1 NR7 ....72 D4
Salamanca Rd 7 NR15 ....106 D3
Salcott Dr NR13 ....152 E5
Sale Cl 5 NR14 ....92 A1
Sale Rd NR7 ....159 D2
Salhouse Dr PE37 ....153 B2
Salhouse Prim Sch
 NR13 ....55 B1
Salhouse Rd
 Great & Little Plumstead
 NR13 ....73 B6
 New Rackheath NR13 ....72 E7
 Norwich NR7 ....159 C2
 Sprowston NR13 ....72 D6
 Woodbastwick NR13 ....55 C1
 Wroxham NR12 ....164 B2
Salhouse Sta NR13 ....54 F1
Salisbury Rd
 Cromer NR27 ....139 D4
 Great Yarmouth NR30 ....169 D6
 Norwich NR1 ....163 B5
 Sheringham NR26 ....138 E7
Salisbury Way IP24 ....176 B4
Sallow La
 Framingham Pigot NR14 ....90 E7
 Snetterton NR16 ....118 B8
Salmon Rd NR30 ....170 D8
Salmons Way NR21 ....141 F5
Salmond Dr 8 IP24 ....125 F6
Salmond Rd 11 IP25 ....84 F3
Salter Ave NR1 ....161 E5
Salter's La PE32 ....48 E4
Salters Rd NR13 ....152 E2
Salters Way PE13 ....152 A2
Salthouse Marshes Nature
 Reserve* NR25 ....8 B7
Saltings The NR14 ....144 A5
Salts Rd PE14 ....59 C8
Samphire 8 PE30 ....147 B7
Sampson Rd NR28 ....151 C3
Samson La NR6 ....129 F4
Samson's La IP22 ....129 C7
Samuel Rd 1 NR1 ....163 B7
Sancroft Way PE20 ....123 A3
Sand Stone Way IP22 ....177 A4
Sandale Rd NR30 ....147 C4
Sandall Rd PE13 ....152 D3
Sandfield Rd 8 PE38 ....172 C6
Sandhole La NR13 ....73 A7
Sandhole Rd NR1 ....163 B8
Sandholme Cl NR1 ....163 B8
Sandover Cl 4 PE33 ....43 F2
Sandown Rd
 Great Yarmouth NR30 ....169 D5
 Wisbech PE13 ....152 A2
Sandpiper Cl 1 NR13 ....170 A5
Sandpiper Ct 13 NR39 ....58 B6
Sandpit La
 Gimingham NR11 ....22 C8
 Saxlingham Nethergate
 NR15 ....107 A8
 Thorpe Market NR11 ....21 F7
Sandringham & W Newton CE
 Prim Sch PE31 ....27 F6
Sandringham Ave
 Great Yarmouth NR30 ....169 D7
 12 Marham PE33 ....63 B4
 Norwich NR2 ....162 A5
Sandringham Cl
 PE30 ....148 D5
Sandringham Ct
 Norwich NR2 ....178 A1
 6 Watton IP25 ....84 D3
Sandringham Ctry Pk*
 PE35 ....27 E7

Sandringham Dr
 Downham Market PE38 ....172 E5
 Heacham PE31 ....133 C4
Sandringham House Mus &
 Gdns* PE35 ....27 F7
Sandringham Private Hospl
 PE30 ....147 E6
Sandringham Rd
 Dersingham PE31 ....140 E2
 Hunstanton PE36 ....132 D4
 King's Lynn PE30 ....147 C7
 Norwich NR2 ....162 A5
Sandringham Way
 PE37 ....153 C2
Sands Cl NR31 ....171 E4
Sandy Cl PE31 ....140 C7
Sandy Cres PE31 ....140 C7
Sandy Hill La NR25 ....8 F4
Sandy La Saham NR11 ....150 B6
 Bacton NR12 ....23 D2
 Barningham IP31 ....127 C4
 Beighton NR13 ....74 D2
 Belton with Browston
 NR31 ....93 F5
 Blackborough End PE32 ....44 C2
 Bradwell NR31 ....94 B6
 Buxton with Lammas
 NR10 ....53 F8
 Canadas NR11 ....10 A3
 Cantley NR13 ....92 E6
 Castle Acre PE32 ....47 A2
 Cromer NR27 ....139 A6
 Denver PE38 ....172 C2
 Dereham NR19 ....154 C8
 Diss IP22 ....177 F4
 Docking PE31 ....134 D6
 East Dereham NR19 ....154 C6
 East Tuddenham NR20 ....69 D8
 Fakenham NR21 ....141 A5
 Fleggburgh NR29 ....75 B8
 Great Massingham PE32 ....46 E8
 Grimston PE32 ....44 C8
 Hardingham NR9 ....86 D7
 Helhoughton NR21 ....30 E6
 Hoveton NR12 ....55 C4
 Ingoldisthorpe PE31 ....140 C7
 King's Lynn PE30 ....148 F1
 Loddon NR14 ....92 B1
 Mundham NR14 ....109 A7
 Norwich NR4 ....162 D1
 Old Hunstanton PE36 ....132 E8
 Oulton NR11 ....35 B7
 Raveningham NR14 ....110 B8
 Rocklands NR17 ....103 A6
 Runton NR27 ....10 C4
 St Mary, South Elmham
 otherwise Homersfield
 IP20 ....123 B3
 Sheringham NR27 ....10 B5
 Somerton NR29 ....57 E6
 South Wootton PE30 ....27 C1
 Southrepps NR11 ....22 B7
 Taverham NR8 ....156 C8
 Thurning NR20 ....34 C8
 West Acre PE32 ....46 B2
 Weston Longville NR9 ....51 D4
 Wisbech PE13 ....152 F4
Sandy La E NR19 ....154 C6
Sandy Way NR11 ....140 C7
Sandygate La PE34 ....144 F5
Sandyland PE13 ....152 B5
Sankence La NR10 ....35 E5
Santon Cl IP24 ....176 A3
Sapiston Rd IP31 ....126 D1
Sapwell Cl NR11 ....150 A6
Saracen Rd NR6 ....157 F6
Sarah W Cl NR22 ....162 C4
Sarah William Cl 2
 NR4 ....161 C5
Sarahs Rd PE36 ....132 C2
Sardis Way NR14 ....109 A8
Saturday Mkt Pl PE30 ....146 D4
Saunders Ct 7 NR1 ....163 A6
Savery Cl NR5 ....161 B6
Savory Cl NR13 ....152 B7
Saw Mill La
 Brancaster PE31 ....3 B6
 7 Great Yarmouth NR31 ....169 B4
Sawmill Cl NR18 ....173 B5
Sawston 1 PE30 ....147 D6
Sawyer's La NR18 ....87 D2
Sawyers Cl NR5 ....156 E1
Saxlingham La NR15 ....106 F7
Saxlingham Prim Sch
 NR15 ....107 B7
Saxlingham Rd
 Blakeney NR25 ....7 C5
 Saxlingham Nethergate
 NR15 ....107 C8
 Shotesham NR15 ....89 F1
Saxon Cres 9 IP31 ....126 B1
Saxon Ct IP27 ....153 D2
Saxon Field PE31 ....3 B6
Saxon Gdns NR30 ....168 D5
Saxon Pl
 8 Thetford IP24 ....176 C3
 Weeting IP27 ....175 A8
Saxon Rd NR30 ....169 D4
Saxon Way
 Dersingham PE31 ....140 D4
 Wormegay PE33 ....62 C6
Saxon Wlk PE26 ....100 A4
Saxonfields NR14 ....90 C4
Sayer Ct NR25 ....9 A7
Sayers St 9 NR2 ....162 C7
Scama La IP20 ....123 B3
Scania Way PE30 ....147 A1
Scarborough Rd NR22 ....17 A8

Scarfield La PE14 ....59 C2
Scarlet Rd NR4 ....162 D1
Scarnell Rd NR5 ....161 C6
Scarning Fen NR19 ....154 C2
Scarning VC Prim Sch
 NR19 ....154 A4
Scarrow Beck La NR11 ....21 A2
Sceptre Cl NR6 ....158 A3
Scholars Wlk IP22 ....177 C5
School Ave NR7 ....163 F6
School Cl
 Kenninghall NR16 ....119 A4
 Knapton NR28 ....143 A1
 3 Ludham NR29 ....56 C5
 Northrepps NR27 ....11 A2
 4 Rollesby NR29 ....57 D2
School Comm Rd NR12 ....24 C3
School Hill
 Reedham NR13 ....93 A4
 Tasburgh NR15 ....106 E6
School La
 Brandon IP27 ....175 C3
 Cantley NR13 ....92 B7
 Colney NR4 ....160 C3
 East Dereham NR19 ....154 E1
 East Harling NR16 ....118 C5
 Gimingham NR11 ....22 E8
 Great Yarmouth NR31 ....170 D6
 17 Harleston IP20 ....122 D2
 Heckingham NR14 ....109 F8
 Little Dunham PE32 ....65 E7
 Little Melton NR9 ....160 C2
 Neatishead NR12 ....55 D7
 North Runcton PE33 ....44 A2
 Northwold IP26 ....99 C7
 Norwich NR2 ....158 B3
 Rockland St Mary NR14 ....91 B7
 Runhall NR9 ....68 F1
 Skeyton NR10 ....37 A5
 Smallburgh NR12 ....38 D3
 Stoke Ferry PE33 ....80 F2
 Swanton Morley NR20 ....73 B1
 Thetford IP24 ....176 D3
 Walpole St Andrew PE14 ....41 E3
 Wereham PE33 ....81 C8
 5 Wisbech PE13 ....152 C5
 Wramplingham NR18 ....69 F1
 Wymondham NR18 ....105 A8
School Loke
 Bodham NR25 ....9 A2
 Hemsby NR29 ....167 A7
School Pastures PE31 ....3 E7
School Plain NR19 ....154 B5
School Rd
 Alburgh IP20 ....123 A5
 Aldborough NR11 ....21 A5
 Ashmanhaugh NR12 ....55 B7
 Bacton NR28 ....23 B4
 Barton Turf NR12 ....22 E8
 Bedingham NR35 ....108 B3
 Beetley NR20 ....49 C5
 Blofield NR13 ....165 B8
 Bracon Ash NR14 ....89 A3
 Bradenham IP25 ....66 D2
 Bressingham IP22 ....129 B8
 Brisley NR20 ....49 A8
 Catfield NR29 ....56 C8
 Colkirk NR21 ....31 D5
 Earsham NR35 ....123 F8
 East Ruston NR12 ....38 E7
 Erpingham NR11 ....21 B2
 Foulden IP26 ....82 A1
 Freethorpe NR13 ....92 F7
 Frettenham NR12 ....54 A4
 Great Massingham PE32 ....29 D1
 Great Yarmouth NR30 ....169 B5
 Haveringland NR10 ....52 D7
 Heacham PE31 ....133 D5
 Hinderclay IP22 ....128 C3
 Holme Hale IP25 ....66 A2
 Horning NR12 ....55 F3
 Kirby Cane NR35 ....109 E4
 Lessingham NR12 ....24 D3
 Lingwood NR13 ....74 A3
 Little Cressingham IP25 ....83 F2
 Little Plumstead NR13 ....73 B6
 Ludham NR29 ....56 E6
 Marshland St James PE14 ....60 B4
 Mautby NR29 ....75 E5
 Middleton PE32 ....44 C2
 Morning Thorpe NR15 ....107 B3
 Neatishead NR12 ....55 D7
 1 Necton PE37 ....65 F4
 Newton Flotman NR15 ....89 D1
 Outwell PE14 ....77 D4
 Potter Heigham NR29 ....56 F6
 Reepham NR10 ....149 B4
 Runcton Holme PE33 ....61 E3
 St Andrew, Ilketshall
 NR34 ....124 E6
 Sculthorpe Airfield NR21 ....15 C3
 Seething NR15 ....108 E8
 Shotesham PE31 ....12 C5
 South Walsham NR13 ....74 A8
 Strumpshaw NR13 ....73 F1
 Swannington NR9 ....52 C6
 Taverham NR8 ....155 F1
 Tibenham IP21 ....120 F7
 Thompson IP24 ....102 B7
 Tilney All Saints PE34 ....42 E4
 Tilney St Lawrence PE34 ....60 C7
 Tivetshall St Mary NR15 ....121 B5
 Walpole Highway PE14 ....59 C6
 Walton Highway PE14 ....59 C8
 Watlington PE33 ....61 D6

School Rd continued
Weasenham All Saints
  PE32 ....47 D8
Weasenham St Peter
  PE32 ....30 D1
West Rudham PE31 ....29 F6
West Walton PE14 ....59 B8
Whissonsett NR20 ....31 E2
Wiggenhall St Germans
  PE34 ....61 B8
Worstead NR28 ....38 A5
School Rd Back 4
  NR30 ....169 C5
School Sq IP24 ....102 E3
School Terr 3 NR14 ....163 B2
School View NR34 ....124 F1
Schoolfield NR10 ....155 C8
Schoolhouse La 1
  NR11 ....150 C7
Scole Comm IP21 ....130 C6
Scole Comm Rd IP21 ....130 D6
Scole Prim Sch IP21 ....130 D6
Scole Rd IP21 ....155 D6
**Scolt Head Island National
Nature Reserve*** PE31 ....3 E8
Sconch Beck Rd IP20 ....123 A2
Scotch Hill Rd NR8 ....155 B1
Scotgate Cl IP24 ....102 E3
Scott Cl IP24 ....176 E6
Scott Rd NR11 ....163 B5
Scott's Cnr NR16 ....105 B4
Scott's Hill NR14 ....24 B8
Scott's La IP26 ....99 A7
Scotter Rise 7 NR26 ....138 C5
Scottow Rd NR10 ....37 B2
Scoulton Rd NR17 ....85 F2
Scratby Cres NR29 ....167 F3
Scratby Rd NR29 ....167 D3
Scroby Ct NR27 ....167 E3
Scrumpy Way NR16 ....119 D7
Sculthorpe Airfield
  NR21 ....15 E2
Sculthorpe Ave PE34 ....146 B5
Sculthorpe Bvd 7 NR21 ....15 C2
Sculthorpe CE VA Prim Sch
  NR21 ....16 C2
Sculthorpe Eastgate
  NR21 ....141 A5
Sculthorpe Rd NR21 ....141 A5
Sea Cl PE31 ....133 B6
Sea Palling Rd NR12 ....39 F3
Sea View Rd
Hemsby NR29 ....167 D7
Mundesley NR11 ....143 B7
Sea View Rise NR31 ....171 E4
Seabank Rd
Heacham PE31 ....133 B6
Wisbech PE13 ....152 F6
Seabank Way PE30 ....146 E7
Seabird Cl 4 NR30 ....168 D7
Seabrook Cl 9 NR5 ....161 A7
Seacliff NR20 ....138 E7
Seafield Cl 2 NR30 ....169 D2
Seafield Rd N NR30 ....168 E6
Seafield Rd S NR30 ....168 D6
Seafields Dr NR31 ....171 D4
Seaforth Dr NR8 ....156 E8
Seagate PE36 ....132 C3
Seagate Rd PE36 ....132 B3
Seagull Rd NR29 ....167 E5
Seamere Rd NR9 ....86 D4
Searle Cl NR21 ....141 F5
Sears Cl NR11 ....150 C6
Seaside La NR12 ....24 E4
Seates The 6 NR5 ....155 D2
Seathwaite Rd NR30 ....147 D8
Seaview Cres NR26 ....138 D5
Seawake Cl NR31 ....170 A4
Seaward Cres NR11 ....143 B6
Seaward Wlk NR30 ....168 E8
Seckar Dr NR19 ....154 C4
Second Ave
Caister-on-Sea NR30 ....168 D8
Wisbech PE13 ....152 D4
Second Dro IP27 ....113 C3
Second Marsh Rd PE14 ....59 A7
Sedge Cl NR21 ....141 E4
Sedge Dro PE38 ....96 C7
Sedge Fen Rd PE38 ....97 B3
Sedge Rd NR19 ....154 B4
Sedgefen Dro PE38 ....112 E7
Sedgeford Rd IP27 ....112 F3
Sedgeford Fst Sch
  PE36 ....13 B7
Sedgeford La 5 PE30 ....146 E4
Sedgeford Rd
Docking PE31 ....134 B4
Snettisham PE31 ....12 D6
Seeche Abbey PE34 ....43 D1
Seething & Mumdham Sch
  NR15 ....108 E8
Seething Old Hall Pk
  NR15 ....108 E8
Seething Rd NR35 ....108 D5
Seething St NR15 ....108 E8
Seeview Cres NR12 ....24 A7
Sefton Ave PE13 ....152 E6
Sefton La NR31 ....169 C3
Sego Vale NR6 ....158 A8
Seagrave Rd 8 PE30 ....147 A8
Selby Pl 10 NR30 ....169 D2
Self's La IP22 ....128 C7
Selwyn Dr 9 NR31 ....94 A5
Selwyn Gdns IP21 ....121 E5

Selwyn Rd NR31 ....170 A5
Semere Gn La IP21 ....121 D2
Semere La IP21 ....121 D4
Sendall Rd NR28 ....151 B3
Sennowe Rd NR20 ....32 F4
Senter's Rd PE31 ....140 D2
Seppings Rd NR21 ....141 A6
Seppings Way NR13 ....72 E6
Serpentine La NR10 ....53 C6
Setch Rd Middleton PE33 ....44 A1
West Winch PE33 ....43 F1
Seton Rd NR8 ....155 E1
Setons Halt Sta NR23 ....5 F2
Seven Sisters Cl PE30 ....146 C4
Seventh Ave PE13 ....152 E4
Severalls Rd IP26 ....98 D5
Sewell Rd Lamas NR10 ....36 F1
Norwich NR3 ....158 C1
Sewell's La NR15 ....90 D3
Sewells Cl 5 NR15 ....89 C1
Sexton Rd NR35 ....108 D2
Seymour Ave
Brandon IP27 ....114 D4
Great Yarmouth NR30 ....169 D8
Shack La NR13 ....165 D6
Shadingfield Cl 10 ....169 D2
Shadwell Cl IP27 ....175 B7
Shakers' Rd
Brandon IP27 ....115 A1
Wangford IP27 ....114 D7
Shakespeare Rd NR30 ....169 E8
Shakespeare Way
Taverham NR8 ....156 E8
Thetford IP24 ....176 E6
Shannock Ct 14 NR26 ....138 D7
Shannon Dr 4 NR30 ....169 E8
Shannons Cl NR17 ....174 E4
Sharman Ave IP25 ....84 D4
Sharmans Loke NR31 ....93 F5
Sharon Cl
East Dereham NR19 ....154 D1
Felmingham NR28 ....37 A8
Sharp St NR29 ....56 C7
Sharpe Way NR29 ....167 B2
Sharper's Cnr IP27 ....113 D2
Sharrington Rd NR24 ....18 B5
Shaw's Yd PE31 ....30 B7
Shawcross Rd NR27 ....10 A4
Shearwater Dr 2 NR31 ....170 A7
Sheddick Ct NR19 ....154 D6
Sheep Mdw Cl NR5 ....156 E1
Sheffield Rd NR18 ....173 C5
Sheldrake Cl NR21 ....141 F5
Sheldrick Pl NR19 ....154 E2
Shelduck Dr 7 PE31 ....12 E5
Shelfanger Rd IP22 ....177 C7
Shelfhanger Rd NR30 ....147 B8
Shell Mus The* NR25 ....7 F4
Shelley Cl NR30 ....168 D6
Shelley Dr NR8 ....156 D8
Shelley Way IP24 ....176 E6
Shelly Cl 3 PE38 ....172 D6
Shelterhouse Cnr
  NR20 ....125 A4
Shelton with Hardwick Sch
  NR15 ....107 B2
Shepheard Cl 1 NR8 ....161 D5
Shepheards Cl NR11 ....150 E8
Shepherd Cl
2 Norwich NR4 ....161 D5
Shepherd's Cl NR30 ....138 B6
Shepherd Way NR8 ....155 E1
Shepherd's Fold PE37 ....153 D2
Shepherd's La NR10 ....36 A2
Shepherds Cl
Cromer NR27 ....10 B5
10 Horsford NR10 ....53 A3
Runton NR27 ....10 B8
Shepherds La
Burgate NR29 ....129 B3
Oulton NR11 ....35 B6
Shepherds Pightle PE36 ....2 D6
Shepherdsgate Rd
  PE34 ....41 C5
Shepley Cres 2 PE30 ....147 D5
Sheppard Way NR17 ....174 C5
Sherbourne Pl NR1 ....178 C1
Shereford Rd
Fakenham NR21 ....141 A3
Hempton NR21 ....31 C8
Sheridan Cl NR8 ....156 F8
Sheridan House Sch
  IP25 ....86 A7
Sheringham Com Prim Sch
  NR26 ....138 C5
Sheringham High Sch
  NR26 ....138 C5
Sheringham Little Theatre
  NR26 ....138 D7
Sheringham Mus*
  NR26 ....138 D7
Sheringham Pk* NR26 ....9 B6
Sheringham Pk Visitor Ctr*
  NR26 ....9 B4
Sheringham Rd
West Beckham NR25 ....9 B3
Weybourne NR25 ....8 F5
Sheringham Sta NR26 ....138 C5
**Sheringham Woodfields Spec
Sch** NR26 ....138 C5
Sheringwood NR26 ....138 F6
Shernborne Rd PE31 ....13 D7
Sherwell Rd NR6 ....157 E6
Sherwood Ave PE13 ....152 D7
Sherwood Rd NR4 ....162 C1
Sheval Cl NR15 ....121 A8

Shickle Pl IP22 ....127 F6
Shillgate Way NR8 ....155 B2
Shillito Rd NR13 ....165 F6
Shimpling Rd IP21 ....121 B1
Ship La PE36 ....2 C6
Shipden Ave NR27 ....139 A7
Shipden Ct NR27 ....139 A7
Shipdham Airfield IP25 ....67 E2
Shipdham Airfield Ind Est
  IP25 ....67 F2
Shipdham Rd
Carbrooke IP25 ....85 A5
East Dereham NR19 ....154 D1
Scoulton NR9 ....67 B6
Shipdham NR19 ....67 E5
Shipfield NR3 ....158 F2
Shipgate Rd NR11 ....23 B5
Shippea Hill Sta CB7 ....112 C3
Shipstone Rd NR10 ....162 D8
Shire Ave 5 NR31 ....94 C8
Shiregreen NR30 ....147 C4
Shires The NR8 ....155 F2
Shirley Cl 3 NR12 ....54 A4
Shoe Devil La NR35 ....124 C4
Shoemakers La PE37 ....64 E3
Shooters Cl NR8 ....155 C1
Shop La Hethersett NR9 ....88 E8
Tunstead NR12 ....38 A3
Wells-next-the-Sea
  NR23 ....136 D6
Shop St NR19 ....68 A3
Shorncliffe Ave NR3 ....158 C1
Shorncliffe Cl 1 NR3 ....158 C1
Short Beck 8 IP26 ....98 E1
Short Dro PE38 ....172 C6
Short Gn IP22 ....120 B5
Short La Billingford NR20 ....50 A8
Feltwell IP26 ....98 D1
Happisburgh NR12 ....24 B3
Harpley PE31 ....29 D4
Mautby NR29 ....75 E6
Swardeston NR14 ....89 C5
Short Rd
8 Attleborough NR17 ....174 C5
Belton with Browston
  NR31 ....94 A4
Short St 8 NR15 ....89 D1
Short-thorn Rd NR10 ....52 F5
Shotesham La NR15 ....107 C8
Shotesham Rd
Howe NR15 ....90 C2
Poringland NR14 ....90 B3
Wootton NR35 ....108 A6
Shotford Rd IP20 ....122 D1
Shouldham Cl NR21 ....140 C3
Shouldham La PE37 ....153 A4
Shouldham Rd
Marham NR21 ....63 A3
Shouldham Thorpe PE33 ....62 C7
Shreeves Rd IP22 ....177 E4
Shropham Rd IP24 ....102 E3
Shrub Cl NR17 ....174 D5
Shrub Dro NR28 ....112 E6
Shrub Hill PE38 ....112 F7
Shrublands The
Horsford NR10 ....53 B4
Norwich NR12 ....162 B6
Shrublands Way IP33 ....170 A8
Sidegate Rd
Great Yarmouth NR30 ....169 C5
Hopton on Sea NR31 ....171 B7
Sidell Cl 10 NR4 ....89 B8
Sidestrand Hall Specl Sch
  NR27 ....11 B2
Siding Rd NR34 ....111 C1
Sidings The IP24 ....176 C5
Sidney Cl
2 Great Yarmouth NR30 ....169 D2
8 Martham NR29 ....57 C4
Sidney Rd
Costessey NR8 ....156 F4
Ingham NR12 ....39 D4
Sidney St NR30 ....169 D1
Sienna Mews 3 NR1 ....163 B7
Sigismund Rd NR1 ....162 D3
Silfield Ave NR18 ....173 D3
Silfield Gdn PE36 ....132 D4
Silfield Rd NR18 ....173 C2
Silfield Sch NR18 ....147 C6
Silfield St NR18 ....88 A2
Silkmill Rd 8 NR18 ....169 D4
Silt Rd Nordelph PE38 ....78 E2
Runcton Holme PE33 ....61 C4
Terrington St Clement
  PE34 ....25 F3
Upwell PE14 ....77 F1
Silver Cour NR27 ....11 A2
Silver Dr PE31 ....140 C4
Silver End NR3 ....162 E8
Silver Gdns 5 NR31 ....94 A5
Silver Hill PE30 ....147 D6
Silver Rd NR3 ....178 C4
Silver St
Attleborough NR17 ....174 F6
Besthorpe NR17 ....104 D7
Fleggburgh NR29 ....75 C8
Garvestone NR9 ....86 C8
Norwich NR3 ....178 C4
South Lopham IP22 ....128 F7
Silvergate La NR11 ....35 F6
Silvertree's Way PE33 ....43 E1
Simon Scotland Rd
  PE30 ....146 F2
Simpson Cl NR28 ....151 B5

Sinclair Ct NR31 ....170 A8
Sir Douglas Bader Espl
  PE36 ....132 C4
Sir Edward Stracey Rd
  NR13 ....72 D8
Sir Lewis St PE30 ....146 E6
Sir Thomas Cl NR14 ....173 C5
Sir William's Cl NR11 ....150 D6
Sir William's La NR11 ....150 D7
Siskin Cl NR31 ....170 A6
Sitka Cl PE31 ....133 C6
Six Crossways NR14 ....91 D3
Sixteen Foot Bank
  PE14 ....77 D1
Sixth Ave PE13 ....152 E4
Skedge Way 6 NR13 ....73 C6
Skelton Cl 1 IP22 ....177 E4
Skelton Rd Diss IP22 ....177 E4
Norwich NR7 ....163 C8
Sketton View NR28 ....151 B3
Skeyton Cl NR11 ....150 C6
Skeyton Cnr NR10 ....37 B6
Skeyton New Rd NR28 ....151 B5
Skeyton Rd
Coltishall NR10 ....37 B2
North Walsham NR28 ....151 A4
Skinner's La IP20 ....122 B4
Skinners La NR12 ....164 B2
Skipping Block Row
  NR18 ....88 B6
Skippon Way NR13 ....72 D5
Skitfield Rd NR20 ....33 E6
Skoner Rd NR5 ....161 B8
Skoyles' La NR9 ....88 A8
Skye Cl NR5 ....161 A8
Slad La NR20 ....50 C6
Slade La
Framingham Pigot NR14 ....90 E6
Old Buckenham NR17 ....104 B1
Wortham IP22 ....129 B6
Slade Rd NR21 ....18 E7
Sleaford Gn NR3 ....158 C2
Sleigh La IP25 ....84 E2
Sleights Dr PE14 ....59 C5
Slessor Cl 2 IP25 ....84 F3
Slip The PE14 ....93 A1
Slip The PE36 ....2 C3
Slipshoe La NR15 ....122 B7
Sloane Way IP24 ....176 B2
Sloe La NR13 ....72 D8
Slopers Rd NR18 ....87 F7
Slough La
Attleborough NR17 ....174 E3
North Tuddenham NR20 ....68 E8
Slough Rd IP22 ....129 A1
Slugs La NR32 ....111 C8
Sluice Dro IP26 ....113 E7
Sluice Rd Denver PE38 ....172 B1
Wiggenhall St Germans
  PE34 ....61 A8
Slutshole La
Besthorpe NR17 ....104 D7
Wymondham NR17 ....105 A7
Small Lode PE14 ....77 F5
Smallburgh Rd
Barton Turf NR12 ....55 E8
Smallburgh NR12 ....38 D2
Smallholdings Rd
  PE34 ....145 D4
Smallworth La IP22 ....128 B7
Smeath La NR12 ....39 E1
Smeat St 2 NR5 ....161 B7
Smee La NR13 ....72 E4
Smee Rd NR13 ....72 F4
Smeeth Rd Emneth PE14 ....59 F2
St John's Fen End PE14 ....60 A5
Smith Ave PE30 ....146 E6
Smith's Dro NR18 ....112 C8
Smith's Loke NR31 ....170 A6
Smithdale Rd NR5 ....157 B1
Smithdon High Sch
  PE36 ....132 D4
Smithfield Rd NR1 ....162 E3
Smiths Dr IP21 ....121 B1
Smithson Cl NR18 ....141 E5
Smithson Cl NR18 ....173 C4
Smithson Dr NR20 ....68 F5
Smithyne Ave
Dereham NR19 ....46 B7
3 East Dereham NR19 ....154 F3
Smithy Cl NR31 ....133 D5
Smithy Rd NR13 ....140 D8
Smock Mill Loke
  NR18 ....173 C3
Smuggler's La NR10 ....149 B4
Smugglers Cl NR26 ....132 F8
Smugglers' Rd IP26 ....100 F8
Snaefell Pk NR26 ....138 B4
Snailgate La Lound NR32 ....94 C2
Topcroft NR35 ....108 A4
Snake Rd PE14 ....77 B7
Snape Hill NR15 ....126 E3
Snape Hill IP22 ....128 C2
Snape La NR28 ....172 B5
Sneath Rd NR15 ....121 A8
Snetterton Circuit
  NR16 ....118 D8
Snettisham Beach
  PE31 ....12 A3
Snettisham Nature Reserve*
  PE31 ....12 A1
Snettisham Pk* PE31 ....12 E4
Snettisham Prim Sch
  PE31 ....12 E5
Snoring Rd NR21 ....17 C3
Snow St IP22 ....177 A6
Snow's Hill 6 NR14 ....92 A2
Snow's La NR14 ....92 A2

Snowberry Cl 4 NR8 ....155 B2
Snowdrop Cl 20 NR31 ....94 C6
Snowdrop Dr NR17 ....174 B4
Snowhill Drift NR19 ....154 D6
Soame Cl NR11 ....150 D5
Soames Pl NR19 ....67 B7
Soanes Ct NR9 ....51 A5
Softley Dr NR4 ....161 C2
Soken Dr 6 Beetley NR19 ....49 C3
5 Gressenhall NR20 ....49 C3
Solace Cl NR35 ....124 C8
Sole Cl 6 NR10 ....53 B3
Soleme Rd NR3 ....158 B1
Solomon Cl NR30 ....168 E5
Somerleyton Gdns
  NR2 ....162 C5
Somerleyton Hall & Gdns*
  NR32 ....111 A8
Somerleyton Prim Sch
  NR32 ....111 D8
Somerleyton St 2 NR2 ....162 C5
Somerleyton Sta
  NR32 ....111 C7
Somers Rd IP21 ....152 B4
Somersby Cl 2 PE30 ....147 A8
Somerset Way NR28 ....155 A1
Somerton Rd
Martham NR29 ....57 D5
Somerton NR29 ....58 A6
Somerville Ave NR10 ....110 B3
Somerville Rd 11 PE30 ....146 E3
Sorrel Cl 2 NR30 ....147 C8
Sorrel Dr
Attleborough NR17 ....174 B4
1 Thetford IP24 ....176 E4
Sorrel La IP25 ....49 C5
Sorrel Rd 25 NR31 ....94 C6
Sorrel Way PE38 ....172 C3
Sotherton Rd NR4 ....161 F3
Soudan Cl 3 NR30 ....168 D7
South Acre Hall PE32 ....46 E1
South Acre Rd PE32 ....46 F1
South Ave Norwich NR7 ....163 E5
Swanton Morley Airfield
  NR20 ....50 B5
South Beach PE31 ....133 A3
South Beach Par
  NR30 ....170 A6
South Beach Pl NR30 ....169 E2
South Beach Rd
Heacham PE31 ....133 A4
Hunstanton PE36 ....132 B3
South Brink PE13 ....152 A3
South Burlingham Rd
  NR13 ....74 B3
South Cl NR25 ....7 A6
South Cnr PE31 ....3 B7
South Creake Maize Maze*
  NR21 ....15 E6
South Croft NR9 ....88 C7
South Denes Rd NR30 ....169 D1
South Everard St
  PE30 ....146 E3
South Gage Cl NR7 ....159 C4
South Gdn NR30 ....170 C1
South Gn
East Dereham NR19 ....154 D3
Terrington St Clement
  PE34 ....144 B5
South Gn Gdns NR19 ....154 D3
South Harford Mid Sch
  NR4 ....89 E8
South Hill Cl NR7 ....163 F8
South Hill Rd NR7 ....163 F8
South Icehouse Hill
  NR31 ....170 D6
South Lynn Plain
  PE30 ....146 E4
South Mkt Rd NR30 ....169 E4
South Moor Dr PE31 ....133 D4
South Pk IP27 ....175 B7
South Pk Ave 2 NR4 ....162 A4
South Quay
Great Yarmouth NR30 ....169 C3
King's Lynn PE30 ....146 D4
South Rd
Great Yarmouth NR30 ....169 D1
Hemsby NR29 ....167 D7
Watton IP25 ....84 D3
South Rise NR28 ....151 B3
South St
Great Dunham PE32 ....47 F1
Hockwold cum Wilton
  IP26 ....113 F6
2 King's Lynn PE30 ....146 E4
Sheringham NR26 ....138 C7
South Walsham Rd
Acle NR13 ....166 A5
South Walsham NR13 ....74 B5
South Wood Dr NR14 ....90 B6
South Wootton Fst Sch
  PE30 ....148 C2
South Wootton Jun Sch
  PE30 ....148 C1
South Wootton La
  PE30 ....148 C1
Southacre Rd PE32 ....65 C7
Southampton Pl 16
  NR30 ....169 D4
Southburgh La NR9 ....86 A5
Southburgh Rd NR9 ....86 A4
Southend
Bradenham IP25 ....66 D3
East Dereham NR19 ....154 D4
Southend Rd PE36 ....132 C3
Southern La IP22 ....128 C5

Southern Reach **7** NR14 ..89 B3
Southerwood **4** NR6 ..158 D5
Southery Prim Sch
  PE38 ....97 A5
Southery Rd
  Feltwell IP26 ....98 B2
  Methwold IP26 ....97 F3
Southfield PE22 ....65 C5
Southfield Dr **8** PE33 ...43 F2
Southfield La NR13 .....55 C1
Southfields
  Downham Market PE38 ...172 B4
  1 King's Lynn PE30 .....147 B6
Southgate **12** IP20 ......122 D1
Southgate Cl NR23 ...136 C5
Southgate La
  Norwich NR1 ....178 C1
  Snettisham PE31 ....12 E4
Southgate St PE30 ...146 E3
Southgates Dr NR21 ..141 B5
Southgates Rd NR30 ..169 D2
Southlands PE37 ....153 B2
Southrepps Rd
  Antingham NR28 ....22 B4
  Gimingham NR11 ....22 E6
Southside PE34 ....79 D8
Southtown Fst Sch
  NR31 ....169 B2
Southtown Rd NR31 ...169 C2
Southwell Rd
  8 Horsham St Faith &
  Newton St Faith NR10 ...53 D2
  Norwich NR1 ....178 A1
  Wisbech PE13 ....152 C7
Southwood Rd
  Beighton NR13 ....74 C1
  Cantley NR13 ....92 C8
Sovereign Cl **2** PE13 ..152 A6
Sovereign Way PE38 ..172 A4
Sow's Loke NR12 ....55 E6
Spa La Aylsham NR11 ..150 B3
  Oulton NR11 ....35 B8
Spalding's Chair Hill
  IP24 ....126 E8
Spar Rd NR6 ....158 C5
Sparhawk Ave NR7 ....159 C4
Sparhawk Cl NR7 ....159 C4
Sparhawk Fst Sch
  NR7 ....159 C4
Sparrow Cl **4** NR31 .....94 C7
Sparrowgate Rd PE14 ..59 C5
Speedwell Cl
  5 Attleborough NR17 ...174 B4
  2 Thetford IP24 ....176 E4
Speedwell Rd NR18 ...173 D4
Speedwell Way
  Norwich NR5 ....160 F5
  IP20 ....122 D1
  13 Redenhall with Harleston
  IP20 ....122 D1
Speke St NR2 ....162 A7
Spelman Rd NR2 ....162 A4
Spencer Ave NR31 .....170 C6
Spencer Cl
  Great & Little Plumstead
  NR13 ....73 B7
  11 Lingwood NR13 ....74 A3
  West Walton PE14 ....59 B8
Spencer Ct **12** IP25 ....84 D3
Spencer Rd NR6 ....158 C5
Spencer St NR3 ....162 E8
Spencers Cl NR20 ......49 E7
Spens Ave NR31 ....170 B3
Spenser Ave NR28 ....151 D4
Spenser Rd PE30 ......148 B1
Spice Chase PE34 ....60 C7
Spicer's La NR16 ....106 B5
Spicers Way IP22 ......127 D2
Spindle Cl NR18 ....173 D4
Spindle Rd NR6 ....158 D4
Spindrift Cl **11** NR29 ...58 B6
Spink's La NR18 ....173 F6
Spinks' La NR35 ....108 D2
Spinnakers Cl NR18 ....88 B4
Spinners Cl PE37 ......153 B5
Spinners La PE37 ......153 B5
Spinney Cl Beetley NR20 ..49 D4
  Brandon IP27 ....175 C2
  King's Lynn PE30 ....148 B4
  9 Long Stratton NR15 ..106 E3
  Norwich NR7 ....163 F8
Spinney Rd NR7 ....163 E8
Spinney The NR14 .....110 B7
Spirkett's La IP20 .....122 D1
Spitalfields NR1 ....163 A7
Spitfire Rd NR6 ....158 C6
Spixworth Fst Sch
  NR10 ....54 A2
Spixworth Rd
  Hainford NR10 ....53 F4
  Horsham St Faith &
  Newton St Faith NR10 ...53 E2
  Norwich NR6 ....158 E5
Splash Leisure Complex
  NR26 ....138 B7
Splashes The PE37 ....153 B7
Spong La
  Carleton St Peter NR14 ..91 D5
  East Carleton NR14 ......88 F4
  Shropham NR17 ....103 C4
Spooner Row Prim Sch
  NR18 ....105 A8
Spooner Row Sta
  NR18 ....105 A8
Sporle Fst Sch PE32 ..65 D6
Sporle Rd
  Little Dunham PE32 .....65 D7
  Swaffham PE37 ....153 C5
Spring Cl PE30 ....148 C1

Spring Gr PE34 ....144 B4
Spring La
  Forncett NR16 ....106 B5
  Hempnall NR15 ....107 E3
  King's Lynn PE30 ....147 C7
  North Barsham NR22 ....16 A7
  Shouldham PE33 ....62 D4
  South Creake NR22 ......16 A6
  Yaxham NR19 ....68 B6
Spring Rd IP31 ....127 A1
Spring Sedge **4** PE30 ..147 A8
Spring View **1** PE31 ...12 D4
Springbank NR1 ....162 E2
Springdale Cres NR13 ..165 B4
Springdale Rd NR13 ...165 B4
Springfield NR13 ....166 C3
Springfield Cl
  Crimplesham PE33 ....80 B6
  Hemsby NR29 ....58 A4
Springfield N NR29 ....58 A4
Springfield Rd
  Great Yarmouth NR31 ..170 D4
  Hemsby NR29 ....58 A4
  Taverham NR8 ....155 C1
  Walpole St Andrew PE14 ..41 D4
Springfield Way NR31 ..86 B5
Springfield Wlk IP21 ..121 E5
Springfields
  Attleborough NR17 .....174 B5
  12 Poringland NR14 .....90 C5
Springfield Cl NR25 .....8 F5
Springles The **6** NR27 ..10 B5
Springvale **3** PE32 ....45 C6
Springwell La NR9 .....51 F6
Springwell Rd NR20 ...31 D2
Springwood
  Taverham NR8 ....155 E1
  Wootton NR35 ....108 A6
Springwood High Sch
  PE30 ....147 C6
Sprowston Fst & Mid Sch
  NR7 ....159 A4
Sprowston High Sch
  NR7 ....159 B3
Sprowston Rd NR3 ....158 F2
Sprowston Ret Pk
  NR7 ....159 C2
Spruce Ave **2** NR29 ...167 A2
Spruce Cl **2** PE31 .....133 B6
Spruce Cres **1** NR14 ..90 C5
Spruce Dr IP27 ....175 D2
Spruce Rd PE38 ....172 B6
Spur La NR14 ....90 C6
Spur Rd NR9 ....69 C2
Spurdens Cres NR28 ..151 D3
Spurge Sq **3** NR18 ...173 E4
Spynke Rd NR3 ....158 B3
Squire's Dr PE14 ....77 E3
Squire's Dro PE14 ......78 A3
Squire's Rd NR13 ....75 A2
Squires Hill PE33 ....63 B4
Stablefields IP26 ....99 C7
Stacy Rd NR3 ....162 E8
Staden Pk NR11 ....11 D1
Stafford Ave NR5 ......156 F1
Stafford Rd NR3 ....169 B2
Stafford St NR3 ....162 B6
Stag Pl PE30 ....147 A7
Stainsby Cl PE31 ......133 D4
Staithe Cl **3** NR12 .....55 E4
Staithe La PE36 ....2 C7
Staithe Rd
  Barton Turf NR12 ....38 F1
  Bishop St Peter NR34 ..111 C3
  Catfield NR29 ....56 D8
  Halvergate NR13 ....166 F1
  Heacham PE31 ....133 C5
  Hickling NR12 ....39 E1
  Langley with Hardley
  NR14 ....91 F4
  Ludham NR29 ....56 C5
  Marthan NR29 ....57 D5
  Repps with Bastwick
  NR29 ....56 F4
  Somerton NR29 ....57 E6
  Stalham NR12 ....39 B3
  Wisbech PE13 ....152 E5
Staithe Stree NR23 ...136 D6
Staithe The NR11 .....150 D8
Staitheway Rd NR12 ..164 C4
Stalham Firehouse Mus*
  NR12 ....39 B3
Stalham High Sch
  NR12 ....39 B4
Stalham Mid Sch NR12 ..39 B3
Stalham Rd
  Ashmanhaugh NR12 .....55 C8
  Hickling NR12 ....39 E2
  Sea Palling NR12 ....24 F1
  Wroxham/Hoveton
  NR12 ....164 D6
Stalland La NR18 ....86 D2
Stalham La NR18 ....86 D2
Stallett Way PE34 ......60 C8
Stan Petersen Cl NR1 ..163 A6
Standard Pl **10** NR30 ..169 D3
Standard Rd
  Great Yarmouth NR30 ..169 E3
  Wells-next-the-Sea
  NR23 ....136 C6
Standley Ct NR18 .....173 B4
Stanfield Rd
  Mileham PE32 ....48 E6
  Tittleshall PE32 ....48 C7
  Wymondham NR18 .....173 F3
Stanford Cres NR13 ....73 B7

Stanford Tuck Rd
  NR28 ....151 B7
Stanhoe Rd PE31 .....134 E4
Staniforth Rd IP24 ....176 B2
Stanley Ave
  Great Yarmouth NR31 ..170 C3
  Neatishead NR12 ....55 E7
  Norwich NR7 ....163 C5
Stanley Cl NR13 ....92 B6
Stanley Dr PE12 ....41 A8
Stanley Rd Diss IP22 ..177 B4
  Great Yarmouth NR30 ..169 C5
  North Walsham NR28 ..151 D6
Stanley St **10** PE30 ...146 E5
Stanley Terr NR30 .....169 D4
Stanleys La NR18 ......173 C2
Stanmore Rd NR7 .....163 E6
Stannard Cl **4** PE22 ..177 C4
Stannard Rd NR4 ......161 F5
Stanninghall Rd NR12 ..54 B4
Stanton Rd
  Barningham IP31 ....127 C2
  Dersingham PE31 ......140 C3
Star Farm Cl **21** NR31 ..94 C6
Star Hill NR12 ....24 C3
Star La
  Long Stratton NR15 ....106 E3
  1 Thetford IP24 ....176 C3
Tivetshall St Margaret
  NR15 ....121 C5
Star Mdw NR21 ....141 B4
Star Rd IP22 ....177 C4
Starling Cl NR11 ....150 C5
Starling Rd NR3 ....162 D8
Starling Rise NR27 .....11 B2
Starston La IP20 ......122 C1
Statham Cl NR4 ....162 B2
Station Appr
  Norwich NR1 ....178 C2
  12 Sheringham NR26 ..138 D7
  Wymondham NR18 .....173 C2
Station Cl
  East Dereham NR19 ...154 D6
  4 Lingwood NR13 ......74 A3
  6 Marthan NR29 ....57 D4
  Sheringham NR27 ....10 A5
  Swainsthorpe NR14 ....89 D4
Station Dr
  Fransham NR19 ....66 A8
  Heacham PE31 ....133 C5
  Wisbech PE13 ....152 C4
Station Gdns PE13 ...153 B5
Station Halt NR13 ......165 B3
Station Hill IP20 ....122 D2
Station La
  Garvestone NR9 ....68 D1
  Hethersett NR9 ....88 E7
  Thetford IP24 ....176 C5
  Thornham PE36 ....2 C6
Station New Rd NR13 ..165 D3
Station Rd Acle NR13 ..166 B2
  Alburgh IP20 ....123 A5
  Aldeby NR34 ....110 F6
  Attleborough NR17 ....174 E5
  Aylsham NR11 ....150 C6
  Barnham IP24 ....125 E6
  Beccles NR34 ....110 D1
  Brundall NR13 ....165 D2
  Burnham Market PE31 ..135 C3
  Burston & Shimpling
  IP21 ....120 F2
  Cantley NR13 ....92 C6
  Clenchwarton PE34 ....145 B4
  Coltishall NR12 ....54 C7
  Congham PE32 ....27 F3
  Corpusty NR11 ....19 F1
  Cromer NR27 ....139 D5
  Dersingham PE31 ......140 B8
  Diss IP22 ....177 F3
  Ditchingham NR35 .....109 B2
  Docking PE31 ....134 D5
  Downham Market PE38 ..172 A5
  2 Earsham NR35 ......123 F8
  East Dereham NR19 ...154 E4
  East Rudham PE31 .....30 B5
  East Winch PE32 ....44 F3
  Ellingham NR35 ....109 D3
  Flordon NR15 ....106 E8
  Forncett NR16 ....106 C4
  Foulsham NR20 ....33 C3
  Fransham NR19 ....66 B7
  Fulmodeston NR21 ......17 F4
  Geldeston NR34 ....109 F2
  Great Moulton NR15 ...121 A7
  Great Ryburgh NR21 ....32 B6
  Great Yarmouth NR31 ..169 B3
  Guestwick NR20 ....33 F5
  Haddiscoe NR14 ....93 D1
  Hardingham NR9 ....86 E8
  Harleston IP20 ....122 D2
  Heacham PE31 ....133 D6
  Hilgay PE38 ....96 C6
  Hindolveston NR20 .....33 A7
  Holme Hale IP25 ....65 F2
  Holt NR25 ....18 C6
  Honing NR28 ....38 C6
  Hopton on Sea NR31 ..171 D4
  Kimberley NR18 ....87 A6
  King's Lynn PE30 ......148 B5
  Lakenheath IP27 ....112 E3
  Lenwade NR9 ....51 E5
  Lingwood & Burlingham
  NR13 ....74 A3
  Middleton PE32 ....44 C4
  Mundesley NR11 ....143 B6
  North Elmham NR20 ....49 F7
  North Walsham NR28 ..151 B4

Station Rd continued
Ormesby St Margaret
  with Scratby NR29 .....167 B2
  5 Potter Heigham NR29 ..56 F6
  Pulham Market IP21 ...121 C4
  Pulham St Mary IP21 ...122 A4
  Quidenham NR16 ....118 E8
  Rackheath/Salhouse
  NR13 ....72 F8
  Reedham NR13 ....92 F5
  Reepham NR10 ....149 C5
  Roydon PE32 ....28 A2
  6 Sheringham NR27 .....10 A5
  Sheringham NR26 .....138 D7
  Snettisham PE31 ....12 D4
  Somerleyton, Ashby &
  Herringfleet NR32 .....111 C7
  South Wootton PE31 ...149 C5
  Stanhoe PE31 ....14 E8
  Strumpshaw NR13 ......91 F8
  Taverham NR8 ....156 F8
  Terrington St Clement
  PE34 ....144 C2
  Thetford IP24 ....176 C5
  Thorpe Market NR11 ....22 A6
  Tilney All Saints PE34 ..144 F2
  Tittleshall St Margaret
  NR15 ....121 B7
  Walsingham NR22 ....16 F7
  Walsoken PE14 ....59 E4
  Watlington PE33 ....61 C6
  Wells-next-the-Sea
  NR23 ....136 D5
  Wendling NR19 ....66 F7
  West Dereham PE33 .....80 B3
  Weybourne NR25 ....8 F5
  Whinburgh & Westfield
  NR19 ....68 A5
  Worstead NR28 ....37 F3
  Wroxham/Hoveton
  NR12 ....164 C5
  Wymondham NR18 .....173 C3
Station Rd Ind Est
  NR17 ....174 E4
Station Rd N
  Belton NR31 ....93 H6
  Walpole Cross Keys PE14 ..41 F5
Station Rd S
  Belton NR31 ....93 F5
  Walpole Cross Keys PE14 ..41 F5
Station St PE37 ....153 B5
Station Terr IP27 ......175 C5
Station Way IP27 ......175 C5
Station Yd PE13 ....153 B5
  Steam Mill La NR31 ...169 B4
Stearne Cl IP24 ....176 B2
Stebbings Cl **3** PE32 ..28 A1
Steel's Dro PE38 ....79 C1
Steepgreen Cl NR1 ...163 C8
Steeple Chase NR8 ...155 F2
Steeple La NR15 ....106 A2
Steeple View PE13 ....153 B4
Steeps The **5** NR30 ..169 D1
Steer Rd PE31 ....27 B8
Stegg's La NR19 ....67 F4
Steggles Dr IP22 ......177 C5
Stephen Beaumont Way
  NR19 ....154 F2
Stephenson Cl
  3 Great Yarmouth NR30 ..169 D5
  West Raynham Airfield
  NR21 ....30 B3
Stephenson Way IP24 ..176 A2
Stephenson Way Ind Est
  IP24 ....176 A2
Stepping La NR1 ....178 A2
Stepping Stone La
  NR12 ....39 A4
Steppings La NR15 ...107 C3
Stepshort NR31 ....94 A6
Stermyn St **22** PE13 ..152 C5
Steven's La
  Ashwellthorpe NR16 ...106 A8
  Wreningham NR16 ....88 E1
Stevens Cl IP25 ....84 D4
Stevens Rd
  Cromer NR27 ....139 C4
  2 Little Snoring NR21 ..17 B3
Stevenson Rd NR5 ....161 B7
Steward Cl **1** NR18 ..173 D5
Steward St **1** NR18 ..162 E8
Steward Way NR19 ...154 C5
Stewards Cl NR10 .....149 C4
Stewkey Hall Drift NR9 ..52 F5
Stibbard Rd NR21 ....32 A5
Stickfer La NR16 ....106 A6
Stiffkey Cl **8** PE33 ....61 D6
Stiffkey Rd Warham NR23 ..5 F5
  Wells-next-the-Sea
  NR23 ....136 F5
Stigand's Gate NR9 ...154 D7
Stile Cl **12** NR18 ......173 E4
Stile La NR18 ....173 E4
Stillington Cl NR7 .....159 B3
Stilwell Dr NR5 ....154 C8
Stirling Cl
  Downham Market PE38 ..172 D6
  Taverham NR8 ....155 F3
Stirling Rd
  Old Catton NR6 ....158 C6
  Scolthorpe Airfield NR21 ..31 C5
Stirrups La NR12 ....38 D3
Stitch The PE14 ....77 B8
Stock Lea Rd **1** NR18 ..173 E4
Stockholm Way NR5 ...160 F7
Stocks Hill NR9 ....160 B5
Stocks La NR13 ....165 C5

Sou - Str **209**

Stockton Rd NR14 .....110 A3
Stody Dr PE30 ....148 E1
Stody Rd NR24 ....18 D6
Stoke Holy Cross Prim Sch
  NR14 ....89 F4
Stoke La NR14 ....89 F5
Stoke Rd
  Barton Bendish PE33 ....81 C5
  Bixley NR14 ....162 F1
  Boughton PE33 ....81 A4
  Caistor St Edmund NR14 ..89 F7
  Methwold IP26 ....90 B5
  Poringland NR14 ....90 B5
  Wereham PE33 ....80 E4
  Wormegay PE33 ....62 A5
Stokes Ave IP25 ....84 C3
Stokesby New Rd
  NR13 ....166 F6
Stokesby Rd NR29 .....75 D6
Stone Breck NR5 ......156 E2
Stone Brigg NR18 ......87 A7
Stone Cl **2** PE33 ....61 D5
Stone Hill Rd NR30 ...168 D6
Stone House Cl NR6 ..158 D2
Stone La Bintree NR20 ..33 B3
  5 Hingham NR9 ....86 C4
  Hoveton NR12 ....164 D8
  Runhall NR9 ....68 F3
Stone Rd **6** Beetley NR20 ..49 D4
  6 Beetley NR20 ....49 D4
  Briston NR24 ....142 E2
  East Dereham NR19 ...154 C2
  Great Yarmouth NR31 ..169 B4
  Halvergate NR13 ....75 A1
  Hockering NR20 ....51 B1
  Mattishall NR20 ....68 C6
  Norwich NR3 ....158 C1
  Strumpshaw NR13 ......73 F1
Stone St IP19 ....124 F1
Stonebridge Rd NR28 ..23 D2
Stonecross Rd PE38 ..172 D5
Stonecutters Way
  NR30 ....169 C4
Stonefield Rd NR25 ....20 A8
Stonegate
  Aylsham NR11 ....150 A3
  Morley NR18 ....87 A3
Stonegate St PE30 ...146 D4
Stonehill Way NR17 ....10 C4
Stonehouse Rd
  Norwich NR1 ....159 B4
  Salhouse NR13 ....72 E5
  Upwell PE14 ....77 E5
Stoney Cl NR13 ....166 F6
Stoney End **2** NR20 ...68 F6
Stoney La Beetley NR20 ..49 B4
  Reepham NR10 ....149 B6
Stoney Rd PE32 ....27 F2
Stony La
  Attleborough NR17 ....174 B6
  Pulham Market IP21 ...121 E7
  Ravenningham NR14 ...110 B6
  Tivetshall St Margaret
  NR15 ....121 B5
Wortwell IP20 ....122 F4
Stores St IP22 ....175 C3
Story's La NR16 ......105 E5
Stow Barn Rd PE33 ....80 A7
Stow Bedon Rd IP24 ..102 C7
Stow Bridge Rd
  Stow Bardolph PE34 ....61 D1
  Wimbotsham PE34 ......79 E8
Stow Gdns PE13 ......152 E4
Stow Rd PE14 ....152 E4
Stow Rd Outwell PE14 ..78 A7
  Runcton Holme PE33 ....62 B3
Wiggenhall St Mary Magdalen
  PE34 ....61 B5
Wisbech PE13 ....152 F5
Stow Windmill*
  NR28 ....143 D4
Stowlay La NR17 ......103 B6
Stracey Rd Lamas NR10 ..36 F1
  Norwich NR1 ....163 A5
Strachan Cl PE31 .....133 C5
Stradbroke CE Prim Sch
  IP21 ....131 E1
Stradbroke Prim Sch
  NR31 ....170 C5
Stradbroke Rd NR31 ..170 C5
Stradsett Cl **4** PE38 ..172 D6
Straight La NR18 ......122 D2
Strangers Hall* NR2 ..178 A3
Strangers Way NR19 ...68 A5
Strasbourg Way NR19 ..154 E1
Stratford Cl
  Dersingham PE31 ......140 E3
  Norwich NR1 ....162 F2
Stratford Cres NR1 ...161 C1
Stratford Dr NR1 ......162 A4
Stratton Cl **6** PE37 ..153 C3
Stratton Rd
  Hainford NR10 ....53 E8
  Stratton Strawless NR10 ..53 E8
  Wacton NR15 ....106 C5
Straw Mus The* NR11 ..21 D3
Strawberry Cl **9** NR13 ..173 E4
Strawberry Fields NR12 ..39 B3
Strayground La NR18 ..173 B2
Street The Acle NR13 ..166 C3
  Alburgh IP20 ....122 F6

Street The continued
Aldborough NR11 ......20 F5
Aldeby NR34 ......110 F4
Ashby St Mary NR14 ....91 C5
Ashwellthorpe NR16 ....106 A8
Aslacton NR15 ......106 A1
Aylmerton NR11 ......10 A2
Baconsthorpe NR25 ....19 F8
Bacton NR28 ......23 B2
Barnham IP24 ......125 E6
Barton Turf NR12 ......55 E8
Bawdeswell NR20 ......50 E7
Beachamwell PE37 ......81 E8
Beeston with Bittering PE32 ......48 C2
Belaugh NR12 ......164 A6
Bergh Apton NR15 ......91 A3
Billingford NR20 ......50 B7
Bintree NR20 ......33 B2
Blo' Norton IP22 ......128 B6
Booton NR10 ......149 E4
Botesdale IP22 ......128 E2
Bracon Ash NR14 ......89 A3
Bramerton NR14 ......90 F7
Brampton NR10 ......36 E3
Brandon IP27 ......175 A3
Bressingham IP22 ......119 D2
Bridgham NR16 ......117 E4
Brinton NR24 ......18 D6
Brockdish IP21 ......131 D6
Brome & Oakley IP23 ....130 C3
Brooke NR15 ......90 E2
Brundall NR13 ......165 E5
Burgh & Tuttington NR11 ..36 E4
Caston NR17 ......102 E8
Catfield NR29 ......56 C8
Claxton NR14 ......91 D6
Coltishall NR12 ......54 E7
Coney Weston IP31 ......127 B4
Corpusty NR11 ......19 F1
Costessey NR8 ......156 E5
Croxton IP24 ......116 C6
Dickleburgh IP21 ......121 B1
Dilham NR28 ......38 D4
Earsham NR35 ......123 F8
East Tuddenham NR20 ....69 C6
Erpingham NR11 ......21 A2
Felthorpe NR10 ......155 C8
Flixton NR35 ......123 E6
Flordon NR15 ......106 D8
Foxley NR20 ......50 D8
Framingham Pigot NR14 ..90 D6
Fulmodeston NR21 ......17 F3
Garvestone NR9 ......68 B1
Geldeston NR34 ......109 F2
Gooderstone PE33 ......83 E5
Great Cressingham IP25 ...83 C4
Great Snoring NR21 ......17 A5
Great Yarmouth NR30 ....76 F5
Halvergate NR13 ......74 F1
Hempnall NR15 ......107 C5
Hemsby NR29 ......167 A7
Hevingham NR10 ......53 C8
Heydon NR11 ......34 F6
Hickling NR12 ......39 F2
Hinderclay IP22 ......128 C3
Hindolveston NR20 ......33 D8
Hindringham NR21 ......17 E7
Hockering NR20 ......69 B8
Honingham NR9 ......69 E6
Horsey NR29 ......40 E1
Kelling NR25 ......8 C5
Ketteringham NR18 ......88 E6
Kettlestone NR21 ......17 C2
Knapton NR28 ......143 B1
Lamas NR10 ......37 A1
Lessingham NR12 ......24 D3
Little Barningham NR11 ...20 B4
Little Snoring NR21 ......17 B3
Long Stratton NR15 ......106 E3
Lound NR32 ......94 C2
Marham PE33 ......63 B5
Market Weston IP22 ......127 E4
Marlingford NR9 ......69 E4
Mautby NR29 ......75 E5
Melton Constable NR24 ..142 A6
Mileham PE32 ......48 D6
Morning Thorpe NR15 ....107 C4
Morston NR25 ......7 A6
Morton on the Hill NR9 ...52 A3
North Lopham IP22 ......119 E2
North Pickenham PE37 ...65 E1
Norwich NR14 ......163 B2
Ovington IP25 ......84 E5
Poringland NR14 ......90 F5
Pulham St Mary IP21 ....122 A3
Redenhall with Harleston IP20 ......122 F1
Redgrave IP22 ......128 E5
Reepham NR10 ......149 C3
Riddlesworth IP22 ......127 D7
Ringland NR8 ......70 B8
Rockland St Mary NR14 ..91 B7
Rocklands NR17 ......103 C7
Rougham PE32 ......47 B7
Ryburgh NR21 ......32 C7
St Margaret, South Elmham IP20 ......123 E2
St Michael South Elmham IP19 ......124 A8
Salle NR10 ......149 D8
Saxlingham Nethergate NR15 ......107 B8
Scoulton NR9 ......85 D3

Street The continued
Sculthorpe NR21 ......16 B1
Sculthorpe Airfield PE31 ...15 B3
Sea Palling NR12 ......40 A5
Shelton NR15 ......122 B8
Shotesham NR15 ......90 A2
Somerleyton, Ashby & Herringfleet NR32 ......111 D8
Somerton NR29 ......57 F6
South Lopham IP22 ......128 D8
South Pickenham PE37 ....83 D7
South Walsham NR13 ....74 A8
Sparham NR9 ......51 B4
Sporle with Palgrave PE32 ......65 C7
Starston IP20 ......122 C3
Surlingham NR14 ......165 B1
Sustead NR11 ......20 E7
Swafield NR28 ......151 D8
Swanton Abbott NR10 ....37 C4
Swanton Novers NR24 ....18 C2
Taverham NR8 ......156 B8
Tharston & Hapton NR15 ......106 C7
Themelthorpe NR20 ......33 F2
Thornage NR25 ......18 E6
Thurlton NR14 ......92 F1
Thurne NR29 ......56 E2
Thurton NR14 ......91 C3
Tibenham NR16 ......120 E8
Tivetshall St Mary NR15 ..121 B5
Topcroft NR35 ......107 F3
Warham NR23 ......6 A4
Waterloo IP21 ......130 C5
Wattisfield IP22 ......128 A1
Wellingham PE32 ......47 F8
West Beckham NR25 ......9 B2
Weybourne NR25 ......8 E5
Winfarthing IP22 ......120 B4
Witton NR28 ......23 E1
Wiveton NR25 ......7 E6
Woodton NR35 ......108 C5
Stretton Sch NR2 ......162 C3
Strickland Ave 9 PE31 ..12 E4
Strickland Cl 8 PE31 ....12 E4
Stringside Dro PE33 ......81 B3
Strumpshaw Rd NR13 ...165 E3
Strumpshaw Steam Mus* NR13 ......73 E1
Stuart Cl Brandon IP27 ..175 C3
Great Yarmouth NR31 ...170 B4
7 Hethersett NR9 ......88 D8
Stuart Gdns NR1 ......178 C3
Stuart Rd
Aylsham NR11 ......150 C7
Norwich NR1 ......178 C1
Stubb Rd NR12 ......39 F2
Stubbs Cl PE38 ......172 E5
Stubbs Gn La NR14 ......109 E8
Sturdee Ave NR30 ......169 D8
Sturdee Cl IP24 ......176 F6
Sturmy Cl 15 NR15 ......106 E3
Stuston La IP21 ......130 B4
Stuston Rd IP21 ......130 B5
Style Loke NR9 ......69 F2
Style Cl NR31 ......170 A4
Styman Rd NR5 ......161 A7
Suckling Ave NR3 ......158 B3
Suckling Dro PE14 ......78 C5
Suckling La
Framingham Pigot NR14 ...90 D6
Hickling NR12 ......39 F3
Suckling Pl NR35 ......108 E5
Suckling La
Suffield Cl
1 Cringleford NR4 ......89 B8
3 Long Stratton NR15 ...106 D3
North Walsham NR28 ....151 A6
Suffield Ct NR6 ......158 D2
Suffield Pk Inf Sch NR27 ......139 C5
Suffield Rd NR11 ......170 C4
Suffield Way PE30 ......147 B8
Suffling Rd NR30 ......170 D8
Suffolk Ave IP31 ......126 B1
Suffolk Cl NR31 ......170 C7
Suffolk Ct IP27 ......175 C4
Suffolk Pl NR14 ......90 C6
Suffolk Rd
Great Yarmouth NR31 ...170 C8
King's Lynn PE30 ......147 C6
Norwich NR4 ......161 C3
Sheringham NR26 ......138 D6
Suffolk Sq NR2 ......162 C5
Suffolk Wlk NR32 ......161 D3
Sugar La NR13 ......140 E4
Sukey Way NR5 ......160 F6
Summer Cl 4 PE14 ......41 E4
Summer Dr NR12 ......164 D6
Summer La IP25 ......85 A4
Summerfield Cl PE13 ....152 A6
Summerfield Rd NR29 ...58 A4
Summerhouse Cl NR27 ......139 A6
Sumpter Rd NR4 ......161 E3
Sun Barn Rd NR10 ......149 B4
Sun Barn Wlk NR10 ......149 B4
Sun La
Great Yarmouth NR31 ....94 C6
Norwich NR3 ......158 D1
Sun Rd NR35 ......109 B2
Sunart Ln NR17 ......174 E6
Suncroft NR1 ......162 F2
Sunderland Cl NR6 ......158 C6
Sundew Cl 6 IP24 ......176 F4
Sunk Rd NR22 ......16 F7
Sunley Cl NR35 ......109 C2
Sunningdale NR4 ......162 A2
Sunninghill Cl 14 NR31 ...94 C8

Sunny Cl NR5 ......157 B1
Sunny Cnr NR28 ......151 B4
Sunny Gr NR5 ......161 B8
Sunny Hill NR1 ......162 E2
Sunnyside
Bedingham NR35 ......108 C4
Diss IP22 ......177 D5
Heacham PE31 ......133 D5
Sunnyside Ave 10 NR14 ..90 C5
Sunnyside Cl PE31 ......133 D5
Sunnyside Rd PE32 ......29 D2
Sunsalve Ride NR19 ....154 C1
Sunset Gdns PE13 ......152 E2
Sunset Wlk NR12 ......24 E4
Supple Cl NR1 ......163 C7
Surlingham Dr PE37 ....153 B1
Surlingham La
Bramerton NR14 ......90 F8
Rockland St Mary NR14 ...91 B8
Surlingham Prim Sch NR14 ......73 B1
Surrey Cl NR7 ......159 C5
Surrey Gr NR1 ......178 B1
Surrey St Cromer NR27 ..139 C7
8 King's Lynn PE30 ......146 D5
Norwich NR1 ......178 B1
9 Wiggenhall St Germans PE34 ......43 B1
Surrogate St NR17 ......174 D5
Sursham Ave NR6 ......158 F4
Sussex Rd NR31 ......170 D5
Sussex St NR3 ......178 A4
Sustead La NR11 ......20 F8
Sustead Rd NR11 ......9 F1
Suters Dr NR8 ......155 E2
Sutherland Ave NR6 ....158 A4
Sutherland Ct Gdns NR27 ......139 C6
Suton La NR18 ......173 A1
Sutton Cres NR13 ......90 B8
Sutton Est PE33 ......135 C2
Sutton Fst Sch NR12 ......39 C2
Sutton Lea PE31 ......133 C4
Sutton Mdws PE13 ......152 A8
Sutton Rd Catfield NR29 ..39 C1
Great Yarmouth NR30 ...169 D1
Hickling NR12 ......39 E2
Swafield PE37 ......153 B1
Terrington St Clement PE34 ......144 A4
Walpole Cross Keys NR14 ..42 A7
Wisbech PE13 ......152 A7
Sutton Windmill & Broads Mus* NR12 ......39 D2
Suttons Cl 1 PE14 ......77 F6
Swaffham Com Hospl PE37 ......153 B2
Swaffham Gap IP26 ......82 C1
Swaffham Greenhoe Mid Sch PE37 ......153 B2
Swaffham Leisure Ctr PE37 ......153 B4
Swaffham Mus* PE37 ...153 B4
Swaffham Raceway PE37 ......64 C4
Swaffham Rd
Ashill IP25 ......84 A7
Barton Bendish PE33 ......63 E5
Cockley Cley PE37 ......82 D7
East Dereham NR19 ....154 D6
Mundford IP26 ......100 B4
Narborough PE32 ......63 F7
Oxborough PE33 ......81 E4
Raynham NR21 ......30 F2
Swaffham PE37 ......64 A4
Watton IP25 ......84 D5
Swaffham VC Fst Sch PE37 ......153 C4
Swafield Rise NR28 ....151 D7
Swafield St NR5 ......160 F7
Swale The NR5 ......160 F6
Swallow Cl 6 NR31 ......170 A7
Swallow Dr IP27 ......175 E3
Swallowfield Rd PE30 ...147 C4
Swallowtail Cl NR5 ......160 F5
Swamp La
Great Ellingham NR17 ...103 F7
Roydon IP22 ......177 A6
Swan Cl Aylsham NR11 ..150 C6
Swannington NR9 ......52 B5
Swan Cotts PE32 ......47 D5
Swan Dr NR20 ......49 C3
Swan Entry 2 IP20 ......122 E7
Swan La
Coney Weston IP31 ......127 B4
Fincham PE33 ......62 E1
King's Lynn PE30 ......147 A6
1 Norwich NR2 ......178 B3
Redenhall with Harleston IP20 ......122 D2
Shipdham IP25 ......67 C3
Swan Loke NR28 ......151 C5
Swan Rd NR19 ......154 E4
Swan St
Horsham St Faith NR10 ...53 D2
Swan Terr 1 PE38 ......172 A6
Swangey La NR17 ......103 D4
Swann Gr NR25 ......137 C6
Swanns Yd NR28 ......38 A4
Swanscroft NR28 ......38 A5
Swansea Rd NR2 ......162 C4
Swansgate NR8 ......168 E6
Swanston's Rd NR30 ...170 D8
Swanton Abbot Rd NR10 ......37 A5

Swanton Abbott Com Sch NR10 ......37 B5
Swanton Ave NR19 ....154 E7
Swanton Cl NR19 ......154 E7
Swanton Dr NR20 ......154 E6
Swanton Gr NR19 ......154 E6
Swanton Morley Prim Sch NR20 ......50 B4
Swanton Morley Rd
Hoe NR20 ......50 A6
North Elmham NR20 ......49 F6
Swanton Rd
Dereham NR20 ......50 A1
East Dereham NR19 ....154 E6
Gunthorpe NR24 ......18 B5
Norwich NR3 ......162 B8
Swardeston La NR14 ....89 B6
Swargate La NR15 ......108 E8
Swash La NR13 ......54 D2
Sweden Pl IP27 ......175 B2
Sweet Briar Rd
7 Long Stratton NR15 ..106 E3
Norwich NR6 ......161 F8
Sweet Briar Rd Ind Est NR3 ......157 F1
Sweetacres 7 ......12 E5
Sweetbriar Gdns NR20 ..49 C4
Sweetbriar La
Edgefield NR24 ......19 D5
Sheringham NR26 ......138 C7
Sweyn Cl IP24 ......176 B2
Swim Rd NR29 ......75 F6
Swinbourne Cl NR6 ....158 E3
Swindells Cl NR5 ......157 A2
Swingy La NR18 ......87 A3
Swirle's Pl 6 NR30 ....169 D4
Swiss Terr PE30 ......146 F5
Sybil Rd PE13 ......152 C6
Sybil Wheeler Cl 8 IP24 ......176 D6
Sycamore Ave
16 Great Yarmouth NR31 ..94 C7
25 Martham NR29 ......57 D5
Wymondham NR18 ......173 E6
Sycamore Cl
Attleborough NR17 ....174 C4
King's Lynn PE30 ......148 D2
8 London NR14 ......91 F1
North Walsham NR28 ....151 D6
Thompson IP24 ......102 A7
Sycamore Covert IP24 ......116 D2
Sycamore Cres NR12 ..161 F7
Sycamore Gn 2 NR31 ..170 B6
Sycamore Gr NR26 ....138 D5
Sycamore Way IP22 ....177 F5
Sycamores The NR19 ...154 E3
Sydenham Cl NR13 ....166 B4
Syderstone Comm Nature Reserve* PE31 ......15 A3
Syderstone Rd NR21 ....15 B3
Sydney Dye Ct PE32 ....65 C5
Sydney Rd 11 NR10 ....54 A2
Sydney St 2 PE30 ....146 E5
Syers La PE32 ......48 D2
Syleham Hall La IP21 ...131 F5
Syleham Rd IP21 ......131 B4
Sylvan Cl NR6 ......157 E6
Sylvan Way
2 Blofield Heath NR13 ...73 C6
Taverham NR8 ......156 E8
Sylvden Dr PE13 ......152 F6
Symonds Ave NR29 ....167 C2
Syon Cl PE38 ......172 B4
Sywell Cl NR6 ......158 F6
Sywell Gr 5 PE14 ......59 A1

T

Tabernacle La NR16 ....105 F4
Tacolneston VC Prim Sch NR16 ......105 F6
Tagg Way 3 NR13 ......72 E7
Talbot Cl NR18 ......173 C5
Talbot Sq NR3 ......178 A4
Talbots Mdw IP21 ......130 B5
Tales of the Old Gaol House* PE30 ......146 D4
Taleworth Cl NR5 ......161 A7
Tallon St IP26 ......82 A2
Tamarind Mews NR4 ...161 E1
Tamarisk PE30 ......148 B1
Tamworth La NR11 ......169 B2
Tan La NR30 ......168 C8
Tanager Cl NR18 ......158 D3
Tanner St 4 IP24 ......176 C4
Tanners Gn NR9 ......68 C3
Tanns La IP22 ......119 A2
Tansy Cl NR6 ......158 D4
Tantallon Dr NR17 ......174 F6
Tar Works Rd NR30 ....169 C6
Target Hill IP20 ......123 B2
Tarragon Cl 7 NR31 ....94 C6
Tarragon Rd PE38 ......172 D7
Tas Valley Vineyard* NR15 ......106 A3
Tasburgh Rd NR15 ....106 F8
Tasman Dr NR11 ......22 F8
Tatterford Dr NR21 ......30 C4
Tattersett Pk Bsns Ctr NR21 ......15 C1
Tattersett Rd IP21 ......121 E5
Tattlepot Rd IP21 ......121 E5
Tavern Cl NR30 ......168 D4
Taverham Chase NR8 ..156 D8
Taverham Hall Sch NR8 ......156 A8

Taverham High Sch NR8 ......155 B2
Taverham La NR8 ......156 C6
Taverham Mid Sch NR8 ......156 C8
Taverham Rd
Felthorpe NR10 ......155 C7
Honingham NR9 ......69 F6
Taverham NR8 ......156 D8
Tavern Cl NR20 ......49 D4
Tavern La Diss IP22 ....177 F3
East Dereham NR19 ....154 E3
Tavistock Rd PE13 ......152 D5
Tawney Sedge 3 PE30 ..147 A8
Taylor Ave 3 NR8 ......89 B8
Taylor Rd Diss IP22 ....177 B4
Norwich NR5 ......161 C6
Taylor's La
Gressenhall NR20 ......49 C3
Norwich NR6 ......158 D6
Trimingham NR11 ......11 E1
Taylors Loke
3 Cley next the Sea NR25 ...7 E6
1 Hemsby NR29 ......167 A8
Taymor Pl PE14 ......95 D4
Teal Cl 8 ......12 E5
Teal Wlk Brandon IP27 ..175 F4
10 Great Yarmouth NR31 ...94 C8
Teasel Cl NR20 ......168 A8
Teasel Dr IP24 ......176 E5
Teasel Rd NR17 ......174 B4
Teasel Rise 4 NR26 ..138 B6
Tebbutt Ave 6 NR19 ..154 C3
Ted Ellis Nature Reserve* NR14 ......91 D8
Tedder Cl
5 Barnham IP24 ......125 F6
15 Watton IP25 ......84 E3
Tee Cl 4 NR14 ......89 B2
Telegraph La E NR1 ....163 B6
Telegraph La W 4 NR1 .163 A6
Telford Cl
King's Lynn PE30 ......147 D4
2 Norwich NR3 ......157 F1
Telford Way IP24 ......176 B6
Temple Cl NR25 ......8 F6
Temple Dr NR13 ......165 B8
Temple Rd
Great Yarmouth NR30 ...169 D4
King's Lynn PE30 ......148 D1
Norwich NR3 ......158 D1
Templemead La NR25 ..137 F8
Ten Bell La NR2 ......162 C7
Ten Mile Bank
Hilgay PE38 ......96 F6
Littleport CB6 ......96 E1
Ten Mile Bank Prim Sch PE38 ......96 F7
Tennyson Ave PE30 ....146 F4
Tennyson Rd
3 Diss IP22 ......177 E4
3 Great Yarmouth NR30 .169 D8
King's Lynn PE30 ......148 F4
Tennyson Way IP24 ....176 E6
Tensing St NR35 ......108 C5
Terence Airey Ct 25 IP20 ......122 D2
Terence Ave NR7 ......159 A4
Teresa Rd 6 NR12 ......39 B4
Tern Cl 9 IP25 ......84 C3
Tern Rd NR31 ......170 A6
Tern Rd NR29 ......167 C5
Terr The 10 NR28 ......151 C5
Terrace Wlk NR1 ......178 B1
Terrington Cl 3 PE14 ...59 D2
Terrington St Clements Sch PE34 ......144 C6
Terrington St John Prim Sch PE14 ......60 B8
Testerton Cotts NR21 ....32 A6
Texas Ave NR21 ......15 C2
Texel Way NR11 ......143 A7
Thacker Way NR5 ......160 F6
Thain's La NR27 ......10 B5
Thames Way 8 NR30 ..168 C6
Thamesfield Way NR31 ......169 B2
Thatchwood Ave PE14 ..59 C2
Theatre Plain NR30 ....169 C4
Theatre Rd NR23 ......136 C6
Theatre St
East Dereham NR19 ....154 D6
Norwich NR2 ......178 A2
Swaffham PE37 ......153 B4
Thelnetham Rd
Blo' Norton IP22 ......128 F5
Hopton IP22 ......127 F5
Theobald Rd NR1 ......89 E8
Thetford Ancient House Mus* IP24 ......176 C4
Thetford Cottage Hospl IP24 ......176 D4
Thetford Gram Sch IP24 ......176 D4
Thetford Priory* IP24 ......176 C4
Thetford Rd
Brandon IP27 ......175 E3
Coney Weston IP31 ....127 B4
Euston IP24 ......126 B6
Garboldisham IP22 ....128 F7
Northwold IP26 ......99 B8
Santon Downham IP27 ..115 B5
Watton IP25 ......84 B2
Wretham IP24 ......117 A7
Thetford Sta IP24 ......176 C5

Wesley Cl
Downham Market PE38 . . .172 B5
⬛4⬛ Mattishall NR20 . . . . . . .68 E6
Mundesley NR11 . . . . .143 D5
Terrington St Clement
PE34 . . . . .144 B5
Wesley Rd
King's Lynn PE30 . . . . .148 C5
Terrington St Clement
PE34 . . . . .144 B5
Wessex St NR2 . . . . .178 A1
**West Acre Gdns*
PE32 . . . . .46 D4
West Acre Rd PE37 . . . .153 A6
West Ave
Great Yarmouth NR31 . . . .170 C3
Ormesby St Margaret
NR29 . . . . .167 A3
West Carr Rd NR17 . . . .174 A4
West Church St NR16 . .119 A5
West Cl NR5 . . . . .157 A2
West Cliff
Cromer NR27 . . . . .139 B7
Sheringham NR26 . . . . . . .138 D7
West Cres NR20 . . . . .50 A5
West Croft NR9 . . . . .88 C7
West Dereham Rd
PE33 . . . . .80 D3
West Dr Brandon IP27 . .175 A2
⬛1⬛ Friday Bridge PE14 . . . .77 A8
West Dro N PE14 . . . . .59 D8
West Dro S PE14 . . . . .59 E8
West Earlham Fst Sch
NR5 . . . . .161 D6
West Earlham Mid Sch
NR5 . . . . .161 D6
West End Briston NR24 . .142 F5
Costessey NR8 . . . . .156 C4
Hilgay PE38 . . . . .79 D1
Northwold IP26 . . . . .99 B8
West End Ave
Brundall NR13 . . . . .165 A4
Costessey NR8 . . . . .156 C5
West End Ct NR2 . . . . . . .84 C3
West End St NR22 . . . . . .162 B7
West Flegg Mid Sch
NR29 . . . . .57 D5
West Gate NR18 . . . . . . .173 B4
West Hall Rd
Dersingham PE31 . . . . . . .140 D3
Mundford IP26 . . . . .100 B4
West Harling Rd NR16 . .118 B4
West Head Rd PE34 . . . . .78 F8
West Herne La IP22 . . . .128 D5
West La NR10 . . . . .53 D1
West Lexham Hall
PE32 . . . . .47 C4
West Lynn Cty Prim Sch
PE34 . . . . .146 C5
West Parade
Norwich NR2 . . . . .162 B6
Wisbech PE13 . . . . .152 C6
West Pottergate NR2 . . .162 B6
West Raynham Prim Sch
NR21 . . . . .30 F4
West Raynham Rd
NR21 . . . . .30 F4
West Rd
Caister-on-Sea NR30 . . . . .168 D4
Dersingham PE31 . . . . . . .140 D3
Great Yarmouth NR30 . . . .168 F1
Norwich NR5 . . . . .157 A2
Ormesby St Margaret
NR29 . . . . .167 A2
Shouldham Thorpe PE33 . . .62 C2
Tacolneston NR16 . . . . . . .105 F4
Watton IP25 . . . . .84 D3
West Caister NR30 . . . . . .168 A4
West Runton Sta NR27 . . . .10 A5
West St
North Creake NR21 . . . . . . .4 D1
Wisbech PE13 . . . . .152 C4
West Stree ⬛18⬛ NR30 . . .169 D2
West Tofts St IP26 . . . . .100 D3
West View
Dereham NR19 . . . . .154 E1
South Pickenham PE37 . . . .83 D7
West View Rd NR13 . . . . .74 A2
West View Rd NR13 . . . .165 E6
West Way
Downham Market PE38 . . .172 B4
Stow Bardolph PE34 . . . . . .61 D1
Tacolneston NR16 . . . . . . .105 E5
Wimbotsham PE34 . . . . . . .79 D8
West Winch Prim Sch
PE33 . . . . .43 E2
West Winch Rd PE33 . . . .43 E2
West Wood Cotts NR21 . . .32 B5
Westacre Dr NR6 . . . . . .158 F7
Westbourne Rd NR12 . . . .54 D7
Westbriggs Dro PE33 . . . .62 B5
Westbrook Ave ⬛2⬛ NR12 . .39 B4
Westcliff Ave NR27 . . . .139 A7
Westerley Cl NR30 . . . . .168 D4
Westerley Way NR30 . . . .168 D4
Western Ave NR7 . . . . . .163 E6
Western Bypass NR11 . . .150 B5
Western Cl ⬛4⬛ IP26 . . . . . .98 D1
Western Rd NR31 . . . . . .170 C4
Westfield Ave NR23 . . . .136 C6
Westfield Cl ⬛2⬛ NR29 . . .57 D1
Westfield Inf Sch IP25 . . . .84 D3
Westfield La NR19 . . . . .154 F1
Westfield Rd
Brundall NR13 . . . . .165 A4
East Dereham NR19 . . . . .154 E2
Swaffham PE37 . . . . .153 B4
Wisbech PE13 . . . . .152 E7

Westfields
Attleborough NR17 . . . . . .174 B4
King's Lynn PE30 . . . . . . .147 C4
Narborough PE32 . . . . .63 E7
Westfields Cl
Terrington St John PE14 . . . .60 C8
Tilney St Lawrence PE34 . . .42 C1
Westgate
Hevingham NR10 . . . . .53 B8
Hunstanton PE36 . . . . . . .132 C4
Norwich NR6 . . . . .157 F5
Shropham NR17 . . . . .103 B4
Walsingham NR22 . . . . .16 F1
Westgate Cl NR2 . . . . . . .162 A4
Westgate Ct NR18 . . . . . .173 B4
Westgate Gn NR10 . . . . . .53 B8
Westgate Rd PE36 . . . . . . .1 F6
Westgate St
Hevingham NR10 . . . . .52 B8
Hilborough IP26 . . . . .83 A3
Holme next the Sea PE36 . . .2 A6
Shouldham PE33 . . . . .62 D4
Southery PE38 . . . . .97 A5
Westhall IP21 . . . . .131 F1
Westhorpe Cl ⬛3⬛ PE30 . .147 A8
Westland Chase PE33 . . . .43 F1
Westlegate NR1 . . . . . . .178 B2
Westmark PE30 . . . . .147 A8
Westmead Ave PE13 . . . .152 E2
Westmead Rd NR21 . . . .141 C4
Weston Cl ⬛1⬛ NR13 . . . . . .73 C6
Weston Ct NR6 . . . . .158 F6
Weston Miller Dr
PE13 . . . . .152 C4
Weston Rd Easton NR9 . . .70 A7
Norwich NR3 . . . . .158 C3
⬛17⬛ Wisbech PE13 . . . . . . .152 C4
Weston Rise NR30 . . . . . .168 D5
Weston Sq ⬛3⬛ NR25 . . . .137 B6
Weston Terr NR26 . . . . . .138 E7
Weston Wood Cl NR7 . . .163 D5
Weston Wood Rd NR7 . . .163 D7
Westry Cl NR13 . . . . .59 C5
Westwick Dr NR28 . . . . . .151 A4
Westwick Rd NR28 . . . . . .37 F5
Westwick St NR2 . . . . . . .178 A3
Westwood Dr NR6 . . . . . .157 D6
Westwood La NR13 . . . . . .46 A6
Westwood La NR21 . . . . . .32 B5
Weybourne Rd
Bodham NR25 . . . . .9 A3
Sheringham NR26 . . . . . . .138 B7
Weybourne NR25 . . . . .8 F5
Weynor Gdns NR25 . . . . . .8 E5
Wharf St PE12 . . . . .41 B8
Wharton Dr NR28 . . . . . .151 E2
Whartons La ⬛5⬛ NR18 . . .173 B3
Wheat Fields NR8 . . . . . .155 F2
Wheatacre Cl ⬛1⬛ NR10 . . .53 A3
Wheatacres IP24 . . . . . .176 D5
Wheatcroft Way NR20 . . .68 A8
Wheatfield Way NR15 . . .106 F4
Wheatfields
Hillington PE31 . . . . .28 B4
Rickinghall Superior
IP22 . . . . .128 E2
Wheatley Bank PE14 . . . .59 C5
Wheatley Dr PE30 . . . . . .148 B4
Wheatley Rd NR4 . . . . . .161 F7
Wheel Rd NR14 . . . . .90 E4
Wheelbarrow La IP20 . . .123 F1
Wheeler Rd NR3 . . . . . . .158 A1
Wheelers La NR15 . . . . . .108 E8
Wheelwright Rd PE30 . . .147 C5
Wheelwrights Cl NR13 . . .92 E8
Wherry Cl NR28 . . . . .151 E7
Wherry Rd
Bungay NR35 . . . . .124 C8
Norwich NR1 . . . . .178 C1
Wherry Reach ⬛2⬛ NR13 . .166 D4
Wherry Way NR30 . . . . . .169 C7
Whiffler Rd NR3 . . . . . . .157 E2
Whimbrel Dr
⬛8⬛ Great Yarmouth NR31 . . .94 C8
⬛1⬛ Great Yarmouth NR31 . .170 A7
Whimpwell St NR12 . . . . .24 C4
Whin Comm Rd
Denver PE38 . . . . .172 D1
Tottenhill PE33 . . . . .61 F6
Whinburgh Rd NR9 . . . . . .71 C5
Whinchat Way ⬛3⬛ NR31 . .94 C7
Whinmere Rd NR12 . . . . .39 E3
Whipp's La NR16 . . . . . .105 F7
Whissler Rd ⬛1⬛ PE30 . . .147 A8
Whissonsett Rd NR20 . . .48 E8
Whistle Dr IP28 . . . . . . .112 D1
Whitby St ⬛3⬛ PE13 . . . .152 C5
White City Rd PE14 . . . . .78 D6
White Clover Rd ⬛5⬛ NR4 . .94 C6
White Cross
Bargh & Tuttington NR11 . . .36 A4
Hardingham NR9 . . . . .86 B8
White Cross Rd PE37 . . .153 C4
White Farm La NR7 . . . . .163 C6
White Gate La NR11 . . . . .11 D2
White Gates NR5 . . . . . .156 C4
White Hall Dr PE34 . . . . .146 C4
White Hart St
⬛2⬛ Aylsham NR11 . . . . . . .150 C7
East Harling NR16 . . . . . .118 C5
Foulden IP26 . . . . .82 B2
White Heath Rd NR15 . . . .91 B3
White Horse Dr PE31 . . . .46 D7
White Horse La
Bixley NR14 . . . . .89 F8
Trowse with Newton
NR14 . . . . .163 A1
Worstead NR28 . . . . .38 B6

White Horse St IP27 . . . .175 A2
White House Ct NR3 . . . .158 B3
White House Dr ⬛23⬛
NR15 . . . . .106 E3
White House Est
NR27 . . . . .139 D4
White House Farm La
IP21 . . . . .122 B2
White House Gdns ⬛12⬛
NR14 . . . . .90 D5
White House La NR17 . . .174 F5
White House Rd CB7 . . . .112 A7
White La PE33 . . . . .63 A3
White Lion Rd
Coltishall NR12 . . . . .54 D6
Wheatacre NR34 . . . . . . .111 B4
White Lion St
Norwich NR25 . . . . .137 B6
Norwich NR2 . . . . .178 A2
White Lodge Bsns Est
NR4 . . . . .89 E8
White Oaks PE37 . . . . . . .65 E2
White Post Rd NR11 . . . . .21 D5
White Rd
Barton Bendish PE33 . . . . .63 D1
Methwold IP26 . . . . .99 A5
White Rose Cl NR5 . . . . .161 D8
White Sedge NR30 . . . . .147 A8
White St NR29 . . . . .57 D5
White Woman La NR6 . . .159 A6
White Woman La Mid Sch
NR6 . . . . .158 F6
Whitecross La PE34 . . . .144 E4
Whitedike Dro PE26 . . . .113 B8
Whitefriars NR3 . . . . . . .158 B2
Whitefriars CE Prim Sch
PE30 . . . . .146 D3
Whitefriars Rd PE30 . . . .146 D3
Whitefriars Terr PE30 . . .146 D3
Whitegates Cl ⬛5⬛ NR18 . .173 B4
Whitegates Rd NR11 . . . .22 B7
Whitehall Rd NR2 . . . . . .162 B5
Whitehall Yd ⬛8⬛ NR26 . . .138 D7
Whitehart La IP27 . . . . . .175 C4
Whitehart St ⬛6⬛ IP27 . . . .6 E1
Whitehorse La NR17 . . . .174 C5
Whitehouse Plain ⬛7⬛
NR20 . . . . .169 C5
Whitehorse St
⬛1⬛ Fakenham NR21 . . . . . .141 C3
Wymondham NR18 . . . . . .173 B3
Whitehouse La
Earsham NR35 . . . . .108 C1
Wicklewood NR18 . . . . . . .87 C4
Whitelands NR21 . . . . . . .141 D5
Whiteplot Rd IP26 . . . . . . .98 D5
Whitethorn Cl ⬛6⬛ NR6 . . .158 D5
Whiteway Rd NR4 . . . . . .161 B4
Whiting's La NR17 . . . . .103 A6
Whitley Cl NR6 . . . . .158 C6
**Whitlingham Ctry Pk*
NR7 . . . . .163 C4
Whitlingham La NR14 . . .163 C4
Whitsands Rd PE37 . . . . .153 A5
Whittington Hill PE33 . . . .81 B2
Whittome Mill PE33 . . . . .79 D1
Whitwell Rd
Norwich NR1 . . . . .163 A7
Reepham NR10 . . . . .149 A2
Sparham NR9 . . . . .51 B6
Whitwell St NR10 . . . . . .149 C3
Whitworth Ave ⬛1⬛ NR17 .174 C5
Whityhead Gdns
IP22 . . . . .177 D4
Wick Farm Cl ⬛3⬛ IP25 . . .84 D2
Wick La NR29 . . . . .57 D2
Wickhampton Rd NR13 . . .93 A8
Wicklewood Prim Sch
NR18 . . . . .87 B5
Wicklewood Rd NR18 . . . .87 B6
Wickmere Rd NR11 . . . . .20 C5
Wicks Yd ⬛5⬛ NR18 . . . . .173 B4
Wiclewood Way PE31 . . .140 C3
Widgeon Cl NR31 . . . . . .170 A6
Wier Ave NR20 . . . . .68 F6
Wigby Rd Norwich NR5 . .161 A7
Quidenham NR16 . . . . . . .118 F8
Wild Flower Ctr* NR25 . . . .7 E3
Wild Radish Cl ⬛15⬛ NR14 .90 E4
Wild Rd NR3 . . . . .158 D1
Wildbriar Cl PE33 . . . . . .43 E1
Wilderness La IP20 . . . . .122 D6
Wildfields Cl PE34 . . . . .145 D5
Wildfields Rd PE34 . . . . .145 D6
Wildflower Way NR35 . . .109 A2
Wilkins Cl NR5 . . . . .161 C7
Wilkins Rd NR14 . . . . . . .72 E7
Wilkinson Way NR18 . . . .87 C4
Wilks Farm Dr NR7 . . . . .159 A5
Willbye Ave IP22 . . . . . .177 E5

William Booth Rd
PE30 . . . . .147 D5
William Booth St NR2 . . .178 A2
William Brown Way ⬛1⬛
IP22 . . . . .177 A5
William Bush Cl NR10 . . . .35 B2
William Childerhouse Way ⬛6⬛
NR5 . . . . .160 E7
William Cl ⬛5⬛ Watton IP25 .84 D3
⬛3⬛ Wymondham NR18 . . .173 C6
William Cowper Cl
NR19 . . . . .154 E1
William Kett Cl NR1 . . . .163 A6
**William Marriot Mus*
NR25 . . . . .137 E8
William Marshall CE Prim
Sch PE14 . . . . .95 D4
William Mear Gdns
NR1 . . . . .163 B6
William O'Callaghan Pl ⬛1⬛
NR19 . . . . .154 D5
William Paston Rd
NR28 . . . . .151 D6
William Peck Rd ⬛7⬛ NR10 .54 A2
William Rd
Fakenham NR21 . . . . .141 F5
Wisbech PE13 . . . . .152 C5
William St ⬛9⬛ NR30 . . . . .146 E3
William Way NR19 . . . . .154 C1
Williams Loke NR7 . . . . .158 F2
Williams Way
⬛3⬛ Holt NR25 . . . . .137 C5
⬛5⬛ North Walsham NR28 . .151 C6
Williamson Cl
Diss NR22 . . . . .177 D6
Norwich NR7 . . . . .159 C2
Williamson Cres ⬛4⬛
IP24 . . . . .176 C2
William Cl NR21 . . . . . . .133 D6
Willis St NR3 . . . . .178 C4
Willoughby Way ⬛5⬛ NR13 .72 E7
Willow Ave NR31 . . . . .94 C7
Willow Cl
Brandon IP27 . . . . .175 D2
Lingwood NR13 . . . . .74 A2
Long Stratton NR15 . . . . . .106 E2
⬛10⬛ Mattishall NR20 . . . . . .68 E6
Middleton PE32 . . . . .44 B4
North Walsham NR28 . . . .151 D7
Wortwell IP20 . . . . .123 A4
Wymondham NR18 . . . . . .173 D5
Willow Cres ⬛3⬛ NR23 . . . .6 E8
⬛8⬛ Attleborough NR17 . . . .174 B5
Beetley NR20 . . . . .49 D4
Willow Dr
Clenchwarton PE34 . . . . . .145 E5
Dersingham PE31 . . . . . . .140 D3
King's Lynn PE30 . . . . .43 F4
Tilney All Saints PE34 . . . .42 E4
West Winch PE33 . . . . .43 F1
Willow Gr
East Dereham NR19 . . . . .154 D2
Sheringham NR26 . . . . . . .138 D5
Willow Heath Rd PE33 . . . .80 B7
Willow Herb Wlk ⬛4⬛
NR18 . . . . .173 E4
Willow La
Bedingham NR35 . . . . . . .108 B3
Broome NR35 . . . . .109 C3
Carbrooke IP25 . . . . .85 B5
Norwich NR2 . . . . .178 A3
Willow Pk PE30 . . . . .147 C8
Willow Pl PE33 . . . . .62 A5
Willow Rd
Downham Market PE38 . . .172 B6
East Dereham NR19 . . . . .154 C2
Hunstanton PE36 . . . . . . .132 C3
King's Lynn PE30 . . . . . . .148 D2
Willow Way
⬛2⬛ Ludham NR29 . . . . .56 C5
⬛3⬛ Martham NR29 . . . . . . .57 D4
Wisbech PE13 . . . . .152 A5
Willow Wlk ⬛5⬛ IP20 . . . .122 D1
Willows Ct ⬛16⬛ NR33 . . . .111 F1
Willowbrook Cl ⬛4⬛ NR33 .111 F1
Willshere St ⬛11⬛ NR30 . .169 D3
Wilson Dr PE32 . . . . .44 F3
Wilson Rd ⬛1⬛ NR1 . . . . .163 B5
Wilson's Dro PE32 . . . . . .45 E3
Wilson's Way NR25 . . . . . .7 D6
Wilton Cres ⬛2⬛ NR10 . . . .54 A2
Wilton Rd Feltwell IP26 . . .98 E1
Norwich NR7 . . . . .159 C2
Wilton View NR28 . . . . . .151 D5
Wimbledon Ave PE13 . . .152 C4
Wimbledon Cl
PE30 . . . . .172 B4
Wimbotsham Rd PE38 . . .172 D4
Wimpole Dr PE30 . . . . . .148 E1
Winceby Cl NR7 . . . . .72 D4
Winch Rd PE32 . . . . .45 D8
Winchcomb Rd NR2 . . . .161 F7
Winchester Twr NR2 . . . .162 C5
Winchester Way IP24 . . .176 B5
Windermere Cl NR15 . . . .90 E2
Windermere Rd NR5 . . . .160 F6
Windle The NR20 . . . . . . .68 C6
Windmill Ave NR20 . . . . . .68 A8
Windmill Cl
⬛7⬛ Poringland NR14 . . . . . .90 C4
Thetford IP24 . . . . .176 D5
Windmill Hill PE31 . . . . . .14 A3
Windmill La
Costessey NR8 . . . . .157 A4
Syleham IP21 . . . . .131 D4
Wretham IP24 . . . . .102 B1

Windmill Rd
Gimingham NR11 . . . . .22 F8
⬛1⬛ Marham PE33 . . . . .63 B4
Norwich NR3 . . . . .158 F2
Worstead NR28 . . . . .38 A6
Wortwell IP20 . . . . .123 A3
Windsor Ave NR30 . . . . . .169 D7
Windsor Chase NR8 . . . .155 D1
Windsor Cl ⬛7⬛ IP24 . . . .125 F6
Windsor Cres PE31 . . . . .133 C5
Windsor Ct ⬛4⬛ IP25 . . . . .84 D3
Windsor Dr
Dersingham PE31 . . . . . . .140 C3
Wisbech PE13 . . . . .152 D8
Windsor Pk
East Dereham NR19 . . . . .154 D8
⬛2⬛ King's Lynn PE30 . . . .146 E3
Windsor Pk Gdns NR6 . . .159 A6
Windsor Rise
Caister-on-Sea NR30 . . . . .168 E6
Cantley NR13 . . . . .92 C6
King's Lynn PE30 . . . . . . .146 E3
Norwich NR6 . . . . .158 A5
Windsor Rise PE36 . . . . .132 C2
Windsor St ⬛1⬛ PE38 . . . .172 A5
Windsor Terr PE30 . . . . .146 E3
Windsor Way NR31 . . . . .170 B4
Windy Cres PE33 . . . . . . .63 B3
Windy La NR15 . . . . .107 B8
Windy Ridge PE33 . . . . . .63 D3
Winfarthing Ave PE30 . . .146 D3
Winfarthing Rd
Banham NR16 . . . . .119 D6
Shelfanger IP22 . . . . .120 B2
Wing's La PE30 . . . . .33 B7
Wingate Way NR2 . . . . . .162 C2
Wingfield PE30 . . . . .147 D5
Wingfield Rd
Lakenheath IP27 . . . . .113 C2
Norwich NR3 . . . . .162 D8
Syleham IP21 . . . . .131 D5
Weybread IP21 . . . . .131 F6
Wings Rd IP27 . . . . .113 E1
Winifred Cl NR26 . . . . . . .138 E7
Winifred Rd NR3 . . . . . . .169 B3
Winifred Way NR30 . . . . .168 D8
Winmer Ave ⬛6⬛ NR29 . . . .58 B6
Winners Wlk NR8 . . . . . .156 E1
Winsford Way NR5 . . . . .157 C1
Winston Churchill Dr
PE30 . . . . .147 C4
Winston Dr NR21 . . . . . . .15 E6
Winter Gdns* NR30 . . . .169 E2
Winter Rd NR22 . . . . .162 A6
Winterton Dures National
Nature Reserve*
NR29 . . . . .58 B7
Winterton Rd
Hemsby NR29 . . . . .167 B8
Somerton NR29 . . . . .57 F6
**Wisbech & Fenland Mus*
PE13 . . . . .152 C4
**Wisbech Castle*
PE13 . . . . .152 C4
Wisbech Gram Sch
PE13 . . . . .152 C4
Wisbech Rd
King's Lynn PE30 . . . . . . .146 D2
Manea PE15 . . . . .95 A2
Norfolk PE38 . . . . .78 D4
Outwell PE14 . . . . .77 F7
Walpole PE14 . . . . .41 D4
Walsoken PE13 . . . . .152 E8
Welney PE14 . . . . .95 D5
Wissey View IP26 . . . . . .100 B4
Wistaria Rd PE13 . . . . . .152 F7
Wisteria Cl NR20 . . . . . . .154 F4
Witard Cl NR7 . . . . .163 D8
Witard Rd NR7 . . . . .163 D8
Withersdale Rd IP20 . . . .122 D6
Withy Way NR5 . . . . .160 E8
Witton Cl
Heacham PE31 . . . . .133 C5
Reedham NR13 . . . . .92 F5
Witton Gn NR13 . . . . .92 F5
Witton La NR13 . . . . .165 A8
Wittons La NR13 . . . . . . .131 A3
Wiveton Rd NR25 . . . . .7 D6
Woburn St NR2 . . . . .162 A4
Wodehouse Cl ⬛1⬛ NR12 . .39 B4
Wodehouse Ct ⬛11⬛ IP25 . .84 D3
Wodehouse Rd
NR28 . . . . .23 D4
Old Hunstanton PE36 . . . .132 E7
Wodehouse St NR3 . . . . .162 E8
Wolfe Rd NR1 . . . . .163 B8
Wolferton Dr PE37 . . . . .153 B2
Wollaston Ave NR7 . . . . .163 E6
Wolseley Rd NR31 . . . . . .169 B2
Wolverton Rd NR11 . . . . . .20 C2
Womersley Cl ⬛3⬛ NR1 . . .163 B7
Womersley Rd NR1 . . . . .163 B7
Wood Avens Way
NR18 . . . . .173 E4
Wood Cl Brandon IP27 . . .175 D2
Hingham NR9 . . . . .119 A4
Wood Dalling Rd
Guestwick NR20 . . . . .34 A2
Reepham NR10 . . . . .149 C6

Wood Dene Sch NR11 .....9 F3
Wood Dr **11** Beetley NR20 ..49 D4
11 Beetley NR20 ....49 D4
Wood Gn NR13 ....72 F8
Wood Hill NR8 ....156 D8
Wood La Aldeby NR34 ...110 E5
Bedingham NR35 ....108 C2
Bradenham IP25 ....66 D4
Bressingham IP22 ....119 E2
Bunwell NR16 ....105 D3
Burgh & Tuttington NR11 ...36 D5
Dickleburgh & Rushall
IP21 ....130 F6
Great Ellingham NR17 ...103 D8
Hepworth IP22 ....127 E2
Holme Hale IP25 ....66 B1
Honingham NR9 ....69 E8
Kelling NR25 ....8 C5
Little Ellingham NR17 ....86 B1
Long Stratton NR15 .....107 A2
Morley NR18 ....87 A1
Pulham Market IP21 ......121 E8
Scole IP21 ....130 F8
Starston IP20 ....122 C5
Strumpshaw NR13 ....73 F2
Swardeston NR14 ....89 C5
Thelnetham IP22 ....128 A2
Wicklewood NR18 ....87 B4
Wood Norton Rd
Foulsham NR20 ....33 C5
Stibbard NR21 ....32 E7
Wood Rising Rd NR9 ....86 A5
Wood St Norwich NR1 ..178 A1
Wisbech PE13 ....152 B6
Wood St Rd NR29 ....56 B8
Wood View NR28 ....151 A4
Wood View Ct NR5 ......157 A2
Wood View Rd NR6 .....157 E5
Wood's La NR20 ....49 B8
Woodbastwick Rd
Blofield NR13 ....165 E7
Blofield Heath NR13 ......73 C6
Woodbastwick NR13 ......55 E1
Woodbine Cl
North Walsham NR28 ....151 F5
Potter Heigham NR29 ....56 F7
Woodbridge Way
PE30 ....147 D4
Woodcock Cl NR3 ......158 D3
Woodcock La PE34 ....61 B7
Woodcock Mews **4**
NR31 ....170 A6
Woodcock Rd NR3 ......158 C3
Woodcock Rise IP27 ....175 F4
Woodcock's La NR9 ......88 A8
Woodcote Pk PE13 .....152 A4
Woodcroft Cl NR7 ......159 E2
Woodend Rd NR21 ......133 E5
Woodfarm La NR31 .....170 A2
Woodfield
Briston NR24 ....142 C4
11 East Dereham NR19 ...154 D1
Woodfield Rd NR25 ....137 C7
Woodforde Rd NR7 .....159 D2
Woodfordes Brewery &
Visitors Ctr* NR13 .....55 C2
Woodgate **12** NR4 ......89 B8
Woodgate La NR20 ......50 B3
Woodgate Rd NR20 ......50 A2

Woodgate Way PE31 ...134 F4
Woodhall Rd PE38 ....97 B8
Woodham Leas NR6 ....158 E6
Woodhill Rise NR5 .....161 C8
Woodhouse Cl **1** NR26 ..138 B6
Woodland Dr
Bungay NR35 ....124 A7
Ellingham NR35 ....109 E3
Thorpe End NR13 ....72 D5
Woodland Farm Ind Units
NR10 ....53 A6
Woodland Gdns PE30 ..148 D5
Woodland La NR24 .....142 F2
Woodland Rd NR6 ......157 E6
Woodland Rise
Sheringham NR26 ....138 E5
12 Tasburgh NR15 ....106 F6
Woodland Rise W
NR26 ....138 D4
Woodland View Mid Sch
NR10 ....54 A2
Woodland View Mobile Home
Pk NR10 ....53 D6
Woodlands
S5 Harleston IP20 ....122 D2
7 Thorpe Marriott NR8 ..155 B2
Woodlands Cl
Holt NR25 ....137 D7
4 Thetford IP24 ....176 E6
Woodlands Cres **1** NR17 .72 D5
Woodlands Ct PE13 ....152 F7
Woodlands Dr IP24 ....176 D6
Woodlands Mid Sch
NR31 ....94 C6
Woodlands Rd NR5 ....157 A2
Woodlands Rise IP27 ..175 A2
Woodlands The IP25 ...84 A7
Woodlands Way Rd
NR12 ....55 D4
Woodlark Cl **2** IP24 ....176 D2
Woodpecker Dr **8** IP25 .84 C3
Woodpecker Mews **5**
NR31 ....170 A6
Woodrising Rd NR9 .....85 D4
Woodrow Ave NR25 ....137 B5
Woodrow La NR15 .....121 A8
Woodrow Pl NR1 ......163 B6
Woodruff Cl **3** NR6 ...158 D5
Woods Cl **3** NR9 ....88 C7
Woods End NR17 ......174 C4
Woodside
Burnham Market PE31 ..135 A2
8 King's Lynn PE30 .....147 C4
North Walsham NR28 ...151 E4
Woodside Ave
Dersingham PE31 ....140 C5
Heacham PE31 ....133 D4
Woodside Cl
Attleborough NR17 .....174 C3
Dersingham PE31 ....140 C5
1 Dereham NR8 ....155 C1
Woodside Ct NR17 ....174 C3
Woodside Fst Com Sch
NR7 ....159 E1
Woodside Pk NR9 ....88 D7
Woodside Pk NR17 ....174 C3
Woodside Rd NR7 .....159 E1
Woodstock La NR15 ...120 F8
Woodstock Way **3** NR29 .57 D4
Woodton Prim Sch
NR35 ....108 C5

Woodton Rd NR35 .....108 A7
Woodview NR28 ....38 A4
Woodview Cl IP25 ......84 C4
Woodview Rd NR9 ....70 B5
Woodward Cl **3** NR13 ..62 D4
Woodward Rd NR3 .....158 B2
Woodwark Ave **3** PE30 .146 E6
Woodyard Cl **9** NR14 ..89 B3
Woodyard Sq The
NR35 ....108 C5
Wooll Dr NR28 ....151 D7
Woolner's La NR14 ......90 E7
Woolstencroft Ave
PE30 ....146 F7
Wootton Rd PE30 ......147 B7
Worcester Cl **3** NR29 .167 A2
Worcester Rd PE13 ....152 C7
Worcester Way
Attleborough NR17 .....174 E4
Great Yarmouth NR31 ...170 B4
Wordsworth Cl PE38 ...172 D5
Wordsworth Gn IP24 ..176 E7
Wordsworth Rd
2 Diss IP22 ....177 E4
Norwich NR5 ....161 C6
Workhouse La
Foulsham NR20 ....33 D4
Tilney St Lawrence PE34 ..42 C1
Upwell PE14 ....77 D4
Workhouse Rd NR12 ...38 C3
Workhouse Rd NR13 ...74 C1
Wormegay Prim Sch
PE33 ....62 A6
Wormegay Rd
Blackborough End PE32 ..44 C1
Wormegay PE32 ....62 D8
Worstead Prim Sch
NR28 ....38 A5
Worstead Rd NR28 ......38 B4
Worstead Sta NR28 .....37 F4
Wortham Cl **3** NR5 ...161 A8
Wortham Prim Sch
IP22 ....129 C4
Worthing Rd
North Elmham NR20 ....49 F7
Swanton Morley NR20 ...50 B6
Wramplingham Rd
NR18 ....173 D8
Wren Cl Brandon IP27 .175 E3
Necton PE14 ....66 A3
Norwich NR4 ....161 E2
Wren Dr
2 Great Yarmouth NR31 .94 C7
Great Yarmouth NR31 ..170 A4
Wrench Cl **4** NR11 ....150 D6
Wrench Rd NR5 ....161 D6
Wreningham Prim Sch
NR16 ....88 D1
Wrens The **1** IP24 ...176 D2
Wretton Fen Dro PE33 ..80 D1
Wretton Rd PE33 ....80 F2
Wretton Row PE33 .....80 E3
Wright Ave NR19 ......154 D1
Wright Cl NR30 ....168 E7
Wright Dr NR19 ....154 C4
Wright's Cl North NR25 .137 C7
North Walsham NR28 ..151 B4
Wright's La PE12 ....41 B8
Wright's Loke NR28 .....22 E5
Wright's Wlk **12** NR19 .154 D5
Wrights Cl NR11 ......150 C7
Wroe The PE14 ....59 C1

Wroo Rd NR17 ....103 F5
Wroughton Fst Sch
NR31 ....170 B6
Wroughton Mid Sch
NR31 ....170 B7
Wroxham Ave PE37 ....153 C2
Wroxham Rd
Coltishall NR12 ....54 E6
Rackheath NR13 ....72 D8
Salhouse NR13 ....54 E2
Sprowston NR7 ....159 C5
Wroxham Sta NR12 ....164 C6
Wyatt St PE30 ....146 E5
Wyatt Way NR24 ......176 B7
Wycliffe Rd NR4 ......161 D3
Wylde Croft NR8 .....155 D2
Wymans Way NR21 ...141 E5
Wymer Dr NR11 ......150 C4
Wymer St NR2 ....162 B6
Wymers La NR13 ....74 B8
Wymondham Abbey (rems)*
NR18 ....173 B3
Wymondham Abbey Sta
NR18 ....173 A3
Wymondham Coll NR18 .87 B1
Wymondham Heritage Mus*
NR18 ....173 C4
Wymondham High Sch
NR18 ....173 C5
Wymondham Leisure Ctr
NR18 ....173 C4
Wymondham Rd
Bracon Ash NR14 ....88 E2
Bunwell NR16 ....105 B5
East Carleton NR14 ......88 F4
Flordon NR15 ....106 C8
Kimberley NR18 ....87 B6
Morley NR18 ....87 A3
Wreningham NR16 ....88 B2
Wymondham NR18 .....105 A8
Wymondham Sta
NR18 ....173 C2
Wyndfields **10** PE37 ...65 F4
Wyndham Pk NR27 ....10 C5
Wyndham St NR26 ....138 D7
Wyngates NR13 ....165 F6
Wynne's La PE34 .....145 C4

Y

Yallop Ave NR31 ......171 D8
Yare Cl
Caister-on-Sea NR30 ..168 D6
Great Yarmouth NR30 ..169 C6
Yare Rd NR31 ....94 A6
Yare Valley Dr NR4 ...161 C2
Yare Valley Rise NR13 .165 C3
Yare View Cl NR13 .....92 F4
Yarmouth Bsns Pk
NR31 ....169 B2
Yarmouth Rd
Blofield NR13 ....165 F6
Broome NR35 ....110 C2
Brundall NR13 ....165 C5
Caister-on-Sea NR30 ..168 E2
Corton NR32 ....171 D1
Dilham NR28 ....38 C4
Geldeston NR34 ....110 A3
Hales NR14 ....109 F8
Hemsby NR29 ....167 A6
Kirby Cane NR35 ......109 E3

Yarmouth Rd continued
Lound NR32 ....94 B3
Ludham NR29 ....56 C5
North Walsham NR28 ...151 C4
Norwich NR7 ....163 E5
Ormesby St Margaret
NR29 ....167 C1
Postwick with Witton
NR13 ....165 A5
Raveningham NR14 ....110 B8
Stalham NR12 ....39 B3
Thurlton NR14 ....93 A1
Toft Monks NR34 ......110 E5
Worstead NR28 ....38 A6
Yarmouth Stadium
NR30 ....168 E2
Yarmouth Way NR30 ..169 C3
Yarn Mews **2** NR3 ...178 B4
Yarrington Way NR5 ..160 E8
Yarrow Cl IP24 ....176 F5
Yarrow Rd Bintree NR20 ..33 B2
2 Dereham NR20 ....68 A8
Yaxham CE Prim Sch
NR30 ....68 C6
Yaxham Rd
East Dereham NR19 ...154 E4
Mattishall NR20 ....68 A4
Shipdham Sta NR19 .....68 A4
Yaxley Way NR5 ......161 A8
Yaxley's La NR11 ......150 C6
Yaxley's Rd NR30 .....169 B6
Yeats Way NR19 ......154 B6
Yelverton Cl NR6 .....157 D5
Yelverton Rd NR14 ....90 E5
Yesmere **16** NR14 ....89 B3
Yew Ct NR7 ....159 C4
Yew Tree Cl **24** NR11 .94 C7
Yew Tree Cl NR20 ......69 B7
Yew Tree Rd NR17 ....174 C5
York Ave PE36 ....132 D5
York Gdns PE13 ......152 D6
York La **19** NR12 ......39 B4
York Rd **4** Cromer NR27 .139 D5
Great Yarmouth NR30 ..169 D3
King's Lynn PE30 ......146 E3
Wisbech PE13 ....152 D6
York Row PE13 ....152 C5
York St NR2 ....162 B4
York Terr Cromer NR27 ..139 D5
Wisbech PE13 ....152 C6
York Villa Cl NR29 ....75 E8
York Way PE12 ....176 B5
Youell Ave NR10 .....170 D1
Young's Cres NR13 .....92 E7
Young's Row PE12 ....41 A8
Youngman's La NR10 ...37 C5
Youngmans Cl NR28 ..151 D3
Youngmans La NR12 ...38 E6
Youngmans Rd NR18 ..173 C8

Z

Zara Way NR19 ....154 C1
Zephyr Cl NR30 ......168 D7
Zig-Zag La NR15 .....108 C8
Zobel Cl NR3 ....157 F2
Zurich Cl NR31 ......171 E4